Eddie — ☆ — Rickenbacker

Eddie — ☆ — Ricke

An American Hero

W. DAVID LEWIS

THE JOHNS HOPKINS UNIVERSITY PRESS

Baltimore

nbacker

in the Twentieth Century

The Johns Hopkins University Press
2715 North Charles Street
Baltimore, Maryland 21218-4363
www.press.jhu.edu

Library of Congress Cataloging-in-Publication Data

Lewis, W. David (Walter David), 1931–
    Eddie Rickenbacker : an American hero in the twentieth century /
      W. David Lewis.
    Includes bibliographical references and index.
    ISBN 0-8018-8244-3 (hardcover : alk. paper)
    1. Rickenbacker, Eddie, 1890–1973. 2. Air pilots—United States—
Biography. 3. Air pilots, Military—United States—Biography. 4. World
War, 1914–1918—Aerial operations, American. 5. World War, 1939–
1945—Aerial operations, American. I. Title.
    TL540.R53L493 2005
    629.13′092—dc22   2005005939

A catalog record for this book is available from the British Library.

Unless otherwise indicated, all illustrations are courtesy of the
Rickenbacker Collection, Special Collections and Archives, Auburn
University Libraries.

For Pat — ☆ —
The Queen of My Universe

No one living has cheated the old grim
reaper oftener than I have.
—*Eddie Rickenbacker*

This thing of being a hero, about the main
thing to it is to know when to die. Prolonged
life has ruined more men than it ever made.
—*Will Rogers*

Contents

— ☆ —

Illustrations follow pages 128 and 352

Preface

— ☆ —

Growing up in my hometown, Bellefonte, Pennsylvania, launched a boy with a vivid imagination on a trajectory that led him to become a historian of aviation and now the biographer of one of America's greatest aerial heroes. Nestled in the Allegheny mountains, Bellefonte was a hotbed of enthusiasm for flight when I was very young. Before my time, in 1918, postal officials had designated its airport as the refueling and maintenance base for the short-range planes that flew the pioneering airmail route between New York City and Cleveland. It was a treacherous domain, an unforgiving expanse of territory mastered only by human daring and a strong will to prevail over natural obstacles. Crossing the Keystone State required a special breed of pilots, whether they carried mail or, like Eddie Rickenbacker, went aloft to satisfy their passion for adventure.

During the 1920s Bellefonte became an aerial crossroads frequented by the most famous flyers of the day. Rickenbacker was one of them. His passion for flight grew out of being a combat pilot in the Great War. Diving from high altitudes with the sun at his back, his machine guns barking and wind whistling through the wires supporting his wings, he became America's Ace of Aces by shooting down twenty-six German aircraft in eight months, though spending much of that time in French hospitals recovering from injuries caused by the inevitable strain his tactics imposed on his ears. Captain Eddie, as his admirers called him, found life barren in the 1920s without taking to the sky and repeatedly flirting with danger. He survived crashes and close brushes with death, some of which occurred on a madcap transcontinental expedition that brought him to Bellefonte in 1922. Many pilots were not so lucky.

Flyers like Rickenbacker were well aware that Bellefonte's airport was a potential deathtrap when fog blanketed the area, a not infrequent phenomenon. Charles Ames, an airmail pilot, was a victim of such conditions, getting lost trying to find the little grass-covered field in October 1925 and slamming into a stand of oak trees 200 feet from a crest in the Nittany Mountains. The site at which he died was so densely forested that it took townspeople, joined by national guardsmen, nine days to find his mangled corpse in a tangle of wreckage four miles from Bellefonte. Because the airport was so potentially hazardous, it was one of the first places on the transcontinental airmail route to be equipped with floodlights, but their beams initially reached only fifteen feet above ground level and did not prevent the tragedy that befell Ames. The government also installed a radio navigational system in 1926, the first station of its type established in the United States. Its early transmissions carried 150 miles, contributing to increased safety in the air and reducing the frequency of fatalities.[1]

The expanded range of aircraft caused Bellefonte's role in aviation to dwindle as rapidly as it had arisen, but during my earliest years, residents looked back proudly at its brief moment of fame, talking about famous pilots who had visited the town and the planes they had flown. Until Charles Lindbergh made his solo flight to Paris in 1927, no aviator of the day commanded greater esteem in Bellefonte than Captain Eddie. His humble origins gave him the image of a "self-made man," epitomizing character traits—raw courage, dogged perseverance, and boundless self-confidence—with which Americans identified strongly at the time. Financial setbacks that left him virtually broke by the late 1920s did not faze him, at least outwardly. They merely made people identify with him all the more because failures were only to be expected in a rough-and-tumble decade marked by frequent gyrations in the business cycle. Pressing ahead without whining or looking back, he went from one achievement to another and became a symbol of the American Dream. In Bellefonte, as everywhere else, his name was a household word. During the 1930s, my first decade of life, I heard his deep bass voice on the radio, saw his lantern-jawed face on Saturday afternoons watching newsreels at the Plaza Theater, and read newspaper and magazine articles sounding his praises. I cannot recall a time when I did not know who he was.

I do remember vividly, however, the exact time when aviation began to preoccupy me, portending my professional future. It happened in 1935, when I was four years old. During a Sunday outing with my parents in their Buick, my mother suddenly exclaimed, "There's a Zeppelin!" and my father stopped the car so we could get out and look at it. As I learned after knowing more about aeronautical terminology, it was not really a Zeppelin, by definition a rigid airship like the *Hindenburg*, which exploded in 1937 before terrified onlookers at Lakehurst, New Jersey. What I saw in 1935 was a nonrigid dirigible, cruising at a low altitude through a break in the mountains between Bellefonte and Milesburg. Its engines hummed with a sound that reverberates in my memory seventy years later. Suspended beneath its elongated gas bag was something that resembled the hull of a ship. Uniformed men stood along its deck, waving and cheering as the aircraft proceeded briskly through the sky. The sound of their voices, echoing as the dirigible disappeared in the west, reaches out to me across the gulf of time that separates me from the child, yet also connects me with a life-altering experience. When I became an adult, I wondered whether it had been only a dream until I saw a photograph from a newspaper of the 1930s, mounted on a wall at a restaurant in Virginia, showing exactly the same type of airship. Men dressed in military garb stood along a railing like the one I had seen, waving at sunbathers looking up from a beach. What I had witnessed as a child was an army dirigible following a flight path across central Pennsylvania, heading for Scott Field in Illinois from its eastern base at Langley Field in Virginia.[2]

My fascination with aviation intensified soon thereafter when I heard on the radio that Wiley Post—the famous airman who wore a patch over a missing eye—had died in a crash at Point Barrow, Alaska, a tragedy that also killed America's most beloved humorist, Will Rogers. Post had flown around the world twice in his Lockheed Vega, the *Winnie Mae*. On the final leg of his first transglobal flight in 1931—I was then only one week old—he flew directly over Bellefonte at nightfall, guided by a revolving beacon light amid the nearby mountains. Years later I noted that Bellefonte was one of a very few American places mentioned by name in the log of Post's navigator, Harold Gatty.[3]

Post was one of the world's greatest aviators, but Rogers was more famous and more deeply mourned. Soon after the crash at Point Barrow, Rickenbacker took charge of a nationwide campaign to honor Rogers by raising funds to help sick and needy children. It may have been at this time that Captain Eddie's name became fixed in my mind. A Latin teacher who lived next door had decided I was ready at a tender age to learn to read and helped me trace letters and words in newspapers while I sat in his lap. I may have seen Rickenbacker's name in a headline during one of my lessons.

During the late 1930s someone gave me a booklet with blank spaces for stickers about inventions that would supposedly change the future. These wonders included a rotorcraft called an autogiro. The accompanying sticker showed an autogiro that could descend to earth and travel on roads like a car. I heard that Rickenbacker, now president of Eastern Air Lines, was using autogiros in an experimental airmail service between the airport at Camden, New Jersey, and Philadelphia's main post office, landing on its roof loaded with mailbags. The service did not last long but aroused a lot of publicity.

Late in 1942, when I was eleven years old, Rickenbacker became a particularly compelling figure to me. Despite near-fatal injuries he had suffered in a crash near Atlanta in 1941, he had volunteered to take a top-secret message to General Douglas MacArthur's headquarters in the Southwest Pacific. On a night flight between Hawaii and Canton Island, a tiny atoll where it was supposed to make a refueling stop, a Boeing B-17 "Flying Fortress" carrying Captain Eddie and seven companions went off course and failed to locate its target. As it ran out of gas, the pilot had to ditch the giant aircraft in a vast, remote, shark-infested expanse of ocean between Japanese-held islands to the north and American supply lines to Australia on the south. Escaping from the aircraft in three tiny rubber rafts, Rickenbacker and his comrades floated slowly westward on sluggish currents (it was a season of doldrums) toward apparent oblivion. Attempts to find them proved fruitless, and a wave of anxiety swept across America about the hero's fate. As weeks passed, many people assumed he was dead. Like millions of Americans, I mourned his loss, only to celebrate when banner headlines and radio broadcasts proclaimed the rescue of Eddie and six of his companions—famished, dehydrated, sunburned, and salt-caked but still alive after a terrible three-week ordeal. At one point in the odyssey, a bird suddenly and uncannily alighted on his hat, seemingly from out of nowhere, miraculously providing food for him and his mates after he wrung its neck, cut up its carcass, and shared it with the men like a priest at a communion service. I felt a sense of wonder at the time. How strange it is, yet natural too because of my childhood experiences, that I should write a biography of Rickenbacker, who became a neglected figure among most professional historians despite the extraordinary life he led and the impact it had on his fellow Americans.

Like every work I have produced, this book springs from memories embedded in my own personal history. Growing up as the son of a correctional official at Rockview State Penitentiary, near Bellefonte, greatly influenced my writing a doctoral dissertation at Cornell University that traced the development of early penal institutions in the state of New York. It became my first published book. Riding a streetcar down the Monongahela Valley in 1949 and seeing Bessemer converters searing the sky with towering flames deeply impressed me, leading ultimately to my writing a book about the history of an Alabama blast furnace complex that captured my attention for nearly a decade.

I am disinclined to write about historical topics that do not evoke my own past. My immersion in Rickenbacker has been the latest result of my passion for exploring what Lincoln called "the mystic chords of memory." I have spent almost fifteen years living with Captain Eddie neither to glorify nor debunk him—for he was and remains a highly controversial figure—but to revisit the wellsprings of my being by writing an accurate and objective book about an endlessly fascinating protagonist who touched my life at a time long ago that remains forever fresh.

Eddie — ☆ — Rickenbacker

A Boy and His Flying Machine

Early in the twentieth century—almost certainly before December 1903 when Wilbur and Orville Wright flew their first successful airplane at Kitty Hawk—a boy made his own attempt to fly in Columbus, Ohio.[1] A few weeks before he had been among the crowd of people craning their necks to gape skyward as a dirigible had sailed over the city, piloted by Roy Knabenshue, a pioneering aeronaut. The aspiring youth, known to his friends as Edd, could not afford to build a dirigible but was sure there must be other ways to go aloft. That night, lying on his bed in a loft under the eaves of the little house on East Livingston Avenue, Edd brooded about the problem before he finally fell asleep.

Wanting a soft place to land, he thought about sand, which he finagled from a contractor at a nearby building site. It took him days of hard labor to carry it, a bucketful at a time, to a spot he had chosen, until the pile was big enough to suit him. Though just a boy, he had already learned that taking risks required some planning—if you tried something dangerous, it was good to have an escape hatch. At an earlier time he and some friends had pushed a steel cart up a pair of rails from the floor of a gravel pit to ground level. After reaching the top, they put chocks under the wheels, and everybody but Edd climbed in. Quickly knocking away the chocks, Edd jumped aboard as the vehicle hurtled down the track. The cart gained momentum, but losing its balance, it turned over and fell on him. A wheel ran over one of his legs, cutting it to the bone. An ugly scar showed how close he had come to being killed. This time he would be more careful.

Edd piled the sand beside a barn that had a steeply pitched roof made of corrugated metal. He borrowed two ladders, one to reach the bottom of the roof and the other to get from there to the peak. He already owned a bicycle and bought a large secondhand umbrella. Wiring the umbrella to the bike, he would lean it against one of his shoulders until he was ready for takeoff. He even took the tires off the wheels, thinking that metal against metal would help him go faster. As the makeshift machine rolled down the roof and gained speed, he planned to adjust the umbrella so that a pocket of air would accumulate under it, as in a parachute. By the time he reached the edge of the roof, he thought he would have gained enough momentum to stay aloft. To make a soft landing, he planned to adjust the angle of the umbrella. If that did not work, the sand pile would save him.

Because his mother would be horrified if she knew what he was up to and his father would beat him, he kept the project secret. But someone *had* to know because he could not push the bicycle and umbrella to the peak of the roof himself. And what good would it do if he flew and nobody witnessed it? So he confided in his friend Sam Wareham.

At the appointed time, Edd and Sam carried the contraption up the ladders to the peak of the roof. Sam held it in place while Edd mounted the seat. The ground seemed so far away it made his head swim, but he had worked too hard to stop now. Away he went. The corrugations acted like tracks and the bare metal wheels rolled faster and faster as the machine approached the edge of the roof, but the umbrella was too weak to withstand the stress and turned inside out. Instead of sailing into the air, Edd, the bicycle, and the umbrella plummeted into the sand pile. Banged up but not seriously hurt, he brushed off the sand and went home. Someday, he hoped, he would really fly.

Chapter 1

— ☆ —

Starting Line

In 1879 a husky young immigrant with a stubborn disposition and vol-
atile temper arrived in Columbus, Ohio. William Rickenbacher had
come far from his native Switzerland. His goal was a better way of life
than eking out a bare existence in Zeglingen, a village in the Germanic
half-canton of Baselland, nestled in the foothills of the Jura Mountains.[1]
In the nineteenth century, Baselland had seceded from the city of Basel,
which then became the half-canton of Baselstadt, to express resentment
of exploitation by Basel's merchants. A rapacious lot, they had long
avoided guild restrictions by distributing raw materials among weavers
in the hinterlands and paying them a pittance for their work. The only
other source of income for Baselland was farming and herding on the
region's steep, infertile terrain. Chronic poverty forced many young
people with no future prospects—William among them—to leave. Most
went to the United States, where the traditions of individual liberty, limited government, and free enterprise reminded them of home.[2]

William's family had been listed in the records of churches near Basel
as early as the thirteenth century. Their name came from Rickenbach
(also Riggenbach), a village located in domains once ruled by the Haps-
burgs but later incorporated into Switzerland. Some members of the
family moved to Basel, a city whose main passion was amassing wealth.
Niklaus Riggenbach (1784–1829) owned a sugar refinery in Alsace. His
son, Anton Ludwig Niklaus Riggenbach (1817–99), became an engineer and invented a cogwheel railway, the Riggibahn, which used racks
and pinions to move trains up and down steep Swiss mountains. The affluent branch in Basel also included Christoph Riggenbach (1810–63),
a distinguished architect, and Christoph Johannes Riggenbach (1818–
90), who taught theology at the University of Basel and was a friend of
the city's greatest scholar, Jakob Burckhardt. Edd may have derived his

lively intelligence, entrepreneurial instincts, and inventive bent from his genetic connection with the Riggenbachs. His father, William Rickenbacher, however, came from a less accomplished family branch that had remained in the countryside. According to William's descendants, he became an apprentice in the building trade. If so, the skills he acquired were probably rudimentary because he spent most of his adult life in Columbus as a common laborer.[3]

Upon reaching America, William headed for Columbus, where an uncle, John Ulric Rickenbacher, had prospered as a tailor. A Republican stalwart in Columbus, John ultimately became sheriff of the surrounding Franklin County. Other Rickenbachers listed in the city directory at the time of William's arrival included Albert, a timekeeper at the Columbus Machine Company, and J. M. Rickenbacher, a bookkeeper identified only by his initials. Both men were likely John's sons, therefore William's cousins.[4]

A depression that had hit the United States in 1873 was over by 1879, and there were jobs for a young man with William's rugged build. He became a laborer for one of many railroads passing through Columbus and boarded at 669 South High Street in an enclave largely peopled by German-speaking immigrants since the 1830s. After the failure of revolutions that swept across Europe in 1848 and a resulting wave of emigration, more houses were built in the city's southern wards than in any other part of town, and the Fifth Ward became heavily Germanic. In 1860 people with that ethnic background constituted about 30 percent of Columbus's population. By 1880 almost 4,500 of its residents had been born in Germany; by 1890 the number reached 7,000.[5]

Important differences separated newcomers from various parts of Germany and those from Teutonic areas of Switzerland, where German was the written language but people spoke various dialects of "Swiss-Deutsch" that were unintelligible outside the cantons where they lived. Significant political and cultural cleavages also divided Germany and Switzerland, a multilingual confederation whose citizens spoke Swiss-Deutsch, French, Italian, or a patois called Romansch. Whatever their ethnic background, the Swiss hated authoritarian government and hereditary monarchy, stemming from bloody wars in which they had freed themselves from the Hapsburg dynasty. Switzerland was also hostile toward the powerful German Empire that emerged from the Franco-Prussian War. To put it simply, people like William Rickenbacher were Germanic but not German, forming a distinct minority among Teutonic immigrants in the South Side of Columbus. Unlike their neighbors, they took no pride in the growing power of the Reich and its Hohenzollern rulers.[6] Edd later called himself a "Heinie" but felt no hesitation about fighting against Germany in two world wars.

Among the Germanic settlers who came to Columbus from Baselland in the 1880s was Elizabeth Basler. In Switzerland her impoverished father, a weaver, made silk ribbons and raised cows, hogs, hay, flax, and food crops to support his growing family. He, his wife, and their ten children lived in three rooms on the bottom floor of a two-story chalet on a hillside overlooking Zeglingen. Liesl, as Elizabeth was known, had flaming red hair and endured a lot of teasing about it. Rebellious and full of mischief, she hated unwinding skeins of yarn from large spools to small bobbins to help weave ribbons on her father's loom and deliberately snagged threads to fight boredom. Because she went to school on weekdays, her father punished her for her mischief on Sundays by locking her in a storage cabinet after the family returned from services at a Zwinglian church. Despite her unruliness, she was deeply religious, and her descendants cherished her baptismal and confirmation certificates.

When Liesl was thirteen, the death of her best friend, Louisa Thommen, dealt her a severe blow. Soon afterward, Louisa's father, Zeglingen's postmaster, adopted Liesl as a foster child, a common arrangement amid the poverty rampant in Switzerland at the time. Glad to have one less mouth to feed, Liesl's parents let her go. In 1881 two of her brothers, Rudolph and Adolf Basler, went to America. Like William Rickenbacher, with whom they may have been friends, they settled in Columbus. Before Rudolph left home, he promised to send money to Liesl as soon as possible to pay her passage to the United States. The speed with which it came convinced her that America was indeed a "land of opportunity." Boarding a French ship in May 1881 with nothing but a round of cheese in her apron, she ate it during the seven-day voyage with hard rolls that she softened in seawater. She stole wine from the men's quarters to share with sixteen women with whom she occupied a nearby cabin. She did not feel guilty, believing her pilfering was justified because of the preferential treatment male passengers enjoyed.

Liesl arrived at Columbus in the middle of the night on a train, clutching a letter in German from Rudolph to show anyone who might be able to direct her to a dairy farm on the North Side where he worked. Unable to speak English, she was terrified by dark shadows cast by laborers in the glare of lights illuminating the freight yards. A ticket agent could not understand anything she said but recognized the Germanic script in her letter and called Sheriff Rickenbacher to the rescue. She never forgot how relieved she felt when John entered the station, greeted her in her native tongue, and took her to the farm where Rudolph worked. She burst into tears when she saw her brother.

"Lizzie," as people called her in Columbus, became a housekeeper at the farm, making $1.50 per week, but soon found a better job at a starch factory. She saved as much money as possible and had little time to enjoy herself. One Sunday evening in 1882, however, Rudolph took her to a band concert at Livingston Avenue Park, where John Rickenbacher introduced her to William. Three years later, in 1885, when William was working at a brewery, they married. Always strong-willed, Lizzie showed her fiancé that she had a mind of her own by having the wedding postponed for six weeks to give the starch factory time to fill her position.

The newlyweds lived in cramped quarters back of the brewery. On 11 July 1886 they recorded the birth of their first child, Mary, in Teutonic script in a large German Bible that had a black cover adorned with gold letters—a prized possession Lizzie had brought from Switzerland. Another entry appeared on 30 August 1887 when a son, named William after his father but called "Bill" to set him apart, was born.[7] William lost his job at the brewery in 1888 when the national economy slumped and had to settle for occasional work as a common laborer. Lizzie later said that financial troubles were "constant companions" at this time. Hoping to build a home, they had saved enough money to buy a plot of land but now had to spend it to survive. They could not afford to have more children until circumstances improved. Late in 1889, after an economic upswing, William got another job at a brewery. On 8 October 1890 their second son, Edward, was born in a house at 247 South Pearl Street, which they shared with William's brother, Herman, who had recently come from Switzerland with a family of his own.[8]

William lost his job soon after Edward's birth and the family moved repeatedly during the next few years. Amid the insecurity, Lizzie decided it was imperative to find a permanent nest. She and William somehow saved enough money to buy two adjoining lots on East Livingston Avenue, where land was cheap. The area had been a swamp, was far from a streetcar line, and had unpaved streets; its prospects improved when the city decided to install paving, but now the couple could not pay assessments on more than one lot. Acting against William's wishes, Lizzie sold one of the lots and used the proceeds as a down payment to start building a tiny frame house on the other. The plan called for only two rooms on the same floor—a parlor about ten feet square and a slightly larger bedroom. Between the eaves would be a loft where the children could sleep.[9]

The cost of the house, $300, was not covered by the down payment, but help suddenly arrived. Lizzie's mother had died and an older sister, Anna, came to Columbus. Their father, once so poor he had given Liesl to foster parents, now visited America to see his daughters and had enough money to pay for his return trip. Lizzie borrowed it without asking William's approval, promising her father to pay it back by the time he left. Using the loan to finish the house on East Livingston Avenue, she took in endless loads of washing and paid off the loan by the time he went home.

William was shocked when Lizzie told him the house was ready for occupancy and that she intended to move into it with the children whether he wanted to go with them or not. Coming from a patriarchal culture, William resented her unilateral decisions. The insult to his self-esteem was compounded by his decline in status from brewery worker to laborer, as well as his inability to be the family's sole breadwinner. The situation had profound consequences for interfamily relationships. William seems to have taken out his feelings of resentment and inadequacy on his children, particularly Edd, whose arrival had set off the power struggle with Lizzie. The move occurred late in 1893, when Edd was three years old. It was one of his earliest memories. By this time another baby, Emma, had arrived on 22 November 1892, followed on 16 March 1894 by Luise, who died 17 September 1896. Three more children, all boys, came by the end of the century. Louis, named for Luise, was born on the day of her death; Dewey arrived 2 June 1898; Albert, on 17 April 1900.

To relieve overcrowding and give Lizzie a place to cook, William, helped by Anna's husband, built a kitchen across the rear of the house. A loft above it provided more sleeping quarters. They also dug a cellar. The house had no electricity, running water, or indoor plumbing. There was a kerosene lamp in the downstairs room where Lizzie and William slept, with another in the kitchen. A stove in the kitchen provided heat. The unheated lofts, one for the boys, the other for the girls, were bitterly cold in the winters. As the boys approached adolescence, there was barely enough room for their beds. The hard-pressed family raised as much food as possible and stored it in a wine vat William buried in the back yard. Almost every available square inch of the lot, 50 feet wide and 208 feet deep, yielded fruits and vegetables. A small barn housed a goat kept for milk and chickens for eggs. Lizzie darned, mended, and handed down clothing from one child to another until it was too threadbare to be worn.[10] It was a Spartan existence, but the Rickenbachers were used to poverty and accepted hard work as the price of survival.

Momentous changes swept across the United States during the 1890s and early 1900s when Edd grew up. Urban growth engulfed a nation once dominated by farms and small towns. Edd belonged to a new breed of future American heroes raised in teeming cities where kids became streetwise at an early age.[11] In 1890, his natal year, Columbus had 88,150 inhabitants. Its population reached 125,560 in 1900 and 181,511 by 1910. It was a tough community. Washington Gladden, a pioneer of the Social Gospel, was appalled by conditions he found when he became pastor of its fashionable First Congregational Church in 1882. Public officials got drunk while sitting at their desks and joked about shootings in broad daylight. Newspapers "supported by blackmail" were "devoted to the vilification and assassination of the character of private persons." So many prostitutes roamed High Street at night that "decent women" could not walk unescorted. Gladden called Columbus "the worst governed of the cities of Ohio."[12]

It was also the capital of the Buckeye State, so the spoils of government, added to jobs created by industry, supported the local economy. A pall of soot and smoke from locomotives and manufacturing plants hung over the city in Edd's early life. Horse-drawn street railways created their own pungent variety of pollution. The Pennsylvania and the B&O were the major rail lines serving Columbus, but the Hocking Valley Railroad was scarcely less important because it provided a vital link to the Ohio River, bringing lumber, coal, and iron from forests, mines, and smelting plants in the southeast corner of the state. Hundreds of shops and factories made agricultural implements, fertilizers, bricks, window glass, paints and chemicals, hydraulic pumps, heating and ventilating apparatus, foundry products, ornamental iron, machinery, leather, shoes, furniture, woodenware, pipe organs—the list seemed almost endless. Breweries like the one where William worked when he married Lizzie made vast quantities of beer. The Jeffrey Manufacturing Company was a major producer of mining equipment. The Columbus

Machine Company, where Albert Rickenbacher was a timekeeper, made steam engines and occupied an entire block along Broad Street. The city's greatest industry, however, which would play a crucial role in Edd's future, was carriage manufacturing, utilizing wood, iron, and leather for bodies, fittings, dashboards, and tops. By the end of the century about one out of every six horse-drawn vehicles in the United States was made in Columbus, which proudly called itself the "Buggy Capital of the World."[13]

The recession that interrupted the growth of the Rickenbacher family in the late 1880s typified Columbus's vulnerability to fluctuations in the business cycle. In May 1893, less than three years after Edd's birth, a panic on Wall Street led to a long depression. William McKinley, who had been elected governor in 1892, repeatedly called out the National Guard to intervene in strikes.[14] The hard times, which lasted until 1897, intensified the poverty in which the Rickenbachers lived. Every member of the family had to contribute to its welfare as soon as they were old enough to help. Mary did housework and assisted her mother in raising the ever-growing brood. Edd and Bill gathered walnuts and scrounged for chunks of coal that fell from cars along railroad tracks to keep the family from freezing in the winter. Like many kids throughout the country, Edd hawked newspapers. When he was only five years old, he got up at four o'clock every morning and trudged two miles to the office of the *Columbus Dispatch* to get on the street before his competitors. He was already smoking and needed money to buy Bull Durham tobacco for cigarettes he rolled by hand. To finance his habit, he collected rags, bones, and rusty nails and sold them to a junk dealer named Sam. (Bones had market value because they could be made into fertilizer by treating them with sulfuric acid.) Noticing that bones he found weighed more when soaked in water, he swished them in mud puddles before selling them to Sam. Suspecting that Sam set his scales to short-weight him, Edd bought his own scales to guard against being cheated.

William was not religious, but Lizzie insisted on saying grace at meals and held evening devotions. It became a coveted privilege for one of the children to fetch the German Bible she had brought from Switzerland. She was particularly fond of the Twenty-third Psalm and paused to explain difficult words to make sure Edd and his siblings understood them. Afterward, the children knelt at their bedsides in the dark attic lofts and said the Lord's Prayer before going to sleep. Lizzie had them attend St. John's German Protestant Evangelical Church on East Mound Street every Sunday, dressed in the best clothes, shabby though they might be, that the family could provide. The church had been founded in 1872 by John Rickenbacher and a group of associates who were barred from other congregations because they belonged to groups with secret oaths and rituals.[15]

Edd and his siblings were christened at St. John's. His baptismal certificate, inscribed in German, is adorned with a depiction of Jesus as the Good Shepherd. Services were conducted in German until after 1897, when Jacob Pister, a new minister, began using English. Pister had a strong influence on Edd, who called him "one of the most forthright and inspiring individuals I have ever known." Perhaps even more inspirational to Edd at the time was Blanche Calhoun, a girl he met at Sunday school.

Growing up in the 1890s—a decade of increasingly strident nationalism—was partly responsible for the patriotic convictions Edd held throughout his life. A vigorous Americanization movement targeted immigrant schoolchildren in Columbus during his formative years, aimed at promoting love of country, loyalty to the flag, participation in public rites and rituals, and respect for traditional values.[16] Edd's parents preached the same message at home. However meager their income, they believed life in America was far preferable to the conditions they had known in Switzerland. To display his gratitude, William tried to enlist at a recruiting office located in a saloon after the outbreak of the Spanish-American War but was turned down because of his age and large number of dependents. Lizzie cried when he set out that morning and was enormously relieved when he came home still dressed in civilian clothes. The choice by the Rickenbachers of the name Dewey for the son born in June 1898, after Admiral George Dewey's victory at Manila Bay, was another sign of their love of country.

Nevertheless, they observed traditions they had brought from Switzerland. William spoke English outside the home, but the family spoke Swiss-Deutsch within it. Lizzie never lost a pronounced Germanic accent. Their diet relied heavily on potatoes from their yard, but she cooked Swiss delicacies, made grape and plum preserves, and administered rhubarb as a spring tonic. Despite their poverty she insisted on buying a Victrola for the parlor, nurturing Edd's abiding love of music.

Edd developed a compulsive need for attention, which was hard to get in a crowded home overrun with siblings. Being among neither the oldest nor the youngest children made it almost inevitable that he would be lost in the shuffle if he did not assert himself, and his parents were too busy making a precarious living to focus on him unless he did something unusual, mostly by misbehaving. His need to stand out aggravated William and Lizzie, and he reacted by getting into even more trouble. The penalty he paid—repeated thrashings by his father—was better than receiving no attention at all.

Proverbially, Germanic fathers treated their children, especially sons, with a heavy hand. This tradition contributed to a family system made up of a punitive father and a mother who comforted her rebellious son, who resented William's abusive behavior and never forgot the pain it caused. When William hit Edd, he hit him hard.[17]

Lizzie, remembering her own contrariness as a girl, probably realized where Edd came by his impulsive nature. Perhaps because she identified with him, she sought to compensate for his father's thrashings and the injuries he suffered in his many childhood accidents. A revealing incident occurred when Lizzie inadvertently hit him with a hoe and cut his head open while he was helping her plant potatoes. He recalled how she scooped him up, ran into the house, tenderly cleaned his scalp, bathed it with ointment, and rocked him gently until he felt better. He was remarkably accident-prone. He ran headlong into the path of a horse-drawn streetcar, fell into a hole and landed on his head, was knocked out in a fall from a tree, and got a foot caught in the tracks when he jumped off a railroad car. Any boy is likely to get hurt in scrapes, but the frequency of Edd's mishaps suggested that something more than bad luck or carelessness caused them.

His vulnerability intensified when he was about eleven years old. In September 1901, an anarchist assassinated President McKinley in Buffalo, New York. McKinley, who tried to identify with workers by favoring high protective tariffs and using slogans like "The Full Dinner Pail," was an idol in the Rickenbacher family. Edd was awed when he heard him speak in Columbus in 1900 during his second run for the White House. McKinley's death confronted Edd with his own mortality. Knowing he would ultimately die, life would continue without him, and he would miss out on "what was happening in the world and all of the wonderful things that would be coming," he took refuge in the barn and sobbed uncontrollably. Coming upon the scene, William tore into him with a switch, scorning him for entertaining morbid thoughts and promising the same treatment if he ever showed them again, predictably driving them deeper into his mind. From then on, Edd was more careful in hiding his fears, but without release they festered inside him.[18]

He also endured frequent humiliation, especially in having to attend school wearing a pair of mismatched shoes, one brown and square-toed, the other tan and pointed, that William had cobbled together. Edd's classmates taunted him unmercifully. They also laughed at the way he talked. Hearing only Swiss-Deutsch at home, he had a hard time speaking English, and his peers ridiculed him for his heavy accent, calling him "Dutchy" and "Kraut." William also mortified him by forcing him to apologize publicly for misdeeds. One time Edd played hooky to help find a lost dog. After whipping him soundly, William made him give an abject confession at school that he remembered with shame as an adult. He was also embarrassed by being short. Only in his late teens did he go through a growth spurt that transformed him into a tall, handsome man whose face became familiar to millions of Americans. Even then, he never forgot the shame of being a runt.

His brother Bill continually bullied him but Edd found a way to retaliate by becoming a master at playing marbles and beating him regularly at the game, offering no quarter and running away before Bill could take back the cat's-eyes and shooters that he lost. Following Bill's example, Edd became a bully to compensate for his feelings of inferiority. When he came home from France as a hero in 1919, Sarah Gifford, one of his former teachers, recalled that he had carried a perpetual chip on his shoulder and constantly got into fights. He hated books and sat in the last row in her classroom with a scowl on his face. Gifford said he enjoyed drawing and arithmetic but did badly in English and geography. He admitted that his conduct had been anything but exemplary.[19]

As he emerged from childhood, he began committing acts of petty vandalism, earning him more beatings from his father. He became the leader of a group of boys called the Horsehead Gang. One evening they pelted the streetlights lining East Livingston Avenue with stones, smashing them and incurring the wrath of the police, who came to the Rickenbacher home and issued a stern warning. When they left, William gave Edd an especially severe whipping, which, as usual, did no good. After he went to bed, Lizzie and William sat at the kitchen table, worrying that he would be sent to a reformatory and ultimately become a convict at the Ohio State Penitentiary. Lizzie cried when neighbors complained about his antics, making Edd feel guilty.

To some degree, Edd's behavior manifested a "boy culture" prevailing in America at the time. Gender roles were sharply polarized and pubescent males were called "sissies" by their peers if they did not meet demanding standards of masculinity, bear pain without flinching, suppress their emotions, defy parental authority, and be cruel to animals. "Crybaby" and "mama's boy" were dreaded epithets.[20] Such expectations must have caused Edd inner turmoil. Turning to his mother for comfort and feeling guilty about making her cry were not considered manly traits by his peers. His memories of boyhood were filled with incidents showing tenderness for goats, chickens, birds, and his pet dog, Trixie, who bit William "on several occasions" when he was administering punishment to Edd and had to be thrown out of the house thereafter to prevent him from defending his young master. Edd fed worms and bread crumbs to robins so often they would perch on his shoulder and eat from his hand. He created a burial plot in the backyard for baby birds that died from falling out of trees when their mothers were teaching them to fly. What if his friends knew about such "weaknesses"?

He also had artistic inclinations that would have made him all the more suspect to members of the Horsehead Gang had they known. Ironically, he did not want to become a warrior but to win recognition as a painter. He shared his ambitions with his mother and visited the municipal art gallery when he got a chance. Poverty prevented him from taking art lessons, but he learned the rudiments of pyrography, artistic woodburning. He indulged a passion for music by fixing a battered violin he bought for a few pennies and learning to play tunes on it.

Above all, he dreaded death—but he found that his obsession with it had a positive side because of the exhilaration he felt when he did something potentially lethal and came out alive. Escaping with nothing worse than a badly lacerated leg from the episode in the gravel pit and landing unscathed in a sand pile after trying to fly off the roof of a barn were early examples of a desire to tempt fate that would ultimately make him a hero. The results, however, would finally catch up with him, haunting him with questions about why God had repeatedly spared his life.

On 18 July 1904, a blazing hot Monday, William, working for a city contractor, was helping some fellow employees lay a cement sidewalk. At noon they sat down by the curb, opened their dinner pails, and ate lunch. While they were eating, an African American who had been laying sod in a nearby yard approached them, asking whether they had any food to share. William retorted angrily that he worked hard for his money and would give anything he had left in his pail to his wife and children. In a fight that followed, the stranger picked up a spirit level, a heavy tool used in laying pavement, and struck William twice, hitting him with such force that he broke his left arm between the elbow and the wrist and fractured his skull.[21]

William Gaines, the assailant, fled the scene but Thomas O'Neill, a detective, caught him in an alley in the northeast part of town. Gaines resisted arrest and tried to grab O'Neill's gun, after which O'Neill hit Gaines with a blackjack, threatened to "blow his brains out if he made further resistance," and summoned a paddy wagon that took him to the police station. Meanwhile, rescuers rushed Rickenbacher, who had been knocked unconscious by the blow to his head, to St. Francis Hospital. He regained consciousness later that day, but physicians held out no hope for his recovery. Roughly interrogated, Gaines pleaded his innocence, claimed he had no criminal intent, and blamed Rickenbacher for starting what had happened by following him across the street, cursing at him, and pulling a knife. Only at this point, and in self-defense, Gaines maintained, did he hit him on one of his arms and "across the back of his head" with "a piece from a fence." He claimed that he had not aimed the second blow at William's skull but at his body. He fled because he was afraid Rickenbacher's fellow workers would gang up on him and resisted arrest by O'Neill because he thought the detective was "one of them Dagoes." Protesting that he had never been in trouble before, he was held under heavy bail pending disposition of the case.[22]

Rickenbacher was reportedly "badly demented" throughout his hospitalization and could not tell his side of what had happened, but his constitution was so strong that he lived much longer than expected. He could eat and drink but momentary hope for his recovery faded as his condition steadily worsened. Concerned neighbors, knowing that Lizzie and her children had been made destitute by the incident, held benefit picnics "from which a large amount of money and many donations of clothing and supplies were derived." The Columbus Light Company provided free transportation to a "lawn fete and dance" at the city's Driving Park. As Edd's father continued to fight for his life, O'Neill swore out a warrant on 5 August charging Gaines with "assault to kill."[23]

William died at 2:00 a.m. on 26 August after lingering in a coma for five weeks. He fleetingly recognized Lizzie and the children before he passed away. A postmortem examination showed an abscessed brain. On 4 September a grand jury, after finding that Gaines "did unlawfully, purposely and maliciously kill William Rickenbacher," indicted him for manslaughter. On 27 October he was convicted and sentenced to ten years in the state penitentiary.[24]

That an African American found guilty of deliberately killing a white man was given only a ten-year sentence for manslaughter, instead of being condemned to death for murder, suggests that the jury, which took more than an hour to reach a verdict, may have given some credence to the story Gaines had told the police. If William's explosive temper was well enough known in Columbus, the jurors may have suspected he had struck Gaines first, or at least provoked him with curses and taunting. Gossip about the case, which newspapers covered in front-page stories, must have been hard for Lizzie to bear. That she and the children felt scandalized seems clear from the fictional account Edd later published in his autobiography about what had happened. His father, now described as a foreman and equipment chief of a company that built bridges in central Ohio, had been hit by a swinging timber while operating a pile driver. He could not admit that his father had been killed by an African American under circumstances sufficiently extenuating to get a black assailant off on a manslaughter charge with only ten years in prison. The episode was difficult enough for a boy to handle, but the burden of shame could only increase as he grew into a distinguished public figure.[25]

After being taken to a mortuary, William's corpse was brought to the little house on East Livingston Avenue. There, two days later, on a Sunday afternoon, Pister conducted a funeral at which Edd and his siblings wore dark clothing that Lizzie, despite the neighbors' earlier generosity, had gone into debt to buy. After the mourners had gone, she gathered the children around the casket to take a final look at their father and told them to watch out for each other's welfare in the future.

Edd could not sleep that night. Hearing a noise, he got up and went down the narrow staircase from his loft into the kitchen, where he found his mother sitting silently at the table holding her head in her hands. Trying to comfort her, he revealed the guilt he felt about complicating her life with his chronic misbehavior by promising he would never make her cry again. After they sat together for a while he suddenly realized— or so he later claimed—that he was sitting in William's chair. Lizzie had already noticed what he was doing but said nothing.

At daybreak, instead of going to school, Edd went looking for a job. By afternoon he found one at the Federal Glass Factory on South Parsons Avenue, where his brother Bill had once worked. He was so eager to take the offer that he did not ask how much the pay would be. From then on he never went back to school, violating Ohio's child labor laws by telling his employers that he had finished eighth grade (he was actually in seventh) and was fourteen years old (he was really thirteen). After agreeing to report for work at six o'clock that evening and spend twelve hours on the night shift, he ran home and presented Lizzie with a fait accompli. Surprised at what he had done, she argued that he should return to school, but he overcame her objections, pointing out that the family needed the money he could earn.

During the past five weeks, while his father was comatose, Edd must have done a lot of thinking about what would happen if the diagnosis that William's case was hopeless was correct. Edd was too intelligent not to realize that the beatings he had endured would end and his life would be dramatically changed. The speed and decisiveness with which he acted as soon as William was buried shows that he had conceived a plan to assume the role his father had played in the home. It is hard to believe he did not know what he was doing when he came down to the kitchen within hours after the burial and sat in William's chair, sending Lizzie a powerful message that he was taking his father's place. He had kept his intentions secret; the object, he realized, was to act first and only then seek his mother's permission. He was not the only sibling who pitched in to help her, but he did not intend to permit Bill or Emma, both of whom worked for a firm that made piano stools, to be the principal breadwinners.

His new job required that he take freshly blown glass tumblers to tempering ovens on a long-handled steel implement shaped like a platter. It was hot, heavy work that made his legs ache and his arms feel as if they would drop off. Somehow mustering the physical and mental stamina required to make it through the night shift despite having had little or no rest since William's funeral, he walked six or seven miles to get home and fell asleep over breakfast. For the next five nights he went through the same grueling stint at the factory, walking to and from work to save the nickel streetcar fare. But he reaped an incalculable reward when he got his first pay envelope, containing three one-dollar bills and a fifty-cent piece. He had never seen so much cash and was filled with self-satisfaction about having earned every cent of it. Lizzie was delighted when he gave her the money, making the toil abundantly worthwhile.

Truant officers came to the house to see why he was not attending school. Lizzie took them upstairs, where they found him asleep in his bed, dead to the world from exhaustion. She told them he had been working all night. Knowing that the family was destitute, they looked the other way and did nothing. Edd's energies, no longer channeled into self-destructive behavior, were now engaged in positive effort, doing wonders for his self-esteem. He became Lizzie's economic mainstay and won her undying gratitude. He had probably always been her favorite child because he was so much like her. If so, Bill must have known about her feelings and been aware of the role reversal that had taken place. Edd was no longer the black sheep of the family but king of the house.

Dropping out of school in the seventh grade was a fateful step but not a severe handicap. That Edd never earned a high school diploma, let alone a college degree, was common for a young man at the time. Public high schools had existed since 1821, but even New York City did not open one until the 1890s, and a majority of American youth avoided enrolling in them until the 1930s. Wilbur and Orville Wright were not high school graduates, nor was Henry Ford. Many people thought secondary education was undemocratic and needed only by members of a few professions. As high schools became increasingly widespread, daughters were more likely than sons to enroll because parents were less likely to depend on them for income than on able-bodied sons. The term "adolescence" was not coined until 1904, when psychologist G. Stanley Hall introduced it, and "teenager" was not yet a generic word for a transitional stage through which youngsters passed on their way to maturity. Males in their early teens were judged as individuals and treated as adults if they proved their ability to do grown-up jobs. Appreciation by successive employers of Edd's talents and drive put him on a career path that might not have been available at a later time, when higher educational levels became a prerequisite for more desirable jobs.[26]

Given prevailing customs, it is doubtful that going to high school or college would have prepared Edd as well for his future achievements as the wide range of on-the-job experience and skills he acquired. But his lack of formal education would become an enduring source of embarrassment, no matter how hard he tried to hide it. His inability to write polished prose was a particular handicap, forcing him to rely on ghost-writers whose contributions to books and articles that appeared under his name he refused to acknowledge. After becoming a powerful business executive and prominent public speaker, he had to interact with people who knew much more than he did about literature, history, philosophy, and other subjects, giving them a sophistication he lacked. He absorbed what he could through self-education, reading books about etiquette and taking lessons in elocution, but his slowness in reading and problems with writing bothered him more than he admitted. As a result he became defensive and dogmatic, concealing his feelings of cultural inferiority behind a crusty, abrasive, and overbearing manner. His arrogance was a defense mechanism.

Nevertheless, he matured almost overnight from a boy to a man. For a few years after his father's death he moved restlessly from one job to another, gaining skills as he went along and impressing employers with his work ethic and innate ability. At first, however, his efforts led only to a series of dead ends. He learned to blow glass into artistic creations that he proudly gave his mother, but he could not tolerate working for low pay on endless night shifts. He increased his earnings by becoming a molder with the Buckeye Steel Castings Company, but could not stand the foundry trade because it was dirty and messy, covering him with sand; a fastidiousness he displayed throughout his life was already apparent. He capped beer bottles at a brewery but the smell of hops sickened him. He made heels at a shoe factory but quit, perhaps because it reminded him of the mismatched footwear his father had forced him to wear. Meanwhile, he spent his spare time trying to invent a perpetual motion machine in a shed back of his home but eventually gave it up.

Still dreaming about becoming an artist, he became interested in sculpture and took a job at a monument works polishing marble. The mixture of water and sandstone he used chilled his hands and splattered him with goo, but he advanced to carving names and symbols and took pride in cutting a headstone Lizzie had ordered for William's (also Luise's) grave at Greenlawn Cemetery. He cut "FATHER" across the top and inscribed an emblem of his own design at the bottom. He also created a representation of a Bible with opened pages and a statuette of an angel, giving both to his mother. Although she was pleased with his workmanship, one day she came to the shop to tell the owner that Edd's lungs were suffering from inhaling dust, a necessary part of the stonecutting trade. He had developed a scratchy throat and a cough, which she could not help but overhear, that kept him awake at night. Because of her anxiety, Edd gave up the job despite an offer of a pay raise from $1.50 to $2.50 per day. It annoyed him that the proprietor could have been paying him the extra dollar all along, making it easier for him to quit, but he feared that leaving probably ended his hopes for becoming an artist.

The episode showed that Edd, like William before him, did not really run the household despite being its main source of money. Lizzie was still in charge, and he did anything he could to please her. Because of his earnings, it was no longer necessary to devote all the available space around the house to raising food, so he landscaped the property by hauling topsoil from a vacant lot, raising the ground between the street and the house, laying sod on the front yard, and surrounding it with a white picket fence. But his mother kept strict control of the purse strings and gave Edd an allowance of only twenty-five cents per week. He usually spent it on Sundays at Olentangy Park; after paying a nickel each way for streetcar fare, he still had enough to ride the Ferris wheel or roller coaster and buy a box of Cracker Jack.

Despite his reservations about quitting his job at the monument works, doing so gave him an opportunity to fulfill his formidable potential. A day after he abandoned the shop, as he walked downtown, he noticed a crowd gathering at the corner of Broad and High streets. As he got closer, he saw the first two-passenger Ford runabout ever to appear in Columbus. It was one of the most beautiful sights he had ever seen. A salesman was touting the vehicle's features, and Edd got up the nerve to ask him for a ride. After thinking things over, the man apparently decided that taking a boy for a spin would assure potential customers the car was safe enough for anybody to buy. Beckoning Edd to climb into the left-hand seat—in those days the steering wheel was still on the right—he set some levers behind the dash, turned on the ignition, ran to the front of the car, and spun the crank. After the engine caught, he hurried behind the wheel and they sped away at what Edd thought was at least ten miles an hour, a speed faster than anything he had experienced up to that time. He never forgot the thrill.

His elation lingered after he found a job at the Columbus maintenance shops of the Pennsylvania Railroad. His first task, cleaning out passenger cars, was more remunerative than the starting pay of $1.00 a day seemed to indicate; looking under the seat cushions and finding loose change doubled or tripled his income. A new assignment, serving as an apprentice machinist, eliminated the extra money but was much more challenging. Indeed, it became the gateway to his professional future. Being trained to operate a lathe introduced him to a new level of fulfillment in the art of cutting metal. Taking a slab of steel and transforming it into a polished object with a practical purpose satisfied his aesthetic instincts as nothing had done before. Besides teaching him how to make machine parts, the men he worked with encouraged him to spend his lunch hours carving canes and baseball bats he could sell for extra compensation.

Edd had discovered "Machine Beauty."[27] He realized that art and technology were closely connected. Had an accident not interrupted his progress, he might have become a tool and die maker, but a wheel fell off a handcar and the load pinned him against a machine, immobilizing him for a few weeks with a severely bruised and lacerated leg. Being bedridden gave him time to think about the relationship between the Ford runabout and the shapes and forms he had turned out on the lathe. Vivid memories of the sudden burst of power after the little auto's engine chugged to life impelled him toward an unforeseen goal. Gaining incremental expertise in all the jobs he had done, however onerous and distasteful they were, had led him to increased self-understanding. He now knew what he wanted to do. As soon as he could go outdoors, he looked for work—any type of work—involving cars. A phase of his life in which motor vehicles would for the first time make him famous was about to begin.

Chapter 2

— ☆ —

Ignition

Edd's search for employment, his first steps on the pathway to fame, took him to the Evans Garage at 140 East Chestnut Street. It was a small shop that repaired bicycles and strange-looking machines that were still called horseless carriages. It also made batteries and rented storage space to people who owned motor vehicles.[1] Peering through the window, Edd noticed several cars, among them a Waverley electric, which had batteries under the driver's seat, a tiller for steering, and a motor mounted on the rear axle. A Locomobile steam buggy had a boiler to provide power for two pistons in a high-pressure engine. The reciprocal motion of the pistons linked with a chain drive connected to the rear axle to move the buggy forward. A third car, a one-cylinder Packard, featured something that would open the door to Edd's future—an internal combustion gasoline engine.[2]

He was looking at the three evolutionary branches of the automobile. Each form of propulsion had merits, but public favor was already turning toward vehicles like the Packard. Electric cars were quiet and easy to drive but their batteries needed frequent recharging, so they were more widely used as taxicabs and short-distance automobiles than as touring cars. They were fine for wealthy people to drive to the opera but had no future for mass markets.[3] Steam-driven vehicles would survive longer than electrics. They, too, were quiet, but faster and more powerful. As Edd would learn, steamers could climb hills that brought other cars to a halt, slither through mud with ease, and accelerate quickly from a standing start to sixty miles per hour. With flash boilers, they could raise steam in two or three minutes. The pistons of gasoline engines had to make many more strokes before turning the wheels of a car than those of a steam engine. The sliding-lever throttles of steamers were easier to use than the gearshifts of gasoline-powered cars. But boilers had to be replenished with water after forty miles—sometimes even after twenty. Their speed tapered off as their water supply dwindled and the pressure declined. The speed of a gasoline-powered auto stayed constant as long as there was a drop of fuel in its tank.[4]

Gasoline-powered cars had many flaws, including polluting the air. At the time, however, this did not seem a serious drawback, given the far more pervasive stench of horse manure and urine in the streets. (The future problem of smog was not even a cloud on the horizon.) Cars with internal combustion engines were much more complicated than their rivals and required an elaborate infrastructure of gas stations, repair shops, and driving schools, but these needs increased their potency for economic growth. Their initial cost was less than that of steamers and their high fuel consumption was a minor consideration in a country where petroleum abounded and gasoline, previously a waste product, was cheap. "Once the gasoline engine had been refined beyond its initial crudity," a historian later stated, "the outcome of the competition was certain."[5]

Filled with excitement, Edd returned to the Evans Garage as soon as he had recovered fully from his injury and asked its owner, William E. Evans, for a job. He came at a good time because Evans ran the shop by himself and needed someone to watch over it while he was out of town. He was tired of working through weekends, holidays, and nights and liked the idea of hiring a helper, but when he learned that this scrawny boy was making $1.25 a day at the Pennsylvania Railroad's machine shops, he said 75¢ was as high as he could go. Edd eagerly accepted the pay cut. At this point he was not interested primarily in money but in learning as much as he could about automobiles. He would earn only $4.50 a week for ten, eleven, or even twelve hours of hard labor each day, but the knowledge he gained would be priceless.[6]

After Edd began working at the shop, Evans explained the mechanical features of the cars stored there, and his young assistant helped him make minor repairs. Edd was awed by the vehicles and could not keep his hands off them. Whenever Evans went on errands, he climbed behind a steering wheel and pretended he was speeding down a highway with the wind at his back and an open road ahead. At first he ran the cars back and forth only a few feet, but he was soon going as far as the confines of the facility permitted. During one of his adventures, while he enjoyed himself at the wheel of a Packard, the engine stopped abruptly because he had driven it too much without adding oil. Guessing that the piston had seized, he opened the crankcase and saw that the engine was dry. Desperate to fix it before Evans came back, he pried the piston loose with a crowbar, filled the crankcase with oil, closed the cover, cranked the engine to get the oil circulating, turned on the ignition, and felt a surge of relief when the motor roared to life. By the time Evans returned, he was innocently patching a bicycle tire. The engine was permanently damaged but Edd's guilt went undiscovered, as did an escapade in which he drove home in a Waverly while Evans was out of town, took his mother and friends for joyrides, and coaxed the car, whose batteries rapidly lost power, back to the garage. He recharged them before Evans returned, none the wiser about what had happened.[7]

Edd had learned his lesson and did not push his luck. Working diligently, he steadily increased his knowledge of automobiles but gradually became dissatisfied with fixing flats and doing repair jobs. He wanted to design and build cars and knew that Evans had no more to teach him. How could he get the knowledge he needed? Both his mother and his former teacher, Sarah Gifford, told him he was too old to go back to school. He soon learned that writing poorly worded letters to universities to ask about their offerings in automotive mechanics was a waste of time. When Gifford suggested that he take a mail-order course, he wrote to International Correspondence Schools (ICS) in Scranton, Pennsylvania, a notable product of the American self-help tradition.[8] He was glad to find that ICS had a mail-order course in mechanical engineering emphasizing automobiles and internal combustion engines. To his relief, the sixty-dollar cost could be paid in installments. The early going, however, was rough for the fifteen-year-old grade-school dropout, and he nearly quit.[9] ICS had high standards and the instructors who administered the course he took had mechanical engineering degrees from Cornell and Penn State.[10] Edd had never developed good study habits nor learned to think systematically. He had nobody to help him as he struggled with assignments and returned them to Scranton for evaluation. It was a lonely battle, but as he persisted, he realized he was learning in a way that had not been possible for him in a classroom, where his self-doubt often had negative consequences. An added benefit was that, after he learned something through his own reasoning ability, the knowledge generally stuck.

Even at this early stage, he discovered, gasoline-powered cars had complicated ignition, transmission, cooling, lubricating, and electrical systems, all with numerous components. An automotive technician had to understand how all of these systems and parts worked, not just singly but harmoniously with one another. He had to deal with a baffling array of chains, gears, pinions, cams, cones, shafts, rods, discs, joints, coils, bearings, valves, rings, bands, pins, springs, and switches. To a mechanic, they were the same as the letters of the alphabet were to a person learning to read.[11]

Mastering automotive technology forced Edd to memorize a mass of details. Timing the opening and closing of intake and exhaust valves was an intricate operation. Valve heads, whether flat or conical, had to be skillfully ground, seated, and adjusted to achieve good compression and quiet operation. Stems, lifters, and tappets (projections touched by cams to impart particular motions) came in numerous varieties, all of which Edd had to know. Almost every maker of gasoline-powered automobiles used a different system to coordinate the operations of flywheels, cams, and crankshafts in four-cylinder engines, the most common at the time. The configuration of crankshafts did not permit cylinders to fire in standard numerical order from the first (in front) to the fourth (nearest the driver) without producing a rocking motion. The firing order was usually 1, 3, 4, 2 or 1, 2, 4, 3. Understanding the dynamics of the process was more difficult with engines that had six cylinders, but these were rare, at least in the United States.

Learning thousands of details in his mail-order lessons required more intense study and mental discipline than he had ever imagined, but it had great potential rewards. Taking correspondence courses, combined with shop training, helped automotive pioneers like Frederick Duesenberg and Jesse Vincent acquire the practical knowledge needed for leadership in motor vehicle production and design. Outstanding men, including Frederick Winslow Taylor, had deliberately bypassed institutions of higher education to be trained in an atmosphere of "Iron, Fire, Sand, and Smoke." Of course, one could learn about automobiles at universities or institutes of technology if they stressed practical aspects of mechanical engineering in addition to their more theoretical approach, but in the early twentieth century it was still common with hands-on training to achieve the status of professional engineer. The American Society of Mechanical Engineers (ASME), founded in 1880, had elected presidents from nonacademic backgrounds for more than three decades. Exponents of "shop culture" training claimed it produced engineers more creative than those from the more narrowly focused and specialized university curricula.[12]

Cultural conditioning has too long associated intellect with verbal ability. Despite his lack of language skills, Edd displayed great intelligence in mastering a formidable body of technological knowledge. Abstracting and internalizing information about mechanical sequences, gear ratios, geometrical relationships, and relative motion require what a later analyst called "logical-mathematical intelligence," a form of thought related to "confrontation with the world of objects."[13] The artistic side of Edd's personality was also an asset in automotive studies. Great engine designers like Harry Miller were artist-engineers who depended heavily on intuition and aesthetic perception.[14]

As he studied his lessons, Edd came to realize even more that he needed better shop training than Evans could give him. Fortunately, he was in a good place to get it because Columbus played an important role in the early American automobile industry. Between 1895 and 1923 at least forty makes of motor vehicles were produced in the city, ranging from single prototypes that were never manufactured commercially to a few cars marketed in large quantities.[15]

A small but high-quality enterprise made automobiles in a plant on the corner of Gay and Fourth streets, near the Evans Garage. Its principal owner, Oscar Lear, had formerly sold typewriters and bicycles. In 1901, however, he created an experimental car with an air-cooled engine. Lee A. Frayer and William J. Miller, also from Columbus, began to design air-cooled engines in the next year. In 1903 Lear, Frayer, and Miller created the Buckeye Motor Company and began designing an engine combining the best features of their respective power plants. Reorganizing as the Oscar Lear Automobile Company, they made a four-cylinder touring car, the Frayer-Miller, selling for $2,500. The performance of the vehicle in the hot summer of 1905 encouraged the partners to begin building the first American six-cylinder automobile. From then on they made both fours and sixes in air-cooled and water-cooled models. "We manufacture the largest air-cooled engine in the world," they claimed, "and challenge comparison with any water-cooled car for efficiency, economy and reliability."[16]

The company's unassuming three-story building stood on a lot measuring only 50 by 100 feet. Despite its modest size, it did not merely assemble components built by suppliers; it made cars from scratch. Edd later recalled that the only components not made in the shop were the rubber tires. The output was about one car per week. Starting in the spring of 1906, he visited the shop whenever possible. Because the only

IGNITION

25

time he did not work for Evans was on holidays, evenings, and Sundays, he quit going to church to hang around the plant, but could not get a job.[17]

Frayer was particularly impressive, being not only chief engineer and engine designer of the firm but also an automobile racer. Born in 1874, he had enrolled at Ohio State University in 1892 and graduated with a mechanical engineering degree in 1896.[18] Like Edd, he craved excitement, which soon led him to start making high-performance cars. In July 1905 he entered a stripped-down Frayer-Miller in a twenty-four-hour marathon at the Columbus Driving Park and went 110 miles before getting a flat tire. The car averaged more than 45 miles per hour on the track, but was badly damaged when Frayer tried to avoid hitting a wrecked vehicle, forcing him out of the race.[19]

Frayer noticed that Edd was always around the shop and called him into his office during one of his Sunday visits, asking him in a kindly way to identify himself and explain what he wanted. Edd brashly said he had already picked out a job that needed to be done, whether or not Frayer was aware of it, and he would return the next morning. With his fastidious eye, he had noticed that the shop needed a good cleaning. Metal and wood shavings covered the workbenches, floor, and machinery. The next morning, without bothering to submit his resignation to Evans, he went to the Oscar Lear plant, arriving at seven o'clock. Grabbing a broom and a brush, he worked furiously to clean up the machine shop on the first floor. Deliberately leaving part of the floor covered with dirt, he cleaned another section as carefully as possible. By the time Frayer arrived, Edd had swept away a large amount of the grime. Amazed at the difference, Frayer told Edd to keep on working. He had his job.[20]

Edd grabbed the offer without asking what he would be paid or what sort of work he would do. He not only obeyed Frayer's every command but also brought his ICS course to work, poring over it at lunch. After he had been on the job for a week or ten days, Frayer, who had been watching him intently, asked to see the lesson he was studying. The workbook was full of diagrams showing how engines worked. Frayer read it intently, saying nothing, but soon gave Edd new duties to match his interests. From then on the young apprentice learned to operate drill presses, lathes, shapers, and grinders and took part in building carburetors, steering gears, axles, transmissions, and ignition systems.[21]

At the time, Henry Ford was merely glimpsing the possibilities of the moving assembly line. The Oscar Lear Company, like all automobile manufacturers, built a car in one spot, bringing parts to it as the process continued. Pursuing the sequence of operations Frayer assigned him, Edd learned how to build a car from the floor up, starting with the front and rear axles and mounting the springs. As Edd had learned from ICS, the components of a car were all systems within systems.[22]

Learning to assemble a car this way gave Edd a far different type of experience from that of later assembly-line workers who robotically performed only one task. He had entered the industry at a time when a worker could still understand a motor vehicle in an intimate, holistic way. Early in his employment with the Oscar Lear Company, he devised a hardwood jig that facilitated drilling multiple holes simultaneously in an airblower component instead of one at a time, increasing productivity and saving money. Working on an assembly line would have thwarted such initiative.[23]

No matter how small or how large, each part had to be made with painstaking care. Edd learned the art of forging engine bearings, starting with making a scraping tool from a file that he ground down to a sharp point, dipped in cyanide, hardened, and honed on an emery wheel. Finding an alloy suitable for bearings, one that could withstand the pressure of a piston hitting like a hammer on the bearing and crankshaft, plagued automotive engineers at the time. Like other firms, the Oscar Lear Company made bearings out of Babbit metal, an alloy of tin, lead, copper, and antimony that had a relatively high coefficient of friction but burned out rapidly under heavy use. Sometimes bearings failed within twenty-five or thirty miles. After becoming a roving troubleshooter for a company that sold cars in western states, where roads were practically nonexistent, Edd learned to take a pocketful of bearings with him on all his service trips. "I'd carry a can of Mobil oil with me or half a dozen cans depending on the length of the trip," he said, "and extra bearings and a bunch of waste." Whenever a bearing failed, he would "take the top of the crankcase off, swab out all of the bearing lead that had been thrown around inside there, clean it out and rinse it out with a little gasoline." After installing a new bearing he would dump a can of oil into the engine and be on his way.[24]

Persons who achieve a rare and elusive quality called "mastery" often mention the benefit of "having a teacher or mentor—a role model who offers invaluable experience, support, inspiration, and guidance."[25] Frayer was the first in a series of mentors who influenced Edd. His combination of university training and shop orientation provided an ideal foundation for Edd's steady progress. If he was not yet a master, he had gained by the time he was sixteen what a student of human achievement later called "competence"—not a sufficient cause of high achievement but a threshold that has to be crossed before greater attainments can occur.[26]

After scrutinizing Edd's performance and seeing his urge to excel, Frayer opened two doors for him. One morning, after Edd had run the gamut of mechanical operations, Frayer electrified him by saying he wanted him to join the engineering department. The company had only a few engineers, whose work was much different from the lower-level tasks he had been doing. They were designers who set the standards and specifications for every car bearing the Frayer-Miller marque. Had this door been the only one Frayer opened, Edd might have become a leading automotive designer or inventor-engineer, but part of his nature would not have been fulfilled by such a career. During the months in which Edd learned the essentials of automotive technology, Frayer was supervising the building of three race cars to compete in the 1906 Vanderbilt Cup Race on Long Island. One fateful day, Frayer asked Edd if he would like to go along with the crew of drivers and mechanics that was about to depart for the event. Frayer wanted to know how fast he could go home, grab some traveling necessities, and return. Edd replied that an hour would be ample. Sprinting all the way to East Livingston Avenue, he stuffed some clothes into a duffel bag that had belonged to his father and ran back to the shop.[27]

And he never slowed down.

Edd was entering a field of mass entertainment that was just beginning to sweep the country. Automobile racing typified the spirit, values, and aspirations of a new age because it embodied the irresistible force of speed. Motor vehicles captured the hearts and minds of people in France, Germany, Great Britain, Italy, and the United States because of their capacity to annihilate distance. By 1906, only two decades after Karl Benz contrived his first gasoline buggy, European cars could go 200 kilometers (124 miles) per hour. According to a French novelist, they had made the human mind an "endless racetrack," a perpetual motion machine. "Everywhere life is rushing insanely like a cavalry charge, and it vanishes cinematographically like trees and silhouettes along a road. Everything around man jumps, dances, gallops in a movement out of phase with his own."[28] Ohio was no different.

The French writer's use of analogies based on horses and horsemanship emphasized the suddenness with which automobiles were taking the place of equines. The railroad, appropriately called the "iron horse," was the first means of ground transportation to transform Western standards of acceleration and rapidity. By the late nineteenth century, express trains roaring though Columbus could travel, under ideal conditions, at more than 100 miles per hour.[29] Railroads, however, forced travelers to conform to rigid schedules. There was a vast potential market for vehicles that could give people freedom to go rapidly wherever and whenever they pleased. At the time, some were not sure how desirable such liberty might be, but individuals captivated by the lure of speed—people like Frayer and Edd—had no doubts.

Bicycles, first mass-produced in the 1880s, gave the first glimpse of the freedom automobile enthusiasts craved. Early bicycles had huge front wheels affording only a precarious perch, leading to dangerous spills, and their hard rubber tires gave enthusiasts a bone-shaking ride. The "safety bicycle," with pneumatic tires and wheels of the same diameter, propelled by a chain and sprocket drive, provided a welcome change in the 1880s. Variable-gear systems mounted on the rear axle facilitated easier pedaling on steep grades. Smaller steel-tube frames put riders close to the ground and gave a more comfortable ride. A bicycle mania swept over the Western world. Lightweight tubing, ball bearings, coaster brakes, improved gear systems, a wealth of accessories, and declining prices came with improved production techniques and attracted droves of consumers in the 1890s. In December 1892 two young men, Wilbur and Orville Wright, rented a storefront in Dayton, Ohio, and developed a lucrative bicycle business despite fierce competition from thirteen other shops. Intrigued by the prospect of human flight, and using some of the same parts found in bicycles, they soon invented the aeroplane, a machine that would powerfully affect Edd's life.[30]

New sporting events capitalizing on the mania for speed provided a popular alternative to horse racing. Many early idols of motor sport began their careers as bicycle racers. Barney Oldfield, whose name became synonymous with speed and against whom Edd later competed, was a case in point. One bicyclist outraced a famous thoroughbred horse by going a mile in one minute, thirty-five seconds.[31]

Bicycles also spawned steam-powered motorcycles, which first appeared in 1869 and had internal combustion engines by 1884. Hot-tube and electrical ignition systems, clutch gears, mechanically operated valves, and other refinements led to increasingly powerful and versatile models by the turn of the twentieth century. Indian, the first great American marque, appeared in 1901, followed by Curtiss in 1902 and Harley-Davidson in 1903. Motorcycle racing on treacherous board tracks, made slippery by leaking oil and grease, became a spectator sport with factory teams and national championships.[32]

Edd was fascinated by bicycles and motorcycles but, through Frayer's influence, gravitated toward automobile racing, which had become widely popular in Europe and America in the 1890s. The sport had broad appeal in the United States, where democratic institutions and values eroded the early identification of motor vehicles with the upper class. As cars became faster and more powerful, fans flocked to speedways to see stars like Oldfield defy danger in arenas where competition was merciless and the prospect of sudden death haunted every turn. In the years before World War I, cars were faster than aeroplanes. The world speed record of 228 kilometers per hour set by Bob Burman at Daytona Beach in 1911, driving a bullet-nosed German racer, the Blitzen Benz, was appreciably better than the mark of 203.85 kilometers per hour French driver Maurice Prevost had posted two years earlier in a streamlined Deperdussin monoplane.[33]

France, which made the finest cars and had the world's best road system, staged the first automobile race in 1895, an endurance contest between Paris and Bordeaux. Italy, a hotbed of futurism, followed quickly with a fifty-eight-mile race between Turin and Asti, but the United States was not far behind. Publishers of newspapers and magazines saw that motor sport made good copy. H. H. Kohlstaat, owner of the *Chicago Times-Herald,* organized the first American auto race between the Windy City and Evanston, Illinois, held on 28 November 1895. Frank Duryea drove nearly nine hours through snow and ice to win the event in a gasoline-powered car he and his brother Charles had built in Springfield, Massachusetts. In 1896 the world's first closed-track automobile race took place at the Rhode Island State Fair. Fifty thousand people saw it, demonstrating that motor sport had mass appeal.[34]

France continued to dominate auto racing, but Americans including William K. (Willie) Vanderbilt, Cornelius Vanderbilt's great grandson, were eager to seize the spotlight for the United States. Willie Vanderbilt epitomized wealthy sportsmen who dominated the early years of American automotive competition. In 1901, at Newport, Rhode Island, famous for its upper-class éclat, he drove a Mercedes ten miles in fifteen minutes. In 1902, driving a Mors, he participated in a road race between Paris and Vienna. In the Circuit des Ardennes, involving six laps on a fifty-three-mile closed course near Bastogne, he finished third, marking the first time an American had placed that high in European competition. In January 1904 he set a record in the United States by driving a mile in thirty-nine seconds.[35]

Without exception, Vanderbilt's cars were made in Europe. The Mercedes was German and the Mors was French. Despite Duryea's victory at Chicago in 1895, American-made automobiles were not ready for prime competition in international motor sport. Wanting to change the situation, Willie decided to create a premier American event by establishing the Vanderbilt Cup Races, to be held every year on Long Island. "I felt the United States was far behind other nations in the automotive industry," he said, "and I wanted the country to catch up. I wanted to bring foreign drivers and their cars over here in the hope that America would wake up." The winner would receive a sterling silver goblet and $10,000 in cash.[36]

Edd knew that the Vanderbilt Cup races were the most prestigious events in American motor sport. The first one had taken place on 8 October 1904 on a tortuous thirty-lap, twenty-four-mile course in Nassau County and the borough of Queens, drawing contestants from England, France, Germany, and the United States. Fifty thousand spectators lined a route full of pot holes, beginning at Westbury Station and bounded by Mineola, Queens, Hempstead, and Hicksville. The event abounded in dangerous incidents that delighted spectators who wanted to see blood and gore. One car crashed on the first lap; others went out with cracked cylinders, twisted drive shafts, ignition problems, and similar mechanical maladies. The race became a two-way contest between George Heath, an American-born driver who ran a haberdashery in Paris, and Albert Clement, a nineteen-year-old Frenchman crouched behind the wheel of a Clement-Bayard Gladiator. Heath, driving a Panhard, won by less than a minute and a half and was lionized by patriotic American admirers who hailed him as "six feet two of magnificent manhood."

The second Vanderbilt Cup race, held on Long Island in 1905, attracted 100,000 spectators, double the number attending the year before. Drivers had to dodge spectators who swarmed onto the road, disregarding mortal danger. After several near-fatal accidents, only eight of the nineteen vehicles that had entered the race were left on the course when Victor Hemery of France won the event at the wheel of a Darracq. Americans rejoiced that a fellow citizen, Joe Tracy, finished third in a Locomobile, the best showing yet for the United States.[37]

Although fully aware of the hazards evident in the first two Vander-bilt races, Edd was overjoyed in 1906 when Frayer invited him to go to the third. The Frayer-Miller Racing Team took three high-performance race cars to Long Island, built under the constant scrutiny of Frayer, who had designed and tested them at a cost of at least $50,000. Naked in their lack of adornment—all they had besides their wheels and frames were bucket seats (with no seat belts) and engines—they epitomized the functionality of modern art. Ike Howard, the firm's mechanical genius, was prominent in the entourage.

Edd's previous life had been bounded by a circle surrounding Co-lumbus with a radius of only a few miles. Nevertheless, as he looked out the windows of the speeding train, the upcoming race was all he could think about. He hardly slept the night after Frayer's team arrived in New York City, went to Long Island by car, and checked in at lodgings amid what was then a rural area. Early the next morning, Frayer handed Edd a leather helmet and a pair of goggles, saying he wanted him as his riding mechanic. He was so dumbfounded that he had to ask Frayer twice before believing him.[38]

Nothing could have pleased Edd more than to be engaged in the most dangerous sport on earth, one even more likely than bullfighting to result in death or serious injury. Safety devices later used to protect drivers did not exist. Racers wore "simple cloth helmets" and protected their faces "from flying gravel and dirt by goggles and cloth masks." Seats were purposely made tight to keep occupants from falling out. Riding mechanics, who sat beside the driver, had the most hazardous job of all. Unlike drivers, they could not brace themselves with the steer-ing wheel if a car went out of control. Indeed, in some race cars a riding mechanic could not sit at all but merely clung to a strap behind the driver's seat, on the right-hand side of the vehicle, and braced his left foot on a projecting piece of metal. In Frayer's racer, Edd sat in a bucket seat, with handles on either side. Like other riding mechanics, however, he stood a good chance of being thrown into the air and killed in a seri-ous accident.

Riding mechanics had arduous duties. Before a race they worked practically around the clock, oiling components and checking connec-tions. At the starting line it was their responsibility to crank the engine. During the heat of a contest, because gravity-feed fuel supply and splash lubrication systems were highly unreliable, their principal duty was to keep gasoline and oil flowing to the engine. Closely monitoring gauges on the dashboard, they vigorously manned bicycle-type air pumps and plungers to maintain fuel and oil pressure when necessary. They also kept an eye out for excessive abrasion and wear on the tires, which were notoriously undependable in the early days of motor sport. Using hand signals, they constantly kept the driver aware of what was happening behind him, especially if another car was about to pass. They had to be ready in an instant for any emergency. If there were blowouts, riding mechanics helped drivers change tires. One of the few detailed accounts of their activities called them the "forgotten heroes of the speedways," saying that they "had to be fearless and possess the overwhelming passion to compete." Because of the degree of bonding required of a driver and his racing mechanic, Frayer was paying Edd an extremely high compliment.[39]

Everything went smoothly on their first trial run. Edd felt the stinging wind hit his face as he monitored gauges and kept an eye on the rear tires, the ones most likely to blow when a car went to seventy miles an hour and hurtled around curves. The second day did not go as well. Frayer entered a sharp curve at such high speed that even a person with Edd's lack of experience could tell he was going too fast. Frayer had the brake pedal jammed down as far as it would go, but the brakes simply gave out. Frayer yelled for Edd to hold on as the car went off the road, plunged into a ditch, climbed out the other side, and headed for an unavoidable sand dune. As the wheels ground into the sand, the car stopped so abruptly that Frayer and Edd were hurled into the air. They escaped with scratches and bruises but no broken bones, and the car was only slightly damaged. After it was towed in, Howard and the pit crew prepared it for another run.

On the next day Frayer successfully rounded the same curve that had been his nemesis the day before. Frayer gunned the engine as he came out, and Edd later estimated their speed at sixty-five to seventy miles per hour, "which was going to beat hell at that time." Elated at beating the curve, they were unaware that a flock of guinea hens was crossing the road directly ahead at just that moment. Amid a flurry of feathers the car collided with the birds, one of which was sucked into the blower. Frayer had not put a screen over the opening in front of the fan and the fowl were torn to pieces. The blower was seriously damaged and the cylinders overheated as the car limped back to its starting place. Howard and the pit crew could tell by the odor that it was near before it came in view. Edd recalled that the engine was festooned with remnants of the hens, requiring a major clean-up.[40]

Howard and his crew once more restored the car to operating condition and readied it for a final qualifying trial that would determine whether Frayer could take part in the cup race. Twelve American vehicles entered, including the three that Frayer and his team had brought from Columbus, but only five could compete in the final event. Edd never forgot the excitement that morning as drivers and mechanics anxiously awaited their turns. Fred Wagner, the official starter of the American Automobile Association, sent them roaring off at thirty-second intervals. Cars from England, France, Germany, Italy, and the United States approached the line, all with drivers and mechanics nervously hoping to make fast getaways. American vehicles included a chain-driven Locomobile and a big Pope-Toledo steamer. The European entries were a Darracq, a Fiat, a Mercedes, a Panhard, and a De Dietrich.[41]

The qualifying runs began as early as possible to avoid the midday heat and protect the highly vulnerable tires. Edd later recalled how poorly tires were made at the time and said getting twenty or thirty miles of wear and tear from them was nearly miraculous, so Frayer's car carried two spares. If Edd noticed that a tire was in dangerous condition, he would give Frayer two taps on the shoulder, as they had drilled for such a contingency. When Frayer's turn to start finally came, Wagner waved his flag and the car sped down the road. Everything went well until the right rear tire blew out as Frayer rounded a curve at too high a speed for its fabric to withstand. The car fishtailed as Frayer, going sixty miles an hour, fought desperately to maintain control. He managed to keep it from veering into some trees and brought it to a stop. After he and Edd had changed the tire, they headed back down the road but went only a short distance before Edd saw that the needle in the temperature gauge was entering the red zone—a sign the engine was overheating. Pumping oil furiously did not correct the problem. Suddenly the engine started to knock, softly at first but with an increasingly ominous sound. As the car slowed down, a big Locomobile came up in back, threatening to crowd it off the road. Edd signaled its approach to Frayer by tapping him on his left knee. Nodding, Frayer allowed the powerful vehicle to pass with a thunderous roar but kept moving ahead until the pounding in the engine became so insistent that he knew one of the pistons was ready to seize. Sighing, he took his foot off the accelerator, disengaged the clutch, turned off the ignition switch, coasted off the road, and sat silently at the wheel for what seemed like an eternity. Finally, he uttered only two words that Edd remembered for the rest of his life. "We're through," was all he said. Edd later realized what Frayer was telling him: give whatever you do everything you have and play to win, but take it like a man and do not cry if you lose.[42]

Only one member of the Frayer-Miller team survived the run and competed for the cup, but he went out with a broken crankshaft in the seventh lap. The race was most memorable for the enormous throng that saw it and the casualties it caused. About 250,000 spectators lined the 29.7-mile course, which was laid out north of the previous ones to reduce the number of dangerous curves. Officials put bales of hay in particularly perilous spots where cars were likely to spin off the road, and banners warned about obstacles that might trap unwary drivers.

The number of mechanical breakdowns was remarkably low but the spectators were less fortunate. The promoters had not expected such a huge number of fans, many of whom would not stay off the road despite the risks they were taking. Sixteen policemen per mile had been stationed along the course but failed to control the crowd. An eccentric spectator, dressed in a Civil War uniform, stepped onto the road after each car had passed and shook his fist, challenging the next to hurry up. He had enough sense to stay out of the way of oncoming vehicles, but other people did not and paid the price for their recklessness. A man who walked in front of an oncoming Hotchkiss was struck, flew through the air, and landed dead at the feet of some terrified women. Two youngsters survived being hit by a Locomobile and a Fiat, but the casualty toll was high. A headline in the *New York Herald* reported "Many Marvellous Escapes." Louis Wagner, a French driver who won the race by pushing his Darracq to an average speed of 61.43 miles per hour, was astonished that "hundreds were not killed."[43]

The dangers inherent in automobile racing, both for drivers and spectators, produced an inevitable backlash. Newspapers across the country denounced the sport not only because of its potential for carnage but also because the rich sportsmen sponsoring races seemed indifferent to the public welfare. Stung by the criticism, Vanderbilt called off the cup race that had been planned for 1907, but the series resumed the following year amid assurances that crowds would be controlled. Under new rules, the Locomobile that had lost in 1906, now using French-made Michelin tires, won in 1908. The victory caused rejoicing in American trade journals, but later cup races continued to be plagued by accidents that killed both participants and spectators. The 1910 event, in which four persons were killed outright and at least half a dozen others were fatally injured, provoked widespread condemnation. Only ten cars remained on the course when British driver Harry Grant set a speed record in his second straight triumph. The crowd that witnessed his victory was so numbed by disasters that "not a cheer burst from the packed grandstand as his winning car thundered over the line."

Vanderbilt, whose grandfather had become infamous by allegedly saying "the public be damned," compounded national outrage by announcing that the tragic spectacle that had just unfolded would not interfere with the running of a race for an International Grand Prix soon to be held on Long Island. His insensitivity produced a mounting chorus of demands that motor sport be banned as "a criminal encouragement of indifference to human safety."[44]

Edd was unfazed by the brouhaha. The thrill of being surrounded by powerful cars and famous drivers at the 1906 race never left him. He could not wait to return to the track and revel in its risks. Four years would pass before he did so, but he would be ready when the time came.

Soon after Frayer returned to Ohio from the Vanderbilt Cup fiasco he made an important career move by becoming chief designer and engineer for the Columbus Buggy Company. Taking Edd along, he gave him a significant boost in professional status by naming him chief testing engineer of a major firm.

Despite its quaint name, the Buggy Company was an important outpost of the early automobile industry.[45] For nearly four decades after 1875, it ranked among America's premier manufacturers of horse-drawn carriages. Starting from humble beginnings before the Civil War as an offshoot of a tannery that became Ohio's first leather trunk factory, it pioneered in the use of standardized parts under the leadership of Clinton DeWitt Firestone, a local entrepreneur who invested $5,000 to help it get through the 1870s when the national economy plummeted. Using convict labor to make carriage parts, it thrived by doing "one class of work in large quantities, and at a price as low as the high quality will warrant." By 1882 it was making 25,000 buggies a year, turning out a finished product "every eight minutes during a ten hour work day." Its plant covered an entire city block and had five buildings, one of which was eight stories high. Like other manufacturers that achieved high output producing bicycles, typewriters, firearms, and sewing machines, Firestone and his business associates pioneered what became known as "mass production" and were among its creators. Harvey Firestone, a sales representative related to the Columbus clan, went into the tire business in the 1890s and may have given a close friend, Henry Ford, some of the ideas his Ohio relatives had developed. Surviving temporary bankruptcy in the depression-wracked decade, the Buggy Company weathered receivership, acquired a New Jersey corporate charter, and entered the twentieth century ready to play a leading role in the motor age. In 1902 it began making an electric automobile and built a new "Model Factory" whose three buildings, each 320 feet long, 100 feet wide, and four stories high, had ten acres of floor space. The owners boasted that the facility, which employed 600 men and had a payroll of $3 million per year, was "the finest equipped and largest carriage plant making high-grade work, known."

In 1906, continuing to make electric cars, the company diversified by introducing gasoline-powered automobiles and launching a big sales campaign. For its initial foray into an unfamiliar market, it took the simple expedient of mating an internal combustion engine with one of its existing horse-drawn carriages, resulting in a product that made business sense by permitting the company's standardized buggy parts to work equally well in a motorized vehicle. It had extremely high wheels with solid rubber tires and wooden spokes and a tiller for steering. It looked antiquated but was well suited for a conservative clientele that wanted to make a gradual transition from an equine age to a horseless future. Although it was a hybrid instead of a true automobile, the company made the best of its virtues by advertising it as "The Car for the Masses," a slogan on which Ford's motto, "The Great Car for the Masses," may have been based.

The Buggy Company's owners knew that the ungainly high-wheeler was not a long-range answer to their desire to make a gasoline-powered car worthy of the name. Needing an engineer who knew how to design and build one, they hired Frayer to create an up-to-date vehicle comparable with the ones he had made for Oscar Lear. Edd was delighted to go to the Buggy Company with Frayer, his mentor and by now his surrogate father. "I would have gone with him as a water boy," he recalled, but "it turned out he had more ambitious plans for me." Frayer showed his confidence in Edd by putting him in charge of the testing department, which had a dozen or so men who were older and more experienced. "As the design for each particular item was finished," Edd stated, "I would take it and make a one-dimensional drawing so that a machinist could reproduce the object in metal. My early interest in art paid off handsomely." His salary, twenty dollars per week, was much more than he had ever made before.[46] In two years he had vaulted from doing odd jobs in the Evans garage to heading an important unit in a big outfit doing standardized high-volume manufacturing. A photograph showed him standing proudly, his arms folded across his waist, amid a group of obviously older men under his command. It was clear who was in charge.

The most enjoyable role Edd assumed in his new position was that of chief test driver, which gave him many opportunities to indulge his zest for danger. Driving the high-wheeler all over town and into the surrounding countryside, he tested a new braking system he and Frayer had contrived. He once took a nasty spill when the brakes failed after he went "lickety-split down a steep hill." The motor buggy overturned while rounding a curve, tossing him into the air and onto the ground. Not seriously hurt, he got up and walked away. Neither this incident nor the unsuitability of a high-wheeled carriage for fast driving stopped him from testing the car more and more rapidly on curves until he "finally reached a speed that would pull a wheel right off." The instincts that would make him a champion racer were clearly evident.

He combined the artistic and intuitive side of his nature with the analytical skills he had learned from correspondence courses and working under Frayer. He had a knack for sensing what was wrong with a malfunctioning engine merely by listening for a strange vibration or a telltale sputter. This talent unexpectedly prepared him for a new role in the company, that of a roving troubleshooter, which satisfied his restlessness better than a more anchored position as head of the testing department. The opportunity arose because Clinton Firestone enjoyed driving one of the high-wheelers from his turreted Victorian mansion on East Broad Street to the Buggy Company's factory by way of a road leading across the spillway of a dam on the Scioto River. One day, summoning Rickenbacher to his office, Frayer told him Firestone had had a mechanical breakdown and needed help. Dropping everything, Edd hurried to the damsite where Firestone was stranded and confidently said he had been sent to solve the problem. The thought that his youth might make a bad impression on Firestone never entered his mind. Flabbergasted that Frayer had sent a stripling to his rescue, Firestone gravely looked up and down at the scrawny teenager standing before him and said he had sent for a full-grown man. Maintaining his poise, Edd took hold of the crank, spun it around, listened to the engine cough and die, and realized that no compression stroke was taking place. Knowing that a lock-

and-spring mechanism governing the intake valve must be out of order, he reached into one of his pockets, took out the replacement parts he needed, installed them, cranked the engine, and had the car running in less than five minutes. Speechless with amazement, Firestone drove off without saying a word. Later that day, however, Frayer told Edd that Firestone thought he was "the seventh wonder of the world." From then on, Firestone looked for the young man whenever he came to the factory and boasted to friends about having his own version of Tom Swift on his payroll. When problems occurred demonstrating the high-wheeled motor buggies in an automobile show in Atlantic City, Firestone dispatched Edd to see what was wrong.

The boy who had suddenly become a man crossed a new threshold. Frayer had become his mentor, but now he had something even more important, a patron. Firestone was the first of many persons to play this role in his life. After arriving in Atlantic City, he quickly diagnosed the problem plaguing the high-wheelers and made an ingenious fix, buying a part from a junk dealer and using it to modify the car's clutch. His creativity made such an impression on visitors to the show that his picture appeared for the first time in a newspaper, making him so proud that he bought a dozen copies to take back to Columbus. Soon he reached another career benchmark when the Buggy Company adopted his new idea as a standard feature and began making thousands of the parts, sending them free to customers for emergency use. He had introduced what historians of technology would later call an innovation.[47]

He consulted frequently with Frayer about the new car he was developing. Possibly because of the debacle at the Vanderbilt Cup Race, Frayer had decided to use a Northway production engine instead of designing a new motor from scratch, but closely supervised the assembly of parts that arrived from the factory. Testing the Northway power plant, Edd learned its intricacies so well that he could tear it apart and reassemble it blindfolded, increasing his ability to diagnose problems in seconds.

After being exhaustively tested, the new car, named the Firestone-Columbus, was ready to debut at the 1909 Chicago Automobile Show, second in importance only to a larger event held in New York City. Emphasizing the marque's superiority over the outmoded high-wheelers, the Buggy Company's advertising division called it "The Car Complete." In his capacity as chief test driver, Edd accompanied Frayer to the Windy City, covering approximately 250 miles of torturous, twisting dirt toads that gave it the ultimate examination of its quality, particularly because the trip took place in the dead of winter. Having no road maps, they had to ask directions at every crossroads as soon as they left familiar territory. They drove in low gear through stretches of mud and occasionally had to be pulled out by farmers with teams of horses. Despite the problems they encountered, they reached Chicago in five days instead of the ten they had allotted. After arriving and restoring the car to pristine condition, they exhibited it in a brilliantly lit floor area draped with patriotic bunting. *Motor Age* estimated that at least 20,000 people attended the show's opening day and took particular satisfaction in the large number from rural areas. The Firestone-Columbus appeared in a pictorial review praising its features and the way it had held up in its muddy trip. While Frayer stayed at the show talking with automobile enthusiasts, Edd gave demonstration rides to potential buyers. His knowledge of the vehicle and his skill in explaining its features resulted in eleven sales, an impressive performance.[48]

The new cars were well proportioned, built along classic lines. They had steering wheels instead of tillers, headlamps instead of the antiquated lanterns on the motorized buggy, gracefully tapering fender lines that created a smart, symmetrical appearance, and shock-absorbing balloon tires on standard-sized wheels. Advertised as "a mechanical masterpiece," the Firestone-Columbus sold for $1,800 and was a significant professional accomplishment for Frayer, who had proved he could design an important new product for a significant manufacturer of motorized and nonmotorized vehicles. By putting it on the market, the Buggy Company was proclaiming it had graduated from the horseless carriage era and was now making real automobiles.[49]

On the other hand, the firm was missing out on an opportunity to which Frayer and Edd seemed as blind as Clinton Firestone and his fellow executives. Had they concentrated on developing the motorized buggy into a simple but sturdy vehicle with greater power and a more substantial body, they might have given Henry Ford, who was now developing his Model T, a run for his money. Instead, they were following the industry's tendency toward what Donald Finlay Davis has called "conspicuous production" by designing an "automobile for the classes" instead of a "car for the masses."[50] Ford had the genius to blaze a different trail, ignoring the virtually unanimous judgment of Detroit industrialists that he was insane.

One of the first places to which the Buggy Company sent the Firestone-Columbus was Dallas, Texas, home of Fife and Miller, one of its

EDDIE RICKENBACKER

premier sales agencies. A week after three of the automobiles arrived by rail, a telegram came back to Columbus saying that they had broken down in test runs after going barely ten miles. Alarmed, Firestone sent Edd to Dallas. It was June, and the heat was intense. Wearing long underwear more appropriate to weather conditions in Ohio, he found a hotel room, freshened up, and reported to Fife and Miller. His youth shocked them, as it had nonplussed Firestone at the Scioto dam. When Fife asked testily what Edd intended to do, the young prodigy calmly told him that he had come to learn what had gone wrong and set things right.

Taking one of the new cars for a drive, he found it performed smoothly until it went about five miles, after which it began to overheat so badly that the engine stopped amid an ominous pounding of pistons and connecting rods. He quickly guessed that because it had been built for weather conditions in the Middle West it was ill-adapted to the searing heat of Texas. Instead of having a force pump to circulate cooling water, it used a "thermo-syphon" system in which water entered the bottom of the cylinder jacket, rose to the top after being heated by explosions of fuel in the cylinders, and passed into the top of the radiator, where it was cooled by ambient air sucked through honeycomb cells with the help of a belt-driven fan and returned to the cylinder jacket. The system obviously—or so it seemed to Edd—could not effectively circulate the hot Texas air being sucked through the radiator.[51]

Having the car towed back to Dallas, Edd made another test run a few days later. Again, the result was the same. This time, however, he was anxious to get back to the city as soon as he could because he had a date that night, so he decided not to wait for help. Seeing some cows clustered at a nearby water hole, he filled his hat with the water they were drinking and poured it into the radiator, taking a chance of cracking the engine block but in too great a hurry to care. As the water boiled out of the radiator, he filled and refilled it until the temperature of the engine subsided. He was greatly relieved the block did not crack. Driving back to Dallas without further incident, he kept his date but kept wondering why the car had not overheated during his return trip. The next day, when he took it out again and repeated what he had done, no overheating occurred, increasing his curiosity. Collecting a sample from the same water hole, he took it to a chemist for analysis. It was merely rainwater.

Reviewing everything he knew about engines, Edd guessed that refilling the cooling system with cold water had microscopically shrunk the tight-fitting pistons so that they now had adequate clearance within the cylinder walls. To test his theory, he took out the other two cars that had been shipped to Texas, drove them until they overheated, refilled their radiators with rainwater from his secret source of supply, and got the same results. He told Fife and Miller he had solved the problem but did not reveal what he had done. Reassured, they ordered another shipment of cars on condition that Edd stay in Texas to give them the treatment that had worked with the first three.

Edd helped the dealership sell off its inventory of the old high-wheeled motor buggies. One of his customers, a physician from Waco, was so satisfied with the one he bought that he wrote testimonials generating additional sales. In Texas, as elsewhere, medical doctors were important users of early automobiles when house calls were still customary.[52] Edd adopted a rule to emphasize the positive aspects of the high-wheelers even when it took ingenuity to overlook their defects. Trying to climb a hill with a prospective customer, and having to stop halfway up, he stressed how effectively the brakes had brought the car to a standstill. Shifting into low gear, he went blithely to the top and got the sale. It did not occur to him or the Buggy Company to ask why the doctor liked the high wheeler so much and to speculate whether the firm was making a mistake by committing itself to Frayer's more complicated and expensive model.

Pleased by Edd's performance, Firestone decided to keep him in Texas for a while to open new dealerships. His monthly salary, $125, gave him enough money to live on and still send much of his earnings home. Before he went back to Ohio, he had retired the mortgage on the little house on East Livingston Avenue, where his mother and some of his siblings still lived.

He showed an instinctive grasp of automobile merchandising in the industry's formative years. Like Ford, he saw that dealers with good service departments sold more cars than vendors who lacked such facilities, and he urged his clients to hire well-qualified mechanics. When establishing new dealerships, he selected aggressive businessmen and went with them to local banks to get loans, not letting his youth deter him from sitting down and dickering with financiers like a seasoned entrepreneur. His ability to raise capital without being fazed by wealthy men was an asset throughout his career.

He also had a flair for advertising. When perennial Democratic presidential aspirant William Jennings Bryan visited Abilene to lecture on the Chautauqua circuit, Edd went to the hotel where he was staying and offered to drive him around town. Bryan, a pioneer in using automobiles for political purposes, accepted the offer, and Edd got valuable newspaper publicity by having his picture taken at the wheel of a Firestone-Columbus while Bryan beamed at spectators from the rear seat.[53]

Selling automobiles required giving customers demonstration rides. Squeezing a wealthy Texas landowner, his wife, and seven children into a five-passenger Firestone-Columbus, Edd set out for a ranch located eighty miles from Abilene on a road barely fit for wagons. Two tires blew out before noon in the unrelenting heat. Near the entrance to the ranch, the front axle failed to clear a six-inch stump in the middle of the road and hit it with a resounding whack, bringing the car to a jolting stop. The axle was too badly bent to continue, so they left the vehicle and went the rest of the way in a horse-drawn wagon. Whooping and shouting, cowboys who had never seen an automobile helped him haul the stricken car into a yard in front of the ranch house. When Edd tried to ride a pony and accidentally kicked its ribs, it threw him over its head. Amused, buckaroos shot bullets into the air and erupted with cries of delight. At daybreak they built a bonfire, removed the bent axle, and helped Edd hammer it back into shape, after which he drove the landowner and his family back to Abilene. Unfazed by the accident, his client bought three cars.[54]

Edd also made a sale to a retired Texas Ranger who lived in Fort Worth. Anticipating the later efforts of Bill Wilson, the founder of Alcoholics Anonymous, he opened his house to drunks and drug addicts and tried to lead them to sobriety. Edd lived with him for a time and decided to "go on the wagon," seeing that socializing with sales prospects was getting him involved in too much drinking—a problem that would recur throughout his life.[55]

Impressed by Edd's achievements, Firestone sent him to Tucson, Arizona, where an agency was trying to cope with the overheating problem that had baffled Fife and Miller in Dallas. In a drier climate where the altitude was higher and water boiled at a lower temperature, Edd found that the simple expedient he had used in Texas did not work. Realizing that the thermo-syphon system was unsuited to the new environment, he devised a forced circulation system driven by the crankshaft. It was a makeshift solution but it worked.[56]

Edd returned to the testing department at Columbus late in 1909. While he was away, he had had a growth spurt. He was now more than six feet tall, and his weight had shot up to 165 pounds, amazing his mother. Soon after he came home, a new opportunity arose when Roy Coffeen, manager of the Racine-Sattley Company, an agricultural equipment firm that sold the Buggy Company's horse-drawn carriages in Nebraska, decided to take on a line of automobiles. Going to Ohio to see the Firestone-Columbus, he went around the countryside with Edd and other test drivers. Impressed, he signed a contract to open a dealership at the Racine-Sattley agency in Omaha.

Firestone agreed to send a representative of Coffeen's choice to Omaha to give him mechanical and sales assistance. Coffeen selected Edd and agreed to pay his living expenses on condition that the Buggy Company would pay his salary—seventy-five dollars per month. Edd had personal reasons for wanting to leave Columbus. While he was in Texas and Arizona, he had thought so much about Blanche Calhoun, to whom he had been attracted in Sunday school, that he bought her a diamond ring. After he returned home and gave it to her, news spread rapidly that they were engaged. Edd later stated he did not realize the implications of what he had meant only as a gift, but he had probably been serious about Blanche and gotten jittery after realizing he had overcommitted himself.[57]

Before he went to Omaha, Firestone had him visit the Buggy Company's five-state north-central sales district, including Iowa, Nebraska, the two Dakotas, and Wisconsin, where a regional manager was having problems making the transition between the high-wheelers and the Firestone-Columbus. Finding that sales operations in the district were slipshod, he taught dealers more effective methods. Pleased by what he had done, Firestone put him in charge of the district, with six salesmen reporting to him, and doubled the salary the company had recently agreed to pay him. Not many nineteen-year-olds earned $150 per month.

Omaha, where Rickenbacher would be based for nearly two years, was a booming city of almost 125,000 people. Teeming with stockyards and slaughterhouses, it was also the headquarters of the Union Pacific Railroad. Evidences of cultural growth included an art gallery, library, an opera house, and Creighton College, named after a pioneering telegrapher. But the city also had a reputation for being a "wide-open town," abounding in gambling dens, bordellos, saloons, and the crime that went with them. Its gaming houses teemed with hard-bitten men playing faro, keno, monte, and poker. Pickpockets and swindlers plied their trade unmolested. Hoboes swarmed into the city on rail cars and congregated in switchyards.[58]

In short, Omaha was even more hard-boiled than Columbus. Not long before Edd went there, kidnappers had abducted Eddie Cudahy, the fifteen-year-old son of a meatpacking tycoon, and threatened to put acid in his eyes unless his father paid a ransom of $25,000 in gold. After he paid the money, they returned the youth unharmed but were caught and put on trial in February 1906. They admitted their guilt but were acquitted by a jury that "felt that if a man could bilk a packer of $25,000, more power to him." Cheers rang out in the courtroom when the verdict was announced. Things had not changed when Edd came to town in March 1910. It was buzzing with excitement about a recent robbery in which desperadoes wearing "long coats, slouch hats, and dark blue polka-dot handkerchiefs" had jumped a train and stolen seven bags of mail before making off in a hail of gunfire. After being apprehended and put on trial in October 1909, they almost escaped when one of them cut a hole in the roof of the jail with a smuggled saw.[59]

Edd and Coffeen had a hard time introducing the Firestone-Columbus in Omaha. Potential customers were unaccustomed to buying cars from an agency that had sold only farm machinery and horse-drawn buggies. Racine-Sattley was also in a different part of town from older dealerships. Coffeen was worried because he had bet his future on selling cars. Groping for a solution, he and Edd devised a plan. Automobile dealers often advertised vehicles by entering them in races, reasoning that "ordinary people would want to watch what their own cars could do."[60] Agencies across the Middle West were competing on dirt-track races at county fairs. What better way to demonstrate the superiority of the Firestone-Columbus to prospective buyers? Frayer had recently shipped an updated model, with a high-speed engine, to Omaha. It had left-hand steering, which Frayer believed to be better than a right-hand drive for judging distance from oncoming cars.[61] Edd stripped it down to the chassis, reinforced the frame at critical points of stress, installed an extra gas tank and bucket seats, and painted the vehicle white, a color that became his trademark. To complement the vehicle's pristine appearance, he chose white coveralls for a uniform. Coffeen had some experience driving race cars and gave Edd lessons on a half-mile dirt track on West Leavenworth Avenue.[62] Looking for an event in which to compete, Edd learned that a twenty-five-mile dirt-track race would soon be held at Red Oak, a town in southwestern Iowa. Responding to the lure of speed and danger, a warrior prepared for battle.

Chapter 3

— ☆ —

Acceleration

The Iowa community of Red Oak, a county seat with about 5,000 people, was wild about automobiles. In 1910 local newspapers were pushing hard to improve the condition of roads leading into town, which became quagmires of mud when it rained. Car ownership, editors believed, would foster competition with the Chicago, Burlington, and Quincy Railroad, Red Oak's economic lifeline, which charged exorbitant prices on short-run traffic.[1] And one way to promote car ownership was to sponsor "hair-raising, hub-shaving" automobile races.

> HONK! HONK! Watch out for the Southwestern Iowa BIG AUTOMO-
> BILE RACES. Red Oak, Iowa, Thursday, June 9, 1910. $600 PURSES
> $600. See the hair-raising, hub-shaving free-for-all. Clean out your
> honker, tie on your hat and come to the carnival of the speed wag-
> ons. Race fiends will be here that will make the timid citizens climb
> telephone poles. There'll be fun. Atlantic, Creston, Clarinda,
> Shenandoah, Omaha, Glenwood, Malvern, and many other towns
> have promised to send delegations with goggles on. You'll want to
> see the crowd of one-lungers, pop wagons, palace cars, fog shoot-
> ers and jack rabbits. The Liveliest, Merriest, Thriller of a Time Red
> Oak ever saw.[2]

Horseracing, a precursor of motor sport, had been a passion in Red Oak from frontier days. Races took place in 1859 at the first Montgomery County Fair. In 1894 Morris Jones, a wealthy equine enthusiast who owned sixty thoroughbreds, built a new track, Pactolus Park, north of town.[3] Edd ran the first automobile race of his career there on 16 June 1910. More than 600 cars brought spectators to town to see the event, and trains from all directions carried passengers to cheer for the contestants.[4]

Edd arrived early, bringing his stripped-down Firestone-Columbus to Red Oak the day before the race. Recalling that Frayer had minutely examined the course as soon as he got to the scene of the 1906 Vanderbilt Cup Race, he went immediately to Pactolus Park to inspect the track, which was flat because it had been laid out for horseracing. Driving repeatedly around the half-mile oval, he took the turns at higher and higher speeds, trying to learn how fast he could make them without turning over. He wondered why competitors were not doing the same thing.

The weather was clear and unseasonably hot. An automobile parade started at 12:30 p.m., giving owners a chance to show off their cars, honking and tooting to the delight of people lining the streets along the route to Pactolus Park. Officials counted 516 motor vehicles coming through the gates. Most of the drivers parked in the infield. About 8,000 people bought tickets, and refreshment stands quickly ran out of beverages, as spectators, wilted by the heat, guzzled tankards of ice water.[5]

The program typified events in which Edd competed during the next few years. Different types of races gave drivers with varying levels of experience a chance to show their stuff. The main attraction, for which Edd had registered, was a twenty-five-mile race with a purse of $225. The preliminary races received little publicity, but the featured event, with its two accidents, gave reporters much to write about. One of them came in the warm-up, involving a Cole Model 36, built by an Indianapolis firm that had entered cars in the Vanderbilt Cup competition. It lost a right front wheel rounding a curve. Its driver, identified only by his surname, Ralston, "was quite seriously injured about the head and shoulders, and was a fit subject for a hospital, but he would not permit his friends to take him from the grounds [and] stayed till the races were over with."[6]

Edd, whom the *Express* called "Ed Reichenbaugh," was the victim of the other accident. Making a fast start, he grabbed an early lead over Walter Smith, who ran an agency for the Chalmers-Detroit Motor Car Company. Edd knew that Chalmers-Detroit models were strong competitors because they had scored five victories in the 1908–9 racing seasons and appealed to discriminating buyers, including, it was said, Vanderbilts and Rockefellers.[7] As the cars careened around the turns, they tore up the flat track and created ridges where the dirt had earlier been level. Not knowing enough about racing to adjust to the changed conditions, Edd kept going around the curves at the same high speeds he had reached while practicing the previous evening. He soon learned why more savvy competitors had not bothered to rehearse, knowing that the track would be too chewed up the next day to gauge what speed to take on the laps. His right rear wheel, the one most affected by the strain of rounding a turn because it had a greater distance to cover than the one at the other end of the axle, buckled on the same curve where Ralston had been injured. Failing to make the turn, the Firestone-Columbus "turned broadside," crashed through a fence, leaped across a ditch, and "landed on the other side, still going sideways." Rolling over, it threw Edd and his riding mechanic, Glen Spies, from the car "with great violence." The *Express* said that "Reichenbaugh was seriously bruised and cut up about the face, but Spies had several ribs broken and for a while it was thought sustained internal injuries, but this proved to be a mistake and he was able to go to his home the next morning." Ignoring his cuts and bruises, Edd examined his car to see what it would take to fix it before he raced again. He knew full well that he would do so.[8]

The race was cut to fifteen miles, possibly because of the accidents. Watching it from the sidelines, Edd, hooked by the thrill of narrowly escaping serious injury, realized that he would never be satisfied selling cars. He was a quick learner and did much better a week later in a two-day series of automobile and horse races sponsored by a jockey club in Atlantic, a town about twenty miles east of Red Oak. The purses, totaling $1,200, were twice as large as the ones at Pactolus Park. Automotive events included two free-for-alls of ten and fifteen miles, a seven-mile race for runabouts and roadsters, and a five-mile race for touring cars. Edd was a three-time winner. The fifteen-mile free-for-all, on 29 June, brought the first victory of his racing career. The next day he won again in the ten-mile free-for-all, taking an early lead that he never lost and outclassing two Model T Fords, one of which threw a wheel over a barn while rounding a turn. Edd's Firestone-Columbus was ineligible for the five-mile race because it was limited to touring cars. Perhaps because of the reputation he had gained by winning the earlier contests, Mike Conway, a local automobile enthusiast, loaned him an E-M-F (Everitt-Metzger-Flanders) Model 30. Driving relentlessly, Edd defeated a Buick by a full lap in the five-lap event. The $275, $225, and $125 prizes he had won left him with a healthy sum after paying his riding mechanic and sharing his winnings in the five-mile race with Conway. For a person accustomed to working for $150 per month, the two-day haul was an eye-opener to the rewards available on the track, intensifying his determination to do a lot of racing. Moreover, the performance of his Firestone-Columbus yielded a sale to a restaurant owner in Atlantic who had already visited the Racine-Sattley showroom in Omaha and been tempted to buy a bright heliotrope-colored car displayed there. The power and speed of Edd's stripped-down version of the same vehicle made him want to buy the snazzier model he had seen. After returning to Omaha, Edd washed and polished it and brought it to Atlantic the next day. The businessman paid him cash on the spot, showing that the strategy Edd and Coffeen had adopted was working.[9]

Edd reveled in his newfound hobby. Automobile companies including Buick, Case, Chalmers, Lozier, Marmon, Peerless, and Simplex sponsored "factory teams" of drivers who demonstrated the speed, power, and endurance of their cars in road, track, and beach races; hill climbs; and twenty-four-hour marathons known as "grinds." Local agents frequently drove the cars they sold in competitions like the ones Edd had entered at Red Oak and Atlantic. He was doing nothing unusual by spending his weekends promoting the Firestone-Columbus on dirt tracks and concentrating on sales during weekdays. It was obvious that winning races was the best type of advertising he and Coffeen could get, but there was no question which role—salesman or racer—he preferred. Exhilarated by the speed and danger of motor sport, he became intimately familiar with dirt tracks within a 100-mile radius of Omaha—some so primitive they were virtual death traps.

Racing opportunities were available in Omaha itself. Promoters had built a new motor speedway in 1910 at an old fairground on West Leavenworth Avenue, with a grandstand for 3,000 people. The formal opening, set for 4 and 5 September, would feature six events each day for purses totaling $5,000. Backers of the facility promised that "professional drivers with national track records will be here with their fast cars." Edd chafed at the delay when rain forced a postponement. As the weather cleared, the *Omaha World Herald* reported that "Hundreds of people have been anxiously waiting to see real auto races, and the management has made every effort to open up the game right, as the future of their new venture depends a great deal on the opening card." On the first day more than twenty-five cars and "a score of motorcycles" roared around the center of town in a parade beginning at the corner of 16th Street and Capitol Avenue.

Edd did not participate in the opening day's races, but the next afternoon he won the first two automobile events, both of the ten-mile variety, dueling in each case with a Staver-Chicago belonging to the Standard Auto Company.[10] "Each time," said the *World-Herald,* "it was a terrific battle." Edd won the first race by about thirteen seconds and the second by a razor-thin eight seconds, increasing his excitement about future prospects. Coming so soon after Atlantic, his victories at Omaha showed him that he had what it takes to be a star.[11]

He proved his ability beyond any doubt a few weeks later with an even more impressive performance in the most important weekend in the Omaha social season, the annual Ak-Sar-Ben (Nebraska spelled backward) Festival. By 1910 the event was so big that it attracted the likes of Theodore Roosevelt.[12] Because of the new speedway, promoters decided to feature two days of auto racing, sponsored by the Omaha Motor Club. Edd swept the field on the first day, 1 October, by winning four consecutive races. The most dramatic victory came in a twenty-mile free-for-all. Smarting from earlier losses to "Reichenberger," a prominent Chalmers dealer named Frederickson drove so furiously "that three times his car almost left the track." Watching breathlessly, the crowd "tried in vain to penetrate the dust clouds that for a few seconds prevented their knowing whether Fredrickson and his car were still in the race or had met misfortune." On the second day Edd won four of five events, losing only a five-mile obstacle race requiring contestants to stop their cars at the end of every mile, kill their engines, recrank them, and jump back in the driver's seat before continuing. The Firestone-Columbus was so fast that Edd overshot each of the first three miles and had to back up after running ahead of his rivals. In any case, winning eight races in two days was a remarkable achievement. The *World Herald* was so impressed that it began spelling his name correctly. "During the two days of the meet," it said, "Rickenbacher won a goodly quantity of glory and incidentally a number of fat purses. The Firestone was unanimously pronounced by the spectators the fastest, most popular and best-driven racer on the course so far."[13]

Edd's racetrack earnings outclassed his salary at the Racine-Sattley agency. He won about $1,500 at the Ak-Sar-Ben Festival even after paying his riding mechanic $200. It was the most money he had ever come close to making in one fell swoop. News of his ability soon got back to Ohio, and Frayer sent him a wire inviting him to bring his car to Columbus and join him in a 100-mile race at the Driving Park. Edd was thrilled by the opening sentence of the message, "How would you like to swap dust with Barney Oldfield?" It was like asking a rookie shortstop if he would like to play on the same field with Ty Cobb. Bernd Eli ("Barney") Oldfield was by far the most famous auto racer in America, a living legend of velocity. In his most recent accomplishment, he had set a world record of 131 miles per hour in Florida on the beach between Ormond and Daytona driving the "Blitzen Benz," a legendary Mercedes with a bullet-shaped snout, a pointed tail, and a 200-horsepower engine. Pulling speeding motorists to the side of the road, cops would ask, "Just who do you think you are, Barney Oldfield?" Naturally eager to compete with Oldfield before the hometown fans but also in front of those who had once taunted him about his poverty, his foreign accent, and his mismatched shoes, Edd jumped at the invitation.[14]

Oldfield brought a high-powered Knox to Columbus to compete with Frayer and Edd. The racing idol was heavily favored to win, but Frayer had conceived a strategy to beat him. Reasoning that Oldfield would underestimate Edd because of his youth and inexperience, Frayer believed the great driver could be victimized by his overweening ego. Knowing that Oldfield could outrun his own car, the "Red Wing Special," and Edd's Firestone-Columbus on the straights, he felt sure that Edd could outmaneuver the bigger Knox on the turns. Thinking that Oldfield would wear out his tires trying to keep up with Edd's pesky vehicle, Frayer told his young protégé to get off to as fast a start as possible and take turns at breakneck speed. Feeling insulted by having a mere novice challenge him, Oldfield would go too fast for the tires of his heavier car to withstand the abrasion and be forced to make pit stops at inopportune times to have them changed, thus losing ground. Meanwhile, Frayer would maintain a steady speed by staying close enough to Oldfield to pass him during his pit stops and win.

It was an excellent strategy. Skidding around turns trying to keep up with Edd, Oldfield blew out two tires and had to pit. As Frayer had foreseen, he lost momentum. Edd's little car, however, had more endurance than Frayer had expected and nearly upset his mentor's plans. Setting a blistering pace, Edd was far ahead after seventy-five miles and still led with only a few laps to go. As Frayer had suspected, however, Edd's smaller car could not take the strain and a connecting rod broke, forcing him out and leaving Frayer to beat Oldfield by a narrow margin.[15]

Edd had nothing to be discouraged about. Coming within a whisker of besting seasoned veterans like Frayer and Oldfield in his first big race did wonders for his confidence, which was never as great as his outward bravado suggested. And he had learned a valuable lesson from Frayer: careful planning, teamwork, and taking advantage of any mechanical or psychological weaknesses an opponent had could lead to victory despite heavy odds. Edd also realized, however, that the outcome of a race hinged partly on luck. If his Firestone-Columbus could have gone only a few more laps, he would have won. Although fortune had not smiled on him this time, it might be kinder in the future. Being superstitious, he hoped to improve his chances by collecting an assortment of good luck charms. But regardless of lessons or luck, the main thing was that he had done so well in the biggest event of his career to date. After the race, Oldfield praised Edd "as a clean, square racing man." "There was no dirty work," Barney declared. "He took his share of the track and no more. The sole of his right foot is as heavy as lead, and it keeps the accelerator pressed into the floorboard."[16]

Soon after returning to Omaha from the Columbus race, Edd suffered an injury that would affect his eyesight for the rest of his life. His sales office at the Racine-Sattley agency was located on the second floor of a building standing beside a railroad track. He was looking out an open window early in 1911 when a passing locomotive blew out a cloud of smoke and soot in his direction and a red-hot cinder hit him in the right eye. An agonizing operation to remove the particle without anesthesia left a hole in his cornea and a permanent blind spot in his field of vision.[17]

But the injury did not deter him from continuing to race. Tasting the thrill of big-time competition made him increasingly bored selling cars. He had also lost faith in the Buggy Company, whose executives were lagging behind the times by standing pat with their existing cars and making only incremental changes. Slow, piecemeal progress was foreign to Edd's outlook.[18] Providentially, another message from Frayer opened up a dramatic new prospect. Frayer was so impressed by Edd's performance at Columbus that he asked him to be his relief driver in a 500-mile race at Indianapolis on Memorial Day. Edd's stripped-down Firestone-Columbus was too light to compete in the event. Indeed, Frayer was unsure his Red Wing Special was heavy enough. But the race would be so significant that Frayer wanted to participate, if only to be able to tell his grandchildren about it. Recognizing that the first Indy 500 would be an automotive milestone, and desperate to get back to the track, Edd quickly accepted the challenge.

On Memorial Day in 1911, 80,000 racing fans gathered at the Indianapolis Speedway to be eyewitnesses at the beginning of a new era in motor sport. Cheering themselves hoarse, they watched the first running of one of the world's greatest automotive spectacles. From the beginning, the Indy 500 was recognized as an ideal expression of the values dominating a culture that worshiped technology, admired masculine virtues, and celebrated the will to win. For motor vehicle manufacturers, the need for cars to make 200 circuits of the 2.5-mile track provided an opportunity to demonstrate the merits of their products in a mercilessly demanding venue. For the road warriors who drove the vehicles, including Edd, the race would be a supreme test of courage and skill in an arena where sudden death lurked around every turn.[19]

The Indy 500 resulted from changes that had transferred power from rich amateurs who looked at racing as a hobby to entrepreneurs who aimed to make money. Racing on enclosed oval tracks like the one at Indianapolis would be much less hazardous to onlookers than road racing but just as dramatic. Cross-country events continued to flourish in Europe and did not entirely disappear in America but became much less frequent as motor sport outgrew its upper-class origins and became a business providing vicarious enjoyment for masses of spectators who had to pay to get into the grounds and were separated from the track by retaining walls. Meanwhile, racing would remain as potentially lethal as ever to competitors like Edd, who became one of a new breed of professional drivers who gradually replaced rich amateur sportsmen.[20]

England created the world's first closed track for automobile racing, the Brooklands Speedway, a giant concrete oval two and three-quarter miles in circumference. Its racecourse, 100-feet wide, had specially banked curves permitting flat-out speeds throughout its entire length. In a free-for-all at the formal opening on 6 July 1907, Lord Lonsdale reached eighty-five miles per hour, after which Europe's best drivers competed in six events including a twenty-four-hour marathon. Commercially, however, the event was disappointing, drawing only 4,000 spectators instead of an expected 30,000. The aristocratic ambience of competitions that followed, sponsored by the exclusive Brooklands Automobile Racing Club, discouraged common folk from patronizing the facility, making it the automotive equivalent of Ascot. The unofficial motto of the speedway, "The Right Crowd and No Crowding," characterized what, from an American viewpoint, was a snooty place best avoided by fans. Cars seemed lost in a vast expanse of concrete, reducing visual stimulation. Not until aviation pioneers A. V. Roe and T. O. M. Sopwith built hangars on the grounds and began to stage air races did Brooklands provide mass entertainment. By 1910 crowds of 50,000 people came to watch pilots vie against one another in frail aircraft that sometimes stalled or crashed into the Wey River. "Brooklands itself was built for the car," said a magazine for flight enthusiasts, "yet it is the aeroplane that attracts most people to its grounds."[21]

In America, unlike England, promoters of automotive spectacles adapted the basic concept of Brooklands to the needs and expectations of sports fans in a democracy. In February 1909 a group of business associates led by Carl G. Fisher, a visionary who paradoxically suffered from extreme myopia, founded the Indianapolis Motor Speedway Corporation, capitalized at $250,000, and started building what became the most famous raceway in the world. Fisher, with whom Edd became closely associated, was a former bicycle racer and Oldsmobile dealer who had made a fortune as president of the Prest-O-Lite Corporation, which manufactured carbide headlamps.

The Indianapolis Speedway was intended partly to provide a proving ground for innovations in automotive technology. Increasing numbers of American designers and manufacturers were building cars specifically designed for racing instead of relying on production models. Nevertheless, the sheer size of the stands at Indianapolis, which could seat 60,000 spectators, showed that the speedway was built primarily to make money. The grounds could accommodate 200,000 fans, and the parking lots had space for 10,000 cars. After a remarkably short construction period, the track formally opened in August 1909, but the crushed stone and asphalt surface could not withstand sustained pounding and was irreparably damaged by the time the races were over. The flawed pavement also caused a crash on opening day, killing a driver, two riding mechanics, and—most important because of the outcry for public safety—two spectators.

Undaunted, Fisher and his partners repaved the track with millions of bricks, giving it the name for which it became famous: "The Brickyard." In mid-December, only sixty-three days after the start of repairs, 30,000 spectators braved freezing weather to see Lewis Strang set a speed record by driving a Fiat 91.81 miles per hour. Dissatisfied with attendance, the Fisher syndicate decided to hold a series of races in 1910 linked to three national holidays: Memorial Day, the Fourth of July, and Labor Day. On Memorial Day, 60,000 people saw a mixture of races ranging from 5 to 200 miles long.

Indianapolis was not the only place in the United States where promoters tried to imitate Brooklands and adapt it to American conditions.

In California, a rival syndicate built a huge board-track raceway at Playa del Rey, near Los Angeles. Fisher and his fellow entrepreneurs knew that the relative lack of friction on boards tightly packed together and laid upright would permit higher speeds than a brick surface would allow. Fearful of being upstaged by the Californians, they decided to create a unique event that would set the Indianapolis Speedway apart as the Mecca of automobile racing. In an inspired move, they would hold a single 500-mile race every Memorial Day.[22]

The basic concept of the race—to test speed, power, and endurance, the three main criteria of automotive excellence—was not without precedent. For almost a decade promoters allied with the American Automobile Association had tried to test the three variables in twenty-four-hour "grinds" held on dirt tracks designed for horseracing. Edd knew about the first event of this type because it took place at the Columbus Driving Park, near his home, in 1905. Twelve thousand diehard fans endured torrential rain as half a dozen production cars slithered through mud and darkness until a Pope-Toledo crossed the finish line after going a mind-numbing 828 miles. Such races jaded drivers and spectators, made virtually impossible demands on cars, and inflicted terrible damage on dirt tracks. By 1910 the grinds were doomed.[23]

Fisher's group, by contrast, created a race of impressive but reasonable distance that lasted a relatively long time but fell within the attention span of most spectators. Instead of taking place on a dirt track designed for equine events, it was held in a facility planned for high-speed cars. Holding the race on a national holiday when people had time off from work attracted large crowds. Starting in midmorning and ending before dark, the new venue made extreme demands on drivers and cars, providing a grueling test of speed and staying power. The soundness of the underlying concept produced what was immediately seen as a great sporting event, explaining why Frayer and Edd wanted to get in on the ground floor.

Edd was fortunate in entering motor sport at a time when it was becoming a business featuring mostly professional drivers. Events like the Indy 500 reflected the declining role played by the Automobile Club of America (ACA), an exclusive organization centered in New York City and dominated by wealthy families like the Vanderbilts. Fisher's entrepreneurial orientation reflected the growing power of the more democratic and inclusive American Automobile Association (AAA), founded in 1902. Needing financial support, the AAA formed an alliance with the Manufacturers Contest Association (MCA), representing automobile makers who wanted motor sport to escape the bad public image of events like the 1906 Vanderbilt Cup Race.

To provide structure and discipline to motor sport, the AAA and MCA formed the AAA Contest Board and put it in charge of regularizing and policing automotive events. In 1909 the Contest Board created an officially sanctioned tour by identifying twenty-six events as "nationals" that would be supervised by starters, referees, scorers, and timers enforcing rules to which drivers, mechanics, and racing teams were obliged to adhere. Drivers engaging in unsanctioned events and breaking the Contest Board's rules could be barred from competition, as Edd was for a short time early in his career. By 1912 the number of AAA-approved closed-track races had increased to ninety-seven and only eight road races remained. The AAA tour attracted the nation's best drivers and a strong group of factory teams representing leading automobile manufacturers. Its officials and elliptical red, white, and blue emblem commanded respect. Its most visible authority figure was Fred Wagner, a starter who signaled for a race to begin, enforced observance of AAA rules, and ferreted out gamblers who followed the tour.[24]

Recognizing the danger to its reputation of "hippodromes" with fixed outcomes, the Contest Board cracked down on promoters like Will Pickens, Barney Oldfield's unscrupulous manager. Despite Oldfield's popularity, the Contest Board periodically suspended him but later re-admitted him to sanctioned events because of his phenomenal drawing power. People who ran county fairs resented the AAA's growing clout because its rules and regulations restricted hawkers and opportunists who contracted with local organizers to provide traveling troupes of drivers with dubious reputations to "put on a good show" without being overscrupulous about observing safety precautions on which the AAA insisted. From the start Fisher's group gave the Contest Board unwavering support. It became proverbial that "As Indianapolis goes, so goes the AAA."[25]

The 80,000 spectators at Indianapolis on Memorial Day in 1911 constituted the largest crowd in the history of motor sport. Edd was awed by the unfolding spectacle as he waited anxiously for the race to begin.[26] Lured by the $27,550 purse, forty drivers, mostly American, slowly circled the arena like Roman gladiators in a ceremonial opening lap while Fisher, wearing pince-nez glasses, led them to their starting positions in a Stoddard-Dayton pace car.[27] Forming ranks of five at 100-foot intervals, they then waited for Wagner to start the race officially by detonating a bomb. Johnny Aitken in a National, Gil Anderson in a Stutz, David Bruce-Brown in a Fiat, Bob Burman in a Benz, Arthur Chevrolet in a Buick, Louis Disbrow in a Pope-Hartford, Ralph De Palma in a Simplex Zip, Ray Harroun in a Marmon Wasp, Hughie Hughes in a Mercer, Ralph Mulford in a Lozier, and Spencer Wishart in a Mercedes were among the fabled drivers revving their engines. Among less heralded drivers was Frayer, crouched behind the wheel of a four-cylinder Firestone-Columbus bearing Ohio State University's colors, scarlet and gray. Harroun attracted the most attention because he was driving without a riding mechanic to reduce weight, relying on a rear-vision mirror, the first time such a device had been used on the tour.

The bomb went off and the race was on. Aitken, Bruce-Brown, De Palma, and Wishart were among the early leaders as the cars sped around the track and the bricks reverberated with a howling sound that could be heard miles away. Frayer, planning to return to the contest in the last fifty laps when excitement would be at its peak, pulled into the pit early and Edd took over in relief, joining the pack just in time to see the first of many fatal accidents that he witnessed in his racing career. As Art Greiner came down the back straight on the thirteenth lap, one of his wheel rims came off and he lost control of his Amplex. As the car spun around, he and his riding mechanic, Sam Dickson, were thrown out. Greiner suffered only a broken arm, but Dickson died instantly as he hit a retaining wall. Soon afterward, Edd found himself in another crisis when the steering mechanism failed on Joe Jaegersberger's Case. As Jaegersberger slowed down in the middle of the track, his mechanic jumped out of the car in a desperate effort to guide the wheels by hand and fell as it lurched toward the pits. As he lay on the bricks, Harry Knight, following close behind in a Wescott, swerved to avoid hitting him and crashed into Herbert Lytle's Apperson while it was pitted for a tire change. The Apperson flew into the air and came down in an adjoining pit as four workers dove for cover, barely escaping with their lives. The impact of the collision threw Knight and his riding mechanic out of the Wescott, which hit a Fiat in another pit. Nobody died, but Knight had a fractured skull and an ambulance took him to a hospital.[28]

The track was quickly cleared and the race continued after a brief slowdown. Frayer took over from Edd after 400 miles and made a better showing than expected by finishing eleventh, but did not complete the entire distance because he was flagged after ten drivers had crossed the finish line. After a duel in the stretch, Harroun garnered $10,000 for coming in first in his Marmon Wasp, followed closely by Mulford's Lozier, Bruce-Brown's Fiat, and Wishart's Mercedes. Harroun's elapsed time of six hours, forty-two minutes, and eight seconds gave him an average speed of 74.59 miles per hour. Observers were proud that a field composed almost entirely of American-made vehicles and American drivers had put on a splendid show, assuring commercial success for automobile racing in the United States.[29]

Sharing in the excitement at Indianapolis only made it harder for Edd to return to Omaha. His efforts for the Buggy Company included selling an automobile to a madam who owned a local brothel. He hung on for a seemingly interminable year, but was bored and frustrated.[30] Frayer again came to the rescue early in 1912 when he decided to retire from racing and offered Edd the use of his Red Wing Special in the second running of the Indy 500. The stands were packed for the drama. Burman was favored to win but Edd was particularly fascinated by a yellow Mercer driven by Hughie Hughes, with a counterbalanced crankshaft to reduce engine vibration—an innovation Edd embraced when he later manufactured a car named in his honor. He also gazed admiringly at a Fiat with large "beer keg" cylinders and a double chain drive, "piloted," in the argot of motor sport, by Teddy Tetzlaff, one of the tour's fiercest competitors. Fisher once again led the pack around the arena in a pace car, this time a Stutz.[31] After completing the circuit he withdrew and the action began. De Palma was in front by the third lap, with Wishart and Bruce-Brown hot on his tail and Tetzlaff fourth. Edd knew from the start that his Red Wing Special was in trouble. Its engine was sluggish, and he soon fell behind by a full lap. De Palma moved relentlessly ahead as other drivers pushed their cars mercilessly. Cylinders blew and connecting rods broke as one vehicle after another was forced off the track. Edd's turn came on the forty-second lap when he went out with a broken valve.

Retreating to the stands, Edd watched a local favorite, Joe Dawson, win in a National, a marque made in Indianapolis. De Palma lost the race because of a mechanical breakdown but became the hero of the day as he and his mechanic, Rupert Jeffkins, attempted, literally, to *push* the race car over the finish line, to thunderous applause from the spectators.[32] The emotional impact of the gallantry displayed by De Palma and Jeffkins made it impossible for Edd to stay at Omaha. By now the Buggy Company was headed for bankruptcy anyway. Quitting his job soon after getting back to Nebraska, he set out on a career as a professional racer. He had a license from the AAA but lacked the financial backing to enter the sport except at the lowest level. Seizing the only opportunity available, he took a job with a second-rate team, the "Flying Squadron," whose name eerily foreshadowed his later career as a combat pilot. Operating out of Chicago, it went from one county fair to another on a treadmill that veteran drivers contemptuously called the "Cornstalk Circuit."[33]

Throughout the summer of 1912, the troupe toured mainly in Iowa, giving exhibitions at fairs in towns like Harlan, Boone, Carroll, Missouri Valley, Mason City, Marshalltown, and Grinnell. Marshalltown, the largest of these communities, had 13,374 people in 1910. Harlan, the smallest, had only 2,570. Several weeks before an upcoming event, the team's business agent, Fred C. Bailey, visited a town where a fair was about to be held and made financial arrangements with its directors. Bailey represented a "Mrs. Marshall"—probably the wife of well-known Chicago architect and automobile enthusiast Benjamin Marshall.[34] Working with local dealers and members of auto clubs, Bailey found places for the team's race cars to be kept and displayed and courted reporters to secure publicity, marveling at the condition of the local track, praising its suitability for a fast race, and intimating that its condition would probably result in speed records. As the time of the fair approached, notices in newspapers heralded the upcoming show and touted the identities and achievements of the team's cars and drivers. Because France was the center of motor sport, Bailey fabricated as many associations as possible with that country. Andrew Burt, driving the "King Dodo," a Cino racer made in Cincinnati, was supposedly the world's youngest French racer. C. W. ("Frenchy") Canner, assertedly Gallic, drove a De Detrich Tornado reputed to have set a speed record at Ormond Beach. Edd's name went unmentioned in advance publicity and rarely turned up in reports of races, showing his lack of star status.[35]

He went like a vagabond from town to town, probably doing maintenance jobs and helping with local arrangements. After arriving by rail (advertisements explained beforehand that the Flying Squadron's race cars, built for special high-speed conditions, could not move under their own power in normal traffic without damaging their delicate components), the monstrous vehicles were taken to showrooms at local dealerships, where auto enthusiasts gaped at them. On the day of a race, they were ceremoniously towed to a fairground, resplendent in gaudy paint schemes, in a festive parade, accompanied by civic dignitaries and a smartly uniformed band. Local automobile owners were encouraged to drive their cars in the parade and invited to participate at the fair in selected events along with the professionals. These venues included a novelty known as a "slow race," in which drivers would vie to see who could go a certain distance at a snail's pace and come in last without stalling. Up to 9,000 spectators paid sixty cents to see the action.

Going all out to please his small-town clientele, Bailey ignored safety regulations stipulated by the AAA. Spectators were permitted to get too close to the track, with disastrous results at Mason City, Iowa, where some drivers failed to negotiate turns and plowed into onlookers.[36] The laxity with which the troupe was run cost Edd his racing license. On 24 October 1912, soon after Canner had a horrendous accident at Blue Earth, Minnesota, the AAA Contest Board disqualified Edd until 1 January 1914 for taking part in unsanctioned meets.[37] Undaunted, he went to Des Moines, where he spent the winter of 1912–13 working as a mechanic for two brothers, Frederick (Fred) and August (Augie) Duesenberg. Fred, the older one, had been a judge when the Flying Squadron visited Marshalltown, which may be where Edd met him. He had little formal education except for courses from Edd's alma mater, ICS. Common bonds probably worked to Edd's advantage in hiring on with the Duesenbergs for three dollars a week, a good deal less than he had made with the Buggy Company but more than enough for a young man who had a passion for automobiles and, above all, was out of a job.

The Duesenbergs had come to America from Lippe, a tiny German principality, to join an older brother living near Mason City, Iowa. Fred became a bicycle and motorcycle racer, fell in love with automobiles, and worked as a mechanic and test driver for a company that made a notable car, the Rambler, at Kenosha, Wisconsin. After Fred returned to Iowa in 1904, he and Augie set up a repair shop in Des Moines and designed the "Marvel," a two-cylinder runabout. Needing money, they got backing from Edward R. Mason, an attorney who lived in Des Moines, and renamed their vehicle after him. Known as "The Fastest and Strongest Two-Cylinder Car in America," it made its debut in 1906 and was famed for its hill-climbing ability and speed. After Mason sold his interest in the venture to Frank and Elmer Maytag, the Duesenbergs moved to Waterloo and built passenger cars named after them, but when the Maytags decided to concentrate on washing machines, Mason brought Fred and Augie back to Des Moines and set them up in a little shop

EDDIE RICKENBACKER

back of a Dodge dealership to build four-cylinder race cars powered by an innovative engine Fred had designed. With Mason's help, the Duesenbergs began competing on the AAA tour. Encouraged by the performance of their new model in the 1912 season, they were building three cars for 1913 when Edd came looking for a job.[38]

Fred was a genius and Edd benefited immensely from his knowledge. Working sixteen hours a day, filing connecting rods from rough forgings and balancing them carefully for smooth operation and maximum speed, he paused only long enough to gulp down a chocolate milk shake containing two raw eggs for lunch.[39] Physically, he felt better than he had in a long time and was full of energy. He had been sober since taking up racing and had also quit smoking. He arrived promptly for work at six in the morning and later recalled that the Queen of Sheba would have been unable to keep him from retiring early enough to get a good night's sleep.

As Memorial Day approached in 1913 the cars were only marginally ready for action, but the Duesenbergs had stretched Mason's funds to the limit and needed the publicity a good showing at the Indy 500 would provide. Even though the racers needed a few finishing touches, they shipped them by rail to Indianapolis. Edd helped paint them a dark tan during the trip and was still fussing with them when the train got to its destination. He later said that entering them in the Indy was foolhardy because they were "so full of 'bugs' that they might well have won first prize as entomological exhibits."[40]

Edd was exaggerating. Willie Haupt, a member of the Duesenberg team, finished ninth out of twenty-seven drivers at the race, winning $1,500. Bob Evans ran 157 laps before going out with a damaged clutch. Jack Tower, at the wheel of the third Mason, flipped over in the 54th lap and broke a leg.[41] The outcome could have been much worse for the "Dutch farmers from Iowa," as racing enthusiasts called the Duesenbergs. The performance of the engines on which Edd had worked impressed experts. About 100 cubic inches smaller than most of the ones used in the Memorial Day event, they performed at least as well, saving weight and reducing costs. The Masons had shown that they could compete with new European cars, including a Peugeot driven by the winner, Jules Goux.

Edd's sour feelings may have been caused by being unable to drive in the race and having to watch it from the sidelines in the pit crew. Soon afterward, however, N. J. Ruggles, president of the Columbus Automobile Club, persuaded the AAA to lift his suspension so he could race as a "native son" at the city's Driving Park on Independence Day.[42] Edd was overjoyed not only because of his reinstatement but also because he could compete on his home turf, with his mother, siblings, and local fans cheering him on. He was also proud to be the teammate of a giant in motor sport, Ralph Mulford, who had won the Vanderbilt Cup. Mulford had raced for the Lozier Motor Company, which went into decline and abandoned the tour, leading him to join the Duesenbergs. He was a devout Christian, admired for his clean-cut image, his abstinence from alcohol and tobacco, and his avoidance of racing on Sundays.[43]

Edd's job in the 200-mile event was to be a decoy for Mulford, the role he had played for Frayer at Columbus in 1910. He got off to a fast start and the partisan crowd cheered wildly as he led Mulford and Ralph De Palma after the first lap, but the furious pace was too much for his Mason and he was forced to leave the track with mechanical problems after going 107 miles. Still, he did a good job for Mulford, who won the race.[44]

Edd's performance gave him a regular slot on the Duesenberg team, far preferable to being with the Flying Squadron. Harrowing experiences in what remained of the 1913 season left him undismayed. On 28 July, in a 300-mile race at Galveston, Texas, one of his tires blew out when he was going 90 miles an hour. Instead of coming off the rim, it got caught and flapped repeatedly across his left arm and shoulder, hitting him like a club. Suddenly, as he considered leaving the race before his arm was fractured, the blows stopped. Climbing out of his seat, his riding mechanic, Eddie O'Donnell, had thrown himself across Edd's body and was absorbing the punishing hits. By the time Edd got to the pit both men had severely lacerated arms and torsos and O'Donnell had a separated shoulder.[45] Edd later had a wreck at St. Paul, Minnesota, that led him to design a special cowl to protect him from being thrown out of his car. The first among a number of inventions he conceived in his racing career, it worked. In November, when he ran a 10-mile race at San Antonio, the track was wet from rain. Disregarding the slippery surface, he took a turn at terrific speed and went end over end. When he realized he was about to turn over, he ducked under the cowl and suffered a separated shoulder but could have been much more badly hurt in the only severe injury of his entire racing career.[46]

Nevertheless, he also savored his first victories since his early days in Iowa and Nebraska, including a 100-mile triumph at Cincinnati. He also placed fourth in the prestigious Elgin Road Race in Illinois. When the AAA published its national standings for 1913, he ranked a respectable twenty-seventh, with 115 points.[47] Considering that his license had been suspended when the year began, things had turned out well despite the shoulder separation that sidelined him near the end of the season. Among his greatest rewards was winning respect from his peers in a hazardous profession in which recognition did not come cheap. After the San Antonio race, Ralph De Palma, talking to drivers in a hotel lobby about Edd's new cowl, praised his combination of audacity and forethought, calling him "the most daring and withal the most cautious driver in America today." Another racer called Edd "the nerviest and most unerring of them all."[48] Nursing his wounds, he aimed to do even better in 1914.

Chapter 4

— ☆ —

Full Throttle

The 1914 season began with a prestigious road race at Santa Monica, California, on 28 February. At stake was the AAA's Grand Prize. An American car—a Mercer, made near Trenton (in Mercer County, New Jersey) by a firm passionately committed to engineering excellence—won the event for the first time. The layout was so treacherous that only five of seventeen drivers at the starting line, including Eddie Pullen, who drove the Mercer to racing glory, finished the course. Rickenbacher, increasingly known as "Eddie" among fans, possibly because his style reminded fans of Pullen's, was among those that dropped out. Rounding a nasty curve, "Deadman's Turn," in the thirty-fourth lap, his car flipped on its side, slid off the road, and careened into a ditch. The crankshaft broke, but he was not seriously injured.[1]

The race marked the last time the cars he drove were called Masons. From this time on they were Duesenbergs, a marque that became world famous. But the brothers were running out of money and the future looked bleak. Turning to Eddie, they showed their respect for his abilities by appointing him manager. Besides overseeing drivers, riding mechanics, and pit crew members, he handled scheduling, business operations, and accounting, drawing on experience he had gained selling cars for the Columbus Buggy Company. Despite his new responsibilities he received no extra compensation other than a larger share of whatever prize money the team won—not much. By May, with the Indy 500 looming ahead, the Duesenberg brothers, still headquartered at Des Moines, faced bankruptcy unless their team won a share of the $39,750 purse—a huge sum at the time.

The stress Eddie felt as he prepared the team for the tour's biggest annual event set him looking for a magic charm. As always, his superstitious nature stood out, even in a fraternity of drivers among whom superstition was rife. Before leaving Des Moines for Indianapolis, he found that a black cat was stuck between the spokes of a wheel in the Duesenberg shop. Incapable of resisting the appeal of animals, he decided to let the cat—a female he named "Lady Luck"—ride with him in a box behind the seat of his racer. Driving a red, white, and blue Duesenberg, he was thrilled to be competing at the Memorial Day classic for the first time in two years. Because of the money Fisher and his partners had put up, the 1914 contest lured European drivers. The unprecedented throng of 100,000 spectators was eager for a good showing by the United States, particularly against France, which disdained American speed records. French drivers set a blistering pace in qualifying runs and held their American rivals, even Barney Oldfield and Bob Burman, in contempt. "We will take your fine money," boasted Jules Goux, who had won the race the previous year.

The contest abounded in thrills and injuries, some fatal, to drivers and riding mechanics. Only thirteen of thirty cars finished as tires exploded, camshafts broke, cylinder bolts came loose, and engines caught fire. When the carnage ended French drivers walked away with most of the purse. Oldfield, recently reinstated by the AAA after being suspended for engaging in unsanctioned events—including racing against Jack Johnson, the first African American to become heavyweight boxing champion of the world—salvaged a vestige of national pride by placing fifth. Eddie made a respectable showing, finishing tenth, but fans were disheartened. "Today has been a bad day for America," lamented a trade magazine. "Our hopes have been crushed to earth."[2]

Despite Eddie's efforts, the Duesenberg team won no prize money, and its hopes of staying solvent were even worse than before. The last chance for survival was a 300-mile sweepstakes on Independence Day at Sioux City. Taking his cat, Lady Luck, Eddie went to Columbus to visit his mother and told her how badly things were going. Steeped in Swiss folklore, Lizzie told him to kill a black bat before the Sioux City race, tie its heart to his right middle finger with a red silk thread, and wear the grisly talisman during the contest. Never was Eddie's superstition more evident. Willing to try anything, he decided to take her advice.

Late in June he put three Duesenberg race cars on a night train from Des Moines to Sioux City and boarded a passenger car with two drivers, four riding mechanics, and Lady Luck. The team's total funds consisted of six silver dollars. Unable to pay garage fees, Eddie parked the cars under the grandstand at the racetrack, which had been built in a cornfield in a tip of South Dakota bordering northwest Iowa. He spent $2.50 for a week's board and lodging at a farmhouse. The rest of the men slept on cots with the cars. Eddie got a restaurant owner to provide meals for the team on credit and agreed to pay the farmer's son his last dollar for a live bat. How they would get back to Des Moines if they lost was a mystery.

Eddie devised a plan for victory based partly on the strategy Frayer had used in the race in Columbus against Oldfield. Knowing that drivers with more powerful cars could outrun him in the straights, he would drive as fast as he could on the turns. Rocks and gravel under the dirt surface of the racetrack formed a mixture that drivers called "gumbo." For protection against being hit as it flew back from beneath the wheels of other cars, he devised a protective wire screen and mounted it on his windshield.

The Sioux City Speedway Association had billed the 300-mile sweepstakes as the biggest event in the community's history. Members had taken out a $25,000 insurance policy with Lloyd's of London in case rain forced its cancellation. To attract the best possible field of drivers the association offered a large purse—$10,000 for first place, $5,000 for second, and $2,500 for third. Lured by the money, Bob Burman, Billy Chandler, Ralph Mulford, Barney Oldfield, Mel Stringer, Howdy Wilcox, Spencer Wishart, and other stars would compete. As the day of the race drew near, local residents spotted cars with license plates from states as far away as New York, New Hampshire, Georgia, and Nevada. The racetrack was in the best possible condition. "Thousands of gallons of boiling oil" had been poured on its surface, "practically petrifying the top soil," a newspaper reported before the qualifying runs began. Ten-ton steam rollers had leveled the surface to make it "as hard as macadam." As a result, some cars went almost 90 miles an hour on the turns and came close to 100 in the stretches. As Fred Wagner weeded out drivers who failed to achieve the minimum speed in practice trials, carpenters built extra seats to bring the capacity of the grandstands to 30,000 people because ticket sales had been better than anticipated.

Eddie survived the qualifying trials but was discouraged by an apparently bad omen when Lady Luck disappeared—to raise a family, he guessed. He had a Catholic priest bless the team and its cars. Finally, incredible as it seems, he implemented his mother's hoary advice. At about ten o'clock on the night before the race, the farmer's son brought him a live bat, "a mean-looking little mouse-colored creature," and he went into town to buy some red thread. Most stores had closed for the night but he found a spool of scarlet yarn at a shop that remained open. Rising at four o'clock, he took the bat, which he had put in a perforated box so it could breathe; decapitated it; cut out its heart; and tied it with the red yarn to the middle finger of his right hand.[3] As he went about his demonic work, thousands of people were waking up in hotel rooms and getting ready for the race. Railroad companies within a radius of 500 miles had brought spectators on excursion trains. People unable to find lodging had slept in wagons near the track, hoping to be first in line to buy tickets when the gates opened.[4]

By noon the expected 30,000 fans filled the grandstand under a broiling sun. Eighteen race cars waited in withering ninety-one-degree heat, ready to explode into a cacophonous roar when Wagner detonated the starting bomb. There was no doubt what the spectators wanted. "In all of its moods and whimsies," said a reporter, "the crowd . . . looked for a tragedy," waiting eagerly for "the thrill of blood." As always, an ambulance was ready to carry off the dead and wounded.

Wagner set off his bomb and the race began. Burman set a torrid pace but blew a tire on the sixteenth lap, after which Oldfield led the pack for about 100 miles before being forced out with a leaking radiator. One by one, cars left as engines overheated, tires exploded, and fuel lines caught fire. "As the race wore on," stated a newspaper, "the strain began to tell on drivers and machines, and all precautions for safety were forgotten by the hooded, begoggled men who crouched behind the steering wheels of their cars urging them to the limit of their capacity. The terrific impact of the machines began to roughen up the track, especially at the turns." Burman went out with a broken steering gear. A clod of earth hit Cyrus Patschke in the face so hard that his goggles were covered with blood and he could barely see. Nevertheless, he crawled along, hopelessly behind. Tom Alley's Duesenberg burst into flames from overheating, burning his head and chest. The ambulance rushed him to a hospital. Ralph Mulford took his place after the car cooled off. Somehow, incredibly, he drove it on.[5]

Halfway through the race the contest was between Rickenbacher and Wishart, a rich young sportsman driving a custom-built Mercer. Following his plan, Eddie tried to keep up on the straights and pull ahead of Wishart on the turns before again slipping behind. Every time Wishart entered a turn he sprayed a stream of gumbo at Eddie, whose left elbow, jutting out of his cockpit, took such a terrific pounding that the pain was almost unbearable. The screen on his windshield did him no good, and flying rocks hit his forehead. Despite everything, he stayed focused.

Abruptly, however, he began losing oil pressure. His mechanic, Eddie O'Donnell, responsible for manually working the oil pump in emergencies, had been knocked out by a chunk of gumbo and was unconscious for five laps. Keeping one hand on the steering wheel, Eddie worked the oil pump with the other. Somehow he held his own against Wishart until O'Donnell came to and started pumping again.

Gaining ground on Wishart every time they rounded a turn, Eddie finally pulled ahead and gained a full lap. From then on he never lost the lead and finished almost two minutes ahead of Wishart, whose fate was sealed when he had to make a pit stop. Still, the end came just in time; one of Eddie's tires exploded after Wagner waved his checkered flag. Had the blowout occurred earlier, Wishart would have won. Instead, Eddie enjoyed his first major victory. Taking his teammates to the finest hotel in Sioux City, he had them soak themselves in hot baths to wash off the gumbo and gave them the best meal money could buy. Mulford had driven Alley's flame-scorched car to a third-place finish, bringing the Duesenberg team's combined winnings to $12,500 and saving its owners from bankruptcy. It was a moment to savor.

The rest of the 1914 season was anticlimactic for Eddie and the Duesenberg team. He placed second and third in two 50-mile races at Galveston but had a series of setbacks caused by accidents and mechanical failures.[6] At the Iowa State Fair, pitting his race car against an airplane, he won a handicap race against stunt pilot Lincoln Beachey.[7] He also won a 100-mile race by ten seconds against Louis Disbrow at Libertyville, Illinois, where he had been victorious a year before. By the end of the 1914 season, he had climbed from twenty-seventh place in the AAA's national standings to sixth, an enormous leap, proving himself to be a champion who could compete with the best the tour had to offer.[8]

Despite his achievements, Eddie looked back at 1914 with mixed feelings. The saddest event occurred late in the season on the eight-mile course at Elgin, where on the fourteenth lap, Wishart paid a price for his "reckless cornering." While trying to pass on a narrow stretch of the course's north leg, he collided with one of his teammates and quickly spun out of control. Plowing through a picket fence and into a farmyard, Wishart injured several spectators, slammed into a tree, and died instantly. Wishart, who had recently married Louise McGawen of Indianapolis, was only twenty-four years old. Eddie and the entire racing community, in which Wishart was extremely popular, deeply mourned his death. Eddie had been forced out in the seventh lap with mechanical difficulties. Not until the twenty-second did he reenter the race to relieve Alley. He was not on the track when the accident happened, but had a close call of his own that same day after taking over from Alley. When Bill Elliott's riding mechanic gave a misleading hand signal, Eddie, who was deliberately trying to set a mark for driving the fastest lap in the race, had to choose between hitting a telephone pole and going into a ditch. Heading for the ditch, he benefited from its V-shape, which prevented him from going out of control, and he survived. But he bent an axle and broke his driveshaft, forcing him out near the homestretch. He walked to the finish line.[9]

He did not know he had gained an important admirer that day. Amid the crowd lining the course was Lowell Thomas, a student at the Chicago-Kent School of Law and part-time reporter for the *Chicago Evening Journal*, accompanied by a friend, Preston ("Cap") Burtis. Thomas, who became one of the most famous broadcasters of the twentieth century, marveled at the élan with which Eddie competed against more-experienced drivers like De Palma and Oldfield. He was awed that a young man "only a year or so older than Cap and I were . . . had already thrown himself into the maelstrom of life, dreaming big dreams, unafraid to test himself against the roughest and toughest."[10]

The 1915 season ended well for Eddie but was flawed by poor judgment on his part. After his breakthrough at Sioux City, he had no trouble finding a backer with deeper pockets than the Duesenbergs. Before the end of the 1914 season, he left their team and found a more prestigious sponsor. The outbreak of war in August of that year shut down race car production in Europe, but Fiat, Mercedes, Peugeot, and Sunbeam continued to compete in the United States. In 1912 Peugeot had introduced a new four-cylinder engine with twin overhead camshafts, hemispherical combustion chambers, and two pairs of elegantly machined valves per cylinder. These features were far ahead of their time; ultimately they became standard in almost all race cars. Further refinements led to vehicles so much admired that a sports writer spoke of the relationship between them and their drivers as "a fitting theme for a word painter like Kipling."[11]

Eddie expected to reach the pinnacle of the racing profession by joining Peugeot. Visiting the offices of the Peugeot Auto Import Company in New York City, he was impressed by a dark blue racer with the same features as one driven by Bob Burman, already a member of Peugeot's American team. Taking it across the continent by rail, Eddie entered it in a 300-mile road race at Corona, California, on 26 November 1914. Because it had been through hard use in France, he had it overhauled at Los Angeles and painted with his signature color, white. As usual, he jumped ahead of the pack to an early lead at Corona, but engine trouble forced him out after 108 miles. It was neither the first nor the last time that his heavy foot turned out to be counterproductive.

The first major event of the 1915 season was the Point Loma Road Race, a 300-mile event at San Diego. While preparing for it, Eddie devised a way to communicate with his riding mechanic above the roar of traffic, using two matching sets of masks and helmets connected by rubber speaking tubes. He also continued to use the weird good luck charm recommended by his mother. In Los Angeles, on his way to San Diego, he bought a bat, took it to a pet store, and asked the owner to keep it until he returned from practicing for the contest. When he came back to claim it, however, the proprietor told him the creature had died in an unseasonable cold snap. Eddie took the news as an ill omen and brooded about it. His fears seemed to be confirmed at Point Loma when a broken connecting rod forced him out after he had taken another early lead. The speaking tubes worked well, but the masks were "unbearably hot and itchy" and he abandoned the invention.[12]

Having failed in two successive races, he decided he had made a mistake by signing with Peugeot. In the worst move of his racing career, thinking his car needed more work than he could afford, he quit the team. Harry Miller, a mechanical genius, overhauled the vehicle, which made racing history in the hands of a more mature driver than Eddie. Dario Resta, a native of Italy, had built an exceptional record after going to England and racing for Sunbeam, which sent him to America early in 1915 to prepare for the Indy 500. Leaving Sunbeam, he joined Peugeot after Eddie left and performed spectacularly at the wheel of his former car after Miller had finished with it. Eddie later publicly admitted that leaving Peugeot was the greatest mistake he had ever made.[13]

He had abandoned Peugeot partly because American fans wanted American drivers to win championships in American cars on the American tour. Reports from Detroit said that Ray Harroun, winner of the 1911 Indy 500 and chief engineer of the Maxwell Motor Company, had designed a new race car with a counterbalanced crankshaft to reduce engine vibration, aluminum alloy parts that gave it an exceptional horsepower-to-weight ratio, and other advanced features permitting it to attain speeds up to 105 miles an hour. It would be unavailable until the Indy 500, but Eddie decided to ignore the delay and joined the Maxwell team, led by Barney Oldfield. Paul Hale Bruske, the team's manager, announced the news by declaring that Eddie's style of driving "resembles, more than that of any other American driver, that of the foreign pilots who have electrified motordom by their wild flights of speed and their reckless daring." Bruske said nothing about finesse, the key element of Resta's style.[14]

The Maxwell Motor Company was all that remained of the United States Motor Corporation (USMC), which had collapsed under the weight of too many ill-assorted marques and models. Eugene Meyer, who later acquired the *Washington Post,* organized a syndicate that bought USMC, mainly to secure the services of Walter Flanders, one of America's greatest automotive engineers.[15] Maxwell's race cars, however, had a major flaw. In an experiment aimed at cost-cutting, Harroun had used kerosene, which vaporized less readily than gasoline, resulting in carburetion problems.[16] Eddie also had to accept second billing behind Oldfield. Along with a third driver, Billy Carlson, who became known as "Coal Oil Billy" because of his association with Maxwell's kerosene-fueled racers, Eddie would be a decoy for Barney, who would hang back and surge to victory in the final stages of a race. He had unwittingly hooked up with a manager who shared Will Pickens's zest for hippodromes.

Weather, kerosene, and carburetor trouble proved fatal to the Maxwells at the American Grand Prize and Vanderbilt Cup races, both held at San Francisco. Resta, so little known in America that gamblers gave fifty-to-one odds against him, won the Grand Prize, driving Eddie's former Peugeot in a torrential downpour. Heavy rain on the day of the race turned the track into a sea of mud, but Resta, who "ignored the rotten weather," took a "terrible beating of the rain in his eyes and face" and amazed fans that marveled at his skill in handling the slippery course. Eddie was forced out with engine trouble after slithering 218 miles.[17]

The Vanderbilt Cup Race began well for Eddie, who got off to his customary fast start and was the first driver to complete a lap, but Resta soon caught up with him and "engaged in a brush which provided some pretty racing on the straightaways." Engine trouble forced Eddie out in the seventh lap after he had gone only twenty-eight miles. An account of the race praised Resta for his "generalship," saying that "Rickenbacher was out to pass the foreign driver and to lap him" but that "Resta was content to speed up only enough to keep himself abreast of his competitor and not to pass him. Resta appeared to drive with his eyes on a stopwatch, Rickenbacher with his eyes on the car ahead of him."[18]

Carburetor trouble traceable to kerosene forced too many pit stops for any of the Maxwell drivers to win the Vanderbilt Cup. After the race, Rickenbacher, Carlson, and Oldfield threatened to quit unless Bruske agreed to modify the engines to use gasoline. After Bruske acquiesced, Oldfield won two races at Venice, California, and Tucson, Arizona. Carlson finished second in both contests. Eddie was fourth at Tucson, overshadowed by Oldfield, who set a world record by making twenty-five laps of the four-mile Arizona desert course without shifting gears or making a single pit stop. Nevertheless, Oldfield remained unhappy with Bruske's management and soon resigned. By this time Eddie was so unsure of himself that he asked Pickens, whose cunning he admired, whether he should retain the name "Rickenbacher" or choose a flashier identity. Pickens told him the key object was to win and everything would be all right.[19]

Ernest A. Moross, a veteran driver and showman, took over the Maxwell team in Oldfield's place and agreed to make Eddie its star driver. Moross's most prized possession was the Blitzen Benz, the German behemoth in which Oldfield and Burman had set speed records at Daytona Beach. To boost Rickenbacher's image, Moross falsely told reporters that Eddie had also made record-breaking runs in the giant car, but Eddie merely drove it as a stunt vehicle in a one-mile race at the Columbus Driving Park, finishing second when a water pump clogged. A photograph, probably from a Columbus newspaper, showed Eddie, wearing a straw hat, driving a car towing the Blitzen Benz. It later appeared in his autobiography with a caption claiming he had set a world speed record with the vehicle in 1912. The persistence with which Eddie clung to the myth does him no credit. It was a claim that he hardly needed.[20]

Eddie won his first victory for the Maxwell team in a 25-mile race at the Driving Park on 16 May 1915. Knowing his mother was among the spectators and not wanting to have an accident that would upset her, it was hard to concentrate, but he won anyway. In a 100-mile race, however, a cloud of dust distracted him and he crashed through a fence, scattering planks and hitting a post that nearly impaled his riding mechanic. After both men climbed out without serious injury, Eddie ran up the steps of the grandstand to tell his mother he was unhurt, but she had already gone home to fix supper.[21]

Eddie had high hopes for the Indy 500, where he would drive one of the new racers built by Harroun, but he could not resist playing a trick that demonstrated his immaturity and cost him any chance of victory. He had noticed that the brick surface of the Speedway was highly abrasive in the initial stages of a race but got smoother as dripping crankcase oil and shreds of rubber from tire wear formed a protective coating. To extend the life of his tires, he devised a system comprising a one-gallon tank, copper tubing, and a pump with which his riding mechanic could spray oil on the two outside tires in the turns to reduce abrasion in the early going. The apparatus did not actually violate AAA rules because nobody had ever thought about it, but Eddie had doubts about its legality and concealed it by hiding the tank under the mechanic's seat.

He continued to rely on the grotesque talisman he had first used at Sioux City. His brother Albert shipped a live bat to Indianapolis, where Eddie kept it in a cigar box. Early on the morning of the classic, preparing for his ghoulish surgery, he opened the box. The bat seemed to be dead but suddenly spread its wings and escaped, which he regarded as an ill omen. Before the race began, members of his pit crew draped their overalls over the right side of his car to prevent officials from seeing the oil-spraying system. Eddie got off to his usual fast start but had forgotten to connect the oil pump to the crankcase as well as to the outer wheels. Midway through the race a crankshaft bearing burned for lack of lubrication, forcing him to leave the track. Noticing oil dripping from the side of the car, officials looked for the cause and readily found it. Grinning sheepishly, an embarrassed Eddie admitted what he had done, the system was disallowed, and he was disqualified. Because there were no specific rules barring the technique, however, he escaped suspension. First place went to De Palma, who won the race in an ardous bout with Resta.[22]

Stung by the debacle, Eddie switched to a new strategy that the AAA could not countermand and the season began to turn around. In San Francisco he had met Harrison (Harry) Van Hoven, a talented young man from Sioux City. Although he was grossly overweight and had trouble fitting into the mechanic's seat in a race car, Eddie hired him as a member of his pit crew. Van Hoven's intelligence yielded important results. As one writer later said, "there was no fat behind his eyebrows." He was an excellent organizer, so Rickenbacher made him pit manager.

Van Hoven believed in scientific management and trained the crew rigorously to perform standardized operations in carefully timed sequences. Under his drilling, members learned to fill the gas tank of a race car, check the oil, replenish the radiator with water, and change all four tires in less than fifty seconds, minimizing the time Eddie had to spend in the pit.[23] After stumbling through the opening months of the season, he now pioneered in adopting time and motion study, which had swept through the automotive and industrial world without being used on the AAA tour.

The results quickly became apparent. Early in July, after Van Hoven had whipped the pit crew into shape, Eddie went to Sioux City for the Independence Day race he had won in 1914. The AAA Contest Board was now featuring several holiday events, and many of the leading drivers on the tour were racing elsewhere. Only 10,000 fans attended the 300-mile sweepstakes, making the stands that had been jammed with spectators only a year before seem virtually empty. Resta had entered the race and was favored to win, but a broken bearing forced him out in the sixth lap.

Sensing a chance to end his string of losses, Eddie raced so impetuously that he violated AAA rules about cutting in and out of traffic. At one point Fred Wagner stopped him for a warning. In another, more regrettable episode, T. C. Cox, driving an Ogren Special, hit one of Eddie's rear wheels a glancing blow, spun out of control, crashed through a fence, and died later that day. Eddie claimed he was so intent on his driving that he did not learn what had happened to Cox until after the race. His statement seemed plausible because even Wagner's warning failed to break his concentration, and he won a stretch duel with his former riding mechanic, Eddie O'Donnell, whom the Duesenbergs had promoted after Rickenbacher left their team.[24] Defeating O'Donnell marked the first time in a year that Eddie had won a major race.

His ability to stay focused was all the more remarkable because of rumors that Maxwell would disband its racing team as a result of disagreements with the AAA Contest Board. After the race, he was celebrating his victory by drinking milkshakes with Van Hoven when a reporter revealed that Maxwell would abandon the tour after the next race, which would be held at Omaha in two days. Just as Eddie was regaining his stride, he was losing his job.[25]

The Omaha race, on 5 July, was the first running of a 300-mile board-track event. Remembering Eddie's victories at the Ak-Sar-Ben festival in

1910, newspapers hailed him as a returning hero. Buoyed by the publicity, he won his second major event in three days, taking the lead at the outset and never losing it. O'Donnell, again his principal opponent, made a long pit stop with engine trouble on the fifteenth lap and finished thirteen minutes behind in second place. Because board tracks (with planks laid side to side with their edges facing up) were exceptionally fast, Eddie's speed averaged 91.07 miles per hour.[26]

Despite savoring the $18,500 he had won in his two victories, Eddie worried about the demise of the Maxwell team. On the other hand, he had regained the aura of a champion, making him more marketable. After going to Detroit to wind up his affairs with Maxwell, he went to Indianapolis to talk with Carl Fisher and his chief partner, Fred Allison. Knowing that increasing problems were affecting American motor sport, he persuaded them to give him an unusual opportunity. Because of the poor showing made by American-made race cars at major events in 1914 and 1915, the AAA was pressuring factory teams to field better vehicles, adding to the cost required for automobile manufacturers to remain on the tour. Maxwell was only one of several firms that had withdrawn from competition because racing was becoming a money trap. At the same time, the European war, now entering its second year, was stopping production of racing vehicles and drying up the supply of foreign champions, many of whom were working in defense-related industries. In the face of this decline, however, the schedule of sanctioned events was expanding because of new speedways at Des Moines, Omaha, and Tacoma, thus increasing the need for cars and drivers. In response, Fisher and Allison were thinking about organizing their own teams and hiring experienced American drivers to staff them. Eddie had gone to Indianapolis at a good time. Knowing that Maxwell's fleet of race cars was for sale, he urged Fisher and Allison to buy them, improve them to meet new AAA standards, and make him manager of a team under their sponsorship. Johnny Aitken, a veteran racer from Indianapolis, had the same idea. After having a disappointing career as a driver, he had become pit manager for Peugeot but wanted to return to competition and win the Indy 500 to make up for previous failures.[27]

Being approached by Aitken and Rickenbacher was a godsend for Fisher and Allison, who saw an opportunity to capitalize on the desire of American fans that American drivers and American cars prevail over European competition. Aitken's association with Peugeot made him a logical candidate to head a team that would use its aging cars against an aggregation headed by Rickenbacher, using upgraded Maxwells. On 14 September 1915, Fisher, Allison, and some associates filed papers to incorporate two new enterprises, the Indianapolis Speedway Racing Team Company and the Prest-O-Lite Racing Team Company, each capitalized at $20,000. The Speedway Team, headed by Aitken, would include a popular driver, Howard ("Howdy") Wilcox, and field two used Peugeots soon to be imported from France, which had no need for them. The Prest-O-Lite Team, managed by Rickenbacher, would have four rebuilt Maxwells.[28]

Eddie agreed to pay Fisher and Allison 25 percent of his team's winnings and defray operating expenses, salaries, and travel and maintenance costs out of the rest. Fisher and Allison would pay for the Maxwell race cars, replacement parts, repairs, and making the vehicles into more competitive models known as Maxwell Specials. Another provision in the contract stipulated that all racers Eddie recruited must be unmarried so they would not have family concerns to worry about as they risked their lives. Otherwise, Eddie would have a free hand. "For a fellow who had landed in Sioux City in 1914 with only six silver dollars," a friend recalled, he "had done very well indeed."[29]

The contract with Fisher and Allison marked the first time that the name "Eddie Rickenbacker" appeared, substituting an anglicized spelling with a "k" for a Germanic one with an "h." It had an appealing sound for an already popular sports personality. Eddie continued to use the regular spelling of his surname for formal purposes, adding "V" as his middle initial after deciding he liked it better than other letters in the alphabet. When he published an article in *Motor Age* in September 1915, depicting riding mechanics as the unsung heroes of motor sport, he used the name "E. V. Rickenbacher." The identity of his coauthor, J. C. Burton, a well-known automotive writer, indicated his rising stature.[30]

Adopting the middle initial "V" suggests that Eddie was searching for a new identity at a time when his fortunes were improving. His parents had not given him a middle name at birth, and it took time for him to decide what V stood for. Decisions loomed on either side of his middle initial as well. Would he use his given name, Edward, his nickname Eddie, or perhaps go with E. V.? And would it be Rickenbacher or Rickenbacker? Circumstances would determine his choice to some degree, of course. But Eddie knew he was changing, emerging from a chrysalis into a brightening future, and wanted to show it.

Returning to the tour in mid-September, he won the first race in which the Prest-O-Lite team competed, a 100-mile contest seen by 40,000 fans at Narragansett Park in Providence, Rhode Island. He was no longer hunting for bats but still relied on a combination of good luck charms and rational planning. Because the Narragansett track had an asphalt surface and the turns were more gently banked than at most other raceways, he saw a chance to go the entire distance with no pit stops if he kept a steady pace and used wide tires instead of the narrow ones, designed to go around turns at high speed, used by most of his peers. He secretly ordered a set of wide tires and had a truck deliver them just before the race. As other drivers looked on in amazement, Van Hoven's pit crew exchanged Eddie's regular tires with the new ones in sixty-three seconds.[31]

Things did not work out exactly as planned. Despite Rickenbacker's hope of finishing without stopping, fouled spark plugs forced him to pit at 15 miles. Van Hoven's team may have been unusually slow, because by the time he got back on course the field had lapped him three times, but he made up for the loss by circling the 1-mile oval in unofficial times of 47 and 48 seconds in his first two laps after being sidelined. By the 30-mile mark he had regained one of the laps; at 56 miles, the second. From then on it was a battle with De Palma, whom Eddie caught at 73 miles, and Burman, from whom he finally wrested the lead at 77. By the 80-mile mark there was no stopping him, and he cruised to a first-place finish in 1 hour, 29 minutes, and 24.70 seconds. His average speed, 67.10 miles per hour, was slow compared with the times achievable on some tracks but commendable for an asphalt surface. *Horseless Age* congratulated him on winning "an uphill race by a splendid exhibition of driving."[32]

Eddie won no more races in the 1915 season, which was dominated by the growing success of Stutz race cars, convincing fans that American-made vehicles were winning their rightful place in motor sport. He did, however, place third in a 100-mile election day race for the Harkness Trophy at an enormous board-surfaced speedway that had recently been built at Sheepshead Bay on Long Island. Resta finished the season ranking first among money winners on the tour, but Eddie advanced from sixth to fifth by earning $24,000. He also won a special award from *Motor Age* for placing first in three speedway events at Sioux City, Omaha, and Providence. The magazine published a photograph of him with a triumphant smile on his grease-streaked face, calling him "unquestionably . . . one of the greatest of American drivers."[33]

Even more would be expected of him the following year. Soon after the 1915 season ended, Stutz withdrew its team from the tour. Part of the price of success on the racetrack was a mounting sales volume that prevented the company from remaining in private hands. Alan A. Ryan, a Wall Street speculator, was poised for a takeover. *Horseless Age* called the action taken by Stutz "a distinct shock to the race promoters who are hard pressed for entries for their long string of 1916 events."[34] It was also a setback for the AAA, which wanted to expand the tour to twenty-five championship races in 1916 and was embroiled in strife with the American Association of Fairs (AAF), whose interests were hurt by the rise of new speedways. At stake was the integrity of motor sport. Everyone knew that races at county and state fairs were often fixed, with artfully staged close finishes that thrilled spectators who did not know what was taking place behind the scenes. The AAA stood for respectability, as shown by its effort to improve American race cars and Wagner's zeal to ferret out gamblers and enforce rules.[35]

The Contest Board could count on unfailing support from the owners of the Indianapolis Speedway and its marquee attraction, the Indy 500. Confronted by the withdrawal of Stutz and other automobile companies from the tour, the battle with the AAF, and the war in Europe, Fisher and Allison believed that vigorous competition between the racing teams headed by Aitken and Rickenbacker, one driving Peugeots and the other representing Uncle Sam with Maxwell Specials, would bring out fans with a patriotic desire to see America win on the racetrack. More than Eddie's personal success was on the line amid preparations for 1916.

Rickenbacker spent the winter of 1915–16 in Indianapolis getting the Prest-O-Lite Racing Team ready for the upcoming season. He wanted to overhaul and improve the Maxwells for serious competition with foreign cars, particularly Peugeots. Although its French manufacturers had made nothing but trucks and military engines since 1914, its prewar racers were still first-class machines.[36] Its American team, led by Burman and Resta, threatened to dominate the tour with Stutz out of the running. If Eddie could transform the Maxwells into better cars, win more prize money, and control costs, he would get 75 percent of the added earnings. He was no longer a racer but a racer-entrepreneur.

Enjoying the backing of Fisher and Allison gave Eddie a chance to change the Maxwells in creative ways. His new sponsors typified men of power and wealth who from this time on backed him because of his demonstrated ability, technological ingenuity, and sheer guts. Fisher, the richest person for whom Rickenbacker had yet worked, had joined an accomplished engineer, Fred Allison, in building Prest-O-Lite into a $6 million business. In 1913 he and Allison had sold Prest-O-Lite to Union Carbide for $9 million under an agreement to retain operating control for four more years. Allison set aside 12,000 square feet of a new Indianapolis plant to overhaul, improve, and create race cars capable of defeating the finest European models, sparing no expense to get the best equipment and technicians money could buy. In his superb facility, Eddie and a team of talented helpers modified the race cars Fisher and Allison had bought from Maxwell.[37]

Eddie's budget enabled him to adopt any idea that might improve the cars. He installed more efficient intake manifolds, a force-fed lubrication system permitting circulating oil to stay cooler, stronger connecting rods, and new valves and lifters. He put streamlined bodies on the old chassis, hoping to add up to twelve miles per hour to the speed of the vehicles. He replaced the stubby rear configuration of the 1915 model with a conical tail containing the main fuel tank. An enlarged inlet permitted more fuel to be pumped into it faster than before. He also added an auxiliary fuel tank that could be accessed by moving a lever under the steering wheel. He put his own signature on the cars, now called "Maxwell Specials," by painting them white with red trim and showed his artistic flair by designing a heart-shaped grill as a distinctive finishing touch.[38]

He drove his staff unsparingly from seven in the morning to late at night. To combat fatigue he brought a phonograph to the shop and played snappy marches.[39] He adopted an incentive program under which anyone on the payroll could win a share of the team's winnings with outstanding performance, and a policy of promoting technicians to riding mechanics and drivers if warranted by their abilities. To show that he meant what he said, he promoted Pete Henderson, a diminutive, baby-faced riding mechanic in 1915, to drive one of the team's race cars in the upcoming season. Henderson could barely see over the cowl but had a fierce desire to excel. Rickenbacker also wrote a detailed list of rules and procedures he expected employees to follow, ending with a blunt admonition to leave the team if they were unhappy with the way it operated.

The rules included getting adequate sleep the night before an event and making a trip to the urinal immediately before it began. "It can be very painful if you get caught during a race," Eddie said, "and it will impair your efficiency and end up in a disaster." Other rules forbade losing one's temper, bragging, and petty bickering. He mandated standardized procedures for pit crews to follow in making repairs or changing tires, and devised twenty-five secret signals that, when combined, formed about 100 messages. Encircled numbers, posted on a blackboard held aloft in a race, would tell how fast a driver had gone in a given lap. A zigzag line meant that "something is dragging under your car; if you don't know what it is, find out immediately."[40]

Rickenbacker's new entrepreneurial role required him to set priorities and allocate resources. Because fewer teams would be available in 1916 for a larger number of races, the AAA had decided to concentrate its schedule by shifting the Vanderbilt Cup and Grand Prize events to November and holding only a few exhibition contests on the West Coast in the early months of the year—the equivalent of baseball's spring training. The first championship race, for the Metropolitan Cup, would be held at the new Sheepshead Bay track on Long Island in mid-May. Studying how to cut costs and maximize profits, Rickenbacker decided to race solely in events that would count in the official standings and skip the openers in California. Forgoing a spring tune-up would give him more time to prepare for meaningful races without incurring unnecessary travel costs. Because the modified AAA schedule concentrated more championship races in a shorter season, he decided to split his fleet whenever two major events took place simultaneously in different cities. Using high-speed rail transport would permit the team to compete in every important race on the tour. When only one event took place on a given weekend, he would take all four cars so that one could substitute for another in case of accidents.

While Rickenbacker got ready, Aitken was doing likewise with his Indianapolis Speedway Team. Fisher and Allison found only two usable Peugeots in wartime France, forcing them to build a pair of clones at the Premier Motor Company, which they controlled. Aitken hired veteran racers Gil Anderson and Tom Rooney to drive them. Implementing the rules the AAA had adopted in 1915 to upgrade American race cars left only thirty-seven vehicles in the United States with the required weight and piston displacement. The Duesenberg brothers had five cars ready for competition, but the disappearance of Stutz, Maxwell, and other factory teams forced greater dependence on rich sportsmen who had dominated American motor sport in its early years. Harry Harkness, an enthusiast whose father had made a fortune in Standard Oil, imported three Delages from France, but fewer cars and drivers would participate in more races than in 1915. Fans worried about declining standards as the European war dragged on and American manufacturers earned more profit from making production cars than staying in racing.[41] The death of Bob Burman from multiple injuries in a California road race that had no bearing on the national rankings cast a pall over the upcoming season before it officially began.[42]

As the race at Sheepshead Bay approached, Rickenbacker seemed to be the man most likely to win the Contest Board's national championship under a point system recently adopted by the AAA. Articles in automotive magazines heralded him as the nation's "most daring pilot" and contained ballyhoo about his personal life, especially his attractiveness to women. Among females supposedly smitten by Eddie was Irene Tams, a leading actress on the silent screen. A columnist wrote that she had sent Rickenbacker a telegram proposing marriage if he would give up motor sport, to which Eddie replied that "a woman is only a woman. My soul mate is a racing car." Undiscouraged, Tams reputedly sent him a photograph that led him to tell friends he was "slipping" and would pack his trunk for a secret wedding at her home in Jacksonville, Florida.[43]

Rickenbacker was probably too busy thinking about Sheepshead Bay to fantasize about marrying a movie star. Living up to expectations, he scored one of the epic victories of his career in the featured 150-mile race for the Metropolitan Trophy. A dramatic moment occurred on the thirteenth lap while he was bunched with four French cars coming into a steeply banked turn. Suddenly the right rear wheel of a Delage driven by Carl Limberg, a member of Harkness's team, came off. As the car flew into the air, the wheel rolled down the slanted surface and narrowly missed hitting Resta's Peugeot. The rear axle and remaining wheel whizzed past Rickenbacker on one side and the rest of the Delage missed him on the other, going end over end toward the infield. Limberg and his riding mechanic were catapulted over the top of the embankment and died outside the grandstand. As wreckage caught fire at the bottom of the curve, black smoke spread across the area where the crash had taken place.[44]

Rickenbacker displayed phenomenal concentration amid the disaster. In the instant that he escaped being hit by the flying debris, he saw Limberg and his mechanic sail over the top of the curve and noticed that none of the wreckage remained on the track. After he rounded the speedway and returned to the same spot, officials were waving warning flags amid the smoke and other drivers were slowing down. Knowing that the track was clear and ignoring the flags, he jammed his accelerator to the floor and drove through the smoke at top speed. Contrary to his later claims, his display of nerve did not in itself lead to victory but did improve his chances of winning. Taking the lead for the first time in the thirty-sixth lap, he fought a spirited battle with Jules De Vigne, another member of the Harkness team, in the next thirty-three circuits. He finally broke away from the French driver in the final six laps, winning the race with almost two minutes to spare. He was lucky to have escaped disqualification for failing to heed the warning flags—possibly indicating how badly promoters wanted an American to win. Of all his victories, this one best exemplified his ability to stay focused and process multiple developments in a single moment, anticipating skills he later displayed as a combat pilot.[45]

Winning the Metropolitan Trophy gave Rickenbacker an early lead in the national standings with 600 points under the new AAA system. Assuming that the Maxwell Special had taken up where Stutz had left off, an automotive journal exulted in the victory, proclaiming that "Once again America has triumphed in the arena of speed . . . against the best that the world could do."[46] Pocketing $10,000 for his victory, Eddie set out for the Indy 500, scheduled two weeks later. At the annual classic he and his teammate, Henderson, wore steel crash helmets for the first time in automobile racing. In another display of creativity, Rickenbacker used radio technology, then in its infancy, stationing an operator with a short-wave sending set in the center of the infield, deploying four observers equipped with telephones at intervals around the track, and putting a receiver in his car. The observers told the operator about the relative positions of other drivers and then the operator radioed the information to Eddie, but to his disgust the message was distorted by static, caused by the sparkplugs and magneto.[47]

The paucity of contestants indicated the problems facing the tour. Because of the war only a few European drivers participated. Eight men who had driven in 1915 had been killed in crashes. Only thirty drivers registered, of whom only twenty-one qualified, the lowest number in the history of what fans derisively called the "Indy 300" because the AAA had cut 200 miles off the distance, claiming that "short, snappy races with plenty of dash and higher speed than the drivers would dare to attempt in a long race should draw large crowds." Numerous empty seats in the grandstand showed the strategy had backfired. Knowing that Fisher and Allison wanted to have a larger field, De Palma, the previous year's winner, had tried to negotiate a deal for merely showing up, but Fisher indignantly rejected it, saying, "If we have to pay Ralph to come here, eventually, we'll have to pay every name driver to appear." The absence of a defending champion detracted from the race before it began.

Like Rickenbacker, Aitken had never won at Indianapolis. Pushing his Peugeot to the limit, he got the pole position by driving it 96.69 miles an hour in the qualifying rounds. Rickenbacker also won a position near the pole and got off to an excellent start by leading the first nine laps, but a connecting rod bearing failed, forcing him off the track. The mishap was actually a stroke of luck because a steering knuckle broke as he drove his car into the pit. Had it fractured when he was at top speed, he and his riding mechanic could have been killed or seriously injured. Aitken was also forced out when he popped a valve, giving Resta's Peugeot an easy victory over Wilbur D'Alene in a Duesenberg, the only American-built car in the top five. Rickenbacker substituted for Pete Henderson in the closing stages and placed sixth. By winning, Resta garnered 900 points in the national championship standings and went ahead of Rickenbacker, who was now in second place. The entire contest was a lackluster affair.[48]

A 300-mile championship race at Chicago two weeks later attracted 90,000 spectators. As at Indianapolis, only twenty-one cars qualified. The weather was clear and the sun beat down unmercifully. A reporter marveled that the Prest-O-Lite pit crew had fifty spare wheels in reserve. After the race got underway, Van Hoven watched intently for any sign of malfunctioning every time Rickenbacker and Henderson passed the pit. At the end of the first, he muttered, "She don't sound right. I thought we had all the 'bugs' out of her, but if I'm not mistaken there's a 'cuckoo' showing up." Soon afterward Rickenbacker pulled in and took off his headgear, revealing "deep red lines on his smeared face where the goggles and helmet have pinched." He calmly observed that a valve had broken 50 miles into the contest but said he had kept going "to make things as merry as possible" for Resta, who won the race and garnered another 900 points in the national standings, giving him 1,800, three times as many as Eddie had to his credit.[49]

At Sioux City Rickenbacker won the annual Independence Day race, now reduced from 300 to 100 miles, for the third straight year. He seemed to be in a class by himself as a dirt-track racer. Local fans were so accustomed to seeing him win that they now called the event the "Rickenbacker Race." Unfortunately for Eddie, who had such affinity for soil-covered courses that he had become known as the "King of the Dirt-Track Racers," it was the last such venue of the season.

At Omaha newspapers again lavished praise on Rickenbacker as a hometown favorite, emphasizing the victories he had won in and around the city early in his career. "His car isn't as fast as some of the others," said one writer, showing that the Maxwell Special's limitations had become common knowledge, "but he's a driving fiend, and he knows how to drive the Omaha track as none of the others do." After showing good sportsmanship by giving Mulford a ride around the course to show him how to take the curves, Rickenbacker smashed a local record in the qualifying heats by coaxing his car to slightly more than 102 miles an hour. The 150-mile championship race, however, was another disappointment as Resta and Mulford won first and second in their Peugeots and Henderson prevented a wipeout for Prest-O-Lite by placing fourth. In a 50-mile free-for-all Rickenbacker took second and Henderson came in third after "a desperate battle for honors with Dave Lewis," who drove for the Crawford team, sponsored by the Crawford Automobile Company of Hagerstown, Maryland. De Palma won the race in a Mercedes, averaging 103.45 mile per hour. It was increasingly clear that the Maxwell Specials, for all the attention Rickenbacker had lavished on them, could not outrace the best foreign cars.[50]

Rickenbacker failed to finish a race at Kansas City, putting him even farther behind Resta in the hunt for the national championship as he prepared for the 300-mile Montmarathon in early August at Tacoma, Washington. The track was made of two-by-four-inch planks with gravel and dirt between them to fill the cracks, a murderous surface for tires. De Palma and his Mercedes seemed likely to provide the main competition. Rickenbacker and Van Hoven had closely observed De Palma's pit crew and thought the Prest-O-Lite team might be able to win if they could limit the Maxwell to two tire changes and refill their gas, oil, and water only once. After the team arrived in Tacoma, Van Hoven and his crew practiced changing tires as fast as possible to shave precious seconds off the time it took Rickenbacker to get back on the track. As he had done in Columbus against Oldfield, Eddie decided to push De Palma as hard as possible on turns to wear down the tires of his heavy Mercedes.

Rickenbacker, not De Palma, blew a tire first, but Van Hoven's pit crew put four new wheels on the car and replenished all its fluids in fifty-nine seconds. When De Palma had a blowout soon thereafter, his pit crew needed a minute and a half to perform the same sequence. It was nip and tuck from then on until Rickenbacker's tires began to fail at 250 miles, and he pitted. Shouting through a megaphone while the crew worked frantically, Van Hoven had Eddie back on the boards in forty-nine seconds. Soon De Palma had another blowout and it took his crew two full minutes to replace the tire. Rickenbacker led the field by a wide margin from this point and won by a half-mile over Tommy Milton and Dave Lewis. De Palma slipped to fourth. It was a heartening triumph, but, as Eddie said, "it was won in the pit, not on the track."[51]

As the season wore down Rickenbacker went to Indianapolis for a "Harvest Classic" of 20-, 50-, and 100-mile races staged by Fisher and Allison on 9 September. At most 12,000 people turned out, showing the tour was fizzling. Aitken took both short-distance races, which Eddie ignored because they were not championship events, but the 100-mile competition, which counted in the AAA standings, was probably the most spectacular contest of his racing career. He and Aitken needed a win to stay in contention for the national title. For 75 miles they were neck and neck, with Eddie losing ground to Aitken's Peugeot on the straights and trying to compensate in the turns. After 90 miles the steering arm on one of Aitken's wheels broke, slowing him down but not forcing him off the track. At this point Eddie began to walk away with the race.

Suddenly, however, with only five miles to go, his right rear wheel began wobbling. He still had an apparently comfortable lead going into the homestretch at the west turn, but half a mile from the finish line he heard what sounded like a rifle shot as one of the wooden spokes began breaking in his left rear wheel. As it continued splintering, that wheel also began to wobble. Officials tried to flag him off the track, but he knew he would lose if he stopped and refused to quit. Aitken was also in extremis at this point because his broken steering arm was dragging on the ground and he could hardly move, even at greatly reduced speed. Cars that Aitken and Rickenbacker had lapped roared around them, adding to the drama. As Eddie entered a turn, his left rear wheel "let go with a helluva bang," and he began spinning around. "His car careened first right, then left, then right again," stated an account of the spectacle. Four cars "seemed about to hit him broadside," but "the Maxwell began sliding backwards and just in the nick of time gave the right of way to the cars bearing down upon it." As Rickenbacker struggled to maintain control, his right rear tire blew out; then he narrowly missed hitting a retaining wall when the front tires exploded. As wreckage scattered in all directions, he came down hard on his brake drums and wound up in a patch of grass beside the retaining wall. Climbing out of the car, he and his mechanic walked to the pit, and the stands erupted in cheering "equal to that ever recorded any winner."

Aitken "drove the last eight miles with only one front wheel attached to his steering apparatus," but mushed across the finish line. "Well, at least I finally won at the Speedway," he quipped. Rickenbacker called the event "one of the grandest free-for-alls" in which he had ever been involved. An account of the race that went out over the wire congratulated Rickenbacker for the "masterly control" he had shown. He, not Aitken, was the hero of the event. But the accolades he earned did nothing to change the fact that he had lost and his chances for a national championship were now virtually zero.[52]

Another championship event, the Chicago Speedway Race, took place on 14 October. Rickenbacker placed third. Feeling the title slipping inexorably from his grasp, he was exhausted and had had enough of the Maxwell Specials. His despair was so great that he abruptly disbanded the team. After paying all his expenses for parts, travel, express car charges, salaries, incentives, and percentages of winnings to other members of the aggregation, his personal earnings were still about $40,000, more than he had ever made on the tour, but he had failed to achieve the national championship, which was more important to him than any financial reward. Resta was again leading the field with the Peugeot that Eddie had given up, and Aitken seemed sure to win second place driving the same marque for the Indianapolis Speedway Team.[53]

It was a bitter experience for Rickenbacker, all the more disappointing because he had supervised the effort to make the Maxwell Specials competitive with Peugeots, still clearly the world's best race cars despite their age. But Eddie's zest for driving was undiminished, and he was already thinking about the 1917 season. Louis Coatalen, chief engineer for Sunbeam, had contacted him with an exciting possibility. If Rickenbacker could not beat Resta and Aitken with an American car, he might do it with a British model. Soon he was on his way to New York

City, preparing to go to England, where a bizarre situation awaited him because of his Germanic name and the wartime anxieties prevailing in Britain. Before he went, however, an unexpected series of adventures would occur in the United States. His racing career was yet unfinished, and aviation was about to become part of his life.

Chapter 5

— ☆ —

Shifting Gears

When he arrived in New York City, Rickenbacker had no reason to suspect that he was approaching a major pivot point in a hero's saga beginning to assume mythic proportions. Although he had never crossed the Atlantic, which in itself would be a novel experience, and despite the unusual opportunities a relationship with Coatalen would give him, what was happening seemed normal and expectable, given Eddie's career trajectory and the internationalism of motor sport. Champions like him would never lack offers from promoters. Because of his close associations with reporters who covered the racing scene and his acute awareness of scuttlebutt passing around the tour, he knew exactly why Coatalen had invited him to England and expected no surprises. On the other hand, there was no telling what exciting developments lay in store for him amid European motordom, and Coatalen was not the only person he intended to visit.

Coatalen, a native of Brittany who had left the French motor car industry because he did not believe it offered him the opportunities merited by a racer and engineer of outstanding promise, had scaled the heights of British motor sport in his rise to power in Sunbeam, making the company a worthy rival of Peugeot. He had a score to settle with Resta, whom he had brought to America in 1915, intending for him to drive a Sunbeam at the Indy 500. Instead, Resta defected to Peugeot after Rickenbacker left its team and Miller overhauled his French-made race car. Resta had consolidated Peugeot's role as the dominant force on the American tour, and Coatalen had every reason to feel betrayed. Sunbeam was now developing a better car than the Maxwell Special for the 1917 tour, and Coatalen wanted Eddie to drive it. Coatalen's commanding status as a world-class automotive engineer was an accolade to the status Rickenbacker had attained in a few short years since breaking in as a lowly member of the second-rate Flying Squadron. Working with Coatalen, "an aristocrat among technologists," as one of his many admirers called him, would be like taking a postgraduate course in race car design. Partly because of Coatalen's French origins, Sunbeam and Peugeot were bitter rivals. After Peugeot improved its already fine racers in 1914, Coatalen acquired one of the new models, took it apart on his living room floor at Wolverhampton, and copied its features. When war broke out later that year and racing ended in Europe, he moved into building innovative aircraft engines but preserved Sunbeam's presence on the American tour. "What the Sunbeam Motor Car Company has achieved in the past fifteen years," stated a historian in 1924, "is mainly the fruit of Mr. Coatalen's manifold genius."[1] Not since working under Frederick Duesenberg had Eddie had a chance to study with a comparable designer.

Rickenbacker, however, received another offer besides the one from Coatalen. Soon after arriving in New York and preparing to sail to England, he got a call from William (Billy) Weightman III, an eccentric Philadelphian whose family had amassed a reputed $80 million in the pharmaceutical industry.[2] Weightman had been a soldier of fortune in Mexico and served with the French army when it turned back the Germans at the Marne early in the European war. After returning from France, he had dabbled in the motion picture industry to promote an actress with whom he was smitten but became more enamored with automobile racing and wanted to compete on the AAA tour.[3]

Weightman had bought two Duesenberg race cars and wanted Rickenbacker to drive one of them in the last three events of the 1916 championship season: the Vanderbilt Cup, Grand Prize, and Ascot races, all scheduled to take place in November in California. Rickenbacker drove a hard bargain but accepted, realizing that if he swept all three races he would still have a slim chance of winning the national title, which Resta had not yet clinched.[4] Postponing his trip to England, he took a train to the West Coast.

Soon after arriving, he went to Riverside, noticed a plane on a grass airstrip near a hangar, and stopped to look at it. Recognizing the visitor's well-known face, the owner of the plane came out of the hangar, introduced himself as Glenn Martin, and offered to take him aloft. It was the first time Eddie had ever had a chance to fly. Ironically, in light of the future awaiting him in aviation, he was so acrophobic that looking down from atop a tall building made him dizzy. He was unaware that seeing the ground from an aircraft did not cause such sensations and had to screw up his courage to accept Martin's invitation. Hiding his fears, he climbed into the plane and was surprised that he enjoyed the thirty-minute flight, during which Martin pointed out landmarks below, shouting above the roar of the engine to make himself heard. Only when the ship came in for a landing and the ground seemed to rise to meet them did Eddie feel an exhilarating sensation of terror.

Martin was one of America's foremost aircraft designers and manufacturers. Thirty years old, he had recently become involved in a merger establishing the Wright-Martin Aircraft Company. He would soon close his Los Angeles factory to move to Cleveland. He and Eddie hit it off from the start, and their paths would cross again.[5]

Rickenbacker soon had another experience with aviation. Driving in a rural area near Los Angeles, he saw a single-seat military biplane whose pilot had been forced down in a pasture. Offering to help, Eddie traced the problem to a coupling in the engine that had become separated from the magneto. The stranded airman was Major Townsend F. Dodd, an officer in the Army Signal Corps, which was in charge of aeronautics at the time. "Turn it over," Eddie said after making the repair. As Dodd swung the propeller, the engine surged to life. Thanking Eddie, Dodd climbed aboard the plane and disappeared into the sky. Like Martin, he too would meet Rickenbacker again.[6]

A stripped gear forced Eddie out of the Vanderbilt Cup race in the early laps. Resta won and nailed down the national championship. Weightman was so avid about motor sport that he drove as a "dark horse" in one of his Duesenbergs. Defying the odds, he finished third and won $1,000. Rickenbacker may have been embarrassed that his patron, a rank amateur, had bested him in a prestige event. Eddie also fared poorly in the Grand Prize Race, when a broken driveshaft forced him off the track in the twenty-sixth lap.[7]

Things went differently at the last event of the season, a 150-mile Championship Award Sweepstakes at Ascot Speedway in Los Angeles on Thanksgiving Day. Because the final rankings had already been decided, Resta and Aitken, assured of first and second place, did not enter. Rickenbacker had clinched third place but competed for part of the $5,000 purse as one of only twelve starters. Eddie Pullen led throughout much of the race, but Rickenbacker forged ahead and crossed the finish line far in front of the pack.[8]

Despite the way it ended, the season had been a bitter disappointment. Resta dominated the final standings with 4,100 points. Aitken had 3,440, Rickenbacker 2,910. The Bosch Magneto Company had offered a trophy and $2,000 to the top driver, $1,000 to the second, and $500 to the third. Not to be outdone, the B. F. Goodrich Company added a much larger sum, $10,000, to the purse, to be split $5,000, $3,000, and $2,000. Resta would receive a cup and $7,000 at a dinner held by the AAA Contest Board at Chicago on 1 February 1917. Aitken would get $4,000, Rickenbacker $2,500.[9]

Eddie, now becoming known on the tour as "Rick," missed the ceremony because he carried out his agreement to visit Coatalen in England. Because he was still on the wagon, he had taken a strong dislike to Weightman, who drank heavily. Although he regarded his wealthy sponsor as "a horrible nuisance," his feelings did not prevent him from making a deal with Weightman, who, like Coatalen, dreamed that Rickenbacker would win the 1917 national championship under his patronage. To attain that dream, Weightman put up the money to send him to other European countries to find a suitable car. By the time he embarked from New York, he carried several letters of introduction from American automobile executives, addressed to foreign entrepreneurs. Reporters speculated wildly about what he would do on his trip. He might acquire a huge chain-driven 300-horsepower Fiat, powered by a dirigible engine.[10] But he might also buy or lease two Sunbeam Sixes and form a team with Joseph Christiaens, a Belgian racer now working for Coatalen. Not knowing what would happen, Rickenbacker did not divulge his plans—or lack thereof.[11]

Taking the Santa Fe Railroad on the first leg of his trip back to New York, he thought about the good luck charms he had used and decided they had done him no good. He recalled that a flying object had nearly hit him on the head after he had deliberately avoided walking under a ladder. Feeling he had been a fool for being superstitious, he went to a toilet compartment and emptied his pockets of an assortment of objects that he was carrying: "lucky elephants and four-leaf clovers; Billikens and tail buttons of rattlesnakes; rabbits' feet and other charms in dozens." Throwing them down the bowl, he pulled the chain and watched them cascade onto the track.[12]

On his way east he stopped at Indianapolis, where rumors were rife about his dealings with Weightman, and at Columbus, where he visited his mother before going to Washington, bearing letters from the Indianapolis Motor Speedway and the editor of *The Automobile,* to obtain a passport, number 41696, on 13 December. He gave his name as Edward Rickenbacker, signed with a distinct second "k," and spelled his father's surname the same way. Besides containing a mug shot, the document specified his physical characteristics: height, 6 feet, half an inch; eyes, brown; forehead, high (he already had a receding hairline); hair, light brown; complexion, fair; face, oval; chin, square; nose, regular. A witness, A. S. Batchelder, indicated that he had known Eddie personally for seven years. An entry visa secured from the British Consulate General in New York City the following day listed Eddie's occupation as "automobile engineer."[13] Soon thereafter he boarded the *St. Louis* and sailed for England, reflecting that he had not previously crossed a body of water wider than the Mississippi River. Now, improbably, an immigrant's son who had only a few years before worked at the Evans Garage was bound for England at the invitation of one of the world's greatest automotive engineers.

Passengers aboard the ship included William Thaw II, scion of a rich Pittsburgh family. He had helped found the famous American volunteer squadron, the Lafayette Escadrille. Others persons on the ship included two men, traveling under the names of Goodyear and Immermann, who were ostensibly involved in the wheat business in Chicago. Rickenbacker noted that they did not have American accents and thought naively that they were probably Canadians. He conversed with them throughout the voyage, joking about the risks people with Teutonic names took by going to England while it was fighting Germany. He did not realize it was no joking matter.

When the liner arrived in Liverpool a few days before Christmas, Rickenbacker noticed that Goodyear and Immermann were not standing in line to have their papers checked. As he tried to go ashore, a "hook-nosed official" detained him. Accusing Rickenbacker of being a German spy, he took him to a cabin where his two traveling companions, now "colder than the god-damndest icicles that you ever saw in your life," revealed themselves to be agents of Scotland Yard. A policeman helped them conduct a brutally thorough strip-search of Rickenbacker. They "rubbed lemon juice and other acids on his skin to bring out any secret writing," wrote a friend he later told about his ordeal. They also refused him permission to contact Coatalen.[14]

Rickenbacker had become an unsuspecting victim of the ballyhoo pervading the racing tour, which thrived on misinformation about celebrity drivers. Instead of telling the prosaic truth, that he was a son of

Swiss immigrants and had grown up in Ohio, tabloids had concocted an elaborate myth that he was Baron Edwardt von Rickenbacher, "a young Prussian nobleman who had fallen victim to the deadly Bacillus Motorus." Crazed by a lust for speed, he had absconded from the Vienna Military Institute in a stolen Mercedes. After reconsidering what he had done and returning to the institute, he was enticed into competing with a famous German racer, Max Sailer, who was "demonstrating a new model for the benefit of a member of the General Staff." Showing his prowess, the young baron left Sailer's car behind, covered "with a lot of dust." Expelled from the institute and disinherited by his father, he went to America to enter the AAA tour, determined to show his father that he "didn't have to starve just because he couldn't wear one of the snappy uniforms of the Imperial German Army."[15]

It was a ridiculous story, but British intelligence had swallowed it whole and filed it along with earlier clippings referring to Rickenbacker by various Teutonic nicknames. His captors told him he would not be permitted to leave the ship until it sailed back to America, threatening to abort his mission before it began, but he talked them into letting him go ashore for Christmas and register at a hotel, at which they took rooms on either side of the one he occupied. After dinner he decided brashly to go for a walk. The streets were gloomy, lit only by "little blue shafts" at intersections. Zeppelins had staged a bombing raid on British coastal and industrial areas in late November, and the city was blacked out.[16] Rickenbacker's pursuers followed him until he reached a dark alley. Sneaking into it, he ran as fast as he could, went around a corner, and stopped in his tracks, wondering why the agents had not tried to shoot him. When they found where he was hiding and apprehended him, he brazenly invited them to a nearby pub and bantered with them over drinks, after which they took him back to the hotel. The next morning, Christmas Day, Rickenbacker phoned Coatalen, who quickly straightened things out with Scotland Yard. A message from London ordered his captors to release him. By afternoon on the following day, after his passport was stamped by the Alien Office in Liverpool, he was on a train bound for the British capital. Coatalen had arranged for him to stay at the luxurious Savoy Hotel, overlooking the Thames near Westminster Bridge.[17]

Rickenbacker arrived at the Waterloo Station after dark. London was shrouded in dense fog. Unable to get a cab, he impulsively decided to walk. He wandered about, utterly lost, until a man appeared out of the murk, told him to grab his coattails, and led him to the Savoy. When they finally got there at one o'clock in the morning his mysterious benefactor refused to accept any pay for his help. "Good luck and God bless you," he said as he disappeared into the night.

But the ordeal had not ended. The desk clerk refused to give Rickenbacker a room until he had registered with the police. A porter took him to a nearby station where he was fingerprinted and given a certificate that had to be stamped wherever he went. He got back to the hotel by three o'clock and crawled into bed, exhausted. Coatalen arrived the next day and arranged to take him to Wolverhampton after the Christmas season.

Nothing in Rickenbacker's previous experience had prepared him for the class-consciousness that prevailed in England. Out of his element staying at the Savoy, with High Tea in the afternoons and room service from staff members accustomed to dealing with a more distinguished clientele, Rick, already indignant because of his treatment by Scotland Yard, began to develop an Anglophobia that remained with him all his life.[18] On the other hand, he was grateful for the pampering the Savoy gave its patrons and enjoyed the Yuletide. On New Year's Day he sent a cable to Artemas Ward, president of the King Motor Car Company in Detroit, which had dealerships in England and for which he had agreed to scout postwar sales prospects. He told Ward about his detainment in Liverpool but said he was now receiving "every consideration." Coatalen was obviously looking out for him. Rickenbacker had examined automobiles on the streets with a practiced eye and said there was "nothing new in body designs that I have run across as yet." Because of the war, no touring cars were being built. "All of England's young men are in khaki and I must admit I feel strange when walking down the street." He told Ward he expected to be in Wolverhampton "for a week or ten days before going to France and Italy."[19]

After the holidays he made weekly trips by rail to Wolverhampton, in England's "Black Country," where he found lodgings near Sunbeam's vast Moorfield Works at Villiers Street and Marston Road. Spending long hours every day with Coatalen and his staff, he checked in at the Detective Office before reporting for duty. Coatalen, whose motto was "Racing improves the breed," remained committed to designing race cars, even though he was now involved in developing aero engines. Under his tutelage, Rickenbacker learned that the excellence of European race cars came partly from high compression ratios and more revolutions per minute, with resulting gains in power. He liked the mechanics and engineers at the plant. Some of them, like racing driver Josef Christiaens, were Belgian refugees. He was, above all, impressed by their devotion to the war effort. Despite his detention in Liverpool and the class consciousness he had seen at the Savoy, his growing friendship with his fellow workers convinced him that America should enter the war against Germany. His changed sentiments notwithstanding, Coatalen told him repeatedly that he was under surveillance and should act accordingly.[20]

On weekends he returned to the Savoy, reporting his whereabouts to the police at the Bow Street Station. His suite gave him a fine view of Big Ben and the Houses of Parliament. What intrigued him most, however, was the sight of airplanes flying up and down the Thames. Asking about them, he learned that they came from Brooklands, where airmen bound for the front now used the infield of the speedway as a training ground for the war in France. Seeing the aircraft made him eager to join the Royal Flying Corps. Unable to restrain his curiosity, he went to Weybridge, where, surprisingly, nobody stopped him from entering the grounds. Hangars where A. V. Roe and T. O. M. Sopwith were making aircraft ringed the track. The infield was a runway for landings and take-offs. Young recruits practiced under pilots who had fought in France and were now flight instructors. Rick was awed by talk about aerial warfare on the western front. When he returned to Wolverhampton, he said he wanted to enlist in the Royal Air Service, but Coatalen advised him to return to America and race for Sunbeam in the upcoming 1917 tour. Rick decided he would become a combat pilot if the United States entered the war.[21]

Prospects for visiting France and Italy disappeared as tensions mounted between Germany and the United States. Throughout January 1917, as Rick shuttled between Wolverhampton and London, Democrats and Republicans were bitterly debating what course of action to take. Led by Theodore Roosevelt, Republicans sneered that President Wilson was a coward for saying a person could be "too proud to fight."[22] When Germany announced it would commence unrestricted submarine warfare at the beginning of February, the United States broke off diplomatic relations. Germany advised Americans abroad to go home within five days and Rick prepared to leave England as soon as possible. Things were "jammed to the hilt" in Liverpool, but an American who was about to embark offered him space in his cabin. Rick said he would "sleep on the god-damned floor if he'd let me sleep there." He had to be in Liverpool before the end of the day, and Coatalen told him to leave immediately. After he hastily packed his bags, Christiaens took him on a hair-raising ride to Liverpool. He arrived and had his papers stamped at the Aliens Office on 3 February, only an hour before the *St. Louis,* the same vessel that had brought Rick across, would sail for New York. In his luggage were engineering drawings he planned to take back to America, along with some letters and a few books to read during the voyage. At the pier the same hook-nosed official who had detained him in December confiscated them. After boarding, Rick was taken to a cabin where Immermann and Goodyear—if such were their names—interrogated him at length, delaying the vessel from leaving port. In the end they allowed him to sail, but he had to send all of his drawings and reading materials back to Coatalen. When he went on deck after his ordeal, he found Gene Buck, a friend from Detroit, lounging in a salon chair. Greeting him, Buck said that there was a German espionage agent aboard. Rick said half-jokingly that he was the spy.[23]

During the voyage, despite his indignation, he thought about a plan to implement when he got home. "If war is declared I will enlist at once for aviation work," he told reporters after arriving in New York, saying he "already had some experience," an oblique reference to meeting Martin and Dodd in California. Because entering the war would "put a damper on automobile racing for the coming season," he planned to recruit drivers and riding mechanics to join him in an aerial unit that would fight on the western front. "We are experts in judging speed and in motor knowledge," he said. "I expect to get up a body of not less than fifty of us who will volunteer if war is declared."[24] Before leaving the city, he talked with Captain W. G. Kilner, commander of an army air unit stationed at Hempstead Plains, claiming he could identify "at least twenty drivers of international reputation who would eagerly join such a body." Kilner told him to go to Washington and talk with the Signal Corps.[25]

Leaving New York, he went to Cleveland and Detroit to begin recruiting racers for his volunteer unit. As he traveled, he wondered if someone was trailing him. By the time he reached Detroit, he suspected that a "blond Englishman" was the person. After visiting his mother in Columbus and going to Chicago for more meetings with drivers and riding mechanics, he continued to Los Angeles, noticing when he checked in at the Alexandria Hotel that the sandy-haired stranger did likewise. Soon afterward, in the lobby, the man introduced himself, told Rickenbacker that he and his superiors had decided he was not a spy, and thanked him for the pleasure of following him all the way from Liverpool.[26]

As he crossed the continent, Rick found that the farther west he traveled, the more remote the war seemed to people he met, but things changed abruptly in early March when Wilson revealed that the British had intercepted and decoded a secret telegram in which German foreign minister Zimmermann had instructed his ambassador to Mexico to offer that country the return of its "captured provinces"—the territory it had lost in the Mexican-American War—if it joined the kaiser in a war against the United States. Suddenly, Rick observed, a war taking place halfway around the globe now seemed to be looming on the Rio Grande. As indignation swept through California, one of the "captured provinces," it seemed clear that hostilities with Germany were imminent.[27]

Feeling he had enough support among racers to implement his plan, Rickenbacker headed for New York to deal with a nagging case of tonsillitis. Dr. Harold Foster, a throat specialist, advised surgery. Coming out of anesthesia, Rickenbacker felt blood gushing from his mouth. Foster was attending another patient, and staff members could not stop the hemorrhaging. Rick sank into a blissful stupor and sensed he was about to die. Mobilizing his deepest inner resources, he demanded to see Foster and fought to survive until the surgeon ran into the room. Shoving a sponge down his throat, Foster, who had accidentally nicked an artery during the tonsillectomy, soaked up as much blood as he could. Clamping the artery shut, he stopped the bleeding.[28]

Events moved rapidly as Rick convalesced. On 2 April Wilson asked Congress to commit America to the holocaust. After heated debate the legislators agreed, and the United States was at war with Germany.[29] As soon as Rick had fully recovered, he went to Washington to present his plan to the Signal Corps. He said he had enlisted some of the nation's best racing drivers, including Earl Cooper, Ralph De Palma, Ray Harroun, and Ralph Mulford, in his projected unit, the "Aero Reserves of America," but got nowhere. Brigadier General George D. Squier and his staff quickly assessed Rick unfit for a military command. His faulty grammar and lack of polish showed that he lacked the educational credentials to be officer material. His interrogators dismissed it as a joke when he answered questions about whether he had a college degree or its equivalent by telling them about the correspondence courses he had taken from ICS. Rejecting the value of his mechanical and engineering experience, they even called it a handicap, saying that a flyer who knew too much about technology would not want to risk his life if he thought something was wrong with his engine. The clinching argument was that Rick was too old—twenty-seven—to meet the age limit for pilots.[30]

Rick had carried out his drive for volunteers out of his own pocket, and his finances were badly depleted. Meanwhile, his hopes of competing for a national championship under the patronage of Coatalen or Weightman had evaporated. As soon as America declared war, Fisher and Allison had suspended the Indy 500 for the duration, and the speedway became an aviation depot.[31] Nevertheless, some racing was still taking place and promoters were planning a 250-mile Memorial Day event in Cincinnati. The winner would get $12,500, a major inducement for Rick considering his dire straits.

During the winter De Palma had designed and built a race car, the "Detroit Special." Rick gladly accepted when De Palma invited him to drive it at Cincinnati. During a trip to Detroit to talk about the car, Mary Alice le Cain, the daughter of a fellow racer, gave him a leather folder containing a Crucifix, telling him no harm would befall him as long as he carried it. He put it in one of his pockets and transferred it whenever he changed clothes.[32] It stayed with him the rest of his life.

For Rick, however, the Cincinnati event would be the race that never was. British and French military officials had visited the United States, saying the situation was so desperate that not only materiel but manpower was needed to prevent a German victory. Wilson decided to send an expeditionary force to Europe under the command of General John J. Pershing, who hastily assembled a staff to sail from New York as soon as possible.[33] More importantly for Rick, Wilson suggested to one of his cousins, John A. Wilson, who was president of the American Automobile Association, that it would be a good idea for the AAA to select a well-known racing driver to go to France as a driver for Pershing. Cousin John relayed the idea to Richard Kennerdell, chairman of the AAA Contest Board, who chose Rickenbacker. Not long after Rick arrived in Cincinnati a phone call came from Major Lewis Burgess, a racing fan helping plan Pershing's departure. Burgess inquired whether Rick would like to go along as one of the general's chauffeurs. Rick asked to think things over. When Burgess called the next day, he said he would come to New York after the race. Burgess said if he failed to show up in New York the next morning, he might as well not come.[34]

Hastily packing his bags, Rick told Van Hoven to get a relief driver and took a train for Columbus for a short visit with his mother. He did not tell her what he was doing, merely saying he was on a business trip to the East Coast. Taking an overnight express train to New York, he arrived as stipulated by Burgess on 28 May 1917. By noon he had enlisted as a sergeant in the Army and was about to embark on the *Baltic,* a twin-funneled ship of the White Star Line.[35] The voyage was supposedly secret, but supplies had been piled at the dock for days, plainly labeled for Pershing's staff. Officers ordered to report in mufti came in uniform. When Pershing finally boarded, the ship cast off in late afternoon on a cold, rainy day. Throughout the night its whistle blew every three minutes as it plowed through heavy fog.[36]

Deep in the steerage, tossing in a hammock in a filthy compartment crawling with bugs, Rick tried to sleep. Leaving racing behind, he went forth to the mighty conflict.[37]

The *Baltic* had an uneventful voyage across the Atlantic. Except for fog lingering along the East Coast, the weather was clear.[38] Unable to stand conditions in the steerage and the sight of maggots crawling out from under oilcloth covering tables at mess, Rick seized the first opportunity to go on deck. A friend from racing days was on the ship, wearing a sergeant's insignia but enjoying much better accommodations. When he said he was a sergeant first class, Rick suddenly realized there were categories of sergeants he did not know about. Fortunately, Major Dodd, Pershing's chief aviation officer, whose airplane engine Rick had repaired in California, was aboard. Thinking one good turn deserved another, Rick asked Dodd for a promotion to sergeant first class. Dodd gave it to him on the spot. He got a comfortable cabin and far better food. Bribing the chef, he took daily baskets of fresh fruit and other food to his former steerage companions.[39]

On 5 June the ship entered perilous waters and began zigzagging. Two American destroyers provided escort at this point, and the *Baltic* ignored distress signals from other ships lest they be fakes sent by German submarines. The U-boat campaign was at its peak. Fifteen vessels went down off the British coast while Pershing and his staff were at sea, but they came through unscathed. Rick later complained that the crossing was "terribly dull," saying that an attack by the "Boche" (uncomplimentary French slang for Germans) would have been a welcome diversion. On 8 June the *Baltic* steamed into Liverpool harbor and, though the landing was supposed to be secret, there was a cordial but low-key reception.[40] "Arrived safe had a bully voyage and am feeling the same,"

Rick wrote in a postcard to Los Angeles, where his message was published in the *Examiner.* Ominously, one of the first persons he met as he came down the gangplank was the same long-nosed sergeant who had arrested him in his earlier voyage to England, who now greeted him in a supercilious manner. That afternoon the Americans took a train to London, where Pershing and his aides were given luxurious suites at the Savoy. Noncoms stayed in the Tower of London, where Rick slept on straw. During the next few days, while Pershing got a gloomy view of the war from notables like King George V and Prime Minister David Lloyd George, Rick and his comrades saw the sights and took a ride on the Thames. Despite enjoying himself, he had an uncomfortable sense of being shadowed. After spending a week in London, the contingent went to Folkestone by rail and embarked for Boulogne-sur-Mer, where they got a frenzied reception on the morning of 13 June. Entraining for Paris, they arrived at the Gare du Nord that afternoon.

Riding through rush-hour traffic in an open car to the Place de la Concorde and the Hotel Crillon, Pershing was astounded by the outpouring of humanity that thronged around him, weeping, shouting, waving American flags, and showering him and his entourage with flowers. "Though I live a thousand years," declared Pershing's chief of staff, "I shall never forget that crowded hour." Rick, using greater economy of words, wrote that there was "a helluva hullabaloo." The top brass settled in at the sumptuous Hotel Crillon. Rick and the other noncoms got quarters at a barracks near Paris.[41]

Rick felt instinctively that he was still under surveillance. Sick of being treated that way, he contacted a high-ranking officer he had known in his racing days. As he suspected, Scotland Yard had sent a lot of poppycock to Washington alleging that he was a German spy, and the Secret Service had ordered one of Rick's fellow drivers to watch him closely. Identifying the culprit, Rick caught him going through his bags. Posing as a friend, Rick led him on a series of snark hunts, helping preserve his sense of humor.[42]

Perhaps because of his European parentage (or so he believed), it was easy for him to learn French. "Whenever I had the opportunity, I always tried to talk French to the French people," he recalled. "I found out that the first thing an American soldier learned in France was how to ask for food and drink. That came very simply." The next thing, he told an interviewer slyly, was learning how to talk with girls, which "was simple too, because if you couldn't talk, at least you could express yourself with gestures which they were very apt at recognizing."[43]

Soon after reaching Paris, he went to the Porte Maillot district, the center of the French racing community. He was glad French fans knew about his achievements. He told a reporter he did not intend to remain a chauffeur any longer than necessary. He would soon "take up flying at one of the American schools in France" and "quickly obtain my license as a pilot." *L'Auto,* a French magazine, praised him extravagantly. "Tall, blond, broad-shouldered, with two large expressive eyes brightening his beardless face, 'Eddie' is the perfect type of American sportsman," it declared, predicting his mechanical knowledge would "be very valuable to his chiefs." *Motor Age* picked up the story in America and said Rick would be a pilot before the end of summer.[44]

Thinking the Crillon too expensive, Pershing moved to sumptuous quarters offered gratis by an American, Ogden Mills, whose father had gotten rich from the Comstock Lode. Meeting with French and British brass including Marshal Petain and Alexander Haig, Pershing made logistical decisions and toured the French countryside to become familiar with the western front. In early September he took permanent headquarters in a chateau at Chaumont, about 150 miles southeast of Paris where the borders of Burgundy, Champagne, and Lorraine met. He had decided on the *Baltic* that the American theater of operations would be in Lorraine, an inactive sector where his inexperienced troops, now dribbling into France and displaying a shocking lack of discipline, could learn to fight before meeting strong German units. Pershing's intentions angered Haig, who wanted as much help as possible on the British front in the north, but delighted Petain, who had recently quashed a mutiny in war-weary French divisions and realized that the American army, when it arrived in force, would bolster his right flank.[45]

Rick later denied he actually drove Pershing on any of his trips, saying the widespread belief he had done so was "a legend that came out of the desire of friends and correspondents . . . to build me up."[46] But he himself had helped create the legend. Writing to the advertising director of the *Chicago Tribune,* he said he had been with Pershing on a trip in which they had seen "the artillery preparation for the last great French offensive at Verdun" from the crest of a hill being bombarded by German shellfire. "Our point of vision was only two and a half miles back of the first line trenches," Rick said. "It is unimaginable—the terrible damage of the shells and the monotonous thundering of the guns which goes on incessantly."[47]

Rick was possibly behind the wheel one day when Pershing and Petain, speeding down a road toward to the front, approached a railroad crossing with open gates. Seeing a train coming, the driver "hesitated, then accelerated, and the car squeaked across just as the train roared by."[48] Pershing may have thought about this incident when he said after the war that he did not like riding with Rick because he was reckless. Quickly sizing up the odds in an emergency and pouring on the gas typified Rick's style on the racetrack.

Another eyewitness was positive Rick drove for Pershing. Late one night, Douglas MacArthur's staff car was blocked by what he thought was a Rolls Royce bearing Pershing's four red stars, stalled in the middle of a road. Pershing's limousine was a Locomobile but looked enough like a Rolls-Royce for MacArthur to mistake it for one. MacArthur "immediately went forward to see if I could be of any assistance" and found the car "empty except for the driver." When he asked what was wrong, the chauffeur cocked an eyebrow and speculated dryly that a hairpin might be stuck in the clutch, reflecting common knowledge among American soldiers that Pershing, a handsome man whose military bearing made him irresistible to women, was having a torrid affair with Micheline Resco, a Romanian beauty he had met in Paris. MacArthur had no doubt that the driver was Rickenbacker, but his comments about the time and circumstances of the encounter are too muddled to verify.[49]

Rick spent much time driving for Major Dodd, who had become subordinate to William B. (Billy) Mitchell on Pershing's aviation staff. Mitchell, who spoke French fluently (he had been born at Nice) was an ambitious career officer and son of a United States senator from Wisconsin. He had become an exponent of aeronautics after being assigned to the army's general staff in 1913. Transferring to the Aviation Section of the Signal Corps, he took flying lessons at his own expense and was sent to Europe in March 1917 to study aerial operations. Starting in Spain, he went to Paris after America entered the war, honed his flying skills, and studied French and British air tactics. Soon after he reached Paris he became a lieutenant colonel, outranking Dodd.[50]

Not long after Pershing moved to Chaumont, Mitchell and Dodd visited the Toul sector, a good place for inexperienced American airmen to learn basic skills of combat flying before fighting strong German squadrons. The two officers rode in Packard staff cars, Rick driving

Dodd's vehicle. They arrived at Nancy as darkness fell and parked on a hill to see a raid by two German bombers. Searchlights probed the sky and French antiaircraft batteries fired ineffectively at the planes, which severely damaged the railroad station, demolished a factory being used to make artillery shells, and set other buildings afire. Seeing the destruction only a pair of bombers could inflict confirmed Mitchell's growing belief, already strengthened by discussions with British air marshal Hugh Trenchard, that American air power should be used in an attack mode and that the Air Service should be independent from the army—an idea that was anathema to Pershing, who strongly believed aviation should support ground operations.[51]

Spending the night at Nancy, Mitchell and Dodd headed for Neufchateau. On the way, Mitchell's car broke down and his driver could not fix the problem. "Dodd suggested that his driver see what he could do," Mitchell recalled. "So the tall, lithe young man dived into the engine and in a moment he had removed the whole carburetor assembly. . . . He found that the needle valve had bent, and in less time than it takes to tell he cleaned it, put it back, and had the engine going. I had never seen a man do anything so quickly with a gasoline engine, or who knew more about what he was doing."[52] Rick's recollections differed slightly from Mitchell's. Water, he said, had gotten into the carburetor. "It was a case of not getting gas through, and the strainer was jammed when I took the bottom off. It only took about five or ten minutes to fix, and sure enough it was all full of water and dirt. I cleaned it out, put it back, and it ran like a charm."[53]

Whatever the details, Mitchell was much impressed by Rick's ability. Dodd told him he had been a champion automobile racer. Pulling rank, Mitchell commandeered his services and from then on Rick drove Mitchell "all over the French countryside." One of their trips was to Rheims, where they visited the cathedral, severely damaged by German shelling.[54] Rickenbacker also drove Mitchell to Issoudun, an ancient town about 150 miles south of Paris. Mitchell inspected a site about 7 miles away where an aviation board had decided the Americans would build a big training base. Construction began on 18 August to transform a barren plain into the massive 3rd Aviation Instruction Center to instruct pursuit pilots.[55]

Mitchell was particularly impressed by Rick's ability on a trip in which a bearing burned out in a Hudson Super-Six. "Billy was in a great hurry, and we were going like hell," Rick said. The engine sounded "like a trip hammer," but he somehow got the car to a nearby village and found a garage. It had no bearings that would fit an American car, but he was equal to the emergency. "I heated some Babbitt metal in a pot with a blowtorch, made a mold from sand and water, and poured the Babbitt into it," he said. The bearing he crafted was "a very crude job, but I trimmed it down, filed it and scraped it, put it in, and by six o'clock that night we were ready to go." Mitchell was astonished. "To think that anybody could make a bearing in a makeshift way in a little wayside garage without any special tools was a superman in his opinion."[56]

Soon afterward Mitchell's admiration for Rick paid off. Strolling down the Champs Elysees, Rick met James E. Miller, a New York banker who had admired him during his racing career. Miller, a founder of the New York Air National Guard, became an officer in the 1st Aero Reserve and went to Europe on the *Baltic,* where he saw Rick again.[57] By the time they met in Paris, Miller had been commissioned as a captain in the Army Air Service and put in charge of the new flying school at Issoudun. When he told Rick that he urgently needed an engineering officer, Rick said he was driving on Pershing's staff merely as a steppingstone he hoped would lead to opportunities in aviation. He struck a deal under which Miller would send him to Tours, where the Americans had taken over a French pilot training base in September. After learning to fly, he would report for duty at Issoudun if Miller still wanted him. Soon afterward, Rick saw Mitchell talking to French officers across the street from the American aviation headquarters in Paris. Approaching them, he waited respectfully for the conversation to stop, saluted Mitchell smartly, and asked for permission to become a pilot. Mitchell hated to lose Rick as a driver but recognized his need for a challenge and asked him if he really wanted to fly. Rick insisted that he did, saying he would be much more valuable as a pilot than as a driver. Anyone, he said, could handle his driving job. Mitchell reluctantly agreed to the transfer. To qualify for pilot training, Rick had to pass a physical exam. When he reported to take it, a doctor who just happened to be a racing fan was in charge, probably reflecting Mitchell's intervention. After pronouncing Rick fit, the physician certified that he was twenty-five, even though he was twenty-seven, two years over the age limit.[58]

Rick went to the 2nd Aviation Instruction Center at Tours for preliminary flight training. Because America's badly understaffed, ill-equipped Army Air Service had neither the instructors nor planes to teach fledgling airmen, it had to use French substitutes. Under French training methods novices began by rolling around a field in "Penguins"—underpowered aircraft with clipped wings, incapable of getting airborne. After learning to taxi without taking off, trainees took short hops of a few yards and gradually up to more than fifty, landed with dead engines, and flew around the aerodrome. The sequence of operations elapsed in a "carefully choreographed aerial ballet" under a *chef de piste* (supervisor of flying). Later the students made longer flights under safe weather conditions. Finally, when judged to be ready, they made triangular cross-country trips linking Tours and two distant airfields.[59]

Rick began with a Moraine-Saulnier, a monoplane with a three-cylinder engine. It reminded him of a grasshopper as it bumped along the field. Being used to a steering wheel, he had to learn to turn the rudder with his feet and hold up the tail with his hands, reminding him of "patting your head and rubbing your stomach simultaneously." After mastering that technique, he advanced to a Caudron biplane with a "tremendous wingspread" and a nine-cylinder Le Rhone rotary engine. It used wing-warping technology invented by the Wright brothers. Experienced flyers made fun of it, but it was highly stable once a trainee had learned to handle the controls.

Rick's first real flight was harrowing. Bumping along on the ground, he accidentally headed straight for a hangar as instructors scattered in all directions. After missing the building by a few feet he bounced across a field, pulled back on the stick, and felt the big wings suddenly lift him aloft. Amazingly, he was flying. He had the presence of mind to remember he was supposed to turn to the right to compensate for the counterclockwise torque of the propeller, but the hole in the cornea of his right eye, which he never mentioned to his teachers, gave him a poor sense of distance. Putting the right wing down and pushing the rudder left, he felt horrified, not only because he did not know how to land but also because he could not tell how far it was to the ground. Remembering what Martin had done during his only previous flight in California, he pushed the stick down to raise the tail, pulled it back so the tail would drop, and anticipated a bump when the wheels hit the ground. But his visual defect caused him to misjudge the distance and he was still about fifty feet above the field. Descending by trial and error, he landed after repeated tries. "I would make a wonderful landing 25 feet in the air," he told an interviewer about subsequent landing attempts, "or head for underneath the ground." He admitted that he never got really good at landing and took a lot of "raspberries" from fellow aviators. He kept the defect in his right eye secret, and especially did not admit to being afraid. Through repeated practice he managed to get on the ground safely by sheer guesswork.[60]

Remarkably, sheer determination and persistence enabled him to finish training in only seventeen days. "I am taking my brevet tests for a pilot's license," he wrote nonchalantly to a friend in Chicago. "You must know that I have already had my thrills in race driving, but the pleasures of aviation cannot be exaggerated." He passed the test before sending the letter. Adding a postscript, he declared, "Now I am a regular pilot." The *Los Angeles Examiner,* to which he sent a Christmas message, reported that "his progress in school was remarkably fast because of his skill with the motor and speed-sense." Upon receiving his *brevet* (license) from the French Air Service, he was commissioned a first lieutenant in the Signal Corps, and Miller sent him to Issoudun as chief engineer.[61]

Only seven months before, officers in Washington had been contemptuous of his aspirations to lead a volunteer squadron. Now he had won a steady succession of victories in his endless quest to achieve whatever he set out to do. It is not strange that Rick became a leading exponent of the American dream. He was living it.

The new base at Issoudun, which had opened in late October, was a quagmire when Rick arrived to take charge of housing, hangars, repair shops, spare parts, the transportation system, and other physical facilities. The French had built seven miles of railways to bring in supplies and provided some aircraft, but barracks were crudely built and roads were not completed before rainy weather set in. Grass had not yet sprouted in recently sown fields and airplane wheels threw rocks and clods of earth at propellers, splintering them almost as fast as they were installed. Machine shops did not exist; all mechanical work had to be done in two specially equipped trucks made in America. It would take a lot of time and effort for Rick to get the base up and running.[62]

Still suspected of being a German spy and shadowed by secret agents, he made frequent trips to Paris to requisition millions of dollars worth of whatever materials he could find. Under his leadership, crews began building a permanent machine shop, a foundry, facilities for acetylene welding and magneto repair, and a place to repair or rebuild instruments. Showing the same ingenuity he had used in racing, he invented a mud guard to protect propellers from being damaged by flying debris. Hamilton Coolidge, a young lieutenant who would become one of

Rick's greatest admirers, marveled at the pace of his progress, noting that heavily laden rail cars were delivering supplies, lumber was piled everywhere, and buildings were going up all the time. Forty-five Bessoneau hangars, made of canvas stretched over wooden frames, were being erected. On all sides, Coolidge said, there was "hustle, activity . . . and loads of mud."[63]

Pilot trainees arrived from America after receiving only ground training because aircraft and flight instructors were unavailable back home. Most came from wealthy backgrounds and had been educated at elite institutions. Soldiers who had risen through the ranks enviously called them the "Million Dollar Guard." Rick resented everything about them: their aristocratic bearing, their superior schooling, and the fastidiousness of their uniforms, which looked like they had come straight from a tailor shop. Determined to get even with them for their superior status, he had them dig latrines and haul buckets of rocks away from the airfields, enjoying hearing them whine about their lot. They loathed him in return and made no secret of their feelings.

Miller lost command at Issoudun after Pershing, a stickler for spit and polish, inspected the base and Miller, "a better banker than a soldier," forgot to salute him. Deciding discipline was lax, Pershing sacked Miller and put Carl A. Spatz, a veteran Signal Corps officer, in charge. Rick was sorry to see Miller go but liked Spatz and felt comfortable with him because of his Germanic descent, noting that the five top men at Issoudun were solidly Teutonic. Besides Spatz and himself, they included an adjutant named Weidenbach (who later changed his name to Willoughby and became Douglas MacArthur's chief intelligence officer), an assistant adjutant named Tittel, and a transportation officer named Spiegel—"all Heinies," as Rick put it. Members of the "Million Dollar Guard" called them "The Five German Spies." Rick loved it and returned their animosity by heaping yet more work on them.[64]

He resented the young recruits all the more because they were supposed to become combat pilots and he was not. He chafed at the prospect of staying at a training school, maintaining buildings and repairing planes, while pampered snobs went to the front. Slinking into classes and standing at the back of the room, he eavesdropped on lectures by French instructors. To sharpen his flying skills, he sneaked airplanes out of their hangars and grabbed as much time as he could get taking them aloft. Besides risking punishment, he was also gambling with his life by trying to fly unfamiliar aircraft. He had no trouble with an older Nieuport model that had a large wing area, but newer types with smaller wing surfaces were harder to manage. He took potentially lethal risks learning how to escape from tailspins, knowing how valuable this ability would be in combat. Day after day, flying where he could not be observed from the base, he summoned more and more nerve, allowing a plane to go deeper and deeper, faster and faster, into the vortex until he narrowly missed hitting the ground before pulling out.

Despite stealing time, he carried on with his regular duties, including keeping numerous planes in repair, without cracking under the stress. One day his temper reached the boiling point when Reed Chambers, a young pilot training at one of Issoudun's scattered airfields, flew in for an overhaul. Chambers, who had gotten into the Signal Corps from the Tennessee National Guard, had a natural aptitude for flying and liked to flaunt it. Instead of obeying regulations by landing on the main airfield and taxiing to the repair hangar, he brazenly landed beside the hangar and stopped his plane smartly among aircraft awaiting service. Rick saw what was happening and flew into a rage. Jumping on a motorcycle with a sidecar, he raced to the scene and demanded to know why Chambers, flagrantly disregarding regulations, had risked damaging planes parked nearby.

Like Rick, Chambers was a first lieutenant, but was wearing a coat hiding his insignia. A sixth sense he had developed in the National Guard told him Rick had been commissioned only recently, and he decided to pretend he outranked him. Snapping Rick to attention, he gave him a tongue-lashing and told him he was thinking about pressing charges of insubordination. Rick fell for the ruse. Flashing his famous grin, he said he wished he could make such a skillful landing and invited Chambers for lunch at the officers' mess. Accepting, Chambers climbed into the sidecar and the two men quickly warmed up to one another. Indeed, Chambers decided at lunch that Rick was "one of the most sincere fellows that I'd ever seen." After Rick fixed his plane, Chambers flew back to his home field and began spreading word that the hated tyrant was "really a swell guy." Nobody believed him, and Chambers wound up being shunned by his comrades. Refusing to knuckle under, he became Rick's best friend.[65]

Rick got tired of hearing young pilots boast what good flyers they were and how few revolutions they had to make getting out of spins. Knowing by this time that he was more skilled in the art of escaping from spins than they were, he decided to show them up and picked a

EDDIE RICKENBACKER

good time to do it. On weekends, trainees who had been sports stars at prep schools and Ivy League colleges played football at Issoudun. Senior officers came from Paris and Chaumont to see them perform. One Sunday afternoon, returning from a flight to Tours, Rick saw a game in progress and decided it was time to act. Diving toward the gridiron until he was about 500 feet from the ground, he stalled his plane and threw it into a spin directly over the startled athletes and spectators. "Everybody ran like the devil in every direction," he recalled. "Frankly, it scared the pants off me too." He pulled out of the spin just in the nick of time, pleased with himself about what he had done. Spatz gave him a severe reprimand and grounded him for thirty days, but he knew he had shown the boss his flying ability.[66]

On 10 December a special order pronounced that fifteen ground officers would be placed "on duty requiring them to participate regularly and frequently in aerial flights." Rick made the list, as did Captain Fiorello H. LaGuardia, stationed in Italy, and first lieutenants Douglas Campbell, Hamilton Coolidge, Quentin Roosevelt, and John Mitchell, based in France.[67] Rick now had a right to practice aerobatics and took full advantage of it. Soon thereafter, when a group of trainees turned up on a list to be sent for gunnery training to Cazaux, a resort forty miles southwest of Bordeaux on the Bay of Biscay, Rick stormed into Spatz's office demanding to know why his name had been omitted. When Spatz said he was too valuable to release him, Rick protested vehemently that Spiegel could do his job just as well, but Spatz refused to back down.

Rick thought up a way to break the impasse by getting a friendly doctor to put him in the base hospital. It was true he had caught a cold from working constantly in mud and was fatigued from practicing aerial maneuvers while doing his regular duties—but he decided to pretend he was even sicker, thinking Spatz would relent if he saw that things went well in his absence. After getting two weeks of badly needed rest with a supposed case of grippe, he went to see Spatz again and found he had already made out orders to send him to Cazaux. Unaware that the doctor had interceded for him, Rick asked Spatz why he had changed his mind. Spatz replied that he knew perfectly well what Rick was doing but also realized that if he wanted so badly to go to Cazaux, he would not be a good chief engineer. Holding out his hand, he wished Rick the best of luck.[68]

On 3 January 1918 Rick went to Cazaux for gunnery training with Oscar J. Gude, Edwin Green, Paul Kurtz, Seth Low, James A. Meissner, and Edgar Tobin, all of whom knew his reputation for slave-driving.[69] The group was quartered in a first-class hotel where they could enjoy life when not practicing. Most of the men ostracized Rick, but Meissner, a gregarious person whose father was an executive with U.S. Steel, decided to give him a break and they became friends. Like Chambers, Meissner was not one of the "Million Dollar Guards" Rick had tyrannized and had no reason to hold a grudge.[70]

Rick was anxious to do well enough in gunnery training to become a combat pilot instead of being assigned to an observation or bomber squadron, a fate disdained by first-class airmen. French instructors gave him a .30-caliber rifle, took him to a nearby lake, put him in a motor boat, and instructed him to try hitting a cigar-shaped canvas sock about 200 or 300 yards away while another boat was towing it fast enough to keep it aloft. Rick had fired a gun only twice in his life. The hole in his cornea was an additional handicap, and he did not even come close in his first few attempts. But he persisted as his instructors counted the number of shots he fired and compared the total with the number of hits. Practicing for hours each day, shooting as many as 800 to 1,000 rounds until his shoulder became almost too bruised to continue, he improved enough to satisfy his teachers.

He next went up in a Nieuport armed with a Lewis gun, which had a circular magazine filled with ammunition. His was supposed to hit a sock, ten feet long and three feet wide, towed by two Frenchmen flying a slow-moving twin-engine Caudron. On his first try, his aim was so bad that the hail of bullets severed the tow rope so close behind the Caudron that the pilots, frightened out of their wits, dove for the ground and the sock fell on the field from which they had taken off. "They raised more hell than seven boxes of monkeys," Rick recalled, shouting "Tirez la" as they pointed to the sock and "Pas la" as they pointed to their plane. After shooting "a few tons of ammunition," he reached a point at which his aim, while not outstanding, was good enough to qualify him as a candidate for training to become a combat pilot.[71]

Together with Meissner, who continued to befriend him, and the other trainees, who did not, Rick went to Paris on leave of absence pending further assignment. On 19 February an order directed him, along with Green, Meissner, and Tobin, to go to a newly established school at Villeneuve-les-Vertus for advanced training.[72] Rick had crossed yet one more barrier, but the United States had no fighter planes and the French had not begun deliveries on an order Pershing had placed long before Rick left Cazaux. Ironically, despite spending months as a staff driver and engineer and being delayed by Spatz from going to gunnery school, he was just as ready as any other American airman to become a combat pilot. The country in which the Wright brothers had made the world's first heavier-than-air flights in 1903 quickly fell far behind Europe in aviation. This was still true as Rick set out for Villeneuve-les-Vertus, a place with which he would become extremely familiar in the weeks ahead.

Chapter 6

— ☆ —

Takeoff

American air power was puny by European standards when Rick crossed the Atlantic with Pershing's staff on the *Baltic*. The aviation branch of the Signal Corps had only fifty-five obsolete aircraft and a dearth of officers and enlisted men at the time the United States declared war on Germany.[1] When Pershing led a punitive expedition into Mexico in 1916 to retaliate for a raid on American soil by Pancho Villa, the 1st Aero Squadron—the only such unit in the Signal Corps—was totally unprepared for the reconnaissance mission it was expected to perform. Its eight Curtiss JN-2s could barely fly. Of ten pilots led by Captain Benjamin D. Foulois, only Townsend Dodd, whom Rick met later that year in California, had ever flown at night. Most airmen got lost on their first mission trying to find Pershing's base in Chihuahua after dark. Inability to cross the Sierra Madre, where Villa was hiding out, limited the squadron to courier service between American outposts.[2] Nevertheless, coping with adversity gave its members an esprit-de-corps that they took to Europe in 1917, even though they brought no aircraft with them. As members of the regular army they were "insiders" and felt superior to idealistic amateurs who had joined the Lafayette Escadrille or been scattered among French pursuit squadrons in the larger Lafayette Flying Corps—no matter how many victories they had won in combat.[3]

Soon after the United States entered the war, Congress appropriated a staggering $164 million to darken the skies of Europe with American-built aircraft, and the Signal Corps called for enlistments that would create "regiments and brigades of winged cavalry," but these grandiose visions never materialized.[4] Planes could not be mass-produced like cars and only relatively few, all foreign models made under license, reached the front by the end of the war. Even after aspiring aviators had been screened to determine whether they were physically fit and had proper social backgrounds, the Signal Corps could give successful applicants only ground training in the United States. It had to send them abroad to learn to fly under foreign instructors, resulting in the "Million Dollar Guard" aristocrats who did menial jobs under Rick at Issoudun. Ground crews and clerical personnel, who could be taught appropriate skills in America, became the first members of fighter squadrons that, as yet, had no pilots.

Pershing detested the army's chief of staff, General Peyton C. March, who remained in Washington. As soon as Pershing got to France, he created a separate United States Air Service, independent of the Signal Corps, and put it under the command of a West Point classmate and personal chum, Brigadier General William Kenly, although he knew nothing about aviation. Pershing also ordered 5,000 aircraft and 8,000 engines from France at a cost of $60 million, doubting that planes would soon—if ever—arrive from America. Billy Mitchell, ranking under Kenly, became chief of a "Zone of Advance" at the front. Mitchell had studied British and French military aviation in actual combat situations and was furious at being subservient to a "kiwi," a term of contempt among pilots for superior officers who could not fly.[5]

Rick got an earful of Mitchell's wrath while driving him around the front. The situation worsened after Rick went to Issoudun. Foulois, who had been brevetted to brigadier general and enjoyed Pershing's confidence because he had served under him in Mexico, arrived in France with a staff of 112 officers and 300 enlisted men. Taking Kenly's place, Foulois made sweeping changes and demoted Mitchell by assigning him to supervise air operations in the 1st Army Corps, increasing his ire.[6]

Foulois reluctantly decided to integrate combat-tested pilots from the Lafayette Escadrille and the Lafayette Flying Corps into the Air Service but had to deal with a ruling by Kenly that these volunteer airmen had to meet certain requirements, including maximum age (many of them were too old) as well as educational requirements (which some of them lacked) required for officer status. Others could not pass physical tests given by military doctors who knew nothing about aerial warfare and had no idea how to measure attributes needed by a combat pilot. In one examination, battle-tested Lafayette flyers like Raoul Lufbery, the Lafayette Escadrille's leading pilot with sixteen victories, had to walk backward in a straight line after being spun around on a piano stool. "When [Lufbery] tried to walk backwards, he nearly broke his neck," a critic of Foulois stated. "When they whirled him around on the piano stool, he fell off it and couldn't get up. And the language he used was awful."[7]

Kenly had also promised to commission Lafayette flyers—who had been noncoms in French service—as officers. Foulois grudgingly complied, although, like other career officers, he was contemptuous of unprofessional adventurers. While Rick was fighting Spatz to let him go to Cazaux, Foulois began in January 1918 to admit Lufbery and his comrades into the Air Service as captains and majors, in each case assigning rank one below what Kenly had intended. Foulois also gave them no formal squadron assignments and let them cool their heels at La Noblette farm, north of Chalons. After more delay, Foulois put them in a newly created unit, the 103rd Pursuit Squadron, commanded by one of their number but functioning operationally within the French 4th Army. None of the victories they had previously won would count in their American service records. The Lafayette flyers resented the shabby treatment.[8]

Nevertheless, the 103rd flew the Spad XIII, the best fighter plane yet developed by French designers. For flyers like Rick and the other airmen trained at Issoudun, who had no aircraft at all, it was highly coveted. Pershing had been promised either the Spad XIII or an even newer plane, but the French had reneged on their contract, claiming that the United States had not supplied war materiel on schedule. The real reason for their intransigence was an impending German offensive that might end the war before enough American troops arrived to avert a catastrophe. The Bolshevik takeover in Russia had led to its withdrawal from the war, releasing many German divisions to fight on the western front, where British and French manpower had been bled white in fruitless offensives in 1917. Allied leaders knew that Erich von Ludendorff, Germany's supreme German field commander, would launch a massive offensive as soon as weather permitted, and the French were not inclined to be generous in supplying the Americans with materiel, aerial or otherwise.[9] It seemed for a time that Pershing would have to settle for an obsolete plane, the Nieuport 27, but the French eventually agreed to give him the more advanced Nieuport 28, which had not seen combat but had performed well in trials late in 1917. Production had only recently begun, and Pershing would have to wait a few months to get the N-28s.[10]

Pershing was still waiting when Rick went to Paris after leaving Cazaux with no assignment to a particular unit. The convoy that brought

Foulois and his staff to France in November 1917 had brought mechanics and support staff for six American squadrons, but not until February 1918 was a group of airmen at Issoudun assigned to the 95th Aero Pursuit Squadron and ordered to go to the 1st Pursuit Group's advanced training center at Villeneuve-les-Vertus, a village in Champagne where the French already had an aerodrome. Miller, whom Pershing had recently cashiered at Issoudun, took charge of the squadron, whose members arrived at Villeneuve weary, dirty, and disheveled after traveling in cold, drafty railroad cars.

Major Bert Atkinson, who had joined the Aviation Section of the Signal Corps in 1915 and served under Foulois in Mexico, had been at Villeneuve since mid-January making arrangements to open the base, assisted by his adjutant, Philip J. Roosevelt.[11] Like Issoudun, it was awash in mud when the 95th arrived and Atkinson marched the pilots to crude, hastily erected barracks. French aviators stationed across the airfield from the Americans had far superior quarters and a well-stocked bar. Above all, they had airplanes, with twin machine guns. Envious, members of the 95th consoled themselves with the knowledge that their unit had been picked to be the first American aggregation to fight against German flyers stationed nearby.[12]

Shortly after the 95th arrived at Villeneuve, Rick went there with Meissner, Green, and Tobin to join the 95th's sister unit, the 94th Pursuit Squadron. Life was miserable for them amid the mud and desolation of the village. Having no planes and still not formally assigned to their unit, they endured gibes from pilots of the 95th, who lorded it over them because they would be the first American airmen to oppose the Germans. Having the friendship of Meissner and Miller helped make life tolerable for Rick, but the other flyers at Villeneuve shunned him because of the way he had acted at Issoudun.

After a long wait, Miller, who had gone to Paris to check on the progress of the Nieuport 28s, returned with word that five of the planes were ready. Four more would become available each day until there were enough for two squadrons. Although the aircraft lacked machine guns, the men could at least learn to fly them. Late in February a group of pilots, including Rick, went to Paris to fetch the planes but a blizzard hit the city immediately after they got there, preventing them from flying back to Villeneuve. Disappointed by the weather, they were also disgruntled because they had hoped for Spad XIIIs and had been obliged to settle for Nieuport 28s.

Rick had dinner with Meissner after arriving in Paris. Realizing he was beginning a significant new chapter in his life, he started keeping a diary.[13] The first entry, on Saturday, 2 March, showed he had spent part of the previous day examining a newly arrived American Liberty engine being evaluated on a test bed. That evening he and Meissner went to the opera for a performance of *Thais* and returned Sunday evening to enjoy *Faust*. The weather seemed to be clearing on Sunday, but it was again "snowing like the Devil" when Rick got up on Monday. He had a date for that evening with an unnamed woman who was "dark and rather small but has a very sweet disposition," but he was sick of the "Battle of Paris" and "crazy to get back to work."[14]

On Tuesday the weather was slightly better and a truck took the fliers to an airfield where the Nieuports awaited them. One pilot took off, but the ceiling was so low that he got lost and the others returned to their rooms. Finally, on Wednesday, 6 March, Rick and fifteen other pilots got off the ground and headed for Villeneuve, only to experience another snafu. Unaware that ground crews at a nearby air depot had put only enough gas in the planes to get them to the aerodrome from which they had started, they had to land for refueling almost as soon as they took off. Rick was one of only seven pilots who made it safely to the training base. Three others crashed while trying to land and six were forced down along the way. All but one of the missing men straggled in the next day, by which time Rick had been formally assigned to the 94th Pursuit Squadron. Major Jean W. F. M. Huffer, an American citizen who had been born in Paris and spoke French as his native tongue, commanded the unit. A personable officer who had served with four squadrons in the Lafayette Flying Corps and flown on the Italian front, he was only twenty-two years old, showing the dire need of the Air Service for airmen with enough experience to lead a unit. At this point the 94th still lacked basic amenities expected by officers; that evening Rick and Meissner went to nearby Vertus to buy beds. Exhausted by the time he got back, Rick set up his bed immediately, "anxious to retire and enjoy its comfort."[15]

He was pleased to have found a home in the 94th, writing that "most of the Boys are good fliers all having gone thru Cazeaux." He did not mention that most of his comrades regarded him as a lowlife and continued to shun him. Reed Chambers had arrived and was assigned to the 94th, giving Rick at least one more friend, but he was an outcast among outcasts. Pilots in the 95th looked down their noses at the new squadron, basking in a "rose-colored fog of content" because they would be first to fly over the front. They invented excuses to sneak off and watch mechanics work on their Nieuports, "tinkering, testing, [and] polishing our little ships till they gleamed in the sun like birds of paradise." Although their machine guns had not arrived, Atkinson sent them on two unarmed patrols of three men each, escorted by French planes, on 15 March, fulfilling their aspirations to be the first American-trained airmen across the lines. The brass at Chaumont debated the wisdom of sending unarmed men on a patrol, but the neophytes were so proud to have flaunted their favored status, even as decoys, that they adopted the duck as a temporary symbol of their unit.[16]

But a tragic loss had occurred that was particularly hard on Rick. On the morning of 9 March, Miller went to Coincy to get a Nieuport 28 that had not reached Villeneuve. Before he left, he told Rick his excitement about a secret pact he had made with Davenport Johnson and Millard Harmon, two American officers still attached to a French squadron that flew Spads. Before flying the Nieuport back to base, Miller said, he would join Johnson and Harmon in a patrol across the German lines near Rheims, but the sortie did not turn out as he hoped. After Harmon turned back with engine trouble, Johnson and Miller flew toward the Argonne Forest, and two German aircraft bounced them. Johnson's guns jammed in the ensuing fight, or so he said. Some airmen at Villeneuve doubted his word and never forgave him for supposedly leaving Miller hanging out to dry, calling him "Jam Johnson." Miller, badly wounded, was last seen spinning out of control behind enemy lines. Word soon arrived that he had died in a German hospital. Terribly upset about losing one of his few friends, Rick decided he could not "cherish friendships with my pilot comrades so intimately that their going would upset the work I had to do."[17]

Amid his grief, however, he gained a mentor. On the morning after he returned from Vertus with his new bed, he drove a motorcycle to inspect one of the planes that had crashed near Villeneuve after the recent flight from Paris. He found it in such good condition that he flew it back. By the time he reached Villeneuve, Lufbery, the legendary dean of Lafayette flyers, had arrived from Issoudun to be a flight instructor. Five years older than Rick, he had been born in France to an American father and a French mother. He had led a vagabond existence, punctuated by a two-year stint with the United States Army in the Philippines. He was in Paris at the beginning of hostilities and joined the Lafayette

Escadrille in 1916. He hated the Germans because a beloved friend, Marcel Pourpe, under whom he had served as a flight mechanic, had died in a crash. Lufbery's skills were extraordinary. Scoring sixteen victories and losing credit for others that were unverifiable because they occurred behind enemy lines, he earned decorations including the Croix de Guerre with ten palms and the French Medaille Militaire. He also became a Chevalier of the Legion d'Honneur, the highest recognition France could bestow. Newspapers were full of his exploits, children were named after him, and he received countless letters from admiring women.

Lufbery came to Villeneuve smarting from being commissioned as a major instead of a lieutenant colonel, which would have been his rank under the Kenly agreement. He had gone to Chaumont expecting to lead the 95th Pursuit Squadron, but Atkinson thought he was too eccentric for unit command. Like Rick, he spoke English poorly, being a Francophone. "Any average judge of character could have known after a five-minute talk with Lufbery that he would never make a paper-work squadron commander," said a friend. "He knew nothing, and wanted to know nothing, about the routine of making reports and of keeping lists and records."[18] Atkinson sent him to Issoudun, where he sat idly at a desk and did not know what to do. Because of his superb combat record, the brass sent him to Villeneuve as a flight instructor.[19]

"Luf," like Lee Frayer before him, became a surrogate father to Rick. Having both been mechanics gave Lufbery and Rickenbacker a natural bond. Seeing that Rick had the aptitude to become a great combat pilot, Luf patiently brought it out in teaching him the idiosyncrasies of one of the most controversial fighter planes of World War I.[20] The Nieuport 28 had clean, graceful lines that made it perhaps the most aesthetically pleasing aircraft of the war and it was highly maneuverable; still, it lacked the power, speed, and structural strength of the Spad XIII, which Rick had ardently wanted to fly. A small, single-seat aircraft, the Nieuport had a sesquiplane design: the lower wings, which contained the ailerons, were shorter than the upper ones. Its noisy 160-horsepower, nine-cylinder Gnome Monosoupape (single-valve) rotary engine received fuel and oil through only one valve port, which was exposed every time the power plant completed a revolution. The entire engine and propeller whirled counterclockwise around a stationary crankshaft, creating a gyroscopic effect that permitted the plane to "turn on a dime." The spinning of the cylinders in the air, combined with fins that dissipated heat, made the engine self-cooling, so that it needed no radiator, giving it a good horsepower-to-weight ratio. Its ample wing area gave it lots of lift and a short takeoff roll. Because a rotary engine needed no warm-up, it could be ready for action at a moment's notice. Its simplicity made it easy to service and overhaul.

Properly handled by an experienced pilot, the Nieuport 28 was a much better plane than Rick and other critics would claim. But it was designed for a type of combat passing out of style by 1918. It was best suited for intricate maneuvers in which a pilot flew tighter and tighter downward spirals trying to get on an enemy's tail and shoot him in the back. To perform effectively, it needed an airman highly adept with stick and rudder. It had a fragile wing structure that permitted it to climb much better than it could dive, and the flawed design of its engine tubing made it fire-prone, giving pilots without parachutes the potential dilemma of jumping to their death or being burned alive.

A fledgling pilot like Rick required a lot of training to master the Nieuport 28's idiosyncrasies. Using a "blip switch" that varied the number of cylinders firing at a particular time was the only way to control its airspeed. Because of the intense heat produced by its engine, the only lubricant it could use was castor oil. Even though the power plant had a protective cowling, the pilot ingested a constant vapor spray that induced nausea, vomiting, and diarrhea. Forward visibility in takeoffs and landings was impeded by the size of the engine, making it necessary to fishtail while taxiing and sideslip when descending toward the ground, looking over the side of the craft to spot obstacles and gauge altitude. As a pilot landed, he slowed the engine by turning the blip switch up and down in rapid succession, causing a series of snorts that were familiar sounds at any aerodrome where the aircraft were stationed.[21]

Rick's inability to judge distance because of his corneal problem was a severe handicap with the Nieuport, requiring many hours practicing basic maneuvers. He also had to learn fundamental rules of combat, many of which had been established by Oswald Boelcke, a superb German fighter pilot who advocated surprising an enemy by spotting him at a distance, gaining altitude on him, coming in from behind, and waiting until the last second to have the best possible shot. Boelcke also trained pilots to keep the sun at their back when they attacked so their opponents would be blinded by its glare. Boelcke died in a collision with a fellow pilot in 1916, but even by then he had seen that a style of combat in which pilots flew alone and won shootouts in one-on-one "dogfights" was no longer effective because of the larger number of aircraft and pilots now engaged in the war and the level of training required for flying more advanced planes. Because it was hard for a flyer to see in all directions and not be surprised by a sudden attack from an unanticipated quarter, a new approach was necessary. In formation flying pilots could watch out for one another. A basic formation was a "V" in which the lead pilot flew ahead at a lower altitude, flanked by pilots flying behind at higher altitudes to prevent enemies from bouncing comrades from above or behind.[22]

Learning these tactics required successful pilots to have a high degree of "situational awareness" or "vision of the sky," the ability to know what was happening at all times and in all places in the thick of combat. As a race car driver Rick had had a riding mechanic to help him keep track of comparable situations, but when piloting a single-seat plane he had to turn his head up and down, forward and backward, and from side to side continuously while air currents or shock waves from exploding antiaircraft shells buffeted his plane. His neck size expanded from such gyrations. He had to maintain such awareness while inhaling castor oil vapor and flying at altitudes at which thin air lessened the amount of oxygen reaching his brain—and despite his unrevealed visual impairment. Through incessant practice, Rick became one of three flight leaders in the 94th in only five days.

His busy schedule notwithstanding, Rick managed to stay in touch with people back home. He tried to write five letters a day but was hard-pressed because his incoming mail sometimes came in at an even faster rate, reaching as many as eight letters per day. He tried to grow a "French mustache," joking that "few of the boys can see it yet," but soon gave up. Petain visited the base to conduct a review. "After much polishing and brushing," Rick wrote, "we marched up in formation and [were] glad it was all over within a few minutes." German bombers came over that night. Searchlights probed the sky and antiaircraft batteries blazed away as members of the squadron dove into trenches until the alert ended.[23]

By 18 March, a Monday, all of the planes had machine guns but could not go aloft because it rained until Thursday. By then Rick had a new aircraft that had just arrived from Paris, armed with a Vickers gun. After Luf "went out to the front without seeing anything," he ordered Rick to make a test flight to see how far and how rapidly he could climb with the new aircraft fully loaded. He got to 3,000 feet in nine minutes and reached 5,000 in twenty-three minutes. Climbing 800 additional feet, he wrote, took seventeen more minutes. He got lost in the process and "just did get home before dark." When he landed, "all the boys were sure I had been out over the Front, which I let them believe." The next day he "tried to have my sights put on plane but [was] unable owing to lack of material"—indicating that logistical problems still bedeviled the base.[24]

Because most flyers in the 95th had not received gunnery training, its cocky members were in for a shock. To their dismay, Atkinson ordered all but two of them (who had already had such instruction and were transferred to the 94th) to go to Cazaux. Miller's death and two subsequent changes of leadership (Lieutenant Seth Low, who took charge immediately after the sortie in which Miller was shot down, was replaced in eleven days by the unpopular Davenport Johnson) had already impaired morale in the 95th. Instead of being the first American squadron to fight, a dispirited group of flyers boarded trucks for a long trip to southwest France. They tried to comfort one another by saying that the squadron had been the first to go behind enemy lines, if only in unarmed planes, but suddenly the 94th would have the coveted distinction of initiating combat with the foe.[25]

On 21 March, on the northern front, Ludendorff launched his long-anticipated offensive. Waves of gray-uniformed infantry smashed into allied lines after a terrific preliminary bombardment, annihilating British units that fought to the last man. Within two weeks the Germans had driven forty miles toward Paris.[26] Because enemy planes outnumbered allied aircraft in the embattled sector, French airmen stationed at Villeneuve expected momentarily to receive orders to go to the front, leaving the 94th in sole possession of the base. Still trying to install his gunsights, Rick wrote on 23 March that the nearby city of Chalons had been "badly bombed last night killing many also wrecking the depot." By Monday, having now regulated his sights, he "went up and tried them out on a small lake not far from here." Papers captured from the enemy indicated that the American 26th Division, posted near Toul, would come under attack. Rick feared that "if they advance here as on the English Front our camp will be in German hands soon." The attack did not come, but German planes bombed Chalons and Epernay and passed over Villeneuve. "Naturally we thot [sic] they would bomb us," he wrote, but they did not.[27]

Amid these ominous developments, Lufbery decided it was time to lead the first patrol over enemy lines before the Germans forced the squadron to retreat. He planned to take two men with him, and everybody was eager to know their identities. "We all had vague ideas of the several kinds of surprises in store for us," Rick said, "and every one of us was keen to get into it." Late on 27 March Luf told Rick and Doug Campbell he had chosen them and ordered them to be ready at 8:15 the next morning. That night Rick wrote he was about to "get the opportunity I have worked so hard for during the past 9 months." He could hardly wait.[28]

"Over the Lines in a Nieuport," Rick scrawled in his diary before going to bed on a day—28 March 1918—that would forever remain etched in his memory. The sky had been "beautifully clear" when he came early to the hangar where his Nieuport was waiting. Wasting no time, he had a mechanic push the plane onto the runway. By 8:15 he and Campbell were dressed in their "teddy bear suits," fur-lined coats and helmets that pilots wore for protection against the extreme cold at high altitudes.[29] Rick puffed on a cigarette as other members of the squadron came out to see them off, "wishing us well, and wondering what they would do with our equipment and personal effects, should we fail to come back." Under the lighthearted banter was an ill-concealed envy of the two men, coupled with an awareness that they might not return. Amid the joshing, Luf came on the scene to lead the patrol, had a few words with Campbell, and walked briskly toward Rick, who was already sitting in his cockpit. Watching Luf approach, he felt apprehensive, like a man in a dental chair awaiting the drill. Death was staring him in the face, he thought, as he snapped on his goggles. The veteran Luf wanted to be sure both men knew what to do if attacked. He reminded Rick to stay near him and not stray from the three-plane formation.[30]

After finishing, Luf strapped himself in his cockpit and signaled for mechanics to swing the propellers (first to prime the engines, with ignition switches off, then to start them with switches on). Linguistic confusion between English-speaking pilots and French mechanics could lead to severed fingers (or death) if the Frenchmen did not get out of the way before the blades began to revolve.[31] Giving the propellers a final heave, the mechanics kicked away wheel chocks and scurried out of danger as rotary engines caught with a roar and tails rose smartly in the air as the three planes moved forward with increasing speed against the wind. Scarves worn to wipe castor oil spray from their goggles flapped around the pilots' faces as they gained momentum. The Nieuports were aloft within a few seconds. Luf's wheels were the first to leave the runway, with Rick's and Campbell's close behind. Climbing into the azure sky, the aviators banked their wings, turned north toward Rheims, and disappeared from sight.

The Villeneuve aerodrome lay near the southern end of the Mountain of Rheims, which had great strategic importance because a German breakthrough in this sector would compromise France's ability to defend the southeastern approaches to Paris. Lookouts stationed on the crest of a hill immediately west of Villeneuve could see the German lines, only eighteen miles away across an expanse of fields that had once yielded abundant crops of grapes ideally suited for champagne. Peasants still tended some of the vineyards, but much of the area was a no-man's-land scarred by the fury of war. Northeast of Villeneuve was Suippes, a market town for which French and German troops had fought savagely in 1917. Observing a French attack in the sector soon after arriving in Paris, Mitchell described it as a fantastic inferno of "smoke, dust, and burning projectiles." Originally held by the French, Suippes was now occupied by a German unit that had positioned antiaircraft guns on a rise about a mile north of town, from which men with binoculars could see all the way to Villeneuve on the southwest perimeter. French and German observation balloons lined both sides of the intervening area, keeping every square yard under surveillance. Chalons, a French rail center, lay in an exposed position north of Villeneuve, within easy range of German artillery and attacked repeatedly by bombers at night. The patrol was no mere training exercise. Now that French aircraft had gone north, it was up to the 94th to assess the security of its base.[32]

The topography immediately west of Villeneuve made it possible for the Nieuports to hide behind the range as they climbed to altitude, temporarily escaping detection by German observers on the opposite front. Luf had instructed his two companions to fly above and behind him, with Campbell on his left and Rick on his right. Rick, however, had trouble getting his plane up to speed and lagged behind when the trio reached Rheims. Below their wings the ruins of the bombed-out city were an awesome sight from their open cockpits in the morning sun. Seeing Rick was not keeping up, Luf banked and led him back into formation. After getting properly grouped they headed for Suippes, flying at 15,000 feet.

It was intensely cold. Rick marveled at the ease with which Luf maneuvered in a corkscrew pattern and tried to follow his example. He worked so hard to stay in formation that he forgot to look at the ground.

When he finally peered down he saw "a devastated landscape full of abandoned trenches and gaping shell holes." In 1917, when heavy fighting had scarred the nightmarish terrain, Mitchell described it as having been scorched by "the blast of a mammoth furnace and withered by giants."[33] Airsickness overcame Rick as he looked at the shattered territory. Wind currents that felt like waves in a terrible storm at sea blew him back and forth, up and down. It took immense determination to keep self-control. Taking his eyes off the ground, he clenched his teeth to avoid vomiting and stared grimly ahead. Experiences like this later led him to make a famous statement, "Courage is doing what you're afraid to do. There can be no courage unless you're scared."[34]

Suddenly the Nieuport shook violently from explosions so close that Rick thought they came from only a few feet behind him. With a jolt he realized that the Germans were sending up "Archy," the British term for antiaircraft fire. It was coming from a battery north of Suippes noted for its accuracy. Rick looked down at the enemy guns while gray-uniformed men looked up at him and tried to shoot him down. Black puffs of smoke rose upward as shells filled with shrapnel exploded under his fuselage. Repeated concussions shook the plane so hard it seemed as though it would break apart. Rick thought about jokes he had heard about the bad aim of antiaircraft batteries and the large sums of enemy money they wasted, but they rang hollow. He was so terrified he had lost all sense of being airsick.

With immense relief Rick saw Luf pull alongside him like an aerial shepherd. His horror gradually subsided as he tried to imitate Luf's corkscrew motion. Suippes receded into the distance and the detonations became less audible. Rick noticed that Luf was leading them home and felt more secure. Then, looking at his instrument panel, he started to worry about his fuel supply. As Villeneuve came into view, Luf began to descend. Following him like chickens staying close to a hen, Rick and Campbell circled the field, looking over the sides of their planes as the ground rose to meet them. As they landed, they repeatedly flipped their blip switches and castor oil vapor blew back in their faces. Comrades who had anxiously awaited their return ran to meet them as they taxied toward the hangar.

Luf debriefed them after they climbed out of their cockpits. They were so inexperienced that they had missed much going on around them during the patrol. Luf asked if they had seen any aircraft and was amused when they said they were positive they had not. Luf glared at them in mock disappointment. Too preoccupied with merely staying alive, they had not seen two formations of French pursuit planes fly directly beneath them. When they turned back from Suippes, Luf said, four enemy fighters of the Albatros type were in their flight path about two miles away. A two-seat German observation plane was even closer, flying at about 5,000 feet. Like a schoolmaster scolding dunces, he warned that they needed to watch the sky surrounding them more carefully. In time they would be able to take in everything at once. Only then would they know what to do, how to react, to prevent some disaster.

Turning to Rick, Luf asked if his plane had been hit by enemy fire. When Rick said it had not, Luf walked him around his Nieuport, poking his fingers where it had been holed. He showed Rick that "one piece of shrapnel had entered my tail, another had gone through the outer edge of my wing and a third directly up thru both wings, not over a foot from my body." Rick turned pale and stayed that way "for a good thirty minutes." Still, he wrote in his diary that evening, the mission "was a wonderful trip." If the weather was good, he wanted to go on another patrol the next day—Good Friday.

It was raining heavily when he woke up—impossible for flying. He was glad his Nieuport was in good shape despite being holed. The morning mail brought letters and a "beautiful ring" from an Elks lodge he had joined in Los Angeles, but he craved action. The downpour continued all the next day, Easter Eve. Accompanied by John Wentworth, an airman from Chicago, he drove a truck to Epernay, where they took a hot bath, ate a good meal, and examined some "new coats we are having made with open collars."

When they returned to Villeneuve that afternoon, they learned that the squadron had been ordered to move to a new aerodrome at Epiez in the foothills of the Vosges near Toul. A few miles north of that city, two National Guard divisions were holding a front between Flirey and Apremont against German forces occupying a bulge called the St. Mihiel salient. Within the enemy-held territory lay the Briey Iron Basin, from which prewar France had drawn much of its ferrous metals and on which Germany was now heavily dependent for war materiel. Little fighting had taken place in the area since 1914.[35] Pershing's aviation advisers thought German squadrons stationed near Toul were "neither aggressive, numerous, nor equipped with the best types of machines," explaining why they sent untested units like the 94th to the area before pitting them against stiffer competition. Rick and his comrades talked excitedly about "doing regular work over the lines" from Epiez at dinner that evening.[36]

But bad weather continued to prevent flying. Rick wrote in his diary that it was "raining to beat the band" when he got up on Easter, forcing postponement of the move to Epiez. A truck convoy loaded with equipment headed out in the downpour, but the pilots had to stay behind with the mechanics, praying the sky would clear. After lunch, while whiling away time playing craps or writing letters home, a cry went up that a hangar was afire. Dashing to the scene of the blaze, they found that "some planes were burnt very badly, mine included," Rick wrote that evening. The inferno had destroyed four Nieuports. A photograph showed the blackened framework of a Bessoneau hangar with bedraggled men, Rick among them, staring helplessly at the wreckage.[37]

By Monday the rain had stopped but the Villeneuve aerodrome was too muddy to leave for Epiez. Huffer went elsewhere, putting Rick in charge. Despite his continuing unpopularity, he evidently had special status, perhaps because he was older than other members of the unit. Why Huffer had not put Luf in temporary command is unclear—maybe because Atkinson held doubts about him. In any case, three of Luf's former comrades in the Lafayette Escadrille—James Norman Hall, Kenneth Marr, and David M. Peterson—arrived that day. Not yet permanently assigned to the 94th, they were reporting for duty as flight leaders, a sign that the squadron would soon be in combat. Hall, who came from Iowa, had graduated from Grinnell College, where he had gained a love of poetry. He was fond of Chaucer's *Canterbury Tales,* which he could read in Old English, and had published a book, *Kitchener's Mob,* about his experiences as a volunteer machine gunner in the British army. Another work, *High Adventure,* telling about his service in the Escadrille, was in press.[38] Peterson, from Honesdale, Pennsylvania, had no zest for excitement. "It may be said without exaggeration that he is the only American who has never had a thrill from his adventures as an airman," said comrades who knew him well. After volunteering for the Escadrille in 1916, he led more sorties than anybody else.[39] Marr, a gregarious individual, came from Alaska, where a French agent had recruited him in 1914 to bring sled dogs to France. Becoming an ambulance driver for the American Field Service, he enlisted in the Lafayette Escadrille as a pilot in 1917. Fellow airmen thought him an authentic sourdough and called him "Siwash."[40]

Another American pilot, John Gilbert (Gil) Winant, flying a two-seater Spad observation plane, made a forced landing with engine trouble that same day. Learning about Rick's reputation as an expert on motors, Winant asked if he could fix the problem, which he did easily. "The minute I opened the throttle," Rick recalled, "I realized that the engine was firing late and no doubt the coupling had slipped at the magneto." After repairing a coupling, he told Winant "to start the engine . . . and it showed full revolution and power." As a reward Winant took him up in the plane and "bounced all over the lot," nearly crashing into a hangar. Like Rick, he had learned to fly at Tours and Issoudun, but his skills were still only rudimentary. Nevertheless, the meeting was a stroke of good fortune because Winant would later be ambassador to the Court of St. James in World War II when Rick made a special mission to England.[41]

Rick's patrol with Luf had confirmed his self-doubt, which increased as the prospect of one-on-one aerial combat loomed in the near future. He was "worried to beat the devil" about his right eye and afraid that the hole in the cornea "might cover an enemy airplane which I couldn't see and would get me first." He "didn't dare tell anybody else" and "was scared to death someone would find out." He was also troubled because, never having killed anybody, he had scruples about taking human life. His solution was to think about shooting down machines, not flyers.[42]

Ludendorff's offensive was stalling, and French planes had returned to Villeneuve. A squadron of bombers took off that night to attack German targets. The presence of the big biplanes created a need for space, making it imperative for the 94th to leave for Epiez as soon as possible. On 2 April, twenty-two pilots, including Rick, made the flight. Everyone but Hall, who had engine trouble and had to land elsewhere, got to Epiez without incident, but the field was muddy from the same storm that had been drenching Villeneuve. Soon after arriving, the men heard the unmistakable roar of a rotary engine from a distance and rushed out of their barracks to see what was happening. It was easy to identify the incoming plane as a Nieuport, and they speculated that a new pilot had been assigned to their unit. When the ship landed, its nose burrowed into the mud seconds after its wheels hit the ground. Flipping on its back, it slid down the field, tail-forward, until it stopped, a twisted mass of wreckage. Thinking the pilot was dead, they wondered who was this blockhead and why had he been added to their ranks—that is, until they reached the wreck and saw Hall, unhurt, hanging from the cockpit and grinning at them upside down. The tragicomic episode reassured Rick, seeing that even a veteran of the famed Lafayette Escadrille could screw up.[43]

Hall reported that a Nieuport left behind at Villeneuve was flyable, and Rick left in a car to fetch it. Approaching Chalons, he and two mechanics who accompanied him saw a German bombing raid taking place and parked on the brow of a hill, watching it unfold. After the raid they stayed in the city overnight and went to Villeneuve the next morning. Retrieving the Nieuport, Rick flew it to Epiez while the mechanics went back in the car.[44]

It was raining again when Rick landed. After lunch he traveled through the downpour to Epernay to get the coat he had ordered on his visit with Wentworth. Fuming about the weather and the deficiencies of the Nieuports, he thought about applying for a transfer from the 94th to the 103rd. "Gee what I would give for such a chance as they are using Spads," he wrote. Still an outcast among most members of the 94th, he thought about getting a fresh start with men who had no reason to dislike him. The 103rd was flying combat missions to help stop the German offensive, and he was wasting time in a "mud hole" waiting to be activated. Before going to sleep that night, he decided to apply for a transfer the next day.[45]

It was still raining when he got up, and the airfield was awash in mud, frustrating him even more. Walter Lovell, a veteran of the Lafayette Escadrille, was stationed at Epiez, helping to put experienced American pilots in newly formed squadrons. Rick was gratified that Lovell sympathized with his feelings. He did not need to be told why Rick wanted to fly Spads instead of Nieuports. In a sortie Lovell had plunged into a pocket of fog to elude a swarm of German fighters, bouncing him from a higher altitude, and the diving ability of the Spad had saved his life. He agreed to arrange Rick's transfer "at once." The 103rd had a Spad nobody was using. "I hope its [sic] for me," Rick wrote.[46]

Transfers were underway because Hall, Marr, and Peterson had been formally reassigned to the 94th and three pilots had to go to the 103rd in exchange. There was no apparent reason to doubt that Rick would be among them. The 103rd would soon occupy a new airfield to join an impending battle on the Aisne River. The more Rick thought about it, the more he longed to go. Huffer, however, did not want to lose Rick and balked at the transfer. On 7 April the 94th was ordered to active duty; no longer a training unit, it was told to move to an aerodrome at Gengoult,

Elizabeth Basler Rickenbacher, mother of Edward Rickenbacher, as a young woman. Her demeanor suggests the sense of determination that enabled her to become the dominant partner in her marriage to William Rickenbacher.

William Rickenbacher, father of Edward Rickenbacher, dressed in his best clothing in a pose that belies his humble status. His huge hands and the fiery look in his eyes reveal both his strength and his temperament, which helps to explain why the frequent beatings he administered to his son Edward left a lasting impact on an incorrigible youth—one whose life might have turned out much differently but for William's death in 1904.

Rickenbacher home at 1334 East Livingston Avenue, Columbus, Ohio. The picket fence, added in 1905, was a result of the income earned by a young Edward Rickenbacher, a symbol of the awakening self-respect he had gained by assuming economic responsibility for the household.

Edward Rickenbacher, working at the Zenker Monument Works, Columbus, Ohio, 1905. His gaze shows the weight of the responsibilities he had assumed as a very young man who had only recently lost his father and was now helping to support his mother and his siblings.

At Col. Buggy Factory Oct 7-08.

Edward Rickenbacher (*standing, fourth from left*) with members of the quality-control staff he headed at the Columbus Buggy Company, 7 October 1908, exuding the sense of authority he had gained in supervising far older and more experienced workers.

Edward Rickenbacher with members of the Mason (Duesenberg) Racing Team, August 1913. *Left to right:* Rickenbacher, Eddie O'Donnell, Billy Chandler, and Fritz Walker, displaying the pride and camaraderie prevailing among competitive young men engaged in a sport that they loved. Walker was killed in 1914 in a crash at Galesburg, Illinois.

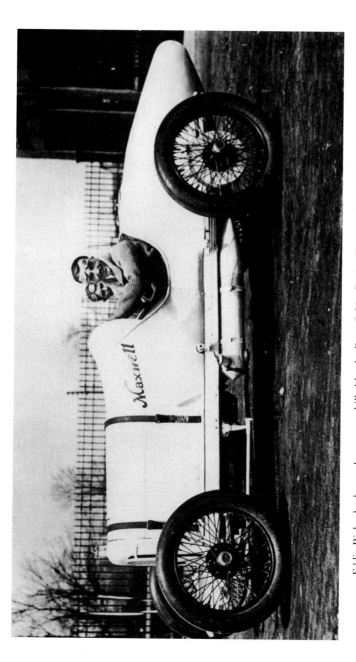

Eddie Rickenbacker, as he was now billed by the Prest-O-Lite Racing Team, and his riding mechanic in a Maxwell Special at Indianapolis, Indiana, in early 1916, with Allison Engineering Works in background. The streamlined configuration, conical main fuel tank, torpedo-shaped auxiliary fuel tank, and other features were designed by Rickenbacker to transform the 1915 Maxwell race car into a faster and more dependable vehicle than the stubby 1915 Maxwell race car. Despite his efforts, the Specials were unable to win consistently against French-built Peugeot race cars in the last season of the AAA tour before the United States entered World War I.

Rickenbacker (holding bottle) and riding mechanic savoring victory in the Metropolitan Trophy Race at Sheepshead Bay, Long Island, New York, 16 May 1916. Rickenbacker's victory in a hotly contested race, marred by the death of Carl Limberg and his riding mechanic, suggested that Eddie might win the AAA national championship as an "American driver in an American car." But his hopes went unfulfilled.

Rickenbacker's grease-streaked face at the peak of his career as an automobile racer, showing his joy in competition and the infectious smile that made him a celebrity on the AAA racing tour. The photograph is undated but may have been taken after one of the victories he scored in 1916 when he managed the Prest-O-Lite Racing Team.

Rickenbacker, wearing the master sergeant's uniform as a member of General Pershing's driving staff in France in 1917. The photogenic style he had honed in his racing career is equally evident here.

Rickenbacker at the 2nd Aviation Instruction Center, Tours, France, standing in front of a Caudron G-3 training plane in which he made his first solo flight, late in 1917. The large wing area enabled the plane to get aloft with ease, but the unexpectedly quick takeoff, combined with Rickenbacker's impairment in depth perception due to his undisclosed corneal defect, could have resulted in a crash at the very beginning of his aviation career.

Members of the 94th Aero Pursuit Squadron, late June–early July 1918. All were lieutenants at the time except for Marr, who was a captain. *First row, left to right:* Leroy J. Prinz, Harold H. Tittman, Frederick L. Ordway, Walter W. Smythe. *Second row, left to right:* William F. Loomis, Chester A. Snow, M. Edwin Green, Alan F. Winslow, Kenneth Marr, Edward V. Rickenbacker, James A. Meissner, Thorne C. Taylor, George W. Zacharias. *Third row, left to right:* Hamilton Coolidge, Arthur L. Cunningham, William W. Chalmers, Joseph H. Eastman, Alden B. Sherry, John Wentworth, Robert Z. Cates Jr., Edwin R. Clark, John N. Jeffers. Reed M. Chambers, Rickenbacker's wingman, was not present at the time the photograph was taken. Marr, who had replaced Jean W. F. M. Huffer at the head of the squadron on 7 June, was ineffective, leading to Rickenbacker's elevation to command on 25 September.

Rickenbacker and comrades at Rembercourt, 18 October 1918, with Rickenbacker's Spad XIII in the foreground and captured Hannover observation plane in the background. *Left to right:* Joseph H. Eastman, James A. Meissner, Rickenbacker, Reed M. Chambers, Thorne C. Taylor. Rickenbacker repeatedly "shot down" the Hannover with the aid of his friends in a filmed mock combat that nearly ended in disaster. Courtesy of Daniel J. Clemons, Escondido, California.

Rickenbacker, wearing the captain's insignia, in front of an operations tent at Rembercourt after receiving his ninth Distinguished Service Cross, November 1918. An official history of the Hat-in-the-Ring unit stated that "Captain Rickenbacker, furnished, by his example, an ideal squadron leader." Colonel Harold H. Hartney, commander of the 1st Pursuit Group, echoed this assessment, saying that "An army of Rickenbackers in the sky would be invincible."

Rickenbacker and "Spad," mascot of the 94th Pursuit Squadron, 1918. The canine was captured from a German unit and became deeply attached to Rickenbacker, a confirmed dog lover. It whined piteously when Eddie had to leave it behind at Coblenz.

Rickenbacker and his mother after he returned from Europe, February 1919, photographed after the surprise reunion arranged by General Charles T. Menoher and Richard Kennerdell, representing the American Automobile Association. The greatcoat worn by Rickenbacker, with its elaborate sleeve embroidery, is the one Rickenbacker obtained in Paris shortly before the end of the war.

Adelaide Frost Durant reading magazines on a park bench prior to her marriage with Rickenbacker in 1922, showing the poise and beauty that Rick found so attractive. The photograph gives no hint that she was five years older than her husband-to-be.

Adelaide and Eddie standing in the plaza of St. Mark's Basilica, Venice, Italy, October 1922. The pigeon perched on Rickenbacker's hat is an eerie premonition of the bird that figured prominently in the raft episode in which he nearly died in 1942.

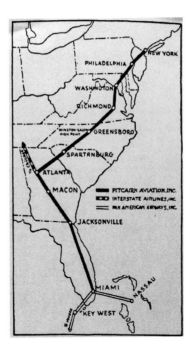

Pitcairn Aviation, Inc., which began carrying airmail in 1928, became Eastern Air Transport in 1930 and Eastern Air Lines in 1934. Pitcairn's mail routes stretched from New York City to Miami and included the Atlanta-Jacksonville-Miami route previously flown by Florida Airways, founded by Rickenbacker and Reed Chambers in 1929. Pitcairn's route system laid the basis for a potentially lucrative passenger vacation trade from northern cities to tropical destinations from which Eastern ultimately profited, particularly because of Pitcairn's connections with Pan American Airways. Courtesy of Stephen Pitcairn.

Rickenbacker, wearing World War I uniform, with his sons, David (*left*) and William (*right*), after he received the Medal of Honor (hanging around his neck) in 1930. Despite the parental intimacy depicted by the pose, Eddie's busy schedule and the self-imposed heroic role model he assumed prevented him from giving the boys, particularly William, the attention they needed.

Rickenbacker, in driver's seat, with his brother Albert at Indianapolis in 1933 for the Memorial Day race held that year. Eddie delighted in presiding over the annual classic but left the day-to-day administration of the facility in the hands of a veteran subordinate, "Pop" Myers.

Douglas DC-1 surrounded by reporters and spectators at Newark, New Jersey, after Rickenbacker's record-setting transcontinental flight, on 18–19 February 1934. Although Rickenbacker hardly touched the controls, he was officially in charge of the flight at the behest of General Motors, which owned the North American Aviation subsidiary controlling TWA, Eastern Air Transport, and the Douglas Aircraft Company at the time. Eddie received a deluge of tributes after the plane set a speed record by flying from Glendale, California, to Newark, in approximately thirteen hours, four minutes.

two miles east of Toul near a front held by the 26th Division. Nieuports that had been reserved for the return of the 95th from Cazaux were now posted to the 94th so every pilot could have his own plane. Hobie Baker, Seth Low, and Richard Johnson went to the 103rd in exchange for Hall, Peterson, and Marr.

Despite his disappointment, Rick made the best of things. The new quarters at Gengoult were much better than at any base where the 94th had been stationed, and he was glad the squadron had finally been activated. "We are going to get started soon so am just as well satisfied," he wrote.[47] Although the Nieuports were not ideal, he had become fairly proficient in flying them, and his personal relations within the squadron were improving. Hall, Marr, and Peterson had never been at Issoudun and had no reason to loathe him. Luf was his mentor. Chambers and Meissner were good friends, as was Wentworth, with whom he had taken a nice walk at Epiez after their trip to Epernay.[48] Another plus for Rick: the 94th was now under the administrative control of the 1st Army Corps, and its chief aviation officer was Billy Mitchell.[49]

Its roster set, the 94th needed appropriate insignia. What symbol best represented its aspirations? The idea of adopting Uncle Sam's stovepipe hat with stars and stripes on the band may have originated at Villeneuve. Rick credited it to Huffer. Gary Walters, the squadron's flight surgeon, thought a ring should be drawn around the hat because tossing a hat into a ring was a traditional American symbol for wanting to fight. The unit adopted the emblem, and Wentworth, who had training in architecture, designed it.[50]

Conforming to Allied practice, the wings of the planes would carry a cockade, or roundel, symbolizing their national identity. France, Great Britain, and the United States all used the same colors, red, white, and blue, but the sequence varied. The center of the American cockade was white, the middle blue, and the outer ring red. The rudders had vertical stripes, with a red stripe on the leading edge, a white stripe in the middle, and a blue stripe on the trailing edge. Pilots could add other decorations. Rick chose posters advertising war bonds and emblems of Elks lodges he had joined in America.[51]

It may have been at this point that he took another step toward clarifying his identity. Writing to a friend back home, he signed the letter "Eddie Rickenbacker," drawing attention to the second "k" by putting brackets around it. Although he had spelled his last name "Rickenbacker" on his 1916 passport, he may have emphasized his choice now because anti-German sentiment was rife in the United States; newspapers picked up the story and said he had "taken the Hun out of his name." He wanted to have Rickenbacker rhyme with "hacker," not "hocker," making it sound less Teutonic and more appropriate for a warrior battling the Boche in a plane adorned with Uncle Sam's Hat in the Ring.[52] It was a fateful move because "Eddie Rickenbacker" stuck with him the rest of his life, not only because he had already used it with the Prest-O-Lite team but also because "Eddie" had an endearing sound. His comrades, however, continued calling him "Rick." Remembering he had once been a runt, he came to dislike "Eddie" because it sounded like the name of a "little fellow," but never got rid of it.

In time he became deeply dedicated to the Hat-in-the-Ring Squadron. More than any other unit in the United States Air Service except the 103rd, it bore the stamp of the Lafayette Escadrille. From the beginning Luf had steeped its members in its heritage and tactics. Adding Hall, Peterson, and Marr intensified the tradition Luf had started. As a result, the 94th developed a collective personality that set it apart, including a special vocabulary used by the Escadrille. The ambition of every pilot was to become a "Gimper," named after a mythical bird "who would stick by you through everything." Rick later told a reporter, "If you were up in the air and ran into a dozen enemies and were getting the worst of it, and the fellow with you stuck with you and gave it to them until they fled, you'd know he was a Gimper. If he didn't have motor trouble, and his gun didn't jam [and] he didn't accept any one of a dozen good excuses for zooming off home and leaving you to do the same if you could get away, he'd be a Gimper all right." His words contained thinly veiled slams at Davenport Johnson, now commander of the 95th, whom pilots like Rick never forgave for leaving Miller in the lurch. "A Gimper is a scout who does everything just a little better than he has to," Rick said. "We call this the Gimper Escadrille because every man has to prove himself by his actions."[53]

Morale in the 94th got a boost on 12 April when Luf went on a patrol, met three German planes, and shot down a two-seater near St. Quentin. Rick spent the same day using his artistic ability painting his Nieuport with the squadron's new insignia. Orders came on 13 April to begin active duty at six o'clock the following morning. When Rick saw the Operations Board, he was overjoyed to learn that he would fly in the first sortie over enemy lines with Chambers as his wingman and Peterson as flight leader. They would spend a couple of hours scouting the area between Pont-a-Mousson on the east and St. Mihiel on the west and intercept German planes trying to observe troop movements behind the American lines.

Rick tossed and turned that night, imagining enemy planes coming at him from all sides and thinking about tactics he would use against them. He dreamed about shooting down one Boche after another and was still firing when an orderly woke him up to get ready for the mission.[54] Time would tell how misleading his visions had been.

It was no secret that Rick wanted the first victory credited to the 94th, which would be a high distinction for a member of the first fighter squadron activated by the Army Air Service.[55] He was in good spirits when he reported for breakfast with Chambers and Peterson. Campbell, Meissner, and Alan Winslow, also present, would stay in the Alert Room until ten o'clock in case the Germans reacted to the patrol by attacking Gengoult. When Chambers left, not realizing how prophetic his words would be, he told Campbell and Winslow that he and Rick "were going out to stir up the Huns and for them to be sure and knock them down."[56]

The field was shrouded in mist when Rick and Chambers reached their planes. Peterson sent them up to estimate visibility at 1,500 feet. After they made a few circuits of the field, Peterson climbed toward them. Instead of making sure what he wanted, Rick kept going up and Chambers followed. Suddenly they realized Peterson had disappeared. Rick guessed he had had engine trouble. As they flew toward the Moselle River, German antiaircraft batteries began shooting. Chambers had never experienced Archy and got so close to Rick as they corkscrewed that he thought they might collide.

After Rick spotted Pont-a-Mousson, they flew back and forth between the city and St. Mihiel under intermittent ground fire but saw no German aircraft. Rick also realized his fuel supply was running low. Fearing they might run out of gas over enemy lines, he led Chambers back toward Gengoult, but they soon encountered fog. Rick later admitted that "my sense of direction in those early days was definitely bad and I got lost several times, particularly if there was any fog in the air."[57] The closer they got to Gengoult the thicker the fog became, and they lost any sense of where they were. Diving through the blanket, Rick checked his altimeter to make sure he was in no danger of flying into a treetop or a hillside and lost sight of Chambers. Fortunately, Rick had scouted the area between Epiez and Toul and made a mental note of a railroad crossing. To his relief, he saw it again just when he needed it. Using the "Y" formed by the rails as a reference point, he flew toward Toul at a low altitude, spotted the aerodrome, and landed, thinking Chambers was close behind him.

After Rick climbed out of his plane, Peterson, despite his reputation for being calm, gave him a tongue-lashing for not realizing he had climbed toward them to abort the sortie because of the fog. Rick quickly took responsibility. He knew he had been impetuous, too anxious to see action. But now he was more concerned about Chambers, wondering if he may have crashed while trying to follow him. Taking off his teddy bear suit, Rick walked glumly to the Operations Room to write a report about a disappointing mission that had gotten him in Peterson's doghouse and may have cost him one of his best friends. Instead of being the first member of the unit to score a victory, he had gotten off to a bad start.

He noticed that Campbell and Winslow were not in the room. They had been marking time by playing cards while Meissner read a book. At about 9:45, only fifteen minutes before their stint would end, an operations officer sounded an alert. An American antiaircraft unit had spotted two German planes flying over Foug, a town west of Tours, headed toward Gengoult. Dropping everything, the fliers raced to their planes. Rick had hardly sat down to write before he heard the roar of engines as Campbell and Winslow took off. Meissner's motor would not start, so he had to stay behind.

Rick ran out of the Operations Room to see what was happening and heard someone shouting that a German plane had just crashed on the field in flames. Looking where the man was pointing, he saw fire and smoke. As he raced toward the crash site, more shouts caught his attention and he turned around just in time to see a second plane, bearing German insignia, plow into the ground near the first one.

What on earth had happened? As Chambers had predicted, the patrol on which he and Rick had flown attracted a response. While they were groping through the fog, the enemy ground units that had shot at them dispatched two fighter planes to the attack. The most plausible explanation for the events that ensued was that, like Chambers and Rick, the German pilots got lost. Failing to spot the Americans, they tried to return to their base but headed in the wrong direction. Thinking they were near Metz, they descended, broke into the clear, and saw an aerodrome they thought was their own, not realizing that it was the one at Gengoult. At this time an American antiaircraft unit saw them and sounded an alert. They were apparently trying to land when Campbell and Winslow, who had just taken off, saw them looming ahead about 500 feet from the ground. Winslow was barely airborne when one of the German pilots veered sharply to avoid him and "came roaring down on me, his guns barking with a volley of lead that screamed by, dangerously near." Pulling back on his stick, Winslow climbed virtually straight up, kicked a rudder, and "went plunging down on his tail, spraying his wings and fuselage with a long rattling burst of fire." His aim was accurate and the plane, an Albatros D-V, "dashed toward earth in an uncontrolled dive," crashing and turning over at the edge of the field. Meanwhile, Campbell, who had been watching the battle, was bounced by the other German ship, a Pfalz D-III. Doug's engine stalled as he tried to open fire and he came within 100 feet of the ground before he got it restarted. Seeing the Pfalz directly overhead, he pulled his stick back, fired a stream of bullets, saw his tracers go into the plane's nose, and watched as it caught fire and fell. The entire episode elapsed within less than five minutes after the alert sounded.

Amazingly, America's part in the air war had begun with a double victory, all the more dramatic because it took place above hundreds of witnesses. Hearing the alert, residents of Toul ran out of their homes, looked up, and saw the battle. Delighted by the outcome, they shouted "Vive la France! Vivent les Americains!" Within minutes crowds of civilians and airmen converged on the field, coming on foot, riding bicycles, and driving cars. The pilot Campbell had shot down was burning alive and dying in "ghastly agony." The other, merely bruised, accepted a cigarette from Winslow, who had been dueling with him only minutes before.[58]

Billy Mitchell was sitting in a nearby office when the episode took place, heard the noise, and dashed to the aerodrome. He later offered a different explanation of what had happened, speculating that the Germans knew they were flying over an American base and were about to strafe it when Winslow and Campbell suddenly met them.[59] If Mitchell was correct, and the enemy pilots had carried out their plan, the patrol conducted by Rick and Chambers (who had found a French base near Toul and returned later that day) would have resulted in a debacle from which the infant American Air Service might have taken a long time to recover. Instead, Rick's error in not realizing Peterson's desire to abort the sortie had led to a spectacular American triumph.

The mayor of Toul had the two wrecked aircraft displayed in the public square. Rick later looked back on what had happened as "a perfect day," but his diary told a different story. His hopes of scoring America's first aerial victory had evaporated, and he had been as much a goat as a hero. His diary showed his feelings. "No flying today, weather is rotten," he wrote laconically the next day as congratulations for Winslow and Campbell poured in from around the world. His entries for the next two days told the same story: "Bad weather nothing doing." "The same today." He did not mention a visit to Gengoult by General Hunter Liggett, commander of the 1st Army Corps, to praise Winslow and Campbell. In short, he seemed depressed. Winslow and Campbell had been in the right place at the right time. He had not.[60]

He craved a chance to get over his feelings, but the weather would not cooperate. Rain fell for three days without letup. Visibility was so bad on the morning of the fourth that there was no point trying to go after a German plane spotted near Gengoult. When another was sighted over Pont-a-Mousson that afternoon, however, the ceiling was higher. Rick and Chambers got permission to pursue it but got lost in the overcast and had to return. Nothing was going right.[61]

Rick got another chance to shine two days later when Mitchell, perhaps knowing how he felt and trying to help, asked him to perform aerobatics during another visit by Liggett. He did his stunts well but overheated his engine, because of which he could not take off when an alert sounded and the squadron was ordered to strafe enemy trenches near Seicheprey, where the first American ground engagement of the war was taking place. German troops had overrun units of the 26th Division in an assault before dawn, withdrawing only after they left 81 soldiers killed and 187 captured or missing. Pilots from the 94th strafed the enemy with "very good effect," but Rick missed the action. "Hard Luck," he wrote in his diary.[62]

His plane was quickly repaired, but bad weather kept him grounded. Two days later, however, on 23 April, he was on duty when an alert sounded. Spotters had seen a German plane "going from west to east over our lines between St. Mihiel and Pont-a-Mousson." Dashing to his plane, Rick went after it alone, but became distracted when he reached Pont-a-Mousson by the devastated cityscape under his wings. When he looked up, he saw what he took to be a German plane heading toward him, but it was a Spad and its French pilot broke off the attack as soon as he saw Rick's American insignia.

By this time the enemy plane Rick had tried to locate had left the area. He resumed his search but, with no luck, returned to Gengoult. When he arrived, members of his squadron congratulated him for scoring a victory. An American antiaircraft battery had seen a German plane fall to the ground, and Rick's comrades assumed he was responsible. He honorably disclaimed credit, and nobody ever received it. "It was a pity to undeceive them," Rick said, "but it had to be done."[63] Had he lied and the truth become known, the consequences would probably have been dire.

His misfortunes continued. The next day observers saw a German plane flying across the American lines near St. Mihiel while everyone at Gengoult except for Rick was having lunch. Taking off alone to intercept it and heading west, he had a sudden impulse to fly north toward Verdun and veer back across the salient, putting himself behind enemy lines where the German pilot would least expect him to be. It was cloudy and the silhouette of his Nieuport against the overcast made him a good target for antiaircraft guns that quickly fired at him. He also sighted what he thought to be an enemy plane heading his direction. After what had happened to him the day before, he wanted to be sure of its identity, thinking it, too, might be French. As he closed in, he saw that it was indeed German, but there was something strange about the way it seemed to be waiting for him, as if its pilot wanted him to attack. At this point he remembered that Luf had warned him about the danger of falling into a trap. Looking over his shoulder, he saw an Albatros coming from behind a cloud, ready to pounce. Abandoning any idea of attacking the plane loitering below him, he wrenched back on his stick and made a steep vertical climb. The maneuver worked beautifully and he was soon behind the Albatros with its tail in his sights. To his surprise, however, he saw a black and white roundel on its wings. Again his mind reverted to the previous day's experience because he had "never been told or had heard of the Boche using anything for insignias other than the Maltese cross."

Deciding the plane had to be German, he cocked his machine gun and was about to pull the trigger when he looked up and saw two more planes heading toward him. Realizing his "inefficiency and lack of experience," he turned tail and headed for Gengoult as fast as he could go. He saw that one of the planes was gaining on him, which shocked him because he had been told that a Nieuport could easily outrace an Albatros. Zooming and corkscrewing, he was relieved to see a cloud in front of him and ducked into the feathery mass. As it enveloped him, he continued zigzagging to confuse his pursuers and hid in the fluff for half an hour before he came out on the other side. Glad that no plane was near him, he flew safely back to Gengoult.

As it turned out, only two of the planes he had met behind the lines were German, and he could have bagged the second one had he not panicked when he looked up and saw two others coming in his direction, not realizing they belonged to his own unit. Soon after he took off on his mission, Campbell and Charles W. Chapman Jr., another former Lafayette flyer now serving with the 94th, had responded to an alert. Going behind the German lines, they saw Rick escape the trap the Boche had set for him and climb rapidly to get on the tail of the Albatros that had been waiting to ambush him. Assuming he was about to shoot it down, they waited to watch his victory and escort him back to Gengoult, only to see him inexplicably break off the fight and do everything he could to elude them. Hiding in a cloud from his comrades gave members of the squadron who already scorned him another reason to ridicule him after he returned to Gengoult. In addition, nobody had ever heard of a German plane with a black and white roundel. Fortunately, an intelligence report verified that an enemy aircraft matching that description, possibly the same one Rick had seen, had fooled the pilot of a French reconnaissance plane and wounded the observer in the rear cockpit before he knew it was an enemy. To that extent, at least, Rick was vindicated, but he continued to feel humiliated.[64]

Three more days of frustration elapsed as rain prevented operations. On Saturday, 27 April, the skies cleared and Rick went over the lines on a patrol with Luf. To Rick's disgust, they saw nothing. It rained again on Sunday and the weather was still bad on Monday morning, but "the sun finally peaked [*sic*] through the clouds shortly after lunch," and the chances appeared increasingly favorable for flying when Rick went to the alert room with Hall in midafternoon. His fortunes were about to turn. Two hours after the watch began, they learned that an enemy two-seater had been spotted "flying south in the region of Beaumont." Running to their planes, they had mechanics swing the propellers but were ordered to wait until Huffer arrived to give them final instructions. Looking at the northern horizon, Rick saw the silhouette of an aircraft and decided it must be the one they were supposed to attack. Huffer had not yet appeared and Rick wondered what he could reveal that he and Hall did not already know. Risking another reprimand in his anxiety to get a victory, he begged Hall not to let opportunity slip through their fingers. Hall, "being a man of unusual qualities and preferring a good fight with the enemy," as Rick later recalled, also "threw caution to the winds" and "gave the signal to the boys to pull the blocks from under the wheels, leaving the camp with me in close pursuit."[65]

Heading toward Pont-a-Mousson, they saw observation balloons hovering above the American lines. Seeing a plane coming toward them, Rick decided that it must be the German aircraft for which they were looking. He tried frantically to get Hall's attention but got no response. Deciding not to wait, he overtook the plane and got under its tail. He was about to open fire when he saw that it was a French three-seater on a scouting mission. He had narrowly averted a terrible mistake.

Breaking off contact, Rick flew west toward St. Mihiel and saw antiaircraft shells bursting around Hall, who was brazenly performing loops, barrel rolls, and tailspins as he showed contempt for the gunners. Seeing Rick coming toward him, he stopped his gyrations, joined him, and led him back toward Pont-a-Mousson, where they saw what they were looking for. It was a German aircraft, and Hall quickly recognized it as such. Signaling Rick, he turned abruptly and climbed toward the sun, which was now setting. His heart pounding, Rick followed. "The Boche, seeing us, turned and also started climbing for all he was worth," he wrote, but the German machine, a Pfalz D-III, was no match for the Nieuports and they soon got above it with the sun at their back.

Knowing he was outnumbered two-to-one, and seeing that the Americans had "at least a thousand feet advantage," the enemy pilot dived toward the German lines but had no chance to outfly the faster Nieuports. According to later accounts, Rick saw in a flash what to do. While Hall fired at the Pfalz, he maintained his altitude, got on the other side of the plane, and cut off its retreat. As he flew past the aircraft, he could see that his adversary, aware of what Rick intended to do, was desperately trying to climb out of range. Banking to his right, just as expected, he plunged and headed for home "like a scared rabbit," giving Rick the opportunity for which he had waited so long. His wartime memoir, *Fighting the Flying Circus*, describes what happened:

In a trice I was on his tail. Down, down we sped with throttles both full open. Hall was coming on somewhere in my rear. The Boche had no heart for evolutions or maneuvers. . . . I was gaining on him every instant and had my sights trained dead upon his seat before I fired my first shot. At 150 yards I pressed my triggers. The tracer bullets cut a streak of living fire into the rear of the Pfalz' tail. Raising the nose of my aeroplane slightly the fiery streak lifted itself like a stream of water pouring from a garden hose. Gradually it settled into the pilot's seat. The swerving of the Pfalz' course indicated that its rudder no longer was held by a directing hand. At 2000 feet above the enemy's lines I pulled up my headlong dive and watched the enemy machine continuing on its course. Curving slightly to the left the Pfalz circled a little to the south and the next minute crashed into the ground just at the edge of the woods a mile inside their own lines. I had brought down my first enemy aeroplane and had not been subjected to a single shot![66]

These words have been reprinted repeatedly and have become a classic passage in the history of aerial warfare, but events did not unfold exactly as stated here. In preparing the published text, a ghostwriter, an army acquaintance with a secure record for promotion and self-promotion, had embellished and distorted the report.

Rick's own version of what occurred said that he and Hall, being "not more than 150 meters apart," headed toward the Pfalz as they both shot at its tail "until only a few hundred meters from the ground, we noticed him apparently lose control and dive behind the woods." French rules specified that pilots involved in a combined victory would each get credit for it. Rick had scored his first official kill, but did not think he deserved it, as a document he gave Driggs after the war clearly shows

> To me, it was a great deal like taking something which did not belong to me rightfully, as I shall always be convinced that it was Captain Hall's victory and not mine, due to his superior marksmanship, for with all my instructions on how to use my sights during my weeks of training at Cazaux and the time and effort I had put forth in arranging same on my plane, I candidly admit that never once did I use them or even realize I had them on my plane, for I was so overcome with excitement and joy at being able to shoot at a Hun, with such advantage, that I aimed entirely by the flashing of my tracer bullets. However, it has always been the rule in all Allied armies on the front that where one or more men had fired on the same plane during a successful combat, those participating were each given credit for a victory.[67]

An entry in Rickenbacker's diary headed "My 1st Victory" is consistent with this modest account: "Was called out on an Alert this evening with Capt. Hall after several minutes maneuvering saw a Hun plane coming from Germany we both attacked and saw the German plane fall to Earth it is my first real fight. We have both been given credit for this Hun."[68] Driggs subtly skewed the postwar account Rick gave him:

The truth was that in the tense excitement of this first victory, I was quite blind to the fact that I was shooting deadly bullets at another aviator; if I had been by myself, there is no doubt in my own mind that I should have made a blunder again in some particular that would have reversed the situation. Captain Hall's presence, if not his actual bullets, had won the victory and had given me that wonderful feeling of self-confidence that made it possible for me subsequently to return to battle without him and handle similar situations successfully.[69]

In short, Driggs altered Rick's words to tell a better story and gave him credit for the victory in a dramatic passage that Rick was incapable of writing. Rick ended his postwar version of the mission by saying that after he and Hall landed, "we jumped out quite happy with glad hands for each other and we were amazed to see the personnel of our Squadron, with their hats and coats off dashing from the barracks across the field to us." American observers had seen the Pfalz coming down and telephoned the result to Gengoult while the rest of the unit was at supper.[70] Even if the victory had resulted from Hall's marksmanship, a huge weight had fallen from Rick's shoulders. Being able to share in a kill after committing a succession of blunders bolstered his self-esteem, which was never as secure as he tried to let on.

Soon after the encounter, he learned he would receive the Croix de Guerre and Palm for his part in it. His first reaction was to think how proud his mother would be. On 15 May, General Gerard, commander of the 8th French Army Corps, which had operational jurisdiction over the Toul sector, visited Gengoult to decorate Rick and other American pilots who had displayed unusual valor in recent engagements. Much joshing took place among members of the 94th about the French practice of kissing the recipient of medals on both cheeks, and the men to be honored carefully shaved and powdered their faces. At about one o'clock three French companies arrived with a military band that joined musicians from the 26th Division. Gerard and his escort came an hour later. As the American band played the "Star Spangled Banner," infantrymen formed a hollow square and snapped to attention. Mitchell gave a brief speech, after which Gerard pinned the medals on the aviators, reading the accompanying citations in French. Rick said that when it came his turn to be decorated he stood on tiptoe "in order to make it impossible for the decorating General to reach me and place the kiss that we might expect on either cheek." After the ceremony ended, having been promoted to flight leader, he joined two other pilots in a demonstration of formation flying, mock combat, and aerobatics.[71]

Although Hall was among the Americans to be honored that day, he was not present for the ceremony, having disappeared while flying on a recent mission. On this day of celebration, his comrades were left to wonder whether he was dead or alive.

Chapter 7

— ☆ —

Learning Curve

Winning an official victory and the Croix de Guerre did not make Rick a seasoned combat pilot. He still made mistakes that could have killed him. Far more experienced airmen flying against the second-string enemy units in the Toul sector were shot down. Rick was lucky to come out unscathed.

In mid-April the 95th Pursuit Squadron, still smarting from being shunted aside, completed gunnery training at Cazaux. Itching for combat, its pilots went to temporary quarters at Issoudun, Paris, Colombey-les-Belles, and Epiez pending assignment to the Toul sector. The meandering route was caused partly by a shortage of aircraft; the 94th had taken all the planes assigned to the 95th, and new ones were not available. Jurisdictional conflicts also caused problems because stationing two squadrons at the same base resulted in a full-fledged Pursuit Group, the first operational unit to be so designated in the history of the American Air Service. Leadership struggles almost inevitably occurred. Only after a fight between Foulois, chief of the Air Service, and Mitchell, who administered American squadrons at Gengoult as aviation officer of Liggett's 1st Army Corps, was the 95th sent to the front, arriving at Gengoult on 4 May.

After enduring the mud and squalor at Epiez, the men were delighted to be based at an aerodrome with decent barracks, concrete sidewalks, and indoor bathing facilities. But they were still angry that the 94th had had the opportunity to score the first official American victories of the air war. In contrast with the planes flown by the 94th, hastily requisitioned ones assigned to the 95th had their camouflage painted in French style, some with American rudder stripes, and none with the unit's insignia, a kicking army mule representing Johnson's status as a West Point graduate. The 94th, once a stepchild, was now cock of the walk at Gengoult, staffed by Gimpers proud to fly battle-tested aircraft adorned with the Hat in the Ring.

Despite its ruffled feelings—perhaps because of them—the 95th lost no time getting into action. One of its members, Lieutenant Richard A. Blodgett, had already been in combat on a patrol at Epiez, near which he had killed a German gunner in a two-seat observation plane. The pilot escaped with the aircraft intact, but Blodgett was proud of dispatching his first Hun. After the sortie he expressed his elation in a letter to his sweetheart: "A fight for life is the most thrilling thing in the world, especially thousands of feet above the earth, alone!" But his glory was short-lived. Less than two weeks after the move to Gengoult, he was killed in a dogfight.[1]

Unlike Blodgett, Rick had no illusions about his profession. "Fighting in the air is not sport," he later said. "It is scientific murder."[2] The 94th escaped fatalities in March and April but the realities of war caught up with it on 3 May when Peterson led a patrol across the lines north of Toul and his flyers met five German planes. During the encounter, Charles W. Chapman Jr., a veteran of the Lafayette Flying Corps, shot down an enemy aircraft but was killed when he dived through a stream of bullets chasing another. It is possible that he blacked out, because he had experienced fainting spells during aerobatics training. "All the Boys feel very blue," Rick wrote, "but same must be expected."[3]

Another loss, however, was harder for Rick to bear. On 7 May, four days after Chapman died, an alert sounded when lookouts spotted four planes that had taken off from the German base at Mars-le-Tour. Led by Hall, Rick and Edward Green took off to find them.[4] As they approached Pont-a-Mousson, Rick saw three antiaircraft shells burst in quick succession, making black puffs in the sky. He recognized that German ground forces were telling fighter units they had seen the Americans. He had already observed the enemy fire one shell higher than others in a barrage to warn a pilot in danger of being attacked from above. Obviously they had developed an efficient system for coordinating ground and air operations. Rick wondered why Americans did not do the same.

Hall's group did not find the enemy fighters because they had returned to the ground to wait for American aircraft to cross the lines. The Americans, however, did notice a German two-seater that appeared to be directing artillery fire. As they headed toward it, the four aircraft for which they were looking, Pfalz D-IIIs, suddenly appeared in the sky about five miles away, climbing in a diagonal formation to block escape to the west. Rick knew their pilots had seen the exploding shells and risen to the attack. Sending them up earlier had been part of a ruse to attract an American response, recall them to see what happened, fire warning shells to signal when enemy planes arrived, and use the two-seater ostensibly directing artillery fire as a decoy. Such tactics were part of a defensive strategy aimed at conserving aircraft, manpower, and fuel.

Rick saw the Pfalzes before Hall did and wagged his wings to attract his attention. Because the Pfalzes were still climbing the Americans were in good position to attack them while they were vulnerable. Rick dived on one of them, got it in his sights, and started shooting after he got within 200 yards. Firing about fifty rounds, he saw his tracer bullets hit its wings. It nosed over and seemed to be spinning out of control. Rick would have followed it down to make sure it crashed but saw another Pfalz maneuvering to get on his tail. Breaking off contact, he climbed steeply to avoid it.

He now saw a Nieuport and a Pfalz in combat about the length of a football field away. At first the Pfalz seemed to be winning, but the Nieuport zoomed upward as if its pilot intended to "loop the loop" and was soon flying upside down above the Pfalz. This tactic, an Immelmann turn, was named after Max Immelmann, a German pilot who had invented it.[5] As the American reached the top of the circle, he kept his engine wide open instead of cutting power to fall off and complete the loop. Executing a half-turn, he rolled right side up, swooped down on the Pfalz, and fired a stream of tracer and incendiary bullets into its fuselage. Bursting into flames, it plunged to its doom.

Admiring this feat of airmanship, Rick assumed that the pilot must be Hall. He searched the sky for Green's Nieuport but did not see it. The victorious American airman turned back toward Gengoult. Because the Nieuports were several miles inside German lines, with shrapnel from enemy antiaircraft batteries flying all around them, Rick thought it was time to get out and followed suit. Overtaking the plane on the way back, he was surprised to see that the pilot was not Hall but Green, but his fuel was running low and it was too late to turn back to look for Hall. Green had bad news after they landed. He had seen Hall going down behind some trees with a Pfalz on his tail and thought he had probably been killed. When he did not return, it seemed that Green was right. "America's greatest loss today," Rick wrote in his diary.[6]

Hall was alive but had been captured by the Germans and was lost for the duration of the war. Neither Rick nor Green knew he had experienced a strange phenomenon that had nearly killed Meissner in an earlier sortie. Spotting a German plane below him, Hall pushed his stick forward as far as it would go, went into a screaming dive, and got his quarry in his sights. He was about to open fire when he heard a loud cracking noise. Looking in the direction from which it came, he saw that the leading edge of his upper right wing had broken away from the ribs and spars to which it had been attached. Canvas was tearing loose and billowing backward in the wind. Fortunately, his lower wings, containing the ailerons, were intact, giving him a slim chance to escape before the pilot he had been attacking turned the tables, but when Hall tried to bank the Nieuport it went into a tailspin. Moving his stick violently to the right, he succeeded in pulling out and headed back toward the American lines amid heavy fire from antiaircraft guns, but he had lost so much speed he was a sitting duck.

Suddenly he heard a loud thump directly in front of him. He did not know that a shell had hit his engine. Had it not been a dud he would have been killed instantly, but it did not explode and lodged in one of his cylinders. The impact of the projectile sent Hall plummeting tail-first toward the ground. The Pfalz he had so recently attacked was now diving at him, trying to finish him off. Hall wrenched his rudder bar with his feet and succeeded in bringing the Nieuport level, but the naked spars in his upper wing snapped under the pressure and the plane stalled as he eased back on the stick. He was only a few feet from the ground, and his wheels collapsed when he touched down, after which the wings tore off as the fuselage hurtled ahead of them. When what was left of the aircraft came to a sudden stop, Hall's face smashed into the instrument panel, breaking his nose. His right ankle, pinned in the rudder bar, was broken and his left ankle badly sprained.

Hall came down in a field surrounded by trees. Miraculously, he missed hitting them before he crashed but was helpless when German soldiers ran out of the woods and captured him. He screamed in agony as they pulled him from the wreckage and tried to make him stand. After they saw that one of his ankles was broken, they took him to a surgeon who set it, bound it to a splint, put a dressing on the sprained ankle, and bandaged his broken nose. At lunch with his captors he learned that Green and Rick had shot down two Pfalzes, but for him the war was over.[7]

Thinking Hall dead, legions of admirers mourned his fate. A former comrade in the Lafayette Escadrille said he was "brave as a lion."

Luf, who had often flown with him, thirsted to get even. Dashing to a Nieuport within fifteen minutes after hearing about Hall's disappearance, he strapped himself in the seat and took off, thirsting for blood. Crossing the German lines, he hunted for an hour and a half and finally found three enemy aircraft, shooting one down while the others fled from the ferocity of this attack. It was the seventeenth victory of his fabled career. His rage expressed how everybody felt. As Rick wrote, "every pilot in the organization that day swore revenge for the greatest individual loss" the Air Service had yet suffered.[8]

Observing the rules of war, the Germans quickly sent word that Hall was alive. After taking him to a prison camp at Karlsruhe, they transferred him to a fortress high atop a hill from which escape was virtually impossible.[9] He could not tell American officials Green and Rick had shot down two Pfalzes, and neither pilot could receive official credit for them. Rick therefore lost a victory that would have been his second of the war. Having seen his victim plunging earthward and feeling certain he had shot him down, he filed a report requesting confirmation. The French 8th Army believed him because Gerard added a palm to a resulting Croix de Guerre with a citation stating that he had "vigorously attacked an enemy combat-plane which he brought down in flames after a brilliant fight," but official credit for the kill remained in limbo.[10]

Rick did, however, take Hall's place as a flight commander. Whatever some of his comrades thought of him, Huffer and Mitchell regarded him highly and gave him the promotion. Soon thereafter, Mitchell invited Huffer, Rick, and a few other pilots to visit Chateau Sirur, an estate about fifty miles south of Tours, where they had tea with a countess who escorted them around the grounds. The tract was heavily forested and a stream flowed through the woods, which teemed with game. It was one of the most enjoyable experiences of Rick's wartime career.

On the trip back to Gengoult, Mitchell took the men to Chaumont for dinner at Pershing's headquarters. When they finally returned, bleary-eyed, at three thirty in the morning, Rick learned he had been ordered to lead a patrol over the lines soon after dawn. He had a hangover that morning and was lucky rain was coming down so heavily that his orderly did not awaken him. The episode showed he had returned to drinking after abstaining from alcohol since he had worked for the Columbus Buggy Company in Texas. He later said he never took a drink within twenty-four hours of a mission, but what happened after his return from Chaumont showed he could not always predict when he would have to lead a sortie. Heavy drinking was endemic among pilots who lived for the moment amid the horrors of war, celebrating victories with mandatory toasts amid drunken revelry.[11] Rick became a flight leader with serious misgivings about the blunders that had plagued him during earlier missions. He knew he was a long way from having Hall's knowledge and maturity and had to be careful to avoid additional slipups. He tried to compensate by pushing himself unmercifully to justify Mitchell's and Huffer's confidence, but trying harder increased the chances for further mistakes. Getting drunk at the wrong time could have been disastrous.

The first man assigned to him for instruction in his capacity as flight leader was Walter Smythe, a New Yorker who had just joined the squadron. Rick took him up for a lesson on the morning of 19 May.[12] Flying west to St. Mihiel, he led Smythe back across the front lines to Pont-a-Mousson. Seeing no enemy planes, he turned northwest over German-held territory toward Verdun, crossing the enemy airfield at Mars-la-Tour. A two-seater Albatros observation plane was flying thousands of feet below at a distance of about two miles, giving Rick an excellent opportunity to show Smythe what to do in such situations. Signaling for Smythe to follow, he flew toward the sun and got into position on the enemy's tail so the glare would blind the gunner in the rear seat. Diving on the Albatros, he sprayed a stream of bullets and watched the tracers dance, but he missed, alerting the pilot and observer to his presence. The pilot, a crafty veteran, outmaneuvered Rick, who forgot that the Nieuport would be less agile in the thin air in which the Albatros was flying. Trying to bank, Rick went into a tailspin from which it took him two revolutions to recover and the Albatros escaped. It was not the tactical exhibition he had wanted to give Smythe, who was flying nearby, taking everything in.

Because they were now far behind the German lines, Rick decided he had imparted enough instruction. Motioning to Smythe, he headed home. On his way back, however, he saw white puffs of Archy coming up from American positions near St. Mihiel and knew an enemy plane must be close by. It turned out to be the same two-seater Albatros that had just escaped him, brazenly returning to the American lines to take pictures. Rick's gorge rose at the thought of the personal insult the German pilot had administered by showing him up in Smythe's presence. Signaling again to Smythe, he turned toward the Albatros, determined to punish it and its crew for making a fool of him, but the enemy pilot

EDDIE RICKENBACKER

had no stomach for a fight and fled. Trying to head the plane off before it escaped for a second time, Rick looked for Smythe. He had disappeared.

Smythe was in no danger. He had developed engine trouble while watching Rickenbacker renew his fight with the Albatros and left the scene. He found a friendly airfield, but not the one at Gengoult. Unaware of what had occurred, Rick jumped to the conclusion that something terrible had happened to his first student. Thinking about the bad reflection that might be cast on him, he stopped chasing the Albatros and headed home. Nearing the aerodrome, he saw airmen and mechanics milling around as if a catastrophe had occurred. Preparing to land, he thought that the hubbub must have resulted from Smythe's apparent misfortune. He was in a panic when his wheels touched the ground, fearing that all the mistakes he had made and the humbling experiences he had gone through in the last few weeks had culminated in a tragedy for which he would be held responsible on his first foray as a flight leader.

Jumping out of his plane, he dashed across the field and asked apprehensively what had happened to Smythe. He was temporarily relieved when nobody knew what he was talking about, but he soon learned that something even worse had happened, leaving him "dumb with dismay and horror." Luf, his beloved mentor, had been killed.[13]

The chain of circumstances leading to Luf's death had begun about ten o'clock that morning when a large black German observation plane was seen coming from the direction of St. Mihiel. At the time it was spotted, only Huffer and Oscar Jay Gude, a member of the 94th who had yet to fly his first combat mission, were on hand to chase it. Huffer took off but engine trouble forced him to return to the airfield. Gude, already suspected of cowardice, stayed aloft but fired at the German plane at such an extreme range that his bullets fell harmlessly to the ground, permitting the intruder to escape.

Gude, a gifted pianist from New York City, was the son of a wealthy pioneer in outdoor advertising.[14] He was "an excellent pilot" but reputedly "unwilling to prove himself as a fighter." Rick had already noted Gude's desire to stay out of harm's way. Now Gude became a scapegoat among comrades who thought that had he gotten closer to the enemy plane he might have shot it down and prevented the ensuing tragedy. A more charitable explanation might be that he was one of many people, both before and since, who cannot bring themselves to take human life in combat, especially when they can see an opponent at close range. Such persons are ill suited to become combat pilots, who above all other flyers must overcome resistance to killing, no matter what.[15]

Luf had watched Gude's fruitless attack from a nearby barracks and was disgusted by his performance. Unfortunately, Luf's own plane was out of commission. Dashing to a motorcycle, he sped to the airfield and commandeered a Nieuport assigned to Philip W. Davis, a veteran of the Lafayette Flying Corps.[16] After mechanics told Luf the plane was airworthy, he took off, caught up with the German plane, and attacked it near Maron (Merthe-et-Moselle), a small town in the Moselle Valley. Evidently his machine gun jammed on his first approach because a witness said he had fired only a few shots before breaking off contact. After clearing his guns he returned to the fight and got under the enemy's tail. A bullet fired by the observer seemed to hit Luf's Nieuport and onlookers saw it turn upside down. Seconds later something looking like a sack fell out of the cockpit. It was Luf, plunging to his doom. The pilotless Nieuport glided for a few hundred yards, hit the ground, and burst into flames.

Luf landed on a picket fence bordering the backyard of a shoemaker's house. One of the pickets impaled his left leg, helping break his fall, but he died on impact when he hit the ground on his back. One of the shoemaker's daughters ran into the yard, tore open his uniform, saw he was wearing his medals, and recognized him from pictures she had seen in posters and newspapers. In May, Maron was ablaze with flowers and blooming trees. Grief-stricken, the girl gathered handfuls of blossoms and heaped them on Luf's body. People arrived quickly on the scene, carried the corpse to the town hall, and reverently laid it to rest for all to see. Debate persisted whether Luf jumped to prevent himself from being burned alive or fell out of the cockpit because in his a hurry to take off he had not fastened his seat belt, but such arguments did not change the fact that he had died a swift and terrible death.[17]

A telephone rang at Gengoult while Rick was listening to what was already known about Luf's final flight. The caller, a French officer, reported where Luf's body had fallen. Joining several other airmen including Huffer and Campbell, Rick piled into an automobile and sped to the scene. By the time they arrived, the corpse was already lying in state, covered with flowers. The plane was a shapeless tangle of burned-out wreckage. There was some consolation in knowing that the German aircraft responsible for his death had been shot down soon thereafter before it could get back to its base. Nothing, however, could compensate for the loss of a man who was not only a beloved warrior but also a teacher able to inspire inexperienced pilots as he prepared them for combat.

Luf's remains were buried the following day. A throng including generals Gerard, Edwards, and Liggett, Colonel Mitchell, and "hundreds of officers, French and American, from all branches of army service on the sector" participated in the ceremony. Late that afternoon a solemn procession marched up a hill to a grave that had been dug in a wooded corner of a cemetery, near the base hospital, where other aviators had been interred. The grave was banked with flowers. Officials gave eulogies and a bugler sounded "Taps," while a musician in the distance echoed the haunting strains. Led by Rick, five Nieuports from the 94th flew over the scene and dropped blossoms in a final salute to the fallen hero.[18]

Luf's death cast a pall over Gengoult. Campbell, who had often played bridge with him, could hardly believe he was dead. "There was nothing he liked better than to help us green pilots just as much as possible," Campbell said. "It is hard to lose him."[19]

On 22 May, two days after Luf's funeral, Rick went on a patrol with Chambers and Paul B. Kurtz, an unseasoned pilot who had joined the 94th on the day before Luf was killed. Knowing Kurtz was unfamiliar with the Nieuport, Rick directed him to fly only as a spectator, avoid combat, and, in case of an emergency, fly in a direction opposite the sun to make sure he was heading west into French-held territory. Flying in a V formation with Kurtz in the rear and above his two escorts, the patrol crossed the enemy lines and met three Albatros fighters that swooped down on Rick and Chambers while Kurtz stayed discreetly at a distance. Fortunately, the German bullets missed their targets.

Climbing, Rick and Chambers pursued the enemy formation in the direction of St. Mihiel as Kurtz joined in the chase. Their flight path took them six miles inside the German lines, emboldening one of the Germans to turn and attack Rick. Again, however, his aim was bad, and Rick gained the advantage by getting on his tail and riddling his plane with a burst of fire from both of his Vickers guns. Rick watched him begin to spin out of control but did not see whether he crashed. As had happened many times before, something shook his concentration.

As the German plane started to plunge, Rickenbacker saw two planes above him. Panicking, he fled for his life, racing for the American lines.

No matter how fast he flew, he could not shake his pursuers, who maintained a higher altitude. Deciding that escape was hopeless, Rickenbacker abruptly turned to fight as one of the planes swooped in his direction. Puzzled that the pilot did not shoot, Rickenbacker held his fire until one of the planes got closer. Just as he was about to pull his triggers, the aircraft banked, and he saw that its wings had red, white, and blue roundels instead of black crosses. Rick had come within seconds of gunning down his best friend, Chambers, at point-blank range. The other pilot was Kurtz. Embarrassed but greatly relieved, Rick joined the pack and headed for Gengoult. The patrol had almost been a replay of the sortie in which he had taken refuge in a cloud to escape from Campbell and Chapman, except that in this case he had decided to fight, with nearly disastrous results. He never knew what had caused him to pause before killing Chambers.

As he approached Gengoult, Rick looked for Kurtz and could not see him. He started immediately to worry about having lost track of another student. Flying this way and that, he hunted until he saw that Kurtz had flown ahead and was far below them, circling the field to land. Suddenly, to his "unspeakable horror," Rick saw Kurtz's plane plunge earthward and burst into flames upon hitting the ground. He thought about landing at the crash site, but it was too full of barbed wire and trenches. Flying as low as possible, he yelled at the top of his voice and waved at a truck driver to race to the scene, but ammunition from Kurtz's Nieuport started exploding in all directions, making it impossible to get near it. Landing as fast as he could, Rick sprang out of his cockpit almost before the wheels stopped rolling, jumped on a motorcycle, and sped to the scene of the wreck. The sight of Kurtz's badly burned corpse haunted him the rest of his life.

The calamity was not Rick's fault. Like Chapman, Kurtz was prone to fainting from aerial maneuvers and wanted so badly to be a combat pilot that he ignored his condition. He did not tell Rick that he might pass out in midair, the apparent cause of his fate. The next day, in a funeral less elaborate than the one held for Luf, Kurtz's charred remains were buried near those of the late, much-lamented hero. Shells flew above Kurtz's grave with an "incongruous whine" in a mordant salute to a young warrior who had risked his life for elusive glory. Rick returned from the ceremony severely shaken. Word awaited him that the German plane he had attacked while flying with Chambers and Kurtz "had crashed to the ground a total wreck." Whatever satisfaction he felt about gaining an official victory was mixed. "I had got my Boche," he recalled, "but I had lost a friend, and he had perished in the manner most dreaded by all aviators, for he had gone down in flames."[20] On the other hand, he was still alive, a remarkable fact considering that he had only recently had a close brush with death in the same type of wing-stripping that ended Hall's wartime career.

The sortie in which Hall became a prisoner of war was neither the first nor the last time American flyers underwent the terrifying experience of shredding wing fabric while executing a sudden maneuver. Repeated instances of this strange phenomenon led to revelations in June 1918 that coincided with a crisis rooted in the chronic animosity existing between Mitchell and Foulois. Until that time airmen misunderstood the cause of wing stripping, attributing it to midair collisions in the close maneuvering that accompanied dogfighting. The discovery that the wing structure of the Nieuport 28 was at fault did not immediately resolve the question of what should be done about the problem because leadership remained fragmented amid conflict between contrasting French, British, and American attitudes about aerial combat. Rick was caught in the middle of the debate, but there was no doubt where he stood because both he and Meissner had been victimized by wing shredding.[21]

The first case of the strange phenomenon came on 2 May. Meissner and Lieutenant Philip W. Davis had escorted a French aircraft taking photographs near Pont-a-Mousson. Sighting his first German aircraft, Meissner carried out a successful attack and saw it go down in flames. While firing and diving, he heard a cracking sound like the splintering of wood and realized it was coming not from the enemy aircraft but from his own. The upper surfaces of his top wings abruptly tore loose, sending him spinning toward the ground. In an impressive display of airmanship, he managed to bring his plane under control and landed it, shaken but unhurt, amid a barrage of German antiaircraft fire, at an aerodrome at Martincourt, just behind the French lines. He was alive only because the Nieuport's ailerons were in its lower wings, which remained unstripped. Meissner thought he had become involved in a midair collision. Because nobody knew exactly what had happened to Hall other than that he had been captured, there was no reason to question Meissner's judgment.[22]

Rick's encounter with wing stripping occurred two weeks later, after he had succeeded Hall as flight leader. Going on a patrol, he and Chambers climbed near maximum altitude and flew over Commercy, Nancy, and Toul. Rick lost sight of Chambers and guessed he had turned back because of engine trouble. Concerned about running low on fuel over enemy territory, he, too, withdrew, only to find himself ideally positioned to attack one of three Albatros fighters. Closing in with a steep, fast dive, he saw a German antiaircraft battery fire a round to warn the enemy pilot, who tried to outdive him. Rick fired about fifty rounds into the plane and watched it spin out of control—until he saw the lead aircraft in the German formation starting to get above and behind him. Without waiting to see what had happened to the Albatros he had been pursuing, Rick yanked back on his stick and climbed steeply to get out of danger.

Just as Meissner and Hall had done, he heard a splintering of wood. The sound came from too close to be coming from anything but his Nieuport. Looking up, he saw canvas tearing loose from his right upper wing. As air blew through the exposed spars, the plane lurched to the left and went into a tailspin. The tail revolved faster and faster around the pivot made by the nose as he tried frantically to level out, but his efforts were fruitless and his momentum increased as he corkscrewed toward the ground. Seeing his plight, the two Germans planes came after him, spraying bullets as he plunged toward apparent death. He recalled thinking they were wasting ammunition when it should have been obvious he had no chance of survival.

Rick's life began passing before his eyes, like a reel of film in a movie projector. He remembered "everything from my childhood days up to that instant, the good and bad things I had done and wondering how Mother would take the news." He felt a rapid succession of bumps as air passed through the naked spars of the upper right wing and formed a cushion under the one on the left, still covered with fabric. He pulled the stick this way and that, pressed his feet against the rudder controls, and shifted his body in a desperate effort to compensate for the gyrations. Looking over the side of the cockpit, he saw a group of uniformed men standing on a road near a line of trucks, staring up at him and waiting for the inevitable crash. He thought he saw his mother coming to the door of the little house in Columbus and being handed a cablegram telling her he had been killed in action. A "spasm of longing" welled up within him to see her face again.

Thinking about her mobilized his will to live as nothing else could have done. Instinctively wrenching the selector switch on the left side of the cockpit, he turned on all nine cylinders of his rotary engine and felt a sudden burst of power that jerked the nose upward. Suddenly he realized he was flying almost horizontally. Yanking the stick with all his strength, he reversed the rudder to combat the gyroscopic effect of the spinning engine and propeller and was enormously relieved to sense that the plane was going forward faster than it was losing altitude.

The front lines were only two miles ahead and he could see Mont St. Michel towering "like a guardian angel" over the Gengoult aerodrome. Archy from enemy batteries exploded all around him, but his pursuers had given up the chase, apparently thinking he was doomed. Nothing he could do with the controls brought the Nieuport completely level, but at least it was flying in a straight line. It was now a race against time to cross the lines before he hit the ground. Elation swept over him as he crossed no-man's-land with a thousand feet to spare. Because all his cylinders were firing, he realized he would probably be killed if he crashed short of the landing field at the speed he was traveling. Had it been even half a mile farther away, he could not have survived. Missing a French barracks by only a few feet, he made a "hot" landing on the runway, too preoccupied with reaching the ground to use his blip switch. Wondering who was trying to land with his motor wide open, French pilots came running out of the barracks as he "pancaked flatly" on the grass. The plane had no brakes but dug into the turf from the force of the landing, slowing his momentum. When it came to a stop, he got out of the cockpit and went behind a wall to puke, after which he walked nonchalantly—but on wobbly legs—to report his "unusual experience" to the operations officer. It would have been unmanly and unworthy of a Gimper to show how he really felt.[23]

Chambers had seen the entire episode from a distance. Landing a few minutes later, he reported seeing only two enemy planes heading back toward Germany and speculated that the absence of the third plane meant that Rick had shot it down. A nearby French antiaircraft battery confirmed within a few hours that its members had seen the Albatros "crashing in a wood just a kilometer or so in their lines," giving Rick his second official victory—actually his third, if the one he had recently scored in the sortie with Hall and Green could have been verified. Shooting down another plane two days later in his ill-fated training mission with Kurtz would have given him four. But his victories were mounting, a sign he was gaining proficiency.

Rick reached the same conclusion as Meissner about why his wing fabric had shredded, speculating in his diary that he had come so close to the Albatros before firing that he "lost my right upper wing in a collision with the enemy plane."[24] Apparently writing about the same episode, Chambers said Rick had "pulled the wing off an Albatros . . . with his tail skid."[25]

Two more wing-stripping incidents occurred on 30 May. In one of them Wilfred V. Casgrain, a pilot in the 95th Pursuit Squadron, went on his first mission in a patrol that met two German reconnaissance planes near Montsec and attacked them. "Casgrain's ship was unable to stand the strain of his initial dive," said one of his comrades, Harold Buckley, writing several months later and knowing the truth about what had happened. "The leading edge of one upper wing caved in, the fabric was ripped off by the rush of air and he was thrown into a vicious spin from which he was unable to come out until he had fallen about two miles." Casgrain made a last-minute recovery and landed unhurt in the no-man's-land between the front lines but was confused about his location. Going in the wrong direction, he found himself near the German trenches, surrendered, and was taken captive. In his confusion, he failed to set fire to his machine, as he was supposed to do to keep it from falling into enemy hands. At the time, the reason for his crash landing was unknown because his plane was not recovered.[26]

Airmen at Gengoult knew more about the other wing-stripping incident because it involved Meissner, who, for the second time in less than a month, nearly met his death while maneuvering violently in a dogfight near Flirey. After executing a sudden maneuver to escape an opponent and avoid hitting a German plane that had been shot down, he heard the now-familiar sound of splintering wood and saw canvas coming loose from both of his upper wings. He was four miles behind the German lines with a densely forested area under him and plummeting to the ground would probably have been fatal. Just as before, however, he used the ailerons on his lower wings to make it back to Gengoult with Rick as an escort. Realizing he had been maneuvering at close quarters, Meissner guessed that a German plane "rammed me, top wings ripped as before, landed O.K. at camp." Rick agreed with Meissner's reasoning, writing in his diary that his friend had lost "most of his upper wings" in a midair collision.[27]

Waldo Heinrichs, a pilot in the 95th Pursuit Squadron, became the next victim of wing stripping in a sortie on 2 June and barely made it back to base. "Leading edge all gone and fabric from topside of wing," he wrote in his diary. "Wonder I ever got home."[28] Because his narrow escape marked the fourth known wing-stripping incident that had occurred within a month, it aroused suspicion that something besides mid-air collisions was to blame. Six days later it finally became clear that the mysterious problem was caused by a structural defect in the Nieuport 28. A French liaison officer serving with the American Air Service issued a memorandum on 8 June stating that a weakness in the ribs between the leading edge of the wings and the main spars to which they were attached caused shearing under excessive strain. A "web" of composite members made of poplar, ash, and birch came apart, causing the leading edge to fold backward, pulling the fabric covering the upper side of the wing with it. The report also revealed other flaws in the Nieuport. The undercarriage was weak, sometimes causing oil lines to rupture in hard landings. Poor soldering made fuel tanks crack from sustained engine vibration. The location of the tanks made them vulnerable to gunfire, turning the planes into potential flaming coffins.[29]

The next day, 9 June, Atkinson confirmed the French investigation and added some criticisms of his own about serious deficiencies in the Nieuports. In Atkinson's view their problems were too numerous to be corrected, and they could never be effective front-line fighters. Huffer joined the chorus, saying (erroneously) that the various types of wood used in building the Nieuport warped at different rates, impairing its structural integrity.[30]

Reports about the Nieuport's shortcomings surfaced amid a serious crisis in the leadership of the Army Air Service and became linked with the tensions accompanying it. Conflict between Foulois and Mitchell climaxed on 29 May when Pershing, who could no longer tolerate the situation, appointed General Mason M. Patrick, another friend from his years at West Point, to replace Foulois as chief of the Air Service. Foulois became chief of Air Service, 1st Army, and Mitchell became chief of Air Service, 1st Army Corps. Foulois continued to outrank Mitchell, and Pershing assigned him Mitchell's office at Toul as his new headquarters. Foulois had actually engineered the shakeup, hoping that controlling aviation in the 1st Army, a larger entity than the 1st Army Corps, and going to Toul in the process would put Mitchell under his thumb. Mitchell tried to sabotage the new arrangement by stripping his office down to the bare walls. When Foulois arrived he found everything gone—maps, telephones, desks, chairs, and the entire support staff. He had to sit on an orange crate. Mitchell said everything he had removed belonged to the 1st Army Corps and was needed for its operations. Livid with rage, Foulois demanded redress from Liggett, commander of the corps, who sent Lieutenant Colonel Frank P. Lahm to Toul with orders that Mitchell give Foulois whatever equipment he needed to perform his duties. Refusing to be mollified, Foulois asked Pershing to cashier Mitchell and send him back to America. Waiting for Pershing to reply, Foulois formally took charge at Gengoult.[31]

Acting on a trumped-up charge by Davenport Johnson that later led to a court-martial, Foulois also removed Huffer from command of the 94th Pursuit Squadron and demoted him to assistant operations officer of the 1st Air Depot at Columbey-les-Belles. Huffer had been an outstanding leader who was popular with his men, and they did not understand why he had been ousted. Foulois apparently thought Huffer was an ally of Mitchell and took Johnson's false accusations at face value. Huffer left Gengoult on 4 June, a day before orders announced his replacement. Kenneth Marr succeeded him as commander of the 94th on 7 June.[32]

Within this emotionally charged atmosphere, Foulois learned about the structural deficiencies of the Nieuport 28. It is possible that he had instigated some of the complaints about the plane because the damaging revelations gave him all the more reason to question the competence of Mitchell, who had praised it ever since the victories won by Campbell and Winslow on 14 April, but Foulois had never been impressed by the Nieuport, thinking it too "delicate" for a front-line fighter. The damaged wing from Heinrichs's plane was prominently displayed in the mess hall at Gengoult when Foulois arrived on 3 June. He had an appointment with Heinrichs that afternoon, and they must have discussed what had happened. Soon afterward Foulois ordered that the Nieuport be abandoned and replaced by the more rugged Spad XIII, whose V-8 engine had much more horsepower than the rotary power plant of the smaller but more agile plane. Until Spads arrived, however, pilots based at Gengoult had to continue flying Nieuports, which did nothing to bolster their morale and combat efficiency.

Most members of the 94th and 95th pursuit squadrons, though not all, were delighted by Foulois's decision. Rickenbacker and Meissner now knew that their harrowing experiences had not been caused by midair collisions but by design flaws in the Nieuport itself. Rick charged that the Air Service had wanted the Spad XIII all along and that the French had always known the Nieuport was a second-class aircraft. His first claim was plausible, the second unfounded. The victories won by members of the 94th in April and May testified to the Nieuport's virtues. Like any product of human ingenuity, it involved trade-offs. Designers had not known the problems the composite materials in the leading edges would cause and had sacrificed structural strength for maneuverability. An admirer compared the plane to "a highbred racehorse, minding the slightest touch of the rider to a heavy draft horse needing a stout hand." Some German experts considered it the best Allied plane of the war, superbly suited for close aerial maneuvering. By contrast, as Campbell stated, the Spad XIII "flew like a brick." Rick was also mistaken that Pershing and his advisers, however much they had originally wanted the Spad, had looked upon the Nieuport 28 as a poor second choice. Its structural flaws were apparent only in retrospect.[33] Rick, who was poor at judging distance to begin with because of his damaged cornea, naturally wanted a stout, powerful plane that he could dive from high altitude with impunity, using it in hit-and-run tactics that did not require the finesse needed with the Nieuport.

Evidence of the Nieuport's virtues was indicated by a firestorm of opposition that erupted in two squadrons, the 27th and 147th, which had joined the 1st Pursuit Group at Gengoult (making it a four-unit aggregation) during the leadership struggle between Foulois and Mitchell. The new squadrons had a British approach to air combat that clashed with the French traditions inculcated by Lufbery, Hall, Peterson, and other former Lafayette flyers. Harold E. Hartney, commander of the 27th, was a Canadian who had served with the Royal Flying Corps and been sent to the United States to train American pilots. An admirer of rotary engines, he compared the Nieuport 28 with the Sopwith Camel, a stubby fighter that could execute phenomenally tight turns and won more victories than any other British pursuit plane. Camels were extraordinarily difficult to handle and notorious for killing pilots who could not master their idiosyncrasies—but Hartney had a typically British attitude, believing high casualty rates were less important than inflicting the greatest possible losses on the enemy in a war of attrition. After coming to France with the 27th, Hartney fell in love with the Nieuport, calling it a "fast moving, fast acting gem" that could "zoom, dive, and about-face" so beautifully that he hated to come down from flying in it. He had known about the fragility of its wings before going to Toul, but regarded this potential problem merely as a challenge that could be overcome with good training and skilled airmanship.[34] Geoffrey H. Bonnell, an American citizen of Canadian ancestry who headed the 147th, admired the Nieuports even more than Hartney and vociferously opposed Foulois's adoption of the Spad XIII.[35]

In the end, to the great satisfaction of Rick, Meissner, and other like-minded pilots, Foulois's decision to switch to the Spad XIII stood firm but would take time to implement. Foulois, however, lost his other battle when Pershing rejected his attempt to remove Mitchell from his post in the 1st Army Corps and send him back to the United States. Pershing had seen the zeal with which Mitchell familiarized himself with aerial tactics and thought he had too much ability to lose him.[36] This development pleased Rick, who had been Mitchell's protégé from the beginning and came out of the leadership crisis feeling doubly satisfied

Chapter 8

— ☆ —

A Matter of Luck

During May, while Nieuports lost wing fabric with distressing regularity and Foulois and Mitchell sniped at one another, a steadily intensifying rivalry unfolded at Gengoult between Rick and Doug Campbell for the honor of becoming the first official American ace of the war. The outcome was decided by luck, which put Campbell, who clearly possessed better innate flying skills than Rick, in the right place at the right time. On the other hand, luck turned against Doug almost as quickly as it had favored him, leaving Rick better off despite the honor that had barely escaped his grasp. The adage "fortune is a fickle mistress" seldom proved more true than it did in the case of the two men.

Like all combat pilots, Rick wanted to be an ace, a distinction given to air warriors who gain exceptional mastery of a merciless game played for lethal stakes. The term may have come from the tennis court or originated in France, after the top cards in a deck. Whatever its derivation, aces had a powerful mystique in the Great War, making triumphal appearances on state occasions, enjoying audiences with emperors and kings, driving expensive cars, and being deluged with letters, some perfumed, from beautiful women. Long rows of medals on their tunics testified to their exploits. "They were a race apart—these knights of the air," said one of many writers who perpetuated their memory long afterward.[1] Among the foremost symbols of their fame was Germany's Orden Pour le Merite, the legendary "Blue Max," a coveted blue and gold medallion featuring a Maltese cross and four imperial eagles. Frederick the Great had created it when French was the language of the Prussian royal court.[2]

Gunners in bombers or observation planes could shoot down enemy aircraft, but, by definition, only a fighter pilot could become an ace. Admission to the club required at least five victories. Germany periodically raised the ante for its *Kanonen*—"top guns"—but Allied nations stuck to the original standard. Though arbitrary, it was well chosen because less than 1 percent of all fighter pilots from World War I through the Vietnam War scored five or more kills. Despite their small number, they accounted for 40 percent of all aircraft destroyed in combat. In military terminology they were "force multipliers," imbued by a "hunger to pursue the enemy through the air, to force a fight under all circumstances, to hound the quarry, and to make the kill."[3]

To become official, combat victories had to be verified under rules reflecting different realities facing belligerent nations. Britain and France collectively produced many more aircraft than Germany and Austria-Hungary and had more manpower to risk. In 1918 alone Britain made 30,671 aircraft for land-based operations and 1,865 for use at sea, more than any other nation. It could well afford to send waves of planes, flown in many cases by poorly trained pilots, across German lines in a calculated war of attrition. Because British airmen often fought where no friendly eyes could see their exploits, rules governing victory claims did not require certification by witnesses on the ground and credited the word of men who saw a comrade shoot down an enemy.[4] France, which had even more pilots than Britain but fewer planes, also pursued an offensive strategy but not so relentlessly or with such callousness toward human life as the Royal Air Service. French rules were much more stringent than British regulations, confirming victories only after they had been verified in writing by independent observers. Locating eyewitnesses, normally in ground units that watched dogfights passing overhead, could take days of search and interrogation. Contrary to British practice, a French win became official only if an enemy plane was actually seen to crash or be captured. Merely sending an aircraft spinning "out of control" did not count. Because American flyers at Gengoult fought under the tactical command of the 8th French Army they were subject to French rules, preventing pilots like Rick from getting credit for victories they could have scored had they flown in the British sector. Rick, for example, could not claim credit for the fighter he saw plunging out of control near Pont-a-Mousson, behind the German lines, on 7 May 1918 in his sortie with Hall and Green. The early victories for which he did receive validation occurred close enough to the front lines to be seen by French observers. French rules were liberal, however, in giving a pilot full credit for a shared victory in which two or more flyers simultaneously destroyed a single enemy plane, giving Rick his first win

EDDIE RICKENBACKER

against a Pfalz that, by his own admission, Hall had almost undoubtedly shot down.[5]

Germany, unable to match British and French manpower and aircraft production, practiced a defensive style of aerial warfare. In March 1918, at the start of Ludendorff's offensive, the kaiser's forces had only 3,668 aircraft on the western front and could maintain superiority only by concentrating air power at points of attack. Observation planes by necessity had to fly over enemy territory, giving Rick and other Americans a chance to fire at them, but German fighter squadrons stayed behind the lines and waited for incursions by enemy aircraft before going up to repel them. This policy explains why the German unit at Mars-la-Tour lured Hall, Green, and Rick over the lines before trying to ambush them at Pont-a-Mousson. Because German combat pilots rarely invaded Allied air space, their victories usually occurred within view of supporting ground forces. Prevailing winds, blowing from west to east, drove Allied planes deep into German-held territory, where wrecked aircraft and dead bodies could be seen and counted.[6] These special circumstances, along with meticulous care in record keeping, increased the chances of a German ace to score verifiable victories.[7]

The acme of recognition was to be an "ace of aces" with more official kills than any other flyer of one's nationality. Manfred von Richthofen's record of eighty wins, the most scored by any combat pilot in World War I, gave him enduring fame. Whatever advantages he may have gained by fighting on his own side of the lines, his record is remarkable considering that many of the planes he flew were obsolescent. (Contrary to a persistent myth, he and Rick never faced each other. Richthofen fought in the British sector and was killed in April 1918, when Rick's combat career had barely begun.)[8] René Fonck, France's ace of aces, had seventy-five official wins and claimed fifty-two more in sorties behind enemy lines that could not be confirmed under French rules.[9]

Partly because of his corneal problem, Rick lacked the skills of many airmen who nevertheless achieved less fame. Nor was he sufficiently ruthless. His qualms about taking human life—his compassion for a German flyer who might burn alive because of bullets he fired—led him to think about shooting down machines instead of men. His view of aerial combat as "scientific murder" set him apart from men with killer instincts like those of Richthofen, a passionate hunter who looked at his victims as prey, or Fonck, a merciless stalker with a cold, calculating nature. The chief assets that made Rick the most accomplished American combat pilot of the war were qualities of mind and spirit that made him a superachiever in whatever he did: his fiercely competitive nature, desire for recognition, relentless determination, unfailing persistence, courage that was more than a match for paralyzing fears, and craving for the elation he felt in cheating death. Deeply imbued with a burning desire for fame, he also realized that money could come with it. As was true of all human beings, he had complex motives.

The chance to become "America's first ace" was an opportunity Rick gained from the decision of the Army Air Service to disallow the transfer of combat records from British and French squadrons to American units, which ignored the achievements of seven United States citizens—Paul Baer, Frank Baylies, Frederick Libby, Raoul Lufbery, David Putnam, William Thaw, and Clive Warman—all of whom had already won five or more victories before the Air Service went into action. Lufbery led the list with sixteen, closely followed by Libby, a cowboy from Colorado who was unique in having scored fourteen kills while flying three different types of planes—observation aircraft, fighters, and bombers. Libby had all the makings of a folk hero, being the first American airman to shoot down a German plane and the first to carry the Stars and Stripes across enemy lines after Congress declared war in 1917. He flew against superb aviators including Boelcke and Richthofen. After transferring to the U.S. Air Service, however, he had the bad luck to be sent home to appear in bond drives, after which he was posted to Hicks Field in Texas as a flight instructor. The sudden onset of a circulatory and spinal illness handicapped him for life, and he faded into oblivion until a book, *Horses Don't Fly,* restored part of his reputation long after he died.[10]

By mid-May 1918 it was clear that either Rickenbacker or Campbell, men with highly dissimilar backgrounds, would become Uncle Sam's first official ace. Doug was sired by a distinguished astronomer and had studied at Harvard. Miller had advanced his career by making him his adjutant at Issoudun at about the time he appointed Rick chief engineer. Campbell had been trained in radio, navigation, and aircraft motors at MIT but never flew a plane before coming to Issoudun, where, like Rick, he schemed for chances to go aloft. When an order from Washington specifically authorized Doug, Rick, and other ground officers to fly, Campbell's innate potential as a pilot became immediately apparent. French instructors started him with a trainer much more advanced than a fledgling could expect to handle. His first solo was so impressive that they gave him even more sophisticated aircraft, which he flew with ease. After he went to Villeneuve, Lufbery recognized his promise, as he demonstrated by taking him and Rick on the first armed sortie across German lines.

Campbell got off to a fast start at Gengoult by scoring the second victory in his and Winslow's famous battle with German intruders on 14 April, but it took him more than a month to shoot down another plane. Rick went ahead of him by gaining his second official victory over the Albatros at which he was diving just before the wing-stripping experience that nearly cost him his life. Campbell pulled even a day later by destroying a two-seat Rumpler observation plane and went ahead with his third victory on 19 May in a "nice fight" with another aircraft of the same type, for which Campbell won the Distinguished Service Cross.[11]

Rick evened the score on 22 May by downing an Albatros in the ill-fated mission in which Kurtz crashed and died, but Doug went ahead by winning his fourth victory on 26 May when he attacked a Pfalz menacing a crippled British bomber.[12] Early the next day, Doug and Rick went on patrol across the St. Mihiel salient toward Pont-a-Mousson and encountered a pair of Albatros reconnaissance planes escorted by four Pfalzes. Maneuvering adroitly, the Americans lured the Pfalzes and one Albatros away from the remaining Albatros and pounced on it after carefully calculating it was too far away from the rest to be rescued. Shooting it down at point-blank range, they watched it crash into a forest and then climbed out of danger amid a barrage of antiaircraft fire. Although both men had taken part in the victory, Rick got sole credit for it because of poor record keeping by the clerk to whom French witnesses had reported it. Doug complained about the mistake in his diary but could do nothing about it. Rick did not correct the error at the time, an indication that his desire to become America's first ace was greater than his sense of fair play, but later admitted that the win belonged to Doug as much as to him. For the moment he was again ahead of his rival.[13]

The duel climaxed a week later. On 30 May, as the Americans at Gengoult prepared to observe Memorial Day, a British unit requested escorts for bombers returning from a raid against a railhead east of Verdun. Two groups of six Nieuports each, led by Meissner of the 94th Pursuit Squadron and John L. Mitchell (no relation of Billy) of the 95th, went to help the Brits. Rick, left behind, decided to go anyway, hoping to score the victory that would make him an ace before Doug could claim the honor. Taking off soon after the planes departed, he intended to join them halfway between Gengoult and the railhead. Climbing rapidly, he wanted to get above whatever took place and be in position to intervene at an opportune time. After getting 15,000 feet above Flirey, he saw a spectacular panorama as the British bombers approached from the east with enemy antiaircraft shells bursting in front of them, a group of German fighters getting ready to attack, and the twelve Nieuports led by Meissner and Mitchell speeding to the rescue. Other enemy planes suddenly came out of the west to intercept the Americans before they could reach the bombers.

Rick saw one of the Nieuports apparently spin out of control with two Germans on its tail but guessed the maneuver was a ruse. Pulling out and climbing rapidly, the American pilot banked toward one of the adversaries and engaged him in a dogfight. Rick got excited as the three planes swirled around one another, seeing that the opportunity he had been waiting for was unfolding right under his wings. It was obvious that neither of the Germans suspected his presence. Plunging into the melee, he poured bullets into one of them and saw it go down in flames toward a forest on the east bank of the Moselle.

Because of Rick's intervention, the pilot in the Nieuport had to dodge the second German plane, an Albatros C, while trying to avoid colliding with the one Rickenbacker had dispatched. As the American, whom Rick could not identify, twisted and turned, the strain was too great for his upper right wing to withstand and canvas began ripping away from its leading edge, billowing in the wind. The British bombers and the remaining Albatros had disappeared. Displaying superb airmanship, the mystery pilot kept his plane under control and flew toward Gengoult. Joining him as an escort, Rick saw as they neared the base that the airman was Meissner, who had survived his second wing-stripping incident.[14]

Rick's kill had to be confirmed before he could take credit for it. He was sure the German must have crashed, but an independent witness had to provide verification. Unfortunately, it was slow to arrive, giving Doug a chance to claim his fifth victory before Rick could get his. On 31 May, the day after Rick had shot down his latest victim—actually his sixth, counting the one still unconfirmed, that he had bagged in the sortie near Pont-a-Mousson in which Hall became a prisoner of war—Doug went on a lone patrol. Disappointed at not finding a German plane, he was returning to Gengoult when he saw a two-seat Rumpler photographing American positions south of Flirey in its descent toward the enemy base at Mars-le-Tour. Flying from east to west and having the morning sun at his back, Doug had the advantage. Approaching the Rumpler, he opened fire, but his Vickers gun jammed after just a few shots that only served to alert the observer in the rear cockpit to his presence.

In the German Air Service an observer, doubling as a rear gunner, commanded a reconnaissance plane. Had this particular observer desired, he could have ordered the pilot to flee while Doug cleared his gun. Instead, he decided to fight, perhaps not only because he did not know whether Doug could fix his jam but also because his own pilot, armed with a Parabellum machine gun that fired through the propeller arc, was skilled in simultaneous maneuvering and shooting. The observer knew his Rumpler was slower and less maneuverable than the Nieuport, but also that it had two guns—his and the pilot's—to Campbell's one, improving the odds.

Clearing his jam and returning to the attack, Doug found himself fighting a worthy adversary. For fifteen minutes the two planes fired at one another in a spectacular display of twisting, turning, banking, and diving. Knowing he was outgunned, Doug, displaying intelligence and self-control, conserved his ammunition, waiting for a good shot before firing short bursts at his opponents. Suddenly he noticed that the German pilot had changed tactics. Instead of maneuvering as before, he seemed intent on keeping the Rumpler's tail out of range. Guessing correctly that the observer was out of bullets and the pilot was trying to protect him, Doug began approaching the aircraft diagonally instead of going above and beneath it. Coming from the side and closing to within fifty feet, he saw the observer standing defiantly in the rear cockpit with his arms folded across his chest, waiting calmly for Doug to shoot. Doug later wrote that he hesitated to kill a helpless man but quickly realized the Rumpler's camera contained exposed film that could cost American lives if developed. On the other hand, he would have been something other than human not to know that his chance to become America's first ace was right in front of his eyes.

In a few moments Campbell killed the observer and pilot, and the Rumpler went down in flames near the edge of the American aerodrome. As the fight unfolded, the combatants had drifted toward the airfield, enabling hundreds of spectators to witness what happened. Verification was immediate. Because Rick's victory the previous day remained unconfirmed, Doug therefore became America's first official ace. If Rick was chagrined that an honor he had craved slipped away, his diary did not show it. "Lt. Campbell shot his fifth Boche today," he wrote, saying that Doug was "certainly going some."[15]

On 5 June, with Rick's recent victory still unverified, Doug and Jimmy Meissner went on a patrol and saw another Rumpler in the distance, flying at an extremely high altitude. It took them fifteen or twenty minutes to get near the plane, which escaped because it had a higher ceiling than the Nieuports. Doug and Jimmy, however, spotted another plane of the same type flying at a lower altitude—perhaps returning to its base—and chased it in a downward spiral, firing as they went. When the two planes were within about 500 feet of the ground, Campbell noticed the observer's gun had jammed. Possibly thinking about his recent victory, he closed in at "a dangerous angle" without realizing that the observer had cleared his jam. Too late, Doug "heard a loud crashing sound" and felt something hit him in the back. Fighting to keep his plane under control, he made a safe landing. Meanwhile, taking advantage of the observer's distraction in shooting at Doug, Jimmy shot the Rumpler down.

A fragment of an exploding bullet had lodged in Doug's back. He gamely refused to take ether, and medics removed it on the spot where he came down after giving him a local anesthetic. "The wound is perfectly clean," he wrote that evening, "and they sewed it up tight."[16] Sharing in the kill gained him his sixth victory. After spending a week at the base hospital he went to Paris and Biarritz, expecting to return after recuperating. Instead, to his disgust, he was ordered to return to America to train future combat pilots.[17]

Bad luck had kept Rick from becoming America's first ace. Had his victory on the mission with Hall and Green occurred where it could be promptly validated, as Doug's fifth victory had been, Rick would have won the honor that went to Campbell regardless of the encounter he won on 30 May. That kill was soon validated and he ultimately got credit for shooting down the German fighter near Pont-a-Mousson after Hall returned from captivity with evidence that the enemy plane had crashed. Rick had therefore won six victories before Doug won five. On the other hand, Rick had admitted that Hall's superior marksmanship was responsible for his shared victory on 29 April, and he was no doubt aware that Doug should have received equal credit for winning the one on 22 May but for bad bookkeeping. Their struggle had come out virtually a dead heat, but now Doug had to return to America. For Doug the war was over. For Rick it was barely beginning.

It would not be long before the 1st Pursuit Group was in the thick of battle. As the jousting between Doug and Rick approached its climax, a titanic struggle began in the northern sector. Ludendorff had failed to end the war before significant help arrived from the United States. By the end of May, 650,000 American soldiers were already in France and many more were about to disembark. Knowing that time was running out, Ludendorff concentrated his forces for a desperate assault. On 27 May a murderous barrage erupted along the Chemin des Dames, a weakly defended ridge named for a road that had been built along its crest for ladies of the French court. After an avalanche of high explosive and gas shells fell on British troops, waves of German soldiers tore gaping holes in their lines. In two days the Germans created a wedge pointed at Paris, where panic reigned in the streets and even among the legislators, who urged moving the government to Bordeaux. As in 1914, the Germans soon reached the Marne, the only obstacle barring the way to Paris.

Recognizing the gravity of the crisis, Pershing committed the 2nd and 3rd Divisions to help stem the onslaught before the Germans could cross the river. Marching rapidly to the front through retreating French units shouting that the war was over, fresh American units sealed the salient in bloody encounters at Chateau Thierry and Belleau Wood, a hunting preserve that became hallowed ground for the Marine Corps. Charging machine gun nests under withering fire, Leathernecks suffered more casualties in a single day than the corps had incurred in its entire previous history. For the first time, Americans were making a difference in the war.[18]

The 1st Pursuit Group was still not ready to face elite German units and stayed at Gengoult while French aircraft left to fight Ludendorff's airmen. With only a bit of additional training, however, the American airmen would be ready for more demanding work. During the week of 17–23 May they flew 293 sorties, took part in 22 combats, and won 5 victories. Meanwhile, German pilots in the sector made 125 sorties and only a single kill. By early June, reinforced by the 47th and 127th squadrons, the Americans had such numerical preponderance that the withdrawal of French planes left the area well protected.[19] Enemy forces confined themselves to missions using Rumpler C-IV observation planes, two-seat aircraft with supercharged engines and staggered swept-back wings. They could climb to about 21,000 feet, well beyond the altitude Nieuports could reach. Superb German cameras and lenses could focus sharply on objects far below. The crews, however, had to deal with anoxia from thin air, which they tried to alleviate by sucking oxygen from bottles. They were also vulnerable against speedier Nieuports while climbing to altitude and descending to return to base before their endurance time—about four hours—expired. If they came down too rapidly, their crews risked the aerial equivalent of the "bends," which may have impaired the judgment of the observer-gunner who risked a duel with Campbell on 31 May and died because he failed to conserve ammunition.[20]

Unlike Doug, who scored four of his six victories against observation planes, Rick had better success against fighter aircraft. On 4 June he took off on a patrol with Walter Smythe, whose Nieuport had two Vickers guns. Rick carried only one gun so he could climb higher and have greater maneuverability. Returning to Gengoult, he noticed puffs of antiaircraft fire rising above Toul and saw a Rumpler taking photographs, flying at an altitude low enough to give him a chance to bring it down. Neither the pilot nor the observer sensed Americans were nearby. Rick got so close to the Rumpler that the upper part of its fuselage, directly in front of the tail, was squarely in his sights. Anticipating an easy victory, he started to shoot but his gun jammed after he had fired only a few bullets—enough to alert the observer, who stopped taking pictures and shot back. As Rick peeled off with tracers streaming past his wings, he saw that the Rumpler was decorated with a rising-sun emblem and a large black numeral, 16, outlined in orange. By the time he cleared his jam, the Rumpler was fleeing. Forgetting about Smythe, Rick went after it, fuming about the carelessness of his armorer and planning to reprimand him when he got back to Gengoult. He overtook the Rumpler, but now it was well behind the German lines, getting ready to land at Mars la Tour. Smythe was too far away to help Rick, who was in such a hurry he was oblivious to the danger of flying at a low altitude, making him vulnerable to attack from above. As he started to shoot, tracers surrounded him, "streaming by my fuselage and cracking all around my plane from above and behind." Knowing German fighters were on his tail, he kicked the rudder control, shoved his joystick, banked as fast as possible, and made a beeline for home. His reflexes were so quick that he escaped before the attackers could pull out of their dive. Almost numb with panic, he resolved never again to lose his temper if his gun jammed in a similar situation. Back at the base, he gave his armorer only a mild reprimand. He was also pleased to learn he had been promoted to assistant commander of the 94th now that Marr had replaced Huffer, giving Rick the right to fly anytime he wanted.

Still waiting to hear whether the apparent victory he had scored on 30 May would be verified, Rick brooded about losing one over the Rumpler that would have made him officially an ace if his most recent victory was not confirmed. When he went to his hangar the next morning, mechanics had already dismounted his gun to see what had caused the jam. Taking advantage of his promotion, he borrowed Smythe's Nieuport for another sortie. Because the plane had two guns, he might have a better chance of success if only one of them jammed at a critical time. Smythe cooperated, not only because he had no choice but also because he suspected his guns were misaligned. Disregarding his concerns, Rick took off. Because French aerial units had left the sector and American trucks were bringing in fresh supplies, he thought the Germans would be curious and send Rumplers up early to take photographs. He would be ready when they came.

Despite the weight of its extra gun, Smythe's plane climbed rapidly and Rick was high above the sector at half past nine when he saw three German planes, including two fighter escorts, coming from the east. He waited for the fighter planes to turn back when they reached the American lines, leaving the Rumpler they were accompanying to climb alone. His anticipation increased when he saw it was the same plane he had failed to shoot down yesterday, with its black and orange 16 and rising-sun emblem shining in the morning light. The pilot and observer did not suspect his presence at such an hour, and he mustered enough patience to follow them until they had climbed a bit higher. Finally, unable to restrain himself, and still well above the Rumpler, he dived diagonally, hoping to unleash a stream of bullets ahead of it in a tactic called deflection shooting, aimed at hitting the plane as it flew through his line of fire. Too late, he realized he should have listened to Smythe's warning; both of his guns jammed after a few shots.

Alerted that he was under attack, the observer popped up and seized his machine gun while Rick tried desperately to unjam his weapons. He managed to get one of them cleared but the other remained stuck. Meanwhile, after coming within a few feet of colliding with the Rumpler, he had lost altitude, and it was now above him. Reversing its course, it started flying toward St. Mihiel, trying to escape. Maneuvering into position for another pass, Rick got under its tail but "was dumfounded to find a stream of fire coming out of the belly of my opponent." He was obviously mistaken because only heavily armored trench-strafing aircraft designed to fly at low altitudes had such guns. Carrying a belly weapon would have increased the weight of an observation plane, decreasing its speed, ceiling, and maneuverability. Probably the observer had swiveled his Parabellum gun into a position alongside the fuselage that made it seem as if it was shooting directly downward when seen from the angle at which Rick was attacking.[21]

Recovering from his surprise, Rick used his one workable weapon to spar with the Rumpler until it jammed again, this time for good. "Not being willing to admit I was helpless," he later said, "I continued to maneuver around as though I was trying to get a position of advantage, hoping to deceive him." The observer and pilot did not fall for the ruse and continued heading home. After Rick followed them back to their lines, the observer fired a burst of bullets in his direction as if to thumb his nose.

Angry and frustrated, Rick had forgotten how long he had been aloft without checking his oil gauge. He had been in the air two hours and thirty-five minutes, twenty minutes longer than the maximum time specified by his instructional manual. Suddenly the oil ran out, and his engine seized. Fortunately he was flying at almost 17,000 feet, and no Germans were in the vicinity as he glided across the lines and spotted friendly territory, looking for a safe place to land. Barbed wire entanglements covered virtually every square foot of space where there were no shell holes, but he finally found a vacant spot just big enough for him. Doughboys who had seen his plight hurried to the scene, thinking he might be wounded, but only his feelings were hurt. Then an officer drove up in a staff car. Leaving one of the soldiers guarding the plane, he took Rick to Gengoult. When Rick arrived, he found that Doug Campbell had been wounded in his battle with another Rumpler while on patrol with Meissner and was about to go to a hospital for removal of the shell fragment lodged in his back. After witnessing the operation and seeing that Campbell was "safely tucked away in bed," Rick and Jimmy went to their quarters.

Knowing that Doug and Jimmy had won an encounter with another Rumpler intensified Rick's determination to try again. He made two more unsuccessful attempts to shoot down the reconnaissance plane that had given him so much trouble before he gave up. Try as he might, he could not climb high enough to get within its range. He took the result like a good sport, saying "should I ever have the opportunity of meeting the pilot or observer who flew No. 16 Rumpler, I would gladly . . . invite him out for a dinner which would be second to none."[22] Ironically, that opportunity would arise soon after the war was over.

He had nothing to blame for the outcome of his battles against the Rumpler except his own bullheadedness. But he was naturally disgruntled despite his good sportsmanship, and it may have been just as well that he caught a virus. Atkinson gave him a leave to go to Paris, his first one since being snowbound in the city in early March. Marr drove Rick to Chaumont on 7 June, and he went the rest of the way by rail, arriving at the Gare d'Est the next day.

Paris presented a much different scene from what Rick had experienced in his earlier visit, confronting him with the "grim horrors of war as I had never seen them before." Trains coming into the city were loaded with "old women, young women, children tugging at their skirts, old men carrying what few belongings they had been able to pack hurriedly before evacuating their homes in the Chateau-Thierry sector." The sun was shining the next morning, but the faces of people walking along the boulevards aroused his compassion. But for the refugees, the city would have seemed half-deserted. Large numbers of people had fled, thinking the Germans would soon arrive. Still, he refused to believe the city would fall. As he continued his stroll, he remembered a poster captioned "Ils Ne Passeront Pas," showing a defiant poilu with a fixed bayonet. Surely, he thought, the French would thwart the Germans, just as troops brought to the front in taxicabs had stopped them at the Marne in 1914.[23]

He was right about the outcome of the crisis, but it was the United States, along with German exhaustion, that turned the tide. The Marines fought so savagely in Belleau Wood that the Germans called them *Teufelhunden* (devil dogs). By 3 June Ludendorff had already decided to stop the offensive temporarily to regroup because his supply lines were overextended. He resumed the drive six days later, but French and American troops quickly repelled it. Ludendorff was dismayed that 250,000 men from the United States were now reaching France every month, a figure the *New York Times* predicted would swell to 1 million by the end of June. German units were also ravaged by a flu epidemic of undetermined origin. It was sweeping through all the combatant armies, but malnourished German troops were especially vulnerable.

More than anything else, however, it was the massive American influx that made situation so grim for them.[24]

Rick left Paris on 10 June, went to a wedding at Chaumont the next day, and returned to Gengoult on June 12. Two developments he learned about buoyed his spirits: confirmation of his victory on 30 May, making him officially an ace, and Foulois's decision to replace the Nieuport 28 with the Spad XIII as soon as Spads were available. Newspaper stories about Rick's achievement had already appeared in America, and congratulations were pouring in by the time he got back to base.[25]

Speculation abounded that the 1st Pursuit Group was about to join the "Big Show" in the Chateau Thierry sector. The rumors, however, were premature because more time was needed to integrate the recently arrived 27th and 147th squadrons, trained in the British style of aerial warfare, with the 94th and 95th, imbued with French traditions. American pilots also had more lessons to learn about basic combat operations and would therefore stay where they were at least for a while. Part of their time continued to be spent escorting British bombers, and a few men, including Hamilton Coolidge, who joined the 94th on 16 June, needed training in protection missions. Soon after Ham arrived, Rick took him on such a sortie, which nearly ended in disaster when Coolidge, unfamiliar with formation flying, missed a signal in a landing maneuver and headed for Germany. Rick saw one of the planes going the wrong way and guessed that Ham was its pilot. Reversing directions, climbing to intercept the novice, and wagging his wings, Rick got his attention and escorted him back to base. Ham thanked Rick profusely for his help.[26]

Like most members of his unit, Rick had little training in close support of ground operations, including "strafing," a German term meaning "punishment." British airmen had pioneered this tactic in 1916 in the Battle of the Somme. Hosing ground forces with machine gun fire panicked German troops. The British also started equipping fighter planes with wing racks and dropping small bombs from them in 1917. The Germans copied the practice, using two-seat planes instead of the single-seaters on which the Royal Air Service usually relied. Utilizing planes including Hannover and Halberstadt Cl-IIs, designated as "attack fighters," the Germans created *Schlachtstaffeln* (attack squadrons) belonging to *Schlachtsgeschwader* (attack wings). In November 1917 the Royal Air Service carried the concept further in the Battle of Cambrai by using low-flying aircraft in close support of tanks. By March 1918 such operations had become standard aspects of both German and Allied air doctrine. Ludendorff used them in his offensives, and the French reacted with low-level bombardment of German troops.[27]

Mitchell had studied strafing and used it in April 1918 when pilots based at Gengoult machine-gunned German trenches near Seicheprey in a sortie from which Rick was absent because he had overheated his engine performing aerobatics. For the most part, however, the Americans had engaged only in air-to-air combat and needed training in close ground support before moving to a major sector. On 19 June flights led by Rick and Jimmy Meissner riddled German trenches and antiaircraft batteries north of Toul from as low as about 300 feet. After running out of ammunition, Rick returned to base, replenished his supply, and strafed an artillery unit. "Undoubtedly my appearance was quite a surprise," he recalled, "for upon diving and shooting at the battery, I was quite amazed to see the battery crew scatter in all directions and leap for their dugouts."[28]

A "dense white fog" that "clung over or blanketed the German lines . . . for at least six kilometers" puzzled Rick during the sortie. He thought the Germans had launched a gas attack and changing winds had blown the fumes back over their own positions. When he returned to Gengoult, a war correspondent told him that he had seen the aftermath of the first American experiment with gas warfare. Conducted at night, the exercise was so secret that even Atkinson had not known when it would occur.[29]

Another operation in which Americans needed practice before moving to the Chateau Thierry sector was attacking sausage-shaped balloons called *Drachen* (dragons) of the type Rick had seen hovering above the German lines in his first patrol across enemy lines with Lufbery and Campbell. The enormous gas bags, filled with hydrogen, which was highly inflammable, floated as high as 4,000 feet above the ground, connected to units below by cables deployed from winches on trucks that could reel them in if they came under enemy fire. Observers hung below the balloons in wicker baskets, using high-powered binoculars to scrutinize Allied positions across no-man's-land, making them effective artillery spotters but also rendering them highly vulnerable, as a result of which they had parachutes that opened automatically as soon as they jumped over the side. Antiaircraft batteries and machine gun nests surrounded balloons to defend them against planes using rockets and incendiary bullets to set them ablaze. "Balloon-busting," requiring a pilot to dive through murderous fire, was extremely hazardous but paid high dividends in blinding the enemy. Because destroying *Drachen* demanded careful planning and great courage, airmen who excelled at it had special status among their comrades and commanders. No activity was more likely to end in violent death or posthumously awarded medals.[30]

Rick spent much of his time in late June organizing an attack on *Drachen* that required much forethought and ingenuity. He hoped its outcome would "be the pinnacle of the Squadron's success in this sector and give the Huns something to remember us by." The key was surprise. Three airmen would divert the attention of crews manning the baskets of five German balloons and their ground defenders by staging an aerobatics display directly across the lines. Meanwhile, Rick and four comrades, having crossed into enemy territory, would swoop down on the unsuspecting foe from the rear, unleash a barrage of incendiary bullets at the gas bags, and make a quick getaway. A major problem would be eliminating the noise made by the rotary engines of the Nieuports. Rick decided the best solution would be for the American attackers to cut off their motors at a high altitude when they got behind the *Drachen,* glide steeply toward them, restart their engines just before reaching them, and climb rapidly out of danger after torching them.

After getting Atkinson's approval for the mission, Rick choose four trustworthy companions—Chambers, Meissner, William Loomis (a former Lafayette flyer), and Thorne Taylor. A French observation squadron supplied photographs of "the five balloons in their lairs." To achieve surprise, the project would be conducted early in the morning, immediately after the *Drachen* were deployed. The attackers would use only incendiary bullets because of moisture the balloons would have absorbed from dew. Three airmen skilled at aerobatics would leave half an hour before the attack force to do their tricks. The weather would have to be ideal if the plan were to succeed. Rick would judge whether or not to go by getting up as early as possible and scouting the prospects for clear skies before arousing the other flyers.

Setting his alarm clock for 2:30 a.m. on 21 June, Rick decided prospects for good weather were not encouraging when he got up. It rained on the morning of the 22nd, again aborting the mission. A party that evening celebrated the impending departure of the 1st Pursuit Group for the Chateau Thierry sector. Because it continued until midnight, it was just as well that bad weather continued the next day, but time was running out. It was still raining before dawn on the 24th, but when the sun broke through the clouds Rick and Reed Chambers took Harold Tittmann, a flyer who had recently joined the squadron, on a patrol to teach him operational procedures. Instructing him to stay out of trouble, the two veterans saw a pair of German observation planes and got so involved in pursuing them that they lost track of Tittmann, who disappeared. He phoned in later saying he had crashed near the Swiss border, and he returned to Gengoult in a few days. Once more, Rick's teaching responsibilities had taken a back seat to his zest for combat.[31]

When his alarm clock rang at 2:30 a.m. on the 25th, Rick decided that the weather was likely to be suitable for the balloon-strafing mission. By 4:15 the five attackers were strapped in their cockpits with engines running. Rick was worried that one of his magnetos was out of order, but luckily the other one restarted his engine as he closed in from behind the *Drachen*. When he attacked a balloon, however, his machine guns jammed. Hurrying back to Gengoult, he found that all of his mates had returned safely. None, however, had bagged a balloon and the mission was a flop. Still, as Rick said, "it was a great relief and weight off everybody's mind, especially my own, and we were all quite willing to admit that, as 'balloonatics,' we were a fake."[32]

That same day, as Rick and his comrades prepared to leave Gengoult, Marines virtually eliminated enemy resistance at Belleau Wood. Pershing's reinforcements had already played a decisive role in stemming Ludendorff's latest offensive. Indeed, the Americans had saved France, and the victory at Belleau Wood had confronted the Germans with the possibility of losing the war.[33]

After getting a taste of combat in the Toul sector, the 1st Pursuit Group was now poised to enter the heart of the struggle. Orders came on 26 June for its four squadrons to relocate to an airfield at Touquin, east of Paris in the Chateau Thierry sector. "Everybody seems real happy to have an opportunity at the Big Show," Rickenbacker wrote in his diary. The next day, however, he came down with a fever more severe than the one he had suffered from a virus a few weeks earlier. Incessant climbing, diving, and flying at extreme altitudes had damaged his ears. Instead of going to Touquin, he went to a hospital at Coulommiers, about twelve miles away from the new base. He felt "rotten" about the situation but there was nothing he could do about it.[34] Considering that his buddies would take on the best airmen Germany had to offer during the next few days, he might have been killed. On the other hand, he may have covered himself with glory in his first encounter with top-flight opponents. Whether his illness was good fortune or bad luck, there is no way of telling.

While Rick was hospitalized, the 1st Pursuit Group, headquartered at a luxurious chateau at Touquin, fought its first battles with elite German flyers. Despite the failure of the recent offensive, Ludendorff still controlled the areas he had overrun, and Allied leaders were planning to reclaim what they had lost. A few days after the transfer to Touquin, American ground forces attacked Vaux, a strongly held village on the south side of the Chateau Thierry salient. Air support from Touquin contributed heavily to the fall of Vaux in a single day, but the success was achieved partly because nearby German squadrons had been caught by surprise. Headquartered not far from Touquin were two well-seasoned *Jagdgeschwader,* one of which had been led by Richthofen before his death on 21 April. It now included a superb pilot, Ernst Udet, who ultimately scored sixty-two wins. Each unit had four squadrons, partly equipped with early models of the Fokker D-VII, which would gain the reputation of being the best German fighter of the war. Enemy aircraft in the sector outnumbered American planes by about five to one. On the day after the occupation of Vaux, two airmen from the 27th Pursuit Squadron were shot down in combat. One became a prisoner of war but the other died.[35]

Rick was already feeling better and reported for duty at Touquin on 2 July but went to Paris with Major Marr and a few other officers for a gala celebration of Independence Day. Marr intended to drive Rick back to Touquin after the festivities, but they missed connections and he stayed overnight in the city. The next day, wondering how to get back, he went to the American Experimental Aerodrome at Orly, a depot where French-made aircraft were inspected before being flown to the front. He later said he was "hoping to find a plane assigned to our Group, which I could return with." Despite the switch to Spad XIIIs Foulois had announced more than a month before, everyone in the 1st Pursuit Group still flew Nieuports. Rick was eager to see if any Spads had arrived at Orly and was delighted to learn from the officer in charge that three of them were there and ready to go. Rick took one up for a trial flight and wrote in his diary that "it certainly is a most wonderful Buss." The depot commander obligingly permitted him to fly the plane, bearing the numeral 1, back to Touquin. "Arriving at our aerodrome, and reporting to Major Atkinson," Rickenbacker wrote, "I found that I had acted unwisely in bringing this Spad out without going thru military channels and that I had upset the Major's plans in so doing." He was in fact risking a court martial. Because of Rick's impressive record, however, Atkinson let him get away with the fait accompli, and the plane was his for the keeping. Two members of the 95th, Sidney P. Thompson, who was killed, and Carlyle Rhodes, who became a prisoner of war, had been shot down while he was gone. He wrote laconically in his diary that their loss was "hard luck," knowing full well that he could have shared their fate.[36]

Waiting for guns to be mounted on his Spad, Rick flew a Nieuport on a patrol on 8 July. When they encountered six Fokkers, "not feeling too sure of myself," and being shaky, he fired "at long range, without results." He hoped to fly the Spad the next day but learned that the entire group had been ordered to move to a nearby airfield at Saints because large numbers of British planes were arriving at Touquin. It was hard for the Americans to leave the beautiful chateau they had occupied. The new aerodrome was much smaller than the one at Touquin, and some of the pilots crashed when they tried to land. Rick and other airmen arranged for billets in private homes, but he called the situation "terrible." He was also disappointed because his Spad did not perform well. When he took it out on 10 July with some Nieuports, a leaking fuel line forced him to turn back. That afternoon he experienced such severe pain in his right ear that he was sent to a hospital in Paris, where doctors found an abscess and told him his eardrum would have to be lanced.[37]

A surgeon performed the procedure on Thursday, 11 July. Rick wrote later that day that he was "receiving wonderful treatment," but postoperative pain gave him a "bad night," alleviated only by attention from an attractive nurse he hoped to take to dinner after he recovered. He felt better Saturday but was still confined to his bed on Sunday, which was Bastille Day; he could only listen to the raucous celebration outside. Detachments from countries allied with France paraded from the Arc de Triomphe to the Place de la Concorde, resplendent in colorful uniforms. Elegantly caparisoned horses pranced, bands played national anthems, cannons boomed, and frenzied crowds yelled "Vivent les Americains!" and "Vive la France!" as if victory had already been assured by the failure of the German offensive.

At the front, however, the Germans were still a force to be reckoned with, as Rick learned to his sorrow a few days later. Quentin Roosevelt, the youngest son of ex-president Theodore Roosevelt, was killed on 14 July when he became separated from his formation behind enemy lines and a German pilot shot him down. Rick felt "deeply depressed" but wrote that "It had always been Lieutenant Roosevelt's method to dash into a combat, showing unusual bravery in a very spectacular manner." He had predicted Quentin's untimely end if he continued these tactics, saying, "The realization that caution is the better part of valor only comes to those who have been more fortunate and had many months experience."[38]

Rick reacted as he did because had been thinking about his own foolhardiness in numerous sorties. He had been too preoccupied with the relentless pace of training, fighting, and trying to survive to have time for reflection. Now, looking back at what had happened in the past few months, he ruminated about the blunders he had made and the crises caused by his impetuousness. Despite being an ace, he was still not a mature combat pilot. Some of his problems had resulted from flaws in the wing structure of the Nieuport or having his guns jam at inopportune times, but he knew he had been at fault more often than not and was lucky to be alive. He resolved to make a new beginning, recognizing the difference between caution and timidity but constantly evaluating his habits and learning from his mistakes. It was the best thing he could have done. Without having the opportunity for introspection, his carelessness might have caught up with him in the vicious aerial combat that took place while he was out of action.[39]

While Rick brooded, Ludendorff prepared for another offensive, code-named *Friedensturm* (Peace Assault). A two-pronged attack, it would cross the Marne at Chateau Thierry, drawing French troops away from Rheims, and sweep through the resulting gap in the Champagne sector. After winning these objectives, Ludendorff would strike against Haig's British forces on his right flank. As a result, the Germans would engulf Paris from three sides and pin the British with their backs to the English Channel. But it was only a pipe dream. Forewarned by accurate intelligence, Allied forces blunted the offensive in intense fighting in which the Americans played a leading role. On 18 July, only three days after *Friedensturm* began, Marshall Ferdinand Foch countered with a force consisting mostly of the American 1st Division and French Moroccan troops which broke through German lines north of the Forest of Retz. Aided by tanks, it overwhelmed the enemy, taking thousands of prisoners and their equipment. Facing disaster, Ludendorff called off a planned assault against British forces to the north, ordered his forces to withdraw, and organized a new line of defense.[40]

The 1st Pursuit Group played only a modest role in the Second Battle of the Marne, as the successful effort to halt the Germans became known. The French had assembled a large number of aircraft in the sector and the British had sent heavy reinforcements, as indicated by the need to give them the aerodrome at Touquin and send Atkinson's force to Saints. Quentin Roosevelt's death was one of the few casualties suffered by the four squadrons in the pursuit group, which flew mostly escort missions to protect Allied bombers. One of the reasons the Americans had fewer planes than normal was because the new Spads awaited by the 94th arrived only a few days after Rick went to Paris to have his abscess lanced. Preparing the planes for action took the squadron out of the fighting. Still flying Nieuports, the 27th, 95th, and 147th bore the brunt of the limited American involvement.

As Rick had already learned at first hand, the Spads had unexpected mechanical problems. They were not only difficult to break in but hard to keep in service before needing repair. Instead of the much simpler air-cooled Gnome-Rhone rotary motors that powered the Nieuports, they had water-cooled, high-compression V-8 Hispano-Suiza engines. Rick had no problems understanding them when he returned to the fighting, but their complexity challenged the skills of ground crews that had to maintain and overhaul them. Reduction gears that did not mesh correctly caused particular trouble. Many Spads were likely to be out of action at any given time.[41]

As he convalesced from surgery, Rick learned that the impending switch to Spads was having serious repercussions in the 27th and 147th squadrons, whose British-trained commanders, Hartney and Bonnell, favored traditional dogfighting tactics. Besides admiring the Nieuport's maneuverability, they liked its short takeoff roll, permitting it to be off the ground within less than two minutes of an alert, and the simplicity of its rotary engine, which required less maintenance and could be quickly overhauled. Hartney was adept at aerobatics and did low-level stunting, which Atkinson thought was excessively hazardous and irresponsible. After he gave him a tongue-lashing for insubordination, Hartney, a realist, swallowed his feelings, and, to preserve his command, accepted the Spads. Bonnell, however, resisted switching to the new planes so vigorously that Atkinson sacked him. Pilots in the 147th were so devoted to Bonnell that they cried when he said goodbye to them. After briefly putting another officer in charge of the squadron, Atkinson changed his mind and transferred Jimmy Meissner from the 94th to head the unit. Jimmy had four victories, only one less than Rick, and was good at getting along with people, qualities that boded well for leading airmen wrought up by Bonnell's dismissal. Surprised by his appointment, he was humble in his first meeting with the pilots, promising he would try to benefit from their experience. His modesty worked wonders, and the flyers adjusted to his authority, which he exercised firmly but fairly. Having nearly lost his life on two occasions because of wing stripping and hating Nieuports as a result, he persuaded most members of the 147th to accept the Spad after new planes began arriving from Paris.[42]

Meissner's departure had unfortunate consequences for the Hat-in-the-Ring Squadron, which was going into a tailspin even before his transfer. Campbell, its first ace, was back in the United States, and Rick, its second, was in the hospital. Huffer, a popular leader, had been replaced by Marr, an ineffective one who had been traumatized by being severely wounded in the Lafayette Flying Corps, drank heavily, disliked flying, and was often away from his desk. Hall was a prisoner of war, Lufbery was dead, and Peterson had taken command of the 95th Pursuit Squadron because of a promotion given to Johnson. The Hispano-Suiza engines baffled mechanics, and some of the new Spads had no machine guns. One that did have them was so badly damaged in combat that it was condemned. Problems multiplied until only thirteen of twenty-five Spads posted to the squadron were still operational by the end of July. Rick, once an outcast, was now sorely missed.[43]

The sad state of the 94th was problematic for the entire group because the British 9th Air Brigade left the Chateau Thierry sector late in July, leaving only three effective Americans squadrons to patrol the entire area. Ludendorff's troops had begun forming new positions while recovering from their crushing loss earlier in the month, and German aerial activity was increasing. In the ensuing fighting, the 27th, 95th, and 147th pursuit squadrons suffered heavy losses against seasoned opposition. Although Mitchell was tactical commander of the 1st Air Brigade, Atkinson's aggregation functioned under the administrative jurisdiction of the 6th French Army. Caught between Mitchell's aggressive leadership and French procedures, Atkinson and his adjutant, Philip Roosevelt, did not know whose orders to obey and lost much-needed supplies. Despite its problems, the group as a whole performed well in its first major effort of the war, scoring thirty-nine victories against the

Germans and suffering thirty-one losses by the time the Chateau Thierry campaign ended in late August. The 94th, however, was in a funk, winning only two encounters and losing five pilots.[44]

Meanwhile, Rick remained in Paris with his ear still draining nine days after his surgery. By this time he had been transferred to another hospital, which was "certainly a pretty place," with "beautiful gardens." He was encouraged to hear about the victories being scored against "Mr. Hun" but felt bored being cooped up in his room and started to venture outside, despite his condition. On 22 July he visited a Hispano-Suiza engine plant and examined a 300-horsepower type designed to use a cannon firing through the propeller hub. Marr visited him the next day, bringing welcome mail from home but also telling him that Fred Norton of the 27th Pursuit Squadron, who came from Columbus, had died after being wounded in combat. Rick heard that "a recommendation for my return to America had gone thru," and wrote, "Well I hope same comes thru last of November then I would be home for Xmas." Nevertheless, he wanted badly to be back with his unit and pulled as many strings as possible to stay in France. Having dinner with the chief engineer of Hispano-Suiza at a chateau on the Seine apparently stimulated him to want to return to his Spad, because afterward he wrote that "the ear is not much better but am going back to the front regardless as there is much work to be done." Marr sent a car to pick him up.[45]

Rickenbacker returned to the aerodrome at Saints on Sunday, 28 July. He was "certainly glad to be back but my ear is no better." Unable to fly, he visited the front north of Chateau Thierry and saw antiaircraft guns shooting at an observation balloon. "Gee but its tough to see ones friends going out, have them come back and hear their stories of fights I should have been in," he complained. On Wednesday he took off on a short hop for the first time in three weeks but felt disoriented. "I'm crazy to get back but don't dare," he wrote. Six men from the 27th were shot down that day. Rick was particularly distressed that Alan Winslow, who had scored the 94th's first victory, failed to return from a patrol, giving the dispirited unit yet another jolt. Winslow was still alive, but had become a prisoner of war, having been shot up so badly that his left arm had to be amputated.[46]

Despite his queasiness Rick could not bear to stay out of action. On 1 August he led a patrol across the lines to help protect American observation planes on what turned out to be "the single worst day of the war for the 1st Pursuit Group." Six aircraft from the 27th alone were shot down in what Rick called a "free for all." A swarm of fighters from four German units attacked the Americans, who lost cohesion. Plainly, Ludendorff's forces were recovering from recent defeats and had not lost their will to fight.[47]

For the next few days bad weather made it impossible to fly, and Rick enjoyed a brief visit to Paris, but when he returned to duty his ear was still causing him serious problems. As the days wore on, he prayed it would "get better soon for if it don't I realize the war is over for me this year."[48] Ignoring the pain, he went on a patrol near Rheims and got into a melee with seven Fokker D-VIIs. Three enemy planes fled but four climbed and dived to the attack. Picking out the leader of the group, Rick got within point-blank range and fired but his guns jammed and the German escaped. Staying in the dogfight lest he confuse his comrades by breaking away, Rick sparred with the Fokkers as if he could still shoot and came close to being hit before the action broke off. Enraged by missing an easy victory, and thinking sarcastically that it was "very exciting to stay on in a combat and dive on a Hun knowing your guns will not work," he lashed out at his gunnery sergeant, Abraham ("Abie") Karp. Blowing off steam led to a productive discussion about why so much jamming took place. Karp suggested making a template to test bullets for irregularities, and Rick conceived the idea of honing bullets down to size if they failed to pass through the device. Karp thought about devising a hammer attached to a leather thong that Rick could wear on his wrist and use to dislodge ammunition that jammed if all else failed. Despite being encouraged by their plans, Rick went to bed tormented by his ear, which continued to hurt when he went up again the next day. "I'm praying to God same will get well soon," he wrote grimly that evening, determined that "I shan't go to a hospital."[49]

Nevertheless, by the next morning his pain was so bad that he lapsed into a "semi-stupor" and had to stay in bed. Eddie Green took his place, leading a patrol including Rick's close friend, Smythe, and Alexander Bruce, who had joined the squadron only a few weeks earlier. Drifting in and out of consciousness after they took off, Rick suddenly had a vision of Smythe plummeting earthward in flames. Soon afterward a report verified that two Americans had collided in midair, tearing the wings off both planes and sending the pilots plunging helplessly to a hideous doom, burning to death as they fell. Green confirmed what had happened after he returned from the sortie and identified Smythe and Bruce as the victims. Rick was deeply affected, not only because of the eeriness of the experience and his feelings for Smythe but also because he thought that parachutes, which German flyers were now wearing, might have saved his comrades. Thinking about the relative costs and values of pilots and parachutes put him in "a very bad state of mind."[50]

There was no longer any doubt that he had to be hospitalized again, and he returned to Paris on 18 August for surgery for an infected mastoid the next day. It proved to have been his problem all along. "It was a success and am feeling quite some better," Rick wrote within hours of the operation. Amid his rapid improvement, he learned the 1st Pursuit Group was about to move to a new aerodrome. Most enemy planes had left the Chateau Thierry sector to reinforce remnants of the German 2nd Army, which had been mauled by Canadian and Australian units in an offensive near Amiens.[51]

A succession of entries in Rickenbacker's diary showed that his condition had finally been accurately diagnosed. "Getting on fine . . . Feeling better today . . . feeling fine and am hoping to be out much sooner than I expected . . . It was a week ago today that I arrived here from the front. My I feel better than then." He sat on a balcony while a band was playing and a pretty nurse told him she wished they could go down to the courtyard and dance. He thought he would "give ten years of my life for the chance. Have seen her only a few times before but always came unto me with a thrill such as has been unknown in my past life. I hardly dare let myself feel she may ever care." She brought him ice cream. Several days later he wrote, "My little girl friend came to the room and we had a very interesting chat. She's a little Dear. [I] certainly would be a happy boy to have such a girl wonder about me now and then."[52]

On 24 August a big idea started to germinate in Rick's imagination when a "Mr. Bradley," representing the "Class Journal Co. of America," asked him to consider writing a book about his experiences as a combat pilot. "A new adventure has been started in my already adventuresome career," he wrote two days later, saying he had begun working on a volume called "War in the Air" and had already completed the first chapter, "Down in Flames." Skillfully edited by a ghostwriter, it would later appear in his famous memoir, *Fighting the Flying Circus*.[53]

Chambers and other comrades visited him from the front, bringing significant news. The 1st Pursuit Group had been released from French oversight and assigned to the American 1st Army. Pershing had rewarded Mitchell's leadership in the air support that helped stop Ludendorff's latest offensive by giving him greater authority, ending the bickering with Foulois. Mitchell had now become chief of the 1st Army Air Service, with headquarters at Ligny-en-Barrois. Atkinson had taken charge of the 1st Pursuit Wing, the largest unit in the Air Service. Hartney replaced Atkinson at the helm of the 1st Pursuit Group. Rick lost no time calling Hartney to let him know that his condition was greatly improved. Hartney agreed to send Rick's Spad to Orly to have a new carburetor installed. Rick had learned about an impending American offensive to eliminate the German-held St. Mihiel salient and was "scared to death" it would start before he returned to duty, the thought making him "sick at heart." When Chambers told him the 1st Pursuit Group had been assigned to a base at Rembercourt, about twelve miles west of St. Mihiel, Rick knew the drive was imminent and pleaded with his physician to release him, telling him he was "crazy to get back." The doctor said he could "leave in a day or two" but would have to take it easy for awhile after being discharged.[54]

Heeding the advice, Rickenbacker left the hospital on 4 September and enjoyed the attractions of Paris for a few days. But he was increasingly impatient. He learned from an officer at Aviation Headquarters that repairs had been completed on a Mercedes belonging to Mitchell, converting a former race car into a powerful roadster with leather seats. Rick eagerly accepted an offer to drive it to Ligny-en-Barrois, about nine miles southeast of Bar-le-Duc. Fetching it the afternoon of 7 September, he set off, taking a lieutenant from the 1st Air Depot along. Swerving to miss a buggy on the first stage of the trip, Rick nearly turned the car over in a ditch, but French mechanics helped get it back on the road. After an overnight stop he did not go far the next morning before a rear wheel came off, "ruining the chain guard" and requiring an hour's worth of repairs. When he finally got to his destination, Mitchell gave him a furious reprimand in the presence of a French officer. Rick thought that Mitchell, who had been assigned a big fleet of French airplanes for the coming offensive, was deliberately flaunting his authority to impress his visitor. He deeply resented the public rebuke but had to take it in silence. Eventually he would have it out with Mitchell, but not now.[55]

After the tirade ended, Rick phoned the aerodrome at Rembercourt and asked for transportation. A car sent for him was so late it was midnight before he reached the base, so elaborately camouflaged in a forest that he had trouble finding where officers of the 94th were staying.[56] Hartney wrote that the airfield "was unbelievably small and incredibly rough. Group headquarters was in a dilapidated shed. Our barracks were roughly constructed shacks hidden among the trees. The officers lived in tents. I had little fear the enemy would find our new location. I could hardly find it myself. It was a mess."[57]

Rick could care less. His comrades welcomed him "with a heartiness known only to flying squadrons." The dispirited unit needed him badly and was overjoyed he was back. Buddies had prepared a bedroll in which he soon fell asleep, "satisfied that I was home again." He had returned in time for the "Big Show." That was all he wanted.[58]

Chapter 9

— ☆ —

Climax

The "All-American drive" Rick had heard about was aimed at removing the Germans from the St. Mihiel salient, a wedge-shaped bulge in the Allied lines, twenty-eight miles wide and sixteen miles deep, anchored by Pont-a-Mousson on the Moselle at the east and St. Mihiel on the Meuse at the west. In August, while Rick was hospitalized, Pershing and his staff planned the impending assault and built up their forces in the area. Mitchell's promotion was part of the preparations. Pershing gave him 1,400 planes, the biggest air armada of the war. Atkinson's and Hartney's promotions were also part of the plan.[1]

Late in August Hartney attended a meeting at Ligny-en-Barrois. He saw Mitchell and other officers studying a huge map, twelve feet square, based on years of French balloon observations of the St. Mihiel salient. It showed virtually every feature of the terrain, including hills, forests, houses, larger buildings, and railroad yards in minute detail. Mitchell showed Hartney a tiny clearing at Rembercourt, six miles from Bar-le-Duc, and asked if he could squeeze an aerodrome into it, with support facilities scattered in the surrounding woods. Hartney promised he was up to the task and moved airplanes and men into the new base by stages lest the Germans see what was taking place. They thought Rembercourt so unlikely a site for an airfield that they never even photographed the locality. Hartney added to the deception by creating a plainly visible dummy aerodrome about four miles away and kept it lighted at night. Falling for the ruse, the Germans bombed it regularly. When Hartney began to experiment with night-fighting operations, the field served as a marker for incoming American planes, whose pilots had ten minutes to land at Rembercourt, which was dimly lit only for a few minutes. Hartney also built what he believed to be the world's first control tower for night flying, "a rough two-by-four scantling affair on top of the Group headquarters shack."[2]

Rick's difficulty finding the airfield typified the secrecy surrounding operations. Men and materiel, including 40,000 tons of ammunition, moved into the sector as stealthily as possible at night, creating mass confusion on roads leading to the front. Bad weather complicated the situation by miring everything in mud. Heavy rain and high winds impeded flying for three days after Rick returned. Only on 9 September could he take his Spad aloft for about an hour. To his disgust he found his machine guns were still jamming and sent the plane to Orly to have one of them replaced.

On 11 September Rick learned that "H Hour" was set for five o'clock the next morning. That night he was awakened by a furious artillery barrage that lasted four hours on the southern face of the salient and seven hours on its western nose. Soldiers waiting near field pieces lined hub to hub could read newspapers by the light of flames from their muzzles. When a whistle blew, thousands of doughboys climbed out of their trenches amid rain and mist, preceded by units equipped with axes, shears, and bangalore torpedoes to cut through barbed wire entanglements.

Rick and Chambers did not go on patrol until early that afternoon, flying low because of restricted visibility. Rick flew a substitute Spad but had wired Lieutenant Cedric G. Fauntleroy, who was coordinating supplies for him in Paris, to get his usual plane, "Old Number One," back to the front quickly. Peering down from his cockpit, he saw Germans retreating and strafed an enemy artillery unit whose members "ran into nearby fields" while horses "dashed madly down the road, causing havoc in general."

The Germans were actually planning to pull out, explaining the minimal resistance. Ludendorff, depressed since the failure of his mid-July offensive and even more disheartened by a setback east of Amiens, lacked enough reserves for a new campaign. He realized victory was slipping from Germany's grasp and saw a negotiated peace as the best hope for ending the war. Trying to avoid catastrophe by concentrating his remaining forces for the best possible defense, he knew that fortifications around the St. Mihiel salient had deteriorated and that troops were not confident they could hold it. The pullout was almost ready to begin when Pershing launched his attack. Some materiel had already been withdrawn, leaving remaining forces, many of which were from Austria-Hungary and secretly sympathized with the Allied cause, highly vulnerable. Defeatism was rampant, and resistance to the Americans was feeble. In one incident 300 enemy soldiers surrendered to a sergeant brandishing an empty pistol. Units that did not give up retreated in confusion, jamming roads and getting trapped.

Mitchell had air superiority from the beginning and fully exploited it, bombing and strafing at will. Mopping-up operations continued until 16 September but the offensive was basically over in two days. Americans incurred 7,000 casualties despite the overwhelming victory, but the Germans sustained many more and 16,000 men were captured. Pershing had restored 200 square miles of territory to France, reopened a long-lost rail connection between Paris and Nancy, and made possible unimpeded river transport on the Meuse. Most important, the Americans had shown they could conduct a major operation, but the cost could have been far higher had the Germans stood their ground as in previous campaigns. Pershing was elated by the outcome, but it had been achieved almost too easily, leading to overconfidence as his troops looked toward an impending offensive in the Meuse-Argonne region.[3]

Besides strafing enemy troops on the congested escape route through Vignuelles, Rick performed reconnaissance useful to the high command. He enjoyed surveying Montsec, a promontory from which German observers had tracked his earlier sorties between St. Mihiel and Pont-a-Mousson, and seeing it in friendly hands. He had a potential disaster on 13 September when a German machine gunner on the ground fired a bullet that hit his plane just under his seat, but he escaped unharmed because, like some other pilots, he had installed a piece of stoveplate under the seat for protection. As weather conditions improved that day and it became obvious that the attack had succeeded, Mitchell began ordering aircraft to fly higher on patrols to protect observation planes. The only victory scored by a plane from the 1st Pursuit Group in the first two days of the offensive occurred on 12 September when Lieutenant Frank Luke Jr. of the 27th Pursuit Squadron, who had been tracking three enemy airplanes toward Pont-a-Mousson, saw a German balloon and set it aflame after its crew had nearly winched it down.[4]

Because of the scope of Pershing's success and improved weather, Mitchell expanded the 1st Pursuit Group's zone of operations on 14 September from Chatillon-sous-les-Cotes to an irregularly shaped body of water, Etaing-de-Lachaussee, which American flyers called the "Three

Fingered Lake." Squadrons in the group flew an unprecedented 123 sorties that day and encountered large numbers of enemy aircraft. Flying on a lone patrol beyond Thiaucourt into what had once been virtually forbidden territory, far behind the German lines, Rick noticed antiaircraft fire near the enemy stronghold of Metz, went to the scene, and saw Allied bombers returning from a mission with four Fokkers hot after them. Their red wings identified them as part of the famed Flying Circus once commanded by Richthofen.

Climbing high above the Germans and maneuvering into position with the sun at his back, Rick pounced on the last Fokker, whose pilot was oblivious to his presence. Rick waited until he had the plane in his sights, fired a stream of bullets, and sent it spinning out of control. Taking advantage of the superior speed and diving ability of his Spad, Rick left the scene, twisting and turning to escape the leader of the enemy formation, who had spotted him too late. Returning to Rembercourt, he requested confirmation of his sixth victory, which soon arrived. He was pleased not only because he had scored it in a way that demonstrated the qualities for which the Spad had been designed but also because he had brought down a worthy opponent from an elite German unit, bolstering his self-confidence.[5]

This victory, the first Rick had won since 30 May, was a significant milestone in his career as a combat pilot. After his self-examination in Paris, looking back at all the previous mistakes he had made, he had resolved to be more patient and calculating, bold in taking advantage of opportunities but avoiding foolhardiness by refraining from encounters he did not have at least a fifty-fifty chance of winning and then getting out as soon as possible. The Spad XIII was ideally suited for this style of attack. Not only because he had ordered a new machine gun from Orly, but also because he and Karp tested and honed every bullet before he went aloft, he had no problems with jamming. A new, mature Rick had evolved from the unseasoned airman whose blunders in April and May had often brought him and his comrades close to disaster.

Rick took the same cautious approach the next day, 15 September. Again going out alone, he saw six Fokkers approaching from Conflans at about the same altitude he was flying. He and the Fokkers immediately started climbing, telling Rick they had spotted him at the same time. "After taking a few short bursts at long range at the rear man," he said, "I decided that it was better to wait for a more promising opportunity," another indication of increased maturity. He and the Germans chased each other around a circle, trying to get an advantage in altitude but failing to do so. Suddenly, far below, Rick saw three Spads that had wing racks and were bombing roads the Germans might use to bring reinforcements to the front. The Germans also saw the Spads, broke off contact with Rick, and dived at them, probably realizing that their bombs would slow them up. In their haste to strike they forgot about Rick, but he did not forget about them. Looking around carefully to make sure no other German planes were nearby, he plunged toward the last Fokker in the group of attackers. It took him more than 10,000 feet to get within firing range but by this time the Spads were less than 1,000 feet below and the Germans were in a frenzy to bring them down. Coming at his target from behind, Rick fired and watched the plane go down in flames. He thought about going after the next nearest one, but the Boche were so startled by his action that they lost cohesion and fled, probably thinking a host of Americans was on their tails. Rejecting the thought of following them behind the lines, and seeing that the Spads below him were safe, Rick returned safely home and drove a staff car to a nearby Allied balloon nest, wanting to see if its crew members might be able to verify not only his latest victory but also the one he had scored the previous day. Although they had seen what he had just done and certified the win, they had not observed his previous one. Luckily, a group of doughboys came along, including a soldier who had seen the battle and attested to its outcome. Rick thereby secured confirmation of his sixth and seventh victories.[6]

He went to so much trouble to verify the results because he knew that David E. Putnam of the 139th Pursuit Squadron had been killed in a sortie on the first day of the St. Mihiel offensive. Putnam had bagged twelve enemy planes, the highest number brought down by a living combat pilot from the Air Service, making him America's ace of aces. Now that Putnam was dead, seven official victories would give Rick the coveted honor. At the same time, he was apprehensive because pilots holding the title had been cursed with a high mortality rate, as if it were a jinx, reinforcing his determination to be careful. When he went on a lone patrol on 16 September he saw three Fokkers near the Three-Fingered Lake and set out in hot pursuit. German units were well informed about the identities of the airmen they were fighting. It is conceivable that the enemy pilots had seen the numeral on Rick's fuselage and knew he was the flyer who had already brought down two of their comrades on successive days. In any case, they fled toward Metz, descending toward the airfield. Rick chased them for four or five miles, firing short bursts to keep them aware he was still hanging around, but it occurred to him that getting too deep into hostile territory at a low altitude was risky, not only because other Fokkers might be in the vicinity but also because he would be increasingly vulnerable to antiaircraft fire. The old Rick might have gone ahead despite the potential consequences but the new one did not. Breaking off the encounter, he returned to Rembercourt.[7]

Rick did not stay America's ace of aces very long because Frank Luke, now known as "The Arizona Balloon Buster," had a much different attitude toward aerial combat and went out of his way to court danger. Destroying enemy balloons was critically important at any time but particularly crucial in the transition to the Meuse-Argonne offensive. American ground commanders in the sector had complained to Mitchell about the accuracy of German artillery and the need to blind the enemy by taking countermeasures against observation craft. After the swift success of the St. Mihiel offensive, Pershing had to move men and materiel rapidly into the Meuse-Argonne region to be ready for another drive he had promised Foch to conduct. Day after day, a stream of men and munitions—approximately 600,000 troops, 90,000 horses, 3,000 field guns, untold numbers of trucks, and huge quantities of supplies—came through or near the area around Rembercourt heading toward the new front. Amid the endless mass was Battery D of the 129th artillery regiment, led by Captain Harry S. Truman. The success of the deployment was partly attributable to excellent staff work done by Colonel George C. Marshall and other American officers who had intensively studied German methods of moving troops and supplies, but its effectiveness also resulted from the heroism of airmen who shot down reconnaissance planes and balloons.[8]

The Germans had good reason to think Pershing would follow his victory at St. Mihiel by continuing toward Metz, a move advocated by Douglas MacArthur and other American generals. The logic of the alternative strategy made it all the more potentially fruitful to keep the impending Meuse-Argonne offensive as secret as possible, preserving the possibility of surprise. At an earlier stage in his career Rick would have been an ideal candidate to risk his life attacking *Drachen* against extreme odds but no longer. His experience and maturity were too valuable to squander, even for such important operations, especially when a willing candidate was waiting in the wings. Nobody did more to confuse the Germans about Pershing's intentions than Luke, who attacked and destroyed balloons with a reckless abandon that made him a legend in the history of American military aviation.

Hartney supported Luke's almost suicidal tactics. Indeed, he helped instigate them. As the success of the St. Mihiel offensive became apparent, Mitchell summoned Hartney to Ligny-en-Barrois and told him it was urgent to destroy German balloons. Reviewing the tactics used in attacking the gas bags, Mitchell said they were relatively ineffective if used in the morning, when balloons were damp and would not burn readily if hit by incendiary bullets. In late afternoon, as the sun went down, it was hard to get close to *Drachen* under its protective glare. Whatever the solution might be, Mitchell said, new methods were needed; it was imperative that they got results, and it was up to Hartney to find them. Cocking his head back and forth and muttering "precisely, precisely," Hartney returned to Rembercourt to do Mitchell's bidding. As a hands-on leader he went regularly among pilots to get their views about balloon-busting. Luke gave him a valuable idea by urging "attacking balloons at dusk—just before it became too dark to see."

Not only because of Rick's age and maturity, but also because of his mechanical knowledge, Hartney, a shrewd judge of character, had already tabbed him for a leadership role and did not want to take unnecessary chances that might cost him his life. Luke, on the other hand, was an unseasoned youth with a different profile. He was expendable to a British-trained commander who had no scruples about incurring high casualties. "If there was any hell-raising to be done, Luke gave it his serious attention," said an admirer. He volunteered for the Air Service after America declared war against Germany, showed skill in stunt flying at Issoudun, and was posted to the 27th Pursuit Squadron in July 1918, but he became unpopular among comrades. Charging that he lied about winning a victory that took place too far behind enemy lines to be verified, they labeled him a coward. He was an odd man out, just as Rick had been at Issoudun and Villeneuve. Luke's only close friend was Joseph H. Wehner, another misfit whose Germanic name, as in Rick's case, had raised unfounded suspicion about his loyalty to the United States, leading intelligence agents to shadow him. Luke and Wehner naturally gravitated together and became inseparable. Hartney had gotten to know Luke and believed his story about shooting down an enemy plane behind the lines. He also realized that a pilot like Luke, who had something to prove to himself and his comrades, might be more inclined to take extremely hazardous chances. Hartney resourcefully hit upon a way to capitalize on Luke's insecurities and the devotion between him and Wehner. Returning to Mitchell's headquarters, Hartney proposed, as a solution to the balloon problem, "to send out only two pilots, one to stay above to protect the other one. The lower one was to fly along close to the ground and shoot the balloon in its nest, just at dusk or even after dark."[9]

Atkinson, whose approach to training American pilots was to bring them along carefully before risking high casualty rates, would have been unlikely to countenance the course of action Hartney planned to take. To him, highly trained pilots represented a large investment in time and money that should not be squandered. Unlike Bonnell, Hartney had kept his command by yielding to Atkinson even though he hated the Nieuports, showing that he would bow to orders, but now an even higher authority, Mitchell, had assigned Hartney a job to do and could be counted on to back him up. Luke was an ideal candidate to do what Hartney needed to accomplish to impress Mitchell. In the upcoming battle against the *Drachen,* Luke would be the low-altitude attacker, Wehner the protective wingman. Hartney provided both airmen with .45 caliber machine guns that fired special incendiary bullets loaded with phosphorous and sealed with an alloy that melted easily when the projectiles were fired. In the days that followed, Luke gave amazing demonstrations in the evenings by diving recklessly and repeatedly at balloon nests through murderous enemy fire, showing utter indifference to danger and torching the hydrogen-filled gas bags while Wehner covered him. Both men came back from their earlier missions alive, but Luke's fuselage and wings were often so badly shredded it seemed impossible he could have survived. There was no doubt he had the recklessness Hartney wanted, and Hartney made the most of it.

On 16 September, the day when Rick had turned back from attacking a group of Fokkers near Metz because he thought it foolhardy to pursue them deeper into German territory, Luke surpassed him as ace of aces. Rick congratulated him but did not admire his heedlessness. As a former misfit who had only recently matured and won the respect of his comrades, Rick understood Luke only too well. Believing that Luke's bravado would kill him, he also saw in him a potentially superb combat pilot and wanted him to be in the 94th, where he could teach him to practice self-discipline—a trait Hartney did not want to encourage.

As Luke's exploits continued, five of his Spads and three of Wehner's became irreparably damaged by enemy fire and had to be replaced. On

18 September the daredevils went on a patrol at dusk in which Luke destroyed two balloons and three planes. Wehner, however, died during the sortie trying to protect his friend from a swarm of Fokkers after he torched the second balloon. Enraged by what had happened to his wingman, Luke shot down two Fokkers immediately after Wehner's death plunge and destroyed a Halberstadt observation plane before leaving the scene. His main fuel tank had been punctured during the fight with the Fokkers. Before seeing the Halberstadt, he had been pumping gas by hand from his reserve supply, but no risk was too great for him to take when he saw a chance for a kill. The Halberstadt was surrounded by four French Spads whose pilots were trying to capture the ship without damaging it, but Luke would not spare the German aircraft. Letting go of a hand pump, he zoomed furiously between two of the Spads, firing his remaining bullets into the Halberstadt and sending it down in flames.

Luke's engine sputtered and died, forcing him to glide to a landing in a field behind the French lines near Verdun. He spent the night in his plane, mourning the loss of his beloved wingman. By this time he had scored fourteen victories in six days. The next morning Hartney and Rick drove to Verdun to see what was left of the Halberstadt and bring Luke back to Rembercourt. Luke still hoped against hope that Wehner was alive but now knew he was dead. That evening the 1st Pursuit Group threw a party for Luke at the mess hall to celebrate his unprecedented feat of scoring five victories in only a few minutes. Rick wrote that "he certainly is a great boy." In his estimation, "there has never been during the entire four years of war, an aviator who possessed the confidence, ability and courage that Lieutenant Luke had shown during the past two weeks." Luke shrugged off the praise poured upon him, disconsolate about losing Wehner and obsessed with avenging his death. Now worried about his state of mind, which could seriously compromise his combat efficiency, Hartney ordered him to take a seven-day leave to Paris to cool off.[10]

Hartney had decided to implement another idea. Rickenbacker had already been urging that the 94th become identified as an elite squadron under his command, hence his effort to have Luke transferred to it. Hartney liked the idea. Seeing Rick as extremely experienced, coldly calculating, a proven organizer, and old enough to be like a father to his men, Hartney appreciated another talent he urgently needed: Rick's mechanical knowledge and ingenuity. Anticipating the Meuse-Argonne operation, he had decided to sack Marr because of his heavy drinking, reluctance to fly, and frequent absences from Rembercourt. The change had obviously been brewing for some time because pilots had been complaining about Marr's leadership and Hartney had been making arrangements to soften the blow to Marr's pride by having him promoted to Major before sending him off. After the party for Luke, Hartney and three pilots left for Paris to participate in ceremonies honoring Marr, leaving Rick in temporary command of the Hat-in-the-Ring aggregation. Rick was aware of Hartney's intentions, writing in his diary that he was "trying my darndnest" to get the 94th "back in shape again." He was in an extremely buoyant mood after Hartney and his companions departed, regaling a reporter with "Gimper" stories and then staging a show by visiting entertainers in a hangar, which he described as a "howling success." He planned to throw a party on the evening of 25 September, when Hartney would be back from Paris.[11]

Hartney was almost desperate about the mechanical problems posed by the Spads, which were so often down for repairs that he could not carry out Mitchell's orders for lack of flyable planes. He saw Rick's grasp of engines and rapport with ground crews baffled by the intricacies of the Hispano-Suiza V-8 as priceless assets. He was also impressed by the coolness displayed by Rick in his victories since returning from Paris. In his memoirs Hartney stressed Rick's patience, contrasting it with Luke's recklessness. He was apparently unaware of the blunders Rick had made before his hospitalizations in Paris gave him time to sort himself out. Hartney saw Rick's age as evidence that he had a maturity lacked by younger pilots. Having laid the groundwork for promoting him before going to Paris, he cemented it on his way back through Chaumont by convincing the top brass that it was the right thing to do.

Hartney had proceeded shrewdly in preparing to complete his plan. His first step was to discuss his intentions with Coolidge, Chambers, and Taylor, who outranked Rick in the length of time they had spent in the Army, to make sure they did not resent being leapfrogged.[12] They unanimously agreed that Rick deserved the post and may have been the three men Hartney took to Chaumont to argue in his behalf. Hartney knew he would have a hard time selling Rick to officers higher up the chain of command. Mitchell had always liked and admired Rick. As Rick surmised, the dressing-down he had given him at Ligny-en-Barrois was merely a way to impress a visiting French officer with his authority. On the other hand, Mitchell was skeptical about "bypassing men with seniority in grade and service." Behind his fears was his knowledge that

Rick was not "regular Army" and his credentials would be suspect to Pershing, Atkinson, and other West Pointers who had been in the Mexican expedition. In his book *Aces in Command*, Walter J. Boyne later sized up the situation by writing that "regular army staff officers did not regard Rickenbacker as 'officer material' and felt that he would be hopelessly out of his element as a CO."

But Hartney was adamant. It is evident from what happened that he put on a persuasive performance at Chaumont. Though a small man, he had skillfully pushed himself up the chain of command despite his diminutive size and could be extremely forceful when he was determined to have his way. It is not clear exactly what he said, but he had ammunition to use and it is unlikely that he did not make the best of it. Unlike Bonnell, he had followed Atkinson's bidding in reluctantly accepting the Spads, but now he could report that they had been mechanically unreliable and that he needed a person with Rick's mechanical genius—with which Mitchell was well acquainted—to keep them in flyable condition. Hartney had come through for Mitchell by identifying Luke and Wehner as a superb team for destroying enemy balloons. Pershing, facing the challenge of his life in the upcoming Meuse-Argonne operation, knew that the 94th was a demoralized outfit. Now Hartney and the pilots he had brought to Chaumont could testify that the unit had welcomed Rick to Rembercourt with open arms, elated to have him back. His performance in the St. Mihiel operation had not only been exemplary but had also shown a high degree of maturity. One of his admirers said that "His mind worked like a cold and efficient steel trap and his indomitable will brought him triumph over many obstacles."[13] In any event, Hartney made his case and announced Rick's promotion as soon as he returned on 24 September. "Was made C.O. of the 94th Aero Sq today," Rick wrote, "which makes me very happy as I have been with this sq for its existence and it was the first American Chase Squadron to do action duty over the lines."[14]

Rick immediately made clear his intention to be a hands-on leader, calling a general meeting of the entire squadron including officers and staff. "In fact, we shut up operations for the moment," he said. One of his most important points was to downplay the niceties of military protocol. "I told them that they had to appreciate that I was in command, that I respected the uniform and all of that, but didn't want any foolishness in connection with the uniform," he later remarked. "I didn't want anybody wasting time saluting somebody else." Instead of going overboard on "military decorum" he wanted results that would restore the 94th to its rightful place as the best unit in the Pursuit Group. He admonished pilots to learn as much as possible about the peculiarities of the Spad XIII and its Hispano-Suiza engine, telling them to "baby" their engines "by not opening them up to full throttle until they needed to do so in actual combat and that if handled properly the power plants would require overhauls after 100 hours instead of the prevailing 20." (He later told an interviewer that the "average life of that engine for the squadron members, all youngsters, in my outfit, was twelve hours before they had either burnt up an engine or misused it.") Meeting with the mechanics who worked on the Spads, he told them they were as valuable to the squadron as the pilots. He recalled that when he and ground crews got together "we'd have sort of a verbal love feast, going over the day's problems and tomorrow's hopes and ambitions." He wanted them to feel like members of his pit crews on the racing tour. Perhaps his greatest selling point was his promise that he "would never ask anybody to do anything that I would not do myself first or do at the same time." Unlike Marr, he would not fly a desk.[15]

Determined to show that he meant what he said, he went on a lone patrol on his first day in command and spotted seven German aircraft, five Fokker D-VIIs and two Halberstadt reconnaissance planes, near Billy-sous-les-Côtes. Despite his feelings about Luke's recklessness, the passion he displayed was worthy of the young pilot's élan. Climbing as high as he could and getting the sun at his back, he dived at one of the Fokkers, raked its fuselage with gunfire, and sent it spinning out of control. Instead of scrambling out of danger, he plunged into the midst of the formation and aimed at one of the two-seat Halberstadts, getting as close as possible and shooting it down in flames. His audacity unnerved the pilots of the remaining five planes so much they became disorganized and withdrew to regroup.

Instead of continuing his attack, Rick flew back to Rembercourt and commandeered a car in which he and Chambers went to the area over which the encounter had taken place to see if they could find the planes he had brought down, but heavy artillery fire forced them to turn back. Nevertheless, the kills Rick had scored were ultimately credited to him as his eighth and ninth victories. He had given the 94th an object lesson in leadership.[16] The sortie would also be of critical importance in his career because it ultimately led to his being awarded the Medal of Honor in 1930.

Luke returned early from his leave of absence, brooding too intensely about Wehner's death to enjoy the attractions of Paris and thirsting to get back at the Germans. Hartney assigned him a new partner, and he continued his twilight attacks on enemy balloon nests, boldly identifying specific targets he intended to destroy and predicting the precise times at which he would set them ablaze. Keeping his word led to evening get-togethers attended by Mitchell and other officers, who would watch the *Drachen* catch fire in succession and marvel at Luke's uncanny ability to perform on schedule. On 26 September, however, trying to protect Luke on one of his daring missions, his new wingman met the same fate as Wehner.

Hartney was no longer under as much pressure to exploit Luke's talents as Mitchell had originally imposed on him. By this time the massive deployment of troops and supplies required for the Meuse-Argonne operation had ended and the offensive had begun. Hartney was also having problems with Alfred Grant, commander of the 27th, who was almost frantic about Luke's recklessness and resistance to orders. Nothing he did or said could rein him in. Rick joined Grant in expressing his feelings, believing he could save Luke from getting himself killed by teaching him the same lessons he was already giving his pilots: never attack an opponent unless the odds of success were at least fifty-fifty, always break off an engagement that seemed hopeless and make a beeline for home, and realize that there was an important difference between cowardice and common sense. These admonitions might be called "Rickenbacker's Dicta," equal in importance to the ones Oswald Boelcke had prescribed earlier in the war. Rick had become a pioneer in what came to be known as "calculated risk management," conserving human resources by minimizing casualties.

Having told Mitchell about his desire for the Hat-in-the-Ring Squadron to be identified as an elite unit similar to the French Cignones (Storks), with whose members Luke liked to hang out, Rick continued to advocate that Luke be transferred from the 27th to the 94th. Hartney was getting so concerned about Luke's increasing mania that he was thinking seriously about approving the transfer. "At this time," Hartney later recalled, "Luke got the idea that he could take on the entire German airplane and balloon services singlehanded, without support of any kind."[17]

Time was running out for Luke. On 28 September he found an enemy balloon nest near Verdun and set it ablaze. Proceeding on another patrol, he developed engine trouble and spent the night at a French base. Against Grant's orders but with the consent of Hartney, who came to the base the next day, bringing Rick with him, the Arizona Balloon Buster took off on his final sortie as evening approached. In the furious action that followed, he destroyed three *Drachen* and shot down two planes, after which he strafed German troops and hand-dropped bombs on them, but antiaircraft fire from a machine gun battery near Murvaux hit him in a lung and he came down in a field behind enemy lines. After climbing out of his Spad, craving water, he staggered toward a nearby rivulet but was intercepted by German troops and ordered to surrender. He responded by drawing his revolver in a final gesture of defiance and died, either in a shootout with the soldiers or, more probably (according to the testimony of three eyewitnesses), from the wound he had suffered. Taking his identification papers and personal effects, the Germans went away, after which villagers put his body on a wagon and buried it in a cemetery. They identified Luke from a note he had dropped near one of the balloons he had torched, explaining who he was and giving his father's name and address.[18]

One of the greatest figures in the history of the United States Air Force had met his doom. Luke posthumously received the Medal of Honor, the only fighter pilot to be awarded it during the war.[19] Hartney's complicity in his fate haunted him the rest of his life. Calling Luke "one of the bravest but one of the strangest men that ever wore the uniform of the United States Army," he tried to justify encouraging him to do what he did by asking, "Did I treat him right? I think so. Did I give him too much leeway? I think not. In any other branch of the service requiring routine discipline he would have been unhappy, unruly, totally lost. In the Air Service his dynamic, rebellious, reckless, fearless individuality found expression."[20]

Rick disagreed, thinking Luke more valuable alive than dead and believing he had taken the loss of Wehner too personally, resulting in a preventable tragedy. Rick later claimed that he had finally succeeded in arranging Luke's transfer to the 94th before his last sortie, possibly explaining why he accompanied Hartney to the French airfield. Had the order authorizing this step come through twenty-four hours earlier, he maintained, he could have prevented Luke from taking off on his fatal flight and thereby saved his life. Had Rick somehow been able to control Luke's "wild, harum-scarum" nature and mold him into a disciplined, mature combat pilot, Luke, not Rick, might have emerged from the war as America's ace of aces, as Rick later hinted at his own Medal of Honor ceremony in 1930. Whether even Rick could have imposed discipline on the impetuous hero, however, is moot.[21]

As it was, Hartney had channeled Luke's recklessness into playing a valuable role in helping to conceal the massive American redeployment after the St. Mihiel offensive. He had also put a much more seasoned and mature pilot than Luke in charge of a unit that would distinguish itself in the Meuse-Argonne campaign. By satisfying Mitchell's wishes and shrewdly playing the cards he had been dealt, Hartney did much to bring the American air war to a successful conclusion. It was unfair of Rick to second-guess him, especially because his argument that he could have tamed Luke was hypothetical and possibly delusory. Great warriors must be who they are and bear the consequences.

Shortly before midnight on 25 September a massive artillery barrage opened the Meuse-Argonne offensive. The initial salvos were aimed at disrupting German supply lines to the rear of the areas where the main assault would take place. Rick slept through the commotion until an orderly awakened him at four o'clock. Thousands of guns were engaged in a furious bombardment that shook windows in Malmedy, twenty-five miles away, where Max von Gallwitz, commander of German forces in the sector, was headquartered. Rick and five of his pilots had orders to attack two balloons to help blind the enemy from observing the disposition of forces conducting the initial assault. After breakfast they arrived at the airfield and saw a brilliantly illuminated horizon that reminded Rick of "millions of electric signs along Broadway." They wanted to reach the *Drachen* at the time their crews were starting to winch them aloft, preoccupied with what they were doing and thus more vulnerable to attack.[22]

As Rick gained altitude he saw the most extraordinary spectacle of his life—"millions of flashes from all calibers of artillery going off all at once" across a wide expanse of territory from Rheims on the west to Luneville on the east. "To me," he wrote, "it seemed as though there was being operated a giant telephone switchboard with thousands of hands putting in the plugs all along this sector."[23] Mesmerized, he circled above Verdun for awhile before remembering what he was supposed to be doing. At first he could not find the balloons he had been ordered to destroy, but suddenly he saw tracer bullets and "flaming onions"—brilliant bursts of phosphorescent shellfire—indicating that enemy batteries were defending the nests. Two enormous sheets of flame showed that his fellow pilots had beaten him to the prey, but he had no time to admire the results because tracers started streaming past his fuselage, making him aware he was under frontal assault. Surprised that enemy fighter planes were up at such an hour, he instinctively pulled his triggers as he saw a Fokker D-VII head directly at him, spewing fire. For a moment it seemed to Rick that he and his adversary were tied together by "flaming red ropes." Which of them would flinch before they collided head-on? Fortunately for Rick it was the German pilot, who suddenly zoomed under his Spad. Knowing that he had a momentary advantage over the enemy, he looped, got on the Fokker's tail, raked it with bullets, and watched it plunge out of control.

Any momentary satisfaction he felt disappeared when his engine began to vibrate so violently it seemed to be tearing loose. He guessed he was at least four or five miles inside the German lines. There was no chance he could glide so far to safety, so he throttled down as much as he could without stalling and headed toward Verdun. Expecting the Spad to shake apart at any moment, he was immensely relieved to reach the emergency field where Jerry Vasconcells, who was leading an experiment in night-fighter operations, was in charge. After landing he saw that half of his propeller had been shot off. Carefully examining the front end of the plane, he counted twenty-seven bullet holes or scratches within a radius of five or six feet. One projectile had gone straight through the center of his windshield. Because of the blind spot in his right eye he habitually aimed through his gunsight with his left. Had he been sighting normally, the bullet—which came close enough to his forehead to singe his leather helmet—would have gone through his left temple, killing him instantly. Instead of costing him his life, as he had so often feared, the blind spot in his cornea had saved it.[24]

Vasconcells, who had just returned from a sortie, had seen Rick's victory and confirmed it. Vasconcells had destroyed one of the balloons Rick had seen going up in flames, enabling Rick to reciprocate by validating his feat. (Because American flyers were no longer under French administrative control, the rules governing verification had been relaxed and both claims stood uncontested.) Vasconcells had a spare propeller. He replaced Rick's damaged one, refueled his Spad, and sent him on his way. When Rick landed at Rembercourt, he learned that Chambers had destroyed the other balloon he had seen explode in a ball of fire. Comparing notes, pilots who had sortied that morning calculated they had won eleven victories. It was an inflated estimate—the actual number was ultimately reckoned at six balloons plus the Fokker Rick had downed—but was still a good morning's work. On the other hand, two pilots from the 94th, Alan Nutt and Alden B. Sherry, had not returned.[25]

For American ground forces, the opening day of the offensive was disappointing. Many of the troops flung into the operation had little training because Pershing had left more seasoned units behind to defend the captured St. Mihiel salient. Supplying the ones now pressing the attack was complicated by miserable roads leading into the Meuse-Argonne area. The Germans, digging in for three years now, could take advantage of the terrain they were defending. The strongest of their fortifications was the Kriemhilde Stellung, which had concrete bunkers from which machine gunners could concentrate fire on troops scaling formidable obstacles to reach positions the Germans were determined to hold at all cost.[26]

Despite Luke's balloon busting, von Gallwitz had been notified that American units were moving north toward the Meuse-Argonne sector but was unsure about the significance of the reports. On the eve of the offensive he still expected Pershing to exploit his recent success by thrusting toward Metz from the St. Mihiel salient and thought an attack across the Meuse near Verdun would be merely a feint. Only five enemy divisions opposed Pershing's far larger forces, but the inexperienced attackers got bogged down and failed to reach the first day's goals. Watching the battle from aloft, Mitchell was appalled by congestion on roads leading to the front. If German aircraft spotted the confusion, even a small number of enemy troops could have torn through the center of the American line. To draw attention away from the area Mitchell had ordered bombers to hit targets in the rear to attract enemy fire. He told Hartney to keep his fighter planes hovering closely above the enemy defenders to prevent their aircraft from strafing American ground forces. "Had we not done this instantly," Mitchell later stated, "I believe that this whole mass of transportation would have been destroyed and burned." As a result of Mitchell's orders the 1st Pursuit Group flew 143 sorties and scored ten victories, both one-day records.[27]

It rained the next morning. Rick set out to find Nutt and Sherry but did not succeed. After the weather cleared up, he went on a patrol and spotted an enemy balloon floating above Sivry-sur-Meuse, well behind enemy lines. It gave him an idea for a sortie he carried out the next day, showing a prudence that contrasted with Luke's impetuousness. Getting up early, he followed the river into German-held territory and tried unsuccessfully to find the nest. Realizing he had gone too far, he turned back toward Rembercourt, carefully observing the roads below in hope of getting an opportunity for strafing. Seeing a German truck, he swooped down to attack and discovered it was towing a balloon. Shifting his aim, he fired a stream of bullets into the giant gas bag and climbed steeply to avoid crashing into it. Suddenly he "heard the rat-tat-tat of an enemy machine gun on the ground and an unusually sharp explosion in the tail" of his plane. Leaving the area as fast as possible, he glanced over his shoulder and saw an observer parachuting to safety from the basket of the balloon as it burst into flames. Realizing that "something unusual had gone wrong," he made it back to friendly territory. After landing and inspecting the Spad, he discovered that a gunner, apparently stationed near the truck, had punctured the bottom of his ship with "six bullet holes in a row equally spaced down the center of my fuselage the first starting only six inches behind my back." The sound he had heard was that of the main strut in his tail being hit by a bullet, but the damage was minor and he flew back to base. Later confirmation of what he had done resulted in his eleventh official victory. Upon returning from his sortie he was delighted to learn that Sherry had phoned in and was safe, but Nutt had been shot through the heart in a fracas with eight Fokkers and crashed in no-man's-land.

It rained most of the day on Sunday, 29 September. Rick did not fly, but one of his pilots, Weir Cook, went up that afternoon and flamed a balloon. Rick wondered what was happening to Luke, who died at Murvaux that evening after scoring the last victories of his brief but tragic career. In sorties on 30 September, Chambers and one of his buddies shot down a Fokker D-VII, adding to the squadron's mounting victory list.

That evening, at dinner, Rick received an important note from Hartney. Mitchell had heard from intelligence officers that eleven troop trains carrying members of the elite Prussian Guards had left Metz en route to the Meuse-Argonne sector. By this time the congestion Mitchell had seen on the first day of the offensive was so bad pilots were dropping emergency rations to troops that had not eaten for two days. Mitchell wanted volunteers to patrol railroad lines deep in German-held territory to see if troop trains were bringing crack enemy units to launch the counterthrust he had been dreading. Taking Cook and Coolidge with him, Rick intently observed the main rail line and saw some trains, but they were obviously not carrying troops. He decided Mitchell's intelligence was "fishy" and returned to base—but not before he nearly ran out of gas and was almost shot down by French antiaircraft fire. Zigzagging frantically, he spotted a signal flare shot from the aerodrome at Rembercourt. Circling the field, he fired "a red Very light, which, if answered from the ground also by a red light meant that the field was clear and to land, which I did, finding Lieutenants Cook and Coolidge had both returned safely." When he phoned Mitchell that no troop trains were on their way, Mitchell said, "Thank God."[28]

The next day, 1 October, after leading a sortie across the lines and seeing many enemy planes that were out of range, Rick thought again about the balloon he had spotted above Sivry-sur-Meuse. He decided to launch a sneak attack by coming at the gas bag from an unexpected direction. Leaving Rembercourt at five thirty that evening, he set out for Pont-a-Mousson. Staying well within friendly territory until after dark, he followed the Moselle River until he was due east of the Three-Fingered Lake. Heading back toward it, he found a road leading to the balloon nest. Following the road, he found the installation without difficulty and fired about 150 rounds of phosphorus-filled bullets into the gas bag, which was lying inert on the ground. He watched with satisfaction as it burst into flames as intense as an exploding ammunition dump. As he sped home, no German batteries shot at him, but French and American units unleashed a stream of incendiary projectiles and tracers reminding him of fireworks on the Fourth of July. Once gain, the batteries missed, and he landed by exchanging Very signals with the ground crew. Mitchell congratulated him, and his victory was later confirmed.[29]

Even though no elite forces were coming from Metz, the American offensive had faltered badly and the Germans were reinforcing the sector. French premier Georges Clemenceau got stuck in a traffic jam trying to visit the front on 29 September and angrily demanded Pershing's dismissal, which would have caused a furor in the United States. Generalissimo Foch wisely countermanded Clemenceau but tried to persuade Pershing to put part of his forces under French command. When Pershing indignantly refused, Foch prodded him to intensify the offensive, putting added pressure on all American units including the 1st Pursuit Group. During early October the 94th was continually in action. Proud of the success he and his pilots were having, Rick lost no opportunity to drill inexperienced flyers in tactics and spur seasoned veterans to greater heights. "At meals there were roundtable conferences of methods, blackboard talks, and ideas for air-battle tactics," wrote an observer. "It resembled a big-time coach and the football team boning up for the season ahead; but it was deadly serious, and, like big-time football, it paid off in results."[30] Well-educated airmen winced at the way Rick murdered the English language but ignored his grammar and syntax because they respected his judgment. A war correspondent wrote that briefings took place in "an air control office where huge charts and blackboards kept track of all planes and records of flights and victories." Rick kept a tally of victories on a blackboard, showing the names of the airmen involved, the dates of the sorties in which they had been flying, the places where the actions took place, and the types of German planes they had shot down.[31]

Rick did everything he could to promote the "buddy system." His efforts to find Nutt and Sherry on 27 September typified his concern for the welfare of his men. He worked hard to help them get their victories verified. Naturally, they did the same for him, helping account for some of the scores that made him America's ace of aces. He continued to ban unnecessary protocol as a waste of time. When Major Maxwell Kirby, being groomed for command of the 5th Pursuit Group, was posted to the 94th to gain combat experience, Rickenbacker made it clear nobody would kowtow to him because they were too busy performing more important duties.[32]

Rick's stress on teamwork paid off in a sortie on 3 October in which he and Chambers jointly attacked a Hannover CL-V observation plane. Both of them experienced jamming and thought they had lost their quarry but found out later that they had killed the observer and sent a bullet through the pilot's face, "badly shattering his jaw." The plane came down behind the American lines, damaged but in flyable condition. Later in the same sortie Rickenbacker emerged from a cloud bank "and to my horror found that I was going head-on into a formation of seven Fokkers, the leader of which was not over 50 yards away." Thinking "my days were ended," he "kicked my rudder hard over and pulled my 'joy stick' back," climbed as fast as possible, looped, and dived at top speed into the midst of the enemy planes. Chambers, leading a formation of Spads, came to his aid and the Germans broke off the encounter, scurrying back toward their lines. Taking advantage of their powerful Hisso engines, Chambers and Rick, having cleared their jams by this time, took off after the fleeing formation, got within range of two stragglers, maneuvered under their tails, and "had the satisfaction of seeing them fall out of control and crash just inside our lines." Each of them got credit for bagging a Fokker and they shared joint credit for shooting down the Hannover.

Pleased by the results of teamwork, Rick organized a balloon strafing mission involving both the 94th and 95th squadrons. Watches were carefully synchronized to make sure all pilots arrived simultaneously at a predetermined location. The plan did not work exactly as planned but resulted in the destruction of one balloon, a victory over an LVG (Luft-Verkehrs Gesellschaft) observation plane shared by Rickenbacker, Coolidge, and Edward P. Curtis of the 95th, and a win Rick scored by himself against a Fokker D-VII. In the same sortie three men from the 94th got joint credit for shooting down another Fokker. Despite being pleased about the multiple victories, Rick was angry that two airmen were shot down and taken prisoner, all because some pilots had arrived three minutes early and disorganized the formation. He blamed the high command for not making effective use of radio-telephone apparatus that might have saved at least one pilot.[33]

He did everything possible to see that his squadron had enough spare parts to keep its aircraft flyable. Cedric Fauntleroy, with whom he had roomed at Tours, was now a staff member at the aircraft acceptance facility near Paris. He was immensely helpful to Rick, making use of his connections with French factories to supply him with engine parts, instruments, and other equipment.[34]

Pilots in the 94th had wanted for a long time to force a German plane down virtually intact, repair it, and see how it performed compared with models used by American units. Rick and Chambers were accordingly delighted that the Hannover they had shot down on 3 October had crashed without sustaining much damage. Two days later they drove a staff car toward Montfaucon, now in American hands. Continuing on foot because of congested supply lines, they found the Hannover in reparable condition, with only a damaged propeller and some broken wing ribs. After turning it over for disassembly to mechanics who had somehow managed to drive a truck through the traffic jam, they set out for Montfaucon but had to dive into a trench because of a sudden German artillery barrage and decided to wait for the truck pulling the dismembered plane. Looking at the sky as they returned to the base, they saw a spirited battle between a group of Fokkers and two Spads that escaped after shooting down two enemy planes. When they got back to

Rembercourt, they learned the victories had been won by John Jeffers and Samuel Kaye Jr., members of their unit.

Mitchell continued to emphasize attacking balloons. Because Cook had shown much skill in this hazardous duty, he and Ham Coolidge received a chance to stand out on 6 October in attacking an installation behind the German lines that had given Americans a lot of trouble. Rick flew at the apex of ten Spads in a V formation led by Chambers. The balloon was poorly defended and Coolidge readily destroyed it. Bad weather prevented flying on the next two days, but on 8 October Rick received confirmation of the victory he had scored a week earlier by flaming the balloon being pulled by a truck west of the Three-Fingered Lake. That evening he went out on patrol and destroyed another balloon that had been reeled in for the night, making two passes at extremely low altitude before setting it ablaze. This time confirmation was swift, coming the next day. On 10 October he went up with a large number of planes from at least three units belonging to the 1st Pursuit Group, looking for more *Drachen,* flying as usual above the formation to play a protective role but still be able to pounce when the time was right. When some Spads from Meissner's 147th squadron strayed from the rest of their formation and were attacked by a swarm of Fokkers, Rick dived at a German fighter bringing up the rear and riddled it with bullets, setting it afire. As it plunged toward the ground he saw its pilot climb out of the cockpit and parachute to safety. Thinking how terrible it was that American flyers were not similarly equipped, Rick was glad to see the enemy airman escape without being burned alive. The next thing he saw, however, was "the most horrible sight I have witnessed during the eight months I have spent at the front." Wilbert W. White Jr., a highly experienced pilot from Meissner's unit, saw a Fokker getting on the tail of a recruit on his first mission. White realized the neophyte was doomed unless he took immediate action and dived head-on into the German aircraft before the pilot could shoot, "with wings and fragments of both planes flying in all directions." The episode was all the harder for Rick to witness because he knew that White, who had a wife and children, had received orders to go home the next day. He had sacrificed his life even though he had his leave papers in one of his pockets. "Greater love hath no man . . ." Rick considered White's intervention the greatest example of heroism he had seen in the entire war.

Soon afterward, Rick noticed a disabled Spad being pursued by two Fokkers. Diving to the aid of his comrade, of whose identity he was unaware, he fired a stream of bullets into one of the German planes and saw it plunge out of control while its companion broke off the attack. After returning to Rembercourt, he learned that the pilot whose life he had saved was Meissner, whom he had already rescued twice before. Rick said that the incident was "the third time together during our association on the front that I had appeared like a guarding angel from heaven in his hour of distress."[35]

Despite Rick's two most recent victories, he could not get what had happened to White out of his mind and needed a break. He took advantage of bad weather on 11 October to get a three-day leave to Paris, where he discussed supply arrangements with Fauntleroy and spent much of his time with Lois Meredith, an actress who had been entertaining troops at the front. Receiving confirmation of his seventeenth victory made him ace of aces among American pilots who had survived up to this point. Reading a newspaper at breakfast on 13 October, he saw huge headlines that Germany had offered to end the war on the basis of President Wilson's Fourteen Points, leading him to think the conflict would soon be over. He was in a much happier frame of mind when he left Paris on 15 October and returned to Rembercourt, but the weather was still too bad for flying. On 17 October he received validation of his eighteenth official victory. Still upset about bad timing in the sortie in which two American airmen had been shot down, he ordered a wireless telephone through Major Kirby, whom he had told to take "those blasted leaves [the gold oak leaf insignia of a major] from your shoulders, and keep them off while you're here. Then no one will have to jump every time you turn around."[36]

Constant attrition had weakened American ground forces to a point at which many of the troops could not continue fighting. Instead of having five divisions in the area at the beginning of the campaign, the Germans now had forty. Pershing's 1st Division—the "Big Red One"—was relieved on the night of 11 October after suffering 9,387 losses—the highest rate of any American unit in the offensive. Two other divisions were also replaced at the same time. American casualties were estimated at more than 100,000. The flu epidemic sweeping across much of the world had taken a severe toll. Cold weather, rain, mud, lack of provisions, and almost universal diarrhea plagued soldiers in what had become a slaughterhouse. Pershing, who himself had the flu and was under mounting French criticism for the limited ground he had taken, removed himself from active command on 12 October, putting Liggett, one of his ablest subordinates, in charge of the 1st Army. Fresh American units, including MacArthur's 42nd (Rainbow) Division, scored limited gains at inordinate cost in a renewed onslaught beginning 14 October, but the initiative soon halted. One American unit that had entered the offensive with 15,000 doughboys was down to 300. Knowing it was imperative to regroup, Liggett permitted exhausted outfits to rest, intending to resume the battle later in the month. Fortunately, the enemy was in a similar condition. "Clouded prospects wherever one looks," wrote a German officer. "Really has everything been in vain?"[37]

Rick and his men took advantage of the reprieve by amusing themselves with the captured Hannover observation plane. Aided by Captain Edward H. Cooper, a military film producer, they staged a mock battle in which Rick repeatedly "attacked" the aircraft while Meissner piloted it and Taylor played the role of gunner, firing bullets deliberately aimed to miss. Taylor had a dummy observer in his rear cockpit and periodically threw it overboard while detonating flares and releasing clouds of lampblack to give the impression that the Hannover was going down in flames. The fun nearly became a disaster when a French aircraft wandered into the area and maneuvered into position to shoot down the captured plane. Signaling frantically, Rick waved him off. Afterward everyone enjoyed a "grand, hearty laugh."[38]

France, Great Britain, and Italy were adamantly opposed to having Wilson negotiate a separate peace. Wilson's reply to the German initiative Rick had read about was unacceptable to Wilhelm II and his advisers, and the war dragged on. Still hoping for a tolerable negotiated settlement, the German high command ordered troops in the Meuse-Argonne and other sectors to continue resisting Allied forces. Cook torched a balloon on 22 October, but Raymond Saunders, another member of the 94th, was killed battling a Fokker on the same day. Trying to avenge his death, Chambers flew a voluntary patrol and narrowly escaped with his life before getting back to Rembercourt. When he landed, Rick and other airmen "noticed that he had lost his customary attitude of self confidence and still resembled somewhat the features of a ghost." The next day Rick saw an American balloon going up in flames and set out to find its attacker. Proving he could still lose his concentration despite his progress in self-control, he strayed too far behind German lines and was surprised by four Fokkers that gave him "the battle of my life." But his superior airmanship paid off in shooting two of them down, after which he sped from the scene and returned to base by "zig-zagging for all I was worth." Bad weather prevented further flying until 27 October, when he noticed a group of American-made De Havilland DH-4 bombers, identifiable by their Liberty engines, heading into German-held territory. He decided to take off to protect them when they returned from their mission.[39] Soon thereafter, he spotted German antiaircraft batteries firing at them as they came back from releasing their bombs. As he hurried to the scene, three Fokkers came after him but he saw them before they got within range. Pretending to flee at top speed, he suddenly executed a backward loop, got above one of them, and shot it down. The other planes retreated.

Rick had not forgotten about the bombers he wanted to protect. Flying toward where he thought they would be, he saw that one of them had engine trouble and was lagging behind its formation, about to be attacked by a lone Fokker that had gotten under it. Getting on the tail of the German plane, Rickenbacker fired a few bursts of ammunition and knew he had an easy victory in prospect when he suddenly saw his opponent's propeller stop spinning and realized its engine had stalled. Knowing that it was helpless, he got the idea of capturing it intact and decided to ride herd on the pilot, letting him know with periodic thrusts and jabs that he could go for the kill any time he chose. Realizing Rick's intentions, the enemy airman glided behind the American lines, looking for a place to land. Excited by the prospect of collecting a trophy and taking the pilot prisoner, Rick suddenly saw that a Spad was flying toward it, getting ready to shoot his quarry down. Furious about the prospect of losing his prize, he dived between the Spad and the Fokker and fired a few short bursts to warn the would-be attacker away. Meanwhile the German had panicked and crashed into the edge of a forest. Seeing the pilot emerge unhurt, Rick circled until he was captured by doughboys and waved goodbye as they took the airman into custody. Returning to Rembercourt, Rick was pleased that he had gained two more victories and spared a human life.[40]

He also learned that his promotion to captain, which had been held up in red tape, had been formally approved, but his elation turned to dismay when Hartney told him that Coolidge had been shot down and killed by German antiaircraft guns. Like Rick, Ham had been trying to protect a formation of Allied bombers. The next day, crestfallen, Rick drove a staff car as close as he could get to the spot where Ham's plane had come down. Sentries stopped him because the road on which he was traveling was so close to the front lines that an automobile was likely to draw shellfire. An officer guided him on foot to what remained of Coolidge and his Spad. Rick wrote later that day that "it was a terrible sight . . . the motor was four feet in the ground and poor Ham on top all burnt to a crisp." After waiting while doughboys dug a shallow pit and interred the remains, Rick returned to the airfield at Rembercourt. On his way back, shells fell around his car, showering it with dirt. Returning safely to the aerodrome, he ordered that a cross bearing Coolidge's name and unit be put at the head of his comrade's grave. He later wrote, "This was indeed a most untimely death, for we all knew that the war was soon to be over." It was only the second time he had heard about an Allied fighter plane being hit by Archy, increasing his fatalistic outlook. He sent a photograph of the grave to Ham's relatives with a letter of condolence.[41]

His grief turned to embarrassment that same day when he read newspaper stories stating he was engaged to marry Priscilla Dean, an actress he had taught to drive during his racing days in California. In September, after his eighth victory, he had received a letter and some photos from her and responded with a message starting "Hello, my California Sunshine!" After thanking her for writing, he said, "Gee, I'd give some years of my life for just one week in dear California—but, no—I must stay to the finish for there's lots to be done." Saying he had been in the hospital with "broken ear drums, which have given me some trouble," he told her, "Gee, I wish you were here to nurse me a wee bit. Hello to mother and all the boys and girls. Write when convenient." After Dean made his message public, newspapers printed two accounts, one saying Dean had already married the "high-powered birdman" in Paris and the other stating they would wed soon after he got home from the war. His comment about his eardrums also led to stories saying he "had been rendered deaf." Rick immediately sent a cable to America denying any intention of marrying Dean. The recipient assured readers that Rick was not deaf but merely had suffered "slight ear trouble."[42]

Rick had sent a stream of letters to people back home knowing and hoping that they would be transmitted to the press, but he had not expected adverse results from his endless quest for publicity. The lesson from distorted accounts of his letter to Dean, however, did not reduce his zeal for self-promotion. On the day Coolidge died, he invited George Seldes, a correspondent for the Marshall Syndicate, to stay "a week or two" with the 94th and sleep on Ham's cot in Rick's tent. Seldes, who had started his career as a cub reporter for the *Pittsburgh Leader,* later said that Rick "became the best friend I had in the U.S. armed forces."[43]

Rick added two more kills to his victory total. The first epitomized the hit-and-run tactics he had perfected since returning from his mastoid operation. Hovering above two of his men, one a newcomer and the other a more seasoned veteran, he watched two Fokkers shadow them. Waiting for the best possible moment, he dived suddenly at terrific speed at one of the unsuspecting German ships and shot it down in an easy victory. The other Fokker panicked and sped behind his lines. Prudently deciding not to chase him into hostile territory, Rick saw an advancing American unit and noticed an enemy balloon observing it. Banking and diving, he raked the gas bag from one end to the other and watched it explode in a giant fireball. Looking at his watch, he suddenly realized he had been aloft for more than two hours and that his fuel supply must be low. He was now about two miles behind the German lines and it was getting darker by the minute. Heading back toward Rembercourt with flashes of ground fire bursting around him, he looked for the searchlight at the dummy airfield that served both as a marker for incoming aircraft and a decoy for enemy bombs, but saw nothing. By this time, he thought, he had only a cupful of gasoline left at best. Convinced he must be somewhere near Rembercourt, he fired two red Very signals and got no response. All he could hope was that his motor would be audible. Suddenly, to his inexpressible relief, a line of white lights shone out of the darkness. Peering under his wings, he saw a road at the boundary of the field. His engine shuddered, backfired, and died as he settled down, stopping about 100 feet from a hangar. Ambling to the mess hall on shaky legs, he tried to act like a Gimper and be nonchalant, but, as a historian of his unit said, "he had stretched things very far indeed."[44]

The war was at last winding down. Liggett's reorganized forces scored limited gains late in October. On the last day of the month Rick flew over the American lines dropping 2,000 copies of *The Stars and Stripes,* a newspaper published for doughboys and edited by a staff including Harold Ross and Alexander Woolcott. Looking into enemy territory he saw a large fire that turned out to be the blaze of an ammunition dump destroyed by retreating German forces. Flying on, he saw horses, trucks, field pieces, and troops moving out of the area and hurried back to Rembercourt to tell Hartney.[45]

In the early hours of 1 November a massive artillery barrage signaled the opening of the last great American drive of the offensive. Noting in his diary the next evening that Austria-Hungary had surrendered to Italy, Rick wrote that he expected the war would end by Thanksgiving. When he went to Paris the next day, he saw captured German equipment lining the Champs Elysees as street lights burned in broad daylight. He had a date with Lois Meredith, drove around the city with her, and bought an elaborate greatcoat for 1,450 francs (probably to celebrate his recent promotion to captain), astonishing himself by his extravagance. Going back to Rembercourt, he went out on patrol but saw nothing unusual. During the rest of the week, things happened indicating that the war was virtually over. Bulgaria and the Ottoman Empire got out; German sailors mutinied at Kiel; worker-soldier governments appeared in cities throughout the Reich; and Colonel House, Wilson's alter ego, was in Paris haggling with British, French, and Italian leaders about the terms of an armistice. Still refusing to abdicate, Wilhelm II left Berlin and consulted with military leaders at Spa. They told him further resistance was impossible because they had no reserves and the army was too badly needed on the home front to put down a threatened Bolshevik revolution. On 7 November Rick heard that German delegates had crossed no-man's-land under a white flag to secure armistice terms from Foch.[46]

By this time a more distinguished visitor than Seldes, whom Rick was thinking about asking to ghostwrite his wartime memoirs, had arrived at the base.[47] Laurence La Tourette Driggs, who first became an important figure in Rick's life at this time, was the son of a timber baron from Oregon and grandson of a congressman who represented Michigan's Upper Peninsula for three terms. Raised in affluence, Driggs was an accomplished lawyer, writer, and Republican politician who had developed a passion for aviation and joined a cousin in developing a gun for use in airplanes. Going to England in 1917, he showed the weapon to military officials and visited aircraft factories and training schools. After coming home, he spent two days in Washington telling officers in the Signal Corps what he had seen. Unlike Rick, who was shunned that same year by the brass because he lacked the proper social and educational credentials, Driggs got a promise from the Signal Corps that he would be commissioned as an officer if the United States entered the war. He published an article in *Outlook* that caught the attention of Theodore Roosevelt, who was trying to form a volunteer unit—an aerial equivalent of the Rough Riders—to fight for the Allied cause.[48] Encouraged by Roosevelt and General Leonard Wood, Driggs recruited a group of wealthy young aviators and was slated to command them with the rank of colonel. He became known as "Colonel Driggs," even though forming the unit was vetoed by Wilson, who disliked Roosevelt and Wood.

Resentful that his volunteer squadron did not materialize, Driggs had sublimated his frustrations by writing articles about the air war for several magazines and collected information for a book, *Heroes of Aviation,* dealing with famous aces. He also created a fictional ace named Arnold Adair and wrote stories about him. Driggs thus became a leading American exponent of the cult of the ace. Eager to play a more active role in the war, he got his wish when Lord Northcliffe, owner of the *Times* of London and British minister of information, visited the United States and played golf with him. After Northcliffe returned to England he invited Driggs to come there as a guest of the British government and be an official observer of military operations. Driggs sailed from New York in July 1918 on a troop transport, joined the Royal Air Force Club, and met prominent British aviation officials. In June 1918 he went to France as an official observer of British air operations and toured bases at Ypres, Vimy Ridge, Arras, Bapaume, and Amiens, visiting forty squadrons to gather information for future books and articles. Mitchell invited him to inspect an American airfield of his choice. Driggs chose the 1st Pursuit Group and came to Rembercourt, where he quickly developed rapport with Hartney. Rick's accomplishments as a combat pilot had been too modest in June for Driggs to include in the first edition of *Heroes of Aviation,* but now his fame as America's ace of aces made him the man Driggs most wanted to see. Hartney arranged for them to meet.

Rick, thinking again about publishing a book about his wartime experiences, knew the limits of his writing skills and needed someone to ghostwrite his memoirs. Seldes had begged off because of other commitments he did not specify. He was secretly hatching a scheme with four other correspondents to enter Germany illegally as soon as the war was over and get interviews with Field Marshal Hindenburg and other leaders.[49] Rick now asked Driggs to help produce his book. He jumped at the chance, and they began working out a contract.

Rick began negotiating with Driggs on 9 November. The weather was bad that morning, but three pilots who knew their chances of winning combat victories were dwindling came to Rick begging to go on patrol. Fauntleroy had been sent to the front and wanted to claim his reward for helping keep Spads in flyable condition. Kirby, who had been gaining experience for a command that never materialized, was also eager to "bag a Hun." Because he was a major, Kirby outranked Rick, making it all the more difficult to deny his request. John De Witt, who had joined the 94th at the beginning of the Meuse-Argonne offensive, had destroyed a balloon on the previous day but wanted one more opportunity for a victory. Because of his experience, Rick thought De Witt would be a good escort for Fauntleroy. Cook, a seasoned balloon buster, volunteered to go along to protect Kirby. Reluctantly, thinking he might be risking four men's lives for no real purpose, Rick allowed them to go and watched them take off in a shower of "blasting sand, water, and mud." Later that day he learned that Cook had glided to a safe landing at a nearby field after his propeller was shot off and that Kirby had reached another base as he was running out of fuel. Fauntleroy and De Witt, however, were still missing. Fearing they might be dead, Rick went through agonies of remorse, such was his concern for his men. Searchlights stayed on at Rembercourt all night, but the two flyers were still not back by morning. A report that a French observation plane and a Spad had collided in midair at Beaumont increased Rick's forebodings.

An award ceremony took place that day—10 November—at which Liggett added two more oak leaves to Rick's decorations, but he went though the motions with a heavy heart. Afterward, accompanying dignitaries to the 95th Pursuit Squadron's well-stocked bar, he was relieved to see the Spad flown by Fauntleroy, who had gotten lost and spent the night at Douaumont but neglected to call in. Soon thereafter De Witt reported by phone that he too had made a crash landing but was safe and would return the next day. Cook was now back and told a harrowing story about the sortie in which he had lost his propeller. Kirby also showed up with even more exciting news. After taking off that morning on his way back to Rembercourt, he had met a Fokker and gotten on its tail. Diving to escape Kirby, the enemy pilot could not pull out and crashed. (Kirby's victory would be the last one of the war for the Army Air Service.) Suddenly all of Rick's worries evaporated. "Gee but I was happy," he wrote in his diary.[50]

Orders went out that evening to stop sorties. As members of the 95th sat in their bar, knowing hostilities would soon end but still unaware when they would stop, a phone rang and a hush fell over the room. John L. Mitchell, one of the squadron's pilots, took the call and tried to keep a poker face as he listened. A radio report had been intercepted that representatives of the German government, already across the lines and waiting in a railroad car at Compeigne, had received instructions from Berlin to sign an armistice the next morning by eleven o'clock. After mumbling something into the receiver, Mitchell turned to his comrades, enjoying the suspense before shouting "C'est le finis de la Guerre!" As bedlam broke out Mitchell called the headquarters of the Hat-in-the-Ring Squadron, where Rick was listening to Cook, Fauntle-roy, and Kirby talk about their recent experiences. Rick took the phone and listened to what Mitchell said. As he turned to tell his friends what he had heard, antiaircraft guns began to roar, indicating what had happened better than any words he could have used. He managed to bring the assembled aviators to observe a moment of silence, raising his glass in a toast to "the boys who are not here," but could do little else to re-strain the pent-up emotions of men who had lived for months thinking they might die at any moment and suddenly realized they were going to live. Running onto the airfield, members of the 94th and 95th began a riotous celebration and were soon joined by pilots and mechanics from other units stationed at Rembercourt. A brass band appeared out of nowhere, adding to the din. "Searchlights danced across the sky, rifles, machine guns, and pistols were fired in every direction," said an ac-count of what happened. "Very pistols were fired into the sky, shedding their bright colors like blooming flowers." Men began taking barrels of gasoline out of storage. Seeing he could not stop what was about to happen, Rick helped airmen roll them across the muddy field and set them on fire.[51] "Everybody was laughing—drunk with the outgushing of their long pent-up emotions." Among the outcries a "whirling dervish of a pilot" yelled "I've lived through the war!" Another airman spoke for millions of men on both sides of the lines, shouting, "We won't be shot at any more!"[52]

The war did not formally end until 11:00 a.m. on 11 November, as representatives of Britain, France, and Germany specified. When Rick awoke, he read an order that no planes from the 1st Pursuit Group were to fly within five kilometers "over what was known to be the front line of the evening previous." Thick fog blanketed the Meuse Valley but Rick ignored the directive, determined to be aloft when the armistice took effect. Getting airborne at 10:40 a.m., he flew toward Verdun "within a few feet of the tree tops in order to distinguish the road, which I used as a guide." A few minutes before 11:00, he turned toward German-held territory "and pulled both triggers until all the ammunition was gone." By the time he quit firing, hostilities had been over for two minutes. Looking below, he saw American troops "jump out of their trenches, firing Very pistols and celebrating the termination of the Great War." Soon German soldiers rushed toward the doughboys and fraternized with them. After returning to Rembercourt, he learned he had been the only pilot to take off in the fog "and woke up to the realization that the war had ended, leaving me hale and hearty and America's ace of aces."[53]

As he had done behind the wheel of a race car, Rick had competed with the best and had tasted victory. But through his heroics in the air, he could now lay claim to what had eluded him on the track—a national championship.

Chapter 10

— ☆ —

Homecoming

The armistice just signed was only the end of hostilities pending a peace treaty. Should fighting erupt again the Allied powers wanted the front lines to be as far inside Germany as possible. Under the agreement Germany consented not only to evacuate the areas held by its armies in France, Belgium, and Alsace-Lorraine but also to remove its troops from the entire left side of the Rhine and a twenty-mile strip on the east bank. The Germans also allowed Great Britain, the United States, and France to occupy bridgeheads on the east bank centered at Cologne, Koblenz, and Mainz. Under these terms Pershing created the 3rd Army of Occupation, composed of troops from battle-tested divisions and an aerial component, to take control of the bridgehead at Koblenz. On 14 November Pershing gave command of the air unit to Mitchell, whom he had promoted to brigadier general for his performance in the St. Mihiel and Meuse-Argonne campaigns. Mitchell chose balloon and fighter units including the 94th Pursuit Squadron to represent the American Air Service, declaring that the Hat-in-the-Ring Squadron had "fulfilled every desire and laid a foundation for the future development of pursuit aviation which will be an example for all to follow."[1]

The 94th had made a remarkable turnaround from the dispirited unit it had been when Rick returned on the eve of the St. Mihiel offensive. "From that point on," Walter J. Boyne has stated, the 94th "became the crack American unit of the war, with more victories and more flying hours over the line than any other."[2] The squadron had officially destroyed sixty-seven enemy planes (of which Rick shot down more than one-third), a total no other aggregation closely approached. Because sharing a kill gave a pilot full credit for a win, the 94th had 84 certified victories. Despite having ten flyers killed in action and five wounded, it finished the war with the lowest ratio of casualties to victories, 1 to

3.9, in the Army Air Service. Its pilots flew 296 sorties, of which Rick carried out fifty, nearly twice as many as the next highest total. Twenty-seven members, not counting those decorated while flying with French units before the United States entered the war, had received medals. Rick again led everybody else, winning the Distinguished Service Medal with nine oak leaf clusters, each representing a citation for the Distinguished Service Cross. He had also received the Croix de Guerre five times. "Captain Rickenbacker furnished, by his example, an ideal squadron leader," stated the unit's official history, stressing that—unlike Atchison, Huffer, and Marr, who viewed their positions as mainly administrative—he had stayed in the thick of combat after assuming his post. "An army of Rickenbackers in the sky would be invincible," declared Hartney, who recommended Rick for the Medal of Honor and promotion to major too late for the top brass to act on his advice before the war ended. Nevertheless, becoming America's ace of aces was what gained Rick enduring fame.[3]

Wanting to capitalize on his record and worried about his financial prospects after the war, he commissioned Driggs to produce the wartime memoirs he had conceived in Paris, telling him his mentor, Lufbery, "had been offered $50,000 by a New York syndicated press for the story of his flying career." Having given most of his earnings in automobile racing to his mother and having come out of the war with glory but no wealth, he hoped to get at least as much financial reward as had been contemplated for Luf. On 16 November 1918 Rick signed a contract under which Driggs agreed to "edit and revamp" his account of experiences in his "aerial career on the Western Front for the purpose of serial stories for magazines and composition for book." Rick's share of the "gross receipts from all sales of such work" would be 75 percent. The contract stipulated that the book and serial stories would be published solely under his name and that he would own all copyrights. The book would contain at least 80,000 words and be completed within fourteen weeks. As Rick's agent, Driggs would not permit the book to be sold for less than $1.50 per copy. Rick loaned Driggs the diary he had kept during the war and agreed to prepare a longer preliminary text of reminiscences already started. A copy of the manuscript in the Library of Congress indicates that Rick dictated it to a staff member—probably an adjutant—who transcribed his words on a typewriter at the end of each day and headed each increment, usually three to five pages, with the date it was prepared.[4]

Rick and other members of the 94th left Rembercourt on 20 November and flew to Longuyon to occupy a former German aerodrome.[5] Meissner had relinquished command of the 147th to rejoin his former comrades, and Thorne Taylor had scoured Rembercourt for the best aircraft to be had. After reaching Longuyon, Rick made one last flight over the battle-scarred terrain he had known so well. It was hard for him to get used to the absence of enemy planes and he kept turning his head in all directions to spot them. It was also unnerving to have no Archy exploding around him.[6]

A few days after the squadron reached Longuyon, a plane landed at the airfield and Campbell emerged "like a bolt from the blue." He had returned to France—just in time—from his duties instructing pilots in the United States.[7] During a brief stay in Paris he met Hall, who had returned from captivity with a statement certifying that German officers from Mars-la-Tour with whom he had talked after being captured had confirmed Rick's victory that day over a Pfalz D-III. Campbell signed the document and gave it to Rick at Longuyon, validating his previously unaccredited twenty-sixth victory. Rick gave the claim to an adjutant who added it to his previous total of twenty-five.[8]

On 27 November Rick learned that orders had reached Mitchell's headquarters directing him, Campbell, and Meissner to return to the United States to sell Liberty Bonds. Mitchell said he would try to arrange a delay. To show his appreciation Rick invited him to spend Thanksgiving at Longuyon, where members of the 94th decorated the mess hall to give the general a banquet. During dinner Rick and Chambers got the idea to ask the army for permission and funding to fly nonstop from America to Paris.[9]

While Mitchell worked on postponing his return home, Rick took the squadron on a spree to Luxembourg, which was interrupted when a phone call summoned him and several other officers to testify at a court-martial at Souilly at which Huffer would face charges brought against him by Davenport Johnson soon after Foulois relieved Huffer from command of the 94th in June. The trial was grounded in resentments that had festered since the formative days at Villeneuve-les-Vertus in March, when James Miller had been killed while flying with Johnson and Millard Harmon. Suspicions that Johnson had hung Miller out to dry mounted at Epiez and Gengoult, possibly because of Johnson's status as a West Pointer who belonged to the regular army and Huffer's having entered the American Air Service from the Lafayette Flying

Corps. Early in June, when Johnson had engineered Huffer's dismissal during Atkinson's absence and then assumed command of the 2nd Pursuit Group, some of his officers threw a party for him at Nancy. Not to be outdone, Huffer, privately wealthy, staged a bash to honor the arrival of the 27th and 147th Pursuit Squadrons. Hartney recalled the affair as a "real blowout," enlivened by the presence of nurses and French damsels Huffer had brought with him. Claiming the woman escorted by Huffer was a "notorious prostitute," Johnson brought charges against him for "conduct unbecoming of an officer and a gentleman." Nothing was done about the matter until after the war, and Johnson offered to withdraw his accusations, but Pershing, puritanical about the sex lives of officers and enlisted men despite his ongoing affair with Micheline Resco, insisted that the trial take place, with Johnson as plaintiff. Driggs agreed to serve as Huffer's defense counsel.

Rick was one of a group of character witnesses who had served under Huffer and detested Johnson. Hartney testified that Huffer would have been a fool to bring a prostitute to the affair, knowing that fellow officers were present. Mitchell made a surprise appearance and spoke on Huffer's behalf. "He was of course young and inexperienced in our methods having recently come from the French whose methods were different from ours," Mitchell said in a delicate reference to French sexual mores. He emphasized how much the Air Service had needed men like Huffer at the time Foulois sacked him on Johnson's recommendation. Impressed by the number of flyers testifying for Huffer, the tribunal acquitted him. Rick rejoiced along with the rest and called the trial a "rotten mess." He was disappointed to learn from Mitchell that his orders to return to America had to be obeyed, but Mitchell had secured a postponement and told Rick to go into Germany with his unit.[10]

Driggs joined the 94th on the rest of its journey, spending much of his time working on the materials Rick had entrusted to him. On 13 December Rick and a small party of Americans reached Koblenz to secure lodgings and an airfield for the squadron, while other members remained at Longuyon. Rick and Driggs occupied adjoining rooms at a hotel with a bath between them and windows overlooking the Rhine. After breakfast the next day, they joined Messner, crossed a pontoon bridge, drove to the top of a bluff, and climbed to the top of an immense fortress, Ehrenbreitstein, to get a spectacular view of the Rhine and Moselle valleys hundreds of feet below. That afternoon they watched the first contingent of American soldiers march across the Rhine to occupy the city and went to an airfield at which German pilots had deliberately crashed their planes rather than see them fall into Allied hands. Rick, in full-dress uniform, was struck by the irony of having shopkeepers admire his decorations without realizing how he had earned them. The next day he was sickened by seeing three mounted French officers use their riding whips to knock the hats off some Germans standing harmlessly on a sidewalk, raising his innate Teutonic sympathies. "No good can come this way," he wrote in his diary.[11]

Rick finished the preliminary text of his experiences—122 pages of single-spaced type—for Driggs on 17 December. Two days later he went to Chaumont, had dinner with Townsend Dodd, now a colonel, and learned that another oak leaf had been added to his decorations. While at headquarters he picked up his orders to return to America, which gave him ample time to return to Koblenz. Arriving there three days before Christmas, he enjoyed an opera, toured the Rhine Valley, and had dinner with Mitchell, who brought him letters from home. During the day he met Lutz Struemer, who had commanded the Rumpler with the rising-sun emblem Rick had tried vainly to shoot down. Struemer gave Rick a bottle of wine as a token of friendship, but there is no indication that Rick treated him to dinner, as he had said he would. Rick also met war correspondent Damon Runyon, with whom he became friends, and played Santa Claus at a Christmas meal at which enlisted men from his unit gave him a silver cup.[12]

Driggs had left Koblenz the day before Christmas to go to Paris and London. British friends put him up at the Royal Flying Club and arranged for him to sail to America on the *Aquitania* about a month later.[13] Rick's return to America could be delayed no further, so he left Koblenz on 26 December with Meissner and Campbell after completing arrangements for an airfield and the transfer of equipment belonging to the 94th from Longuyon. He was reluctant to leave the city so soon and unhappy he would be unable to welcome his unit when it arrived. He also felt bad about having to give up a captured German police dog, "Spad," that had been his mascot in the Meuse-Argonne campaign. "The night that I was packing up to go to Paris on my way home," he said, "the dog knew that something was happening, knew I was leaving because he hung around and cried and licked my hand and whined." Chambers, now commanding the 94th, accompanied Rick and his companions to Bar-le-Duc; from there they continued to Paris, dined at Ciro's, and went to the Folies Bergère. Rick had a "wonderful visit" with Hall the next day, during which Hall expressed interest in the book Driggs was writing and offered to help find illustrations for it. On a side trip to Tours, Rick and his buddies got orders permitting them to stay in England for a while before going home. When they returned to Paris a cable was waiting from the *New York World* wanting "exclusive rights on my book and serial stories." On 31 December Rick wrote he was "positive the coming year will not hold as many thrills for me as the one just past thru." The next morning the party went to Le Havre to board a steamship bound for Southampton.[14]

It was raining when they left port, and the ship was jammed with British officers and enlisted men going home. Rick felt nostalgic about leaving France after twenty months. It was a "terribly rough night" and nearly everyone got seasick except for Rick, who credited his "good night's rest" to his flying experience. After disembarking in England, he and his companions went to London, where the Waterloo Station reminded him of arriving there in 1916 and wandering for three hours in the fog before finding the Savoy. This time—with difficulty because accommodations were scarce—the three men found rooms at the YMCA officers' quarters. After checking in, Rick visited Driggs, who was continuing to ghostwrite his wartime memoirs at the Royal Flying Club. While they drank Scotch and soda—which Rick did not like—he learned that Elsie Janis, an entertainer who had raised morale among doughboys in France, was in London giving a hit show, *Hello, America*. He phoned her and got front-row tickets for himself, Driggs, Campbell, and Meissner the next evening.[15]

Among the reasons Rick had gotten his orders changed to go through England was to retrieve the briefcase and engineering materials confiscated by Scotland Yard in 1917 before he returned home after working with Louis Coatalen. He got them back but did not want to leave England before seeing Coatalen, who had been designing airship engines at Wolverhampton. Zeppelins were constantly in the news because of an epic flight in November 1917 in which a giant German dirigible, L-59, had carried a twenty-two-man crew and thirty tons of supplies from Bulgaria deep into central Africa to relieve a garrison besieged by the British. The captain, Ludwig Bockholt, turned back at Khartoum under the mistaken impression that the defenders had surrendered. By the time the aircraft returned to Bulgaria it had made a 4,200-mile round trip in ninety-five hours with ten tons of fuel to spare. Had it been headed west it could have gone all the way to Chicago.

The aborted mission produced a sudden public awareness that large rigid airships could make transoceanic passenger flights. While Rick was in London, work was in progress on the R-34, a long-range dirigible modeled on a captured German zeppelin, preparing for a round-trip transatlantic flight that would ultimately result in a stunning success in July 1919. Coatalen had designed its five Sunbeam V-12 engines, and many of its other parts came from Wolverhampton.[16] Knowing what was happening Rick wanted to learn about Coatalen's visions for a new era of commercial lighter-than-air flight. Thinking Coatalen would be at Wolverhampton, Rick telephoned him there but found he was in London and paid him a visit at which Coatalen invited him to come to the Sunbeam works. Rick gladly accepted and went to Wolverhampton five days later. After having lunch at Coatalen's home, they drove to the plant, where Coatalen showed Rick "several new engines and drawings for new airships." At dinner they talked about the possibility that Coatalen might bring his "entire staff" to the United States to "build Zepps for America." Before returning to London the next day, Rick had another tour of the plant and "received many drawings and information on Zepps from Coatalen," who came to London two days later for another discussion. Although nothing came of the project, Coatalen and Rick were clearly interested in renewing their relationship.[17]

Driggs planned to return to America with Rick on the *Aquitania* and booked passage for Campbell and Meissner on the same ship.[18] Soon after returning to London from Wolverhampton, however, Rick learned that the *Aquitania* would be delayed "owing to labor troubles which I firmly believe will be the reason for terrible things in England during the next 12 months." Deciding not to wait, he got a berth on the White Star liner *Adriatic* (sister ship of the *Baltic*), which was scheduled to leave for New York on 20 January and arrive by the end of the month. Driggs went with Rick to Liverpool and stayed overnight in his "very nice state room" before the vessel headed out to sea. "Had a very bad night," Rick wrote in his diary. "Driggs and I were not made for the small bed as my knees were always in his back."[19]

Before coming aboard, Rick wanted to see if the "long-nosed sergeant" who had treated him so humiliatingly on his first arrival in Liverpool and had disrespected him at the time he came ashore from the *Baltic* in 1917 with Pershing's entourage would still be at the dock. "Sure enough, he showed up," Rick recalled, with "the same old expression." When the sergeant repeated his familiar statement, "Ah, I see you're back again," Rick replied, "Yes, I've got my briefcase, and that isn't all I've got." Wearing his dress uniform, he stuck his chest under the official's nose "with a certain amount of ego" and enjoyed receiving congratulations for his decorations "after the grueling tests he put me through." Praise from the obnoxious sergeant "made up to some extent for all the brow beating and insults that were heaped on my shoulders by the Scotland Yard boys."[20]

After Driggs went ashore, the *Adriatic* left the ship channel. "And very happy was I," Rick wrote in his diary.[21] A national hero was going home in triumph.

What would he do when he got back? Before Rick left Koblenz, he and other members of his squadron had answered questionnaires about postwar occupations they hoped to pursue. American newspapers were already speculating that Rick would resume his racing career, but his response to the questionnaire cast doubt on such predictions. "Automobile racing will be pretty slow for me hereafter," he said. "I may start an aviation school or interest myself in the manufacture of airplanes." A reported offer of $200,000 to return to the AAA tour did not change his mind.[22]

Rick was considering a nationwide campaign to educate citizens about the need for air power. "America's future depends upon its air service," he told newsmen aboard the ship on his way home. "The biggest army and the biggest navy in the world would be useless in modern warfare without the largest air service." The United States "should be able to mobilize within 24 hours 10,000 aviators with five high-class planes for each man." Aircraft construction and control of an air force should be separate, but the government should be "vitally interested in both." It was rumored that Rick and other American aces would help "build a national flying school to rank with West Point and Annapolis." The plan was said to be endorsed by two wealthy veterans of the air war, Charles J. Biddle of Philadelphia and William Thaw of Pittsburgh, along with John D. Ryan, formerly a member of the Manufacturers' Aircraft Association. "While the school would be one of military flying," it was reported, "the school also would have a department for the study of the mechanics of airplanes, aerial engines, and other equipment of the aviator."[23]

Despite Rick's lack of interest in returning to racing, the AAA planned to hold a lavish banquet in his honor at the Waldorf-Astoria. It was scheduled for 3 February, a date to which the AAA (having sold

600 tickets and made arrangements with speakers including Secretary of War Newton D. Baker) had been forced to commit itself while he was still at sea, still without knowing whether he could attend. A reporter wrote that Rick would "be greeted by the whistles of all automobile, tire and accessory manufacturing plants" when the *Adriatic* reached port.[24] After it docked on the evening on Friday, 31 January, journalists swarmed aboard but Rick was more interested to hear that his "Dear Ole Mother and Sister Emma had come from Ohio."

He could not leave ship that night and had to report to the army debarkation center at Hoboken the next morning before doing anything else. For reasons that he did not understand, General Charles T. Menoher had ordered him to report directly to his office, so he donned his full-dress uniform. Waiting in suspense with Menoher were Rick's mother and sister and representatives of the AAA, including Richard Kennerdell, who had chosen Rick to represent the racing tour on Pershing's staff at the invitation of President Wilson. "We could hear Rick's heels clicking as he came down the hall," wrote Christian ("Chris") Sinsabaugh, a journalist who had covered automotive events since the inception of the industry. "The door swung open and Rick, in a swagger aviation uniform, came through it, stopped, saluted the general, and for the first time saw his mother, who rushed into his arms." He was too busy to write much in his diary for the next two days except to say that he spent a "wonderful" weekend.[25]

The annual New York Auto Show was in progress. On Monday Rick was guest of honor at the banquet at the Waldorf-Astoria sponsored by the AAA, which had paid for his mother and sister to come and put them up at the Hotel McAlpin.[26] A galaxy of officials and drivers including Kennerdell, Wagner, Oldfield, and De Palma attended the "Standing Room Only" event. Among dignitaries at the speaker's table were Secretary of War Baker, who would deliver the principal address; Representative Clifford Ireland, head of the House Ways and Means Committee and a staunch aviation enthusiast, who was toastmaster; and Henry van Dyke, a Francophile and master of florid eloquence who would introduce Rick as "America's ace of Hearts," in a speech stressing America's historic ties with France. Most importantly, Rick's mother, whom a reporter called "a little woman in black silk whose beaming eyes shone proudly through gold-rimmed spectacles," sat in the gallery with Emma. Baker's address was mainly a defense of the American aircraft industry against a storm of criticism about the slowness with which it had produced planes for the war effort. As former mayor of Cleveland, however, Baker also dwelt at length on Rick's Ohio origins, calling him "one of the real crusaders of America, one of the truest knights our country has ever known." Rick, seated next to Baker, saw a good opening to try to sell him his idea of flying with Chambers from New York to Paris assisted by the War Department, but Baker vetoed it—which would return to haunt Rick because Raymond Orteig, a wealthy hotel owner of French birth, was present at the banquet and was so inspired by the tributes paid to his homeland that he conceived the Orteig Prize, in quest of which Charles A. Lindbergh would fly nonstop from New York to Paris in 1927.

Rick recalled being so overawed by van Dyke's eloquence that he could hardly speak when Baker gave him a pair of wings containing 156 diamonds and 62 sapphires, set in platinum and gold. All he could manage to do was wave the wings in the direction of Elizabeth, saying "For you, Mother"—a simple tribute that brought down the house. But that is not what happened. The *New York Times* reported that Rick spoke at some length upon receiving the wings. After telling the audience how Chambers had rescued him in a sortie when his guns jammed— a comment perhaps aimed at Baker—he talked about the many times he had "gone out into the front line trenches and sat with the chaps who lived in six to ten inches of water and suffered without a murmur more discomforts than the average American dreams of." He added that "every man who went through the trench life in France should have some decoration." Possibly he was embellishing a bit about fraternizing with doughboys before they went over the top to attack the St. Mihiel salient. The *Times* failed to mention his extending the wings in the direction of his mother, if indeed he did, but another account said that Rick envisioned a future in which aircraft would link the world's peoples in peace—a statement that may have contributed to Orteig's thinking about the $25,000 prize he would announced publicly on 22 May 1919. Whatever happened, Rick was overjoyed by the banquet, writing later that evening that he had had the "most wonderful day of my life."[27]

Despite rebuffing Rick's plan to fly the Atlantic with Chambers, Baker invited him to come to Washington to discuss aviation with military and political leaders. He went there several days later and got a royal welcome in a reception at Congressman Ireland's apartment the evening of 10 February. The rules were suspended the next day when he went to Capitol Hill and appeared in the House gallery during a debate on naval appropriations. Rising to their feet, congressmen "applauded vociferously for a full minute," after which Rick "came to attention and stood at salute." In a week of lobbying he bluntly asserted that American aeronautics "was inferior to that of England, France, Germany, even Italy." Despite being honored at a St. Valentine's Day dinner held in observance of Ireland's birthday, at which Rick met former speaker of the House "Uncle Joe" Cannon and the entire Illinois congressional delegation, nothing tangible resulted, either from his efforts on behalf of air power or from a renewed attempt to gain support for a New York-to-Paris flight.[28]

On his last day in Washington, Rick was guest of honor at a "tea party" thrown by a wealthy socialite who had been an avid supporter of the Lafayette Escadrille. It was "worse than an engagement with seven Fokkers" as far as he was concerned, and he left hastily, arriving at Union Station in the nick of time to board a train bound for Columbus, where citizens were preparing to shower him with adulation. During the trip passengers besieged him to sign bills of various denominations to keep as souvenirs, which he considered a waste of money. Crowds lined the tracks as the train approached Columbus. Within seconds after he arrived "a woman in Red Cross garb planted a smacking kiss" on one of his cheeks. "That was the beginning of an awful barrage of kisses," wrote a reporter. "Eddie was kissed from the train steps to the upper platform, with workers in the Red Cross canteen leading the attack." Officials from the Columbus Automobile Club elbowed through the crowd to extricate him from the adoring females and took him to his mother, whom he greeted with "a huge man-hug and kiss." An automobile covered with patriotic bunting took him through the streets of the city at high speed to a country club to get dressed for a parade that afternoon. Braving snow and sleet, crowds lined the parade route along Mound, Broad, and High streets to cheer Rick and members of his family as they rode in five automobiles to the Capitol, where Governor James M. Cox came to Rick's car. "In the name of Ohio and the 5,000,000 people it contains," Cox said, "I am glad to welcome you back."[29]

Rick could not stay long because of other commitments and took a train back to New York City to attend a charity ball at Madison Square Garden sponsored by the Knights of Columbus, where he and Governor Al Smith would be guests of honor. He also needed to talk business with Driggs, now in America. Driggs later recalled that he "had worked steadily on Rick's book" throughout his voyage on the *Aquitania,* finally deciding to call it *Fighting the Flying Circus*. Far more polished than the diary and reports Rick had given Driggs in Europe, the manuscript contained much material Driggs had added on his own initiative, along with skillfully embellished accounts of Rick's sorties. Whatever the historical limitations of a work that aficionados of aerial warfare later took as gospel, Driggs had written an elegant narrative amply fulfilling his side of the contract he had signed with Rick. As it stipulated, Driggs took no credit for authorship but contributed a foreword under his own name, praising Rick's prowess and recalling how he had met him at Rembercourt. Acting as Rick's agent, Driggs turned down $10,000 offered by the *New York World* and accepted $25,000 from the McClure Syndicate for serial rights. He also negotiated a contract with the Frederick A. Stokes Company to publish the book, starting with a $6,000 advance. Rick signed the deal with Stokes on 26 February, calling it "the first business I have done in two long years." The book ultimately yielded about $25,000 in royalties.[30]

Getting back into civilian clothes gave Rick "the most wonderful feeling I have ever had." He spent much of his time preparing for the fifth Liberty Loan Drive, for which the War Department had called him home from Koblenz. Regarding himself as a "flat and dull" speaker, and knowing that his grammar and wordsmithing were badly flawed, he dreaded the impending campaign and turned for help to Damon Runyon, also recently returned from Europe. Runyon had been so impressed by Rick at Koblenz that he had hoped to launch him on a political career leading to the White House. After hearing him stumble through an "Ode to America" he had prepared for him to deliver, however, Runyon saw that the Ace of Aces was not presidential timber. Besides trying to improve his speaking skills by having him write key ideas on index cards and slip them into a pocket as he went from one point to another, Runyon also prevailed upon Rick to take lessons from a "Madam Amanda," who taught voice production at the Metropolitan Opera.[31]

With Runyon's help Rick wrote an article about the joys of flight for the *New York American*. Confessing that aerial warfare was "scientific murder," he also described "something spiritual—I don't know what else to call it—in the feeling you get up there . . . I expect to keep on flying and I expect a part of the future of flying to lie in the scope it gives to the initiative of the American boy in the sort of thing that hunting used to mean to him in the day when there was hunting close at hand."[32]

His schedule was unrelenting. On Friday, 28 February, temporarily interrupting his stay in New York for a whirlwind trip, he took an overnight train to Washington to confer with government officials about the upcoming bond drive and show congressmen slides he intended to use.[33] On Sunday morning he left for Detroit, which gave him a homecoming celebration comparable with the one in Columbus. Newspapers called him "Edward Victor Rickenbacker," indicating he had decided on a middle name appropriate to his wartime exploits. A headline called him "Vic." Henry Leland and other industrialists took him to an automobile show that he described as a "peach," and 500 guests attended a banquet held in his honor at the Pontchartrain Hotel on Monday evening. After receiving a platinum watch and chain, he dashed "madly" to the railroad station and left shortly before midnight to go back to New York.[34]

The day he spent in Washington may have cleared the way for him to seek compensation for the slide-illustrated speeches he planned to give in the bond drive. Only one day after returning from Detroit, he discussed a deal with "Pond and Wagner" (the B. P. Pond Lyceum Bureau) to sponsor his appearances. "Proposition looks good," he wrote in his diary. Two days later he had lunch with Charles Wagner and Glenn Frank, "Editor of Century Magazine who is going to fix up my lecture." On Saturday, 8 March, which Rick called "The Day of Days for me," he reported signing a contract with the Pond agency for $10,000 a week, "which I hope works out" suggesting that military officials had to approve the deal. It is hard to believe, especially considering that most of his speeches were poorly attended, that he got such a fantastic sum, but he worked steadily during the next few days "trying to get my lecture together, which is some job." He buttressed his financial prospects on 12 March by arranging with the McClure Syndicate "to handle my story, believe I have a good proposition. Had several of the boys up here last evening to handle my lecture including Damon Runyon of the American, he has agreed to write same for me." Two days after consulting with an official representing McClure he "talked to Gen. Mitchell at Washington about 94th Sq.," perhaps to verify information he planned to use.[35] He wrote nothing about what happened in the following week, but on 22 March he made the first entry in an engagement book that he kept throughout the coming months: "Tonight I am starting for Boston then to Pittsfield Mass where I lecture for the 1st time in my life and it is the start of a tour [on] which my future depends."[36]

"The Arena of the Sky," which Runyon had helped him to prepare, recounted Rick's wartime experiences and featured live action films of aerial warfare. The tour, scheduled to last through May, would take him to cities scattered throughout New England, the Middle Atlantic States, and the Midwest. Rick set forth with glowing testimonials from Senator Warren G. Harding, General Pershing, and Secretary of War Baker.[37] Nevertheless, he faced two obstacles, his fear of public speaking and America's deep war-weariness, which made people unenthusiastic about another bond drive.

Audiences were smaller than anticipated, starting with poor turnouts in Pittsfield and Hartford, but things went better in Boston. Speaking to businessmen attending a luncheon at the Victoria Hotel on 25 March, he urged that they band together to build an airport, predicting that within a few years "all the fast long-distance travel from Houston to New York, to Chicago and even to California will be through the air." That evening he presented "The Arena of the Skies" at Symphony Hall to a packed house. "Scared to death," the honored guest listened as Massachusetts governor Calvin Coolidge introduced him, speaking "in a high, whiny voice," Rick recalled, his delivery "worse than mine. If he could get to be governor, I had no worries." Rick called the audience "very appreciative" and said "my voice was good." The *Boston Transcript* agreed, saying that he "held the closest attention of his audience for more than an hour, as he related some of the most remarkable of the aerial activities in which he was engaged or was an eye-witness." Nevertheless, contributions for the bond drive, about $800, were disappointing.[38]

At Springfield the Knights of Columbus sponsored Rick's presentation but few people came. "I would rather meet the whole German Air Corps than lecture to a small audience," he wrote after garnering only $190 for the bond drive. A critique of his performance, however, stated that "he has a clear, resonant and attractive voice, which, as he spoke last night, simply and without gesture, could be heard in the farthest corner of the Auditorium. Calmly, and without a raise of voice, he gave his audience an insight into the lives of those men who sweep the skies where it is so high they can 'see the sun rise for the day after tomorrow,' and who do battle in the face of certain death." A blizzard the next day did not help Rick's mood, nor did another small turnout at Worcester. He demurred when the Columbus Gas Company offered him $5,000 to use his name for commercial purposes, but wrote, "Did I make a mistake?" A handful of people heard him speak at Providence. Glad to leave New England, he returned to New York City wearing a brave face, saying he was "feeling very fit and hope to stay so."[39]

Although "scared stiff," Rick made an excellent impression on 1 April in a very well-attended appearance at the Metropolitan Opera House. "The Arena of the Skies" was the main attraction in a program to benefit the American Fund for French Wounded. Van Dyke chaired the event, and the hall was filled to capacity despite prices running as high as $100 for box seats. Reviews the next day were uniformly positive. "An attractive personality and a natural modest gift as a story teller made him an ideal man to relate to an audience one of the most fascinating chapters of war—that of battle in the air," a critic wrote. "The self-possession of Captain 'Eddie' had another sort of test last night and he came through with flying colors to the great delight of the large audience."[40]

Rick's favorable reception by metropolitan reviewers was not surprising. Van Dyke's florid rhetoric was going out of style, and sophisticated listeners wanted something more down to earth. One of Rick's biographers, Finis Farr, later likened him to Ring Lardner, whose mastery of the American vernacular had created a sensation in 1916 with the publication of *You Know Me, Al.*[41] Appreciation for a homespun approach, full of grammatical errors and faulty word use, lay behind the phenomenal popularity of Will Rogers, whose *Illiterate Digest,* published only a few years after Rick's tour, received plaudits in the *Saturday Review of Literature.*[42] If Rick lacked the wit of Lardner and Rogers, the sincerity of his expository style helped him become a respected public speaker.

Nevertheless, audiences dwindled as he spoke in a seemingly endless list of venues. Albany, Utica, Syracuse, and Buffalo across New York; Harrisburg, Johnstown, and Pittsburgh in Pennsylvania; then Cleveland; on to Kalamazoo, Grand Rapids, Lansing, Saginaw, Battle Creek, and Ann Arbor in Michigan; back to Akron, Ohio; next to Hopkinsville and Owensboro, Kentucky; Rock Island, Illinois; Kansas City and Wichita, Kansas; and Muskogee, Oklahoma—the grind went on and on. A few bright spots included meeting De Palma at a party in upstate New York. In Chicago he "auctioned off one of my Boche chassis"—apparently part of an enemy plane he had brought back to America—"for $30,000 worth of Liberty Bonds." He tried to keep his chin up.[43]

A highlight of the campaign came at Dayton, Ohio, where he met Orville Wright. "I have talked about you, heard about you, read about you, and dreamed about you," Rick told him. "And I expect there have been times when you and the rest of the flyers have wished that they had never heard about me," Wright responded. At lunch that day Rick "declared it was a burning shame that the people of America, both officially and otherwise, were not at this moment taking their rightful leading places in the development and manufacture of airplanes." How ironic it was, he said, that the Wright brothers had been "compelled to go to European powers to get encouragement and finance to carry on their all-important work." He pleaded for American investors to "wake up" and predicted that within the next few years airplanes "would become as common as automobiles."[44]

Even so, Rick drew "little more than 300 people" when he presented "The Arena of the Air" at Dayton's Memorial Hall that evening. Perhaps because he was inspired by meeting Wright in one of the foremost citadels of aviation, he made a strong impression. A review called him "a polished speaker, with a sure command of his subject, and a graphic sense of the vivid." His lack of pretense was appealing. After a lecture at the Detroit Opera House, a reviewer wrote about his extreme modesty and noted that he spoke about his own exploits "usually as backgrounds for the achievements of his comrades."[45]

Rick was exhausted as the tour wound down in late May. He canceled an appearance in Duluth after speaking in Minneapolis against a doctor's advice. Commenting that he had "spoken seven nights a week, and every night in a different city," the *St. Paul News* said that "Captain Rickenbacker's strenuous career in the clouds over the battlefields of France failed to unnerve him or to 'wear him down,' but a two months' lecture tour proved his undoing." He could barely speak above a whisper and considered going home to Columbus. Nightmares hounded him. One night, dreaming he was in "a terrific dogfight in the skies over France," he fell from an upper berth and landed on the floor of a railroad car. A rumor circulated that he had suffered a "nervous breakdown" in Oklahoma City after canceling another appearance.[46]

Somehow he hung on. At Little Rock the city went all out to welcome him with a long, noisy parade while aircraft from Ebert Field flew overhead. On 27 May, traveling north on the "Sunshine Special," he was happy to have "only three more days of this chorus-girl life for me." The tour ended in Ohio two days later and he gratefully headed his diary entry for 29 May "The Last" after giving his final lecture at Toledo to the "best crowd" since the start of the campaign.[47]

The marathon thus ended positively. As Farr later wrote, "It had been hard work, it had nearly worn him out; but he had derived education from these recent experiences, not so much in the college of hard knocks as in the university of public relations."[48] Besides the financial rewards from his contract with the Pond agency, whatever they were, Rick had gained an opportunity to develop his speaking skills and lose his fear of audiences. Apparently satisfied, the army released him from further duty and promoted him to major, but he spurned using the title, preferring "Captain Eddie," a nickname that clung to him the rest of his life.[49]

At last he could enjoy being a civilian. From Toledo he went to Indianapolis to see the first running of the Indy 500 in three years. The AAA had failed repeatedly to lure him into competing, and he sat in the stands. Fisher had patriotically billed the race as the "Liberty Sweepstakes," but it became a carnival of death when two drivers and a riding mechanic died in crashes.[50]

That same day, 31 May 1919, 17 pilots and 179 enlisted men of the 94th Pursuit Squadron arrived home from Koblenz. Campbell, whom a reporter called "the Douglas Fairbanks of the air," met the men as they debarked at Hoboken, New Jersey. On 3 June the squadron held a Farewell Dinner at the Commodore Hotel. Rick sat at the center of the main table, flanked by Meissner, Chambers, and Elsie Janis. Rumors flew that she and Rick would get married. "There's not one iota of truth in it," Janis said. "I only wish I could make such a nice announcement. I'd shout it and sing it and maybe weep it to all the world, in my joy." She neglected to add that a marital relationship with Rick was impossible because she was a lesbian.[51]

Fighting the Flying Circus was now in print and getting good reviews. Driggs had negotiated a price of $1.50 per copy, the minimum figure Rick had counted on to yield the royalties he wanted. "The story is an inspiration to red-blooded Americans," said one critic. "The reader will not wish to lay down this book until he has finished it." A trade journal said the narrative would "make an American leap with patriotic joy," but a perceptive writer noted that it was easy to see the "experienced hand" of Driggs "driving the pen held by Eddie Rickenbacker."[52]

Driggs had foreseen it would be hard for Rick to adjust to civilian life. Near the end of *Fighting the Flying Circus*, speaking for Rick but drawing on his eyewitness impressions of the riotous festivities at Rembercourt on the night before the Armistice was signed, Driggs wrote, "It was to us, perhaps unconsciously, the end of that intimate relationship that since the beginning of the war had cemented together brothers-in-arms into a closer fraternity than is known to any other friendship in the whole world." He recognized that "The most significant community for a combat veteran is that of his surviving comrades," as an expert in counseling ex-servicemen later confirmed. For Rick, as for his buddies, returning home left a void that was extremely hard to fill.

Rick was outraged by an impending ban on alcoholic beverages, decrying "the tactics of the Anti-Saloon League in fastening prohibition upon this country when he and his fellows were fighting for liberty in France."[53] Legally, consumption of alcoholic drinks would not end until midnight on 17 January 1920, but it was obvious that the Eighteenth Amendment was a fait accompli, made all the more bitter to Rick because of his ethnic and urban background. Anti-Germanic sentiment during the war had been a powerful force in making the outcome a foregone conclusion, affronting city dwellers who, like Rick, came from beer-loving Teutonic enclaves in a nation where state legislatures that ratified Prohibition were dominated by overrepresented rural constituencies.

Combat veterans dreaded what was coming because they needed what a later analyst called "chemically induced forgetting" to dull the memory of the horrors they had experienced.[54] Rick's unsuccessful efforts to develop a taste for Scotch and soda in London on his way home showed he was continuing to drink alcohol. When he was on leave in Paris, wine flowed like water. Beer was an everyday staple in places like Koblenz. Rick never tired of denouncing Prohibition as a blatant violation of individual liberty, an invitation to gangsterism, and a threat to family life in homes where parents made bathtub gin and had stills in their cellars. He did not intend to obey a law violating the freedom for which he had fought.

A more welcome development came in May 1919 when veterans met at St. Louis to establish an organization providing a sense of solidarity that was ebbing with the arrival of every incoming troopship. Within a month approximately 353,000 individuals who had undergone what a historian of the movement called "life-changing experiences" in the war joined the American Legion, headquartered in New York City. Rick, a charter member, joined its first unit, the George Washington Post. Within less than a year the Legion had 700,000 members. By offering "cut-rate bars and drinking clubs" in defiance of Prohibition, it gave veterans making an often painful transition from battle to a strange new peacetime environment a chance to work off frustrations and inhibitions by sharing their experiences with buddies who knew war at first hand. Rick described an early national convention as "one of the wildest affairs any of us had seen or been a part of."[55]

New York City became Rick's temporary base. "Slept until noon means I am beginning to relax and forget the world," he wrote. He knew from traveling around the country that a career in aviation might take time to materialize, and he should keep other options open. Serial and book royalties from *Fighting the Flying Circus* freed him to wait until he found something of compelling interest.[56]

He had reestablished relations with his former pit crew director, Van Hoven, and made him his personal secretary and business agent. During the closing stages of the bond campaign, in Chicago, Rick and Van Hoven talked about a motion-picture contract offered by a person Rick mentioned only as "Brunner." Rick had Van Hoven set up a meeting with Brunner in New York City. He predicted that the project would "no doubt . . . prove a failure," noting he had publicly spurned "all efforts to make him into a matinee idol."[57]

Brunner was waiting for Rick in New York. "Van is trying to get movie proposition fixed up," Rick stated. "I have decided it must be a $50,000 cash offer or nothing and so it stands." He met Brunner at least twice, saying he made the motion-picture agent "a proposition of 40,000 and 20%. He is going to think same over [and] let me know in a day or two." Torn by mixed feelings about acting on the silent screen, Rick said he was "Just trying to make a decision on my future and it's nearly impossible. Van insists a picture is the thing. . . . Everybody else seems to feel different no doubt when the time comes everything will work out o.k." Brunner agreed to wait while Rick made a trip to Ohio, but Rick doubted that "we will ever get together." Meanwhile, an unnamed party in California, possibly another movie agent, had offered him "$20,000 for 30 days work" of an unspecified nature.[58]

These diary entries are the only documented basis of claims Rick later made that Carl Laemmele, a German-born film magnate with a huge studio at Universal City, California, had pursued him relentlessly in 1919 to sign a contract. Brunner may have represented Laemmele, whose name is unmentioned in Rick's engagement book. Laemmele's notoriously stingy business tactics raise doubt whether he would have offered Rick a certified check for $100,000, as he later claimed. Explaining why an acting career did not appeal to him, he said that the amorous footage typical of the silent screen would degrade his heroic image and set a bad example for America's youth. A greater deterrent may have been that Priscilla Dean, with whom his name continued to be romantically linked, had switched from Biograph to Laemmele and was starring in films including *The Brazen Beauty* and *The Wicked Darling*. In any case, Rick claimed he had to threaten a lawsuit against Laemmele to end his pestering.[59]

A visit to the Pond Lyceum Bureau led nowhere, possibly because Rick had been such a poor draw in most of the cities he had visited on his recent tour. He also had a long discussion with promoters about holding an annual "Rickenbacker Race," either at Chicago or New York, but could not resolve a dispute between rivals from the two cities. After returning to New York from autographing copies of *Fighting the Flying Circus*, he left for Columbus in mid-June to participate in a charity drive to endow beds in a new hospital. Spending a few hours with his mother, he gave a speech at a ceremony at which Mayor Karb gave him a jeweled Hat-in-the-Ring emblem. That evening he took a train to Chicago, attended an air show in the Windy City, and left for a big reception planned for him in Los Angeles.[60]

Crossing the continent, he admired the scenery from the deck of an observation car. Notifying the mayor of Los Angeles when he would arrive, he said the prospect of returning to "dear old California" made him "happier than you perhaps will ever know." By 20 June he was in the Golden State. "Gee, but it's great to be in Southern California again," he told reporters. "I've been looking forward to this ever since I got home from France, and I'm hoping on my next visit out here to bring my mother along, because this is where we propose to make our home."[61]

An estimated 300,000 people, the largest crowd in the city's history, lined the streets to see a parade in his honor. The festivities began when he reached the Southern Pacific Station at one o'clock on 21 June, wearing a "full dress uniform with Sam Browne belt, breeches, high laced boots, wings above his left front jacket pocket, one line of campaign ribbons, but no medals." Airplanes from Rockwell Field in San Diego flew over the parade and showered spectators with flowers. Crowds lining the streets pelted Rick with bouquets, threw hats in the air, and blew kisses at him. Bands, fife and drum corps, drill teams, firemen, cowboys, tanks, trucks loaded with wounded veterans, and delegations from civic organizations passed by the crowds and bombs exploded at various places, "adding 'war color' to the scene." Rick called the frenzy "the greatest ovation I have been given anywhere. . . . Never for a moment did I expect anything like this. It was magnificent, and the best part of it was that they must have meant it. People can't pretend that sort of thing. I knew I loved Los Angeles and Southern California, but I never really knew how much."[62]

He later claimed that waving to crowds in Los Angeles from a flower-bedecked mock airplane made him feel "like an idiot," but contemporary accounts show that he enjoyed himself immensely. He had planned to leave on 24 June but stayed two extra days. Going to Hollywood, he met Douglas Fairbanks and Charlie Chaplin and hammed it up with Mack Sennett.[63] He finally left on the evening of 26 June on a train for San Francisco, where he spoke at a luncheon at the St. Francis Hotel, sponsored by the local Motor Car Dealers' Association. He said nothing about automobiles except that he was through with racing, but talked a lot about aviation. "Within ten years transcontinental railroads will be used only for produce and the Panama Canal for slow freight," he predicted. After telling the people of Los Angeles he planned to move there, he now said he wanted to settle in San Francisco and make it an airline hub. "The time is just about upon us when commercial aviation will be the thing," he stated. "San Francisco can take the lead by starting now. I am figuring strongly on making this my headquarters in an enterprise along such lines. With 5 per cent of the expenditures for the upkeep of road in this country we could establish airdromes in every principal city in the United States."[64]

By the end of June, accompanied by Van Hoven, he was bound for Tacoma, where he had beaten De Palma at the Montmarathon in 1916. Van Hoven, who had played a crucial role in the victory with an outstanding demonstration of time and motion study, looked forward to a resumption of the racing event on the Fourth of July, with Rick as a referee. After stopping in Portland to admire Mount Shasta, they arrived in Tacoma, where aircraft manufacturer William E. Boeing took them to Seattle on his private yacht, the *Taconite*. That evening, at a large open-air enclosure among 500 revelers, Rick was feted at a dinner sponsored by Boeing and the Seattle Flyers' Club, whose members came in uniform. Eddie Hubbard, Boeing's chief pilot, flew overhead, took photographs, and performed aerobatics. After returning to Tacoma, Rick was guest of honor at a banquet sponsored by the Commercial Club, arriving "amid a deafening din of Klaxons, hundreds of horns and the cheers of 300 husky-voiced men." During his speech he said, "There is no thrill in the world like that of the air. . . . I expect to devote myself to commercial flying, probably in the manufacturing end."

A record crowd jammed the Tacoma Speedway on Independence Day to see Ralph Mulford win one of three scheduled races and Louis Chevrolet take the other two. Rick, in his military uniform, drove around the arena in a flag-bedecked Buick bearing a wreath identifying him as America's ace of aces. He was so exhausted by the pace he had been following that he turned down a proposition to pay him $15,000 plus expenses to fly over Mount Tacoma.[65]

Two days later, Rick and Van Hoven took a pleasure boat, the *Princess Patricia,* to Vancouver. Priscilla Dean was visiting the city and Van Hoven spotted her ahead of Rick in the registration line at their hotel. Shoving a newspaper in Rick's face, Van Hoven hustled him into a corner until the danger of being seen with Dean had passed. Rumors were still circulating that he was romantically involved with Elsie Janis.[66]

Leaving Van Hoven behind, Rick headed for the Canadian Rockies on a train carrying the wealthy Bill family of Hartford, Connecticut, headed by electricity magnate Charles G. Bill and including two sisters, Dorothy and Ruth. Rick found Dorothy especially attractive. Riding in an observation car, he marveled at the splendor of the mountains and forests but saved his highest praise for Lake Louise, which had "the most beautiful scenery I have ever seen." He spent much of his two days at the Chateau Lake Louise taking a boat ride and walking in the woods with Dorothy Bill. "Oh how enchanting," he wrote, calling the resort "a most wonderful place to fall in love with a fair maiden." He was sorry to see the Bills leave on an excursion train, saying goodbye "as tho' I was a newly wedded man."[67]

He went from Lake Louise to Banff to give a speech about aviation at the Banff Springs Hotel. Entitled "Predictions," and obviously prepared with much care, possibly with help from Van Hoven, it dealt with the future of aviation, describing it in glowing terms as a new mode of mass transport.[68] Flying, he said, was "in its infancy," requiring government aid in plotting air routes. Now that the war was over, commerce should be the chief focus of aeronautics. Among other marvels, he predicted air routes fanning out from nodal cities like spokes of a wheel. They would be alphabetically designated, have navigation markers, and provide fields for emergency landings.

Discussing the fundamentals of flight, Rick said that airplanes were currently best suited for short-range operations and dirigibles for long-distance passenger and cargo flights. Ultimately, however, he foresaw multiwinged passenger planes "having an immense body similar to a fish," with only one engine of "several thousand horsepower" in the center, turning multiple propellers. Pilots would use instruments to control them. Besides having "cabins and salons," they would feature "promenades" on which sightseers could stroll "without affecting the stability of the ship."[69] Aircraft of the future would have a range of 5,000 miles; dirigibles would be "up to two thousand feet long" and carry "from five to six hundred passengers and their baggage." Used primarily for transoceanic flights, they would fly from New York to London in twenty-four hours on regular schedules, offering all the conveniences of ocean liners. After they docked at mooring masts, passengers would exit on elevators. Aircraft engines, "previously based on water-cooled automotive designs," would be air-cooled or use turbines. Ultimately, however, all engines would be electric, drawing power from wireless stations on the ground.

Air travel, he asserted, would be safe. Pilots would use "wireless controlled compasses" operating on "special electric wave lengths" to navigate between large cities. Planes would have to "register in and out without stopping, by number, owner's name, speed they are traveling at and their altitude." Personnel in control towers would track their progress to keep them separated. Weather conditions would be monitored and forecast. Planes and pilots would have to be licensed by the government and examined regularly for airworthiness and physical fitness. Insurance policies would be issued, just as at present in railroad and steamship travel. Every city should have a large municipal airport, centrally located to integrate it with other modes of ground transport. Cities located on bodies of water should build airports beside them to maximize accessibility to highways and railroads. Otherwise, a large city should "have a landing field on the roofs of its buildings in the down town districts. They eventually will be built of universal height with the streets bridged over for many square blocks—making it possible to land within fifteen or twenty minutes ride of your office or destination." New York City, he said, should construct a "massive building" up to sixty stories high, "covering Central Park." The top of the building would be a gigantic airfield providing connections with all parts of the world, and the top ten stories would be used exclusively for hangars.[70]

Rick foresaw a need for international aeronautical associations, meeting annually to deal with problems caused by technological innovation.[71] National governments "should encourage commercial aviation by using it for delivery of mails, thereby giving them a force of pilots and mechanics that could be turned into war pilots overnight." There would be no reason for planes to be idle at any time except for "repairs or overhauling." Rick's presentation ended with a vision of a giant aerodrome ten years in the future, painting a vivid picture of a huge pressurized airliner that had flown in from Japan taking off from Seattle and flying at 34,000 feet across the country, reaching New York City the next morning.[72]

Rick accurately anticipated many future developments. Some of them were already materializing in Europe, but Canada and the United States were lagging far behind. As he prepared to leave Banff on 12 July the Bill family arrived, and he had the unexpected pleasure of spending one last afternoon with Dorothy.[73] When he left that evening on an eastbound train, he had other things to think about. Much as he wanted to build a career in aviation, it was not clear when, or even if, it would come to pass. For the time being he might have to settle for something else. Leaving his visions in Banff, he turned to a more prosaic but also more pressing matter: making a living.

Chapter 11

— ☆ —

Domestic Front

In 1965, looking through a rear-view mirror at his quest to start a career, Rick told an interviewer that at some point late in the summer of 1919 he sought refuge in a desert, where he slept outdoors under the stars, marveling at their radiance and wondering what the future might hold. It was then, he said, that he had pondered a cherished goal of manufacturing a high-quality automobile he had envisioned during the war. Sometimes he said the desert was in Arizona, at other times in New Mexico, but in any case he spent six weeks in solitude, clearing his mind of war and calming his nerves after the frantic pace of his life since returning from Europe.[1]

Rick may have had such an experience, but it could not have happened so soon after he came home from the war. Newspaper clippings and his engagement diary for 1919 show where he was every day until early November. He had no time to go to Arizona or New Mexico even briefly, let alone for six weeks.[2] Perhaps he went there late in the year, but reliable sources show he had no intention of manufacturing automobiles when he came home from Europe. For six months he proclaimed the gospel of flight and his desire for a career in it. In Los Angeles he declared he would build "a plane that will cross the Pacific Ocean" to claim a $50,000 prize announced by film magnate Thomas H. Ince. "I am now on my way East and one purpose I have in view is the selection and construction of an airplane, built according to my specifications, with which I hope to win the honors of this international event."[3]

Winning prizes was about the only way to make money in aviation. The market was glutted with surplus military planes, mostly Curtiss JN-4 trainers, selling for cheap prices. They were used mainly for barnstorming by pilots that had flown in the war, now making a precarious living by taking people for joyrides or risking their lives in death-defying stunts.[4] Airmail routes existed, but the Post Office Department operated them, employing pilots to fly in weather conditions so hazardous that some died in crashes. Passenger operations flourished in Europe with government subsidies that were anathema in the United States. Because of constitutional scruples, no federal policy existed for regulating commercial aviation. Aerial mapping and photography, crop dusting, surveying pipelines, and skywriting were sources of precarious income, and bootlegging was available for unscrupulous entrepreneurs with the onset of prohibition. The military was the only possible source of funds for large-scale aircraft production, but fiscal retrenchment was the order of the day. There was also strong opposition to Billy Mitchell's ambitions for a strong, separate air force.[5]

Nevertheless, none of these considerations prevented Rick from seeking opportunities in aviation. He seriously considered an offer from Curtiss to sell airplanes for a $25,000 salary and a $10,000 expense account but backed off, saying he might be interested later. "It was hard to turn down $35,000 for the coming year," he wrote, "but truly I don't want the job." No wonder—Curtiss had lost about $75 million in canceled wartime contracts, was constrained by a competitive bidding system under which the government refused to recognize proprietary rights to new designs, and was deeply in debt. Because prospects were bleak in aviation Rick had to consider other possibilities. He pursued sales positions in the oil, tire, and automobile industries, but his efforts led nowhere.[6] Instead of occurring to Rickenbacker during the war, or in a desert, the idea of an automobile named in his honor first surfaced on 10 June 1919 when two promoters from Sandusky, Ohio, approached him, wanting to build a car and call their enterprise the Rickenbacker Motor Company. Rick wrote that "their proposition was to give me two dollars per car royalty and 10% of the common stock . . . or I could join the organization and be part of same." He turned them down because Sandusky seemed like a bad place to make cars and he did not like the entrepreneurs, but their proposition simmered in his mind until 6 October, when "a Great Idea came to me of a Rickenbacker Motors Corp." while having dinner in New York City with Harry Cunningham, a racer-turned-engineer with strong connections in Detroit.[7]

Within a few days Rick was in the Motor City. On 10 October he sounded out industrialist Walter Flanders, whom he had known as the principal investor in Maxwell Motors. Flanders referred him to Byron F. ("Barney") Everitt, a multimillionaire with whom he and yet another

Detroit businessman, William Metzger, had developed a car called the EMF (Everitt-Metzger-Flanders). Rick had lunch with Everitt, who seemed "interested in the proposition."[8]

Flanders now ran a farm in Virginia and came only intermittently to Detroit, but loved automobiles too much to stay out of the industry. Everitt had several phone conversations with Flanders after meeting Rick. Both men saw great potential for a high-quality car named for a national hero. By the end of October they shook hands on an agreement with Rick to go ahead.

Everitt and Flanders belonged to what one automotive historian has called a "Detroit Elite" that practiced "conspicuous production" by making expensive cars, leaving the low end of the market to mavericks like Ford.[9] One of the reasons Rick approached Flanders was because he wanted to make a classy automobile that would compete with Cadillac, Packard, and Lincoln but cost less. The main problem with his strategy was that the bracket he aimed at was already congested.

Rick, evidently free from an enforcable contract with Everitt and Flanders, helped develop his new car by sending mechanical drawings to Cunningham, who had worked for EMF and Maxwell. Cunningham soon started building a prototype at a shop in Detroit. Because Everitt had an existing factory that could take care of coachwork, Rick and Cunningham were concerned only about the mechanical components that would set the Rickenbacker car apart from other makes in its price range. One feature was a crankshaft with flywheels mounted at both ends to eliminate "periods of vibration" in certain speed ranges among four- or eight-cylinder engines. Rick later claimed he had observed the "tandem flywheel" feature during the war when he inspected a captured German fighter plane with a counterbalanced crankshaft and immediately realized it was intended to make the engine run smoothly. He and Cunningham also aimed for an extremely strong chassis with frame channels that would endure punishing road conditions. An early advertisement for their car said, "Brooklyn Bridge does not provide such a factor of rigidity and strength." They agreed that the vehicle should have a low center of gravity, with elliptical springs cradling the frame in the front and rear, helping it cling to the road on curves. A feature Rick wanted but did not get, because Everitt and Cunningham thought it too radical for a new marque, was a four-wheel braking system Rick had admired on the racetrack.

When the prototype was finished Rick began torture-testing it under extremely challenging conditions, ignoring pressure from Everitt to make production cars as soon as possible. He later claimed to have driven approximately 150,000 miles across rugged terrain in varied weather and temperature ranges, especially in western states where roads were characteristically bad. He traveled incognito, avoiding publicity, experimenting with gear ratios, depending on whether he was driving on sand, gravel, gumbo, or other surfaces, and replacing parts that broke or wore out. He said he could have built three more cars with used-up parts. Perhaps it was during this period that he went to the southwestern desert to meditate for six weeks. His whereabouts were not clear on any given date, but there was enough time for such a sojourn. At the end of the trials, incurring further displeasure from Everitt, he demanded even more testing so the car would be easy for inexperienced to drivers to operate, thereby preventing it from being marketed until 1921—a benefit, Rick claimed in hindsight, because of the economic downswing that took place in 1920.[10]

Given that he had not yet signed a binding agreement with Everitt and Flanders, a better explanation of his dilatory conduct was that aviation still attracted him and he was playing for time. In December 1919, Chambers, now leading the 1st Pursuit Group at Kelly Field in Texas, began urging Rick to join him in aircraft manufacturing. Chambers believed Mitchell's dreams of an independent air force would soon materialize and money could be made filling orders for military planes. Legislation was pending in Congress to create a separate air arm. Asserting that "we have connections with the best talent in the game," Chambers was confident existing planes could be substantially improved and "we can find the engineers that can get the results." Aircraft that survived rigorous testing would be "purchased in a large quantity if the separate Air Service goes through," and "we are in a position to bring considerable pressure to bear in the right spot if necessary." Potential partners who were "itching to get into the game" included Rudolph ("Shorty") Schroeder, formerly chief test pilot at McCook Field, who had recently become the first man to fly an aircraft with a supercharged engine and had also set a world altitude record by reaching 28,900 feet in a one-man flight. Chambers said advanced aircraft were unlikely to come from existing manufacturers including Curtiss, Martin, and the army's own facility at McCook Field. He reminded Rick that "the early bird catches the worm."[11]

When Rick failed to respond, Chambers became all the more insistent. He said Alfred Verville, a distinguished aircraft designer, was interested in his plan. Schroeder and Verville, he intimated, wanted to start building a scout plane Verville had designed, theoretically capable of reaching 200 miles per hour. Chambers seems to have learned by this time about Rick's automotive plans. "I think we can put out planes worthy of the name Rickenbacker," he said. "And I think your name will sell for more when connected with airplane[s] than in any other business." Chambers wanted to leave the Air Service and intimated that Harold Hartney did too. "Now answer this by return mail and give me your ideas," Chambers admonished.[12]

Chambers had hit Rick in his ego, where it counted, by raising the possibility that an advanced "airplane worthy of its name" would be a good substitute for a car of the same description. "We can do experimental work for the government sufficient to give us all a good income," he wrote in April. "It will be a business that we will like better than anything we can get into. I don't believe there is any doubt in any of our minds but what it holds wonderful opportunities for the future and that we can build up the strongest organization of its kind in the U.S."[13]

It is not clear what happened when Rick, Chambers, Schroeder, and Verville met face-to-face early in May 1920 at Dayton, Ohio (not Detroit, showing that Rick did not want Everitt, Flanders, or Cunningham to know about it), but events soon afterward cast doubt on Chambers's optimism. The National Defense Act (also called the Army Reorganization Act) passed in June 1920, though perpetuating the Army Air Service and giving it modest encouragement, fell far short of what Mitchell had wanted. Despite this "crushing defeat," he was still determined to proceed on his quest.[14]

Nevertheless, Chambers had rekindled Rick's desire to find opportunities in aviation. He immediately took a strong interest in the Junkers F.13, a five-passenger low-wing monoplane that had recently been introduced in the United States. Built by a brilliant German designer, Hugo Junkers, it was the world's first all-metal airplane, featuring a fuselage and cantilevered wings made of duralumin, an aluminum alloy combining low weight with great strength.[15] Believing the F.13 had great promise for both military and commercial applications, John M. Larsen, a Danish-born entrepreneur with whom Rick was friends, bought the American patent rights to the aircraft, which he renamed the Larsen JL-6, and imported several of them to sell to the armed forces and the

Post Office Department. Brigadier General Charles T. Menoher, chief of the Army Air Service, liked the plane, as did Hartney, who was now heading training and operations and thought it suitable for bombing, pursuit, or reconnaissance.

Believing the JL-6 opened new vistas in commercial aviation, Rick helped Hartney organize a cross-country flight to demonstrate its potential. Hartney flew with Rick in a three-plane flotilla of JL-6s with Bert Acosta, an airman with a penchant for flying under bridges, and airmail pilot Samuel C. Eaton Jr. Rick persuaded Edward E. Allyne, an executive in the aluminum industry, to come along, accompanied by his wife and daughter. After an accident in Cleveland, in which Hartney hit a telephone pole trying to take off over some railroad tracks, the little fleet, now reduced to two planes, flew on to Chicago, Des Moines, and Omaha, landing in the center of the racetrack where Rick had starred at the Ak-sar-ben festival. Atmospheric conditions at Omaha were unfavorable for takeoff, causing Rick's plane, with Hartney aboard, to crash before it could lift off a runway. After plowing into a ditch, it hit a house so hard that a two-by-four went through the side of the fuselage, missing Rick's head by inches but not seriously injuring him or Hartney. Fortunately, the occupants of the house had been outside watching the attempted takeoff and were not hurt. Undaunted, Rick and his friends had another JL-6 flown in from New York and continued but had another brush with disaster flying over Texas. The engine overheated while cruising at altitude on benzol and forced Rickenbacker to make an emergency landing. Coming down on its nose, the plane needed further repairs, but Rick and Hartney were lucky it did not explode in flames.

Somehow they reached the Pacific Coast, flew from Oakland to Los Angeles, and headed back east. Engine problems resulted in near-fatal takeoff at Tucson, and a broken fuel pump caused a sudden loss of altitude over mountains near Roswell, New Mexico. With Eaton at the controls, furiously manning a hand pump, Rick barely cleared the summit of a range, as the patched-up plane scraped against the treetops. Ultimately the planes reached western Pennsylvania, where fog forced them down in a field near Du Bois in the Allegheny Mountains. Leaving Acosta to guard the aircraft, Rick and other members of the party hitchhiked to Bellefonte, whose airport was a refueling stop for mail planes flying between New York City and Cleveland. The next morning, waiting for help, they heard the roaring of an engine overhead and saw

Acosta, a notorious womanizer who had a date that evening, flying high over the airfield, ignoring their plight. Disgusted he had stranded them, they took a train to New York.[16]

Catastrophic or near-fatal accidents involving the JL-6 resulted when benzol, which could burn through rubber tubing, leaked from joints in rigidly connected copper pipes because of engine vibration. If too much fuel was lost, backfiring could cause benzol that collected under the engine block to burst into flames, which would erupt under the cockpit floor. Soon after his cross-country flight, Rick heard that an airmail pilot had been charred beyond recognition in the crash of a JL-6. Going to the scene, he was horrified by what he saw and wondered how he and his friends had flown almost all the way across the country and back without having a similar fate.[17]

Taking the JL-6 on a long junket to assess its suitability for commercial use soon after his meeting at Dayton with Chambers, Schroeder, and Verville shows that Rick had not abandoned his dream of pursuing a career in aviation. Exactly what business relationship he was seeking with Larsen—perhaps to help him sell JL-6s to the military, postal officials, or other buyers—is unclear. A partner with Rick's fame and contacts would have been valuable to Larsen. Taking Allyne on the flight suggests that Rick wanted him to help manufacture the JL-6 under license in America. Because of what Chambers had said about Hartney's intention to leave the army and go into business, Rick may have thought about forming a partnership with his old commander. The seating capacity of the JL-6 could have interested them in launching an airline.

Rick had another aerial opportunity in 1920 when asked to fly Republican presidential candidate Warren G. Harding to various stops on the campaign trail. He eagerly consented and arranged to have a war-surplus De Havilland DH-4 specifically modified with a rear canopy for the tour, but it fell through when Harding's managers decided the cost Rick had specified—$500,000—would seem extravagant to voters accustomed to traditional front-porch appearances. After winning office, however, Harding asked Rick to fly a message to a Masonic conclave in San Francisco. Taking Eaton along as copilot, Rick set out for California in a DH-4 provided by the postal service. Things went well until they made an overnight stop at Elko, Nevada, and got up to find the ground covered with snow. After helping shovel a narrow path down the runway they tried to take off, only to skid into a snowbank and roll the plane over before they could stop. Uninjured, they secured another DH-4 and got airborne but had an even worse accident when they landed to re-fuel in a blizzard at Reno, demolishing the aircraft but again escaping unhurt. Rick finally delivered the message after reaching San Francisco in a third DH-4, quipping that losing two planes had saved the cost of sending it by airmail.[18]

While Harding was still giving speeches on his porch in Marion, Ohio, Rick eliminated an obstacle that would have made it hard to deal with Mitchell if the battle for a separate air force succeeded. Despite their mutual respect, Rick still resented the way Mitchell had embarrassed him in the presence of a French officer on the eve of the St. Mihiel offensive. An opportunity to clear the air arose when the Cleveland In-dians and Brooklyn Robins (not yet called the Dodgers) won pennants in 1920 and the World Series began in Brooklyn on 5 October. Rick invited Mitchell to join in the festivities. As usual, Mitchell arrived in full military regalia, "hot as a pistol," but Rick insisted he wear civilian clothes. After the first game was over, they caroused from one speakeasy to another, but Rick missed his chance to confront Mitchell about his behavior in France. He was about to broach the subject at a dive in Greenwich Village when Mitchell suddenly apologized for the incident, giving Rick the opportunity to forgive him.[19] If Mitchell's dream of an independent air arm materialized, they would be on good terms in the project into which Chambers had inveigled him.

Although things did not work out as Chambers had hoped, Rick had finally found how to combine his passion for aviation with making auto-mobiles if he had to honor his verbal commitment to Everitt. From the beginning he had thought he could best contribute to the new motor company in marketing. At some point in 1920 he decided that he need-ed more experience in selling cars, which he had not done since his days with Firestone-Columbus in Omaha. Looking around, he learned that a mid-priced four-cylinder car, the Sheridan, selling for about $1,700, had been introduced by General Motors in September 1920 to fill the price gap between the Chevrolet and the Oakland (succeeded by the Pontiac).[20] Intrigued, Rick looked for a vacant distributorship and found that GM did not yet have an agency in California. Applying, he got it and estab-lished his headquarters in San Francisco because its central location afforded potential access by air to all parts of the Golden State.

Leasing a single-seat Bellanca inexpensively because it had a suppos-edly inferior Hall-Scott engine, Rick flew to Bakersfield, Stockton, and other places interviewing dealership applicants. After choosing winning candidates, he took out full-page ads in local newspapers announcing in big letters, "Sheridan Is Coming." When a dealership was about to open, he would publish a similar notice with the message, "Sheridan Is Here," fly to the community, and land in a field where the dealer he had selected would meet him in a pristine Sheridan, thinking reporters and photographers would come to write articles and take pictures, stirring up publicity. With such tactics, Rick built a sales network with twenty-seven dealers, to whom he sold more than 700 cars.

When a recession hit in 1921, Sheridans did not sell as well nationally as in California, leading GM to cut prices by $200. The decision threatened to ruin dealers who had bought Sheridans from Rick at normal wholesale prices. Taking a train to New York City, Rick stormed into the office of Pierre S. Du Pont, who had temporarily assumed the presidency of GM, demanding that his dealers be protected from impending losses. Relenting, Du Pont promised to take care of them. Nevertheless, GM stopped producing the Sheridan on 1 August 1921 and sold the marque to William C. Durant, who soon abandoned it. Even though it had existed for a single model year, it served Rick's purposes as a vehicle with which to renew his marketing skills.[21]

That same year Rick had another chance to indulge his passion for flying. In May 1921 Mitchell invited him to attend a banquet that would take place in Washington to commemorate the fourth anniversary of the sailing of the *Baltic* for France. Accepting with alacrity, Rick decided to attempt a transcontinental speed record by flying from the West Coast to Washington in a De Havilland DH-4 fitted with extra gas tanks and loaned to him by Captain Henry H. ("Hap") Arnold, commander of the army's San Diego Air Station. Adding a further challenge, Rick planned to make his official start at San Francisco, crossing the Sierra Nevada range to see how well it would climb with so much fuel aboard. Taking off at San Diego, he tried to cross the Tehachapi range, but a "violent snowstorm" forced him to retreat to Los Angeles, where it had been raining heavily. The airfield was muddy and the De Havilland turned turtle after landing, smashing its propeller and wingtips. Uninjured, he flew to San Francisco at noon the next day, after the damage had been repaired, and got there in six hours. He took off into a heavy fog at 4:00 a.m. the following morning to maximize daylight before reaching North Platte, Nebraska, 1,600 miles away, where he planned to spend the night. Once again he had bad luck, getting lost, narrowly missing the top of Goat Island in San Francisco Bay, and having to land at Redwood City airfield. At 8:30 a.m. an opening in the clouds above the Sierras encouraged him to try again, but he had trouble gaining altitude, doing figure-eights before finally crossing a pass at 11,000 feet with his tailskid almost scraping the trees.

By the time he reached Salt Lake City, he realized that he could not get to North Platte by dark because of his late start. Cheyenne, Wyoming, seemed to be the best place to spend the night. As daylight waned, he descended to follow some railroad tracks, but as he approached Cheyenne he saw no automobile headlights, which he had arranged to illuminate the spot where the airfield was supposed to be located, and realized he was off course, heading for Denver. Hurrying back toward Cheyenne, he made out the headlights for which he had been looking but found when he landed that they had been poorly positioned. Flying with the wind instead of against it, he could not stop at the end of the runway. Plowing into a ditch, he demolished the plane and found himself hanging upside down in his safety belt. In his haste to escape, he undid the catch and fell on his cranium but was not badly hurt and decided not to give up his quest after flying almost thirteen hours. The next morning, after telephoning Mitchell, he shipped out of Cheyenne as cargo on a mail plane bound for Omaha, where he caught another one and flew to Chicago, having made arrangements to have a fresh DH-4 ready for him. Airborne early the next morning, he made it to Dayton and took on enough fuel to complete the remaining nine-hour trip to Washington nonstop.

By the time he got to Wheeling, however, he encountered heavy storm clouds that got so thick he could not climb over them. Realizing he would have to land or risk hitting a mountain, he descended below the murk and went to and fro trying to find a place to land, following the Monongahela River and coming dangerously near some electrical lines. Caught in a downdraft and disoriented, he had to land or crash and found a clearing near Hagerstown, Maryland. When he set the plane down, it slid to a stop on a slope at the far end of a rain-soaked pasture. As a crowd gathered around the aircraft, he realized that his chances of getting to Washington in time for the banquet were dwindling and thought he would be disgraced if he failed to appear. Getting out of the plane, he kept the engine running for fear nobody would know enough to help him get started again by swinging the propeller. To his horror, a girl was walking toward the whirling blade, but somebody stopped her, and he shouted at the top of his voice for the spectators to stay back.

When he finally got in position to attempt a takeoff, the aircraft could not leave the soggy turf because it had too much fuel. Before he made a second try, farmers helped him drain seventy-five gallons of gasoline from the tank into milk cans. Having never taken part in such an activity, they thought he wanted to sell it to them and were surprised to learn he was giving it away. He also decreased his tire pressure to get better traction and felt a surge of relief when the plane struggled aloft, lopping off the tail of a dog in the process.

Despite everything, he reached Bolling Field with almost an hour to spare before the banquet would start. His clothes were soaking with sweat as he saw his steadfast supporter, Congressman Ireland, waiting to meet him. After changing to dinner attire at Ireland's apartment he strolled nonchalantly into the Metropolitan Club at seven o'clock as if nothing unusual had happened, showing he was still a Gimper.[22]

Ireland's position as chairman of the House Ways and Means Committee made him a powerful force. His presence at Bolling Field indicated that Rick had political reasons as well as sentimental motives for attending the reunion. Mitchell, still trying to marshal public opinion behind his campaign for a separate air force, was in the final stages of a successful effort for authorization to bomb—and, he hoped, to sink—captured German warships, including the battleship *Ostfriesland,* in a demonstration of what air power could accomplish even against capital vessels supposedly invulnerable to air attack. Tension was rife between Mitchell and the army's chief of staff, General Charles T. Menoher, over Mitchell's attempts to buck the military establishment by willfully antagonizing the navy. Rick had published statements in a veterans' journal, *U.S. Air Service,* going out of his way to criticize Pershing, who now presided at the Fourth Reunion dinner, for opposing Mitchell's ideas.[23] Critically important issues affecting the future of military aviation were on the line in Washington in an atmosphere of backstabbing and intrigue. It was an ideal time for Rick to make whatever influence he possessed felt among the powerful, especially those who would decide what would be done about military aviation. His presence at Mitchell's behest makes it hard to believe he was not there for ulterior motives. The outcome of the ongoing debate would decide whether there was any chance of success for the aircraft manufacturing project into which he had been at least partway lured by Chambers.[24]

It was also make-or-break time for the automotive project with Everitt, who had wanted to begin producing the Rickenbacker car as soon as possible in 1920 and waited impatiently while Rick found one reason after another to demand more time for testing a prototype. By the time Rick attempted to set a transcontinental record from California to Washington in May, no final action had yet been taken to incorporate the motor company that would bear his name. Time was pressing for the first vehicles to be assembled to have any chance of introducing them at the New York Automobile Show in January 1922. Everitt was running out of patience.

The denouement came quickly. The Rickenbacker Motor Company received a charter of incorporation at Lansing, Michigan, on 1 July 1921. Two days later, Everitt began organizing the firm, which was capitalized at $5,000,000, personally subscribing $2,499,400, representing 249,940 shares of common stock. Six other investors, including Cunningham, Flanders, and Rickenbacker, held ten shares each. An application to the Michigan Securities Commission listed assets of $3,550,000 and liabilities of $3,500,000, including $2,500,000 worth of stock not yet issued and a $1,000,000 land contract. On the same day, 3 July, Everitt wrote a letter to Rick stating that he and Cunningham had spent $545,654.21 for "materials, traveling expenses and wages during the time that has elapsed since we had our memorable meeting at the Hotel Statler in 1919." Everitt pointedly noted, "You have never furnished us with any of the money that has been expended and it is my understanding that you are adjusting this account today by giving me a note payable on demand for one-third of this amount, which note is in the sum of $181,884.73." The letter assigned no monetary value whatever to the time and effort Rick had spent in testing the projected automobile or organizing dealerships. Everett ended the letter saying he hoped Rick would "never regret having entered into this agreement." Two days later, after Rick had endorsed a promissory note Everitt had specified, he also signed an agreement to serve the corporation for a five-year term, at $20,000 per annum, "to be paid in semi monthly apportionments." Under the contract, Rick, as "Party of the Second Part," was "to devote his entire time to the business of the Party of the First Part," Everitt.[25]

In a development that had possibly forced Rick's hand, Pershing, a vigorous opponent of Mitchell's aspirations for an independent air force, succeeded Menoher as the army's chief of staff on 1 July, the same day the motor company was incorporated. Rick must have been aware Pershing's appointment was forthcoming. Because there was no chance Pershing would appoint Mitchell to head the Army Air Service, the visions Chambers had set forth a year before would go by the boards. On 28 September 1921, in a foregone conclusion, Pershing chose his friend Mason Patrick for the post Mitchell had coveted. Rick reacted by saying, "General Patrick is a capable soldier but he knows nothing about the Air Service," adding a gratuitous slap that "the appointment is as sensible as making General Pershing admiral of the Swiss Navy."[26]

Rick was now living in the Motor City at the prestigious Detroit Athletic Club, whose luxurious new building, erected in 1915, had replaced the Pontchartrain Hotel as the favorite watering hole of the city's automotive titans. Membership in the club was limited to 2,500 and at least that many people were on its waiting list. Their chances of admission, one writer said, were "so remote that they might just as well have filed their applications in the archives of the Library of Congress." Obviously Rick had become a star in Detroit's pecking order by knuckling under to Everitt.[27]

On 5 August the Michigan Securities Commission approved Everitt's application for incorporation, giving him permission to sell $2.5 million worth of common stock and validating the total capitalization of $5 million. Among the assets Everitt listed was a factory he owned on Harper Avenue, which, according to a trade journal, "will afford the Rickenbacker company sufficient working space for the production of 20,000 to 25,000 cars a year." The "land contract" to which Everitt referred in the same document was "unoccupied acreage . . . to permit of tripling or quadrupling present capacity should it be required." Removal of present equipment from Everitt's plant would be done rapidly, after which "the installation of the Rickenbacker machinery will follow at once." Everitt was also negotiating to buy the former Disteel Wheel factory of the Detroit Pressed Steel Company, located on twenty-seven-and-a-half acres five miles from the center of the city on Michigan Avenue. It had 380,000 square feet of floor space, enough to produce 200 cars per day. Everitt obviously intended to return to the automobile business in a big way.[28]

The corporate hierarchy included Everitt, president; Flanders, chairman of the board; Rick, vice president and director of sales; and Cunningham, secretary and treasurer. The distribution network would include the Flanders-Rickenbacker Company, managed by Walter Flanders's son, George, which was given exclusive rights to sales in Maryland, the District of Columbia, and Virginia. Cunningham would take charge of sales in Michigan. The company was looking for distributors to handle other territories on a noncancelable five-year basis.

Three models were scheduled to appear early in 1922: a five-passenger Phaeton selling for $1,495, a four-passenger Coupe for $1,885, and a five-passenger Sedan for $1,985. Both open and closed models would be available. All cars would be of the six-cylinder type and feature Rick's concept of "dynamically balanced" tandem crankshaft flywheels at both ends, supported by three main bearings. "The frame is very deep and wide, and the long springs with a novel shackling arrangement at the rear add to the easy-riding qualities of the car," an advertisement stated, listing other features including an "all walnut steering wheel" and headlights like those on a Rolls Royce. Publicity contained an ironic statement about the severe testing the car had endured. "The original chassis and body traveled over 80,000 miles! Was ever a car so exhaustively and so expensively tested? No—but Capt. Rickenbacker laid down the rules and his rules *ruled!*"

The first pictures of the new cars appeared in *Motor World* in December 1921. The three vehicles displayed at the New York Automobile Show constituted the firm's entire output to date. The event, in which ninety-two car manufacturers displayed their marques, occupied four floors at the Grand Central Palace, decorated with red velvet and gold trimmings. The Rickenbacker was among nine marques that appeared for the first time, competing for attention with Ambassador, Bournonville, Durant, Frontenac, Handley-Knight, Kelsey, and Wills-St. Claire.[29]

It made a hit among the new entries. Visitors liked the value it offered for the money and ordered more cars than the company could supply at the time. After the New York show, Rick traveled from Boston to Texas to attract customers and candidates for marketing outlets. Based on his experience with the Sheridan, he had conceived a five-year plan beginning with appointing distributors in "a strip of territory, roughly 500 miles wide, right across the country, from Boston and Philadelphia on the east to San Francisco and Los Angeles on the west," which he called "The Highway of Progress" because "it is the wealthiest, most progressive, most highly developed, most thickly populated part of the country." He hoped 5,000 cars would be produced in the first model year, requiring twenty-five distributors. His plan called for more sales representatives to be appointed in the second year in all places with populations of 5,000 along the "Highway of Progress," associate distributors north and south of it in the third year, and representatives in foreign countries thereafter.[30]

As he had done with the Sheridan, Rick traveled around the "Highway" by air. The chief engineer of the airmail service had redesigned the Larsen JL-6 to eliminate its dangerous features, but the Post Office Department had abandoned the plane in 1921 after further accidents, one of which cost the lives of three pilots.[31] Undaunted, Rick chartered a JL-6 owned by Eddie Stinson, a barnstormer who had become one of Detroit's leading aircraft manufacturers, to fly him from one potential distributor to another. Stinson and Rickenbacker handled the dual controls. Steve Hannagan, who had previously handled publicity for the Indianapolis Speedway and was now serving as Rick's press agent, went along for what turned out to be a harrowing trip. The plane ran out of fuel during a flight to Cleveland, requiring an emergency landing in a wheat field. Lightning hit it on the ground in Detroit, knocking out two mechanics, who survived the incident without further harm. An oil line ruptured over Ypsilanti, Michigan, and water leaked from the cooling system in a flight to South Bend, Indiana, necessitating more stops to repair the damage. The plane was also forced down when the engine froze over Iowa. After reaching Omaha, Stinson crashed the plane trying to take off with overloaded fuel tanks. Nobody was seriously hurt, but Hannagan, who had never flown before the trip, was terrified by the incident, and Rick had seen enough of the JL-6 to realize it was still a hazardous airplane. He and Hannagan finished the trip by rail.[32]

Tooling up for production at the factory provided by Everitt required much time and effort. As 1922 began, it was hard to fill orders resulting from the New York Automobile Show and Rick's sales efforts. Only 27 vehicles rolled out of the plant in January but output multiplied steadily, reaching 18 cars per day on 11 March. The 1,000th vehicle, "a coupe decorated with pennants and ribbons," came off the assembly line on 10 May in the presence of corporate officers and invited guests. In June the firm made 533 cars, a figure hailed by a leading trade journal as a triumph for Rick and his associates. By September production reached 2,500 and a Rickenbacker went 246 miles on 7.01 gallons of gasoline in an economy run, averaging 35.08 miles per gallon and using only a pint of oil.[33]

Amid these developments Rick gave an address, broadcast 21 June 1922 by Los Angeles radio station KHJ. He began by declaring that "The entire history of the world's progress has been in the main a history of transportation," and told listeners how the automobile had radically increased the delivery radius within which a business could operate since the days of horse-drawn vehicles, saying, "Cities are laid out with suburban residence districts served by the automobile and by no other means."

But that was basically all Rick had to say about automobiles. The main theme of his message was the way aviation was transforming human life "in far greater proportion than any previous transportation invented." The airplane was "a thoroughly practical vehicle" that had in a few short years become "400 per cent advanced" over types used in the war, and it would soon be "many times more efficient than it is today." The reliability of airmail had already been "established beyond that of the railroad in the accomplishment of mail delivery under all weather conditions. Its cost has been cut to a point where we can now deliver a ton of freight from Los Angeles to San Francisco in four hours on sixty gallons of gasoline." Taking aim at the industry he had just entered, Rick asserted that "One can build a five-passenger airplane in equal quantities for as little or less than it costs to build an automobile of the same class. It is as easy to fly a plane as it is to drive a car, once one has gone through the preliminary instruction of about eight hours. There is less mechanism to take care of in an airplane than in a car and less upkeep per mile, while the gasoline consumption per mile will soon be less than in the average motor car of today."

Rick was just hitting his stride. He spoke glowingly about the promise of commercial aviation, admitting that "the ships being used are of the old inefficient type, but the pilots and those interested are holding on at a no-profit stage, waiting until the new planes on which they can make money, are produced." He forecast a vast increase in aircraft production and said its "superdevelopment" was vitally important to America's place in the international economy. Aeronautics had a mighty mission to fulfill. Today's children, "the men and women of tomorrow . . . will, through their support of aviation, reduce the size of the United States to the size of Texas in hours of travel."[34]

It was a curious speech coming from a man who had just signed a five-year contract to make "A Car Worthy of Its Name." Obviously Rick's passion for the sky was greater than his love of the road. He was committed to the automobile industry for the short term, but what then?

In 1922 he made a much more lasting commitment by getting married. Steve Hannagan said that women chased Rick constantly after he came home in 1919, but "it meant nothing to him." According to his biographer, Finis Farr, "Rick was moving too fast to settle down with a wife. Sometimes . . . he would go for two weeks, passing as many nights in Pullman cars as in hotels."[35] Things were now different. Walking along Fifth Avenue during a visit to New York City in 1921, Rick encountered Adelaide Frost Durant, with whom he had been on familiar terms during his years on the AAA tour. At that time she had been the wife of racing driver Russell Clifford ("Cliff") Durant, son of General Motors founder William C. ("Billy") Durant.[36]

Adelaide grew up in Grand Rapids, Michigan, where her father, Stoel Meech Frost, was a wholesale grocer. Her mother died during her childhood, and she was raised by a grandmother, becoming an alluring woman with a beautiful singing voice. Cliff, an accomplished musician, was smitten after he heard her perform at a cabaret, and they married in September 1911. Cliff, who had divorced an earlier wife, was a heavy drinker and womanizer. Adelaide's life with him was marred by physical abuse and his extramarital affairs. She had a number of miscarriages and finally had a hysterectomy after deciding she did not want to start a family with such a man.

Adelaide was surrounded by carefully manicured grounds, costly antiques, and exquisite works of art at her husband's 470-acre estate in Oakland, California. Despite the luxury in which she lived, her marriage became intolerable. In July 1921 a California court granted her an interlocutory divorce decree on grounds of "extreme cruelty," but she probably became separated from Cliff as early as May 1918, when her wealthy father-in-law, who was extremely fond of her and knew she was not at fault for the failed marriage, bought her a house. "I think it is about time you were 'settling down' and am going to make you a present of a home if you can find one 'ready made' to suit you," Billy Durant wrote her from his executive suite at General Motors. "A not too large, well arranged and well located place, costing from $25,000 to $30,000, is my idea, and if you can locate it and will 'send the wire,' I will 'send the check.'" As a Christmas present he deposited $100,000 worth of securities for her on 21 December 1918 at the Bankers Trust Company of New York. Ten days later he established a fund for her at the Guaranty Trust Company, based on 4,200 shares of General Motors and United Motors stock valued at $120,000.[37]

Adelaide went from one place to another after abandoning Cliff. She lived for a time near the Grand Canyon with a friend, probably an Ethel Wilhelm to whom she was closely attached when Rick renewed his acquaintance with her in New York. She traveled abroad with Wilhelm, visiting France, Italy, and Morocco before returning to the United States. She claimed to have sent Billy a Moroccan motif that became the famous Chevrolet bow tie.[38] She was on a shopping spree in Manhattan when she renewed acquaintances with Rick in 1921. He invited her to dinner, and she agreed if Wilhelm could come along. According to Isabel Leighton, a writer who later interviewed Adelaide in connection with a film about Eddie, "He gulped but made a gallant attempt at convincing her that nothing would please him better than to take them both to theatre and supper."[39] On the evening they were to spend together, Wilhelm was "unexpectedly and urgently called home. This provided Eddie with his first romantic break where Adelaide was concerned. He professed great concern over Mrs. Wilhelm but his heart was singing." After they saw a play and went dancing, he asked Adelaide whether he could see her "whenever he came down from Detroit . . . on business of course." She accepted.

After this time Rick found as many opportunities as possible to go to New York. He and Adelaide spent New Year's Eve together, and "he took her to the Beaux Art to meet some of his friends," Leighton wrote. "She wore her newest Paris creation for even then she had a feeling that somehow, in her life, this was an event." Rick later said it was during this visit that he fell in love with her.[40] He sent her flowers—always red roses—and gave her a diamond pin. Finally, he suggested to her that "I can't keep on making excuses to come to New York on business . . . so you'd better marry me and come to Detroit." They could not tie the knot until her divorce decree went into effect, but they became engaged and she began apartment hunting in the Motor City, where she soon took up residence.

Rick's friends were already suspicious about his frequent trips to New York. Adelaide's visits to Detroit and her decision to live there aroused further curiosity. Rick wanted to keep their relationship secret because of unwelcome publicity about his earlier affairs with women, real or imaginary. Adelaide, "deeply hurt" by her awkward position, "felt that there should be some announcement of their engagement to put an end to the tongue-wagging." Deciding that Rick "was ashamed to admit that he was in love with her," she got "thoroughly fed up with the situation" and sent him a telegram calling everything off. Alarmed by the prospect of losing her, he backed down and went public with their intentions, setting off what Adelaide called "an avalanche of unpleasant notoriety . . . a rehash of all his so-called former romances, escapades that didn't make very agreeable reading." She decided he had been right about being tight-lipped and told Leighton that she had "never since . . . tried to sway him against his better judgment."[41]

After Adelaide moved to Detroit, taking Wilhelm along, Rick introduced them to Everitt and his wife, Donna. They dined at the Athletic Club but from then on usually had home-cooked meals "where prying eyes couldn't find them and gossip-mongers couldn't make something of it." Occasionally the Everitts took them somewhere to eat, but they left hastily if anybody recognized them. "One night they ate their dinner in three separate places," Leighton said, "a course in each restaurant."[42]

Adelaide told Rick about her hysterectomy and offered to release him from the engagement if he was troubled by her inability to bear children. He assured her that it was of no concern to him. His only reservation involved how keenly he felt about the difference between his limited financial means and Adelaide's wealth. Wilhelm later said that "In the early days Eddie found it very difficult to reconcile himself to the fact that she had been used to a kind of luxury he couldn't provide." When he finally gave Adelaide a simple engagement ring, of which he felt ashamed because he could not afford anything better, he said that it would give him "something else to work for." According to Wilhelm, he was "a very possessive person. He never manifested his jealousies during their engagement but his point of view about even having her talk to other men showed in his eyes."[43]

After her divorce became final in July 1922, they decided to get married on 16 September at an Episcopal church in Greenwich, Connecticut. Hannagan, Rick's best man, and Wilhelm, Adelaide's maid of honor, were among the few witnesses present at the wedding. Jacob Pister, Rick's childhood minister, assisted T. B. Barney, rector of the church. "It was a quiet ceremony but impressive," Rick wrote in a diary he began keeping that day. "Adelaide looked beautiful and inspiring."[44] They drove immediately to New York City, obtained passports and visas, and went to a pier to board the White Star liner *Majestic,* bound for a two-month European honeymoon. "It's the happiest day of my life," Rick wrote in the diary.

"Like a child with its first real toy am I, only the most beautiful toy, not in the true sense of the word but in the form of a wonderful Pal to share and suffer through life alike," he wrote the next day when the *Ma-*

jestic was at sea. During the six-day voyage he repeatedly expressed his delight in being married to the woman of his dreams. "Adelaide looked stunning and was admired by all," he wrote after their first dinner in the grand salon. When weather permitted they strolled around the deck, made friends with other travelers, lounged in deck chairs, took pictures of one another, and gazed at the ocean. They slept late mornings and thought they were "the laziest people on board."

Nearing the end of the voyage, they packed their trunks to disembark at Cherbourg on 21 September. Rick was sorry to see land, writing, "it has been like a dream, and am not certain yet it is not, for our companionship seems so perfect and the one I have secretly longed for so many years." The first discordant note came after they reached Paris that night and checked in at the Continental Hotel. "Adelaide lost a $325 fur neckpiece," Rick wrote. "I think it was left in the taxi—this upset the both of us." Something more serious than a lost fur was bothering him. He was afraid Adelaide's "love for fine clothes and jewelry" was greater than her feelings for him. She wore a ring he thought made the one he had given her look cheap, and wished she would take it off, "if only out of courtesy to me."

They moved to the Hotel de Crillon the next day and filed a police report about the lost fur. After an interview with a reporter, Rick took Adelaide to a show and decided to tell her how he felt about the rings. "Enjoyed a real chat with Adelaide today," he wrote, "and am certain we are both better acquainted with my faults." On Sunday they went to Fontainebleau Castle, had a "wonderful lunch," and explored the woods. "It's just a dream," Rick commented. "I wonder at times if it can be true, there seems so much happiness in life." Back in Paris, they dined at a café, danced, and walked back to the Crillon "to end a perfect day," but trouble was still brewing in paradise. "Then something happened and as I write this it seems untrue," Rick wrote, hoping God would "never let it happen again or let this occasion ever mar the love and happiness of Adelaide and me for it means much." He would not put in words whatever distressed him so badly.

"Adelaide shopped all morning and expects to this afternoon," Rick wrote the next day. He was becoming troubled by the abandon with which she spent money. Making arrangements to fly to Germany, he thought the price, $500 for two passengers, too high, and was put off by the slowness of French business dealings. "It's simply impossible to get started before 10:00 a.m.," he wrote, "and then it takes five times as long to get anything done as in America." But he felt better that evening after he and Adelaide had dinner brought to their room, declaring, "It's just like real home life and I love it."

Tuesday, 26 September, was the fourth anniversary of the start of the Argonne offensive, bringing back memories of aerial combat. He had lunch with some buddies who were visiting the city, and "enjoyed fighting the war over again." He planned to take Adelaide to the Coupe Henri Deutsch de la Meurthe air races at Etampes, honoring one of France's greatest aviation promoters. After dinner they went to the Alhambra Theater to see a performance by a Spanish actress whom Adelaide admired, but another sour note appeared in Rick's diary after they packed their trunks to visit areas where he had fought. "Adelaide just had a shock that she lost the diamond shoulder pins until I remembered they were in a gown last worn on the *Majestic* which made her happy," he wrote. "She has a bad habit of mislaying things and losing them." He wrote that she should "attach everything with rubbers so they will fly back in place."

Things kept dampening his mood. Before leaving for the battlefield excursion on Wednesday morning, Rick learned from a former flight instructor at Issoudun that "the monument to the boys who were killed in training had been neglected shamefully." It was foggy and raining when he and Adelaide set out at ten o'clock, but the sky brightened as the day went along. At Chateau Thierry, "most of the wounds of 1918 had been healed by Mother Nature." At Coincy the aerodrome where he had been stationed "was nothing more than a fertile farm field, no more signs of aviation than the White House." At Rheims he was impressed by "the spirit to rebuild," seeing nothing of "the days when wrack and ruin dominated, but instead a happy, hard working people." On the other hand, he was disappointed to see that little had been done to repair "the beautiful cathedral, few outward improvements have been made in rebuilding God's art." At Chalons they visited the hotel where he had stayed during the war when he retrieved a plane from Villeneuve and witnessed German bombers attacking the city. Entering the Argonne Forest made him feel "as if I were in a dream living again days of 1918." He and Adelaide were "tired but happy" when they reached Verdun after dark.

On Thursday Rick had "an uncanny feeling to again see the Verdun airdrome with its wrecked hangars and buildings." At Fort Danaumont, they saw heaps of skulls and bones and headed for Montfaucon, where they visited the place where he and Chambers had brought down a Hannover observation plane virtually intact and used it for a theatrical exhibition. At Rembercourt they saw "nothing but fertile fields." They dined at Toul amid familiar surroundings but could not find a room with a bath and drove on to Nancy, reminding Rick how he and Mitchell had parked on a hill to observe a German air attack when he had driven Mitchell around the front. That night Rick and Adelaide found acceptable lodgings at the Grand Hotel.

When they returned to Toul the next day, Rick was shocked to see the rundown appearance of the aerodrome at Gengoult, noting that "the old hangars had the covering removed and frame work had collapsed from lack of attention and old age." The stone structures at which he and his comrades had marveled after living in mud and squalor at Epiez were still as he remembered them, but empty. His nostalgia turned to rage when they "drove over to the hospital where our early boys were buried." He "had hoped to find a neat little graveyard well taken care of, where we had placed the bodies of Lufbery . . . and a dozen others," only to learn the corpses had been exhumed and taken to Thiaucourt. Making matters worse, the French had built a rifle range where he had dropped flowers on Luf's grave after his beloved mentor had plunged to his death at Maron. By this time Rick had seen enough, and they returned abruptly to Paris. Having visited hallowed places "where so many gave their lives to war," he wrote, "I am sad but more vindictive toward those in power—*statesmen* who make and stop wars with the masses and their meager wealth . . . the fallacy of war is livid and I am certain though I may never see the day, it will come when instead of people being the victims of government, statesmen and government will be their victims, letting those who suffer also profit." He was still in dudgeon on Saturday when they attended the air race at Etampes. "All went well until our arrival at the field when the ladies were forced to ask where the lavatory was," he wrote, disgusted to find that "typically French it was along side of the men's *open air* lavatory. How these fool Frenchmen can be so immodest and yet be insulted by being called *pigs* is beyond me."

They spent much of the following day packing to leave for Berlin that evening. Because the airfare had been too high to suit him—Adelaide could easily have paid for it but he chose to assert himself—they got a bad bargain taking a sleeper train. During the night "customs officials and fool train men" repeatedly woke them up. The "coffee was bad and service worse" at breakfast. His pride in being Germanic surfaced as they rolled through the countryside, which seemed "green and prosperous, what a relief the clean villages after passing the manure piles in the front yards of France." But it did not take much to make him feel depressed. The passengers included a businessman they had met on their voyage to Europe. "Since he was on board *Majestic*," Eddie observed sourly, "we naturally spoke, quite interesting but typically Jewish." When he exchanged currency, he was outraged that the steward cheated him by almost 500 marks, but felt better on learning he had lost only 28¢ in American money. Hyperinflation had become so severe the Germans were spending "a basketful of money to get a pocket full of bread."

"After a stupid day on the train, which was very cold," they arrived at Berlin's Friedrichsstrasse depot and went to the luxurious Adlon Hotel, where they paid 14,000 marks, about $8.50 in the constantly gyrating price levels, for a "nice suite of rooms" and had a dinner for $3.50 that would have cost $25 in New York. Adelaide scolded Rick when he tipped each of the waiters 50 marks, only recently the equivalent of $12.50; realizing he had given them only 6¢, he went back and gave them more. Afterward he and Adelaide took a stroll on once magnificent streets that now looked dilapidated. Pitifully ill-clad, undernourished children were trudging along with sad-looking faces and no soles on their shoes.[45]

Dealers still sold automobiles amid the squalor. Visiting showrooms the next day, Rick criticized "the lack of improvement in bodies and chassis," saying they were too "high and heavy." At dinner that evening the businessman they had encountered on the train introduced them to a Mr. Rachman, "a Jew promoter of picture fame." He had invested in gliders and "in his characteristic way promised to make me millions, also wants to tie up Zeppelin patents for America." Rick discussed Rachman's ideas at lunch the next day with Foulois, who had reverted to his prewar rank of major and been posted to Berlin. Although the Treaty of Versailles prohibited Germany from making military aircraft, Foulois reported that the Junkers and Zeppelin companies were still making money building them in exile.

Rick later revealed that Ernst Udet, a crack German pilot against whom he had fought, had learned he was in Berlin and invited him to dine with former enemy combat pilots. The setting was a squalid room in a dingy basement. Rick later said, "we had a nice dinner, and you would never have thought I was a former enemy but one of them." He conversed with Udet, Hermann Goering, who was obviously the leader of the group, and Erhard Milch, who would play a major role in creating the Luftwaffe, recalling that they communicated well in English. He saw fire in their eyes as they boasted about how Germany would regain its status as a formidable military power. Goering revealed how Germany would rebuild its air force by encouraging gliding and creating commercial airlines whose planes could be readily converted to wartime use, after which an imperialist Germany would rise again. Curiously, Rick did not mention the meeting in his diary, perhaps because "It was a secret dinner, had to be," but he later emphasized it in an interview with Booton Herndon, the ghostwriter of his autobiography, who made much of it in the book.[46]

After a few days he and Adelaide had seen enough of Germany and took a train back to Paris. Before they left, he distributed about 1 million marks—$20 in American currency—in tips at the Adlon. Again they were kept awake by German and French customs officials, who "would walk in unannounced and have no respect for men or women alike." What they had seen in Berlin made them glad to be in Paris, where Adelaide examined the latest fashions in haute couture while Rick attended an automobile show. He also went to Le Bourget and pronounced it the finest airport he had ever seen. Workers were erecting hangars, office buildings, and a big new hotel as passengers, amid a swarm of baggage handlers, deplaned from airliners that had arrived from London and Brussels. As Rick was well aware, nothing comparable was happening in America.

Sunday, 8 October, was Eddie's thirty-second birthday. "What a change," he wrote, "now happily married and on my honeymoon in Europe—may it always be as today." He enjoyed going to a horse race with Adelaide that afternoon, but she felt ill at dinner and could not dance. Her sickness, however, whatever it was, did not prevent her from shopping for new clothes the next two days while Eddie went to more automobile shows. On Wednesday evening they went to the opera to see *Thais*, reminding him how he and Meissner had heard the same music in 1918 during the blizzard that delayed their flying to Villeneuve in the newly acquired Nieuports. This time Rick complained about the "rude habit Frenchmen have in all theaters by standing up with hats on and reviewing the audience." His Francophobia erupted again after he and Adelaide had dined with a couple from the United States, both "real good Americans, she having been here three years hates the French."

Seemingly endless rain, "morning night and noon," produced more bile because it delayed a flight Rick wanted to make over wartime battlefields. When the weather finally cleared up, he and Adelaide took a taxi to Le Bourget, where they learned that tickets would cost 2,400 francs instead of 1,600 as Rick had expected. "I told them to go plumb to hell," he wrote. "This is typical of the French businessman and a damn good reason why Americans hate to do business with them. They have absolutely no business ethics. . . . Whatever these words may convey of my ideas of the French, they are nothing compared with my thoughts, to cancel one penny of the war debt would be too good and foolish. Make them pay."

Preparing to leave the French capital, they packed to tour southern France and Italy in a Packard driven by a chauffeur named Pierre. Their itinerary took them to Nice, Monaco, Rome, Naples, and Capri, after which they returned to Paris by way of Florence, Venice, Turin, Avignon, and Lyons. Rick was awestruck by the beauty of the French Alps and the countryside along the Mediterranean coast. Drawing on Adelaide's wealth, to decorate their projected home in Detroit, they bought a hoard of antiques and art works in Italy that Rick could not possibly have afforded. Adelaide's shopping sprees became so incessant that they had to strap an extra trunk to the top of their car and eventually had to pay for 1,400 pounds of excess baggage to fly from Paris to London. Great paintings, statuary, and architectural wonders reminded Eddie of his boyhood aspirations to become an artist and made him regret they had not materialized. A village near Naples where Enrico Caruso had been born was so squalid that Rick called it "Stinkville." From a veranda of a restaurant atop a hill near Capri, he painted a postcard-sized watercolor for his mother. Revealing an intuitive grasp of three-point perspective, it depicted a bluff and a hillside dotted with houses overlooking a bay far below, curving gently out to sea.[47]

They saw history in the making at Naples on the eve of Benito Mussolini's "March on Rome," being present when the future dictator delivered an impassioned oration. In Venice Rick fell in love with the canals and gondolas but saw with a knowing eye that out-of-plumb buildings were slowly sinking into the waterlogged ground. A highlight of the trip was a visit to the huge Fiat factory at Turin, where he saw automobiles being manufactured, mostly for export, and swarms of black-shirted Fascisti, many carrying guns, preparing to go to Rome in the wake of Mussolini's takeover. Despite his frugality he considered the cost of renting the chauffeur-driven Packard—8,165 francs—a bargain in light of everything he and Adelaide had seen and experienced.

Getting back to Paris on 3 November, they spent a few more days there. The Folies Bergère struck Eddie as "truly a folly because the chorus girls are simply disgusting. . . . Give me the American women and their sense of modesty, even though it is only skin deep." Nevertheless, he called "Oh, How Naked," a show at the Theatre Royal, "the most daring and artistic I have ever seen," praising three actresses who performed "in nude and perfect figures." Adelaide bought "new gowns which are beauties" at Lanvin's, while Rick attended more automobile shows.

Determined to fly instead of hazarding a rough voyage across the English Channel, he made reservations to go London on a Handley Page airliner. After taking care of tickets and baggage, he colluded with the American Embassy to ship "2 bottles of tangerine liqueur" to the United States by diplomatic pouch to avoid inspection by revenue agents. After he tipped the "Guard of Departure" at the Crillon—"chamber maids, valet, waiters, boot blacks, head waiter, telephone girls, elevator boys, door boys, door man, concierge, porters, in fact everybody but the owner of the hotel"—they went by bus to Le Bourget, where officials stamped their passports, and boarded a twin-engined airliner waiting on the concrete runway. "The motors were run up, signal OK given by pilots and mechanic, the wheel blocks were removed and off we taxied to far end of field, turned around into the wind and were off in 1/3 of the field, it was hard to believe but true."

The flight gave Rick a favorable impression of the strides commercial aviation had taken in Europe while the United States lagged. The plane climbed to 1,000 feet as they watched Paris recede into the distance and flew over northern France at ninety miles per hour. Shining through clouds, the sun made "uncanny shadows below, then the shore line one hour later starting across just below Boulogne for Folkestone." Heavy clouds and mist hung over the English Channel, forcing the pilot to descend to 800 feet to get below the weather, but the sun shone again as they crossed the shore, "showing us the winding roads and green fields of England." Rick noticed an emergency field at Lympne and saw that communities along the route were "well marked in large letters" painted on rooftops. As they approached London, they encountered the "pea soup" mist for which the city was famous. Despite the murk, a Fokker from Amsterdam had just landed at Croydon, and a French airliner was close behind as their plane touched down with great precision. A friend took them to the Savoy, where they dined after a "huge day."

After awaking the next morning, Rick went to yet another automobile show, where the only cars that impressed him were French and American. "The English don't seem to have an artistic sense in their body," he wrote, noting that the British models were smaller than the others. Saturday, 11 November, was the fourth anniversary of the armistice that had ended the Great War and people were wearing red poppies to honor the dead, but that evening, when a big celebration took place at the Savoy, where "every inch of space was utilized for guests, all decorated in their best, beautiful women and handsome men." Rick wrote that "it was a gala night for all but the poor and unemployed." His heart went out to "ex-soldiers selling post cards, shoe strings and matches," and he thought about "how the spirit of humanity would be benefited if the millions spent on pleasure could be given to a better cause and the spenders stayed a night at home." Walking through thick fog along the Strand brought back memories of how badly Scotland Yard had treated him in 1916. His Anglophobia was showing, and he wanted to get back to America. "Here it is cold and damp, fogs most all winter, slow moving people, while we have all that's good."

The flight from Paris had intensified his longing for a career in aviation. He met Sir Sefton Brancker, "a real live wire" who headed the Air League of the British Empire. Two officials took him to Farnsborough, the main experimental station of the Royal Air Force. "They have an abundance of junk and successfully kept their new things under cover," he observed, "which is foolish for we have nothing to fear from them or anyone else excepting the Germans." His meeting in Berlin with Goering, Milch, and Udet, along with what Foulois had told him about the work of Junkers and other expatriated German aircraft manufacturers, had impressed him strongly. When he visited another British air base, his hosts were more obliging, taking him up in advanced aircraft that could reach 200 miles per hour and climb 15,000 feet in eight minutes.

After returning to London, he attended a show with Adelaide. They would have gone dancing except for a midnight curfew imposed by blue laws that seemed to him "rather foolish but one must remember that they are English." On Sunday a French airplane designer showed Eddie some patents for which he was considering buying the American rights. On Monday he visited the Handley Page plant at Cricklewood, which impressed him because of its size but seemed to have a "lack of activity." Thinking as always about how to combine aeronautics and automobiles, he "decided to have a 3 motor plane built which will have the body hinged at the rear of wings and large enough to transport one of our cars ready to drive away from landing. This will be one of the greatest advertising stunts ever put over in the auto industry." He went to Wimbledon for discussions with an inventor who had developed a "bird glider, a very interesting piece of work, also his lifting wing." He met again at the Air Ministry with Brancker, who was considering visiting America, and he talked with another aircraft designer about "some plane designs he wishes to sell."

Returning to the Savoy on the last day he and Adelaide would spend in London, he began packing for the voyage home. He had arranged to meet a photographer at six thirty that evening and forgot a dinner engagement. Posing for pictures in the lobby when their guests arrived, he had to dash upstairs and dress in the bathroom while they waited for him. "Adelaide was furious," he said, "but we had a nice dinner and finished packing."

Needing to reach Southampton the following afternoon to board the *Olympic* for their homeward voyage, they went to the Waterloo Station. Whatever the frustrations and disappointments he had experienced, Rick wrote that evening that the trip "had been a huge success for I have never been any happier in my life and I hope Adelaide feels the same way. To me it is like starting a new honeymoon for we are returning to Detroit and our little home, which with Adelaide's taste is going to be a real love nest."

The voyage home was punctuated by animated conversations with fellow passengers, including Canadian ace Billy Bishop and a test pilot who had bought the American rights to an all-metal Dornier plane. Rick and Adelaide also had champagne with a "Mr. and Mrs. Lipsner," who were "Jews but seem very decent." He wrote that *"everyone has their pet Jews,"* underscoring the statement for emphasis. As they approached the North American coast, he got a message that Everitt would be at the dock in New York and heard by radio that a representative of Automotive Industries wanted to meet him. His honeymoon diary ended abruptly—evidently he was too busy to keep it any longer. He wanted to be on native soil and get back to work.

In Detroit the Rickenbackers set up housekeeping at Indian Village Manor on 8120 East Jefferson Avenue, the city's "most exclusive apartment building." It was only twenty minutes from the heart of the business district and offered a sweeping view of the Detroit River overlooking

Belle Isle and Lake St. Clair. "Nature has endowed this location with an attractiveness seldom equaled elsewhere," stated a brochure, stressing the "beautiful lawns and landscape gardening" enjoyed by residents. Leases ranged from $300 to $600 per month, a lot of money in the 1920s.[48]

The "love nest" about which Rick had dreamed was elegantly furnished and featured the artworks that he and Adelaide had collected abroad. Adelaide soon became accustomed to his frequent absences. Starting in December 1922, he spent at least half the time traveling, making two transcontinental trips and inspecting 75 percent of his company's 400 dealerships. He also "met face to face at luncheons, dinners, and other affairs, at least two-thirds of the 7,000 Rickenbacker owners." A writer who pinned him down for an extended interview reported, "He attracts publicity as rapidly as a flame attracts moths" and had "a single consuming hobby: 'filling each unforgiving minute with sixty seconds worth of distance running.'"[49]

The company ended 1922 on an upbeat note. On 24 November, soon after Rick's return from Europe, Everitt announced a 5 percent cash dividend on the year's earnings, $360,806 before taxes. "Our finances are in excellent shape," Everitt stated. "Our company has borrowed no money from banks or from other sources. We have always discounted all our bills and we have on hand a cash reserve large enough to handle our business in a successful and economical way."[50] At the first annual meeting, he stated that the company had begun making money within ninety days of beginning production. Every month had shown a profit, and 5,000 cars had been manufactured in 1922.[51] This figure was inflated; a reasonable estimate, made by *Moody's Industrials,* was 3,709 vehicles.[52] On the other hand, as 1923 opened the company had a large backlog of unfilled orders. A single distributor in Los Angeles claimed to have sold 204 Rickenbackers in 165 days and could have "moved twice that many if they had had the cars to sell." Increasing its rate of production, the company planned to manufacture 500 cars in January and 750 in February. Partly because of Rick's strenuous sales efforts, it reached an output of 1,040 in April. In March the Michigan Securities Commission authorized it to increase its capital stock by $2.5 million "on the ground of increased business . . . with consequent expansion of plant and equipment." A milestone was reached on 10 July 1923 with the production of the 10,000th Rickenbacker.[53]

The 1923 model had much the same body style as in 1922 but offered a number of improved mechanical features. Testimonials to its quality came from a physician who bought two Rickenbackers; the president of a coal company, who wrote he was getting fuel consumption of 19.6 miles per gallon; and a journalist who stated, "My Rickenbacker has lots of pep and hills do not seem to trouble it at all."[54] In May the company made a major policy change by announcing it would make open cars only on special order and regular production would be limited to closed bodies, now favored by 80 percent of its customers. A balance sheet for the first three months of 1923 showed that earned surplus had risen to $511,630.[55]

At the beginning of June the company took a momentous step by announcing that four-wheel brakes would become optional on all of its cars. In August it revealed that this feature would become standard equipment on all automobiles by 1 January 1924. The driving force behind the change was Rick, who had wanted four-wheel brakes from the outset but had yielded to advice from Everitt, Flanders, and Cunningham that the dual-flywheel system was sufficient to set the automobile apart from other cars and adopting four-wheel brakes would be too radical a move for a new marque.[56]

Four-wheel brakes were unusual at the time but not new, having been used in European automobiles since 1909. Rick had seen them on foreign race cars in his years on the AAA tour and admired them in France during the war, making him want them included in the 1919 prototype built by Cunningham in Detroit. In 1920 the Kenworthy Line-o-Eight introduced them in the United States, followed by the Duesenberg Model A race car; in 1921 the Heine-Velox, a San Francisco marque, introduced a hydraulic four-wheel braking system developed by Malcolm Loughead (who changed his surname to Lockheed) but never sold any cars.

Seeing no less than forty-two types of four-wheel brake systems at automobile shows in Paris during his honeymoon rekindled Rick's determination to include them in Rickenbacker cars after he came home, and he pressed hard for the board of directors to add them. The disclosure in June 1923 that they would be available starting in August for an extra $150 and standard on all cars by the beginning of the 1924 model year was a victory for him but may have been hastened by Packard's announcement two weeks earlier that it planned to adopt four-wheel brakes on all eight-cylinder models. Cadillac, Chalmers, Elgin, Marmon, Oakland, Locomobile, and other marques joined the bandwagon soon after Rickenbacker. Rick and his cohorts had not quite "scooped the industry," as they tried to claim, but by a narrow margin offered the first American production car to use four-wheel brakes and pioneered making them universal throughout its line.[57]

The company published a clearly written, well-illustrated eighteen-page booklet explaining the innovation to prospective customers, stressing that the technology was strictly mechanical, using differential gears, pull rods, and cams putting greater pressure on the rear wheels to insure that the front ones would not lock when the driver brought the car to a stop. The brakes would halt a car "on wet asphalt quicker than 2-wheel brakes do on dry" and "ensure absolute uniformity and smoothness of operation," providing a safety margin "100 per cent more than you have been accustomed to."[58]

Besides promoting the new system in advertisements in hundreds of newspapers, magazines, and trade journals, the company painted brake drums orange-red and enclosed the rear-mounted spare tires in a fancy covering featuring a Hat-in-the-Ring emblem with "4-WHEEL BRAKES" emblazoned in large letters and numerals. Introducing the new system in the middle of a model year, however, was an act of business warfare and rivals caught with large inventories of cars reacted by charging it was inherently unsafe. Studebaker led the attack with full-page advertisements in early October, listing six reasons why prospective buyers should beware of the innovation and charging that front-wheel locking and skidding could result in serious accidents. "Studebaker engineers have been studying, experimenting with, and testing four-wheel brake mechanisms for two years, the ad asserted. "These tests merely convince us that four-wheel brakes are unnecessary, mechanically impracticable, and dangerous in the hands of unskilled drivers." The full-page text ended with a pledge that "The 1924 Studebaker cars are not, and will not be, equipped with four-wheel brakes."[59]

Rick later dwelt heavily on the adverse impact of the publicity battle but took responsibility for pushing the system through, putting other companies in an awkward position because they could not install it on cars already in production. Damaged by bad publicity, he charged, his company had incurred a catastrophic drop in sales.[60] Yet there is no convincing evidence to support his claim that he was a victim of zest for technological pioneering. He admitted that the decline of his company's fortunes was attributable to other developments, one of which happened on 13 June 1923 when Flanders was killed in an automobile accident, depriving the Rickenbacker Company of its board chairman and most distinguished director. The impact of Flanders's death is hard to gauge; he was an absentee owner living in semiretirement near Newport News, where he devoted most of his time to running a plantation and raising prize-winning animals. Nevertheless, he was an extremely enthusiastic promoter of the Rickenbacker and was engaged in establishing a high-powered agency with exclusive rights to sell the marque in Virginia, Maryland, and the District of Columbia.[61] His untimely death cost the company sales along the East Coast and deprived it of an automotive genius who might either have restrained Rickenbacker from introducing four-wheel brakes at a bad time or, because of his prestige, blunted attacks by endorsing them. Automotive historian Beverly Rae Kimes is justified in saying that the impact of Flanders's death on the fate of the Rickenbacker motor car, "although unmeasurable, was very real."[62]

In any case, Rick's self-serving emphasis on the perils of innovation was overdrawn and misleading. The public reaction to the introduction of four-wheel brakes in August 1923 was by no means negative. Sales that month were the highest in the company's history to date, going up 20 percent and raising it to nineteenth place in the industry, a huge leap from starting out eighty-third in 1922. Insurance companies gave a 10 or 15 percent discount on coverage for collision, liability, and property damage to owners of cars featuring the new system. Sales for 1923 climbed to 8,539 units, more than doubling the level reached in 1922. The company made a $407,175 profit and paid investors a 6.5 percent dividend. Besides having a constantly expanding number of dealers in the United States, it now had agencies in five foreign countries. Nearly half of America's automobile makers introduced four-wheel brakes in 1924, showing where the market was headed.[63]

Much of the controversy swirling around the new system late in 1923 passed over Rick's head because he went to Europe to inspect the latest motor vehicles displayed in Paris and London, also visiting Germany, Switzerland, and the Fiat factory in Turin. Contrary to Studebaker's claims, he found that leading British manufacturers that had not previously used four-wheel brakes were adding them to their product lines for 1924. An upbeat article he wrote for a leading trade journal after coming home showed no concern about criticism of four-wheel brakes in the United States.[64]

His trip had a lasting sequel that proved beneficial to his career. Before leaving, he had asked for a new secretary who had a strong work ethic and was not contemplating matrimony in the near future. During his absence the company hired Marguerite Shepherd, a Canadian whom he soon called "Sheppy." Her work was so outstanding and her loyalty so pronounced that he promoted her to office manager and accountant for himself and Adelaide. She became almost like a member of the Rickenbacker household.[65]

Another significant development was a Christmas present from Everitt. "It is almost three years now since I took your note for $181,884.73, and at the time of taking it I appreciated the fact that you were going to be a valuable asset to the corporation and to me in carrying out our plans, but I little appreciated the undaunted desire to work and the strength, will power and drive that you would put into your new position," Everitt wrote on 24 December 1923. "My share of the world's goods at the present time is sufficient for me and I want you to have an opportunity of going on and growing into a position where you can take over a large share of the burden of this company and I don't want you to be fettered with financial burdens. I have always intended, if you made good, to give you your share of the money that was spent in building this car. Therefore, you will find enclosed your note, which has been cancelled by me and I hope that this will give you added incentive to go on and complete the work that is now before you."[66]

Buoyed by this vote of confidence, Rick unveiled the company's Model C series in mid-January 1924 at the New York Automobile Show. It was available in four body styles priced from $1,595 to $2,135.[67] All models had six cylinders and four-wheel brakes. Buyers could choose among three colors, black, blue, and maroon, and benefited from formerly optional improvements that were now standard. The new line included the Model C "Opera Coupe" and a rakish Sport Roadster, with beveled glass windshield wings. Advertising director LeRoy Pelletier, who had created the slogan, "Watch the Fords Go By" and worked for Everitt and Flanders at EMF, displayed a characteristic fondness for alliteration by calling the Roadster "a modern chariot for the man who still retains his boyish enthusiasm, or for the boy who has inherited all the vim, vigor, vitality, verve and vivacity of his sire."[68]

But a bold new competitor was now on the scene that would have much to do with the swift demise of the Rickenbacker car. The Chrysler Model 70 was the most significant vehicle introduced in 1924, with "many boldly innovative features and panache unmatched by other cars in its price range, starting at $1,395."[69] Catching the automotive world by surprise, it offered exceptional fuel economy, low maintenance costs, and a cruising speed of seventy-five miles per hour. The *New York Times* praised it in glowing terms, and 32,000 of the new cars were rolled out in its first year.[70]

It was the Chrysler—not the campaign against four-wheel brakes—that threatened the future of the Rickenbacker, demanding a swift response. Launching a campaign to arouse its dealers to greater feats of salesmanship and service, Rick's company adopted new standard equipment including the Skinner rectifier (a device that removed impurities in oil to prevent fouling of spark plugs, scoring of cylinders, and other problems) and a new type of clutch. But a much more important and unfortunate change was brewing. In June, again in the middle of a model year, the company suddenly announced a new Series 8-A automobile with a straight eight-cylinder, 268-cubic inch engine. Among other features, it had a counterbalanced crankshaft supported by nine main bearings, a camshaft continually immersed in oil, a dual-throat carburetor, and a high-pressure oiling system. The price of the vehicle, a considerable bargain, ranged from $2,195 to $2,795, indicating that the firm was trying to deal with Chrysler's challenge by moving up to a heavier, classier automobile with advanced features at a cost it hoped would be irresistible to discriminating buyers.[71]

Meanwhile, showing alarm, Everitt pursued merger opportunities. In addition to the Chrysler menace, fluctuations in the national economy were producing a shakeout in the motor vehicle industry. Eleven marques had died in 1923 and fourteen more faced extinction in 1924. Bargains were available for the taking, and safety might be found in horizontal integration, yielding economies of scale. A potential combination in April 1924 would have consolidated Rickenbacker with seven other firms: Dort, Gardner, Gray, R&V Knight, Stephens, Stutz, and Velie. Stutz, the most famous marque involved in the deal, was controlled by steel magnate Charles Schwab, who wanted to sell it. The famed Bearcat, with which the company's name was indelibly linked, had its last model year in 1924. Other firms included in the merger plan were moribund, but, if successful, it might have resulted in a mixture of high-and low-priced cars based on the strategy followed by General Motors.[72] But it soon collapsed when satisfactory terms could not be worked out.[73]

In October 1924 Everitt pursued another merger, this time with Gray, which was at the low-priced end of the automotive spectrum, and Peerless, made in Cleveland, Ohio, which was considered a worthy rival of luxury cars like Packard, Pierce Arrow, and Cadillac. Everitt also wanted the deal to include the Trippensee Closed Body Company, which he and other investors had founded in Detroit in May 1923. The resulting company would reportedly be worth $23 million. After a promising start, things fell apart amid rumors that Cleveland bankers did not want to see Detroit get another plum. All that resulted was a total buyout of Trippensee, which was already making all closed bodies for the Rickenbacker.[74] The deal gave the company four additional buildings with a total area of 1,071,000 square feet. A new main plant was built at 4815 Cabot Street on Detroit's west side. It occupied twenty-nine acres and had 350,000 square feet of floor space, abounding in specialized precision machinery for turning out finished automobiles on "progressive assembly lines" where "each important operation is performed by skilled workmen and checked by competent inspectors." Completed cars came through an arched doorway surmounted by a large Hat-in-the-Ring emblem to receive at least fifteen miles of road testing. A two-story administration building flanked by a large white-bordered area displayed the words "Rickenbacker Motor Company," with another Hat-in-the-Ring symbol on the ground. A photograph of the plant showed a biplane soaring above ultramodern structures, symbolizing connections with Rick's exploits in World War I.[75]

The Trippensee facility, where all bodies were built, was larger than the main plant, with 721,000 square feet of floor space, but older and less imposing. Kiln-dried hard maple frames (hard oak was used for floorboards) were made by hand and metal panels were manually hammered on jigs. Forty preliminary subassembly areas converged in eight major stations that met "at the main buck or jig where the final assembly is completed." The system exemplified an era when, as a trade journal stated, "men who can or will frame an entire body are becoming scarce."[76] By comparison with the methods introduced much earlier by Henry Ford, it was costly and cumbersome.

The company began to falter in 1924. Rumors of impending mergers were unsettling, but making two important changes—four-wheel brakes and the new eight-cylinder model—at midseason in successive years created uncertainty and grumbling among dealers. Introducing an eight-cylinder car required curtailing production of six-cylinder types to a few hundred per month and only a small number of distributors could get them. Suspicions that the six-cylinder model would soon be discontinued caused so much discontent that Rick persuaded the board of directors to back down, but he intensified bad feelings among dealers by stipulating that they sell two six-cylinder models for each eight-cylinder vehicle marketed. Continued protests caused him to assert that the firm could not be "led by the whims, desires, and opinions of our Distributors" and that the two-to-one ratio "must be lived up to religiously," but he seemed willing to yield to agencies that sold the company's products exclusively.[77] He tried to reassure distributors skeptical about the new eight-cylinder line that it placed them "in an enviable position in your community, as this product's individuality, merit and value will have a tremendous effect psychologically in lifting the standard of our Six Cylinder models to a position that their merit and value justly entitles them." Many dealers found such logic dubious. The new Series 8-A, Rick argued, was in a class with the Packard, widely regarded as the premier car in the industry, but cost $1,000 to $1,500 less. Customers unable to afford the 8-A could have the prestige of owning a Rickenbacker by getting the six-cylinder model for less money.[78]

Instability began pervading the company's sales network while the Chrysler continued upsetting the market. The resignation of sales manager A. J. Banta on 20 December 1924 indicated the situation was getting serious. Another sign of trouble was an announcement by Everitt in January 1925 that he would defer paying a 2 percent dividend, significantly lower than the one of 6.5 percent declared a year earlier. Meanwhile, operating surplus had slipped to about $46,000. "The automobile business is a seasonable business and your company will need all the money at its command for the next four months," Everitt said. He tried to compensate by promising that semiannual dividends would begin being paid by July, but his concern was transparent when he urged that stockholders hold onto their securities and not permit "false representatives" to "take your holdings in Rickenbacker away from you."[79]

Everitt tried to prove that the company was not abandoning six-cylinder cars by introducing a new Series D with that type of an engine at the 1925 New York Automobile Show. "As a matter of fact," he declared, "the Six always has been, and will in my opinion continue to be our standby, with production three to one of the eight, which latter model will necessarily be, in price, within the reach of a more limited number of buyers." The new series came in five body styles including a "Coach-Brougham" that accounted for 60 percent of sales in 1925, sporting a two-tone paint scheme and extra oval-shaped window at the side of the rear passenger compartment. All of the company's cars now had a larger piston displacement, increasing horsepower. The most important change, however, was that many parts of the sixes and eights were inter-changeable, resulting in price reductions ranging from $200 to $600 on three of the five models in the Series D class.[80]

Rick tried to gain publicity by associating the company with news-worthy events. In 1924, when the Army Air Service sent four Douglas seaplanes on a round-the-world flight, he made Rickenbackers avail-able to the pilots engaged in the venture. Open-top luxury models bearing the Hat-in-the-Ring emblem were waiting at Boston when the "World Cruisers" arrived back in the United States.[81] Early in 1925 Rick began an even bolder search for publicity by commissioning Erwin G. ("Cannonball") Baker, America's best-known long-distance automobile and motorcycle driver, to set speed records in a six-cylinder Model D stock car. The campaign began with an impressive display of Baker's determination. Two days before he set out from New York to Califor-nia, carrying two passengers and three sets of luggage, a blizzard swept through the Middle Atlantic States. Disregarding the hazards, he bulled his way across the country despite horrendous weather, roads, and ter-rain. When he reached Los Angeles, he had gone 3,106.5 miles in 71 hours and 33 minutes of actual driving time, averaging 43.4 miles per hour. Disassembling the car at the end of the trip he found "all parts in perfect working condition without a single adjustment . . . on the best 4-wheel brakes in the world." He had not changed a single tire. To fur-ther demonstrate the virtues of the Series D, he set record times in trips between Vancouver and Tijuana, Jacksonville and Miami, and other city pairs. Pelletier advertised the car as a "Performing Fool."[82]

The new Series D and the publicity stemming from Baker's record-setting runs seemed to remove doubts that had been nagging the com-pany's dealers, leading Rick to send stockholders an upbeat booklet, *The Whole Works,* in March 1925. He declared the firm had enough or-ders to keep it running full blast for sixty days and might be forced to have its employees work overtime to keep up with demand. It had 100 dealerships in large cities throughout America, 600 "associate distribu-tors" in small towns, 12 dealers in Canada, and 11 scattered elsewhere. Rick scored another coup when he drove a four-door open-top Vertical 8 Phaeton as the official pace car at the 1925 Indy 500, resplendent in a two-color paint scheme and prominently displaying the Hat-in-the-Ring emblem.[83] If he was worried, his family life did not show it. Early that year he and Adelaide adopted a son, whom they named David Edward, through an agency in New York City.[84]

In July 1925, however, again in the middle of a model year, the company made another mistake by slashing prices on its eight-cylinder automobiles by $200 to $600, depending on the model involved. A press release said the reduction was possible because of economies achieved in making various components of the six-cylinder and eight-cylinder models interchangeably, but the decision cheapened the image of the company's top-of-the-line cars. Moreover, it infuriated dealers who had bought them at original prices and now had to sell them at a substantial discount. Other than sheer desperation, the motives underlying the price reduction are not clear, but it seems likely that there were two rationales: giving consumers more quality for their money and stimulating demand by all possible means. Whatever the reason, the new policy was counterproductive. Rick later tried to explain its failure with the excuse that "the country entered a recession in 1925, and sales in general went down," but the economic slide did not begin until late in the year, during which car sales rose to 4 million and the industry earned $331,391,000. An automotive historian has stated that in 1925 "there was still room for nearly everybody not merely to get along but to register new records in sales and profits." Conforming at least partly to the trend, Everitt's firm sold 9,270 cars in the first ten months of 1925, and its earnings increased to $247,563 in the same period, but this performance was unimpressive considering the industry's record as a whole.

Everitt was obviously dissatisfied by how things were going. One sign of his frustration was his addition in September 1925 of an estimated $1.5 to $2 million in working capital, achieved by appointing two new directors representing Noyes & Jackson, a banking enterprise. Another sign of change was that Everitt planned to produce 30,000 cars in 1926, causing Beverly Rae Kimes to speculate later that he was changing his mind "about the cut-off point incompatible with quality." If Everitt was indeed planning to increase output at the expense of quality, he was on a collision course with Rick, whose ego was invested in making cars exemplifying engineering excellence, believing that "the road to sales success lay in continual refinement and increased value."[85]

In an obvious gesture of defiance, Rick threw his weight behind the creation of a breathtaking vehicle, the 107-horsepower Super Sport 8, which debuted at the New York Automobile Show on 8 January 1926. Admirers hailed it as "America's fastest and most beautiful stock car." The boat-tailed wonder was designed to cruise at ninety to ninety-five miles per hour; in one demonstration, Rick drove it a measured mile in thirty-eight seconds. Its exterior features included a "torpedo-shaped rear deck, aerofoil bumpers, cycle fenders of laminated mahogany, brass-bound and with wood inlay ornaments, bullet-shaped headlamps, safety glass all around," wire wheels, and, to enhance speed, no running boards. The interior was likewise designed for the most fastidious buyer, with a dashboard similar to that of an airplane cockpit, "lush Spanish grain leather" seats, and windows trimmed in teak. All hardware was gold-plated, with silver an option. The price, $5,000, identified it as a luxury vehicle far beyond the reach of ordinary buyers.[86]

The introduction of the Super Sport at the beginning of a slowdown in the national economy was an aesthetic triumph but a financial disaster. At most, 14 Super Sports found buyers. Meanwhile, total sales of Rickenbackers for 1926 plummeted to 5,400—perhaps even to 4,050 according to some estimates. Everitt denied in April that the company was planning to build "a little cheap six," but quickly slashed prices to the bone. Despite the recession, economic conditions did not alone account for the company's plight. Its network of dealers never recovered from feeling betrayed by the price reductions that obliterated distinctions between six- and eight-cylinder cars in mid-1925.

Bickering ensued between rival cliques backing Everitt and Rick, whose five-year contract would expire in July. It was hopeless to oppose Everitt and the Super Sport had been a colossal failure. Once free of legal obligations, Rick decided to quit in September 1926. Because reorganization was already underway, his exit may have been a preemptive strike. Cunningham and Rick's close friend, Pelletier, resigned as a reshuffling of positions got underway favoring executives who had sided with Everitt. In November the company went into receivership under an arrangement that left Everitt in temporary control, but a new line of cars with high-sounding British names that came out in 1927 failed to attract sales. In February the firm's assets were put up for auction, but the bids were so low that a master in chancery threw them out. Everitt later acquired what remained as an "undisclosed buyer" for a knockdown price, $600,000. Ironically, considering Rick's earlier dalliance with Chambers, Verville, and Schroeder, Everitt now began building airplanes designed by Verville.[87]

Rick emerged from the debacle with debts totaling $250,000. He later told an interviewer he had borrowed to the hilt to help dealers who had suffered from price cuts in 1925 for which he felt partly responsible. "No automobile manufacturer is stronger than his dealers," he said.

"When the dealers are solvent, the company is solvent; when the dealers go broke, the company goes broke." He never considered the possibility of bankruptcy "because I knew that that was bad for anybody to have a blot like that on their reputation." He told creditors he would pay them back, and they seemed to have taken him at his word.[88]

Soon after Rick got out, Frank Blair, chief executive of the Union Guardian Trust Company, called him aside and told him he was sure he would find fresh opportunities. When this happened, Blair stood ready to help. Rick walked out of Blair's office glad that at least two people believed in his future, even though one of them was buried under a mountain of debt.[89] He was already trying to make a comeback, but it would not turn out as he hoped and years of frustration lay ahead.

Chapter 12

— ☆ —

Frustrations

To what extent had Rick himself caused the mistakes that undermined the Rickenbacker Motor Company? Of course, Everitt had to approve any major action the firm took. Still, Rick's passion for aviation helped lead the enterprise into dubious ventures and undercut the attention he paid to strictly automotive matters. When he went to Butte, Montana, to speak at the American Legion Post in 1923, startled citizens read a newspaper headline about a new vehicle that "Flies like a bird, rides water like a duck, covers land like an auto, and it's coming out fall of 1924."[1] The hyperbole referred to Rick's latest brainstorm: creating a hybrid airplane-automobile selling for about $1,500 with an engine accounting for no more than $1,000 of the price. Glenn D. Angle, a highly regarded aeronautical engineer, helped Rick create the power plant, which became known as the Rickenbacker engine. Angle patented it in May 1928, based on a specification filed three years earlier.[2]

This low-cost, light, simple, robust, air-cooled engine, which went through months of testing, was built for an aircraft similar to a "flying flivver" Henry Ford was creating at the same time. Planning in earnest for producing the engine began at the Rickenbacker plant early in 1926. The accompanying airframe was built at Dayton by Ivan H. Driggs, reputedly "the foremost light airplane engineer in America." After signing a contract with Rickenbacker in June 1926, Driggs unveiled plans for the "Driggs Coupe," a high-wing, closed-cockpit monoplane that was only twenty-two feet long, with a wingspan of thirty-five feet. Its maximum airspeed was set at ninety-five miles an hour and its ceiling would be 5,000 feet. Its high-lift wings would have trailing flaps designed for quick takeoffs, and its landing speed would be extremely low, thirty-five miles an hour. It would stop in the same distance as a car, and its wings could be folded quickly against the sides of the fuselage by removing two pins on the front wing spars. It could be towed by a car and parked in a garage.

The plane made its maiden flight in October 1926 when test pilot Jack H. Laass flew it from Dayton to Detroit, going 226 miles in two and a half hours and cruising at a speed averaging 80 miles per hour. Gasoline consumption averaged 15 to 16 miles per gallon, and the aircraft used only one pint of oil. Rick accompanied Laass. Glowing with pride, he stressed that the aircraft was a civilian model, priced at about $1,500 and designed without any compromises for the sake of military use. He claimed it was the world's first roadable aircraft. Land it in a field or on a highway, furl the wings, disconnect the prop, and away you went.[3]

But only a few of the new aircraft, at most, were produced. Angle and Rickenbacker sold their patent rights to the LeBlond Aircraft Company of Cincinnati, Ohio, which invested $500,000 in having Angle explore its potential. Meanwhile, Audi bought foreign rights to the engine. Rickenbacker later said he had profited from these transactions.[4]

Rick probably allowed the venture to wither on the vine because he was too busy pursuing a more exciting project. While plans for the new aircraft were proceeding, Congress had decided in was time to privatize airmail and passed the Airmail Act of 1925 (Kelly Act), permitting contractors to fly all federal mail routes except a transcontinental artery from San Francisco to New York City. In 1926 the Air Commerce Act established a sound regulatory base for commercial aviation long advocated by businessmen, giving the government power to aid navigation, license aircraft, certify the airworthiness of planes, and promote air safety procedures. As amended in 1926, the Kelly Act attracted a swarm of applications from prospective contractors to be paid per pound-miles of mail they carried. The rates set by 1927 yielded $3.20 per pound-mile, a bonanza to entrepreneurs as monthly contract miles burgeoned from 328 to 4,713.[5]

While still employed by the Rickenbacker Company, to which he had agreed in 1921 to give his undivided time, Rick seized the opportunity to become a mail contractor as a silent partner with Reed Chambers, who had resigned his military commission to sell corporate securities in California. The two men jointly applied for an airmail route between Atlanta and Miami, creating an entity called Florida Airways. Wealthy investors including Henry Ford, Richard F. Hoyt, Anne Morgan, Percy Rockefeller, and Charles A. Stone and George Mixter of the Stone & Webster banking house in New York subscribed for shares in the venture. Ford's stake was four Ford-Stout 2-AT monoplanes, single-engine all-metal corrugated-skin aircraft. The other subscribers, including Rick, collectively signed up for $300,000.[6]

As a silent partner still committed to Everitt, Rick had to be circumspect about the role he played, but the enterprise was headquartered in Detroit and he sat on its board of directors. Exactly how much actual cash he put up is unclear. Despite playing a covert role, he was as active as possible and worked closely with Chambers establishing the airline, traveling back and forth between Michigan and Florida and combining his trips with promoting the interests of the Rickenbacker Motor Company. He actively pushed for airport development and persuaded municipal officials in Tampa to acquire a cow pasture for this purpose.[7]

He also helped Chambers assemble a formidable executive team. Chambers became president, assisted by Vergil E. ("Vic") Chenea, who had helped him sell securities on the West Coast. William A. Robertson, a West Point graduate who had led aviation departments in the Border and Forest Patrols, became vice president for operations. Pilots included Carl Ben Eielson, who had flown in the Arctic. A knowledgeable observer said Florida Airways had "the finest aggregation of flying men and flying craft ever assembled for a commercial venture."[8]

Rick and Chambers wrote a prospectus asserting that Florida's weather and topography were ideal for year-round scheduled operations. They also cited remarkable population growth in the Sunshine State since the war. Highways and railroads, they said, were too congested to meet the needs of Jacksonville, Tampa, Fort Myers, and Miami, which were far apart and could be reached more quickly by air than otherwise. Their financial forecast for the first year estimated gross revenues of $1,032,804, against only $288,944 in operating costs. Even allowing reserves for depreciation, insurance, and deferred charges, they predicted a net profit of $531,693.[9]

Florida Airways was part of a much more ambitious plan. Chambers intended it to form the "opening wedge for a great airways transportation system that will cover the entire south and connect with Chicago and Washington on the North," serving Detroit, Cleveland, Chattanooga, Nashville, and Louisville. The four Ford-Stout 2-ATs were the nucleus of a fleet that would soon have six more such aircraft. According to Chambers, "22 eastern and Detroit multi-millionaires" would finance the "huge program."[10]

Florida was a good place for Rick and Chambers to become active in commercial aviation because Rick's friends, Carl Fisher and Fred Allison, were partly responsible for its burgeoning growth. Attracted by south Florida's economic potential from the time of his first visit there in 1910, Fisher had built Miami Beach into a flourishing resort and promoted the Dixie Highway to connect it with the Midwest. Fisher's promotional genius underlay a real-estate boom cresting when Florida Airways began operations. Miami's population had reached 75,000 and people were sleeping on porches because construction lagged behind growth.[11]

Unlike carriers handling only airmail, Florida Airways aimed to combine mail with passenger and cargo service. Rick helped secure a corporate charter in Michigan on 3 November 1925. On 28 December, 5,000 people, including Henry Ford, braved subzero weather at Dearborn Field to see the four 2-ATs, with arched windows and seats for six passengers, begin their southbound delivery flight. When they landed to refuel at Nashville, another throng waited to see them leave for Montgomery, Alabama.

Then disaster struck. As lead pilot Lee Schoenhair increased power for take-off in *Miss Fort Myers,* the craft fishtailed and hurtled toward a grandstand where Nashville's mayor and other dignitaries were sitting. Desperately maneuvering his rudder, Schoenhair crashed into *Miss Tampa* and *Miss Miami,* "ripping a big hole in the wing of the former and smashing a wing tip of the latter." Only *Miss St. Petersburg* escaped harm; *Miss Fort Myers* had a "broken propellor, damaged radiator and motor mount, and damaged wing tips." Nobody was seriously hurt, but the airline had gotten off to a bad start. Chambers made the best of things, saying newspaper articles about the debacle were "several hundred per cent exaggerated. They will make old men out of us yet if they don't get the facts."[12]

Despite this bravado, the damaged fleet was only partly repaired when three 2-ATs—the fourth was cannibalized for parts—arrived in Florida in February 1926 to begin service. The contract with the Post Office Department stipulated that service from Jacksonville to Miami would start by 1 April and mandated flights to Atlanta by 1 June. Poor performance by civic leaders who had promised to prepare airfields complicated the situation. "The field at Fort Myers was little more than a hollowed-out section of a pine forest with a surface of unprepared, soft sand," said one account. "On a trip into Fort Myers to show off the new airplanes to Thomas A. Edison and his wife, the takeoff, though successful, offered thrills to even experienced pilots."

Other cities were equally unprepared for operations, causing over-head to escalate before the first load of mail left the ground. To per-suade civic organizations to take remedial action, Chambers hired Ar-thur R. Brooks, a veteran of the Army Air Service who had also worked for the Commerce Department's Airways Division, as public relations assistant. Chambers also arranged for convict labor to improve the Tam-pa airfield. To compensate for damage to the 2-ATs, but also because Jacksonville's Paxon Field was too small for them anyway, the company acquired a Curtiss Lark called *Miss Tallahassee,* and two Travel Air bi-planes.

Somehow the enterprise met the April deadline and became the sec-ond contractor (after Henry Ford) to carry mail under the Kelly Act. Brooks prepared for the event by printing 20,000 ceremonial envelopes. All inaugural fights were successful, carrying 24,000 pieces of mail and earning $1,900 in postal revenue, but much of the mail was first-day-of-issue traffic and subsequent volume was poor. Suffering from a "cross between malaria, flu, and hookworm" and worried about the airline's financial prospects, Brooks resigned, and a Tampa newspaperman suc-ceeded him.[13]

Passenger operations began 1 June 1926, the first time travelers had flown a federal airmail route. The airline said patrons could save eight hours and fifteen minutes from Jacksonville to Miami and five and a half hours between Jacksonville and Tampa flying instead of going by ground, but anticipated traffic failed to develop. "People were just plain scared," Chenea stated. "We had to lock the door on [a plane] before we started the engine." Fewer than 1,000 travelers flew the firm's air-craft in its entire history.[14]

The opening of the route from Jacksonville to Atlanta was postponed because Candler Field, built on the infield of the Atlanta Speedway, was unready. William B. Hartsfield, chairman of Atlanta's aviation commit-tee, helped Rick solve the problem. On 15 September a Stinson De-troiter, *Miss Atlanta,* inaugurated service from Jacksonville with a load of mail and three passengers (all airline officials), marking the first scheduled passenger and mail operations to reach Georgia's capital. A crowd of 15,000 saw the plane land. Thirty aircraft, some military, some civilian, gave demonstration flights and took people for joyrides. "What a day it was!" said a witness. "Hundreds of whistle blasts pierced the afternoon calm, a council proclamation having requested every factory and every siren in the city to blow simultaneously for a full minute." A celebration greeted another plane, the *Miss Tallahassee*, when it arrived in Jacksonville from Atlanta with 10,000 pieces of first-day mail, after which a Travel Air took the load on to Miami.[15]

First-day-of-issue mailings were too infrequent to give the airline the postal revenue it needed. Inability to fly at night created problems because a mail train leaving Miami just before midnight could arrive at Atlanta before an aircraft that left Miami the next morning. Discouraged, Robertson resigned as operations head, and Chenea took his place.[16] As autumn approached, employees began using a tactic widespread on airmail routes by soaking blotters to double their weight and increase revenue under the per-pound system. Bricks worked even better, but a postal inspector vetoed this scheme.[17]

On the night of 18 September 1926, only three days after service began to Atlanta, a fierce hurricane came ashore on southeastern Florida's Gold Coast. Blowing with a "far-shrieking scream," winds reaching 130 miles per hour pummeled the area, tearing boats from their moorings in Biscayne Bay and depositing them inland. Victims of the catastrophe included about 400 dead, 6,300 injured, and 50,000 homeless.[18]

Florida Airways lost a 2-AT in the storm. Anchored on a concrete apron, the plane was battered for seven hours before being torn from its moorings, swept 500 yards across a field, and wrecked. Nevertheless, the airline rendered notable service. A Stinson Detroiter flew $2 million, the largest dollar amount carried by air up to then, to restock the Bank of Biscayne as soon as news of the catastrophe reached Atlanta. Getting to the beleaguered city when no other form of transport could do so, the carrier doubled its schedules to Miami and airlifted food and other supplies. Postal receipts reached their highest levels since service had opened in April.

Business, however, slackened the rest of the year, and Florida Airways faced insolvency. The last hope was establishing connections with Cuba and other Caribbean points, a goal sought by Rick and Chambers. Hoyt, their principal Wall Street backer, was active in the sugar trade, and they hoped to reconstitute Florida Airways into Atlantic, Gulf, and Caribbean Airlines with his help. In June 1926 the two comrades flew to Havana hoping to secure landing rights from the Cuban government as the first step toward a route to the Yucatan Peninsula and the Panama Canal Zone.

They failed because Florida Airways was not the only contender for mail connections with Latin America. A syndicate headed by John K.

Montgomery, a naval aviator with strong connections in New York City, founded Pan American Airways, Inc., and sought a mail route linking Miami, Key West, and Havana. Behind Montgomery's efforts were Air Corps officers including Major Henry H. ("Hap") Arnold, who thought about leaving the army and entering private business. Arnold was concerned about a supposed threat to the Panama Canal from a German-backed Colombian airline, Sociedad Colombo-Alemana de Transportes Aereos (SCADTA), which wanted to establish a mail route from Venezuela to Miami via Colombia, Panama, and Cuba. Rick and Chambers were playing for high stakes in a game with economic, diplomatic, and military considerations.

The most formidable competitor was a syndicate including Juan Trippe, an extraordinary entrepreneur who held a secret trump card. In December 1925 Trippe, backed by financiers including Cornelius Vanderbilt Whitney, had flown to Havana with Anthony Fokker, who was introducing his airplanes in the United States. During the visit, Trippe negotiated an agreement with Cuban dictator Gerardo Machado, giving him sole landing rights on the island. Neither Rick nor Chambers knew about the deal when they visited Cuba.

Events began moving beyond their control as officials in Washington, worried about the German threat to the Panama Canal, forced the three contending groups to cooperate. Trippe, a Yale graduate, made the most of his connections with alumni in the State and Post Office departments. Although distrusting Trippe, Hoyt, heavily involved in the battle, endorsed his selection as president and general manager of Pan American Airways, the operating subsidiary of the involuntary alliance. After Pan Am won a contract to operate between Key West and Havana, Trippe rented a Fairchild monoplane and delivered a load of mail to Cuba in October 1927, barely meeting a crucial deadline. In the following months Trippe and his associates maneuvered skillfully to win permanent airmail rights in the Caribbean under a foreign airmail bill passed in March 1928. Under its provisions, Pan Am won lucrative routes that made it the "Chosen Instrument" of American commercial aviation outside the United States.[19]

Florida Airways was defunct before the denouement. In January 1927 Hoyt told Chambers and Chenea "it was no use and that they must throw in their lot with the Trippe-Whitney group." Soon afterward, Chambers gave the Post Office Department a required forty-five-day notice to end existing airmail operations, and Florida Airways disappeared 9 June

1927.[20] During its brief history it flew 259,924 scheduled revenue miles and 22,984 in special operations after the Miami hurricane. It carried 13,200 pounds of mail and 938 passengers and completed more than 90 percent of its missions. There were no accidents apart from the Ford airplanes lost on the ground at Nashville and Miami. Nevertheless, final operations occurred on 31 December 1926. After vacating the contract for the mail route between Atlanta and Miami, Rick and Chambers hoped to obtain new financing to get it back after an airmail route materialized to Atlanta from the north, but the attempt failed. Harold Pitcairn, owner of a fixed-base service in Pennsylvania, bid successfully for a route from New York to Atlanta in September 1927. Two months later he took over the dormant Atlanta-to-Miami contract previously held by Florida Airways.[21]

As much as it hurt to see another dream die, Rick may have been more distressed in May 1927 when Charles A. Lindbergh, a former barnstormer and airmail pilot, flew nonstop from New York to Paris. Previously unknown, Lindbergh became America's greatest hero and most famous aviator overnight.[22] Being eclipsed by an upstart, coupled with the other setbacks he had suffered in recent years, could not help but lower Rick's spirits. It was not mere coincidence, soon after Lindbergh's flight, that Detroit congressman Robert Clancy launched a campaign to have a Distinguished Service Cross Rick had earned for his sortie of 25 September 1918, the day he took command of the 94th Pursuit Squadron, converted into the Medal of Honor.[23]

Nonetheless, 1927 ended on an upswing when Rick acquired the Indianapolis Speedway. Fisher, preoccupied with the Florida real-estate boom, wanted to sell the racetrack, which was rundown and needed $200,000 worth of repairs. His losses from the Miami hurricane made it imperative to unload what had become an albatross. Allison suggested that Rick, who needed a new challenge after Florida Airways failed, might be interested. "You are the only real life looking customer at this time who understands the business and could handle the proposition," Fisher told Rick.

The asking price was $650,000 plus interest, a total of $672,690.92. Allison gave Rick an option to buy the property and extended it for thirty days after he had trouble raising the money. Developers were waiting to tear down the racetrack as the option came within a whisker of expiring. At this juncture, Blair, the Detroit banker who had promised Rick help if he needed it after the Rickenbacker Motor Company folded, organized a $700,000 bond issue that went over the top at the last moment. Rick took 51 percent of the resulting common stock as a bonus. The deal became final on 1 November 1927.[24]

Acquiring the Speedway renewed Rickenbacker's spirits, but managing the racetrack, which he delegated to veteran manager T. E. ("Pop") Myers, was routine except in May. Late in 1927 General Motors made Rickenbacker an offer that would keep him busy during other months of the year. He had returned to the automotive world but was as much as ever in love with the sky. How long he would stay grounded was moot.

Rick's ties with General Motors, starting with his Sheridan dealership in 1921, became an asset after the Rickenbacker Motor Company and Florida Airways failed. Alfred P. Sloan, GM's chief executive officer, was fond of Rick.[25] Adelaide's shareholdings in GM from Billy Durant provided another connection. During the late 1920s GM became an important part of Rick's life.

In March 1927 General Motors unveiled a new marque, the LaSalle. Sloan had long wanted to make GM's products visually appealing. Cars with closed tops were increasingly popular and steel companies had learned to roll continuous sheets in alluring shapes. In response, GM, which had invested in the Fisher Body Corporation in 1919, acquired it outright. In 1925 Sloan appointed Lawrence P. Fisher, a member of the family that had built the body company, to head GM's Cadillac division. Fisher was as eager as Sloan to emphasize styling and was dissatisfied with the marque he inherited, which devolved from a model introduced in 1915 and had become increasingly stodgy.

Fisher began a $5 million expansion program. Deciding it was "high time Cadillac had a design department," Fisher approached Harley Earl, who had created flamboyant coachwork for the Don Lee Corporation, a California distributorship catering to movie stars. Instead of using wooden or metal forms, Earl worked with modeling clay, creating a sculptured style emphasizing curved surfaces. Fisher brought him to Detroit to design a vehicle that would make a fashion statement.

Earl admired the Hispano-Suiza, a Spanish luxury car, and had the "Hisso Look" in mind when he designed the LaSalle to fit the market niche between Buicks and Cadillacs. The LaSalle's louvered hood panels, bowl-shaped headlights, elegantly curved fenders, elaborate chrome, winged radiator cap, and two-tone color scheme set it apart as an American car with Old World flair. Detroit had never seen anything like it. Sloan admired it so much he put Earl in charge of his own department, the Art and Color Section, under Sloan's direct control. It became known in GM as the "beauty shop."[26]

The LaSalle made a sensational debut. Motorists flocked to salesrooms to admire and buy it. The price, in the mid-$2,000 range, made it a bargain for a luxury vehicle. A newly designed 303-cubic-inch, seventy-five-horsepower engine increased its appeal. A LaSalle roadster impressed Rick when it became the pace car at the 1927 Indy 500.[27] He bought a LaSalle and drove it thousands of miles. As sales neared 12,000 toward the end of the 1927 model year, Fisher organized a major marketing campaign and asked Rick to direct it. He accepted, provided he would remain owner of the Indianapolis Speedway and spend each May preparing for the Indy 500. On 1 January 1928 he joined GM's Cadillac subsidiary as assistant general manager for sales.[28]

Fisher wanted Rick to visit every Cadillac-LaSalle dealership in the country by the end of March, reaching seventy-five cities in eighty-one days. He would have preferred to fly but went by train because GM was not renowned in aviation. Starting at the Chicago Automobile Show, he crossed the continent to Portland, Oregon, flew to San Francisco (being already behind schedule) and proceeded to Los Angeles, Denver, Kansas City, St. Louis, San Antonio, Fort Worth, Dallas, Houston, and New Orleans, then across the Southeast, up the East Coast to New England, and across the upper Midwest to Detroit, meeting Fisher's deadline.

Throughout the grueling tour he smarted from his recent setbacks and precarious financial state. Besides the $250,000 debt he had refused to duck after the automobile company failed, he had assumed a mortgage of almost $700,000 on the Indianapolis Speedway. Furthermore, he knew his nationwide tour was being overshadowed by a goodwill flight around the Caribbean by Lindbergh, whose name came up everywhere Rick went. While the Lone Eagle was mapping air routes, the Ace of Aces was back hawking cars as he had done for the Columbus Buggy Company, caught on a treadmill.[29]

Had the War Department supported Rick and Chambers in 1919 when they wanted to make a transatlantic flight, Lindbergh might still be the name of a little-known barnstormer turned airmail pilot. Since the hoopla surrounding Rick's return from Europe, his life had been a series of flops. "Naturally, I felt the pang that sticks you in the left side," he recalled, being "worse off than broke." He talked about "being in the gutter and having to crawl out myself."[30]

His frustration came out at dealerships he visited. Before his tour, Fisher had ordered him to shift his focus to drooping sales of Cadillacs, which had sunk from 27,771 in 1926 to 8,599 in 1927 in the shade of the LaSalle, which was doing so well that it scarcely needed special promotional efforts. Being abruptly upstaged by Lindbergh led Rick to identify with a venerable marque that had once set the American standard for excellence and was now overshadowed by Earl's brainchild. He was angry when he saw Cadillac showrooms and repair shops that were not up to snuff. Like a drill sergeant he upbraided salesmen and mechanics, leading them abjectly around unkempt facilities and preaching to them with what Finis Farr called "Pauline fervor." Where was the passion for excellence Cadillac had once stood for? What had happened to the proudest marque in the nation?[31]

Lunches and dinners were more enjoyable because they gave him a chance to talk about wonders of the future. In Milwaukee he predicted that in two decades Americans would own 50 million cars and travel on "super-highways with no speed limit," crisscrossing "both continents of the Western Hemisphere." At Houston he envisioned a dozen such routes across the United States, divided into 100-foot-wide sections to separate eastbound and westbound traffic. Underpasses would lead cars to lanes on which they would move safely at speeds approaching 100 miles per hour, protected by four-wheel brakes, low centers of gravity, advanced steering systems, improved tires, and smoother road surfaces. Cities would have parking garages fifteen stories high.[32]

Despite his enthusiasm he frequently browbeat his listeners, particularly when speaking about aviation, where his deepest passions lay. Frustrated by dimwitted audiences that could not see scenarios apparent to him, he vented the same anger he displayed when visiting badly run dealerships. In southern California he denounced "the backward position of Los Angeles, without a mile square municipal airport," calling its plight "really pathetic from a civic standpoint." A single terminal, however large, would not suffice. "One airport won't take care of air traffic of the future any more than an alley will take care of your downtown traffic of today." Los Angeles would need "a dozen airports, and wherever you build them community centers will grow and property values leap. It is the duty of every city official to work for a great municipal airport and they will be damned if they don't."[33]

Change was inevitable, and people better get ready for it.[34] He got particularly abrasive when he visited New England, which he deemed too set in its ways. Speaking in Rhode Island and southeastern Massachusetts, from which the textile industry was migrating south, he fulminated that "You people are historical and traditional. That's bad. Tradition is the most deadly thing that ever happened to mankind. You have lost industries by your lack of vision."[35] "You gentlemen," he told businessmen in Boston, "have no conception of the leaps and bounds that have been made in the airplane industry," telling them about a huge German aircraft, the Dornier D-OX, that would soon fly 100 passengers across oceans and discussing the U.S. Navy's plans to create "a giant dirigible that will carry an entire squadron of scout planes in its stomach, launch them in midair, refuel them and send them out again." Cities that did not change would suffer the fate of communities once bypassed by railroads.[36]

Despite the way he had carried on at dealerships, trade journals confirmed that Cadillac sales were up by the time he returned to Detroit. Stylistic changes wrought by Earl, not his harangues, were responsible. Abandoning the dowdiness of previous Cadillacs, Fisher had introduced a "low, long, fleet and beautifully balanced" car, the 341-A, with a ninety-horsepower engine and "elegance to match its engineering."[37] A much-improved business climate was helping sales. The American economy was emerging from a recession, and a roaring bull market soon drove securities toward dizzying heights at the New York Stock Exchange, encouraging affluent consumers to buy big luxury cars. During the model year 40,000 Cadillacs and only 16,038 LaSalles rolled off the line at the Clark Avenue factory in Detroit. The advent of the Model A Ford helped automobile production surge from 3,083,000 in 1927 to a record 4,012,000 in 1928. Even so, output barely exceeded the 3,949,000 cars made in 1926, but few business analysts sensed danger.[38]

Amid the flush times the Rickenbackers moved from Indian Manor to a large house in Grosse Pointe. They also decided 1928 was a good year to adopt another child, whom they found in California, where Dame May Whitty, a well-known actress, made a hobby of finding parents for babies in need of homes. Whitty, a Christian Scientist, belonged to a church where she had met Lillian Tolliver Montgomery, nee Beecher, descended from the famous New England evangelical family. A gifted pianist, Lillian had been born in Missouri in 1893 and taught school in Kansas before moving to Los Angeles and marrying Fred Montgomery, a railroad clerk, in 1916. The relationship ended in divorce, after which she became romantically involved with Ralph Peterson, a brilliant linguist of Swedish descent who shared her cultural interests. She became pregnant by him while doing secretarial work for Whitty in 1927 and gave birth to a boy on 16 March 1928. Because of her straitened finances, she could not keep Isaac, as she named him. Knowing that Rick and Adelaide were child hunting, Whitty contacted them about Isaac's availability. Coming to California, they claimed him in early April, took him to Detroit, renamed him William Frost—after his paternal grandfather and Adelaide's maiden name—and adopted him formally on 2 December 1928.[39]

Whatever satisfaction Rick felt in having another son and seeing automobile sales reach new heights was outweighed by being mired in a position he did not like. Being assistant general manager for sales at Cadillac was only a way to mark time until he could return to aviation, now reaping the benefits of the Air Commerce Act and Lindbergh's flight to Paris. Making occasional speeches to promote aeronautics was incomparable with what Lindbergh was doing, and Rick was desperate to get back in the game. All he had to do to see what he was missing was to read articles about the Lone Eagle's activities. President Coolidge had decorated him with the Medal of Honor, which Rick wanted intensely but had not yet received. Plans were afoot to enshrine the *Spirit of St. Louis* in the Smithsonian. Lindy also accepted a generous offer of cash and stock from Juan Trippe, who had courted him since his return from Paris. Soon America's idol became Trippe's "technical adviser," boosting the prospects of Pan American Airways.[40]

Rick would have given anything to be in a similar situation, and his frustration showed. Even when he got chances to preach the aerial gospel, his evangelism was tinged with the bitterness he had vented on his nationwide tour for Fisher. When he spoke to the Washington Board of Trade in November, he lashed out at the District of Columbia's lack of an airport, calling it "a source of shame to every Washington citizen, member of Congress, and to the country at large." He warned that the cost of such a facility would be "nothing compared with the cost of the penalty which you will pay for failure to provide it." As always, however, faith in progress cut through his abrasive rhetoric. "We are on the threshold of a new era," he proclaimed. "There has come into our lives a science which is going to be a blessing to every human being, the science of aviation. . . . This new science will someday be the biggest industry in the world."[41]

The Indianapolis Speedway was the only source of excitement in an unfulfilling year. Owning the Brickyard brought back memories of his racing career. With Pop Myers's help he rebuilt the retaining walls of the aging facility, laid steel rods under the track, and changed the angle at which the curves were banked, all to enhance driver safety. Experts helped him plan an eighteen-hole golf course to make the property useful throughout the entire year. He conceived having the Indy 500 broadcast on radio and invited Merlin H. Aylesworth, president of NBC, to attend it as his guest. Despite rainy weather, fans created a massive traffic jam and it took three hours to fill the parking lots. The race was so exciting that Aylesworth agreed to Rick's idea.[42]

Unfortunately such experiences did not happen often enough. Seeking relief, Rick turned increasingly to alcohol. One evening, heavily stressed after three days of sales meetings, he decided to "get a little bun on" and stayed out long after midnight. Driving home in his LaSalle, he collided with a sanitation vehicle, hitting his emergency brake so hard that he "cracked my chin and my chest hit the wheel." He blamed the incident on "a couple of darkies" who cut in front of him. "There were egg shells and lettuce leaves and coffee grounds and banana peelings all over the front of the car." After parking the vehicle in his garage and going to bed, he began to wheeze and Adelaide noticed his chin was bleeding. Suspecting he had been in an accident, she went to the garage and gagged at the smell of the garbage festooning the LaSalle coupe. She promptly summoned two physicians, who gave Rick an injection, took him to a hospital, x-rayed him, found his clavicle cracked, and heavily taped his chest.

Wanting to protect his privacy, the doctors did not check him in, but Adelaide indiscreetly mentioned the cause of the accident to a telephone operator. A few days later, while Rick was preparing to go to Los Angeles for a meeting, a reporter called his office to find out what had happened. "Sheppy" Shepherd did a masterful job covering for him, saying it could not have been serious because he was about to catch a train for the West Coast. The newspapers failed to pick the story up and it died. Rick was lucky not only to escape publicity but also to avoid legal repercussions. Ironically, the owner of the Indianapolis Speedway, who had also become chairman of the AAA Contest Board, had not deigned to get a driver's license.[43]

Rick reentered the aviation industry in 1928. Soon after he acquired the Indianapolis Speedway, his former patron, Fred Allison, died from a heart attack and the Allison Engineering Company (AEC) went on the block to settle his estate. The property available included the repair shop in which Rick had transformed Maxwell racers into Maxwell Specials in the winter of 1915–16. Since then Allison had gone into making bearings, superchargers, and reduction gears for aircraft engines. Following the bidding closely, Rick got control of AEC by borrowing $90,000 but realized that he lacked the financial resources needed to administer its affairs. Still, he came out ahead by selling the company to the Fisher Brothers Investment Trust, which in turn sold it to GM. Rick got an ample finder's fee from the transaction, helping him retire some of the remaining debt hanging over from the failure of the Rickenbacker Motor Company. He also enjoyed the satisfaction of nudging General Motors, which had acquired the Dayton Wright Airplane Company in 1919, deeper into aeronautics.[44]

GM's willingness to take control of Allison showed the aviation boom was whetting Sloan's appetite. As the 1929 model year opened, automobile sales continued to climb at a record pace. By year's end Americans had bought a record 4,445,178 cars. Sales might have mounted higher but for the October stock market crash, which dampened demand.[45]

But Rick had long since lost interest in such things. After he sold the Allison works to GM, he prodded the colossus into a transaction that made it for the first time a major force in aeronautics. On 17 May 1929, after a spirited battle on Wall Street, GM bought a 40 percent interest in the Fokker Aircraft Corporation of America (FACA), the world's largest producer of commercial and military aircraft. Soon afterward, Charles E. Wilson, who had taken charge of GM's aviation program, invited Rick to become FACA's vice president for sales. Jumping at the opportunity, he sold the Grosse Pointe home, moved Adelaide and the boys to New York City, and assumed his new post on 1 July, thrilled to have escaped from the automotive wilderness. At last he was back where he belonged.[46]

Joining FACA brought Rick into a business relationship with Tony Fokker, the aircraft designer against whose D-VII fighter plane he had contended on the western front. They had much in common: stubborn dispositions, a consuming interest in aviation, entrepreneurial instincts, and a strong problem-solving orientation. Rick had Swiss ancestry and Fokker was Dutch, but they shared Teutonic roots, Germanic but not German. Rick had been friends with Fokker since 1922 and was an ideal intermediary when GM rescued FACA from financial straits in 1929. It was only logical for him to join the executive team that took control of FACA after the bailout.

Fokker, born in the Netherlands East Indies, did not give up his Dutch citizenship when he became a designer and builder of military aircraft for Germany during the war. With the connivance of the new government that came into power after the armistice, which had no immediate prospect of rebuilding an air force and realized that Fokker could be more useful outside the country, he smuggled six trainloads of equipment from Schwerin to Amsterdam and reopened his business. He built civilian and military planes for the Dutch Air Corps and Royal Dutch Airlines (KLM), which began operations in 1919, but being based in a small country with limited markets made it imperative for him to get into the export trade. The American Air Service acquired a Fokker F.IV, a single-engine plane that set a transatlantic speed record in 1923. Other Fokker aircraft wound up at a secret base in the Soviet Union where Germany was rebuilding an air force in violation of the Treaty of Versailles. Bringing out a proliferation of designs, Fokker rejected the all-metal concept pioneered by Hugo Junkers and Claude Dornier, clinging to wooden structural members and fabric-covered fuselages. He sold most of his output to military customers but also became a strong presence in commercial aviation.[47]

In May 1922 Fokker visited America to test the waters for manufacturing aircraft there. After delivering two torpedo planes to the U.S. Navy, he decided he wanted to enjoy the Indy 500. Hotels in Indianapolis were jammed, tickets were scarce, and a mutual friend asked Rick to help. He had never met Fokker and knew he was unpopular in America because of the role his planes had played in the war, but cooperated because he was curious to meet the "aeronautical genius against whose planes I had fought." Rooming with Fokker for three days led to an unexpected friendship. "Few men have had the privilege in so short a period of time," Rick said, "of hating and appreciating one another through imaginary as well as actual contact."[48]

Fokker could see that the same circumstances that had led Rick into the automobile industry made it premature to attempt manufacturing aircraft in the United States, and he went home but with plans to return if the situation improved. By 1925, when the Kelly Act opened airmail routes to private enterprise, he knew the time was ripe. Opening a sales agency in New York City, he leased a vacant factory at Teterboro, New Jersey, where he built a passenger plane, the Fokker F.VIIa-3m. Typical of Fokker's composite construction methods, it had a fuselage of duralumin tubing covered with fabric, a high wooden wing, and three 200-horsepower Wright Whirlwind radial engines. Fokker entered it in the first of a series of "reliability tours" sponsored by the Ford Motor Company, in which judges, including Rick, rated it the best of sixteen aircraft.[49]

Edsel Ford bought the plane, named it the "Josephine Ford" after one of his daughters, and commissioned Richard E. Byrd, already gaining a reputation as an explorer, to fly it to the North Pole with Fokker's name in giant letters. After Byrd returned, the aircraft flew all over the country, bringing Fokker the recognition he coveted. In September 1925 Fokker bought a factory near the Teterboro Airport at Hasbrouck Heights, New Jersey, and established the Fokker Aircraft Corporation (FAC). The performance of his planes in long-distance flights attracted orders from Western Air Express (WAE), which had established a route between Los Angeles and San Francisco under a grant from the Guggenheim Foundation, and also from Pan American, stemming from a favor Fokker had done for Trippe by accompanying him to Cuba on the flight in which Trippe got a lock on landing rights from Machado. Among Fokker's chief competition, Boeing's twelve-seat Model 80 biplane attracted few buyers; however, the Ford Trimotor, a rugged high-wing passenger monoplane that looked a lot like one of his planes but was made entirely of metal, won widespread popularity. Fokker and Ford soon became the "two main pillars of civil aviation in the United States."[50] Rick watched these developments with great interest.

Becoming an American citizen, Fokker reorganized his company as the Fokker Aircraft Corporation of America and added new plants at Passaic, New Jersey, and Glendale, West Virginia. In 1928 one of his planes, the three-engine "Southern Cross," made a 7,000-mile flight from North America to Australia. In 1929 the army set a duration record of 150 hours with a Fokker C-2A, and WAE bought a huge new Fokker F.32, with seats for thirty-two passengers. As Rick was aware, however, FACA, now capitalized at $1 million and employing more than 900 workers, was expanding too rapidly and running short of capital to fill its orders. Ford had much greater resources and a wave of mergers was producing giant holding companies including Curtiss-Wright, Detroit Aircraft, and United Aircraft and Transport, with which FACA could not compete. A bidding war on Wall Street portended a hostile takeover. General Motors, recognizing that automobile markets were becoming saturated and eager to diversify, was a logical white knight. Prompted by Rick, working with GM executive Charles E. Wilson, it offered to buy 400,000 shares in FACA at less than the going market price, but the prospect of securing $5 million in badly needed cash was too great for the company's directors to resist. Fokker, who had little to do with the deal, received a titular post, chief engineer, with no real power.

GM's financial analysts soon realized FACA was in even worse shape than they had thought. Fokker had skimped on research and development to skim profits from sales and his planes were increasingly outmoded. Tightening its grip on FACA by acquiring additional stock, GM made it a subsidiary of a new entity, General Aviation Corporation, thereby consolidating its increasing holdings in aeronautics. Amid these developments, GM rewarded Rick for his role in its diversification by giving him a managerial post he eagerly accepted. Soon after joining FACA, Rick pushed GM even further in the new direction it had taken. After acquiring the Pioneer Instrument Company, which became better known as Bendix Aviation Corporation, he sold it to GM. He kept the details of the transaction secret, but whatever he did saved him taxes while yielding a commission with which he retired his remaining debts from the failure of the Rickenbacker Motor Company. In a remarkably short time he had figured significantly in the emergence of GM as a major force in American aviation.[51]

Finally solvent and liberated from the automotive industry, Rick was in a buoyant mood. The satisfaction he took from being back in aviation was evident in a photograph showing him posing with a group of executives and directors standing under the nose of FACA's most impressive product, the four-engine F-32. Wearing his trademark, a straw hat, he stood next to renowned Antarctic explorer Hubert Wilkins, who had been associated with Fokker in the "Southern Cross" expedition. Rick's sense of satisfaction pervaded an article he wrote for a trade journal. "When one compares the giant Fokker transports of today with the war-time Fokkers we boys of the A.E.F. fought against," he stated, "one hesitates to prophesy in any detail as to what the airplane of the future will be." It was clear to him, however, that the future would be extremely bright and that the adage "the sky's the limit" was an understatement. "Who knows what the 'sky' is in aviation?" he chirped. "Even with minor improvements in airplanes the altitude records are being broken from month to month for various classes of planes and with these new records the field of usefulness of the planes concerned is being constantly

extended." Variable pitch propellers, monocoque fuselages, new aluminum alloys, and advanced propulsion systems would permit aircraft to
fly at extremely high altitudes. "Designers have already made important
steps in building wings that can be varied in camber so as to alter effective flying speeds," he declared, emphasizing for safety's sake that the
top cruising speed of the F-32 was "three times its landing speed."[52]

Rick was writing before the stock market crashed in October 1929.
During the ensuing winter, too happy to be unduly troubled by the debacle, he flew 12,000 miles and "made stops at all the important market
centers of the nation." Speaking in March at a banquet, he scoffed at
"idle gossip" that recovery from the panic sweeping the country would
be slow and warned that pessimistic talk could delay the return of pros-
perity. The next few months, he said, would see "a race between sunshine and conversation."[53]

The McNary-Watres Act, passed in April 1930, heartened him because
its aim of inducing airmail contractors to buy bigger planes capable of
carrying larger numbers of passengers seemed to guarantee expanded
markets for the giant Fokker F-32.[54] Believing the law portended the
end of reliance on governmental subsidies, Rick wrote another article,
"We Can Go Forward without a Nurse," predicting the statute would put
airlines on a "sound economic basis." The F-32, he stated, would come
into its own in the new era not only because of its large capacity for
passengers but also because its massive size and accoutrements would
enhance its appeal to the traveling public. An F-32 displayed at a recent
air show in St. Louis was a case in point, "painted outside in a brilliant
and thrilling design in black and yellow and upholstered within in har-
monizing tones in silk and damask."

He called the F-32 an aerial Pullman car well suited to compete with
the railroad for long-distance transport. Capable of cruising at 125
miles per hour and having a seven-hour range, it could be "furnished
with comfortable sleeping quarters for sixteen passengers, including
dressing and toilet facilities." A passage about night flight, in which he
referred to the "soporific effect" of high altitudes, contrasted "the dust,
heat, grime, and swaying motion of the railroad" with the comfort of
basking peacefully in "the full sized three-quarter beds" of the F-32. As
a bonus, the giant airliner could achieve costs comparable with those of
railroads. "Essentially there is no reason why the cost of transportation
by air should be higher than by rail," he claimed. "There are no right-
of-way and maintenance-of-way charges. The mechanism of an airplane

is after all a lighter, even a simpler, contrivance than a Pullman car and locomotive."

Illustrations he chose for the article showed the luxurious accommodations offered by the F-32, including a table tastefully set for dinner, an easy chair, and draperies. The cabin of an F-32 flown by Western Air Express had padded chairs, a kitchenette, dressing rooms, couches for lounging, and cozy bunks. Rick ended by stressing the need to provide more frequent schedules so that a prospective passenger could "journey at a number of times to suit his convenience." By rewarding airmail contractors for the amount of space they provided, the McNary-Watres Act would "enable operators to venture on these new runs."[55]

The ebullient tone of Rick's article contrasted with concern among FACA's new owners that the F-32 was a defective product. One of the giant planes, which had made its inaugural flight from the Teterboro airfield on 13 September 1929, had crashed two months later, bursting into flames after hitting some houses. Instead of being the airliner of the future, the F-32 seemed more and more like a dinosaur as the economic downturn went on and on. Even a cut-rate price tag of $110,000 made it a risky investment for airlines facing what now loomed as a major depression. Its four tandem engines, two tractor type and two pushers, created excessive drag and made a terrible racket that could be alleviated only by cutting back on power. As Rick already knew, the engines had a nasty tendency to blow off their cylinder heads. If this situation occurred in one of the tractor-type engines mounted on the front of a wing, the cylinder head could hit the rear engine's propeller, which could hurl it anywhere, with potentially disastrous results. The rear engines with the pusher propellers were prone to overheat, and pilots also had a hard time keeping the plane in trim.[56]

In May 1930, the same month in which Rickenbacker hailed the F-32 as the airliner that would lead to a new era, higher management told him to cut prices drastically on all FACA products. The Standard Universal and Super Universal, each with seven seats, came down from $15,000 and $21,800 to $11,000 and $17,500. The nine-seat F-14A Mailplane, which had sold for $26,500, could now be had for $22,500, and the eight-seat F-11A Flyingboat, previously priced at $40,000, for $32,500. The F-10A Trimotor, FACA's most popular aircraft, which had cost $67,500, now sold for $54,500.[57]

Amid the gathering gloom, Rick received extremely welcome news. After an uphill battle by his stalwart supporter, Congressman Clancy, the War Department announced on 14 July 1930 that Rick would, at long last, receive the Medal of Honor. Clancy had adroitly overcome objections by Prohibitionists, who knew about Rick's drinking habits, but other opponents were harder to convince. The General Staff had been offended by Rick's outspoken defense of Mitchell when he was court-martialed in 1925, calling the outcome a "crime against posterity." Hiram Bingham, a senator from Connecticut with much influence in aviation-related matters, charged that Rick was unworthy of the nation's highest military decoration because he had prostituted the 94th Pursuit Squadron's Hat-in-the-Wing emblem for personal gain by putting it on his cars. Other detractors claimed that the "voluntary patrol" in which Eddie had single-handedly taken on seven enemy planes after taking command of the 94th had been "only what might have been expected of him in his regular work." Clancy had won approval of two affirmative resolutions in the House of Representatives, only to be blocked in the Senate. Reacting vigorously, Rick's former comrades-in-arms rallied to his cause, as did Lindbergh and Byrd. The American Legion joined the battle, as did Michigan's governor, Fred W. Green. Such pressures finally persuaded the Senate to relent after Bingham and other critics grudgingly withdrew their opposition, and the War Decorations Board ratified a joint resolution of the Senate and House of Representatives to confer the country's highest honor on Rick.[58]

Congratulations swamped Rick's office after the announcement, saying the award was long overdue. Hartney said it had always been "no small chagrin and discouragement to me to have had your great efforts go unrecognized." "With all due respect to those who have flown from Long Island to Paris," wrote one admirer in a slap at Lindbergh, "that flight is a joyride compared to the flights you made day after day in the face of a wartime enemy." A veteran who had disliked seeing Rick upstaged by the Lone Eagle wrote that "it gives some of your old friends a personal delight to know that Uncle Sam eventually recognizes some of the men who, while they did not fly to Paris, kept a lot of Germans from flying to Paris."

The award ceremony took place at Bolling Field on 6 November 1930. F. Trubee Davison, assistant secretary of war for air and a strong supporter of air power, was master of ceremonies. Major General James E. Fechet, chief of the Army Air Corps, read the citation: "For conspicuous gallantry and intrepidity above and beyond the call of duty in action against the enemy near Billy, France, September 25, 1918. While on a voluntary patrol over the lines, the then Lieutenant Rickenbacker attacked seven enemy planes (five type Fokker protecting two type Halberstadt). Disregarding the odds against him, he dived on them and shot down one of the Fokkers, out of control. He then attacked one of the Halberstadts and sent it down also." President Hoover slipped the ribbon to which the medal was attached over Rick's head, saying, "Although this award is somewhat belated, I hope that your gratification in receiving this Medal of Honor will be as keen as mine is in bestowing it to you. May you wear it during many years of happiness and continued usefulness to your country." In a brief reply, Rick said, "I should be ungrateful if I failed to recognize this great honor as a true tribute to my comrades-in-arms, soldiers and sailors, living and dead. In peace and war they have contributed their share." Rebuking opponents of air power, he said that members of the armed forces "have perpetuated the traditions and high ideals of the United States in the air as they have on the land and the sea." He also modestly included a veiled statement that Luke, whom he did not name, might have become ace of aces had he lived.

Aircraft from three units including the 94th climaxed the festivities by performing aerobatics and maneuvers. Hoover reviewed the aircraft "in mass and line," and Rick shook hands with current officers from his old unit. He beamed for photographers who took pictures of him wearing the decoration he had wanted so long, but there was a sour note. Despite strenuous efforts by Rick and his supporters, Mitchell's enemies had prevented him from being invited to attend, showing the hatred they felt toward him. Hartney, who had recommended Rick for the Medal of Honor late in 1918, was present and congratulated him warmly.[59]

But Rick's post at FACA was increasingly unfulfilling. His efforts got a contract from the army for fourteen twin-engine bomber-reconnaissance aircraft. The coast guard bought five GA-15 flying boats for rescue work, but the transaction resulted in a loss. Meanwhile, sales of commercial aircraft continued to sag despite the steep price cuts he had put into effect. FACA even offered an installment plan similar to those with which GMAC sold automobiles, but to no avail. Rick sold only two F-32s, both to Western Air Express. Universal Aviation Corporation canceled orders for five others it had contracted to buy before the Depression hit. Fokker himself acquired one of the big planes as a personal "air yacht." The rest, in the words of his biographer, Marc Dierikx, became "white elephants that had trampled on the house of their creator." One suffered the indignity of becoming a gas station.[60]

Rick fought disillusionment in his usual way by hitting the bottle. Unlike the cover-up of his collision with a garbage truck in Detroit, however, the publicity was nationwide. One night in September 1930, after imbibing too heavily, he returned to his suburban residence at Bronxville and went to bed. While sleeping off the effects of the bender, he got up, walked through a pair of French doors onto a second-floor balcony, and fell over the railing onto the ground twenty feet below, landing on his back with such force that the impact knocked him out. Adelaide and a maid were leaning over him when he came to and managed to get him back to bed. Feeling "sore and stiff" at breakfast the next morning, he ignored the pain and kept an appointment with friends at the Winged Foot Golf Club, but by the time he got to the fourteenth hole he felt as if "a million needles" were going "up and down my back and hips." Acting like a Gimper, he finished the course, "had a couple of highballs, and came on home" but felt the same sensations that evening when he and Adelaide had dinner with one of his golfing buddies. After he went to bed, the pain became so severe he "decided to be x-rayed to see if there was really anything wrong with me." As he later recalled, "there were three little prongs off my spine that were floating around in my back, separated probably an eighth of an inch. They had cracked off. They wound me up in tape from my hips to my armpits, and I went about my business, and that was that."

When he came to work the next day heavily taped up, there was no way to hide what had happened, as Shepherd had done after his accident in Detroit. Newspapers picked up the story from coast to coast and published it for everybody to see. Rick said he had merely been sleep-walking and that somnambulism had been a problem throughout his life, but his excuse did not satisfy skeptics who guessed what had happened. Will Rogers wrote a memorable quip: "Captain Eddie shouldn't go to bed without wearing a parachute."[61]

Disaster hit FACA on 31 March 1931 when one of TWA's Fokker F-10A Trimotors crashed near Bazaar, Kansas, en route to Los Angeles. Looking skyward as a roaring of engines became increasingly deafening, witnesses saw the airliner come out of a low cloud formation and bank as if preparing to land. "Then they heard a loud bang as a section of the Fokker's wing separated from the fuselage and fell to earth," said one account. "The airliner's nose dropped, and the plane dove 1,500 feet into the ground, crashing into a cow pasture." Onlookers watched in horror as five passengers fell out of the plane and plunged to their death. The impact was so great that engine parts were found buried two feet under the ground and there were no survivors. Among the victims, his body "terribly mangled," was Knute Rockne, Notre Dame's famed football coach, who had been flying to Los Angeles for speaking engagements and an advisory role in making a film. But for his presence on the aircraft, the tragedy might not have riveted Americans, who responded with "a huge outpouring of grief."[62]

Even before the crash, the wing structure of the F-10 had caused speculation about design flaws. Tests at Wright Field had raised questions about its wooden spars and internal bracing, resulting in proposals to adjust its ailerons to "relieve tail heaviness." The navy had twice rejected the plane because of its alleged instability. Airline pilots had noted that its wingtips fluttered in turbulent weather and that the engines backfired when throttled down to overcome the vibrations. After a bungled investigation of what became known as the "Knute Rockne Accident," the Commerce Department's Aeronautical Branch offered a series of specious explanations. Charging that improper gluing of wooden components in a wing had caused it to separate under compressive stress, the bureau ordered that thirty-five F-10s made by supposedly inexperienced workers at the West Virginia plant be grounded until unspecified "maintenance problems" were resolved. A thorough inspection of the wing structure, however, was inconvenient because a wing had to be torn apart to determine where it might fail. Most of the F-10s ultimately returned to service, but their reputation had been irreparably hurt. Objecting bitterly to the way the investigation had been conducted, Fokker resigned from FACA under terms that permitted him to retain his patents and use his name on aircraft built in the Netherlands. Returning home, he resumed his career in Amsterdam.[63]

An increasing prejudice against wood as an antiquated and inferior material for use in aircraft construction compounded the bad reputation of Fokker's designs. All-metal construction seemed safer and more modern than his composite models.[64] GM recognized the need to adopt the new technology, but Herbert V. Thaden, president of a metal aircraft company GM had acquired in 1929, did not provide the needed leadership after becoming chief engineer in July 1931. Meanwhile, FACA groaned under an inventory of F-10As for which Rick could find no buyers. As losses mounted, GM decided to close its three existing Fokker plants, consolidate operations under a new name, General Aviation Manufacturing Corporation, and transfer workers and staff members to a former Curtiss-Caproni facility at Dundalk, Maryland, a suburb of Baltimore. Executives in Detroit initially told Rick that the sales office would stay in the General Motors building in New York City, but finally told him he would have to join the exodus to Maryland. Too fond of the nation's largest metropolis to consider living on the shore of Chesapeake Bay, he refused. On 31 March 1932, exactly a year after the tragedy in Kansas, he resigned, hating to leave GM but feeling he had no alternative.[65]

Another venture in aviation had ended badly and his future was uncertain. But he believed New York City was too vital a nerve center of aeronautics for a charismatic figure with his credentials to remain idle for long. And he was right.

Chapter 13

— ☆ —

Comeback

No sooner had Rick left one hornet's nest than he stepped into another. On 29 April 1932 he became vice president for governmental relations of American Airways, which had a hodgepodge of routes and a motley fleet of aircraft. It was losing money at an alarming rate. Under the McNary-Watres Act, Postmaster General Brown had awarded it a southern transcontinental airmail route and another potentially lucrative artery from Chicago to New Orleans via St. Louis, hoping to wean it from depending on mail revenue by making it better able to attract passengers. Despite this largesse, American lost nearly $8 million in the next two years.

American had a parent company, the Aviation Corporation (AVCO), doing business as American Air Transport (AAT) and consisting of thirteen previously separate entities. Hit hard by the Depression, AAT was in sad shape. W. Averell Harriman and Robert H. Lehman, the chief stockholders, tried to get General Motors to take control, but Sloan refused. In March 1932, after a crash in California, Harriman and Lehman sacked chief executive Frederick G. Coburn and replaced him with Lamotte T. Cohu, head of Air Investors, an underwriting group worried about how things were going.[1]

By the time Rick came aboard, AAT had avoided a hostile takeover by Errett L. Cord, a wily entrepreneur he knew well because he had raced against him before the war. Harriman and Lehman made a strategic mistake in the process by agreeing to buy out two airlines owned by Cord, who now joined AAT's board of directors and became an even more serious menace, like the proverbial camel sticking his nose under a tent. Getting an inside look at the firm's inept management merely emboldened Cord, who continued scheming to take control. Seeing what was coming, Hainer Hinshaw, a veteran lobbyist, resigned as public relations representative in Washington, thereby creating the opening Rick filled and giving him Hinshaw's former place in the corporate boardroom. Rick had probably known about Hinshaw's impending departure before he left FACA and been looking forward to succeeding him, thinking he could placate his old friend Cord and keep things from falling apart.[2]

Ostensibly aligning himself with Harriman, Lehman, and Cohu, he played his own game. He felt no animosity toward Cord, who kept buying as much company stock as possible and made a pest of himself at board meetings. Some of his ideas were constructive, as in prodding the directors to promote Cyrus Rowlett ("C. R.") Smith, a young Texan who ran one of AAT's numerous subsidiaries, to president. Cohu resisted but made Smith vice president, after which finances began to improve.[3]

AAT had a brief moment of glory soon after Rick came on board. On 1 July 1932 the Democratic national convention nominated Franklin D. Roosevelt, New York's reform-minded governor, for president. Abandoning the time-honored practice of waiting coyly to be officially notified, Roosevelt decided to break tradition by flying to Chicago to accept the party's choice in person. Knowing a public relations bonanza when it saw one, AAT ferried a Ford Trimotor to Albany, which was normally served by smaller Curtiss Pilgrims. At 7:30 a.m. on 2 July, Roosevelt, his wife Eleanor, four of their children, and a party of advisers and speechwriters took off for the Windy City. After refueling in Buffalo and Cleveland, the plane encountered turbulence and arrived in Chicago three hours late. Cheering throngs lined the route to the convention hall as FDR showed his ability to do multiple tasks at once, doffing his hat and beaming at the crowd while reading and rejecting most of a speech his advisers had prepared on the plane. He began his address by joking about having "no control over the winds of Heaven."[4]

Affairs at AAT were no less turbulent than the weather through which FDR had flown. Amid bitter strife with Cord, Harriman resigned as chairman of the board to devote more time to the Union Pacific Railroad, which had risen to greatness under his father but had not paid dividends since the start of the Depression. Harriman's absence from board meetings weakened Cohu's ability to withstand Cord's increasing attacks.

Rick added fuel to the fire by urging the airline to acquire Eastern Air Transport, whose routes ran north and south, and integrate it with AAT's mainly east-west system, thereby eliminating wasteful seasonal variations in traffic patterns and increasing revenue. In November 1932, on Rick's motion, a majority of the board voted to acquire North American Aviation (NAA), a vast holding company now in receivership, whose assets included Eastern, TWA, the Curtiss-Wright Corporation, and a substantial block of shares in the Douglas Aircraft Company. Cohu and other board members who were allied with Harriman and Lehman supported the plan not only because of the benefits Rick pointed out but, even more significant, because an influx of new stockholders would dilute the increasing shareholdings of Cord, who had by now acquired 25 percent of AAT's outstanding stock. Vigorously opposing the plan, Cord began campaigning for proxy votes to defeat it and secured a court order to stay its implementation pending a special stockholders' meeting. Rick tried to work out a compromise that would satisfy both sides and keep his plan alive, but Cord refused to be deterred and spearheaded a reorganization of the board, reversing the decision to acquire NAA. Cohu thereupon resigned and Richard F. Hoyt replaced him to implement Cord's takeover.[5]

Rick also decided to get out because he had been on the losing side. Holding no grudges against him because he valued Rick's friendship and business ability, Cord asked him to stay. Rick agreed to remain temporarily but changed his mind when Cord decided to move AAT's headquarters to Chicago. On 18 February 1933 Rick resigned, leaving without qualms because he had already seen another way to put together an aerial empire including North American. On Christmas Day 1932, before Cord's victory was assured but after it seemed inevitable, Rick and Adelaide visited Ernest R. Breech, general assistant treasurer of General Motors, and his wife, Thelma, at their residence in the affluent New York suburb of Larchmont. It was not merely a social call. Breech, a wizard in cost accounting, was a rising star in GM's corporate affairs and also a director of TWA. Before leaving, Rick asked Breech for an appointment the next morning. At the meeting he told Breech that AAT's projected merger with North American was doomed and proposed that GM acquire the bankrupt holding company. Breech liked the idea.

Rick and Breech persuaded Sloan and other GM potentates that acquiring NAA made sense to climax GM's diversification into aviation. Early in 1933, while Cord was cementing his victory, General Motors negotiated with the trustees controlling North American's assets. J. Cheever Cowdin of Bancamerica Blair, who brokered the deal, had reservations about its scope, causing Rick to worry that it might fall through, but Breech agreed to spin off some of North American's properties, making sure, however, to retain Eastern, TWA, and the shares in Douglas. Catching wind of what was happening, Edward A. Deeds, a crafty financier who had close ties with United Air Lines, TWA's chief competitor, threw sand into the gears by acquiring $1.9 million worth of North American stock, but Breech agreed to seek reimbursement of that amount from GM if Deeds withdrew his objections. Securing the money required approval from the Du Pont Company, which had a controlling interest in GM. Going to Delaware, Breech persuaded Walter F. Carpenter, chairman of GM's finance committee, to approve buying Deeds off. Everything worked out, and GM formally acquired North American on the same day that Rick parted company with Cord, still on amicable terms with him. Breech was eager to become involved in aviation and had himself appointed president of North American. One of his first steps was to appoint Rick vice president for public relations. Once more back under the GM umbrella, Rick returned to the familiar surroundings of the General Motors Building on Broadway.[6]

GM's buyout of North American was an enormous victory for Rick, climaxing his campaign to get GM to diversify into aeronautics and giving a great boost to the airline industry as it struggled to survive the Great Depression. As historian Robert F. van der Linden later stated in an authoritative study, "The entry of GM clearly demonstrated that aviation was finally a serious, full-scale enterprise, capable of producing profits for the investor and operator alike." The takeover, however, aroused an outcry for the Justice Department to investigate GM for infringing the Sherman and Clayton antitrust acts. Owners of small airlines saw the deal as further evidence that Hoover and Brown had delivered commercial aviation into the hands of big business, which was battening on huge governmental subsidies. The chorus of complaints was heard in the White House, now occupied by Franklin D. Roosevelt after his landslide victory in the 1932 election. As Rick settled into his new position, battle lines were already being drawn and the airline industry would soon face the biggest crisis in its history. Nobody would figure more prominently than Rick in the impending fight.[7]

Sweeping changes introduced under the New Deal quickly offended business leaders who had supported FDR's campaign under the mistaken notion that he was fiscally conservative. Especially alienated were members of the Du Pont corporate family that had played major roles in the Democratic Party during the 1920s, when it was out of power. As

Wilsonian progressivism waned after the war, strict constructionist doctrines deeply embedded in the party's Jeffersonian heritage resurfaced. The increasing power of big business made John W. Davis, a prominent corporation lawyer, the Democratic nominee for president in 1924 after a marathon deadlock in balloting at the national convention. Support for the Eighteenth Amendment by Hoover and other Republican leaders changed the party affiliation of "Wets," including family patriarch Pierre S. Du Pont and his right hand man, John J. Raskob, who, like Rickenbacker, regarded Prohibition as a blatant infringement on individual liberty. In the 1928 election Du Pont and Raskob strongly supported Al Smith, a "Wet," in his hapless run for the White House. Raskob resigned his position as a vice president at GM to chair the Democratic National Committee. After Smith lost, Du Pont and Raskob joined him in plans to create the Empire State Building.

FDR had become estranged from much of big business even before his nomination, but Du Pont, Raskob, and senior officials in GM supported him because the platform under which he ran opposed Prohibition and condemned Hoover for increasing federal power to fight the economic downturn. FDR soothed conservative feelings in campaign speeches designed to woo southern Democrats and businessmen. Rick voted for Roosevelt in 1932, thinking he would curtail federal spending and govern with a strict constructionist view of the Constitution. Confronted by the worst economic crisis in the nation's history, however, FDR went far beyond constitutional limits that Rick and the Du Ponts held sacred. They were pleased by the repeal of Prohibition but disappointed by the creation of a powerful Federal Alcohol Control Administration. Pierre S. Du Pont, who had contributed heavily to FDR's campaign, turned against the National Recovery Administration (NRA) after being appointed chairman of the Industrial Advisory Board (IAB) and named to the National Labor Board (NLB). Disturbed by mounting bureaucracy and the spread of federal agencies, Du Pont resigned from the NLB because it did not protect workers from "exploitation," which to him (and Rickenbacker also) meant pressuring workers to join unions. Du Pont, speaking for people like Rick, regarded the NRA as "a conspiracy on the part of the New Dealers to change permanently the traditional balance between federal power, state prerogatives, and private business." His disenchantment, shared throughout the General Motors hierarchy, led to the Liberty League, an ultraconservative coalition financed mostly by Du Pont.[8]

Rick unhesitatingly made common cause with his friends and associates in GM and the Du Pont family, later charging that, soon after taking office, FDR made an about-face toward collectivism.[9] On the other hand, the league and its members, including Rickenbacker, did not want to move precipitously into declaring outspoken enmity against Roosevelt personally, preferring to say that he was ill-advised. Rickenbacker's attitude hardened early in 1934, however, when a special congressional committee headed by Senator Hugo Black of Alabama began inquiring whether Hoover's postmaster general, Walter F. Brown, had committed serious improprieties in awarding airmail contracts under the McNary-Watres Act. Whatever Rickenbacker may have felt about Brown's heavy-handedness, he believed a strong airline industry promoted national defense and there was consequently nothing improper in the exercise of centralized federal power to foster the industry's growth. He also saw that commercial aviation had made great strides in combining passenger and airmail operations under Brown's leadership, flying 200,000 miles and carrying 500,000 passengers per day, pioneering communications innovations including two-way radio, and developing larger, faster, and safer aircraft. He was enraged in February 1934 when FDR, responding to evidence the Black committee had unearthed, canceled existing airmail contracts and ordered the army to fly the mail. He was not alone in his attitude. Lindbergh sent a public letter to FDR charging that the cancellation failed to "discriminate between innocence and guilt" and condemned "the largest portion of our commercial aviation without trial." *Fortune* charged Roosevelt had "kicked askew the underpinnings of a $250 million investment shared by 200,000 stockholders."[10]

Rickenbacker believed that canceling contracts was by itself a grave offense against business ethics, but replacing seasoned airline pilots with military airmen who lacked training in commercial operations was nothing short of criminal. Speaking to reporters in New York City on a foggy morning, he expressed strong forebodings about "what is going to happen to those young Army pilots on a day like this. Either they are going to pile up ships all the way across the continent, or they are not going to be able to fly the mail on schedule."

When three pilots crashed and died on their way to pick up mail for their first day of operations, Rickenbacker, now in California, spoke impulsively about "legalized murder." His words inevitably made headlines and led to a persistent but mistaken impression that he applied them directly to FDR. As quoted on the wire services, he was more carefully nuanced, saying that "legalized murder has just begun and I fear for the future," without holding FDR personally responsible for the tragedies. This distinction was not mere hairsplitting. Like Pierre S. Du Pont and the Liberty League, he was trying to be outspoken but respectful to Roosevelt. On the other hand, reporters ignored the fine line Rickenbacker was trying to draw because it attracted attention to do so. Rickenbacker himself later went along with the story that he had accused FDR of "legalized murder" because he came to hate the president and wanted it to seem that his statements in 1934 were consistent with these feelings.[11]

Rickenbacker had flown to California to prepare for a transcontinental flight that he and TWA's vice president and general manager, Jack Frye, had planned to express the indignation felt by North American and its financial backers about the cancellation of airmail contracts. They also wanted to prove what high operational standards the airline industry had achieved in recent years. The plane they would fly was a revolutionary new airliner, the Douglas DC-1, which epitomized GM's foray into aeronautics. The Douglas Aircraft Company, partly owned by North American, had built the airliner in response to a letter Frye had written to stave off a potentially devastating threat to TWA posed by the introduction of the world's first really modern passenger plane, the Boeing 247, and by the stranglehold on orders that United, Boeing's ally, enjoyed. Unlike the boxy, noisy Ford Trimotor, the industry's principal airliner, which was slowed down by its exterior bracing, corrugated skin, and thick wing, the 247 was streamlined and could cruise at a previously unattainable speed. United's lock on production of 247s made it imperative for Frye, another Breech protégé, to find an aircraft able to compete against them. Although Douglas had previously built mostly military planes, its connections with North American made it the most logical candidate to create the design Frye had in mind.[12]

Douglas and his engineers accepted the challenge, proposing a twin-engine aircraft, the DC (Douglas Commercial)-1. It would have greater speed, power, and carrying capacity than the 247, which had the fatal flaw of being underpowered. Strongly influenced by its pilots, United had chosen to use a Wright Whirlwind engine instead of the Cyclone, a new model that would have increased the 247's size and passenger-carrying capability, limited to ten seats. The 247 also had a main spar running all the way across the wingspan, creating an annoying hump in the floor of the passenger cabin that travelers had to step across.

Douglas's design, however, was opposed by Lindbergh, TWA's technical adviser, who believed a more conventional three-engine plane was needed for safely crossing the rugged terrain between Winslow, Arizona, and Albuquerque, New Mexico. For this reason, General Aviation, the GM subsidiary that had supplanted FACA, worked on a trimotor design until the debate was resolved. Douglas settled the question by showing that a single Cyclone engine with a variable-pitch propeller could carry its new airliner across the mountains even if the other one failed. As president of North American, Breech aborted the General Aviation project, in which GM had invested $800,000.[13]

Rickenbacker, as a vice president in North American, outranked Frye, the operational head of its subsidiary, TWA. He was also a highly visible national hero, whereas Frye was modest and shrank from the limelight. Breech therefore put Rickenbacker officially in command of the effort to set a transcontinental record, even going to the extent of ignoring his lack of a pilot's license. Pilots from TWA would get on and off the plane during fuel stops, making it unnecessary for Rick to take the controls. Critics would later complain that Rick received credit for setting the speed record, but his status as senior officer was based on sound reasoning, given the publicity motives underlying the flight.

Rickenbacker gave a radio address on the evening before takeoff. Honoring the wishes of the Du Ponts and higher-ups in General Motors not to attack FDR personally, he toned down remarks about the airmail cancellation while making it clear he strongly disapproved of it. As he and Frye breakfasted at Glendale the following day, 18 February, reports of a storm gathering in the East prompted suggestions that he call the venture off. A postponement would have killed it because the army was about to take over the airmail service. After checking with TWA's weather forecasters, Rickenbacker demonstrated his authority by deciding the DC-1 would proceed as planned.

Later that day, at 8:56 a.m. (PST), a crowd of 15,000 people saw Rickenbacker and Frye take off from Glendale, carrying five news reporters and Paul Richter, TWA's western division superintendent. The DC-1, named *The City of Los Angeles*, was bound for an initial refueling stop at Albuquerque. Following a radio beam, they used a Sperry automatic pilot almost all the way across the continent, stopping only about eight minutes in New Mexico to top off their tanks for the second stage of the trip. As they flew over the Rockies and the Great Plains, passengers slept in the soundproofed cabin, undisturbed by shifting cross-currents that the plane, still on automatic pilot, handled with ease. There was only a meager tailwind, however, and Rickenbacker decided it would be prudent, especially with a storm brewing ahead, to make a fuel stop at Kansas City instead of proceeding to Chicago. After the landing, which took place at 6:02 a.m. (CST), Richter got off and Larry Fritz, superintendent of TWA's eastern division, came aboard. Thus far the flight had covered 1,574 miles in less than seven hours. Servicing the ship and transferring personnel at Kansas City required only fourteen minutes.

The DC-1 reached the western edge of the predicted storm as it crossed Illinois and the weather got steadily worse as it approached the next refueling stop, Columbus, Ohio. But the plane was up to the challenge. Ordering a change in the pitch of the propellers and relying on the supercharged engines, Rickenbacker got the aircraft back to 14,000 feet, putting it above a blizzard howling under its wings. Snow covered the apron as the plane sat in front of the main terminal at Columbus, 660 miles east of Kansas City. After refueling and spending an extra ten minutes taking on hot meals, they began the final leg to Newark, now less than 500 miles away. The storm intensified after they left Columbus, paralyzing traffic on the roads below. "It couldn't stop our ship," Rickenbacker reported after they reached their goal. "We set the automatic pilot . . . and started climbing on the radio beam. Up, up we went until it seemed that storm simply had no top anywhere." After they reached sunlight at 18,500 feet, Rickenbacker ordered oxygen tanks brought out to give everyone an "occasional shot." During their descent they encountered the hostile elements, but, just as meteorologists had predicted, they reached the eastern edge of the storm about 50 miles from their destination and had clear sailing the rest of the way. They landed at Newark less than a minute after 1:00 p.m. (EST), setting a record of 13 hours, 4 minutes, and 20 seconds, shattering the previous record of 18 hours, 13 minutes. Because the rated speed of their plane was 180 miles per hour, the flight might have taken 15 hours, but they had averaged 210.12, at times reaching 255 miles per hour.[14]

Headlines across the country hailed the feat, and Rickenbacker received a deluge of congratulations.[15] Speaking on behalf of the airline industry, he said, "We hoped to be able to bring forcibly to the attention of the nation, and of the world, what we had accomplished through years of endeavor and the unbounded confidence of the men in our organization." He called the DC-1 a "pip" and predicted that the time currently allotted for crossing the continent would soon be cut in half.[16]

He freely admitted he did not have a pilot's license and said he had handled the controls for only a few minutes from the copilot's seat. Indeed, he spent the last leg writing a speech to deliver at Newark. Frye and other pilots flew the ship when it was not on automatic pilot. Later criticisms that Rickenbacker was unjustified in accepting plaudits for the feat were beside the point.[17] He was in command at all times, following a script designed to maximize publicity, which Frye could not have generated.

Rickenbacker had increased his stature by bringing General Motors into aviation and leading a flight resulting in a new transcontinental speed record. Meanwhile, FDR had made a serious mistake, the first in his administration. One of the worst winters on record killed ten army pilots and seriously injured others. Retreating in the face of public outrage, FDR returned airmail routes to private carriers, which alone had the capital and experience to fly them.[18] Nevertheless, a new, punitive airmail act aroused indignation among businessmen. Testifying at hearings led by Senator McKellar of Tennessee, Rickenbacker lashed out against the impending legislation but chose his words carefully and did not attack FDR personally, praising him for "wonderful accomplishments" and blaming advisers who were making "slanderous charges incapable of proof and seriously damaging the airline industry." His words carried no weight and did not prevent reporters from saying he had accused FDR of treason.[19] The Air Mail Act of 1934 slashed mail pay and denied route awards to carriers guilty of participating in so-called spoils conferences held by Brown in 1930. It also proscribed executives who had supposedly used their powerful positions in mail-carrying enterprises to collude with Brown. Postmaster General Farley, knowing the ban on airlines could not be implemented because only existing companies had the aircraft, facilities, pilots, and expertise needed to carry mail effectively and efficiently, conducted a charade in which established carriers posed as new entities by changing their identities. Eastern Air Transport became Eastern Air Lines (EAL) and TWA added "Inc." to its corporate name. Executives present at Brown's "spoils conferences," however, were treated more rigidly, ending several outstanding careers.[20]

The new law also banned airframe and engine manufacturers from holding stock in companies that flew airmail. Nevertheless, the wording was too vague to prevent General Motors from retaining Eastern Air Lines, which continued to carry mail under GM's umbrella despite its continuing control of subsidiaries that made airplanes and power plants. By disposing of its Douglas stock, GM could maintain that it made only military planes, obviating conflict of interest in commercial aviation. Selling TWA to protect Eastern from potential antitrust prosecution, Breech won back EAL's previous airmail contracts, albeit at much lower rates. On the other hand, Richard Robbins, previously head of TWA, and Thomas B. Doe, Eastern's former chief executive, had to resign their posts. Breech, who appointed Frye president of TWA before selling it, personally assumed control at Eastern. Terminating the existence of General Aviation, he closed its manufacturing plants, moved its equipment and staff to Los Angeles, and made James H. ("Dutch") Kindelberger, its former general manager, president of a new GM subsidiary, North American, Inc., confined to military aircraft manufacture. Allison, run by GM, still made engines, and Pioneer Equipment, renamed Bendix Aviation, continued to produce instruments as a GM subsidiary. The government conveniently looked the other way.[21]

"What a crazy quilt of policy, with each new patch more ludicrous than the last," Rickenbacker, who became Eastern's vice president for public affairs, wrote William Randolph Hearst. "If this sorry mess is an indication of what may be expected from State socialistic management of public service enterprises, there can be no better illustration of the superior advantage of the American system of individualism."[22] On 8 November 1934 he won a triumph even more impressive than his recent record-setting flight across the continent in the DC-1 by overseeing delivery of a DC-2 (an improved version of the DC-1) from Burbank, California, to Newark International Airport in twelve hours, three minutes, and fifty seconds, cutting more than an hour off the mark he had set in February. On 13 November he commanded the same DC-2, now called the "Florida Flyer," in an attempt to set another record by flying from Newark to Miami and returning the same day before nightfall. Headwinds put the plane behind schedule, and it did not reach Miami until 2:45 p.m., delaying its return to Newark until 11:27 p.m. Nevertheless, the plane had set a record by flying a Newark-Miami-Newark round trip within a single day. Rick took the "defeat" cheerfully, hailing "a triumph over obstacles and another indication of what aviation can do."[23]

The flight led to an exciting opportunity for Rickenbacker. Breech regarded it as a convincing demonstration of his hard work and organizing ability. Soon afterward, Breech became chief financial officer to John Lee Pratt, a venerable figure second only to Sloan in GM's corporate pecking order. The promotion made it impossible for Breech to run Eastern's day-to-day affairs, so he became chairman of the board and appointed Rickenbacker general manager. Sloan wondered whether Rick was up to the job, but Breech, who would stay in Manhattan at the General Motors Building, promised to keep an eye on him.[24]

At last Rick was in charge of an aviation enterprise. He was thrilled by the chance Breech had given him, similar to the challenge presented in 1918 when the brass at Chaumont resisted Hartney's intention to assign him command of a unit. He had transformed the downtrodden, dispirited 94th Pursuit Squadron into the most honored unit in the Air Service. Now he intended to make Eastern America's best airline.

Chapter 14

— ☆ —

Apex

Taking charge of Eastern's day-to-day operations on 1 January 1935 marked Rickenbacker's coming of age as an entrepreneur. Having already made a great contribution to the aviation business by prodding General Motors to enter the industry on a large scale, he would transform Eastern within five years into the most profitable carrier in the American sky. If he retained rough edges traceable to his climb from poverty to the pinnacle of managerial excellence, he was not alone; the same could be said of many unquestioned masters of enterprise. A crustiness that impressed many of his critics as arrogance shielded the sensitive inner core of an abused child who had reached success in a fiercely competitive culture, one in which men were expected to fight their way to the top without giving any quarter to rivals. As he had shown in leading the 94th Pursuit Squadron and would once more demonstrate to subordinates who winced under his abrasive tongue, he was a warrior with a compassionate heart. Ethnic, gender, and racial biases abounding in his makeup, however unfortunate they may have been, could be traced to the social context within which he had grown up. Despite his lack of formal educational credentials, his intelligence and ability shone through his limitations, and his courage and perseverance were undeniable. The status Eastern won under his leadership could not have materialized under a lesser man.

The enterprise he inherited was born in 1925. Aided by aircraft designer Agnew Larsen, Harold F. Pitcairn, a protégé of Glenn Curtiss, developed a small but sturdy plane, the Mailwing, which helped him win an airmail contract in February 1928 for a route between New York City and Atlanta. Later that year he extended his operations to Miami by acquiring the dormant route vacated by Florida Airways.[1] He became captivated, however, by the autogiro, an aerial hybrid with a rotor for lift and a propeller for thrust. In January 1930, after securing an American license to manufacture autogiros from Spanish inventor Juan de la Cierva, he sold Pitcairn Aviation to a Wall Street mogul, Clement M. Keys, who renamed it Eastern Air Transport (EAT) and grafted it into his giant holding company, North American Aviation Corporation (NAAC). Postmaster General Brown made EAT a major component of the route system he created under the McNary-Watres Act of 1930.

Operating up and down the Atlantic Coast gave Eastern outstanding prospects for future growth. It began carrying passengers in August 1930, using Curtiss Condors for flights between New York and Washington and smaller Curtiss Kingbirds from there to Miami. Mailwings continued to carry letters and packages. In 1931 Eastern acquired New York Airways, giving it access to Atlantic City. By the end of the year it had 2,876 miles of routes linking New York, Philadelphia, Baltimore, Washington, Richmond, Norfolk, Raleigh, Charleston, Savannah, Atlanta, Jacksonville, Daytona Beach, Orlando, Tampa, St. Petersburg, and Miami. By 1932 all of its domestic routes had beacon lights for night flying, radio equipment for aerial navigation, and Teletype systems for weather reporting. Ties with NAAC's Sperry Gyroscope subsidiary facilitated instrument flying.

After Keys went bankrupt and GM acquired NAAC, Breech expanded EAT's fleet by adding updated Condors with extended range, improved navigational equipment, roomier fuselages, leather seats, and lavatories with hot and cold running water.[2] Unfortunately, because Boeing's 247 appeared at the same time, the portly twin-engine biplane, with a fabric-covered fuselage, water-cooled engines, and modest cruising speed, was already obsolete when it debuted in January 1933. Nevertheless, it helped EAT transport 63,504 passengers that year, all in multiengine planes, significantly exceeding 27,791 in 1932. Acquiring the Ludington Line, a Philadelphia-based enterprise with no airmail contract, further strengthened EAT in its first year with GM.

Cancellation of airmail contracts in 1934 forced Breech to make severe cutbacks. Limiting regular passenger service to seven cities, he cut the payroll to less than 300 employees. After privately owned carriers regained contracts, Breech recaptured most of EAT's former routes by submitting low bids under the punitive Black-McKellar Act. Eastern Air Lines (EAL), as it was now called, flew only 11,660 miles of scheduled passenger service, and mail payments shrank to unprofitable levels. It lost valuable connections when Breech sold TWA to his friend John

Hertz, founder of the Yellow Cab Company, and jettisoned GM's former holdings in Douglas Aircraft.

The forced retirement of Thomas B. Doe, a holdover from the Keys era, was a blessing in disguise, helping Breech prune dead wood from EAL's management.[3] He increased efficiency and lowered costs by improving maintenance and weather forecasting and reorganized the airline into three divisions—New York–Miami, Chicago–Miami, and New York–New Orleans. He began replacing outmoded airliners with DC-2s, updated DC-1s whose air-cooled Wright Cyclone engines permitted accommodating fourteen passengers, along with 1,740 pounds of baggage, mail, and freight. The first of the new planes arrived in October 1934. Its maximum speed, 196 miles an hour, made possible Rickenbacker's second record-setting transcontinental flight and the round trip between New York and Miami in a single day.

Considering everything Breech had done, Rickenbacker's assertion that Eastern "was in bad shape and getting worse" when he became general manager was much too harsh. His claim that the carrier had lost $1.5 million in 1934 was probably exaggerated. More dependable evidence indicates that the actual deficit was $709,700.35. Whatever it was, the shortfall could be traced largely to FDR's cancellation of airmail contracts and the low bids, averaging about 19.5¢ per mile, that Breech had been obliged to submit to regain Eastern's former routes under the Black-McKellar Act.[4]

In short, Rickenbacker inherited a solid foundation on which to build. Nevertheless, he did an admirable job after taking command. Eastern had never earned a profit on passenger operations since its inception in 1930, and he was determined that it do so. After touring the route system, he fired nineteen station managers, showing he meant business. In 1935 he eliminated all Mailwings, Kingbirds, and Condors. Completing the transition to DC-2s, he added ten orders to four already placed by Breech. For short-route segments he bought five Lockheed L-10 Electras, sleek all-metal planes introduced in 1934. Carrying ten passengers and cruising at 180 miles an hour, they showed his determination to use only the most up-to-date equipment.[5]

Realizing that aircraft made money only when they were in the air, Rickenbacker maximized fleet utilization, gambling that increasing the frequency of flights would boost passenger revenue without incurring unsupportable costs. Starting in May 1935, he scheduled fifteen round trips per day between New York City (Newark International Airport) and Washington, D.C., starting a "Merry-Go-Round" that provided what Eastern touted as "the most frequent service between any two cities in the world." DC-2s made the strategy possible because they could fly the one-way distance in eighty minutes instead of ninety-five with Condors. Because of the DC-2s' speed and carrying capacity, Rickenbacker also increased service on the Newark–Miami route, which they could fly in ten hours despite intermediate stops. To Eastern's former twice-daily round trips, he added three extra southbound flights on Wednesdays and Thursdays and three northbound ones on Sundays, permitting passengers to plan minivacations to Florida. The public response was phenomenal. Soon after the program began, Eastern sold every available seat on the artery in one week, with 50 or more passengers on waiting lists. Northbound traffic began averaging about 500 passengers a week. Capitalizing on the speed of the DC-2s, EAL began to advertise eight-hour service from New York to New Orleans and nine-hour trips from Chicago to Miami. By the end of 1935 traffic on EAL's 3,143-mile system averaged 7,000 passengers a month, turning the 1934 deficit into a $38,000 profit.[6]

Despite being quickly overshadowed by its remarkable successor, the DC-3, the DC-2 was a revolutionary airplane. It helped stanch the flow of red ink because it was not only fast but also rugged, dependable, and economical. All of its features reduced costs. Its supercharged air-cooled radial engines used high-octane fuel from a separate tank during takeoffs but switched to cheaper lower-octane gas after reaching cruising altitude. Streamlined engine cowlings and baffles between cylinders stopped overheating, requiring less maintenance. Variable-pitch propellers, adjustable for climbing and cruising, yielded further savings. With a maximum range exceeding 1,000 miles, and the ability to fly 500 miles when fully loaded, the DC-2 was the most economical airliner yet designed. The smaller Lockheed L-10 Electra was also cost effective. Using DC-2s and Electras, EAL flew an extra 3 million route miles in 1935 with about half the planes it had used in 1934.[7]

Passengers liked the DC-2 because it gave them unaccustomed space at a time when flights between widely separated destinations were extremely long. Unlike the Boeing 247, the DC-2 had no hump in its central aisle, making it easier for passengers to move about the cabin. DC-2s, however, did have limitations. Like all airliners deployed before 1940, they were unpressurized and passengers were uncomfortable if they flew much above 8,000 feet, making it impossible for pilots to escape turbulence. The heating system was noisy and deicing equipment primitive. Even so, though not an ideal airliner, the DC-2 was a genuine breakthrough.[8]

Charles Froesch, Eastern's chief engineer, played a strong role in advising Rickenbacker to abandon Condors and Kingbirds and adopt DC-2s and Electras. They had met each other at FACA, and Rick admired the way Froesch managed spare-parts inventories. When Froesch refused to move to California after Breech consolidated General Aviation and North American, Rick quickly hired him.[9] Froesch, a heavy-set, bespectacled man with a German accent, recommended that EAL acquire an even better aircraft, the DC-3, that Douglas was developing, and Rickenbacker began switching to it in 1936. Cord's protégé, C. R. Smith, who became president of American Air Lines in May 1934, was the driving force behind the new plane. Like EAL, American had an excellent chief engineer, William Smallwood, who advised Smith to abandon outmoded Stinson Trimotors and lumbering Condors that were no match for the DC-2s used by TWA on cross-country routes. Even after Smith acquired DC-2s, however, Smallwood urged him to look for a bigger and better airliner. In response Smith turned to Donald Douglas, who was too well satisfied with orders for DC-2s to want to build a new plane, but Smith persisted in a marathon telephone conversation in 1934 lasting more than two hours and costing an astronomical $335. A Texas Democrat with powerful friends in Washington, Smith found enough money to justify the expense of the retooling and redesign work Douglas had to incur by persuading Jesse Jones, a native of the Lone Star State who headed the Reconstruction Finance Corporation, to loan American a whopping $4.5 million. The result was a revolutionary plane known as the DST (Douglas Sleeper Transport) when built for night flight and, more famously, the DC-3 when designed for daytime operations. The DST could carry fourteen passengers, the DC-3 twenty-one. On 25 June 1936 American's first DC-3, *Flagship Illinois,* took only three hours and fifty-five minutes in a maiden flight from Chicago to Newark.[10]

Capable of producing a profit without carrying a pound of mail, the DC-3 launched a new era in commercial aviation. Its rounded fuselage, twenty-six inches wider than that of the DC-2, had space for seven rows of three seats, two on one side of the aisle and one on the other. Its wingspan, almost ten feet wider than that of the DC-2, made possible larger fuel tanks, yielding a 1,200-mile range. Its larger tail surfaces, after the addition of a dorsal fin, provided greatly enhanced stability and helped

APEX

make the plane highly forgiving of pilot error. One airman called it a "contented cow." The DST, while not as popular as the DC-3, had larger and more comfortable bunks than those of the Condor and could cross the continent three hours faster from east to west against prevailing headwinds.[11]

Like most other airline executives, Rickenbacker ordered DSTs and DC-3s with alacrity. After he prodded Douglas to rush production, Eastern took delivery of its first DC-3 in December 1936. The speed with which Rickenbacker acted to acquire the plane Smith had spearheaded may help explain the smug and condescending attitude Smith took toward him, beginning about this time. On the other hand, Rickenbacker was scaling financial heights impossible at American, which had not recouped the enormous losses of the early 1930s. The arrival of Eastern's DC-3 climaxed a brilliant year in which the airline broke all previous records by carrying 102,606 travelers, flying 45,435,175 revenue passenger miles, and transporting 1,787,611 pounds of mail. Its net profit of $182,534 far exceeded its 1935 earnings. Even more important, passenger income, $2,573,045, more than doubled $1,250,328 in mail revenue, a historic watershed.[12]

Froesch was not the only member of an excellent managerial team responsible for Eastern's progress. Noticing Sidney Shannon's fine performance as station manager at Richmond, Rickenbacker put him in charge of operations. Paul Brattain, a former public relations officer at TWA, began an enduring role at Eastern as assistant general manager and head of the traffic department. Beverly Griffith, an ex-cameraman in the film industry whom Rick had met in his racing career, became director of public affairs. A corpulent man weighing nearly 300 pounds, Griffith had shot aerial films of Pershing's punitive expedition in Mexico and served as manager with Fox and Universal studios. He was constantly alert for new ideas, as was Brad Walker, Rickenbacker's press agent in the 1920s, who now supervised Eastern's advertising. Walker conceived "The Great Silver Fleet," the name by which EAL's airliners became known, and suggested using the duck hawk (peregrine falcon), supposedly "the fastest-flying bird in the world," as its corporate symbol.[13]

Rickenbacker, a relentless self-promoter, tried to take credit for Walker's ideas, but attracted attention to Eastern on his own merits. Soon after Wiley Post and Will Rogers crashed to their deaths in August 1935 near Point Barrow, Alaska, Rick became head of the Will Rogers Memorial Commission, which helped crippled children as a fitting tribute to the beloved humorist. He commissioned famed aviator Frank Hawks to make a national publicity and fund-raising tour. Through rigid cost controls, Rick ensured that only minimal sums would be spent covering administrative expenses.[14]

By contrast with his parsimony in administering the Rogers drive, Rickenbacker spent what was needed to surround EAL with glamour and excitement. A company magazine, *The Great Silver Fleet News*, which first came out in September 1936, teemed with photographs of celebrities including First Lady Eleanor Roosevelt, who flew EAL's "Silverliners." Nobody, however, brought the airline more publicity than Henry Tyndall ("Dick") Merrill, a Mississippian who had served briefly with the Army Air Service in France but did not fly until after the war, when he bought a "Jenny" for barnstorming. Showing instinctive control of stick and rudder, he joined Pitcairn Aviation and developed a reputation for surviving near-death experiences flying Mailwings through thunderstorms and doing flamboyant but illegal stunts after winning his commercial pilot's license. Addicted to gambling, he excelled in poker and craps, was a familiar figure at horse races, flaunted wads of money, wore flashy clothing, used expensive cologne, and adopted lion cubs, dogs, and flying squirrels as mascots. Strangely, however, he shunned alcohol and tobacco, which his mother had taught him to abhor.

Merrill transferred to Eastern Air Transport when Keys bought Pitcairn and became so adept at instrument flying that he instructed fellow airmen in the demanding art. Switching from Mailwings to flying passengers, he abandoned stunting and took pride in reassuring nervous travelers, treating them courteously, giving them the smoothest flights possible, and being a goodwill ambassador for the airline. Radio commentator Walter Winchell thought he was the world's best pilot and did not want to fly with anyone else.[15]

Rickenbacker made Merrill a symbol of EAL, appointing him chief pilot on promotional flights and sending him on special publicity-generating missions. When a famous explorer, Lincoln Ellsworth, got lost in an Antarctic adventure in 1935, Rick put Merrill on leave to fly a Northrop Gamma along South America's Pacific coast and across the Andes Mountains to the Strait of Magellan. After four days of perilous landings in Ecuadorian and Peruvian jungles, crossing jagged cordilleras in blizzards, Merrill delivered the plane to another celebrity explorer, Hubert Wilkins, who used it to search for Ellsworth. Merrill survived two crashes returning home, where Captain Eddie gave him the good news that Wilkins had found his man.

Merrill won more publicity for Eastern in September 1936 when Broadway entertainer Harry Richman bought a single-engine low-wing Vultee V-1A and invited Merrill to join him in attempting the first two-way Atlantic crossing. The aircraft's 1,000-horsepower Wright Cyclone engine, secretly developed for the army, had not been out of the country. Boasting a cruising speed of about 215 miles per hour, it would assertedly enable the Vultee to reach England in eighteen to twenty hours. Rickenbacker enthusiastically supported the venture and went to Floyd Bennett Field to see the plane, now called the *Lady Peace*, take off with Merrill at the controls. The wings were full of ping pong balls, which would supposedly provide superior flotation in case of a crash in the ocean, and cameramen from Movietone News were on hand to film the action. William Rickenbacker, Eddie's ten-year-old son, worshiped Merrill but was ill at the time and summoned him to his bedside to give his idol a playing card—the ace of spades—for good luck, unaware that many fliers thought it a bad omen. As throngs watched in suspense, Merrill had trouble getting the plane, carrying excess fuel, off the 4,000-foot runway. Barely clearing Flatbush Avenue and heading northeast over the Rockaway Peninsula, he noticed a DC-2 escorting him. Captain Eddie, who was aboard, waved his familiar straw hat as the *Lady Peace* climbed to altitude and faded into the distance.

Adverse weather, radio malfunctioning, and fuel problems forced Merrill to land in a cow pasture in Wales. Disappointed by not reaching London's Croydon Airport, he and Richman were nevertheless pleased they had set a record by crossing the Atlantic in eighteen hours, thirty-six minutes. After spending two weeks being lionized in London and Paris, they took off for home from a beach near Liverpool. The plane was carrying extra fuel to battle headwinds. Afraid it might be too heavy to get off the ground at Croydon, they made a successful takeoff from a longer beach with hard-packed sand. During the ensuing flight they encountered a storm, and ice accumulated on the wings. Descending to warmer air, Merrill realized that his gasoline was almost gone and thought something was wrong with his fuel system. Spotting the coast of Newfoundland, he made a quick emergency landing in a bog near Musgrave Harbor. As the wheels sank into the soft earth, the engine nosed into a muddy morass, burying the propeller and leaving the flyers dangling from their safety belts as villagers hurried to the rescue.

Rickenbacker was waiting in suspense at Floyd Bennett Field. When Merrill sent radio messages about what had happened and where he was, Captain Eddie could not resist joining a rescue mission in a DC-2 loaded with extra fuel and emergency supplies. In his haste he forgot that weather conditions in Newfoundland would be much colder than in New York City and wore only a blue serge suit and his usual straw hat. His teeth were chattering when the DC-2 landed near Harbor Grace, the only community near the crash site that had an airfield. Taking a motorboat to Musgrave Harbor, he found Merrill and Richman sitting on an improvised raft trying to keep their relatively undamaged plane from sinking into the bog. Inspecting the belly, Rickenbacker saw that a dump valve had partially opened during the return flight, causing about 200 gallons of fuel to leak out. Working feverishly, rescuers built a corduroy road and tugged the plane to a nearby beach. To keep its weight down, they loaded it with just enough gasoline to reach Harbor Grace. Eddie said he came close to coronary arrest as it struggled aloft.

At Harbor Grace Merrill and Richman had to wait for high winds to subside, after which they took off and flew to Floyd Bennett Field. Radio broadcasts kept a gathering crowd notified about their progress. Amid the throng were William and Adelaide, who was upset about the ace of spades her son had given Merrill. Completing the 1,150-mile flight from Harbor Grace, the *Lady Peace* landed in mid-afternoon on 21 September 1936, nineteen days after its departure. Unaware that grass along the runway was soggy from recent rain, Merrill taxied into a wet area and got stuck. A tow truck had to pull the plane out. After the fliers exited the cockpit, Merrill gave William a bear hug but Adelaide apologized profusely about the "omen of ill fortune" he had given the famous pilot, spoiling the occasion for the boy and permanently scarring his memory of what had happened.[16]

Knowing that the misadventure in Newfoundland had only intensified public acclaim for the first flights across the Atlantic in opposite directions, Eddie put a more positive spin on things. His DC-2 had peeled off to land at Newark, and he rejoined Merrill and Richman to bask in their accomplishment. "The boys have made an epochal flight, and they've gotten back without harm to themselves or to the plane," he told reporters. "What more can be asked?"[17]

When George VI was crowned king of England in June 1937, the event provided yet another opportunity for Merrill to make headlines for EAL. It was also a bonanza for William Randolph Hearst, with whom

Rick had close connections. Using a Lockheed Electra owned by Harold S. Vanderbilt, Merrill flew to London, got a scoop for the Hearst chain by securing films taken in Westminster Abbey, and rushed them back to America ahead of other newspapers. Rickenbacker followed the Electra in a DC-3 when it took off from Floyd Bennett Field. Merrill's mission was the first transatlantic round trip by air for business purposes and won the Collier Trophy. FDR presented it to Merrill in a ceremony at the White House.[18]

It had been another great year for Eastern. The airline's performance in 1937 eclipsed all earlier records. It now owned ten DC-3s and had carried 126,334 passengers, up more than 23 percent from 1936. Selling three DC-2s (leaving only eleven) and jettisoning all five Electras left twenty-one aircraft that earned a net profit of $196,982.[19]

Relations between Rickenbacker and Breech soured despite Eastern's success. Breech denied Eddie $820.20 he claimed for expenses in his mission to Newfoundland.[20] More signs of estrangement surfaced in a dispute about secretarial services at EAL that Breech considered excessive.[21] Breech also rejected Rickenbacker's desire to compete with American and United in the New York–Chicago market. Coupled with a route from Miami to New Orleans, the concept would have given Eastern a "figure eight" route system, greatly increasing aircraft utilization. Nevertheless, Breech concurred when Rickenbacker negotiated a merger in 1936 in which EAL acquired the Wedell-Williams Transport Corporation, which flew between New Orleans and Houston, giving Eastern direct connections all the way from New York City to Texas. Harry P. Williams, who owned the line, had bought automobiles from the Rickenbacker Motor Company. After protracted discussions with Rick, Williams sold his enterprise to Eastern for $160,000.[22]

Early in 1938 Rickenbacker was surprised to learn from Leslie Gould, a financial analyst for the Hearst chain, that Breech was planning to sell EAL, removing it from GM's corporate empire. The maneuver stemmed from changes in General Motors after William S. Knudsen became president in May 1937, creating a possibility that Breech would be transferred from New York to Detroit. Breech did not want to move because he was fascinated by the airline industry and had a new home in Scarsdale. To forestall the transfer, he tried to buy EAL with the help of John Hertz, a partner in Lehman Brothers. Breech and Hertz had been friends since the merger of the Yellow Cab Company with GM's Truck Division in 1925, and Breech had arranged Hertz's acquisition of TWA.[23]

Sloan did not want to lose Breech. After some crafty maneuvering, he persuaded him to abandon his plan, intimating he might soon become a vice president at GM. Breech agreed to move to Detroit at least temporarily, though still hoping he might someday acquire EAL and return to New York. To keep that possibility alive, Breech hatched a plan to have GM sell EAL to Hertz, from whom he might reacquire it in the future. At the time, TWA was losing money and would benefit from combining its east-west line with Eastern's north-south system. Hertz accepted Breech's offer.[24]

Rickenbacker knew nothing about these machinations and was astounded to learn from Gould about Breech's move to have GM sell EAL to Hertz for $3,250,000. Eddie realized that Hertz did not like him and that fruition of Breech's plan would end his tenure as general manager of Eastern. Wanting passionately to control the airline and realizing that GM had considered selling for $1,000,000 in 1934, Eddie knew it could not have been worth $3,250,000 had it not grown dramatically under his management. His indignation mounted soon after he heard about the impending sale. One evening the phone rang at Rickenbacker's Bronxville residence. The call was from Hertz, who had dialed the wrong number and thought he was talking to Breech. Only after Hertz had delivered a long diatribe about Rickenbacker did Eddie reveal his identity.

After consulting with Henry M. Hogan, GM's general counsel, Eddie capitalized on his long ties with General Motors by going over Breech's head and contacting Sloan, asking for a chance to raise enough money for a counteroffer. He had no way of knowing—but Hogan probably did—that he was playing directly into Sloan's hands. As a special inducement to Sloan, he proposed to buy Eastern for $3,500,000 in cash. Hertz had offered $1,000,000 in cash and $2,250,000 in notes, so Rickenbacker's ante was substantially better for GM than the one on the table. Eddie also pleaded his case with other GM executives, including Knudsen and Donaldson Brown. Sloan was pleased to have him in the picture and gave him thirty days to come up with the funds.[25]

Working furiously against time, Eddie persuaded John Schiff, Hugh Knowlton, and Frederick Warburg, the three chief members of the Kuhn, Loeb banking empire, to put up the cash if he could organize a group of backers willing to subscribe for enough stock to initiate the transaction. A public stock offering would be necessary to provide the rest of the money required. Laurance Rockefeller, beginning his career as a venture capitalist at the time, played an important role in the developments that followed. "We are making considerable progress in the Eastern Air Lines matter and an unusual amount of interest has developed," William Barclay Harding of Smith, Barney & Company (who was helping Eddie put the deal together) told Rockefeller at an early stage. "It is our desire to restrict the sale to a small group of purchasers who are agreeable to each other and who have an understanding of the business." By mid-April Harding had organized a syndicate including Paul M. Davis (Nashville), George Howell (Tampa), Wiley Moore (Atlanta), Jack Peabody (Chicago), Walter Pyron (Houston), and J. Ford Johnson Jr., Knowlton, Rockefeller, and Harold S. Vanderbilt (all from New York City).[26]

The climax came at a stormy meeting at the General Motors Building pitting Eddie and his lawyer, Alexander B. Royce, against a group representing Hertz. Breech, realizing that he would lose any future chance of acquiring Eastern if Rickenbacker won, sided with Hertz, prompting Eddie to call Knudsen to remind him that he and his backers were offering more money than Hertz and his team. Knudsen knew what was going on and assured Rickenbacker he would take care of things. What happened in the next few hours is not clear but easy to guess. Breech folded, and GM accepted Rick's deal.[27]

Complex financial and legal legerdemain was involved in completing the transaction. Because Eastern was not a separate corporation, North American had to constitute it as one and register its stock with the Securities and Exchange Commission. If the SEC approved, Smith, Barney & Company and Kuhn, Loeb would "go through the motions of buying the stock," *Business Week* reported. The magazine also stated that a victory for Rickenbacker would make things easier for the government because "Washington, either for anti-trust or airmail reasons, might not have looked kindly on a working agreement between Eastern Air and Transcontinental & Western [TWA]."[28]

Rickenbacker still had to guarantee he had the cash in hand by six o'clock on Sunday afternoon, 22 April. If not, his option would expire, and he fretted about whether the money would materialize. When Saturday evening came and he still did not have it, he had the temerity to call Sloan's apartment in New York City as the powerful executive was getting ready for bed, asking to "come over for a few minutes." Sloan, wearing pajamas when Rickenbacker arrived, told him not to worry, but he got little sleep that night. Early the next morning Warburg called, inquiring when and where he wanted the money. Eddie specified ten o'clock on Monday morning at one of Eastern's hangars at Newark International Airport. Warburg brought the funds at the appointed time. Later that day, Rickenbacker gave Sloan a certified check for $3.5 million. "Congratulations, Eddie, and God bless you," Sloan said. "I wish you every success in the world."[29]

Kuhn, Loeb had put up the cash intending to sell 416,000 shares of the newly created Eastern Air Lines Corporation stock in a public offering at $10 per share, yielding a substantial profit. Expectations ran high that the offering would be oversubscribed, but Hitler complicated things by marching into Austria on the day the sale was announced and only half of the shares were sold. Rickenbacker himself had to help peddle the securities, but the issue ultimately went over the top. He celebrated the end of the struggle by writing twelve resolutions that he called "My Constitution." The first pledged, "My goal will be to do a good job and sell, sell, sell Eastern Air Lines at all times." The rest set forth various ways he would fulfill his mission. Tenth was a statement, "I will always keep in mind that I am in the greatest business in the world, as well as working for the greatest company in the world, and I can serve humanity more completely in my line of endeavor than in any other." He ended with a motto italicized for emphasis: *A winner never quits and a quitter never wins.*"[30] Having reached the greatest milestone in his life, he was off and running.

Free from Breech's restraining hand, Rickenbacker could now move boldly in his new capacity as Eastern's president and chief executive officer. The takeover that put him in uncontested power coincided with two historic milestones. On 29 April 1938 Eddie cut a giant birthday cake at a dinner celebrating Eastern's Tenth Anniversary.[31] On 15 May, the twentieth anniversary of the U.S. airmail service, one of its "Silverliners" retraced its original route between New York to Washington. Rick commanded the flight, Merrill was at the controls, and Postmaster General Farley was aboard. At 12:15 p.m. on the same day another of Eastern's DC-3s flew over Kitty Hawk and broadcast a radio program about the history of aviation and the birth of the airmail system in 1918.[32]

Rickenbacker did not let these events pass without a cautionary note, admonishing Eastern's employees that "We are no longer under the protective wing of General Motors and North American Aviation. We are absolutely on our own—out there on a limb where all may take a shot at us."[33] But, as he knew, it was a very strong limb. The board of directors resulting from his takeover included Harold S. Vanderbilt, whose name was synonymous with wealth; George B. Howell, president of the Bank of West Tampa and head of the Florida Bankers Association; Wiley L. Moore, an oil magnate from Atlanta; Stuyvesant Peabody, head of a firm that mined 15 million tons of coal per year; and Edwin C. Romph, President of the First National Bank of Miami. The most important board member was Laurance Rockefeller, who started with an investment of only $10,000 but soon became Eastern's largest stockholder. An avid aviation enthusiast, he often showed up at Newark International Airport, conversing on familiar terms with couriers, mechanics, dispatchers, and pilots, many of whom he knew by name. He later said his attitude toward Rickenbacker at the time was one of "hero-worship."[34]

While the new order began at Eastern, leaders in Washington created one for the airline industry as a whole. A fact-finding committee appointed by FDR urged that carriers be removed from the sway of the Post Office Department and controlled by a unified "Air Commerce Commission." Wrangling between Congress and the White House made it impossible to determine what powers the agency might wield, but the momentum of change was irresistible. The industry's infrastructure needed serious attention. Federal budget cutting had prevented improving the nation's airways, contributing to a spate of accidents. One crash aroused particular concern because it took the life of a popular United States senator, Bronson Cutting of New Mexico, but eight fatal episodes took place in 1936 alone. Passenger revenue fell sharply every time a plane went down because worried travelers chose other modes of transport, forcing airlines to seek higher mail pay to survive. In 1936 nineteen carriers formed the Air Transport Association (ATA) to lobby for their interests. Edgar S. Gorrell, its president, was a veteran of the Army Air Service who had been trained at West Point and MIT and had an impressive record as an automobile executive. Gorrell obtained federal appropriations to improve radio navigation systems, but the industry's woes, exacerbated by low airmail rates, continued.[35]

The advent of the DC-3, the first airliner that could make money simply by carrying passengers, brought things to a head. The only leverage the government had over airlines was the Post Office Department's power to award airmail contracts. If these were no longer needed for survival, interlopers could buy a few DC-3s and have an open field. Carriers that had depended for more than a decade on mail pay cried for protection against "unfair competition." Because 1938 was a congressional election year, public concern about crashes intensified pressure for airline regulation. The Republicans expected major gains in the wake of a sharp recession in 1937 and the unpopularity of FDR's recent attempt to pack the Supreme Court.[36]

Congress acted by passing a legislative landmark, the Civil Aeronautics Act, which became law in June 1938. A single government agency, the Civil Aeronautics Authority (CAA), was established to control the allocation of air routes, fix mail rates, and prevent unnecessary competition. An administrator, cooperating with the CAA but not under its control, represented the executive branch of the government. A three-member Air Safety Board (ASB) would investigate accidents and determine their cause. Established airlines heaved a sigh of relief, but critics of the bill objected that the Post Office Department still paid for mail transport and supervised scheduling. In 1940, acting under a recently passed government reorganization law, FDR replaced the CAA with an even stronger body, a five-member Civil Aeronautics Board (CAB), which exercised both economic supervision of airlines and the functions previously vested in the ASB. The CAB functioned under the aegis of the Commerce Department but in fact was an independent regulatory agency.[37]

Under the CAA or its successor, the CAB, no airline could henceforth carry airmail or passengers across state lines without a Certificate of Public Convenience and Necessity (CPCN). After securing a route, a carrier could not abandon it without official permission. Airlines had no control over fares for transport of passengers or cargo. Mergers could not take place without the consent of the CAA or CAB. Various types of questionable practices, including rebates, were illegal, and the government could scrutinize airline records. Airlines could arrange schedules and select aircraft but do little else without permission from Uncle Sam.

On the other hand, the airlines derived substantial benefit from the new order. Certification to fly routes was now permanent. Indeed, a route franchise became a form of property that one airline could sell another, subject to government approval. Permanent certification greatly enhanced an airline's ability to obtain long-term credit from financial institutions. Existing carriers could automatically secure grandfather certification of their existing routes simply by proving they had provided satisfactory service between 14 May and 22 August 1938. CPCNs, however, were nonexclusive, and the CAA or CAB could admit additional carriers to existing or future routes. Because these bodies controlled fares, airlines could compete only by acquiring faster or more-comfortable aircraft, offering superior passenger amenities, and improving the convenience of their schedules. Service competition was in. Price competition was out. As airline historian R. E. G. Davies has succinctly stated, "the prospect of an open free market, in which all could participate under a benevolent and indulgent bureaucracy, was removed."[38]

Rickenbacker scored a notable triumph before the Civil Aeronautics Act went into effect and the Post Office Department lost control of routes. Through adroit lobbying in Congress, he secured passage of an act authorizing the Post Office Department to open bidding on service between Houston and Brownsville, Texas. The winning airline would be in a strong position to obtain a route to Mexico City if the government chose to end Pan American's privileged position. In a furious battle between Eastern and Braniff, Rickenbacker undercut Braniff's bid to transport mail on the Houston-Brownsville route for $0.0001907378 per pound mile by offering to perform the same service for nothing. Braniff protested vehemently that the bid was illegal, but Postmaster General Farley's advisers found Eastern's bid unexceptionable. Learning that Thomas Braniff planned to make a speech to the Houston Chamber of Commerce saying a victory by Eastern would destroy his airline, assertedly "a Texas operation," Rickenbacker went to Houston, crashed the meeting, pointed out Braniff was based in Oklahoma City, and argued that Eastern offered superior connections with major metropolitan centers. Impressed by his arguments, the chamber endorsed Eastern, and the Post Office accepted its bid.

Rickenbacker's victory, giving Eastern's passengers through service all the way from New York City to the Rio Grande, confirmed his wisdom in acquiring the former Wedell-Williams route from New Orleans to Houston. Without that step, Eastern would not have been in position to win the Brownsville award, which added San Antonio and Corpus Christi to its domestic system. Establishing connections with Pan American's existing route from Brownsville to Mexico City also significantly enhanced Eastern's revenue potential. As a columnist pointed out, someone leaving Newark International aboard an Eastern evening flight could eat lunch in Mexico City the next day and soon be "winging his way across the mountains of Latin America." Winning access to Brownsville also raised Eastern from fourth to third place, ahead of

TWA, among the so-called "Big Four"—American, Eastern, TWA, and United—in total route mileage.[39]

Despite his reservations about centralized government, Rickenbacker had no objections to the Civil Aeronautics Act. His belief that a strong airline industry was essential to national defense was consistent with his support of the statute as a way to prevent unfair competition from "wildcat" airlines threatening existing carriers with chaos. Eastern's annual report for 1938 anticipated "sound regulation" under the new law. Like other airlines, Eastern enjoyed a honeymoon from 1938 to 1940 with the CAA, which had every motive to treat the industry with kid gloves. Under its benevolent care, carriers won twenty-two new routes, and airlines became generally profitable.[40]

Eastern was a prime beneficiary. Soon after the Civil Aeronautics Act took effect the CAA granted Eastern a CPCN for service to Florida's West Coast, creating an Atlanta-Tampa route via Tallahassee and Albany, Georgia. It also gave Eastern another plum: a route extension from Tallahassee to Memphis, Tennessee, via Montgomery, Birmingham, and Muscle Shoals, Alabama.[41]

Lavish celebration in April 1939 heralded Eastern's new ties with Mexico City via Brownsville and Pan American. The Mexican government permitted one of Eastern's DC-3s to fly from Newark International Airport to Mexico City, stopping along the way to refuel and pick up dignitaries. When the plane landed at Mexico City on 6 April, it was greeted by an estimated 5,000 people. A motorcade hustled the passengers, led by Rickenbacker, to a cocktail party thrown by Erwin Balluder, divisional traffic manager for Pan American. During the next two days Rickenbacker received lots of attention and went back to New York after what *The Great Silver Fleet News* called a "perfect trip."[42]

On 6 July 1939 Eastern established the world's first regularly scheduled airmail service with rotary-winged aircraft on a six-mile route from Central Airport at Camden, New Jersey, to the rooftop of Philadelphia's 30th Street post office. John M. ("Johnny") Miller, who had defeated Amelia Earhart in a quest to be the first person to fly a rotorcraft across the United States and back, piloted a Kellett autogiro that reduced the time needed to transport mail between the two terminals from forty-five minutes by ground to less than ten minutes by air. "Eastern Air Lines is proud to be in the forefront of this progressive, pioneering movement," Rickenbacker proclaimed when the route was inaugurated, but the CAA denied permanent certification a year later, ending the venture.[43]

As the denial indicated, Eastern's relations with federal regulators did not always go smoothly. In 1939 the CAA initiated a proceeding to determine whether the airmail rates paid to Eastern and several other airlines were "fair and reasonable." Eastern was receiving $1.20 per ton-mile, the lowest rate earned by any domestic carrier. Although opposed to subsidies, and willing to carry mail for nothing if it suited him, as he showed in the Houston-to-Brownsville case, Rickenbacker believed an airline was entitled to fair compensation for services rendered. He protested vigorously in 1940 when examiners representing the newly established CAB proposed a 50 percent reduction in Eastern's mail rates and a recapture of fees totaling $2.5 million for the past three years. Telling stockholders the proposal "completely failed to recognize the efficiency of your Company's operations," he won a concession when the CAB dropped the recapture demand, but the board cut EAL's mail rate in half.[44]

Nevertheless, the CAB continued to expand Eastern's system. On 28 June 1940 it gave Eastern two new routes, one from Birmingham to Chicago via Nashville, Louisville, and Indianapolis, and the other from St. Louis to Miami via Evansville, Nashville, and Atlanta. The route from St. Louis to Miami was particularly valuable, giving Eastern three lucrative vacation routes to Florida (it already had operating authority from Chicago to Miami via Louisville), funneling additional traffic to and from the Caribbean and South America through the Miami gateway via Pan American. Only one segment of Eastern's entire route system—New York to Washington, shared with American—was open to competition. Because Rickenbacker excelled at holding down costs, Eastern had a virtual license to print money.

Eastern's balance sheets reflected its increasingly favorable route structure. Its net profit for 1939 after taxes was $883,823.73, dwarfing all previous figures. Its twenty-seven DC-2s and DC-3s flew 11,281,333 miles and carried 231,215 passengers between forty-seven cities. Earnings in 1940—$1,575,455.65—nearly doubled as Eastern added fourteen DC-3s and five DST sleeper transports and sold ten DC-2s, increasing both seating capacity and operational efficiency. By the end of the year only four DC-2s remained and ten additional DC-3s would soon join the Great Silver Fleet. The CAB closed a gap between Atlanta and Birmingham and added Brunswick, Georgia (whose airport served the adjacent Sea Island resorts) to the New York–Miami route. Applications to serve Raleigh, Knoxville, Charleston, Orlando, and other cities were pending.[45]

Eastern continued to thrive despite a downswing in 1941. In June, *Aviation Week* reported that domestic carriers had sustained operating losses of more than $2,000,000 before taxes in the first three months of the year, blaming the situation on inflationary trends caused by American preparations to enter the war now raging in Europe. Eastern's profits shrank by about half, to $762,121, but American was the only other airline to generate profit at all, earning $93,459. TWA and United lost $987,998 and $1,104,461 respectively. Eastern was in a class by itself, being by far the most profitable carrier in the industry—a tribute to its route system, its lack of competition, and Rickenbacker's careful management.

Eastern's name was misleading. "Southern" would have been more appropriate because more than 90 percent of EAL's income came from below the Mason-Dixon Line and the Ohio River. Rickenbacker, who called black people "darkies," kept Eastern lily-white except for baggage handlers and custodians. It adopted a corporate flag featuring crossed American and Confederate flags in the center and the banners of all the states served by the company, mostly in Dixie, along the edges. A photograph in *The Great Silver Fleet News* showed Rick presenting Eastern's flag at a meeting of the United Daughters of the Confederacy.[46]

Eastern's system grew so large that Rickenbacker divided it into seven divisions. The most important nodal points were New York City (served by Newark International Airport), Atlanta, and Miami. In July 1935, six months after becoming general manager, Rickenbacker concentrated all but routine maintenance and operational facilities at the 36th Street Airport in Miami, making the Florida city a second corporate headquarters. Eastern's vice president for operations, Sidney Shannon, moved his office there from Manhattan, emphasizing the company's southern orientation. The complex at Miami included a print shop producing almost all the company's tickets and forms, a communications system operating a three-kilowatt radio station, WEEM, and a pioneering aeromedical facility at Coral Gables administering physical examinations to pilots and performing health-related experiments. More than 360 employees and 30 pilots were posted at Miami, the largest concentration at any point in the system.[47]

Atlanta, however, was the heart of Eastern's system, where seven of its routes converged as of December 1938. Eastern's weather-forecasting, dispatching, and pilot-training facilities were located in the Georgia capital, which was also the hub of Delta Air Lines, a considerably smaller enterprise functioning partly to funnel traffic into Eastern's system. The two carriers had twenty-eight arrivals and departures at Atlanta each day, twenty by Eastern and eight by Delta. Long-range radio receivers and transmitters at Atlanta, staffed around the clock, handled message traffic throughout Eastern's entire system. Pilots were trained at nearby Hapeville, using a Link trainer called the "Hapeville Clipper."[48]

New York City was Eastern's central administrative and financial center. The General Motors Building continued to house the executive offices after the 1938 takeover; Rickenbacker and his secretarial staff, including Shepherd, had Breech's former suite on the eighteenth floor. Other parts of the building provided space for the accounting, traffic, and engineering departments.[49] In July 1940, however, Rickenbacker completed negotiations for a transfer to Rockefeller Center, where occupancy at a new building was plummeting because the Netherlands had been conquered by Hitler's legions, removing anchor tenants including the Dutch consulate and KLM airlines.[50] Rickenbacker thought EAL's office space in the General Motors Building was too cramped and was infuriated when he heard Juan Trippe hoped to move Pan American's New York City offices into Rockefeller Center. Taking advantage of the Dutch exodus, Eddie persuaded Laurance Rockefeller that Eastern's corporate headquarters rightfully belonged in the vast complex that bore his family name. A resulting agreement gave the carrier the top ten stories at 10 Rockefeller Plaza, henceforth called the Eastern Airlines Building. The ten-year lease negotiated by Rickenbacker was signed aloft in a DC-3 Silverliner.[51]

Eastern's new corporate home was dedicated on 15 October 1940. Fiorello LaGuardia, mayor of New York City, lauded "the progressive pioneering of the nation's air transport industry," and Laurance Rockefeller emphasized "that the structure is the only building in the world bearing the name of an air transport company." Rickenbacker, now at apex of his career, presided over the proceedings.[52]

"Eddie is always on the go," stated a feature article about Rickenbacker in *Life* magazine. Saying he "lives to run his airline," it reported he had logged 75,000 miles supervising its system in 1938. Photographs in *The Great Silver Fleet News* showed him seemingly everywhere, presiding at banquets, presenting awards, starring in ceremonies marking the inauguration of service in new cities, shaking hands with celebrities, and inspecting every aspect of the airline's operations. He worked sixteen hours a day and slept only four or five hours a night—even less on weekends. According to Shepherd, he was at his desk even on Sundays.[53]

Rickenbacker's marriage suffered from the unrelenting pace of his business life, which had left Adelaide to her own devices since they returned from their 1922 honeymoon. Addicted to clothes, jewelry, art, and furniture as ever, she shopped and played bridge while he was almost constantly away. She had her own friends and Eddie had his. Despite being able to live the life-style of a corporate magnate only because of her wealth, he never discussed business affairs with her. The romance they had experienced before and during their honeymoon was long past. As Eddie wrote before their marriage, he had been looking for a "pal." What he got was a woman who was hard as nails (a nephew later called her a "very tough lady") and determined to follow her own inclinations. There is no evidence that she cared much about aviation, the passion of his life. The DC-3 "Silverliners" he was so proud of were unimpressive compared with the majestic ocean liners that were her natural habitat when she traveled. He was an extremely frugal man who guarded his funds carefully. She was rich, ostentatious, and flung money at expensive furs, jewelry, and fine clothing. In short, they had little in common. Adelaide also knew that his adoration of his mother went much deeper than his feelings for her. "If anybody ever had an Oedipus complex it was Eddie," said one of her daughters-in-law. Probably the warm climate of southern California was not the only reason why he kept his mother there, living with his brother, Dewey. Her presence in New York, close to Adelaide, could have been uncomfortable for both women.

Adelaide thought about divorce and traveled to Europe by herself to sort out her feelings, but continued the marriage, perhaps because of the boys but probably because she still cared for Eddie, as she would demonstrate forcefully in two future traumas in which her firmness and resolution saved his life. The most likely reason for her fidelity to the marriage, however, was that she knew she could control her famous husband, about whom she had no romantic illusions. In an interview he granted late in his life, William was asked whether there was anyone his father ever feared. "Yes—my mother," he said instantly and with great emphasis. Asked why, he said in dark tones that "*She had his number.*" Asked again to clarify his statement, he repeated, slowly and deliberately, "She–had–his–*number,*" emphasizing the final word. Refusing to elaborate, he died too soon afterward to entertain further questions.

What was Eddie's "number"? Perhaps it was a realization on Adelaide's part, going back as far as their 1922 European honeymoon, that he was not as self-assured as his outward behavior suggested—that there was a vulnerability so deeply hidden that it was known only to those closest to him, his mother and the less-forgiving Adelaide.[54]

Living in separate worlds, Eddie and Adelaide were too wrapped up in their own concerns to give David and William the parenting they needed. The boys were reared mostly by nannies, one of whom was abusive to William. The boys went to boarding schools at relatively young ages and came home only for summers, holidays, or vacations. This type of situation was common in socially prominent families but took a heavy toll on William, who longed for an intimate parental relationship. David may have felt equally neglected but was less demonstrative. William deliberately broke things and at one point ripped off the wallpaper in his room. When Adelaide tried to punish him by shutting him in a closet, he defiantly burst into song, "never minding the least bit."[55]

David and William had strikingly different personalities and orientations. David was mechanically gifted and built Adelaide a radio. His academic performance was never better than average. William was intellectually and artistically gifted, made excellent grades, and had a remarkable talent for playing the piano before his feet could reach the pedals. He loved the music of Johann Sebastian Bach, which Adelaide could not stand. To please her, he learned pieces by Chopin and Rachmaninoff and developed such formidable skills that he won a competition sponsored by the Steinway Company. He had a fierce rivalry with David, whom he despised for his lack of cultural interests. Meanwhile, William lived in awe of his famous father but could not break through to him emotionally. He later remembered that sitting across the breakfast table from him was like looking at the Washington Monument.

Eddie loved the boys and tried in his own way to relate to them. When David was four or five years old, he gave him an electric train for Christmas and got down on the floor with him to play with it. Although his musical tastes ran to ballads like "Moonlight and Roses," his favorite song, he wrote a touching letter encouraging William's efforts to master a piano sonata by Beethoven that he performed in a recital. Eddie instructed his sons in shooting air rifles, taught them golf, and gave up matches against better players to go on the links with them. He took them to the Indy 500, where they met famous drivers and sat in a race car, wearing helmets and goggles. Still, something was missing because his attention was limited to short periods of time when they were not away at school.

Eddie could be a strict disciplinarian but avoided the child beating he had suffered from his father and rarely administered physical punishment. The only spanking he ever gave William was for ruining a cake Adelaide had baked for a party. Remembering the episode haunted William for life. Extremely sensitive to the slightest rebuke, he had an unhappy childhood and resented being sent to private schools, which, as one of his admirers later wrote, was "a poor substitute for a home."[56]

David got no special favors when he became old enough to take a temporary job with Eastern. Eddie had him assigned to cleaning out the toilet compartments. He endured merciless hazing from employees. When he went to the locker rooms where he and fellow workers changed their uniforms for street clothes at the end of the day, he would find water bottles emptied into his pockets and shoes. "Being the Captain's son didn't rate him anything," said a witness to the pranks. "Nobody could have blamed him if he'd gone back to his father and had told him that there was much more kidding going on than there was work done."[57]

Eddie was generous with gifts but could not bring himself to tell people how he felt about them unless he had something negative to say, in which case he showed a rare talent for invective. During the many years Shepherd was his secretary, he never told her he was "even mildly satisfied with her work." An interviewer reported she had "resigned times without number when he's barked at her in irritation. Once, she got so angry with him she picked up her notebook and threw it at him. He merely picked it up from the floor and threw it back at her." Both of them burst out laughing, and Rickenbacker apologized. He was actually deeply fond of her and appreciated her contributions to his welfare. One day when she called in sick, he went to her apartment to see whether she was in fact ill, afraid she was merely unhappy about a recent disagreement. He was vastly relieved to find that she was in fact sick and not angry at him. When Shepherd's brother got hurt in an automobile accident, Eddie "insisted that she leave everything and go to the boy," which he also did when her sister became ill, saying she "needs you more than I do." Despite his dependence on Shepherd, he arranged for her to go to Canada. The compassionate side of his nature was evident in his actions, if not in his words.

Although he dictated many letters and gave many speeches, which Shepherd possibly wrote for him—just as Driggs had ghostwritten his wartime memoirs—Rickenbacker never overcame his limited formal education. Despite his keen intelligence, he disliked intellectual discourse, preferring what he called "horse sense." It was an indication of esteem if he sat with someone for a long time and said nothing, merely listening. He would stare out a window for hours without making a sound, smoking cigarettes incessantly. When thinking intently about something, he twisted his eyebrows and ran his fingers through his hair. He hated to be disturbed when he was deep in thought reading newspapers, which he preferred to books, or ruminating about business matters. He had phenomenal powers of concentration and tried to keep his mind uncluttered with past failures. If something was troubling him, he arose before sunup and tried to erase it from his mind, never to be recalled. He had his father's stubborn disposition; if he thought he was right, nobody could persuade him that he was wrong. He did not expect to be repaid for his acts of kindness, which were legion, and did not seek consolation from others when suffering, preferring to bear his burdens alone. On the other hand, there were times when he craved companionship, always male. His favorite radio program was *The Lone Ranger.*

He had few material wants. Achievement meant more to him than money. His wardrobe was limited but of high quality, and he took excellent care of what few clothes he had to make sure they lasted a long time. He habitually wore a blue suit, always made by the same tailor. He was as parsimonious in personal expenditures as in his managerial style. He abhorred debt and told his sons never to buy what they could not afford. He prized neatness and tried to clear his desk by the end of a day at the office.

He took much satisfaction in inspiring youth to fulfill their talents and ambitions. He received, on average, thirty letters a week, largely from "young admirers who want to fly and ask about the ships they will be expected to pilot." He answered them by himself, "sitting at his desk in a little den crammed with war and racing pictures and containing a big elaborate album of citations." He enjoyed being a hero and took the role seriously. "You know, boys need heroes," he said, and he was always on the lookout for youngsters who showed traits he liked. In 1937 his caddy told him he was financially unable to accept offers of admission from two schools to which he had applied. Rickenbacker said nothing until the end of the season, when he gave him a "whopping big tip" and an envelope containing a letter to one of EAL's field managers recommending him for a job with the company. He was hired within a few weeks.[58]

Hanging on a wall in Rickenbacker's den, where he answered fan mail, was a huge painting of him by Howard Chandler Christy, an artist and illustrator famous for the "Christy Girls" in World War I recruiting posters. Christy's patrons included Calvin and Grace Coolidge, Amelia Earhart, and Herbert Hoover. The canvas he painted of Eddie showed him wearing the large, flamboyant greatcoat he had acquired in Paris late in 1918. It was embroidered with piping near the wrists and had big lapels to which Christy gave special prominence. A Sam Browne belt girded Rickenbacker's torso, and a campaign cap was pulled down at an angle above piercing eyes that looked as if they could cut steel. His right hand was thrust into a pocket in a way suggesting enormous strength. His left hand, more relaxed, carried a pair of gloves. His chin was as rigid as a block of granite, his lips firmly pressed together in a straight line under his prominent nose. His captain's bars were visible on his right shoulder and the Medal of Honor hung from his chest, some-what incongruously considering that he had not won it until 1930 and that the action shown behind him had occurred in 1918. The underlying rationale of the painting was the connection between the medal and the sortie near Billy-sous-les-Côtes that ultimately brought him the nation's highest military honor. He was sitting on a rocky eminence set against an acrid pale yellow sky laced with dark puffs of Archy above his head. His Spad XIII was diving above his right shoulder with its propeller whirling furiously. Christy painted its wings as if they were stretching backward to suggest the great speed at which it was plummeting toward its prey. Flanking Rickenbacker were the two German planes he had shot down in his mission. Both were on fire and one was trailing dense clouds of smoke. High in the right corner, barely visible, were the five enemy aircraft that had become disorganized under the fury of his attack, disappearing into the distance.

Rickenbacker believed the painting distorted his chest, explaining he had been too busy to pose for the hours Christy needed to paint his likeness and a female model had substituted for him, resulting in a torso looking "too full and bulgy."[59] Christy, however, knew what he was doing, having opened the left lapel so the Medal of Honor could be clearly seen. The "bulge" about which Rickenbacker complained was actually a dark shadow intended by Christy to give the medal added prominence. Everything about the canvas suggested enormous power; it was a far more successful work of art than a bronze bust, also displayed in the den, which made Eddie's face seem pinched. He knew it was an inferior likeness.[60]

Rick's desire to inculcate his beliefs among American youth led him to create a fictional character, "Ace Drummond," typifying a genre of "juvenile aviation adventure stories" popular in the 1930s, preaching traditional American values involving success, bravery, hard work, moral virtue, and technological ingenuity.[61] Drummond was a handsome lad whose father, a combat pilot, had been killed in the Great War. "No flyer in France could equal your dad till the day he died fighting a whole squadron of enemy planes," said Ace's sidekick, Jerry, a garrulous Irish companion steadfastly loyal but lacking Ace's leadership skills and obviously inferior to him in intelligence and judgment. Mary Lou Goodman, a beautiful young lady with whom Ace was in love, was the daughter of Horace Goodman, president of Super Air Lines. It carried airmail but its operations were plagued by Air Pirates, led by two evil men within the enterprise: its superintendent, Mr. Snyde, and his henchman, Stony. In 1935 Eddie wrote what was known at the time as a "Big Little Book"—a thick, compact volume designed to be easily carried in a boy's pocket or schoolbag—about Drummond, spinning a dramatic tale and illustrating it with his own drawings. Ace, a "born pilot" despite his youth, defeated Snyde and Stony in a series of desperate encounters. Ultimately he won a $25,000 reward for tracking down the evil pair and used it to design an experimental aircraft with which he rescued an elderly gentleman and his daughter, trapped by a forest fire. The father turned out to be a rich investor who backed Ace in building a swift airplane, the "Rainbow," in which he won a transpacific race.[62]

Drummond, who became the subject of a radio series, had much in common with the hero of a story by Horatio Alger, but he was essentially a projection of Rickenbacker's inner vision of himself, living out a fantasy life based on his own experiences and his faith in technology as the master key to progress. "Rick is now enjoying his boyhood vicariously," said a magazine article that called him an "Air Lines Wizard" and held him up as a role model for Americans, admiring his zest for achievement, his optimism, and his visionary nature. "Men smile when they hear Rick predict that the airplanes of the future will be almost as big as the Queen Mary," the writer continued, but he said that many of Eddie's predictions came true. Rickenbacker's constant message, he declared, was that "we must eliminate our weak thinking, put aside sinister philosophy that the government owes us a living, roll up our sleeves and go to work."[63]

He drank heavily to deal with the demands he imposed upon himself but was not alone among harried executives. "Booze was big then,"

344   EDDIE RICKENBACKER

wrote William Randolph Hearst Jr., about the supercharged business environment of the late 1930s. Whereas matadors showed their courage by fighting bulls, Hearst noted, American executives proved their masculinity by demonstrating how much they could drink and still seem to be sober, gulping "four or five martinis for lunch" and returning to their offices as if nothing had happened. After leaving work they would continue to imbibe. "It was a hail-and-slap-me-on-the-back era in which liquor seemed to be the oil that greased much of Manhattan business."[64]

Even in the hard-driving environment of Rickenbacker's time, however, his thirst for alcohol concerned Eastern's directors. "Since seeing you I have thought considerably about the serious problem of our President's overworked condition, complicated by his tendency to compensate therefore in the traditional manner," Laurance Rockefeller wrote to Romph early in 1939. Rockefeller said he had "discussed this matter at length" with another director, Moore. "Apart from cutting down on the drink," Rockefeller confided, "Wiley suggested that a position such as Assistant to the President might be created to relieve Eddie of a lot of the running around which he now does."[65] Rickenbacker evidently resisted Moore's idea because it took a year to implement it. On 20 February 1940 Eastern appointed Leslie P. Arnold to the position Moore had suggested. Arnold had served in the war and been one of the army's Round-the-World Flyers in 1924 before launching a career in commercial aviation with TWA and Pennsylvania Central Airlines.[66] Predictably, the move did little to slow Rickenbacker down, indicated by reports of his activities in *The Great Silver Fleet News* throughout the rest of the year.

When he was not away on his incessant trips, Rickenbacker reveled in the vibrant, kaleidoscopic ambience of the world's greatest metropolis. "If you had a job and money in those days," Hearst wrote, "Broadway and midtown Manhattan offered great restaurants, theater, and nightclubs. With safe streets and no television, the best of these places were often packed until well after midnight."[67] Sherman Billingsley's Stork Club, gossip columnist Walter Winchell's favorite base of operations, was one of the places where Rickenbacker dined with close friends including Damon Runyon. Both men were heavy drinkers and understood each other at a deep level. Rickenbacker's favorite haunt, however, was the Louis XIV restaurant, where a table was reserved specifically for him. There he would hold meetings with staff members, pilots, and mechanics, always with a bottle of liquor close at hand. In Rickenbacker's view, alcohol made it easier for him and his friends to talk frankly about work-related issues and problems. He also enjoyed reminiscing with wartime buddies who came to town and was a soft touch for money when they were down on their luck.[68]

Although he delegated the day-to-day administration of the Indianapolis Speedway to a staff led by "Pop" Myers, the responsibility of owning it was never far from his mind, intensifying the other stresses with which he lived. To prod manufacturers into producing better engines, he prohibited oil changes during the Indy 500, which also cut down on crankcase drippings that made the track slippery. Motor companies squawked about the change, but he stuck to his guns on this and other rulings. The twenty-first running of the race in 1933, which took place soon after he had helped General Motors acquire North American Aviation, was a case in point. He later claimed that a popular racer, Howdy Wilcox II, had diabetes, impairing his driving ability. George Seldes, who became increasingly critical of Rickenbacker after visiting the 94th Pursuit Squadron during the war, put a different spin on the situation, saying Wilcox had been trying to organize a labor union among racing drivers, but Rickenbacker had good reason to be concerned about safety. Heavy rains had fallen during the qualifying runs, swamping cars and producing such severe flooding that people paddled canoes around the edge of the slippery track. Ostensibly acting on the advice of physicians, Eddie banned Wilcox from competing and arranged to have another driver, Mauri Rose, substitute for him. The decision aroused strong opposition among contestants sympathetic to Wilcox, who had been runner-up the previous year and placed sixth in preliminary runs.

A showdown occurred on the morning of the race when supporters of Wilcox threatened to pull out unless Rickenbacker reinstated him. Rick responded that he would call off the race and explain his decision on the public address system and national radio. His ultimatum worked, and the race began on schedule. Rickenbacker recalled that he watched it in an agony of suspense, thinking fatal accidents would occur because of the treacherous conditions. He was right. Two drivers, both rookies, and a riding mechanic were killed.[69]

The authoritarianism Rickenbacker displayed at the race, mingled with compassion for the men who died and their families, characterized the benevolent but sometimes abrasive despotism he exercised over Eastern's affairs. Demanding unquestioning loyalty, he had what one writer called "the capacity for striking hard, fast, and quickly when he believes that there is anything that deserves to be struck." But he went out of his way to demonstrate concern for his employees, always in a patriarchal way. The widow of one of Eastern's captains remembered how Rickenbacker slipped an envelope with a generous amount of cash into his hands when he was hospitalized. Like C. E. Woolman, the affable general manager of Delta Air Lines, he was a father figure exemplifying a style of management prevalent in the South, where all of Delta's and most of Eastern's operations were concentrated. Woolman was modest and homespun, Rick egotistical and often arrogant, but both men looked upon their companies as extended families, knew their employees by name, and kept track of their personal lives.[70]

Rickenbacker made it his business to know about the sexual habits and financial problems of employees. "A word from him has blighted more than one unconventional *amour* and propped up more than one pilot's faith in matrimony," said one observer. In 1940 Dick Merrill married actress Toby Wing, who gave up her screen career after the wedding. Rickenbacker tried to stop Merrill's gambling by suggesting to Wing that she get her husband to buy a home. "It would be a good investment," he urged, "and if Dick had to meet a big payment every month, I don't think he'd take a chance on gambling it away." Soon thereafter the couple bought an expensive dwelling in Miami Beach. "It was a beautiful place, with a mortgage in proportion," Eddie said. He attended the housewarming and was glad "Dick had to forego the ponies" to pay for the homestead.[71]

One of Rickenbacker's first decisions when he became general manager at Eastern in 1935 was to give employees a pay raise and improve working conditions to bolster morale. Breech had denied employees time off when they were ill, given them no paid vacations, and forced flight crews to work more than the eighty-five hours per month stipulated by federal regulations. Compensation began when a plane took off and stopped when it landed. Rickenbacker was indignant about these policies and vowed to change them if he became chief executive. Nevertheless, he kept wages and salaries "among the lowest in the industry" after taking complete charge in 1938.[72] He claimed he did so not simply to control costs but also because he did not want to encourage employees to spend money frivolously. During the late 1930s he launched a series of innovations, which, though unusual in the airline industry at the time, were characteristic of "welfare capitalism," aimed at controlling labor and averting radicalism by providing benefits and amenities.[73]

Rickenbacker's playbook was derived from self-help manuals he read and distributed among Eastern's employees. He established credit unions to make loans to employees for "provident or productive purposes."[74] Late in 1938 Eastern created a "Christmas Appreciation Fund" of $40,000 to be distributed among employees earning $300 or less per month, based on length of service. Early in 1939 Rickenbacker announced a plan under which workers could buy 25,000 shares of stock in the company, in installments at $10 per share, with a provision that the stock could be used as collateral for long-term loans. At going rates, a share in EAL was worth $17.75 at the time the program began. "If it develops that selling these shares will bring in a profit and you need that money to buy a home or pay medical bills or take care of some extreme emergency, then I won't object," Eddie said at a staff meeting. "But if I find anybody selling his stock to buy a big red automobile or something equally frivolous, I warn you right here and now I'm going to be mad as Hell!" He established the first pension plan in the airline industry with the Connecticut Mutual Insurance Company. Employees could designate a planned retirement age and specify premiums to be withdrawn from their paychecks to yield whatever annuities they desired when they stopped working. Eastern also became the first carrier to mandate a forty-hour week for maintenance workers.[75]

Rickenbacker's efforts to promote employee welfare did not stop unionization. The Air Line Pilots Association (ALPA), an elite labor organization founded in 1931, flourished among Eastern's captains and copilots. Merrill was a stalwart member. No love was lost between Rickenbacker and David L. Behncke, a United Airlines pilot who had conceived the ALPA and guided it through a series of victories, culminating in provisions in the Civil Aeronautics Act of 1938 that assured the union of representation on the Air Safety Board. Despite his feelings about Behncke, Rickenbacker made no effort to suppress Eastern's ALPA chapter and would have been ill-advised to try.[76]

His relationship with mechanics was more complicated. In November 1937, after a union organizing drive he opposed, Rickenbacker quelled a brief strike by mechanics at Newark International Airport by bringing in skilled personnel who were loyal to management from other stations, and the disaffected workers returned to their jobs. But he also recognized the necessity for accepting a union, partly because of the 1935 Wagner Act that protected employees' rights to engage in collective bargaining and partly because the Rockefeller family, which never forgot the Ludlow Massacre that occurred in 1914, would not countenance union busting. Accordingly, he reached an agreement with the craft-oriented International Association of Machinists to organize Eastern's mechanics.[77]

Rickenbacker tried to maximize profits by emphasizing fleet utilization. Subscribing to the principle that an aircraft was not earning money unless it was flying, he achieved the distinction of having his planes in the air longer per day—twelve hours, forty-five minutes by 1941—than any other carrier in the industry. He required employees to know the cost of a given operation or piece of equipment, not only in dollars and cents but in mills. Nothing above fifty dollars could be spent for anything without his written permission.[78]

He stressed economy as a reason for abandoning the use of "hostesses" on Eastern's airliners and hiring male stewards in their place. He argued that female cabin attendants too often got married soon after they began working for the company, which lost the money it had invested in training them. *The Great Silver Fleet News,* arguing that "service rather than glamor and silk stockings" was the best way to please passengers, featured photographs of snappily dressed graduates of the steward-training program, wearing military-style caps, white jackets, contrasting bow ties, brass buttons, and blue trousers with red stripes. Pan American's use of stewards was probably another reason for his decision, promoting EAL's elite image as Trippe's chief domestic ally.[79]

As demonstrated by his fondness for Merrill, Eddie was proud of his pilots, particularly airmen who attained the coveted status of "million milers," of whom EAL had fifty-four in 1939. He believed in the "spiritual brotherhood" of "men who live in the heavens" but had an idiosyncratic outlook about the equipment provided to them. He particularly opposed the use of "automatic pilots" to relieve them of spending time at the controls. An incident that occurred over Richmond, Indiana, on a flight from California while the company was experimenting with such devices gave him a particular reason to dislike them. When part of a propeller blade broke off and hit the fuselage with a "terrible bang," Rickenbacker thought that the cockpit crew was suspiciously slow to feather the engine, which was shaking violently. Feeling that dependence on the automatic pilot had dulled their reflexes, he bellowed his displeasure at the guilty crewmember and he abruptly discontinued using it. He said he wanted his pilots, and especially copilots, to work constantly at honing their skills. It became a standing joke among Eastern's flyers that Eddie would not permit the use of any instruments that had not been in a Spad XIII.[80]

Rickenbacker had no doubts, however, about equipping planes with the best safety features available. Existing systems of radio navigation were obsolete and remained so from 1933 to 1938 despite complaints by federal aeronautics chief Eugene L. Vidal, who called for improved equipment that existed but was unobtainable due to budgetary stringencies.[81] Besides advocating static-free transmitters, Rickenbacker wanted planes equipped with homing compasses so pilots could tune in on an unvarying radio signal and calculate where they were. He also wanted to eliminate danger to radio antennas from ice formation. On one occasion a DC-2 on which he was flying lost contact with the navigational beam in a snowstorm because its antennas had snapped under the weight of ice. Coached by Rickenbacker, the pilot got safely to Toledo, Ohio, with less then ten gallons of gasoline in his tanks by glimpsing the glow of the city's lights under conditions of nearly zero visibility. Eddie's fears were intensified by the crash in 1936 of a DC-2 piloted by Merrill. Descending into Newark International on a flight from Miami, it brushed against treetops on a mountain near Port Jervis, New York, and came down in dense underbrush after losing radio contact in a blinding snowstorm with heavy ice formation. Thanks to Merrill's flying skills, nobody aboard the plane was killed. Hastening to the scene with a rescue party, Eddie was amazed that Merrill had merely suffered a broken ankle in the crash. In a vigorous statement to the media, he reiterated his previous demands, called for changes in the DC-2's deicing system, and urged improvements to its primitive low-frequency radio receivers to eliminate static caused by precipitation. He wanted weather balloons to be sent aloft at specific intervals, equipped with transmitters to provide pilots information about wind conditions. He also had Eastern's engineers design a spring-loaded tension reliever to shake ice particles from antennas.[82]

In January 1937 he set forth a four-point plan he believed would reduce the number of air accidents by 75 percent if enacted by Congress. It proposed that the Department of Commerce take action to raise navigational standards and modernize all aids required to attain them, that planes be required to have shielded antennas and radio compasses to facilitate triangulating their positions, that cities be obliged to establish twenty-four-hour ground stations transmitting a unique identifying signal, and that such stations must have radio direction-finding aids and provide trained personnel to determine a lost plane's position. California congressman J. F. Dockweiler pushed for the adoption of Rickenbacker's program, which resulted in a $7 million modernization program after a spate of accidents. Vidal mandated the use of shielded antennas and direction finders before he was forced out of office in March 1937.[83]

Rickenbacker crusaded for the improvement of existing airports and the creation of new ones. On 29 September 1937, sitting in his New York City office, he "tapped a telegraph key, closed an electric circuit, and fired a cannon 1,271 miles away," formally opening a new airport at Grand Island, Nebraska. He was responsible for persuading Houston to build a new airport and campaigned for a bond issue to improve air terminal facilities at Beaumont, Texas. He strongly supported a drive by the Virginia Aeronautics Association to upgrade the state's air safety infrastructure. He fought strenuously for a new airport on Philadelphia's south side. *The Great Silver Fleet News* abounded in articles about airport development, almost always with help from the Works Progress Administration (WPA). Whatever his feelings about the New Deal, Rickenbacker approved the WPA's efforts on the grounds that all citizens benefited from air transportation. He also stressed the relationship between aviation and national defense at a time when war was looming in Europe and the need for preparedness was becoming increasingly urgent.[84]

Enhancing safety was a constant theme in his efforts to improve airports and airways. Knowing how precarious flying could be, he refused to use the word "safe" in Eastern's advertisements even though the airline went from 1930 through 1936 without a single passenger fatality in 141,794,894 miles of operations. In 1937 the National Safety Council gave an award to EAL for this accomplishment, but the string snapped on 10 August of that year when one of Eastern's DC-2s crashed near the end of the runway at Daytona Beach. Taking off before dawn, it smashed into an emergency electrical pole the Florida Power and Light Company had installed directly in its flight path only hours before the aircraft was scheduled to depart for Miami at four o'clock. Nobody had thought to notify Eastern's local traffic manager or any of the other airlines using the terminal. Rickenbacker flew to Daytona Beach immediately after the crash and subsequently spread the news to cities and power companies on EAL's route system about what had taken place and why. Despite the accident, EAL received consecutive awards for safe operation from the National Safety Council from 1936 through 1939 and was the first carrier to receive the distinction.[85]

Such things did not happen by chance. They reflected Rickenbacker's determination to track every detail of EAL's operations. Like Delta's C. E. Woolman, he tried to read every piece of mail sent by passengers, whether they patted the company on the back or complained about its service. Woolman, however, was genial, whereas Rickenbacker was abrasive. He did not suffer fools gladly and dealt caustically with travelers who pushed his temper to the boiling point, telling them he did not want their business.[86] Whatever his flaws, Rickenbacker built Eastern into the most profitable carrier of his day. A tribute to him declared, "Eddie is that rarity among mortals—the romantic and romanticized daredevil who has successfully managed the evolution into the solid man of affairs."[87] In an era in which airlines were struggling to establish themselves against other modes of transportation, as Robert Serling has said, they "needed their Rickenbackers with their heavy-handed strength, their single-minded determination, their dogged resilience under the worst adversity."[88] And the worst adversity was yet to come.

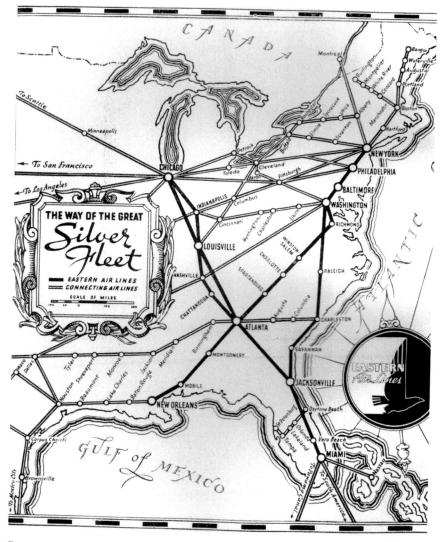

Route map of Eastern Air Lines in 1936, the year after Rickenbacker became general manager of the carrier. Because of his desire not to compete with TWA, Ernest Breech vetoed Rickenbacker's long-standing hopes, going back to his association with American Airways, to establish a route from New York City (Newark airport) to Chicago, which would have smoothed out Eastern's regional traffic flows. Nevertheless, except for the short stage between New York and Washington, which it shared with American, Eastern monopolized potentially lucrative vacation routes from New York and Chicago to Miami, which Rickenbacker quickly developed with Douglas DC-2s that had the range, passenger-carrying capacity, and operational costs required for profitability, funneling passengers into the Latin American route system of Pan American Airways. Source: *The Great Silver Fleet News* 1, no. 1 (September 1936): inside front cover.

Douglas DC-2 airliner, which entered service with Eastern Air Lines in 1935, looming over maintenance staff in a hangar at the Newark airport. Despite being quickly overshadowed by the larger and faster Douglas DC-3, the DC-2 represented a remarkable forward step in American commercial aviation. Fast by the standards of the time, rugged, dependable, cost-efficient, and able to fly 500 miles when fully loaded, it was the most economical airliner yet designed, making it possible for Rickenbacker to transform Eastern for the first time into a profitable enterprise. Source: *The Great Silver Fleet News* 4, no. 7 (November 1939): 30.

Rickenbacker with his sons, David (*left*) and William (*right*), at the Indianapolis Motor Speedway.
Once again Rickenbacker is playing a parental role that was less intimate than the photograph
suggests, but there is no reason to question the sincerity of his love for his adopted sons, who had
differing personalities and disliked one another.

Portrait of Rickenbacker by Howard Chandler Christy hanging in the entrance hall of the apartment occupied by the Rickenbackers on East End Avenue in New York City. The painting is based
on the sortie near Billy-sous-les-Côtes on 25 September 1918 in which Rickenbacker, just placed
in command of the 94th Pursuit Squadron and determined to show that he would lead by example,
took on seven German aircraft single-handedly and shot down two of them, causing the other five to
regroup from the ferocity of his attack while he escaped unharmed. Rickenbacker ultimately won
the Medal of Honor in 1930 for gallantry in this action.

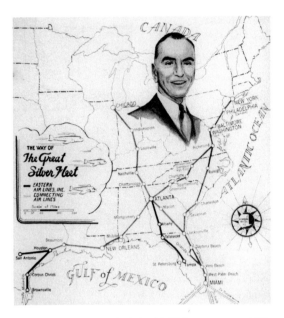

Route map of Eastern Air Lines in 1938, shaded to highlight two recent additions. Service linking Houston, San Antonio, Corpus Christi, and Brownsville, Texas, won in a hotly contested struggle with Braniff, permitted connections (via Pan American) with Mexico and South America's West Coast. But for the bargain Rickenbacker had made in 1936 by paying $160,000 for the Wedell-Williams Transport Corporation, with its route from New Orleans to Houston, service between Houston and the Rio Grande would not have materialized. The other addition, granted to Eastern by the Civil Aeronautics Authority, linked Atlanta and Tampa via Albany, Georgia, and Tallahassee, Florida. Rickenbacker's smile reflects the satisfaction he took in Eastern's growing stature. Source: *The Great Silver Fleet News* 4, no. 1 (September 1938): inside front cover.

Rickenbacker signing a ten-year lease to new headquarters of Eastern Air Lines at 10 Rockefeller Plaza, 14 June 1940. Lawrence A. Kirkland (*left*), rental manager for Rockefeller Center, and Laurance S. Rockefeller (*right*) are looking over his shoulder in the cabin of a Douglas DC-3 Silverliner in what was believed to be the first execution of a lease for office space ever signed aloft.

Route map of Eastern Air Lines in 1941, showing how much the company had grown since 1938. Linking Atlanta to St. Louis via Evansville and Nashville was a particularly important step, opening a lucrative new vacation artery from the Ohio and Mississippi river valleys to Miami. Other major additions included Memphis, Tennessee, and Birmingham, Alabama. A direct connection between Louisville and St. Louis via Evansville facilitated connections with routes leading to the Pacific Coast, and a direct connection between Birmingham and Atlanta further integrated Eastern's sprawling southeastern system around the Atlanta hub. Access to wealthy Sea Island resorts adjacent to Georgia and South Carolina further stimulated vacation traffic to Miami and Latin America through connections with Pan American. The network that Rickenbacker developed, linking critical markets and destinations, made Eastern the most profitable privately owned airline of its day. Source: *The Great Silver Fleet News* 6, no. 2 (Summer 1941): back cover.

Wreckage of Douglas DST Silversleeper that crashed in a forest near the Atlanta airport with Rickenbacker aboard, 27 February 1941. Despite the life-threatening injuries he suffered, Rickenbacker survived a fierce struggle for life in Piedmont Hospital. Along with the twenty-one-day raft ordeal he suffered in the Pacific Ocean in October–November 1942, the Atlanta crash began a turning point in Rickenbacker's life that changed him from a pragmatic, though highly opinionated, executive into a controversial advocate of political and ideological causes.

Cartoon, "The Ace Turns Up!" after Rickenbacker's rescue from the Pacific raft episode. Banner headlines exploded across the country greeting the news the Rickenbacker was safe, providing a "national Christmas present" at a time when the course of war against Germany, Italy, and Japan was shifting in favor of the United States and its allies after an initial string of discouraging setbacks. Source: *Washington Post*, 16 November 1942.

Rickenbacker, wearing a pith helmet, smiles broadly while pointing at a photographer after returning from his Pacific Mission in December 1942. The photograph is signed, "All of America glad to see the Indestructible 'Eddie' return," by Major General Barney M. Giles, United States Army. Rickenbacker's popularity reached its peak after he survived the ordeal but waned in the postwar period as he struggled to find a sense of purpose after concluding that God had spared his life in repeated close encounters with death.

Rickenbacker with Adelaide and New York City mayor Fiorello LaGuardia at LaGuardia Field upon Eddie's return from the Pacific Mission, 19 December 1942. The two men, both veterans of aerial combat in World War I and fellow devotees of Billy Mitchell, were good friends despite political differences and Rickenbacker's questioning of LaGuardia's judgment in building a major airport on a swampy site in Queens.

Rickenbacker (*left of center*) standing near the microphone with N. Dreystadt, general manager of Cadillac Division, General Motors Corporation, at the initial "Hat-in-the-Ring Squadron" ceremony on 22 January 1943 to discourage absenteeism and promote job performance. Eddie and plant personnel have thrown their headgear into the circle on the floor. The campaign, conducted amid impassioned attacks by Rickenbacker on labor tactics that he felt undermined the war effort, was unsuccessful.

Rickenbacker addressing American airmen at Kweilin, China, during his visit to that country in 1943. Rickenbacker willingly assumed a role that made him unpopular among airmen, telling them on General Eisenhower's behalf that they would not be permitted to return home after completing twenty-five missions or 200 hours of combat flying, as they had been promised. Although Eddie deeply admired the Chinese people, he bitterly criticized Chiang Kai-Shek's corrupt regime.

Rickenbacker, with Adelaide registering mock disapproval and William relishing the occasion, pretends to quaff a goblet of vodka "straight up" after returning from the Soviet Union in 1943. A well-seasoned drinker, Rickenbacker impressed Russians with his ability to down repeated toasts without showing ill effects, contributing to the success of his mission. He made himself useful not only by showing the Soviets how to better utilize aircraft supplied to them under Lend-Lease but also by telling them about the Boeing B-29 Superfortress being developed in the United States.

Rickenbacker sitting at his desk in his office after the appearance of his article, "Why I Believe in Prayer," in the first issue of *Guideposts* magazine, prominently displayed in the foreground. Rickenbacker's humanity shines through this photograph; his crusty manner masked a softer side of his personality that was warm and compassionate. His survival of the raft ordeal contributed to a spiritual conversion that made him feel divinely ordained for a mission he tried hard to find, leading him to become closely associated with religious leaders, including Norman Vincent Peale, the editor of *Guideposts*.

Cutaway view and photograph of Lockheed L-1049 Constellation, which entered service with Eastern Air Lines in 1948. The Constellation, stretched into a larger and longer configuration, was one of the most aesthetically striking airliners in the history of American commercial aviation because of its gracefully curved fuselage and triple tail. Its range, seating capacity, and operational characteristics made it possible for Eastern to compete with airlines utilizing such planes as the Douglas DC-6 in an era when federal regulators were opening routes formerly monopolized by single carriers to increasing numbers of commercial airlines. Source: National Air and Space Museum, Smithsonian Institution (SI 77-5795).

Residence at Bear Creek Ranch near Kerrville, Texas, which Rickenbacker acquired in 1949. Rickenbacker bought the ranch partly as a potential place of refuge from an atomic war, but enjoyed using it to entertain members of Eastern Air Lines' board of directors. He ultimately gave much of the ranch to the Boy Scouts of America.

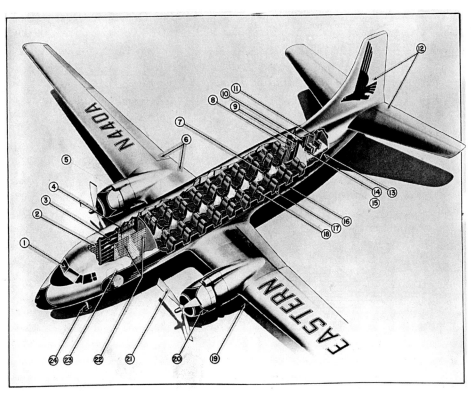

Cutaway view of Martin 4-0-4 Silverliner, which entered service with Eastern Air Lines in 1952. Providing a decade of dependable service without a single significant accident on midrange routes, the 4-0-4 saved Eastern from serious financial difficulty after a series of disasters accompanying the introduction of an earlier model, the Martin 2-0-2, to which Eastern had committed itself but fortunately never used. Rickenbacker and Laurance Rockefeller, with help from bankers and government officials, negotiated a plan to redesign the 2-0-2 into the 4-0-4, but the deal forced Glenn Martin to yield control of the company he had founded in the earliest days of the American aircraft industry. Source: National Air and Space Museum (NASM 00069738), Smithsonian Institution.

Rickenbacker with Thomas F. Armstrong (seated at right), Sidney Shannon, vice president in charge of operations (looking over EVR's shoulder), and Paul H. Brattain, vice president in charge of traffic (standing at right), in 1953 after Armstrong was named president and Rickenbacker was appointed chairman of the board and chief executive officer of Eastern Air Lines. Armstrong's promotion was a titular move that left Rickenbacker in control of the carrier.

Rickenbacker, grand marshal of the Tournament of Roses Parade, rides with Adelaide at his side in Pasadena, California, on 1 January 1957. Being chosen for this honor indicated his continuing popularity as a national hero and oracle of anticommunism in the postwar era.

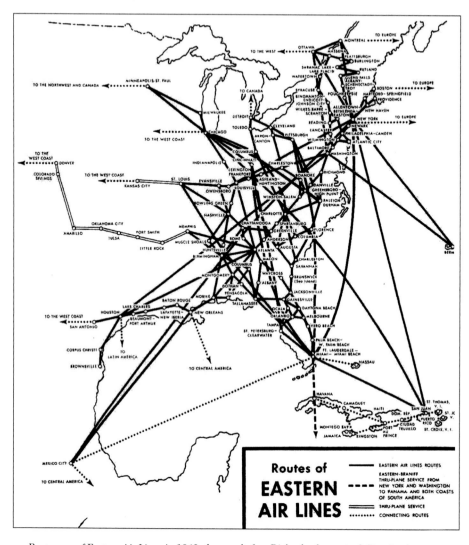

Route map of Eastern Air Lines in 1962, the year before Rickenbacker retired. Despite the super-ficial impressiveness of its system, Eastern suffered from having a hodgepodge of relatively short routes that were unprofitable to operate and too few long, nonstop routes capable of yielding costs and traffic levels to compensate for them. The company's failure in 1961 to win transcontinental routes to markets on the Pacific Coast, partly attributable to the way Rickenbacker had alienated federal regulators, was a shattering blow to Eastern that helped lead to Eddie's forced retirement in 1963. Source: Annual Report of Eastern Air Lines, 1962.

Rickenbacker posing with a copy of his autobiography in May 1968. Booton Herndon, a veteran freelance writer, wrote the book after a series of sometimes stormy interviews with Eddie in 1965. Although the work contains many inaccuracies and distortions, Herndon registered an outstanding performance as a ghostwriter by recognizing Rickenbacker's achievements and producing a work that honored him despite personality traits that Herndon strongly disliked.

Rickenbacker greeting chief executives of major airlines at a banquet sponsored by the Boeing Aircraft Company and held at the 21 Club in New York City, 25 May 1972. *Left to right:* Rickenbacker, Charles H. Dolson (Delta), William A. Patterson (United), Charles Tillinghast (TWA), C. R. Smith (United), and Juan Trippe (Pan American). Whatever mistakes Rickenbacker may have made at the helm of Eastern Air Lines, he was one of the outstanding figures in the history of American commercial aviation.

Chapter 15

— ☆ —

Pivot

As one of America's foremost military heroes, Rickenbacker inevitably became involved in debates about a steadily worsening international situation in the 1930s as war increasingly threatened to engulf a nation desperately unprepared for a major conflict. His position was paradoxical in that nobody did more to beat the drums for air power but nobody was more reluctant to use it. Ardently antifascist, he was prepared to wield the sword for freedom but anticipated later doctrines of deterrence by preaching that being armed to the teeth was the best way to guarantee peace.

On 28 January 1936 Billy Mitchell, whose increasingly outspoken views had alienated even many of his supporters, contracted influenza at his Virginia farm and was rushed to Doctors Hospital in New York City, where Rickenbacker visited him. Friends on Capitol Hill had recently tried but failed to restore him to brigadier general and give him a colonel's retirement pay. Mitchell died on 19 February. A posthumously published article he wrote for *Liberty* stated his epitaph, which could just as well have been Rickenbacker's: "The cause of right cannot be furthered by a defenseless, unarmed country."[1]

Rickenbacker did not always agree with Mitchell. In October 1934, when they testified in Washington before the President's Aviation Commission, Mitchell called for vesting control of military and commercial aviation in one government department. Captain Eddie—testifying as "Edward Bernard Rickenbacker," showing he was still unsettled about his middle name and had not yet adopted his final choice, Vernon—differed, arguing that airlines should be regulated by a "non-political" agency "similar to the Interstate Commerce Commission." Mitchell believed in preparing for war against Japan, but Rickenbacker said America should "use planes to make love to Japan" by creating a transpacific air transport system linking the two nations via Hawaii and the Philippines.[2]

Nevertheless, he remained one of Billy's greatest champions. After Mitchell died, Rickenbacker helped carry the fallen warrior to a train that would take his body, dressed in civilian clothes, to Milwaukee for burial, feeling unspeakably bitter as the footsteps of the pallbearers reverberated eerily throughout the catacombs of Grand Central Station to a waiting railroad car. He accompanied Mitchell's body to Milwaukee and was the first person to step down when the train reached the station.[3]

Rickenbacker worried about the state of American air power as the world drifted toward another global war. He believed the nation's airmen were unexcelled but the United States was woefully behind in equipment and materiel.[4] His assessment was confirmed in 1935 when he and Adelaide went to Europe together for the first time since their honeymoon, taking David and William along. In London, before visiting Germany, Rickenbacker had lunch with influential publisher William Maxwell Aitken, now Lord Beaverbrook, who wanted a firsthand report as soon as Rick returned to England.[5] The growth of American commercial aviation amazed officials with whom the Rickenbackers talked in France and Italy, but Eddie knew that Ernst Udet, with whom he had become friends at American air shows, would try to overwhelm him with the power of the Luftwaffe, whose existence was formally announced in 1935. Udet did not admire Hitler but had taken charge of design and supply for the resurgent Nazi air arm.[6]

Erhard Milch, the "prime architect of the Luftwaffe," and Udet welcomed the Rickenbackers when they deplaned in Berlin. Contrasting with their shabby clothes when Eddie had last seen them during the 1922 honeymoon, they were resplendent in Nazi regalia. After they escorted the visitors to their hotel in an impressive motorcade, Udet took his American friend to a ceremonial luncheon at the Air Service Building, which covered an entire city block and had a thick concrete roof. Hermann Goering, whom Hitler had appointed supreme commander of the Luftwaffe, made a brief appearance and asked if Eddie remembered the predictions he had made about the future of German air power at their previous meeting. When Rickenbacker assured him he did, Goering told Udet to give him a grand tour to see for himself what had been achieved. Eddie later said he knew that Goering was too proud to hold anything back and wanted to overawe him.[7]

Udet took Rickenbacker to the headquarters of Richthofen's former unit, located about thirty miles outside Berlin. Eddie was interested to see that the twelve fighter planes and two trainers bore the same insignia, including bright red noses, which they had displayed in the war. They were scattered throughout a pine forest in the most effective display of camouflage he had ever seen. Udet told him that, to conserve manpower, the Luftwaffe was training every man in a squadron, however humble his status, to learn to fly. This idea seemed sensible to Eddie because he himself had been a mechanic before becoming a pilot. They toured the BMW Engine Works and aircraft factories, one of which had an advanced wind tunnel for testing tailspins. Udet showed him the latest German engines and instruments and revealed designs still being planned. At Friedrichshafen they toured the Zeppelin and Dornier plants. None of the people he met tried to hide their overriding objective—to regain imperial Germany's former greatness by force of arms. Eddie believed that Germany did not really consider the United States an enemy, as it did England and France, but he felt threatened nevertheless.[8]

The next day Nazi bigwigs treated the Rickenbackers to lunch at the Aero Club in Berlin. That afternoon Udet threw a cocktail party for them at his apartment. He repelled Adelaide by showing off his gun collection and displaying his marksmanship, shooting at targets in one of the rooms and making so much noise she was afraid the neighbors would "think someone is being liquidated."[9] Escorting them to a restaurant, Udet ushered them into "a private dining room, small and stuffy, with portieres closely drawn." Adelaide recalled that the walls were unadorned except for a huge picture of Hitler. They ate "pressed duck, and innumerable other dishes that one considered delicacies even in other times." Adelaide thought it scandalous that they had so much to eat when many Germans had so little. "The room reeked of cigar smoke and was unbearably hot because every window was tightly shut to guard against the ever-present possibility of assassination." After the meal, Udet, a talented cartoonist, drew caricatures on smoked dinner plates with a burnt match, a "cruel and horrible one" of himself and "a kindly and pleasant one" of her husband. The proprietor coated them with varnish and gave them to the Rickenbackers.[10]

Eddie and Adelaide returned to London about a month later, and he went to Chelsea Square to dine with Lord Beaverbrook as promised. The number of political potentates present, including virtually every member of Stanley Baldwin's cabinet except the prime minister himself, surprised Rickenbacker. The main question on everybody's mind was how soon the Germans would be ready for war. When Eddie predicted five years, Foreign Undersecretary Vansittart, an ally of Churchill and the only person in the room who believed Germany was conducting a military buildup aimed at world dominance, said it might take only two, causing Eddie to think that he was unduly alarmed but still on the right track.[11] Eddie concluded the Brits could not distinguish between preparedness and warmongering. After drinking cocktails and sitting down to eat, he recalled saying to himself, "Rickenbacker, just be a country boy. Keep your damned mouth shut and your ears open, and maybe you will learn something."[12]

Rickenbacker returned to America even more deeply convinced that the United States was far behind in building an air force even remotely comparable with the one Germany was creating, but senior officers in the Army Air Corps turned a deaf ear to him. Hap Arnold was not alone in refusing to believe that mechanics and other support personnel could become pilots. Rickenbacker protested that he himself had made such a transition, but decided his listeners were "too obtuse to see the peril America was facing."[13]

Rickenbacker's fears became increasingly plausible as the world slid closer to war. Beginning in 1936, Charles Lindbergh made repeated trips to Germany, confirming the alarming progress of Nazi air power that Eddie had already observed.[14] FDR was hamstrung by neutrality acts he signed because Americans did not want to make the same mistakes that had dragged the country into the Great War. The situation increasingly impaled Rickenbacker on the horns of a dilemma. Like many Americans, perhaps a majority, he believed that Europe was decadent and that the Western Hemisphere had a separate destiny. Nevertheless, he abominated Hitler and felt strongly that the United States should prepare to defend itself, the sooner the better. He was not an isolationist but a noninterventionist. Had Mitchell's warnings been heeded, he thought, Germany would have been too awed by American air power to threaten world peace.[15]

An extended cruise with his family to Norway and other European countries in mid-1938 confirmed Rickenbacker's opinions about the direction America should take.[16] The Great War, whose horrors he had seen at first hand, had not made "the world safe for democracy," as Wilson had hoped. French morale had wilted, and Britain lacked the will to win a war against the German juggernaut he had seen taking shape in 1935. Meanwhile, Eddie's aversion toward FDR, which was shared throughout much of the airline industry, was intensified by the court-packing episode and the president's verbal jabs at "Economic Royalists" with whom Rickenbacker was closely allied.[17]

What could be done? Rickenbacker doubted public opinion would tolerate a massive military buildup. Casting about for ideas that would keep America out of war, as he strongly wished, but build the foundations for a strong air force that could be a bulwark for peace, he proposed a plan published by *Collier's* in April 1939. He noted that FDR had recently called for the production of 10,000 military aircraft and the capacity to build 20,000 more but had settled for only 6,000 planes.[18] Because the will to build large numbers of military aircraft was obviously lacking, Eddie advanced a proposal to build 50,000 *commercial* ones to carry all first-class mail and large amounts of cargo to every part of the nation. Assembly-line techniques already used in the automobile industry could achieve this goal, he asserted, but only if the country had a much larger aviation infrastructure and trained many more pilots and technicians. "Consider what a different situation we would have with fifty thousand airplanes all in common use," he urged. "Then we would have the finest training fleet for pilots in the world, a fleet that would fly every day and every night, over every section of the national terrain, in all weathers."

Legislation was already pending in Congress to appropriate $300 million for aerial rearmament.[19] Rickenbacker estimated his own project would cost $500 million but perhaps could be done for less when mass-production techniques were perfected for making airplanes. The fleet he wanted would create jobs for "more than a hundred thousand men in factories alone, to say nothing of the necessary construction of new airfields, and airways," stimulating commerce in every field of business that used airmail.

Rickenbacker candidly admitted that the aircraft he envisioned, costing about $10,000 each, would have only limited utility in an all-out war, but said something was better than nothing. They could not be used as fighter planes, but might be upgraded into small bombers capable of overwhelming invaders by sheer force of numbers. They could also perform reconnaissance. Their chief value, however, would lie in "a wealth of uses in civil transportation behind the lines, cadet training, hauling of light materials and air-corps supplies and the patrolling of our immense coast line, or communications to the interior and speedy service to bases of operations." The tools, jigs, dies, and updated drawings required to produce them would contribute to mounting a major effort to manufacture more-advanced military aircraft if need arose.

Eddie had more than domestic uses in mind for the armada of planes he wanted the nation to create. It would provide the basis for a "merchant marine of the air" under twenty-five-year reciprocal franchises with England, France, the Netherlands, Scandinavia, Germany, and the Soviet Union. "This program would insure to the United States not one company but half a dozen transatlantic services." At the very least, it would stimulate airmindedness in the United States and train large numbers of pilots. "The only way to make our people unconquerable in the air," he said, "is to give them the habit of the air."[20] His project was consistent with the a proposal to create a Civilian Pilot Training Program advanced early in 1939 by Robert H. Hinckley, a New Dealer from Utah who had strong connections with Harry Hopkins and the WPA.[21]

As the threat of war intensified, the Rickenbackers took yet another cruise to Europe in the summer of 1939. Norway was their principal destination but Germany was the first place they visited. Early in a detailed diary of the trip, Adelaide described a festival in Hamburg celebrating a bountiful wheat harvest, noting that the city, which had been a hotbed of anti-Nazi sentiment because of the damage Hitler's policies had done to its international trade, was full of storm troopers and awash with flags, banners, and floats adorned with swastikas. Rickenbacker visited Udet while she kept the boys occupied with sightseeing. After going briefly to Sweden, they enjoyed a long excursion, mostly by boat, along the Norwegian coast before going to Copenhagen, Amsterdam, and London. After conferring with airline executives in the British capital, Rickenbacker flew back to New York on one of Pan American's clippers, leaving Adelaide, David, and William behind to continue touring England and France.

Things had been idyllic up to this point but became much less so after Eddie went home. Adelaide saw "gorgeous oaks" uprooted in London to build bomb shelters and noticed signs asking whether citizens had obtained gas masks. Paris was seething with panic when she and the boys ascended the Eiffel Tower and looked down on parks "simply honeycombed with bombproof shelters." As war became imminent because of Hitler's threat to Poland and an Anglo-French guarantee to defend it, she did not know whether they would be able to return home from Cherbourg as planned. When they arrived there, the lobby of their hotel was "completely filled with stranded Americans left high and dry" because the *Hansa,* the liner on which they had hoped to sail, had been recalled to Germany. After a determined campaign by Adelaide to get other accommodations, they finally embarked on a Polish ship, the *Batory,* which providentially arrived from Gdynia and Copenhagen after going through dangerous waters without lights. The vessel was so jammed with passengers when it left Cherbourg that she had to share a room and bath with a general from Warsaw who had been sent to America on a secret mission. German troops stormed into Poland while they were at sea, and the war everyone had dreaded now erupted. Adelaide was immensely relieved when the liner finally reached New York on 5 September. Eddie, waiting at the dock as she and the boys came down the gangplank, had worried intensely and regretted he had not brought them back to America when he left England. Adelaide said he was surprised the war had begun so soon, giving Hitler "credit for a more normal brain than he has."[22]

Pressure mounted for repeal of an arms embargo mandated in the latest neutrality act passed by Congress. Rickenbacker thought the United States would do well to husband its own resources and strongly opposed such a step, receiving many messages supporting his stand.[23] On 26 September, three weeks after his family returned home, Rickenbacker broadcast a strongly noninterventionist speech from radio station WJZ in New York City, carried by the NBC Blue Network. Speaking "without political ambitions or selfish motives," he said he was merely "a private citizen of this country who loves his heritage, as well as the liberties and opportunities it offers with a passion that knows no bounds." In 1917, he asserted, "Americans entered the World War with a profound conviction that we were fighting for the preservation of Democracy." The result had been bitter disillusionment and a "realization that the winner and the loser of such a conflict must suffer the consequences alike." Participation in the war had resulted in "the complete disruption of our economic machinery" and "ten years of depression."

He estimated the Great War had cost America $250 billion, a staggering sum that could have been used to enhance the welfare of its citizens and people in other countries. He feared the effect of regimentation upon American youth. Disclaiming "ill will towards the people of any of the belligerent countries," he said, "My heart bleeds with sympathy for all of them. But this can be no justification to me for our involvement again, with the horrible consequences of the probable loss of millions of our young men, and billions of our wealth." His military record proved he was "not a pacifist in any sense of the word." He simply wanted "preparedness to insure against foreign invasion, by having, primarily, a peace time aviation industry, developed through peace time service, that will give us an adequate military aviation reserve for defensive purposes only." He would offer his services and "any worldly goods I may possess to protect and guard our institutions" if need arose, but demanded "KEEP US OUT OF THIS WAR," emphasizing his point with all capital letters in the published text.[24]

Listeners sent an outpouring of letters and telegrams, mostly favorable and praising the evident sincerity with which Eddie spoke. A journalist said he wished he knew "of some way to compel every man, woman and child in the United States" to read a text of the address, which he called "the greatest talk ever made over the radio." "Never was I jolted so severely nor so actively by a radio speech," said a broadcaster from Colorado. Particularly pleasing to Rickenbacker was a letter from Daniel Willard, president of the Baltimore and Ohio Railroad. "Your remarks were more illuminating and stated in a more convincing manner than anything I have heard," Willard said. "You performed a real public service and I congratulate you."[25]

Many Americans, however, were changing their minds as Hitler's armies overran Poland from the west and Stalin's forces invaded from the east, resulting from a Nazi-Soviet Pact negotiated earlier in the year. Alarmed by the speed of the German onslaught, Congress repealed neutrality acts that had prevented the British and French from buying arms in the United States. During the winter months, as Hitler bided his time and a "phony war" settled upon Western Europe, the Soviet Union attacked Finland, whose resistance against overwhelming odds inspired American admiration. After the Finns capitulated in March 1940, attention shifted to Scandinavia, where Hitler launched a sea and air attack on Denmark and Norway in April. Denmark fell quickly, and Norway, a country the Rickenbackers loved, was completely in Nazi hands by mid-June. Belgium and the Netherlands fell, followed quickly by France.[26]

The rapidity of these developments, and particularly the speed with which French resistance had collapsed, forced Eddie into an agonizing reappraisal of American neutrality. On 3 June 1940, still arguing that the United States should stay on the sidelines, he pleaded for a national preparedness program including 50,000 warplanes, 150,000 pilots, and 500,000 ground mechanics. Only a few days later, however, as the French war effort crumbled, he began to sense that mere preparedness was not enough and that the United States would have to enter the conflict. Speaking at New Orleans, he predicted intervention would come if Britain and France could somehow hold out another three months, but the fate of France left the British Commonwealth facing the Germans alone. "If England lasts through the winter," he told a crowd at Evansville, Indiana, "we'll be in the war by April"—taking care to add, "though I'm against it." Despite his lingering reservations, he was being forced to become increasingly realistic. "Britain can not defeat Germany alone," he said, "but Germany can not defeat Great Britain with the United States behind her." Finally, reluctantly, speaking at St. Louis, he candidly admitted that England could not survive without American "money, munitions, and men."[27]

In August, while Rickenbacker was still wavering, General Robert E. Wood, chairman of the board of Sears, Roebuck and Company, invited him to join a committee devoted to the principles that "the United States must now concentrate all its energies on building an impregnable American defense," that "American democracy must be preserved by keeping out of the European War," and that "further extension of 'aid to the Allies' beyond the limitations of cash and carry weakens our own defensive strength and threatens to involve America in war abroad." An "Emergency Committee to Defend America First" would launch a national radio campaign, issue "advertisements timed to counteract rising hysteria at times of crisis urging Americans to keep their heads," and send out letters making a "simple statement of our objectives," using mailing lists compiled by senators Robert A. Taft of Ohio and Burton K. Wheeler of Montana.

Wood asked for Rickenbacker's permission to use his name in organizing the committee. He included a broadside urging that the United States "build at once the greatest air force in the world," a goal Eddie had tirelessly advocated. Another enclosure stated it was "time we started believing that within the boundaries of the United States are every material resource, every economic, military and naval skill required to see us safely through anything," and that "the way to defend America is to defend it ourselves," echoing convictions Rickenbacker had already stated. The text counseled resistance to "prophets of doom" who "would see us drain the resources of America—our steel, our airplanes, our chemicals, our food, through the harbor of New York, rather than to employ these sinews of war on western hemisphere defense." Such sentiments were congruent with fears already expressed by senior officers in the Army Air Corps, including Arnold, who believed that sending too many American combat planes abroad would compromise the nation's ability to defend its own territory. Nothing in Wood's statements conflicted with Eddie's expressed opinions, despite his growing sense that the United States would ultimately have to enter the war, and he sent a brief reply to Wood on 19 August 1940 endorsing his views.[28]

Early in September, R. Douglas Stuart Jr., a law student at Yale University and the son of a Quaker Oats Company executive, notified Rickenbacker that the name of the venture described by Wood had been changed to the "America First Committee" (AFC). Stuart's letter contained a list of distinguished citizens "balanced equally as to Republicans and Democrats," who had agreed to speak on behalf of the goals Wood had expressed in his previous message. The document included Burton K. Wheeler, Arthur H. Vandenberg, Henry Cabot Lodge, Robert M. LaFollette, Robert A. Taft, Bennett Champ Clark, Hiram W. Johnson, Gerald P. Nye, and General Hugh Johnson, who had headed the National Recovery Administration in the early days of the New Deal. Most important for Rickenbacker, however, was the left-hand margin of the letterhead on which Stuart's message was written, listing persons who had been appointed to a "National Committee" of the AFC. The names included Avery Brundage, John T. Flynn, Alice Roosevelt Longworth, Oswald Garrison Villard, Mrs. Burton K. Wheeler, General Wood—and Eddie Rickenbacker.[29]

There is no evidence that Rickenbacker had asked to be appointed to this "National Committee." In all likelihood, the inclusion of his name had been a fait accompli by Stuart and Wood. He did not object—but there were limits beyond which he was unwilling to go. On 3 December 1940 Theodore Roosevelt Jr., and John T. Flynn, a perennial critic of FDR, wired Rickenbacker inviting him to chair the America First Committee in New York, stating that "we will do all the work and get [an] active vice chairman." The telegram put Rickenbacker, increasingly convinced that the United States would have to enter the war to rescue the British from defeat, in an increasingly uncomfortable position. After spending almost a month deciding what to do, he finally sent Roosevelt and Flynn a message on 27 December, while vacationing in Mexico, declining to serve "due to lack of time and possible complications."[30]

Rickenbacker had done nothing more than tacitly permit the AFC to use his name. He had never been an admirer of Hitler and had been troubled by German preparations for war from the time of his visit to

Berlin in 1935. His public statements in late 1940 had shown an unmistakably interventionist trend. He was deeply inspired, and said so, by England's heroic resistance to relentless attacks by the Luftwaffe. "Should these gallant British withstand the terrific onslaught of the totalitarian states until the summer of 1941," he declared on 10 December at a meeting of the New York Economic Club, "it is my sincere conviction that by that time this nation will have declared war." That is what he had been saying for months, but his rhetoric had a new edge. "I say to you and the rest of my fellow Americans," he declared, "we had better prepare to die fighting, rather than fight dying." If Germany won the war, the United States would have no choice but to become the world's "greatest militaristic nation" and incur huge burdens that would "inevitably mean a loss of American liberties." In a stopover at Atlanta en route to Mexico, he issued another dire warning by telling reporters that "if England is defeated Hitler will certainly turn to South America as a convenient road for delivering an attack on this continent." Upon arriving in Mexico City to celebrate Christmas, he predicted that "the collapse of England would mean the removal of the British government to Canada and a merger of the English-speaking peoples in the defense of their way of living." In such a case, he foresaw an interminable "war of attrition" against the Axis "in the air and on the high seas."[31]

Soon after returning to New York City, in a telegram dated 16 January 1941, Rickenbacker formally resigned from the AFC, a fact that historians who later linked him with the organization have failed to acknowledge.[32] Meanwhile, during Eddie's brief period of membership, FDR, needing the cooperation of American industry to prepare the nation for war, had steadily taken a more conciliatory attitude toward big business. In June 1940, in a move aimed at national unity, he appointed two strongly interventionist Republicans, Henry L. Stimson and Frank Knox, to his cabinet as Secretary of War and Secretary of the Navy respectively. Testifying before the Senate as his nomination was being considered, Stimson said the United States would not be safe from invasion "if we sit down and wait for the enemy to attack our shores," a position toward which Rickenbacker himself was being inexorably drawn. After being confirmed by the Senate, Stimson and Knox used their power to favor large corporations with which Rickenbacker was associated or allied. Their influence was present in a revenue bill, passed in July 1940, full of loopholes for aircraft manufacturers that would enable them to escape excess profits taxes. As Stimson wrote in his diary, "If you are going to try to go to war, or to prepare for war, in a capitalist country, you have got to let business make money out of the process, or businessmen won't work, and there are a great many people in Congress who think they can tax business out of all proportion and still have businessmen work diligently and quickly. That is not human nature." Rickenbacker was not privy to Stimson's diary but held the same views. Eastern Air Lines was among the corporations benefiting as mammoth defense plants run by industrial giants like General Motors, Ford, and Chrysler started producing munitions and the American economy began booming for the first time since 1929.

Typical of persons who now began to appear in government service was one of Rickenbacker's close friends, William S. Knudsen of General Motors, who had helped him defeat Breech in 1938. Equally characteristic of the times was the waning influence of Sidney Hillman, who represented organized labor in Roosevelt's inner councils and was outraged by "big business's use of the war emergency to render New Deal labor laws ineffective." In December 1940 Stimson named Wall Street banker Robert S. Lovett, a former naval pilot in World War I, assistant secretary of war. Lovett had recently completed a study of the air power needed for war against Germany and was prepared to go all out to fill the sky with planes, as Eddie had been urging all along.[33]

In a radio broadcast delivered on 29 December 1940, Roosevelt declared that America must become "the great arsenal of democracy."[34] His speech was the kickoff for a drive, strongly supported by Stimson, Knox, and other Republicans, to promote a new concept of transferring military equipment, "Lend-Lease." Rickenbacker's resignation from the AFC coincided with the beginning of a heated debate in Congress to implement the president's new program against determined opposition from Wheeler, Nye, Lindbergh, and other isolationists. As his recent speeches indicated, he had jumped ship. Had a life-threatening crisis not intervened, he would have been in the thick of the fight supporting FDR's plan.

On the evening of 7 October 1940, a group of Rickenbacker's friends and business associates gathered at the 21 Club, on West 52nd Street between Fifth and Sixth avenues. The occasion, which came as a surprise to Eddie, was a "Golden Birthday Anniversary" celebration in his honor.[35]

At a time when men who had lived half a century looked old, Rickenbacker was in the prime of life, radiating vigor and good health. Considering his many close scrapes with death, he had survived with hardly a scratch. With unflagging energy he traveled throughout Eastern's system, presiding over ceremonial events, cutting ribbons, posing for cameramen, giving interviews, keeping track of all the data an airline president had to have at his fingertips. During the Yuletide season late in 1940, dressed as Santa Claus, he announced at a company dinner that $70,000 would be distributed among employees in that year's "Christmas Appreciation Fund." Early in 1941 he was the focus of attention when EAL celebrated the opening of "the world's first Airlines Terminal," a block-long Art Deco structure at 42nd Street and Park Avenue. He demonstrated his dedication to the gathering war preparedness effort at about the same time by speaking at the unveiling of the Army's "Flying Cadet" poster, "Wings over America," depicting military aircraft soaring in the company of a fierce-looking Bald Eagle. Anticipating the passage of the Lend-Lease Act, Rickenbacker sold Eastern's remaining DC-2s to Australia. In another move of great importance to the company, he accepted joint occupancy with Canadian Colonial Airways of a giant hangar costing $1.3 million at a sprawling new airport at North Beach in Queens. The hangar was dedicated by the man most responsible for its construction—New York City's feisty mayor, Fiorello H. LaGuardia.[36]

No one in the metropolis, Rickenbacker included, had more energy than LaGuardia. A progressive Republican who had become mayor in 1933 after the scandal-ridden administration of Jimmy Walker, he worked wonders in modernizing municipal government after decades of venal machine politics.[37] LaGuardia and Rickenbacker had much in common. They were both self-made men who worked themselves to near exhaustion, hated pretense, spoke bluntly, and expected unquestioning obedience from their subordinates. Like Rickenbacker, LaGuardia had been an airman in World War I, leaving the House of Representatives to become a pilot-bombardier on the Italian front. After returning to his desk, he became known as the "Flying Congressman." Rickenbacker and LaGuardia both admired Billy Mitchell and were not afraid to challenge senior military officers who opposed his desire for a separate air force. Above all, LaGuardia and Rickenbacker shared a passionate commitment to commercial aviation.[38]

One of LaGuardia's most cherished goals after becoming mayor was for New York City, served by Newark International Airport, to have its own commercial air terminal, and he lobbied incessantly to build one.[39] He recognized that the location of Floyd Bennett Field, an hour distant from downtown Manhattan, made it unsuitable for expansion into the major facility he desired. At first he looked with favor on Governors Island but ultimately chose an area, partly marshland, on North Beach in Queens, between Flushing Bay and Bowery Bay. It had been used for amusement parks since its initial development in the 1880s until the Curtiss-Wright Company bought it in the late 1920s and built a small private airfield, Glenn Curtiss Airport, for wealthy flyers. A major drawback of the site was that it overlooked a noisome municipal garbage dump on Riker's Island. Among its advantages, however, was its proximity to midtown Manhattan. LaGuardia's ally, city planner Robert Moses, had led construction of the massive Triborough Bridge, leading directly into the area. Another point in its favor was that New York City would open a huge world's fair in 1939 on 1,216 acres of nearby reclaimed swampland in Flushing Meadows.

LaGuardia got what he wanted in August 1937 when the city acquired the 105-acre flying field from Curtiss-Wright for $1.3 million and made plans to fill in 453 acres of adjacent marshland with vast quantities of refuse from Riker's Island to create the most up-to-date airport in America. Rickenbacker steadfastly opposed the site, not because he objected to creating a new airport with a more convenient location than Newark but because he thought garbage a poor material on which to base runways that would sink into the muddy bottom of the marsh and require constant rebuilding. In future years, landing surfaces would have to be continually renewed and elevated, confirming his foresight.[40]

Despite his friendship with Rickenbacker, LaGuardia would not be denied. To finance the project, he wrung every available dollar from municipal, state, and federal agencies. His main source of support was the WPA, headed by one of FDR's chief lieutenants, Harold L. Ickes.[41] Preparations for the terminal required transporting 17 million tons of refuse across a causeway to the site where it would stand. To complete the job, at least 15,000 persons worked around the clock in three eight-hour shifts, six days a week, for two years. "A thousand carloads of cement, 3 million gallons of asphalt, 200 miles of cable, 25 miles of underground piping, 20,000 tons of steel, and enough electrical power to provide street lighting for 14,000 city streets went into the project," states a biographer of LaGuardia. The dedication ceremony on 15 October 1939 attracted 325,000 people. Few of them knew how much the airport had cost—the most accurate guess was $40 million—but it was commonly known the figure was enormous.

TWA began regularly scheduled service when an incoming DC-3 arrived at 12:01 a.m. on 2 December. American Air Lines inaugurated outgoing service soon thereafter. By this time the facility's original name—New York Municipal Airport—had been changed to LaGuardia Field. American shifted operations from Newark to the terminal as soon as it was ready for traffic.[42] For reasons easy to understand, Rickenbacker moved more slowly. Eastern had deep historical ties with Newark International. It had flown airmail from Newark since February 1929 and started passenger operations there in April 1930. It had a heavy investment in facilities at the field and had made it a major base of operations. About 240 of EAL's employees worked there in 1939: accountants, couriers, ticket clerks, dispatchers, transportation agents, maintenance personnel, meteorologists, radio operators, stockroom helpers, a Link trainer instructor—the list went on and on.[43] Transferring staff members and equipment from Newark to LaGuardia in March 1940 (EAL continued to use Newark for a number of flights) was an arduous undertaking.[44]

Eastern's first scheduled flight at LaGuardia began on the evening of 1 April 1940 when a Douglas DST Silversleeper, the "Mexico Flyer," took off for Washington, Atlanta, New Orleans, and Brownsville. Rickenbacker hosted a gala dinner before the event, with explorer Sir Hubert Wilkins among the guests. Mayor LaGuardia handed a steward a gift-wrapped package containing a silver replica of the DST for Raul Castellaños, his counterpart in Mexico City, and a basket of American beauty roses for senora Castellaños. LaGuardia then smashed a bottle of champagne against the plane as Rickenbacker and Captain E. H. Parker, its pilot, looked on. Floodlights swept the sky as the plane rolled down the runway and took off, bound for the Rio Grande.[45]

Shifting personnel from Newark to LaGuardia, starting operations at the new terminal, moving EAL's headquarters from the General Motors Building to Rockefeller Center, and inaugurating new routes to Miami took place from March through September 1940. Eastern opened new overhaul and maintenance facilities at LaGuardia Field and showed them off to municipal officials and reporters from Baltimore. Mayor LaGuardia spoke at a luncheon. As always, Rickenbacker's schedule was unrelenting, and he had no idea of the tragedy about to overtake him.[46]

On Wednesday, 26 February 1941, cold rain spattered against the windows of Rickenbacker's executive suite on the sixteenth floor of 10

Rockefeller Plaza. The day had begun crisp and clear but a low-pressure trough that had stalled over the Great Lakes earlier in the week had moved eastward and reached the Atlantic seaboard sooner than expected. A storm front loomed along the Appalachian Mountains.[47]

Late that afternoon a telephone rang on Rickenbacker's desk, and the voice of an angry state governor came over the line. As daylight receded and evening descended on Manhattan, Rickenbacker set out on a trip he did not want to make. After packing his bags, he headed for LaGuardia Field to board the Mexican Flyer, which would leave that evening for its overnight run to the Rio Grande.

Rickenbacker planned to deplane before the ship reached Brownsville, spending the first three stages of the flight doing paperwork and getting off at Birmingham in the early hours of the morning to catch some sleep. At noon he would speak at a luncheon hosted by the municipal aviation committee, talking about Eastern's plans to improve service from Alabama to the Great Lakes and Gulf Coast. A day later he had to make an important presentation in Miami, asking directors to approve spending $5 million for new aircraft and equipment.

Speaking in Birmingham would force Rickenbacker to backtrack to Atlanta to catch a plane for south Florida. He wanted to be at his best in Miami and could not afford last-minute complications. For weeks he had resisted increasing pressure to give an address at the luncheon, but Birmingham's pleas had been too persistent to overcome. Its leaders were obsessively jealous of Atlanta, EAL's southeastern hub. The two cities were almost the same size but had little in common. Atlanta, basking in the afterglow of *Gone with the Wind,* which debuted there in 1939, was the urban center and financial capital of the South. Birmingham, Alabama's major industrial city, was dirty, smoky, and down at the heels. It had suffered greatly during the Depression and was fearful about the future. Its power brokers, known as Big Mules, wanted assurance that they would share with Atlanta in the upswing resulting from the preparedness drive.[48]

Rickenbacker was forced to yield to Birmingham's pleas when Alabama's governor, Frank W. Dixon, called from his office in Montgomery late in the afternoon. Dixon charged angrily that Eddie looked down his nose at Birmingham and felt too big to bother with Alabama. Like Rickenbacker, Dixon was a much-decorated veteran of World War I. As a volunteer in the Lafayette Flying Corps, he had lost a leg in combat while serving as an aerial observer and machine gunner. He received the

Croix de Guerre and was a Chevalier of the Legion of Honor. Rickenbacker could not ignore a verbal thrust from a worthy peer and agreed to speak at the luncheon.[49] Shepherd had never seen him so agitated as he dashed around Eastern's headquarters, barking last-minute commands before bolting out the door.[50]

The storm moving into the southeast was bringing a mixture of rain and sleet. Rickenbacker thought about going to Birmingham by rail to get a better night's rest before arriving the next morning. Penn Station was only a few minutes away from Rockefeller Center and a Pullman train left for Dixie every evening. Liquor would be served in the club car as soon as it reached the middle of the railroad tunnel under the Hudson River and crossed the New Jersey line.[51] The thought of having a few drinks before crawling into a berth was tempting. Domestic airlines did not serve alcohol.[52]

Taking the Mexico Flyer had another disadvantage. All of the DST's sleeping accommodations had been reserved for passengers originating in New York and a few who would board the plane in Washington. As a result, Eddie would have to spend a stormy night with bumpy air sitting in a small compartment behind the cockpit. He thought about the jokes Big Mules would tell if Eastern's CEO pulled into Birmingham the next morning on a Pullman car. He simply had to fly.

Amber boundary lights ringed the perimeter of LaGuardia Field as Rickenbacker approached it on the Grand Central Parkway in Queens.[53] High atop the control tower a revolving beacon, the largest and most powerful airport searchlight in the world, swept across the darkening sky with the radiance of 13.5 million burning candles. Its rotating beams illuminated the hulls of ocean liners berthed along the East River, the Triborough Bridge, and Flushing Meadow Park, where the New York World's Fair had closed a few months earlier. The Trilon and Perisphere still dominated the abandoned fairgrounds. The front had passed through, and the weather had cleared as night fell upon the world's greatest city.[54]

On his left Rickenbacker passed a huge five-sided marine terminal used by Pan American's clippers on flights to Europe. A curving driveway led off the Grand Central Parkway to LaGuardia's three-story central terminal. Its walls, faced with buff and black bricks, were half-hidden in the searchlight's penumbra, but the stainless-steel marquee of the domed rotunda reflected the beacon revolving overhead. Eight hangars, each bigger than Madison Square Garden, flanked the building, four on a side.[55] One of them was the cavernous building Eastern shared with Canadian Colonial. Under a steel-girdered ceiling, surrounded by a sea of floor space, ground crews swarmed around a DST, preparing it for the run to Brownsville. It had fourteen sleeping berths, seven up and seven down. Small, oblong windows, situated above larger ones below, were designed to protect travelers from claustrophobia in the upper berths after the curtains were drawn. Looking through the narrow panes of glass on cloudless nights, passengers could gaze at the stars before falling asleep.[56]

The main doors of the administration building opened into the airport's vast rotunda, which contained the world's first airport bank, a stock exchange, restaurants, barber shops, and booths where passengers could purchase newspapers, magazines, and gifts. Curved desks of the five airlines using the terminal—American, Eastern, TWA, United, and Canadian Colonial—lined the walls. People waiting for overnight flights crowded the floor. A 700-pound copper globe hung from the ceiling. Its burnished surface showed the world's landmasses in relief. Behind the building, floodlights illuminated a 2,500-foot concrete apron, from which intersecting taxi lanes led to four runways, 4,500 to 6,000 feet long. Even after dark, throngs of spectators stood on an observation deck overlooking the apron to watch takeoffs and landings. Large letters spelled "New York" in grass plots between the runways.

The "Mexico Flyer" was now poised on the apron to enplane passengers for Flight 21 to Brownsville.[57] James A. Perry Jr., a twenty-nine-year-old Georgian who had been a captain for only a year, would pilot the plane. Rickenbacker later called him "a fine young man" who had an excellent record, but the word "young" meant "inexperienced." Perry had logged more than 3,000 hours with Eastern since May 1937 but had spent two-thirds of them as a copilot before moving into a captain's seat. Rickenbacker later put it mildly by acknowledging that his presence on the plane was stressful for Perry. Everyone knew the boss had a caustic tongue.[58]

Rickenbacker was not the only celebrity boarding the plane. Among other passengers was Drew Pearson, an investigative reporter whose column, "Washington Merry-Go-Round," kept him constantly embroiled in litigation with people whose secrets he unearthed. Pearson had originally planned to fly to New Orleans but canceled a speech there because a libel suit filed against him by Congressman Martin Sweeney, an Ohio Democrat, had lasted longer than anticipated. As a result Pearson would now get off at Washington.[59] Also aboard were Clara Savage Littledale, editor of *Parents* magazine, and her husband, H. A. Littledale, a writer for the *New York Times*. Several businessmen were flying to Atlanta or New Orleans.[60]

The DST's "Sky Lounge," which Rickenbacker would occupy, was aft of the cockpit on the starboard side of the cabin. Originally intended for honeymooners, it had two facing double seats that could accommodate four people if not made into a bed. Tonight Rickenbacker had it to himself. Sitting by the window, he opened his briefcase and took out papers regarding the equipment purchases he wanted the directors to authorize at Miami. High above his head, in the airport's control tower, authorities speaking a "queer, staccato language" to cope with the volume of traffic coming in and out of the field were communicating with pilots, including Perry, as they prepared for takeoff. After the DST reached an altitude of a few thousand feet they would turn it over to Air Traffic Control, located in the same terminal and run by the Civil Aeronautics Authority. Eight federal employees with headphones had continuous access to five large panels showing the positions of all commercial aircraft flying in the eastern United States. One of their tasks was to keep airliners, which flew at staggered altitudes depending on where they were heading, separated from one another. Perry had already filed the mandatory flight plan.[61] Rickenbacker was studying data for the Miami meeting when the Silversleeper's twin fourteen-cylinder Pratt & Whitney Wasp radial engines, each rated for 1,200 horsepower at takeoff, throbbed and lifted the 25,000-pound plane off the concrete airstrip.

Aboard the ship were thirteen passengers and a crew of three. Copilot Luther E. Thomas, a thirty-one-year-old Texan, had been a barnstormer and a member of the U.S. Air Corps' Seventh Bomb Squadron before joining Eastern in 1940. Steward Clarence Moore was smartly dressed in the snappy red, white, and blue uniform Eastern had copied from Pan American Airways.[62] The plane was ten minutes late when it took off at 7:21 p.m. Perry probably worried about the delay because Rickenbacker, always in a hurry, demanded on-time operations. Because the sky had now cleared along the East Coast, Perry would have contact flying all the way to Washington, cruising at an altitude of 4,000 feet. The flight lasted about an hour and thirty minutes and everything went smoothly. Rickenbacker was still absorbed in his work when the plane crossed the Potomac and landed at Washington-Hoover Field.[63]

If LaGuardia represented commercial aviation at its best, Washington-Hoover exhibited it at its worst. Located next to Arlington National Cemetery at the Virginia end of the 14th Street Bridge, the 146-acre terminal was fourteen acres shy of meeting a minimum area standard for American airports set in the 1920s. Many airmen thought it was the most dangerous airfield in the United States. Everyone in the industry was glad the field would soon be abandoned. Nearby, at Gravelly Point, workers were rushing a new facility, Washington National Airport, to completion, but it would not open until 16 June 1941, when the Pentagon Building would be built where Washington-Hoover had once stood. The old terminal was still being used in February when the DST landed on its gravel airstrip.[64]

After the plane stopped, Pearson, who would be grateful Congressman Sweeney had sued him, deplaned and walked across the apron toward a two-story Art Deco terminal building that could have fitted into the rotunda at LaGuardia. Three new passengers boarded the aircraft, including William D. Byron, a Maryland Democrat serving in the House of Representatives. Byron planned to join his wife, Kathleen, in New Orleans, where she was at Mardi Gras, and take her on a vacation to Mexico.[65]

Weather reports indicated the plane would "encounter a general lowering of ceilings" as it flew toward Atlanta on a trip scheduled for three hours and thirty-two minutes. Federal traffic controllers had designed a flight plan to spare it as much danger as possible, directing Perry to skirt the Blue Ridge Mountains on the east at 4,000 feet, cruising at 165 miles per hour. The plane had been refueled at Washington-Hoover with 650 gallons of gasoline, enough to turn back if the southeastern storm became too threatening. Perry took off at 9:05 p.m., EST. At 9:22 the aircraft was seen crossing its first check point at Mason Springs, Maryland. As he headed for Atlanta, he flew over Richmond, Greensboro, Charlotte, and Spartanburg within three minutes of schedule.[66]

By the time Perry reached Spartanburg he started to worry about rapidly deteriorating weather conditions in the Atlanta area as the storm front moved in from the west. Leaving Thomas in the cockpit, Perry came back to the Sky Lounge to share his concerns with Rickenbacker, still preparing for the meeting in Miami. Perry wanted to know whether the boss thought he should turn back and land at Charlotte for the night. Eddie recalled having been kind and gracious to the young pilot, empathizing with an inexperienced skipper facing the likelihood of an instrument landing with Eastern's chief executive aboard the plane. He told him he could return to Charlotte if he felt it necessary.[67]

Rickenbacker, however, was probably irritated by Perry's indecisiveness. He had reason to be annoyed about being interrupted when he had important business on his mind. He paid his pilots to make their own decisions and had a policy of trusting the judgment of the professionals who flew Eastern's ships. After asking Perry some routine questions about visibility at Atlanta, estimated to be about one mile with a ceiling of 500 feet, he told the jittery pilot to decide what to do. Returning to his work, Rickenbacker remembered the weather forecast for Atlanta wasn't really too bad despite the oncoming front, calling for overcast skies, occasional light rain, and fog, all of which a capable pilot should be able to handle.

Returning to the cockpit, Perry continued heading for Atlanta.[68] He had an overriding responsibility to do everything he could to keep his passengers safe. On the other hand, he was also expected to stay on schedule if possible. He had the right to turn back if that was what his best judgment dictated, but available evidence told him landing conditions at Atlanta were at least marginally safe. Pilots were expected to be prudent, but Eastern's airmen had a reputation, conforming to the hard-nosed attitude of their boss, for boasting about flying in weather that shut other airlines down.[69]

Perry stayed on course as the weather deteriorated. When he reached the Atlanta area near Stone Mountain, a regional traffic control center switched him to the airport tower operator. Rain, turning to sleet, was now falling and visibility getting steadily worse. Preparing for an instrument landing, Perry contacted the control tower at Atlanta's Candler Field at 11:38 p.m., CST (Atlanta was then in the central time zone), reported his altitude (still 4,000 feet), and told the operator, C. M. Pruitt, that he was ready to begin his descent. After giving Perry an altimeter reading, based on the atmospheric pressure currently prevailing at the airport, Pruitt told him the ceiling had now dropped to 300 feet—the absolute minimum for operations. Visibility was one mile at best. The wind was coming from the northeast, its velocity ten miles per hour. Delta, an airline less hesitant than Eastern about canceling operations, had already diverted two inbound flights to other airports. Nevertheless, another plane had just gotten down safely, showing that landings could be made. Pruitt cleared Perry to land at 11:44.[70]

Like all scheduled airliners, the DST had a loop antenna coiled inside a doughnut-shaped aluminum shield to receive low-frequency directional signals from an airport's homing transmitter. The signals were relatively static-free even under severe weather conditions. To get a bearing a pilot hand-cranked an antenna-turning mechanism until the volume of the signals peaked, showing that the loop was pointing directly at the ground station. An indicator needle, mounted on a compass card, registered the position of the loop. Eastern used two altimeters, both of which had three pointers registering barometric pressure in thousands, hundreds, and tens of feet. When preparing to land, the cockpit crew set one altimeter at the altitude above sea level and calibrated the other one to correspond with the current altimeter reading at the airport. The second altimeter would register zero when the plane landed.[71]

Following the airport's northeast radio beam, also known as a "range leg," Perry made his approach. While flying immediately above Candler Field, as expected, he encountered a "cone of silence" because of his momentary inability to pick up radio signals coming from directly below. After picking up the southeast range beam, he went a prescribed distance, made a 180-degree turn, came back on the beam, and started his glide toward the runway.[72] Even under normal conditions it was hard to make a night landing in Atlanta because Candler Field was located on a slight rise and a pilot might not see the runway until he was almost above its outer perimeter. On this night conditions were far from normal.[73] Candler Field was not well equipped for instrument flying. A federal official later testified that the airport needed five new radio receivers, a more sensitive tower altimeter, and a light gun for signaling to aircraft, but said that Atlanta's City Council had not provided the necessary funding. No commercial airports in the world had radar at the time.[74]

Apparently Perry and Thomas did not set their two altimeters correctly. Both instruments were later recovered and neither showed the numbers inspectors anticipated. One of them bore a reading that "would have resulted in the altimeter showing an altitude of 883 feet greater than was actually the fact." Consequently the plane was "39 feet below the elevation of the airport" when it came to earth far short of the runway. To federal investigators, everything pointed to pilot error.[75]

Rickenbacker had finished his work by the time the plane began its descent and was talking with Moore. He was sitting by the window of the Sky Lounge, Moore by the aisle. Looking out, Rickenbacker saw points of light from Atlanta's federal penitentiary shining through the falling rain. Suddenly, as Perry let down his left wing to go into a turn, Ricken-backer felt it hit something, which turned out to be some pine trees. He could tell that Perry was feeling the same thing as the left wing went up and right wing went down. Eddie knew that the best place to be in an emergency was near the rear of an aircraft. Knowing instantly that the plane was going to crash as it lurched off course, he reacted swiftly and instinctively by jumping up and moving aft as fast as he could.[76]

He made it only to the aisle when the right wing became entangled in some trees and was torn away from the DST, causing the aircraft to veer in the direction of the impact. Memories of World War I flashed through his mind as he thought how stricken comrades had deliberately inhaled fire to shorten their agony while plunging toward certain death in bullet-ridden Nieuports and Spads. He decided to do the same thing if the DST caught fire.[77] Fortunately, such drastic action was not needed. In the last few seconds of his life, one of the men in the cockpit had the presence of mind to cut the electrical system. Had he not done so, Rick-enbacker and everyone else on the plane would have been incinerated. Neither Perry nor Thomas, however, had had time to cut the engines, and the plane was still flying under power when it smashed into a pine forest near Morrow, Georgia, with a roar audible for miles.[78]

The impact was so severe that the plane cartwheeled. Shearing off seven pine trees, it came to rest on its roof after burrowing into the earth with such force that the nose and cockpit were jammed backward under the inverted top of the fuselage. Perry and Thomas were instantly crushed to death. When the DST was found the next morning, the front third of the fuselage was a grotesque mass of metal, twisted and shred-ded so violently it would have been hard to identify as part of an airliner except that the rest of the plane was sticking out of the ground at a 45-degree angle.[79]

Some travelers bunked near the rear of the plane were extremely lucky. George Feinberg, vice-president of a textile firm in New York City, was sleeping so peacefully that only the sound of the crash awakened him. Tumbling out of his bunk, he landed without injury on the in-verted ceiling of the passenger cabin and crawled out of the wreckage through a crack in the side of the plane. He told reporters he was "ma-rooned all night in my underwear, wandering in the underbrush and shouting for help as long as I could." Nils Hansell, a civil engineer, and Jesse S. Rosenfeld, a clothing merchant from New Orleans, were only slightly hurt.[80] Eight people survived, but nine did not. Byron was killed;

other fatalities included Juan Gadala Maria, son of a millionaire in El Salvador; Allan Lebowitz, an Atlanta businessman; and B. C. M. Van der Hoop, vice-president of the Tin Processing Company in Scarsdale, New York. Moore, who had joined Rickenbacker in dashing toward the rear of the plane, was also dead. He had landed on top of Rickenbacker in the aisle after the airliner cartwheeled. Birdie Bomar, a nurse who helped care for Rickenbacker during his subsequent hospitalization, later speculated that being protected by Moore's corpse saved his life.[81]

Of all the survivors, Rickenbacker was the one most badly hurt. When the crash occurred he had reached the section of the plane just aft of the area that had been twisted apart when the ship slammed into the earth, causing him to lose his footing and fall with such force against a seat arm that his left hip was severely fractured. He found himself caught tight in a mass of debris when the cacophony of the crash stopped, his head fastened between a bulkhead and a fuel tank. His forehead was badly bruised and he felt as if his skull had been dented. Something he had hit had creased the area above his left eye. The entire left side of his body was mangled. His left arm was completely immobilized (he had sustained a shattered elbow and a crushed nerve) and the hand projected grotesquely from the jumble of wreckage in which the arm was embedded, causing him intense pain. He had multiple rib fractures and jagged rib bones protruded from his skin. His left hip socket and pelvis were smashed, a nerve torn apart, and his left knee splintered. His right hip and leg were jammed in place but not fractured. Only his right hand and forearm had some small range of motion.[82]

Soaked with blood and aviation fuel, he lay in pitch darkness, writhing in excruciating pain. The stench of gasoline was overpowering. Passengers were groaning and crying out in agony. Both of Clara Littledale's legs were broken and one of her feet was wedged under her body. She was screaming at the top of her lungs. Freezing rain fell through exposed parts of the cabin. As Rickenbacker silently thanked God that the gasoline had not ignited, a male voice came out of the night. Somebody had climbed outside the plane and was telling other survivors to build a fire in the freezing cold. Ignoring pain from his cracked and broken ribs, Rickenbacker yelled at the person not to light a match and warned him about the danger of setting fire to the gasoline that had escaped from the fuel tanks.[83]

Soon after this outburst Rickenbacker wrenched his body upward, trying to get out from under Moore's body. The thought went through his mind that if he was going to die he would meet death trying to escape the living Hell in which he was trapped. As he jerked himself upward he did not know a jagged piece of metal was pointing at him from directly overhead. It ripped open his left eyelid and the eyeball popped from its socket, falling on his cheek. When he struggled again to get up by exerting force with his shoulders and chest, his ribs snapped so loudly that he could hear them breaking apart. Every breath he took tormented him. He prayed in vain to pass out. Unable to move, he lay where he was throughout an interminable night, half-crazed by his suffering. Despite his agony he continued to encourage passengers who were still alive and barked out orders as interminable hours wore on, preparing survivors for the rescue effort he surmised was already underway.[84]

He was correct that a search was in progress. One of the people involved was Bishop Simpson, a mechanic at one of Eastern's Atlanta hangars, who had gone to bed about eleven o'clock that night. Soon after he fell asleep a phone call awakened him, telling him Flight 21 was overdue and presumed down near Morrow. Hurrying to the airport, he joined about fifteen employees. Dividing an area around the Jonesboro courthouse into five sections, they set forth in automobiles in groups of three, taking "kerosene lanterns, flashlights, whatever you had." They planned to have five cars stay on the roads while the rest of them scoured fields and woods looking for wreckage. Simpson was with a pilot, Perry Hudson, and a fellow worker, Curtis Wright. If one of them found the crash site, he would signal the nearest car, and its driver would blow his horn, calling the rest. "We looked all night," Simpson recalled, "and just about daybreak we heard a horn blowing. We were not too far from it. We had gone, I'd say, within 50 feet of the wreckage and it's a good thing we didn't find it at the time because some of the guys had kerosene lanterns and probably the fumes would have ignited, but anyway, about daylight one of the boys . . . saw something glistening up in one of the trees—the sunlight was just coming up and it was a piece of metal."

Peering through early sunbeams, rescuers located the wreckage. A ravine between the nearest road and the crash site made it impossible to reach the tangled ruin by car. Rain had fallen steadily throughout the night and they slithered through mud, underbrush, and stumps to reach the crumpled remains of the DST, hearing moaning as they approached and began looking for survivors. They found Rickenbacker where he lay. "The floor had broken and it was between his legs." Thomas was lying, dead, on top of Eddie's feet. "Rickenbacker could talk," Simpson recalled. "We had to tear out a place inside and got to him and his one eye was way down on his cheek, he was all bloody and he said, 'If you'll just let me hold onto you, maybe I can pull myself out.' Well, the aircraft was crushed at the point you couldn't get out and there happened to be a stump close by. We figured out we could use the stump as a fulcrum and pried the fuselage up enough that we got him out."[85]

Forgetting his warning to survivors during the night, Rickenbacker asked for a cigarette. "Captain, you can't smoke here," Simpson said. Remembering the danger of fire, Rickenbacker apologized. A newspaper photographer arrived on the scene and tried to take a picture of him but Paul Charles, one of the rescuers, "pasted him hard and smashed his camera." Ambulances had now reached the site. Medics gave Rickenbacker "a couple of shots" to knock him out, but he remained conscious. They managed to put him on a stretcher but had a hard time carrying him up the muddy bank of the ravine; he nearly slipped off before they got him to the nearest road. When they reached the ambulance, it was already full of dead bodies. Rickenbacker later said Georgia law stipulated paying $200 for hauling a corpse and only $50 for someone who was alive. He had to wait almost an hour for another ambulance.[86]

Two rescuers, one of whom got sick to his stomach from looking at Rickenbacker, accompanied him in the ambulance to Piedmont Hospital, at that time located on Capitol Avenue in Atlanta. Despite heavy sedation he remained rational. After they reached their destination, attendants engaged in triage decided that Rickenbacker was unlikely to live and devoted their attention to other survivors. When one of them tried to summon a Catholic priest to give him last rites he angrily declared that he was a Protestant, showing them that he was still alive. Realizing that he might not die despite his massive injuries, staff members telephoned the hospital's chief surgeon, Dr. Floyd W. McRae Jr., who came rushing from his home. By a strange coincidence, McRae's father, an intern in Paris, had participated in Rickenbacker's mastoid operation in 1918.[87] McRae pushed Eddie's dangling eyeball back into position and sewed his eyelid without benefit of anesthesia, causing him to unleash a torrent of profanity. Responding in kind, McRae told him to shut up. The medics, uncertain whether Rickenbacker would rally, decided to postpone invasive action and, instead, wrapped him from head to foot in a cast. The next day, when McRae inquired whether he wanted to eat, he asked for a ham and egg sandwich and some beer.

EDDIE RICKENBACKER

After McRae got six bottles of beer, Eddie quickly quaffed two of them. McRae falsely told reporters he had given Rickenbacker Coca-Cola, and the Atlanta-based firm sent a refrigerator full of it but Eddie turned it away.[88]

Dr. Ralph Green, head of Eastern's medical department at Miami, flew to Atlanta. Adelaide, who was visiting friends in Charlotte, also rushed to Eddie's side. Meanwhile, David and William, now students at the Farragut School in Asheville, sped to Atlanta with a police escort. After observing her husband's condition and thinking he was rallying, Adelaide sent the boys back to Asheville on a bus and moved into the hospital to stay close to him. Abruptly, however, Rickenbacker's condition worsened, and an alluring sense of death overcame him. Reporters passed word of his condition to Walter Winchell, who asserted that evening on his radio broadcast that Eddie had died, but he spoke too soon. Infuriated, Rickenbacker, who was listening, threw a pitcher of water at the radio and hit it head-on. He demanded that Adelaide call the media to tell them he was alive and determined to stay that way. She humored him by pretending to place three long-distance calls on a disconnected telephone, and he fell asleep. Meanwhile, fearing that he might really die, she had reestablished contact with the boys. A police car again rushed them back to Atlanta, its siren going full blast. When they stopped at a gas station, an attendant told them they were too late but the troopers brought them on anyway. When they arrived, Eddie was hallucinating. Grapes were hanging over his bed—the proximity of death perhaps recalling to his fevered mind the vineyards of France—and he asked David to pick them. David knew he was not in his right mind, but William wondered why the fruit was invisible and asked Adelaide if his father was going crazy.

As Rickenbacker's fate hung in the balance, McRae and Green put him in an oxygen tent on the second floor. One night Adelaide awakened with an overpowering sense that he was dying. Dashing up a flight of stairs and down a hallway to his room, she found an attendant asleep at the door and saw that Eddie had ripped the tent apart in the ferocity of his struggle to live. After saving him from suffocation, she exploded at the staff for its negligence.[89]

As Rickenbacker rallied, therapists set his hip, administered heavy doses of morphine, and gave him frequent blood transfusions. Despite his torment, he protested against sedation and eventually persuaded McRae he could do without it, saying that he was "allergic to dope"—

possibly because he knew he was becoming addicted and, combined with his existing dependence on alcohol, drugs could ruin his career. He later recalled hallucinations in which he thought he was at LaGuardia Field trying to prevent a snowfall from damaging a Douglas DC-4, a plane then under development, and trying vainly to call a taxi to return him to his apartment. He wrenched a cast off his left wrist with his teeth. He accused nurses and medical attendants of mistreatment and then recanted when his senses returned and he realized the charges were baseless. Meanwhile, the hospital received thousands of letters, telegrams, and flowers from persons including Ernst Udet, J. Edgar Hoover, and Wendell Willkie.[90]

The ordeal made Eddie think more deeply about life and death than he had ever done before. Eventually he got better, at least as far as his injuries permitted. He persuaded McRae to allow him daily visits by an osteopath, Alexander Dahl, which Rickenbacker found extremely helpful. Seeing a paralyzed girl passing his door in a makeshift "kiddie car," he sketched it, added modifications, and had some of EAL's mechanics create one for him. After initially seating himself and moving it with his feet, he stood in it, grabbed hold for support, and walked gingerly with its help. Relearning to use his legs, he went from crutches to canes and forced himself to walk for hours.[91]

McRae finally discharged him on 25 June. Gaunt and ashen-faced, he went to the Atlanta Airport looking like the wrath of God and prepared to board a Silverliner bound for LaGuardia Field, where his ordeal had begun four months and two days earlier. His left leg was now shorter than the other and had a permanently severed nerve. He was still in great discomfort and walked with a cane. After posing with McRae and other persons, he slowly mounted the steps, turned when he reached a door leading into the fuselage, smiled, waved his straw hat, and took off for New York. That afternoon, at LaGuardia, a crowd of more than 200 people, including buddies from the Hat-in-the-Ring Squadron, cheered as David and William helped him get off the plane. EAL's mechanics gave him a bottle of champagne. He told reporters "he had a few aches and pain but no complaints."

The next day EAL announced that employees had contributed $3,100 to establish a Rickenbacker Blood and Plasma Bank in tribute to the role Piedmont Hospital had played in saving his life. Attached to the bequest was a message from Eddie to McRae: "Regardless of the years ahead, I shall always look back on the four months I spent with you and your associates as a most pleasant period in my life, in spite of the suffering endured, as it gave me an opportunity to know the true souls of men and women under most adverse circumstances." McRae wrote back. "Through your misfortune we were permitted to know you, your family, and those closely associated with you and we had the privilege of ministering unto you for four months. During this period we learned to love and respect you and our lives have been enriched as a result of this opportunity and privilege to serve."[92]

Rickenbacker's spirit seemed enriched by his suffering, and he was in a good mood when he began an arduous convalescence at Candlewood Lake in Connecticut. He worked on his golf game with David and William, who observed that "he doesn't swing 'em like he used to," but that "what he lacks in power he more than makes up for in direction. He doesn't slice 'em as of old!"[93] Neither Rickenbacker nor Eastern blamed Birmingham for the part its aviation committee had unwittingly played in his ordeal. Eastern now scheduled ten flights a day from the Alabama city to Washington, New York, New Orleans, Houston, and San Antonio. An article in the spring 1941 issue of the company magazine stressed the contribution made by steel to the national defense and announced the establishment of a "crack sales team," the "Flying Vulcans," to promote Birmingham's commercial interests.[94] In a special message to Eastern's employees, published soon after his return, Eddie left no doubt about what was uppermost in his mind. "This is no time to waste time!" he declared. "In National Defense, the fateful eleventh hour is at hand." Day and night, Eastern's planes and facilities were "being regularly utilized both by captains of industry and officers of the Army and Navy in saving previous hours of traveling, shipping and mailing time . . . *and you could do no better for your country than to follow their example!*" One would never have known from his actions that he had belonged, albeit briefly, to the America First Committee. He knew that the nation was headed for war and was eager to do his best. With characteristic determination, he persisted and joined the struggle.

Chapter 16

— ☆ —

Call to Duty

Rickenbacker made much greater contributions to the war effort than might have been expected. Despite his injuries in the Atlanta crash, he refused to be sidelined and went on special missions to the ends of the earth. Even being marooned for three terrible weeks at sea in 1942 slowed him down only temporarily. But the effects of what he went through made him a different man, bringing out aspects of his makeup that were present all along but which he had kept under control up to now. A degree of pragmatism he had managed to blend with his other characteristics gave way to a nature that was less willing to compromise, and his strong views made him an increasingly controversial person to whom historians have still not accorded the recognition merited by his achievements. An embodiment of the American dream became a protagonist well suited for a Greek tragedy. His fate, however, lay hidden in the future as he survived his ordeal in Atlanta.

While Rickenbacker went through his more personal agony at Piedmont Hospital, the British Empire continued to fight alone against the fascist powers. As he had hoped, Congress passed the Lend-Lease Act on 11 March 1941, but it was debatable how long Churchill's struggle would continue until Hitler diverted his attention to the Balkans and, like Napoleon, committed the blunder of invading Russia. On 22 June 1941—three days before Rickenbacker left Atlanta—millions of German troops, supported by thousands of tanks and airplanes, stormed across the Soviet border. By the time he reached LaGuardia Field on 25 June, "pale and thin and limping slightly" from his ordeal, the Nazi juggernaut had annihilated two Russian army corps and almost wiped out two others. Competent analysts predicted the USSR would last only a few months, but the tide was in fact turning against the Axis.[1]

When Rickenbacker deplaned in New York, reporters asked him if the United States would enter the swiftly escalating war. "We are in it and have been in it for a year," he declared. "A lot of people don't realize that. The sooner everybody knows we are in the better it will be. The sooner we crush Hitler the better." *The Great Silver Fleet News* was steadily proclaiming Eastern's role in preparing America for war, and Eddie contributed a lead article about the preparedness drive to the summer issue. "Over a period of years," he wrote, "Eastern Air Lines has built up routes and schedules covering that great section of the country in which the major portion of our national defense program is being carried out. Day and night its facilities are being regularly utilized by captains of industry and officers of the Army and Navy." Eastern was cooperating with Pan American in providing the means of war to British forces, flying munitions and supplies to Miami, from which a Pan Am subsidiary took them abroad.[2]

Rickenbacker was in step with fellow veterans rallying to the British cause. The American Legion abandoned nonintervention at a convention in Boston in September 1940 and declared support for FDR's policies. Legionnaires rebuked the America First Committee's efforts to gain support for the isolationist message passionately articulated by Lindbergh, who held England "largely responsible for the mess we are being dragged into."[3] Once a national idol, he was now reviled by millions of citizens as an admirer of Hitler, with whom he advocated a negotiated peace. His refusal to return a medal awarded him in Germany in 1938 and his apparent insensitivity to atrocities perpetrated against Jews led to his portrayal as a Nazi sympathizer. After he began his crusade in 1941, FDR publicly questioned his loyalty, comparing him to the Copperheads that had opposed Lincoln. Indignant, Lindbergh responded by resigning his commission as a colonel in the Air Corps Reserve. Speeches in New York City, Philadelphia, St. Louis, Minneapolis, Los Angeles, and San Francisco—some of them twisted and misinterpreted by the Lone Eagle's enemies—produced mounting vilification. Invective intensified after he spoke in Des Moines, identifying Jews as one of three main forces—along with the British and the Roosevelt administration—that were dragging the country into a war in which millions of American mothers would lose their sons. The America First Committee considered disbanding amid a firestorm of charges that Lindbergh was anti-Semitic. Seldom had a hero sunk so far so fast.[4]

Rickenbacker's support for Britain and fortitude in surviving the Atlanta crash enhanced his image, while Lindbergh's reputation plummeted. An Atlanta VFW post tried to have Lindbergh Drive, linking Peachtree Street and Piedmont Avenue, renamed Rickenbacker Drive. In September a new airport at Marietta in nearby Cobb County was named Rickenbacker Field. When Eddie returned to Atlanta that month for the first time since leaving in June, 500 people, including invited guests from Piedmont Hospital, gave him a standing ovation at the Ansley Hotel, where Eastern held its annual dinner.[5]

Rickenbacker stayed mum about Lindbergh's disgrace but would have been blind not to recognize the role reversal taking place. Since 1927 Lindbergh had been America's foremost oracle on air power. His repeated assessments of the Luftwaffe, made in the late 1930s at the behest of the American military attaché in Berlin, received respectful attention in Washington, whereas Eddie's visit in to Germany in 1935 went largely unheeded and even Hap Arnold ridiculed some of his views. Now, Rickenbacker's connections with General Motors and the Rockefellers, together with his success in running an immensely profitable airline, gave him credibility in the nation's capital, where Republicans were running the War and Navy departments and giant corporations FDR had once scorned received huge orders for armaments.

Rickenbacker's status as America's Ace of Aces, his identification with Mitchell, and his unstinting support for expanding air power in the budget-starved 1930s assured him cooperation from the Army Air Forces (AAF), as the Air Corps had become known in June 1941. The main question about his role in the coming war was his health. Knowing people were concerned about it, he tried to look increasingly robust. His appearance in Atlanta was only one sign of his recovery. He showed vigor by chairing a subcommittee in LaGuardia's campaign for reelection as mayor and participated in a drive to enlist 100,000 men in the Civilian Pilot Training Corps.[6] Nevertheless, despite outward appearances, he was not doing as well as he let on. His limp was barely noticeable only because he wore a special shoe with an elastic clog in the heel, hiding it when he posed for photographs. He needed daily massages to relieve stiffness and pain. He was drinking more heavily than ever. Nevertheless, he was determined to become involved when his services were needed.[7]

He could see the United States moving inexorably into the maelstrom.[8] The American occupation of Iceland in July to free British troops for other roles and protect convoys showed him where things were heading.[9] In August FDR and Churchill met in Newfoundland and proclaimed an "Atlantic Charter" emphasizing the principles for which they would fight against Germany. When U-boats attacked three American destroyers, FDR ordered warships to "shoot on sight" if threatened. Meanwhile the USSR stayed in the war despite huge losses of manpower and materiel, encouraging Roosevelt to send Harry Hopkins to Moscow and provide $1 billion for Lend-Lease aid to Russia. Despite his hatred of the Third Reich, Rickenbacker would have been chagrined to know that Hitler's inability to defeat the Soviets was caused partly by poor management of aircraft production by Udet. The old pilot shot himself in November but, with the bogus announcement that he had died in a plane crash, still received a hero's burial.[10]

Rickenbacker was well aware that American embargoes on scrap iron and petroleum were hurting Japan. Instead of going to war in Europe, as most people had thought, the United States became a formal belligerent when the Japanese attacked Pearl Harbor on 7 December. Rickenbacker heard the news that afternoon at his office in Rockefeller Center and hurried home to be with Adelaide. Listening to the radio late into the night, they did not know the full extent of the disaster, which FDR kept under wraps, but the next day EAL employees in Washington said the damage was heavy.[11] When Roosevelt asked Congress for a declaration of war, Lindbergh, feeling there was now no alternative but to fight, canceled an address he had planned to deliver in Boston. The America First Committee stayed precariously alive for a few days because hostilities had not yet begun with Germany. Hitler removed any doubt on that score by declaring war on the United States on 11 December, and the AFC went into oblivion.[12]

Rickenbacker thought the war would last a long time. Speaking to a "hushed audience" of about 500 persons at the Waldorf Astoria, he said there was "no prospect of victory in less than four years." He predicted the national debt would mount to a "staggering figure," $300 billion, and said the United States would need "at least 30,000 bombing planes capable of 300 miles an hour."[13]

Among his first decisions was to close the Indianapolis Speedway, which he put in the hands of his brother Albert as a caretaker. Eddie believed that shortages of alcohol (used for racing fuel), rubber, steel, aluminum, and other strategic materials would doom the Indy 500 for the duration. The engineering knowledge of drivers and mechanics was urgently needed for more important tasks. He knew he was not ready for the burdens ahead but was determined to get into the best possible shape, so he headed for Florida, where he owned a houseboat, to soak up sunshine in Biscayne Bay.[14]

Meanwhile, Lindbergh went to Washington to offer his services to Arnold, who had valued his advice about the Luftwaffe in the late 1930s while making light of Rickenbacker's suggestions to give mechanics pilot training.[15] Arnold liked Lindbergh and was grateful for his help, but his hands were tied by FDR's hatred toward him. Only one major industrialist dared to employ the Lone Eagle. In March, after gaining approval from Undersecretary of War Lovett, Henry Ford hired Lindbergh to be an adviser at his giant Willow Run plant, which was making B-24 Liberators.[16]

Rickenbacker received much better treatment. While he convalesced in Florida, Arnold was too preoccupied with high-level planning to do anything for him. In February Hap was named to the newly constituted Joint Chiefs of Staff, joining General George Marshall, Admiral Ernest J. King, and Admiral William D. Leahy, FDR's personal military adviser, at the apex of the military establishment. In March, after becoming commanding general of the Army Air Forces, Arnold finally had time to think about Rickenbacker and asked him to make a 15,000-mile tour of army bases. Morale was sinking among airmen resulting from the disorganization rampant amid the sudden, massive expansion of the Air Forces. Arnold wanted Eddie to put fire in their bellies. He wanted leeway for time to recuperate and said he would be ready in ten days, but Arnold told him some flyers would be going overseas in that amount of time. If Rickenbacker didn't go now, there would be no reason for him to go at all. Eddie decided to go immediately.[17]

In announcing Rickenbacker's appointment, Arnold said nobody was better qualified than the Ace of Aces to instill a fighting spirit in America's fledgling aviators.[18] He also appointed Frank O'Driscoll ("Monk") Hunter, who had scored eight kills in World War I, to accompany him on his mission. Like Eddie, Hunter was in pain, having recently suffered a fractured spine. He had also been promoted to lieutenant colonel. (Rickenbacker could have become a two-star general, but accepted Arnold's assignment only on condition he would retain civilian status, giving him immunity from taking orders and permitting him to speak his mind.)[19]

Rickenbacker had plenty to say and knew it would be controversial. While German submarines sank cargo ships in full view of the Atlantic seaboard and the Japanese ran amok in the Far East, FDR believed it necessary to downplay the magnitude of the damage the United States fleet had sustained at Pearl Harbor, making reassuring statements that victory could come within two years. This stance did not galvanize public opinion. After an initial period of hysteria on the West Coast, a "slackening of resolve" took place among a citizenry that was "not despondent and defeatist so much as it was overconfident and blasé." Critics were increasingly worried about a failure of presidential leadership. "Give us the facts and figures. We can take it," said an exasperated writer. Walter Lippmann joined in, saying the White House was being dishonest with the people.[20]

Rickenbacker was determined to tell the truth. Instead of confining himself to teaching airmen what Arnold called "combat psychology," he would confront them, and the nation as a whole, with harsh realities. "Don't think that after the first fifty, hundred, or two hundred hours in the air you're a helluva good flyer," he told pilot trainees bluntly on the eve of his tour. "In the last war we found that some of the greatest stunters of them all flopped when they faced combat."[21] The odyssey began on 10 March when Rickenbacker and Hunter, like "two battered old retreads," landed at Tampa's McDill field in a converted bomber to make their first presentations.[22] During the next two weeks they and their entourage visited bases from Georgia to the Pacific Coast. Limping with a cane, Rickenbacker talked with officers and trainees up to eight hours per day, doing his best to bolster their spirits. "American war planes have proved good—more than a match for the enemy planes they have met to date," he told flyers. Nevertheless, he warned about the hazards of cockiness. "Don't let your plane bite you by getting complacent and careless," he said. "An airplane is a dangerous thing—it is like a rattlesnake and it will bite you if you are not careful." He told recruits to "study the mechanics of your plane even in your spare time" and to be "clean physically and mentally. Airmen must be alert, for more than other fighters he must go on his own." His speeches bristled with patriotism and encouragement. "You fellows are the best fighters in the world," he told cadets at Barksdale Air Force Base in Shreveport. "One reason for that is that flying is a free man's game. You have to be a leader by yourself and the type of life we lead in America fits you for this job. That was proved in the First World War and it is being proved in this one."[23]

It did not take him long to learn why Arnold was receiving complaints about morale. After visiting half a dozen bases, he found that a shortage of planes, ammunition, and supplies was limiting flying time and gunnery practice. There were not enough mechanics and spare parts to maintain aircraft that had already arrived. Technicians, he said, should be moved out of the automobile industry, where they were no longer needed for making cars. Inspectors should be withdrawn from "trying to police the airlines" for the CAB. High schools and colleges did not give enough accelerated aviation training.[24]

He was proud to visit the 94th Pursuit Squadron at March Field in Long Beach, California, on 26 March. He marveled at the horsepower and firepower of the Lockheed P-38 Lightnings and Republic P-43 Lancers flown by the men, dwarfing planes he had flown in France. He told the airmen it was up to them to "bring back greater traditions" from the current war. He heard complaints about bad food and insufficient flying time that he had already picked up elsewhere, but was especially dismayed to find that the Hat-in-the-Ring emblem he and his comrades had made famous had been retired. The airmen now wore the Indian-head symbol of the 103rd Squadron, harking back to historical connections with the Lafayette Escadrille. He protested vigorously to Arnold, saying, "You would make this squadron of officers and enlisted personnel tremendously happy and proud if you would take it upon yourself to see that they are permitted to use the old insignia immediately, and it would stimulate their fighting spirit beyond words."[25]

He sought out reporters and spoke at public forums. One of his constant themes was the need for self-sacrifice. "Today . . . it's a case of gimme gimme," he said at New Orleans, "what can I get out of it, instead of what I can give." He battled complacency and emphasized the work ethic. "We can get licked—and don't think we can't," he admonished people at Oklahoma City. "Any man who works longer will find himself on top. . . . The same thing applies to a nation!" Working only forty hours a week could "defeat America." On 26 March he gave a mordant luncheon address to the Los Angeles Chamber of Commerce at the Ambassador Hotel, attended by his mother, his brother Dewey, Babe Ruth, and Barney Oldfield. Rickenbacker declared the war might last five to eight years and said that "we'd better put some of our liberties in escrow now so we can have them later. We've got to learn to slave voluntarily before we become involuntary slaves." He became more caustic as the trip continued. His feelings boiled over in a letter he wrote to the *New York Journal American* from the Pacific Northwest. "Tell the public," he urged, "that the boys on the front are not taking out an hour for lunch, or quitting at four and going to work at nine. . . . Do you think France and Belgium and Holland have a 40-hour week now?" Visiting the Boeing aircraft plant, he said Seattle could be bombed. "We're madmen if we don't get down to business," he warned. "War is a cold, heartless business of killing men and destroying property and it can't be won on a part-time basis. If American's don't slave now—voluntarily—they'll learn to slave under the whip-crack of dictators who sneer at our freedom and standards of living."[26] He wrote to Arnold about learning from Boeing executive Philip Johnson that "unless something broke loose soon in the raw material bottlenecks, he would have to cut down to three or four days a week. It is hard to believe, Hap, but true, and again dangerous and pathetic in view of the fact that the B-17s are worth their weight in gold."[27]

He assured Arnold that his "rattles and squeaks are improving slowly but surely," but observers noted he looked gaunt and tired. Nevertheless, his aches and pains had at least one good effect: his "stove-up" appearance, as one reporter described it, gave him the aura of an Old Testament prophet as he thundered Jeremiads. Seeing people going about life as usual disturbed him deeply. An interviewer in Denver saw scorn in his eyes as cars moved up and down the streets as if nothing had changed. "This can't continue," he said. "We've got to wake up. People think they can drive their cars today as they did last year and the year before. But we are going to see between seven and ten million cars taken off the highways, and soon." He would not equivocate about the war in the Pacific. "Hell, we underestimated the Japs in everything," he declared. "We were supposed to have their navy wiped off the seas in three weeks—but it is still out there. The Japs have won enough in Malaya, Burma and Java to enable them to fight on for 25 years—maybe 50 years. They've got the oil, the rubber, the tin. We have most of the gold in the world. But, hell, you can't make battleships or bullets out of gold." Winning the war would require 10 million fighting men, 300,000 pilots, and untold years of struggle.[28]

He met a storm of criticism from people who thought he was exaggerating the crisis facing the country. An article in California called one of his speeches "disheartening, coming, as it does, from a man whose fighting qualifications put him in the front rank, but, after all, his prediction is only one man's opinion and we don't have to accept it if we don't want to." The writer was "convinced in my own mind that the war will be over not later than 1943 and maybe sooner than that. It doesn't hurt to be optimistic." A columnist said, "Even if Capt. Rickenbacker did have a superhuman gift of foresight, we would not care to believe him."[29]

Admirers, however, thought Eddie's trenchant remarks had aided the war effort by awakening the country to sobering realities it needed to hear. "The lads on Bataan Peninsula and in Australia don't need to be told of their country's peril," said the *Spokane Chronicle* after Rickenbacker spoke at a nearby air base, "but the same message should be burned home in the minds of men who are walking off the job, of factory managers whose war plants are not running full time, of industrialists who are piling up profits with more zest than they are piling up war materials, of congressmen who are trying to find which way the wind is blowing instead of showing courageous leadership." A letter in a Los Angeles newspaper said Eddie was "doing his part in saving us from destruction as he limps his way with his tortured body throughout the land to arouse us. He is grim, powerful, determined."[30]

On 12 April, exhausted from flying long hours in a stripped-down military plane, he ended his tour at Mitchel Field on Long Island after visiting forty-one bases in thirty-two days. He reminded 700 airmen present for his speech that they were being trained to be killers. "It is cruel, but that is what war is for—to kill," he said. "We can lose this war, damn it, we have lost it to date. You are fighting fanatics. If you don't kill them first they will kill you."[31] Here was the essence of what Arnold called "combat psychology." Arnold had written Eddie the previous day "to publicly commend you for the valuable work that you have done in forwarding the interests of the Army Air Force. . . . Your recent epic trip throughout the entire length and breadth of the United States was an inspiration to us all in the way you overcame the handicap recently imposed upon you by your serious accident in Atlanta." Ordering that the Hat-in-the-Ring emblem be returned to the unit Eddie had "commanded with such distinction," Arnold said his "magnificent record during the last war has been splendidly carried on in this fine piece of work that you have just finished, and we all salute you."[32] A battered hero who had recently survived a close encounter with death had shown that he could contribute valuably to the war effort. And he would continue to do so.

While Rickenbacker made his tour, German submarines were feasting on American shipping. People living along the Atlantic coast saw the destruction at night as flames leaped into the air from torpedoed vessels before they sank. In April 1942 alone "wolf packs" commanded by Grand Admiral Karl Doenitz claimed 74 ships; in May, 125; in June, 144. Vessels were sunk faster than they could be launched. German production of 20 or more U-boats each month made the situation only worse.[33]

In July the Senate Subcommittee on Military Affairs, chaired by Josh Lee of Oklahoma, and the Senate Special Committee to Investigate the National Defense Program, chaired by Harry S. Truman of Missouri, began hearings on how to solve the problem. Production genius Henry J. Kaiser advocated a solution that attracted widespread support. Kaiser had astonished the nation by the speed at which he could turn out standardized cargo vessels known as "Liberty Ships." In June he had contracted with the navy to make escort carriers the same way. He saw no reason why his techniques would not work equally well in building giant seaplanes to airlift massive cargo loads across the oceans in total immunity from submarine attack, ultimately replacing seagoing ships entirely. He proposed converting six of his shipyards on the West Coast to build 5,000 seaplanes, each weighing 200 tons and being capable of carrying 75 tons of war materiel. He estimated it would take six months to retool for the project but said the planes could be in full production in ten months. Ample raw materials and labor could be found, he declared, to make his plan feasible. A possible prototype already existed in the "Mars," a giant seaplane being developed by the Glenn L. Martin Company in Baltimore.

Two principal opponents of the Kaiser plan emerged in the debate. Howard Talbot, chairman of the War Production Board's Air Transportation Committee, argued that vital materials, including tungsten, manganese, vanadium, and particularly steel for engine parts, were too scarce to implement it. These high-priority commodities, Talbot said, had already been committed to fighter and bomber production through 1943. The other person who attacked Kaiser's ideas was Rickenbacker, who argued that production of existing transport planes including the Curtiss C-46 Commando and the Douglas C-47 should be greatly increased and development speeded of the Douglas DC-4, a prototype of which had been flown in February 1942. Rickenbacker marshaled statistics showing that the C-47 and DC-4 could carry one and one half and four and one half tons of war supplies respectively for 2,000 miles. The rugged C-46, he said, had a more ample fuselage and a service ceiling even higher than that of the C-47 and was well suited for supply lines like the one across the "Hump" from India to China. He calculated that the C-46 could carry six tons 1,000 miles, four and one half tons 2,000 miles, or two and one half tons 3,000 miles, allowing for the amount of fuel carried proportionate to the distance flown. An untested and untried monster would divert production from warplanes and take too long to become fully operational. It would be far preferable to stick to modern transports immediately available for mass production. In the future, he urged, 20 percent of all American military aircraft production should go into transports, leaving the remaining 80 percent for fighters, bombers, and other combat planes.[34]

Rickenbacker advanced other arguments. There was "a hell of a lot of difference between shipbuilding and airplane building. When you figure down to an inch in building ships, you must figure down to minute fractions in aircraft." Shipyards were not well laid out for making aircraft and hard to revamp for such a task. He declared, "if you're going to have thousands of big planes, you're going to need thousands of crews to handle them and they don't grow on trees." One of his most telling points was that giant seaplanes of the type Kaiser wanted to create would be limited to harbors on seacoasts, whereas large but more-modest-sized transports like the C-46 and C-47 could fly all sorts of places using hastily prepared airstrips. Kaiser's energies, he said, should be channeled into building destroyers and subchasers to attack U-boats.

Truman told reporters that Rickenbacker's ideas did not "carry much weight with me," suggesting that "the same things were said about the automobile industry," referring to skeptics who had doubted the feasibility of mass-producing cars in the early twentieth century. A supporter of Rickenbacker's views, however, was Undersecretary of War Patterson, who urged that "production of cargo planes for emergency transportation of supplies must be balanced against the need for combat aircraft." Kaiser's plans, Patterson said, would divert production away from warplanes. Rickenbacker's proposals, by contrast, would supplement but not unduly impede the manufacture of bombers, fighters, scout planes, and reconnaissance aircraft.[35]

Hundreds of newspaper articles debated the issues at stake. Kaiser's supporters stressed his uncanny abilities, affirming Truman's belief that he could do anything to which he committed himself if given enough public backing. But Eddie's arguments attracted widespread support. An Oregon newspaper compared the difference between building cargo ships and air transports to "constructing a steam shovel and a watch." A New Jersey newspaper said that a "doer in one line is not necessarily a doer in another." Walter Lippmann warned against diverting scarce resources from building bombers. The *Philadelphia Evening Bulletin* stated, "The practical aircraft for carrying freight is the landplane of transport size, already in steady production. Planes leased from civilian air lines are already doing it." Rickenbacker's suggestion that 20 percent of American aircraft production be allocated to existing types of cargo planes was "a practical program," whereas it was "not practical to attempt to win a war with an airplane which has not yet been invented or which cannot be produced until two years from now."[36]

Attempting to settle the controversy, War Production Board head Donald Nelson asked Kaiser to submit his plan to a four-man committee including Donald Douglas, Glenn Martin, Grover Loening, and John Northrop. Nelson called the resulting report "somewhat unfavorable but not necessarily fatal." Kaiser continued to press his case, announcing he would not use Martin's "Mars" as a model and saying that Howard Hughes would take charge of engineering and design. Kaiser was certain he could overcome shortages in materials and labor required for his program, but Rickenbacker countered that it would take too much time to build the giant planes Kaiser proposed, regardless of what materials were used. Even if they could somehow be created more quickly than he anticipated, they would be doomed by fundamental geographic realities. "If we build 5,000 of them right now," he said, "you couldn't find enough land-locked harbors and lakes on the shores of America to get them out."

Nelson finessed the issue by awarding Kaiser a contract to build a prototype from "nonstrategic material" but accelerating the production of existing transport planes as Rickenbacker had advised. Soon C-46s, C-47s, C-54s (a military version of the DC-4), and C-69s (the future Lockheed Constellation) were coming off assembly lines in record numbers and the Air Transport Command was using them around the globe in one of the greatest success stories of the war. General Eisenhower ultimately listed the C-47, along with the ubiquitous Jeep, as one of the chief "weapons" that defeated the Axis. If so, Eddie had served his country well by leading the opposition against Kaiser's ideas.

Meanwhile, the prototype Nelson authorized Kaiser to develop was a spectacular flop. Told by Nelson to use a nonstrategic material, Kaiser and Hughes chose birch veneer as the basis for a monster aircraft officially designated the HK-1. As its future became increasingly problematical, Kaiser quit the venture and critics began calling it the "Spruce

Goose," a rhyme that misidentified the material used to build it. The single prototype finally produced by Hughes had a 320-foot wingspan, 218-foot hull, and eight Pratt & Whitney engines, each rated at 3,000 horsepower. Hughes made a brief and very low altitude test flight, after which it returned to its hangar, never to fly again. It became a tourist attraction after the war.[37]

Events proved Rickenbacker right in arguing that there were better ways to combat the submarine menace than building thousands of monster seaplanes to fly above it. By April 1943—at about the time that Kaiser might have begun production of the giant aircraft—the tide had turned in the battle against the U-boats. "Looking backwards," Samuel Eliot Morison later observed, "we can see that the peak of enemy success came exactly halfway between the winter and the summer solstices of 1942–1943. More danger lay ahead, but the darkest days were over."[38]

Given Rickenbacker's eminence in commercial aviation and time-tested skills as an often very public controversialist, the airline industry and its military allies had probably handpicked him to combat Kaiser's plans. Airline operators and aircraft builders had everything to lose and nothing to gain from the shipbuilder's ideas but had everything to gain and nothing to lose from producing thousands of conventional passenger and cargo planes that could fill the skies with commerce after the war. The Army Air Forces also had every reason to oppose Kaiser because implementation of his ideas, as Talbot and Patterson indicated, would have seriously, and perhaps fatally, disrupted the creation of an enormous bomber fleet that would rain destruction on the Axis nations and the equally large number of fighter planes needed for escort, pursuit, close battlefield support, and other operations.

Rickenbacker's success in the Kaiser battle led to an assignment from Arnold after it ended. Calling Eddie to his office, Arnold showed him a thick file containing hundreds of letters from parents alleging that pilots and aircrews were going to battle in inferior aircraft. Not only parents were involved; congressmen, newspaper columnists, and a host of other critics were complaining about the quality of American aircraft and decisions Arnold and other officials had made in prewar selection and procurement. Arnold needed a public defender. Fresh from defeating Kaiser, Rick was his choice.

To answer Arnold's critics, however, Rickenbacker had to violate his own convictions. Having only recently toured air bases and listened to scuttlebutt among pilots, he knew the charges against Arnold were soundly based. Because experts at the Air War College were so heavily committed to strategic bombing, they had disregarded critics, including Claire Chennault, the officer in charge of fighter training, who departed in 1937 to train combat pilots in China for Chiang Kai-shek. Only belatedly did the United States begin to improve fighter planes to the level of the best British, German, and Japanese models. People who had underestimated Japan as a technologically incompetent country now believed, with some cause, that the Mitsubishi Zero was superior to the fighters the Army Air Forces were using in the Pacific Theater. Rumors were spreading that Bell P-39 Airacobras and Curtiss P-40 Warhawks Arnold had helped select were being left uncrated in England because American pilots knew Spitfires were better. Even America's best bomber, the Boeing B-17 Flying Fortress, once touted as virtually immune to attack, was not fulfilling British expectations.

Rickenbacker was not totally disingenuous. He admired much about the P-40, which reminded him of the Spad XIII because it was a rugged, well-armored plane with little maneuverability but good firepower. Like the Spad, it could dive into a melee, wreak havoc, and leave the scene to fight another day, as Chennault had proved in China. Eddie also had a sincere belief in the superiority of American ingenuity and was confident the nation's technological prowess would enable the Army Air Forces to win the battle for the skies, however bad things seemed at the moment. Most important, he saw another chance to be useful in defending the military establishment, as he had done in fighting Kaiser, and strengthening his influence in the process. Riding to Arnold's rescue, he changed from a Jeremiah into a bearer of good tidings.[39]

He had to be selective in the evidence he used. At the time that Japan attacked Pearl Harbor, Gerald Astor has stated, "the entire U.S. Air Force hardly deserved the name, so deficient was it in terms of . . . combat aircraft performance capability and qualified airmen compared to enemy forces." B-17s sent to Britain under Lend-Lease had missed their targets in the first raid assigned to them. Their machine guns had frozen at high altitude and their lack of tail guns made them highly vulnerable from behind. Consolidated B-24s shipped to England had been relegated to antisubmarine patrol because the British believed their lack of defensive firepower made them unsuitable for long-range bombing missions.[40]

It was similarly hard for Rickenbacker to argue against critics of

American fighter planes. As he knew, Arnold and his friends had helped create the situation for which angry citizens were now nailing them. Until awakened by the Spanish Civil War, in which Germany's Kondor Legion introduced the superb Messerschmitt Bf-109, framers of American air doctrine had believed that high-altitude heavy bombers would be invulnerable to attack. Consequently they devoted relatively little attention to what they still called "pursuit planes" that, in their estimation, were chiefly valuable for low-level warfare. They only belatedly began adopting enclosed cockpits and retractable landing gear in the Seversky P-35 and Curtiss P-36, which were still standard equipment in 1939 despite being vastly inferior to their German and British counterparts. Warned by Lindbergh about the capability of aircraft being used by the Luftwaffe, Arnold was told by the Kilner Board, which he appointed in May 1939, and its successor, the Emmons Board, that the United States should have state-of-the-art fighter planes, including escort fighters with a range of up to 1,500 miles. The two boards, however, had listed improving such aircraft only as third and fourth priorities, and the pace of further development was slow, reflecting continued emphasis on strategic bombardment.

By the time the United States entered the war, the Army Air Forces had only two relatively modern fighter planes in quantity production. One, the Bell P-39 Airacobra, could have been excellent but for engineers at Wright Field mesmerized by its thirty-seven-millimeter cannon firing through the propeller hub. Despite the speed, climbing power, and agility of a prototype introduced in 1938, capable of reaching almost 400 miles per hour, the army had decided to cast the Airacobra as a ground-attack plane, eliminated a turbocharged engine in the original model, and made other changes resulting in a relatively slow maximum speed, a low ceiling, and poor maneuverability. It could defeat Zeros only at low altitude and then only if American pilots did not try to outmaneuver them. Almost as unfortunate was the history of the Curtiss P-40. What could have been a great fighter aircraft was only a good plane, lacking the speed, high-altitude performance, and dogfighting capability of superior British, German, and Japanese models. Among the reasons for its defects was its lack of more powerful engines with turbochargers—but these would have required tungsten alloys reserved for large, four-engine bombers prioritized by Arnold and his supporters.[41]

Three better fighters were still in final development when Rickenbacker accepted Arnold's assignment. The most innovative was the

Lockheed P-38, which Eddie had admired in his recent tour, noting its two booms, twin engines, counterrotating propellers, high-lift flaps, and tricycle landing gear. It was hard to control in a dive. If equipped with turbochargers, as designers wished, it was deemed too hard for one pilot to fly. On the other hand, its long range made it a promising photo-reconnaissance craft. The British used it without superchargers and gave the plane its abiding nickname, "Lightning," but were so unimpressed that they stopped ordering it after getting the first batch from the United States. Arnold thought seriously about killing production but permitted 300 P-38s to be sent in November 1941 to units including the 94th Pursuit Squadron, which was using the plane during Eddie's visit in March 1942.

Rickenbacker knew that Arnold could claim no credit for another fighter, the P-51 Mustang, whose inception had been initiated by the British in cooperation with North American Aviation. Its radiator positioning below the fuselage, which reduced drag, and its smooth, square-cut wings, designed to facilitate laminar airflow, seemed initially unpromising to British officials who failed to appreciate its potential for much higher speeds if equipped with a more powerful engine. They thought it best suited for low-level ground attack or dive-bombing, which is how an early model, the A-36A Apache, was used. Arnold and his advisers had no idea of its potential as an escort fighter, a concept foreign to experts who believed unescorted high-altitude heavy bombers would penetrate the strongest defenses, but they were not alone because the concept of the long-range escort fighter was not current anywhere.

Eddie appreciated the promise of another American-built fighter aircraft, the Republic P-47. At Arnold's insistence, it had a phenomenally large air-cooled radial engine because Hap did not want to limit himself to water-cooled power plants. Arnold's advisers wondered whether the P-47's thin wings would support its machine guns and ammunition without fluttering, but liked its ability to reach altitudes up to 42,000 feet. In any case, as Rickenbacker was well aware, it did not reach large-scale production until July 1942 and was still untested in combat.[42]

Ironically, the best way to defend Arnold was to use the same type of arguments Eddie's opponents had used against him in his recent speeches, particularly that criticism of American aircraft was bad for morale. His first speech against Arnold's detractors was a radio broadcast on NBC in late August, claiming that "destructive criticism of American plane performance does Hitler's work" and "destroys our confidence."

He then switched to the standard Air Forces doctrine that the B-17 was invulnerable to attack at high altitude. Talking about the first raid the fledgling 8th Air Force had staged with England-based B-17s on railroad yards at Rouen on 17 August 1942, Eddie described "German fighters trying desperately to attack the B-17s at 35,000 feet. When the German fighters tried to do battle in that thin air they dropped off and lost up to 2,000 feet of altitude. But the B-17s flew right on. When some Germans did get close the B-17s delivered withering crossfire from their power turrets and shot down Germany's latest and fastest fighters—Focke-Wulf 190s." This was sheer poppycock. Rickenbacker also denied that Spitfires accompanying the B-17s to Rouen were really needed; instead, they went along simply because so many of them were available in England, practically behind every bush. Spitfires, he said, were inferior to American fighter planes, which "were shooting down Zeros at a rate of 3 to 1." Rejecting claims that the United States had no high-altitude fighters, he said that the Republic P-47 Thunderbolt "goes to 40,000 feet, and this surpasses the ceilings of enemy planes." He did not say that it was not yet in service for combat, as he knew perfectly well.[43]

In short, Rickenbacker's arguments were specious. The attack on Rouen had taken place only in response to severe pressure from British officials who wanted to see B-17s get into action but doubted the American doctrine that they should be flown in broad daylight and expected them to be decimated by the Luftwaffe. Fortunately, the twelve Flying Fortresses that took part—the only ones that had yet been successfully ferried across the North Atlantic—had met little resistance. The yards at Rouen had been chosen as the target precisely because the city was only thirty-five miles inland from the English Channel, which was as far as the Spitfires, piloted by Americans who had served as volunteers in the Royal Air Force (RAF), could escort them. The damage inflicted on the enemy was minimal and quickly repaired. At most only one German fighter was shot down in crossfire that existed only in Rickenbacker's imagination. His statements about the ratio of victories over Zeros made sense, if at all, only by taking into account the performance of Grumman Wildcats used by the navy and Marine Corps, for which Arnold could take no credit. The P-47-B Thunderbolts he mentioned did exist but were not ready for action and had serious problems that would not be eliminated until March 1943. Nothing in Rickenbacker's broadcast disproved that aircraft currently used by the Army Air Forces were woefully inadequate in quantity and quality. Like a good debater, he did his best for Arnold with what little evidence there was and stretched the truth when he had to.[44]

After making a second presentation on NBC in Chicago, largely repeating what he had already said in New York, Rickenbacker flew west for a final broadcast at San Francisco. Stopping at Denver, he disregarded the barrage of complaints he had heard in his recent tour from airmen who were getting little flying time due to a severe lack of aircraft. "Our boys are getting the finest training and the finest ships American ingenuity can provide and there's nothing finer," he stated. "Don't let the armchair strategists tell you otherwise." Based on nonexistent evidence, he said that daylight precision bombing was "changing the whole course of air warfare."[45]

After arriving in San Francisco, Rickenbacker stressed to reporters the P-40 was better armored and had greater firepower than the Zero. "Sure, anybody can build a kite," he said. "The Zero has no armor plate, low firepower, not even a parachute. Sure it will climb and maneuver, but it's finished when it's hit. Our planes are well built, rugged. Sometimes they come back looking like a screen door, but our boys come back to live and fly again." He said that no bomber could take as much punishment as the B-17 and "return safely to base."[46] This claim was justified by future events, but there was no evidence at the time to support it.

He saved the best for last, ending his tour with a rousing speech to the San Francisco Chamber of Commerce on the evening of 10 September. Again broadcast nationally by NBC, it was a masterpiece of selective evidence and rhetoric that skirted important issues. Starting by pointing out that American workers were now manufacturing 4,000 aircraft per month, one every ten minutes, and would soon be producing 10,000, one every four minutes, he cleverly spoke to an imaginary audience, the "Unholy Three"—Hitler, Mussolini, and Tojo. "It takes a little while for a peace-loving democracy to gird itself for battle," he said. "But once we hit our stride—we'll be hitting harder and harder until we knock you down—down and out." "Don't, for a moment, believe those who try to tell you that the planes we are turning out are lame ducks and easy pickings," he told his invisible listeners, charging that "some of those analysts who give you Axis leaders the greatest encouragement are a hundred per cent in error." He talked sarcastically about "aviation experts" who, from "the stratosphere of their desks," had "a bird's eye view of war in the air," comparing them to the parrot, "a very inexpert flyer" that did "more talking than any other bird."

Drawing upon his "lifetime of experience" and reminiscing about his days as a combat pilot in World War I, he gave a lesson in aeronautics ostensibly meant for the "Unholy Three" but designed for domestic consumption. Different planes, he said, were built for different purposes. Some, like the Spitfire, were specifically created for taking off rapidly and climbing swiftly to fight intruders at short range. Others, like the P-40, were heavily armored to maximize pilot protection and intended to be "fast, shifty, and tough." American warplanes were designed for versatility in all sorts of climatic and geographic conditions. "Therefore," he said, "when American pilots fly Spitfires over England, the Channel and France just remember [that] American fighter planes are at work elsewhere. They are not only patrolling 6,000 miles of coast-line in the United States, they are also on duty in Alaska—in the Caribbean—in Iceland—Honolulu—Australia—and Russia. They are spreading over the world in steadily increasing numbers and are giving a good account of themselves wherever they go." He gave an engineering lesson by stressing the importance of trade-offs. "No one plane can do everything," he said. "Each plane is built to do a specific job. The fastest plane may not be the best. Other things being equal, a light plane can out-climb a heavy one. But a heavy one can out-dive a light one. A plane designed to fly at high altitude is usually at a disadvantage at lower altitudes against planes designed to fly close to the ground."[47] Everything he said was true but skirted issues that were highly pertinent at the time.

It was a brilliant display of debating strategy and had the effect Rickenbacker intended. Lecturing to Hitler, Mussolini, and Tojo went over extremely well, and discussing trade-offs carried a ring of authority coming from America's Ace of Aces. A cascade of congratulatory letters and telegrams poured in from every part of America. Parents thanked Eddie for reassuring them that sons serving in the Army Air Forces were well equipped and in good hands. Newspapers teemed with articles, columns, and editorials praising his performance. Rickenbacker's judgment, said an Ohio newspaper, "should be preferred to that of loose talkers who compare planes that are not comparable." An article in the *New York Journal American* called the speech "one of the most stimulating the American people have received since the start of the war." Comparing Rickenbacker with an earlier proponent of air power, the author recalled how Mitchell had been stymied by "tradition-bound brass-hats of the Army and Navy" and "peace-blinded and penurious politicians." Now, however, Rick was "happy to report a transformation in American

400   EDDIE RICKENBACKER

military aviation." Banner headlines across the nation cheered his remarks. A column in South Carolina, headed "U.S. Airplanes Are Tops," was typical, saying: "There's no worry about our planes: they are delivering the goods."[48]

Actually, it was Rickenbacker who had delivered the goods, in spades, for Arnold at a time when the navy had provided most of the encouraging news the nation had received to date: providing the platform for Doolittle's Raid, turning the tide in the Pacific at Midway, and defending Henderson Field on Guadalcanal with Grumman Wildcats in the first American offensive of the war. The Army Air Forces had accomplished little at the time he spoke, but he made it seem like a lot. Arnold owed Eddie a great deal for the victory he had won for the AAF in the war of public opinion and would owe him even more in the future for detailed analysis of flaws in American planes that needed modification. Nevertheless, he said nothing about Rickenbacker's help in his wartime memoir, *Global Mission,* including the service Eddie had rendered in correcting the underproduction of military transport planes, which reflected badly on Arnold's judgment in the prewar era.

Amid all the reactions to what he had accomplished, one stood out. Writing from Washington on 14 September, two weeks after the San Francisco speech, Secretary of War Henry L. Stimson, who knew the true state of affairs as well as Rickenbacker, praised him for the "magnificent job" he had done in "evaluating the fighting spirit and training" of airmen in his tour of army air bases and asked him to undertake the same mission among American flyers abroad. What he really wanted, as Rickenbacker's subsequent report indicated, was dependable information about the 8th Air Force, its equipment, and the morale of its personnel. Saying that he wanted "a first-hand report by a non-military observer"—spurning a two-star generalship had paid off for Eddie—on how airmen were "getting along," Stimson stated that "No one could be better equipped to undertake this mission than you, not only because of your distinguished aviation record and profound aviation knowledge, but also because of your clear and sympathetic understanding of human problems in military aviation. I am certain that your visit itself will serve as a welcome message from home. Therefore, if you accept this assignment, as I hope you will, I am happy to authorize you to proceed to England and visit the various AAF stations. On your return to this country, you would report to me directly."

Accompanying the letter was a cachet giving Eddie extraordinary clout. Addressed "To Whom It May Concern," it stated that Rickenbacker would "visit the stations and installations of the Army Air Forces in the British Isles for such purposes as he will explain to you in person. Captain Rickenbacker, in this capacity, as Special Consultant to the Secretary of War, is to receive every possible assistance in the performance of his duties, by all commanders concerned, and he is to be provided with such transportation both ground and air as he may need and such accommodations as may be available under the circumstances." As Rickenbacker said, it was this "sweeping communication" that "raised the eyebrows" of officers who read it because of the authority it gave him. Armed with Stimson's stamp of approval, Rickenbacker prepared for a mission attesting to the respect he had earned at the pinnacle of the War Department for everything he had said and done in recent months.[49]

Not the least of Rickenbacker's aims in England was to gain support for doctrines that the Army Air Corps had formulated in the 1930s—doctrines that had been responsible for the critical lack of advanced fighter planes in 1942 he had noted in his tour of American air bases and that were now under fire from British critics. In the months before and during Rick's visit, leaders in Washington were reevaluating strategy. The opening phase of America's part in the war had been different from what strategic planners had envisioned. Prior to December 1941 they had thought Europe would come first in a war against the Rome-Berlin-Tokyo axis. Operations against Japan would be defensive until Germany, the main enemy, had fallen. The emotional effect of the attack on Pearl Harbor and a stunning Japanese offensive that swept everything before it for several months created an unanticipated situation forcing America to redistribute its resources.

For a time it seemed that the Japanese onslaught would overrun Australia and New Zealand, leaving the United States and Great Britain without a base of operations west of Hawaii from which to counterattack. Then, swiftly, came a turnaround beginning with Doolittle's Raid on Tokyo in April, the Battle of the Coral Sea in May, and the enormous victory in the Battle of Midway in early June. If the Japanese had not been defeated, their campaign had been blunted. On 7 August 1942 came the first American offensive of the war as Marines invaded Guadalcanal to prevent construction of a Japanese air base that threatened supply routes to the South Pacific. For about six weeks it was unclear whether a tiny beachhead would hold, but by mid-September reinforcements—men, materiel, tanks, and General Roy Geiger's "Cactus Air Force"—had arrived. By October the failure of a massive Japanese supply effort encouraged further optimism, and "Bull" Halsey was boasting, "We've got the bastards licked!" Doolittle's Raid would have been impossible without army bombers, B-25 Mitchells. As Rickenbacker learned in a future mission, the Army Air Forces played an important role in New Guinea and the Solomon Islands when an imaginative general, George Kenney, cobbled together a makeshift air force and devised new equipment and tactics to go with it. Basically, however, naval aviation provided the air power chiefly responsible for turning the tide.

Good news from the Pacific made it increasingly hopeful when Rickenbacker arrived in England that "Project Dog," the main effort against Germany, could be carried out.[50] Hitler had withdrawn from the Battle of Britain and was tied down in the Soviet Union. The way was clear to turn Great Britain into a bastion from which massive Allied forces could attack the Reich, but when, where, and how such an invasion would proceed was bitterly debated by American and British leaders. From Chief of Staff Marshall on down, the U.S. Army wanted to move directly across the English Channel. The British, however, did not want to send an expeditionary force into France and hoped to attack Germany elsewhere, preferably in the Mediterranean theater against weaker—principally Italian—opposition.

Representing a point of view that Rickenbacker would hear a lot about in England were leaders in the AAF who believed that air power could win the war alone with waves of high-altitude, high-speed, four-engine strategic bombers, invulnerable to attack, that would pummel the Germans into submission. Arnold and his disciples thought the AAF would not need to practice indiscriminate terror bombing of civilians, which became the main British tactic, because it could hit rail yards, factories, and other enemy installations in broad daylight with great precision by using the Norden Bombsight, which could assertedly "drop a bomb down a pickle barrel." This doctrine was ultimately traceable to Rickenbacker's mentor and friend Billy Mitchell, who had advocated an independent air force relying on strategic bombing to destroy enemy forces far out at sea. Beginning with the Martin B-10, introduced in 1930, American air planners had secured the weapon they wanted by the middle of the decade—the Boeing B-17 "Flying Fortress." Supposedly invulnerable to defensive attack, it was the world's heaviest four-engine bomber when World War II began. Another big strategic bomber, the Consolidated B-24 "Liberator," was also in service by 1941, but its potential was not fully appreciated. By the time Rickenbacker arrived in England, Arnold had dispatched two generals, Carl Spaatz (who now spelled his last name with two *a*'s) and Ira B. Eaker, to build the 8th Air Force into a powerful armada capable of carrying out a massive strategic bombing campaign with B-17s—but the execution of the plan would have to be postponed because of an invasion of North Africa that Spaatz and Eaker did not want.

Rickenbacker knew that British air marshals, disciples of "Boom" Trenchard, the father of the RAF, also advocated strategic bombing but had experienced bad results in daylight attacks that did not come near hitting their targets and resulted in heavy losses of aircraft and crews. Arthur Harris, now chief of Bomber Command, devised an alternate approach: sending huge numbers of planes to attack German cities at night, using "area" or "carpet" incendiary bombing against heavily populated centers that could hardly be missed. Although he recognized that large numbers of civilians would be killed and residential areas burned out, he followed Italian theorist Guilio Douhet, who had argued in his 1919 treatise, *Command of the Air,* that the fastest way to win a war was breaking an enemy's will to resist by terrorizing noncombatants who would demand surrender.

It would be hard for Rickenbacker to overcome doubts about the American doctrine of daytime precision strategic bombing among Brits who had tried similar tactics and failed. They were also unimpressed by the B-17, telling him it was too slow to elude German antiaircraft batteries and fighter planes in broad daylight and poorly armed against attack from various vantage points, particularly from the rear and head-on. On 30–31 May 1942 Harris sent 1,158 bombers against Cologne, burning out 600 acres of the city, destroying 13,000 homes, and killing and wounding thousands of people—the Germans said 459 died and more than 4,000 were injured—at the cost of 40 attacking aircraft. Arnold called Operation Millennium "bold in conception and superlative in execution," but Rickenbacker doubted its efficacy. Despite his enthusiasm for air power, he did not think strategic bombing alone could defeat Hitler. "We could send ten times that many over Germany and still I don't think we would be able to bomb them out of the war," he declared. "We must have command of the air, of course, over the land or the sea, but this isn't enough. When the time comes we must send an army into Germany and defeat her on land." Nevertheless, Eddie

supported American air doctrine to the extent of believing a successful land campaign required control of the air. "The enterprise which
begins on land or sea without air superiority," he said, "is foredoomed
to failure. The enterprise which starts with air control is already on the
high road, or the sky road, to success."[51]

Rickenbacker was in England by 25 September 1942 and began making
a detailed survey of the 8th Air Force and its problems. His findings were
the basis of a long report he gave Stimson after returning to the United
States. Sharing Arnold's disappointment that Spaatz and Eaker had not
mounted many air attacks on the European mainland, Rickenbacker
noted that meteorology was partly responsible. The weather, the worst
in recent memory, had been so bad that missions were possible on only
a few days. He realized that B-17 crewmembers, trained in clear desert
skies over Arizona and Texas, had little opportunity in England to practice the precision daylight bombing techniques they had learned.[52]

Rickenbacker also saw that the number of bombers available to Spaatz
and Eaker was far less than American planners had hoped to provide.
Not until after the victory at Midway were B-17s sent to Britain. Once
they were available, ferrying them across the North Atlantic through
Greenland and Iceland had proved much harder than expected. Only
twenty of the first thirty-one B-17s sent to Britain in July arrived safely;
eleven were lost trying to cross the Arctic ice cap. Arnold had considered dispatching B-17s on ships instead of ferrying them but rejected
the idea as too slow. Because of the U-boat menace, now fading but still
present, it was also too dangerous. Harassed by the same critics he had
appointed Rickenbacker to help silence in his American speaking tour,
Arnold had compared Spaatz to the dilatory General George McClel-
lan of Civil War fame, but Eddie realized that Spaatz was doing the best
he could with what he had. On 4 July, before any B-17s arrived, Spaatz
had mounted a small raid against Dutch targets, using twin-engine A-20
Bostons belonging to the RAF and bearing British insignia. The results
were negligible. The B-17 raid on railroad yards at Rouen on 17 August,
about which Rickenbacker had boasted in radio broadcasts, was another
hurry-up job, more of a propaganda stunt than anything else, and was
only marginally more successful. Reports to Arnold that the operation
had gone well were aimed mainly at discouraging him from sending
what few bombers Spaatz had to North Africa to support a provisional
invasion, code-named Operation Torch, that FDR hoped might score

a badly needed victory in a strategic location where the Axis least expected to be hit. Roosevelt had already agreed with the Brits that a cross-channel invasion was not feasible at this stage of the war. Without it, and without effective American bombing of the European mainland, it was difficult for Spaatz to resist diverting B-17s to Torch.[53]

Nevertheless, Rickenbacker learned that things were not completely bad for Spaatz and Eaker. Dwight D. Eisenhower, who had arrived in London in late June to command American forces in the European Theater of Operations, had kept the 8th Air Force from being absorbed by the RAF and sucked into nighttime area bombing raids that might have completely negated American plans for daylight precision operations. Despite British skepticism about daylight attacks, friendship also existed between Eaker and Spaatz on one hand and Harris on the other, stemming from previous meetings when Harris had visited the United States. When Eaker had arrived in England early in 1942, preceding Spaatz, Harris headquartered him at a former girls' school at High Wycombe and, with Churchill's consent, set aside East Anglia and large parts of Norfolk and Suffolk for Americans to build airfields from which giant bombers could conduct future operations. By the time Rickenbacker arrived, earthmoving equipment sent from the United States was stripping grass and topsoil from what had once been verdant fields, covering vast areas with concrete for the long runways required by B-17s and B-24s. Incessant rain had caused the "Battle of the Mud," reminding him of Issoudun, but he could see that a basis for a strategic bombing campaign was slowly taking shape.[54]

Wanting to support Arnold, Spaatz, and Eaker despite his skepticism about the efficacy of strategic bombing, Rickenbacker put the best face possible on what he saw, reporting to Stimson that the Brits were "swinging around to the appreciation of our ideas of daylight precision bombing" and that around-the-clock bombing would take place "as more equipment and personnel become available." Hoping to discourage the diversion of scarce aircraft to North Africa, he said that "we have every right to feel that we are on the right track, provided we here at home do everything within our power to produce planes and equipment at the greatest speed possible and give those materials absolute priority in reaching their destination, which would be England." As Stimson must have recognized, Eddie was saying as diplomatically but as firmly as possible that Spaatz and Eaker wanted Washington to live up to Arnold's promises about building an air force in Britain. He also told Stimson he was "impressed by the truly wonderful relationship that exists between the Americans and the English from the top down to the lowest ranks." As he knew, this statement was full of hyperbole because many British officials remained convinced that high-altitude precision bombing would not work, were skeptical about both the B-17 and the B-24, and had little faith in American airmen with little or no combat experience. Resentment was rife among crewmembers in the RAF about the high pay earned by American GIs, who "monopolized the girls and guzzled the beer in record time." Rickenbacker told Stimson only part of the truth.[55]

Armed with the authority Stimson had given him, Rickenbacker visited American air bases and had many talks with British and American leaders, a number of which dealt with the merits of specific aircraft. He met for several hours with Trafford Leigh-Mallory, chief of the RAF's 11th Fighter Group, who had led air units in a disastrous raid on Dieppe in August.[56] Like other British air officers, Leigh-Mallory was enthusiastic about the North American P-51 Mustang but believed the Douglas A-20 attack bomber was of "limited value until bases are established closer to the enemy where its effectiveness could be proven only in short-range support." Seeing the bias against daylight strategic bombing underlying Leigh-Mallory's remarks, Eddie disagreed with this dismissive view of the A-20, telling Stimson about talking with a wing commander who boasted about the twin-engine De Havilland Mosquito. Featuring wooden stressed-skin construction, it was highly esteemed both as a night fighter and an attack plane because of its high speed, ability to fly up to four hours without refueling, and heavy firepower. Rickenbacker got the commander to admit that many Mosquitoes had been lost to antiaircraft fire because of their wooden construction. Seizing on this observation, Eddie repeated a theme he had used in radio broadcasts back home, reporting to Stimson that the A-20 could "take much greater punishment from enemy flak and return to its base because it was made of metal." He was characteristically American in thinking it axiomatic that wood was inherently inferior to metal for airplanes.[57]

Harris lectured Rickenbacker about the terrible impact of night area bombing, saying that "large bombs were doing great damage to German morale by blowing out the window panes of homes, factories and buildings for blocks around. This is particularly effective during the cold winter months due to the lack of labor and material shortages." Rickenbacker wrote dismissively to Stimson about Harris's claim that about half of Bomber Command's recent missions had hit their targets and provided useful information by revealing that the British had been losing 6.5 percent of their planes per raid, of which about half were brought down by night fighters and half by antiaircraft guns. Four or five months earlier, Harris said, about two-thirds of the losses had been caused by flak, indicating that the Germans now had better interceptors for night operations. He expected losses from night-fighting aircraft to increase in the future. At present production rates, the British could replace only about 200 bombers per month. Harris told Eddie he was optimistic about new devices that could detect the approach of enemy planes from 1,000 yards away. Because human eyes were capable of concentrating for only fifteen or twenty minutes in darkness, this equipment would give gunners a welcome respite from being continuously alert. Harris also said the British were developing new techniques for jamming enemy radio transmissions. Rickenbacker had thus obtained useful data for Stimson.

Churchill, fresh from a recent visit to Moscow, visited Harris's headquarters while Eddie was there and invited him for lunch at Chequers. He said he would be keenly interested to hear what Rickenbacker would find when he visited other theaters of war, echoing a request that Stimson had already made to Eddie and that Churchill obviously knew about. Churchill repeated several times, "Give me a thousand more heavy bombers and two hundred destroyers now," saying that "this would not change the trend of the war but certainly would shorten the length of it." More significantly, however, instead of trying to convince Rickenbacker that night area bombing was superior to daylight precision operations, Churchill said that round-the-clock bombing "would do more to break the morale of the German people than any land offensive that might be initiated." This concession to American air doctrine stemmed from a recent visit to Moscow in which Churchill had promised Stalin to devastate Germany with massive day-night bombing to substitute for opening a second front in Europe. The prime minister's statement may have been the most important piece of intelligence Rickenbacker reported to Stimson, helping explain his optimism that British leaders were recognizing the merit of the American air doctrine. At the time, Spaatz and Eaker were worried about whether Churchill would endorse a twenty-four-hour "combined bomber offensive" at an upcoming conference at Casablanca in January 1943 and thought he made an "astonishing surrender" when he did so.[58] Because of what Rickenbacker reported about his meeting with Churchill, Stimson was aware of the direction of the prime minister's thinking long before the conference took place and had undoubtedly transmitted the information to FDR.

Rickenbacker was delighted to visit John Gilbert (Gil) Winant, American ambassador to Great Britain, for the first time since repairing Winant's Spad at Epernay in 1918. After returning to America from France, Winant had served three terms as governor of New Hampshire, chaired the Social Security Board, managed the International Labor Organization, and succeeded Joseph P. Kennedy at the Court of St. James in February 1941. Rickenbacker appreciated that, like Stimson, Knox, Patterson, and Lovett, Winant represented an influx of Republicans into Roosevelt's circle of advisers after the fall of France.[59] Putting in a good word for his old friend, Rickenbacker told Stimson that the United States was "very fortunate in having such a man as its Ambassador," but his report on the conversation dealt largely with the anguish Spaatz and Eaker felt about having the 8th Air Force diverted to North Africa and was deliberately conceived to encourage support in Washington for the desire of the two generals to keep airplanes flowing to England despite Operation Torch. Eddie told Stimson that Winant believed the British were starting to appreciate the effectiveness of daylight precision bombing and, like Churchill, feared that Hitler would center his efforts in the coming spring on England. Accordingly, Winant argued, the 8th Air Force should be "prepared for combat not only in quality but in numbers."

Rickenbacker conferred with another old friend, W. Averell Harriman, reminding him of his days with AVCO. Harriman now directed Lend-Lease operations in England and had asked Churchill to invite Eddie to lunch at Chequers. He told Rickenbacker that the prime minister was worried about whether the United States was doing its best in the war effort, echoing a theme Eddie had stressed in his tour of American air bases for Arnold. Harriman did not discuss strategic bombing, however, and was mostly concerned about how the Americans and Brits should use gliders against the Axis.

Rickenbacker had wanted to meet Lord Hugh ("Boom") Trenchard, the father of British air power. Unfortunately, Trenchard was not in Britain at the time but had left a copy of a secret report for Eddie, who regarded it as extremely important and attached it as an appendix in his report to Stimson. Predictably, Trenchard, an arch-advocate of strategic bombing, lamented the diversion of bombers, which constituted only 10 percent of Britain's "operational strength," to other functions including defense against U-boats, impeding its primary mission of raining destruction on Germany. Predictably, he said that air power, properly used, could decide the outcome of the war by itself and warned strongly against becoming involved in land campaigns that would fritter away resources better spent on aerial bombardment. Up to now, he stated, British use of air power had been "half-hearted and feeble," and "Bomber Command is the Cinderella of our forces," used in "tiny packets here there and everywhere." Three months of "ruthless bombing of Germany on the Cologne scale," he believed, could work wonders in determining the outcome of the war.[60]

Rickenbacker's comments on Trenchard's memorandum about not frittering away bombers to support land operations, and his action in passing it along to Stimson, were intended not only to emphasize the anxieties of Spaatz and Eaker about diverting aircraft to North Africa but also to underscore his own conviction, which Stimson shared, that Germany should remain the primary target of the Allied strategy. "Air power is striking power but its blows become feeble and ineffective unless that power has the maximum combination of quality and quantity," he said, echoing what Trenchard had written. "By that is meant that bomber and fighter planes, no matter how far and fast and high they fly, how well they shoot, or how well they bomb, are weakened by attrition in their numbers." He stated pointedly that it took "at least two months to train air and ground crews to serve under actual combat conditions." He cautioned that large-scale raids should remain within range of fighter escort until experienced gunners could be provided, but said, "As soon as a strong enough force is available, not less than 200 planes with seasoned gunners, we should strike at the vital enemy targets such as aircraft factories," especially in Germany itself instead of occupied countries like France, Belgium, and the Netherlands. The thrust of his advice to Stimson was clear: give Spaatz and Eaker the airplanes they needed and let them to do their job as they saw fit.

Rickenbacker argued against opening up a second ground front in Europe in the near future, however, strengthening his case for supporting the 8th Air Force in a strategic bombing campaign against Germany instead of diverting its already scarce resources to North Africa. The fiasco at Dieppe, he urged, had made it clear that the Germans were well prepared to resist a cross-channel invasion. Nevertheless, "The trend of the war on the Western Front clearly indicates that the European theatre is and will remain an air theatre until we have secured superiority over the German Air Force and paralyzed the production capacity of the German aircraft industry." Knowing from what Churchill had said at Chequers that the prime minister was moving toward accepting round-the-clock air operations, Rickenbacker told Stimson that it was "no longer a question of day bombing or night bombing, but rather a matter of precision bombing and area bombing—both are vital and effective." Reflecting Churchill's intimation that B-17s might be used by day and B-24s by night, Eddie said that British heavy bombers were best suited to operate after dark but there was no reason why four-engine American planes could not operate both night and day because of their "speeds, altitudes and terrific defensive fire power." Pointing out that the range of American and British fighters now available limited them to short-range escort duty, he suggested using heavy bombers built specifically as escorts, giving them enough ammunition to shepherd stragglers home after finishing raids. Because Spitfires had reached the limits of their development, he urged that the United States speed up production of P-38s, P-47s, and P-51s.

Rickenbacker said there was a "crying need for vital airplane and replacement parts" and commended General Tony Clark for doing "an exceptionally fine job in setting up an organization in England." He wanted to give logistics "the highest priority possible" but also shared another concern with Stimson, saying that "U.S. Air Forces are in exceptionally good shape with respect to high command leadership" but "concentrated effort should be put forth in the selection of flight, squadron, and group leaders who should be developed to the highest point of efficiency before arriving on the front."[61] He recommended that pilots be "taken out of combat service after every 50 missions or 150 combat hours in the air," urging that they be brought back to America to train cadets.

Rickenbacker's report abounded in specific criticisms of existing American aircraft and recommendations for their improvement, based on what Spaatz, Eaker, and other officers had told him, and his own observations from talking with lower-ranking personnel and witnessing mock combat at American fighter and bomber bases already in operation.[62] He made no less than thirty-eight suggestions and recommendations with regard to the B-17. Its center of gravity was "too far aft." Shifting it forward would increase the bomber's speed by twelve miles per hour. Its oxygen supply was inadequate and should be increased two- or threefold for long missions. Rubber oxygen masks worn by its crews froze to the skin at high altitudes. Electrical generators could not provide enough heat to permit crews to wear lightweight flight suits instead of heavy, bulky ones. Increasing electrical power would also help prevent gun turrets from freezing at high altitudes. Based on his interviews with gunners, Eddie recommended that B-17s carry heavier machine guns and more ammunition on missions and called for the repositioning of armor plate. He also made recommendations involving instrumentation, autopilots, navigation aids, and bomb-loading equipment.

Like other experts, Eddie did not foresee the development of long-range escort fighters, explaining why he thought some of B-17s should be equipped with more machine guns and fewer bombs and used as escorts. Nevertheless, he was extremely enthusiastic about the North American P-51 Mustang, which became the best escort fighter of the war but was not yet used by the 8th Air Force. He told Stimson presciently that the P-51 had "the greater potentiality by far as a fighter plane than any other English or American plane now in production" and that, even with its present 1,150-horsepower Allison engine, it outperformed "all other fighter plane types in England." Giving it a Merlin 61 or a 1,450-horsepower Allison engine, he said, would enable it "to out-perform any single engine fighter made."[63]

Rickenbacker told Stimson that British pilots liked the way the Lockheed P-38 had performed in mock battles with British or captured German planes. He passed along complaints, however, about a lack of vision to the left and right because of the twin booms on either side of the cockpit and also rated frontal and rear vision in the P-38 as only fair. He later claimed that his report was instrumental in saving the plane, which Arnold did not like and was considering eliminating from production.[64]

Finally, Rickenbacker pointed to a feature of all existing fighter planes that in his view required immediate improvement. In World War I, he said, open-cockpit planes offered superior visibility, permitting pilots to look around the sky. He was puzzled why closed-cockpit models used since 1935 did not have the rear-vision capability needed to spot enemy planes coming from behind. Better cockpit canopies, he urged, would provide such visibility. New canopies later used in such planes as the P-47 Thunderbolt showed that his advice was taken seriously.[65]

Rickenbacker's report was notable for its comprehensiveness, its sensitivity to ongoing debates about the use of heavy bombers, its detailed recommendations for the improvement of aircraft, and the intelligence it provided about shifts in British policy that proved correct at

Casablanca. He also effectively communicated the anxieties Spaatz and Eaker felt about the diversion of scarce resources to North Africa and stressed the legitimacy of their needs. Even though the die had already been cast for an invasion of North Africa, he went as far as he could in asserting that Northern Europe should continue to be the main theater of operations and that the best hope of winning the war, at least for the present, lay in inflicting maximum damage on Germany with heavy bombers. Never afraid to express his opinions, he had done what Stimson had asked him to do.

He also had one more task. On 26 September, soon after Rickenbacker arrived in England, Eisenhower was authorized to set the date on which the impending invasion of North Africa would begin. He chose 8 November. During Eddie's visit, Ike's staff worked up to fourteen hours a day planning the operation.[66] When Rickenbacker called at Eisenhower's headquarters before leaving on 8 October to return to America, Ike gave him one of three sets of the final invasion plan, which were being sent to Washington in triplicate by separate routes to make sure at least one arrived safely. After a rough, bone-chilling flight across the North Atlantic with stops in Ireland, Iceland, Greenland, and Canada, Rickenbacker delivered the plan to Stimson, together with his own report.[67]

Stimson must have been pleased by what Rickenbacker had done because he confirmed his intention to send him around the world on a tour of American air bases in every theater of combat. It would begin with a secret mission of a highly sensitive nature. Disregarding his fatigue and debilitated condition, less than a week after returning to America Rickenbacker set out on an expedition that would include an ordeal as terrible in its own way as that in Atlanta, greatly increasing his infirmities and profoundly affecting his state of mind, not only in the immediate aftermath but for the rest of his life.

Chapter 17
— ☆ —

Pacific Mission

Rickenbacker's new mission for Stimson was not merely to tour air bases around the world, which the two men had already discussed, but also to deliver a secret message to Douglas MacArthur, supreme commander of Allied forces in the Southwest Pacific Theater. Its contents were too sensitive to put on paper; Eddie had to memorize it and deliver it orally. It was so top secret that Stimson did not share it with Chief of Staff Marshall, who occupied an adjoining office in the Munitions Building. Stimson normally shared everything with Marshall—but not this time. Shutting the door to the general's office, usually kept open, he gave Eddie the message in a hoarse whisper: a withering reprimand to MacArthur not only for publicly criticizing the Roosevelt administration and its Germany-first strategy for winning the war, but also for sending cables disrespectful to Marshall.[1]

Partly because of his relentless self-promotion, pompous manner, and gift for words, but mostly because Roosevelt and the War Department had proclaimed him a military genius to boost morale, MacArthur had a godlike status on the homefront late in 1942 despite the overwhelming defeats the Japanese had inflicted on his forces. Republican admirers in both houses of Congress worshiped the general's image, but top-level administrators in Washington despised him and seethed with frustration while supporting the myth in public. Nobody disliked him more than Stimson, who deeply resented his conduct, stopping just short of insubordination, and his outspoken criticism of Roosevelt. In a conference with Arnold in September 1942, MacArthur called the plan to invade North Africa "a waste of effort" and shifted the blame for reverses in the Pacific by calling the existing defense system there "old and out of date as a horse and buggy." He sent petulant and implicitly disrespectful messages to Marshall, who had done his best to send supplies and reinforcements to MacArthur's beleaguered forces in the Philippines early in 1942 and even arranged to give him the Medal of Honor. Geoffrey Perret, a biographer of MacArthur, later called his cables to Marshall "melodramatic," "hysterical," and "a farrago of empty threats and surrealistic demands."[2]

Stimson admired Marshall greatly and was galled beyond endurance by the disrespect MacArthur showed for him. Because Marshall was an extremely private person, Stimson did not want him to realize he was cutting through the chain of command to rebuke MacArthur, now headquartered in Brisbane leading American forces he considered woefully inadequate and Australian troops whose fighting abilities he deemed inferior. Roosevelt had once called MacArthur one of the two most dangerous men in America—the other was Louisiana senator Huey Long—and wanted to keep him as far away as possible because MacArthur clearly wanted to run against FDR for president in 1944. Indignant about his effrontery but hamstrung by the administration's adulatory policy, Stimson could only slap his wrist in private, probably knowing MacArthur would ignore his rebuke but at least giving him the satisfaction of administering it.

Rickenbacker was an ideal emissary for Stimson. He could keep secrets. He had a razor-sharp tongue and a legendary ability to use it. He did not admire MacArthur, with whom he had crossed swords when the general was a member of the tribunal presiding over Mitchell's court martial. MacArthur, as chief of staff under Hoover and FDR, had also voiced doubt about the importance of air power. Rickenbacker's civilian status, self-assurance, and unwillingness to take anybody's guff insured that MacArthur's exalted rank and imperious manner would not overawe him. As America's Ace of Aces and a winner of the Medal of Honor, Rickenbacker was a worthy peer of the egotistical general. Stimson had no doubt about Eddie's support for the "Germany First" strategy and admired the effectiveness with which he had already carried out important assignments. Sending him to tour air bases also gave Stimson a cover story for his ulterior purpose, and Eddie gladly accepted the assignment.[3]

Because Rickenbacker was a civilian, he had to have a military aide escort him to battle zones. He chose Colonel Hans C. Adamson, who had served him in the same role during his tour of American air installations and his recent trip to England. The two men left New York City on 17 October on an overnight flight to Los Angeles, where Eddie visited his eighty-year-old mother and his brother Dewey, who continued to look after her. Proceeding to San Francisco, they boarded a Boeing B-314 Clipper on 19 October, bound for Hawaii on the first leg of their mission. The four-engine flying boat, built for Pan American's prewar transpacific operations, regularly shuttled dignitaries between California and Honolulu.[4] Despite its spacious and comfortable accommodations, Eddie twisted and turned during the fifteen-hour flight to keep his aching muscles from cramping.

Evidences of the Pearl Harbor attack were still present when they arrived in Hawaii—bullet holes pockmarked hangars, sandbags surrounded public buildings, and armed patrols enforced nightly blackouts. Most of the ships the Japanese had damaged were back in America undergoing repairs or had already rejoined the fleet, but a huge crane was righting the capsized battleship *Oklahoma* and divers were exploring the hull of the irretrievably sunken *Arizona*.[5] On 20 October, ignoring his aches and pains, Rickenbacker inspected air units stationed on Oahu. That evening he and Adamson went to Hickam Field, where Brigadier General William L. Lynd had promised to have "a good ship and a top-notch crew" waiting to leave at 10:30 p.m. on the island-hopping remainder of their trans-Pacific trip. Instead, Lynd gave them an obsolete B-17C slated to return to the mainland to be used for training purposes. Canton Island, an atoll in the Phoenix archipelago where Pan American had established a base in 1938 after the United States asserted sovereignty over it, would be their first stop.

Rickenbacker had hoped for a newer, roomier, and more comfortable B-24 and was disappointed to see an obsolete B-17 with a cramped fuselage waiting for takeoff. He was also unimpressed by the crew, whose members had recently ferried a B-24 from Australia to Hawaii. Expecting to go home on leave, they were naturally disappointed about being delayed. Sergeant James W. Reynolds, the radio operator, had planned to get married soon after his return. The flight mechanic, Private John F. Bartek, had recently lost a sister and wanted to return home to console his family.

The pilot, twenty-seven-year-old Captain William T. Cherry, from Texas, had been a copilot for American Airlines before the war. Rickenbacker would have been more impressed if he had been a full-fledged captain. Nevertheless, Cherry had made seven flights between Hawaii and Australia and flown 500 hours in B-17s and B-24s. The crew, accustomed to his leadership, admired him, but he sported a Vandyke goatee, wore cowboy boots, spoke with a slow southern drawl, had a deceptively lazy manner, and lacked the military polish Eddie expected. The copilot, Lieutenant James C. Whittaker, nearly forty-two years old, was a powerful, rugged-looking man who had flown light planes before the war but had virtually no experience in four-engine aircraft. Eddie doubted he belonged in the cockpit of a B-17 and thought him too old for an important mission.

The navigator, twenty-three-year-old Lieutenant John J. De Angelis, was slightly built, had a swarthy complexion, and wore a pencil-thin mustache. Fellow crewmembers praised his skills and said he had the instincts of a homing pigeon, but he had received little training for his difficult job. Until the fall of Singapore and the Dutch East Indies, supply routes to Asia had followed land-hugging routes linking Trinidad, Brazil, Central Africa, the Middle East, India, Malaya, and Java, with open water limited to the waist of the South Atlantic. Before the war, Pan American was alone in having flown long transoceanic routes. As of 1942, military navigators received minimal instruction before being thrown into roles demanding the use of delicate and sophisticated equipment that had to be handled with extreme care. The octant, the optical device that they used to take sightings from the sun and stars, contained a complicated array of prisms, mirrors, lenses, gears, calibrators, a bubble chamber, control knobs, and eyepieces that had to be kept in perfect alignment to work properly for accurate celestial observations. A chronometer helped calculate airspeed and ground speed, based partly on star positions but also on winds affecting an aircraft. Even slight errors could yield cumulatively large mistakes. Herbert S. Zim, an expert on navigational techniques, estimated in 1943 that a navigator had to make at least fifty observations before he could get even a rudimentary feel for his instruments.[6] De Angelis did not meet these standards.

Reynolds and Bartek, in their early twenties, rounded out the crew normally carried by the plane. Bartek, skinny, redheaded, freckle-faced, and speaking with a high-pitched voice, was an avid photographer and the youngest man aboard. Despite his youth, he had already served a stint with the coastal artillery before reenlisting in the Army Air Forces and being hastily trained as a flight mechanic. Eddie had qualms about his age and experience. Before the war, flight engineers of four-engine aircraft received eighteen months of training; Bartek had only four. Because he had no experience flying on B-17s, General Lynd had assigned a sixth, better-trained airman, Sergeant Alexander Kaczmarczyk, who had serviced Flying Fortresses on a ground crew in the Panama Canal Zone, to help Bartek if he encountered unfamiliar problems.[7] Unfortunately a recent illness and an appendectomy from which Kaczmarczyk had not fully recovered rendered him unfit for the long, potentially demanding mission. Rickenbacker later described the crew Lynd had provided as "second line."[8] He did not know the B-17C had been in a hangar since the attack on Pearl Harbor and was poorly maintained.

Bartek was startled by Rickenbacker's gaunt, emaciated appearance and wondered why a "cripple" had been given a transoceanic assignment.[9] The engines were already idling when Rickenbacker and Adamson boarded the aircraft through the tail, and the cabin was too dark for more than perfunctory introductions. They went forward through the bomb bay and radio compartment and sat on jump seats in the cockpit behind Cherry and Whittaker. Eddie was immediately put off by Cherry, but the pilot and copilot were too intent on their business to give more than a nod. After the control tower gave Cherry clearance for takeoff, he switched the four engines from idling to taxiing speed and the B-17 moved down the uneven runway, "bumping and thumping," as Adamson remembered. When it reached the end of the field, Cherry turned it around to go forward on the takeoff roll. It reached about seventy-five miles per hour and was almost ready to leave the ground when an expander tube burst on the starboard wheel, causing the plane to lurch with inadequate brakes to keep it under control. Cherry struggled with the engines and rudder to avoid crashing into a hangar and succeeded, but the B-17 was now headed for the harbor until Cherry, in Adamson's words, went into "a ground loop that almost tore off a wing and nearly knocked the engines out of their mountings." Unbuckling his seat belt, Cherry joked that the incident was "the longest no-hop crash landing I've ever made," and for the first time introduced himself and Whittaker to the startled visitors. "Any landing you can walk away from is a good one," Whittaker quipped. Ambulances and crash vehicles circled the plane with their lights shining through the windows as Lynd yanked open the tail entrance and yelled to know if anybody was hurt. He was relieved that everyone seemed "all right."[10]

Bartek stayed aboard as the plane was towed back into its hangar, thinking the mission would be postponed until the next morning, but he was wrong. During Rickenbacker's childhood his father had warned him repeatedly not to waste time, reinforcing his admonitions with thrashings he felt as if they had happened only yesterday. Determined to reach his destination without delay, he responded gladly when Lynd told him another ship was available. It turned out to be a B-17D nearly as obsolete as the other one, but a ground crew rolled it out of the hangar to prepare it for takeoff as soon as possible. Like the plane used in the aborted takeoff, it had been scheduled to be returned to the United States for use in training inexperienced crews. Its magnetic compass had been swung only for an eastward flight and its direction finder, a doughnut-shaped loop mounted outside the cockpit, had to be hand-cranked from inside the plane to put it in the proper position to receive signals from a ground transmitter, depending on the direction in which the aircraft was flying. Nobody knew it was jammed.

Returning from the hangar in which he had left the B-17C, Bartek was amazed to see the second plane warming up. He heard that Cherry had protested vigorously about taking it aloft before having a chance to check its airworthiness, but Lynd had overruled him, saying if he did not fly the plane he would get somebody else to do it for him.[11] Realizing that disobeying orders would ruin his career, Cherry had no choice. He could not check the direction finder because no radio stations in Hawaii were broadcasting so late at night. De Angelis was even more worried than Cherry because he had not stowed his octant securely before the aborted takeoff, and it fell from a plotting table in the nose compartment, where a bombardier would have been stationed had the flight been a combat mission. When Cherry ground-looped the plane, the delicate instrument bounced and clattered amid the surrounding plexiglass. De Angelis had had no time to recalibrate it before taking it aboard the B-17D.

Rickenbacker and Adamson waited in Lynd's residence while the ground crew hastily fueled the B-17D and prepared it for takeoff. They returned at 1:30 a.m., by which time members of the flying crew had taken their places for a second attempt to get going. Filled with misgivings, Cherry sped down the runway, the wheels left the ground, and the aircraft climbed to 10,000 feet, headed for a refueling stop at Canton Island, about 1,650 nautical miles southwest of Hawaii. Cherry and Whittaker had been poorly briefed and did not know where they would be told to go after they reached the atoll. They were unhappy when Eddie told them he and Adamson were headed for Brisbane. Whittaker tried to calm Cherry and other crewmembers by saying the mission would be "more fun than a barrelful of monkeys."

After a brief conversation, Rickenbacker went aft to sleep on a cot in the bomb bay. He was extremely cold lying under a thin blanket and rested only fitfully as he shifted positions, trying to keep from stiffening up. He fretted that the tailwind was much stronger than predicted. He later learned from a pilot who had taken off from Hickam only a few minutes earlier that he was correct. Instead of being ten knots per hour, the tailwind was closer to thirty. Possibly because of the discrepancy, De Angelis did not take accurate star fixes during the night and miscalculated the plane's position and ground speed as it flew onward under a clear sky.

Daylight came at about 6:30. Rickenbacker went forward to the cockpit, where Cherry told him "everything seemed to be going on serenely." Adamson joined them as they breakfasted on coffee and sweet rolls and smoked cigarettes. Whittaker was manning the controls, but Cherry took over about an hour before the estimated time of arrival, 9:30 a.m. Nudging the yoke forward, Cherry put the plane into a long, gradual descent toward their tiny target, only about eight miles long and three miles wide, with three coral islands clustered around a lagoon. Although Canton is the largest of the eight atolls in the Phoenix archipelago, it is a mere speck in a vast expanse of ocean, rising to no more than twenty feet above sea level at its highest point. Because it was barely visible from the air at even a modest distance, finding it remained a textbook exercise for navigators well into the postwar period and was an even harder one in World War II, especially for a navigator with De Angelis's limited training. Even so, hundreds of military planes had successfully landed at Canton by this time in the war, and the B-17 appeared to be on course when it passed Palmyra Island, about halfway between Hawaii and Canton. In a routine communication, radio operator James Sinott, stationed at Palmyra, received a message from the aircraft requesting a directional bearing.[12]

Cherry descended toward the assumed location of Canton but it was nowhere in sight. He tried to get a bearing with the direction finder but it wouldn't budge "more than an inch or so," only a few degrees of the circle it was supposed to describe. Pounding Morse code on the radio key (no voice communication was possible), Reynolds contacted the operator on the island, who supposedly—some sources say implausibly—told him he could not give bearings to incoming aircraft because equipment that had recently arrived had not yet been uncrated. Leaving Whittaker in charge, Cherry lowered himself into the nose compartment to talk to De Angelis, who was already anxiously coming up to meet him. Increasingly frantic, he suspected his octant was out of adjustment, making the celestial observations he had made during the night useless. Solar computations had turned out no better. De Angelis was bitter about being unable to check the octant before the second takeoff.

In the cockpit, Whittaker tried to reassure Rickenbacker and Adamson that De Angelis had a wonderful sense of direction, but when Cherry returned with a troubled look on his face it was clear something was wrong. A cold sensation crept up Rickenbacker's spine, as happened in emergencies. Thinking about the tailwind seeming faster to him during the night than predicted, he suggested the plane had overshot the island and was now south of it. Because Canton did not or could not provide a bearing, Cherry contacted Palmyra, which had the necessary equipment to determine their location, but the radio operator confused the position of the B-17 with that of a B-24 approaching Canton at the same time from another direction and gave Cherry an incorrect heading. As disaster became increasingly probable, Eddie recalled that bursting antiaircraft shells had been used for signaling in World War I and recommended that Reynolds radio troops at Canton, asking for projectiles to be fired, set to detonate at 7,000 feet. The gunners complied, shooting for about half an hour, but nobody on the B-17 saw the explosions. Using an ancient navigational technique, Cherry began "boxing the compass," flying west, north, east, and south for an hour in each direction, but did not have enough fuel to complete the circuit. Staring at the ocean, everybody began experiencing "island eyes," seeing specks of land that were only mirages.

Knowing about the impending invasion of North Africa and unable to share their secrets with the crewmembers, Adamson and Rickenbacker whispered to one another about what might happen if the plane went down in Japanese-held waters and they were captured. Talking about the possibility of torture, Adamson told Rickenbacker about intelligence briefings in which he had heard about "truth serum" Japanese interrogators might use to loosen their tongues. Upon learning what they knew, officials in Tokyo would tell Berlin what was about to happen in Algeria and Morocco, resulting in disaster for Eisenhower's expedition. Rick and Adamson decided that if the B-17 had to be ditched and they were forced to take refuge in life rafts, they would have no alternative but jumping overboard and drowning if Japanese ships or planes spotted them.[13]

By midafternoon the B-17 had been aloft for more than fifteen hours and was running out of gas. Opening a hatch, Rickenbacker and Kaczmarczyk heaved all unnecessary objects into the sea, not only to conserve fuel by lightening the plane but also to reduce the impact of the crash-landing attempt that now seemed inevitable. As far as anybody could recall, no B-17 had ever accomplished such a feat without breaking apart. Various items, including six bags of priority mail, splashed into the waves, along with an expensive Burberry coat Eastern's employees had presented to Eddie. Acting on an impulse, he decided to save five silk handkerchiefs Adelaide had given him, thinking they were too light to make a difference.

After jettisoning everything that could be spared, Rickenbacker and Kaczmarczyk filled thermos bottles with water and coffee and put a box of emergency rations in the radio compartment, which had an overhead escape hatch. Everybody donned Mae West jackets. Rickenbacker cautioned the men not to inflate them until they were out of the plane. Cherry and Whittaker remained at the controls, and Bartek stood behind them to pull levers that would deploy two five-man life rafts from compartments in the fuselage that would pop open, causing the rafts to inflate automatically. He also prepared to release a smaller raft designed to hold three occupants but actually only big enough for one. Reynolds continued to send SOS signals on the radio but got no response. Rickenbacker stationed himself beside a window to estimate the plane's altitude as it descended. Adamson, De Angelis, and Kaczmarczyk lay prone beside parachutes that would hopefully cushion the impact when the plane hit the waves. While moving toward the cockpit, Bartek noticed that Adamson's body was pointing the wrong way and feared he would be injured, but he had never met an officer higher than a major before the mission and the discipline he had been trained to observe prevented him from daring to rebuke a colonel, so he said nothing. Bartek also wondered why Rickenbacker had wrapped a long coil of rope around his waist. Most of all, he thought about possessions he had thrown overboard to lighten the plane. The most valuable was a camera—a Leica—that had cost almost $500, an enormous amount of money at the time. He decided to keep a small book of Scriptures given him by members of a church he had attended when stationed at Roosevelt Field on Long Island.[14]

Cherry expertly guided the ship toward the ocean, realizing he needed to ditch it in a trough between two waves because hitting the water near the crests might cause it to break apart. He also wanted to come down tail first to lessen shock on the fuselage and wings. Seated by his window, Rickenbacker called out estimates of the distance between the plane and the water. Cherry had already cut the two inboard engines to conserve fuel and had just enough gas left in the outboard ones to make a powered entry. As he had intended, the B-17 came down tail first, making a thunderous roar as it plowed into a trough between two swells.

The tail broke apart from the force of the impact, and water began pouring into the cabin. Bartek had been too weak to pull the levers controlling deployment of the two main rafts, and Whittaker had helped release them in the nick of time for them to inflate before the B-17 hit the water. The smaller raft had also been ejected and was bobbing up and down on the ocean. Climbing through the plane's two escape hatches, the men were buffeted by towering waves that made it extremely hard to get to the wings. Following time-honored tradition, Cherry got out last. As Bartek had feared, Adamson's back was severely injured from lying in an improper position, but he got out successfully. Reynolds also exited, but his face had smashed into the radio as he sent his final SOS. His lacerated nose was bleeding profusely. A piece of jagged metal cut one of Bartek's hands to the bone as he tried to disengage one of the rafts from a line with which it was fouled. Rickenbacker cut the line with a six-inch knife Cherry had brought from the plane. Blood flowed from Bartek's wound, increasing the danger of shark attack. Floundering desperately, the men lashed the three rafts together with the rope Rickenbacker had tied around his waist and drifted away from the B-17. Sharks had indeed sensed the blood from Bartek and Reynolds getting into the water. Circling around the party, they bumped against the sides and bottoms of the little vessels. Fortunately everybody got safely aboard, having no idea where they were, lost in an endless expanse of heaving salt water.

Bartek later recalled that the crewmembers had expected to be rescued quickly because Rickenbacker was on the plane. Surely, he thought, a massive search and rescue effort was underway. Spirits remained high even when the survivors discovered that the food, water, and coffee Rickenbacker and Kaczmarczyk had stored in the radio compartment had been left behind in the commotion after the plane hit the water. They decided not to attempt retrieving the provisions because they thought the B-17 would sink rapidly. Actually it stayed afloat long enough to bring out the emergency rations, then slowly sank tail upward beneath the waves, leaving them suddenly aware that their only food consisted of four oranges Cherry had stuffed into his pockets. Some chocolate bars they had also brought on board had been saturated with salt water, making them inedible.[15]

The two main rafts were seven feet long and four feet wide on the outside. Their interior dimensions were considerably less, five and a half by two and a half feet. The third raft, which the men called "The Doughnut" because it was round, was much smaller. As planned, Cherry, Whittaker, and Reynolds got into one of the larger rafts, and Rickenbacker, Adamson, and Bartek took the other. Because De Angelis and Kaczmarczyk were shorter and smaller than the rest of the crew they occupied the tub, so tiny they could fit into it only by draping their legs over each other's arms and shoulders, making it inevitable they would get muscle cramps in the coming ordeal.

Cherry's raft led the little flotilla, with Rickenbacker's second and the tub containing De Angelis and Kaczmarczyk third. The rafts had blue bottoms to blend with the sea and not attract fish that might attack and puncture them. The sides and floors were painted bright yellow to stand out against the water and attract notice from overhead. The larger rafts had aluminum oars and survival gear including two knives, two hand pumps, a pair of pliers, two bailing buckets, a first-aid kit, patching equipment, and a Very pistol with eighteen flares, twelve of which turned out to be duds. Cherry and Adamson had revolvers that became useless because salt water got into them. Repeated efforts to keep them workable by taking them apart and lubricating them with oil that members of the party scraped from the backs of their ears were fruitless. Eventually they threw the weapons overboard.[16] Some watches worn by the airmen were still working after the crash, but two were out of commission because of broken mainsprings. Whittaker's timepiece was the best and lasted throughout the entire ordeal. It showed it was 4:32 p.m., Honolulu time, when the men began shoving away from the stricken B-17.[17] De Angelis had two fishhooks and some green cord he had found in a parachute in the bomber, but there was no bait to go with them. Adamson recalled that it was "almost homicidally maddening for the men to look into the sea from the rafts and watch fish swimming all around them," but nothing, including paper wadding or a "trolling gadget" that Eddie made from Adamson's key chain, attracted bites.[18]

Adamson was in agony from the outset because of his back injury. Reynolds had not broken his nose from banging into his radio set, as

Rickenbacker had feared, but was a "gruesome looking spectacle" when the blood dried on his face.[19] Bartek's fingers were slow to heal because salt water washed off iodine from the first-aid kit, intensifying the pain from his cuts. Of all the men, however, Kaczmarczyk, already weak at the outset of the mission, was in the worst shape. He had swallowed salt water climbing into the tub he shared with De Angelis and was violently seasick from swells acting like elevators, lifting them up and leaving their stomachs in midair before dropping them back onto the ocean. His thirst became unendurable as the ordeal dragged on. Despite warnings from Eddie, he drank seawater and hallucinated.

The men speculated where they might be in the endless expanse of ocean. Adamson had a map that became unreadable because of exposure to the elements but was legible early in the ordeal. De Angelis had a compass that was soaked by salt water but was useful for a time. With these meager aids, and by observing the stars at night, Cherry and Rickenbacker correctly surmised they had come down west or southwest of Canton Island. Actually, the B-17 may have come within about 150 miles west of the atoll; if this is true, De Angelis had not been as far off course as Rickenbacker thought.[20] In any case, they were in an oceanic no-man's-land, borne slowly westward by prevailing winds and sluggish currents at seven or eight degrees south latitude between the Phoenix and Ellice Islands, with no bodies of land, however small, anywhere in the area. Because of the remoteness of their location and the vastness of the uninhabited waters surrounding them, they floated interminably without being spotted by search planes. They were north of the American supply route going through Samoa, the Fiji Islands, and New Caledonia to Australia, but too far south and east of Japanese bases in the Gilbert and Marshall Islands from which enemy patrols might have seen them, leading to captivity and a fate worse than death. There was no reason for ships, friendly or hostile, to intrude upon the waters in which they were marooned, moving slowly toward oblivion. Rickenbacker tried to lift their spirits by saying they might be headed for the Fiji Islands. As the ordeal continued he kept predicting they would land on them any day, knowing it was only a dream.

Sharks followed the men from the moment they had struggled into their rafts and paddled away from the stricken B-17. They were very lucky the menacing creatures had not attacked them before they made it to the rafts, floundering in blue-green waves already splotched with blood from Bartek's and Reynolds's wounds. Sharks have a phenomenal sense of smell and can detect blood in concentrations of less than one part per million. Had great white sharks, makos, tiger sharks, or hammerheads been lurking where Cherry had ditched the B-17, Eddie and his companions would probably not have lived to tell the tale, but the sharks surrounding them were more benign. After the men got underway the creatures did not bother them and seemed to be more curious than malevolent, possibly because they were accustomed to feeding on marine life teeming in the seawater. Because of the remoteness of the area where the flyers were marooned, they may never have come in contact with humans and did not know what to make of aliens suddenly appearing out of nowhere.[21] Whittaker later wrote that the "shark escorts" were "good-humored beasts in their uncouth way and as playful as a pasture of calves. We didn't mind the little ones, but the big 12 foot fellows had a disturbing habit of scraping the barnacles off their backs on the bottoms of our boats. After a dash to gain momentum they scooted under us, rubbing their backs and giving a flip of the tail as they left each boat. The man sitting on the canvas floor got a wallop that jarred him to the teeth."[22]

Swells continually buffeted the rafts, soaking the men and forcing them to bail at least every two hours. "The breakers would come up and slap us and go over the roll," Rickenbacker recalled, saying "It was like being doused with a bucket of ice water." For the first few nights the sky was clear except for scattered clouds, and the stars shone vividly, with a full moon increasing the wonder of the spectacle. To Eddie it seemed as if the clouds were forming "unusual pictures—beautiful women, elephants, birds." One cloud looked like a "wild boar," others like trees. Thinking he was hallucinating, he kept his thoughts to himself for a few nights but finally shared them with Adamson, who admitted seeing the same things. He had been in charge of a planetarium after Trubee Davison became director of the Museum of Natural History and led discussions about the star formations the men had seen as they lay awake at night. His lectures helped pass the endless hours of freezing darkness and broiling sunlight.[23]

At times they had no sense of forward motion. On the second day "a terrible calm started which made the sea just like a glassy mirror," Eddie remembered. "The sun was horribly hot. The glare was terrific and terrible on the eyes, and most of the boys fell into a doze or sort of stupor." Hunger pangs had now begun tormenting them and they decided to eat one of the oranges every other day to stretch their meager food supply.

Eddie tried to divide the fruit into equal portions with Cherry's knife. "When you have got seven pairs of hungry eyes watching you, you can't help but do a pretty good job of carving," he recalled. His method was to "cut the orange in half first, then take those halves and cut them in half, and then take those halves and cut them in half. In that way I could get pretty close to the correct proportions. They got the skin as well as the heart of the meat. It was surprising what that one little bit of orange would do for you."[24] Trying to maintain discipline, the men waited two days to share the second orange but became so ravenous they ate the rest on the fifth and sixth days.

Because of Rickenbacker's importance they continued to feel sure a search must be underway and clung to hope that they would soon be found. Surely newspapers must be filled with speculation about what had happened to them (as indeed they were), and Eddie's army of admirers must be in an agony of suspense (as was also true). The men constantly scanned the horizon for any sign of a ship and waited expectantly for the sound of engines indicating a plane was about to appear in the sky, but help did not come and they felt an increasing sense of abandonment. A search was actually taking place, but their position, far out in the middle of nowhere, made it unlikely that the limited number of vessels and aircraft that could be spared would find them in the vast expanse of the remote area in which they had disappeared. Mere specks in an endless seascape, they had no chance of being detected at night and only the slimmest hope of being discovered by day.

Searing heat returned after each successive dawn and the men felt the pain of badly sunburned skin. Before leaving the plane Rickenbacker had put on an old gray hat he had for some reason thought to bring with him. Repeatedly dipping it into the ocean, he pulled it over his ears and felt momentary relief as cold salt water cascaded over his head and shoulders, but the brine that encrusted him only made things worse in the long run. Remembering he had saved the five silk handkerchiefs Adelaide had given him, he shared four of them with his mates (three already had handkerchiefs). "The other five, including myself, used what I had," Eddie recalled, "and we put them over our noses bandit-fashion to shield our faces."[25]

Rickenbacker had been wearing a summer-weight suit—inevitably blue, as was his custom—and a tie at the time he boarded the B-17 in Hawaii. He kept the outfit on during the flight and his escape from the plane. Only his hands were directly exposed to the sun. "They swelled and blisters would raise and then break. Then the salt water would get into them, and they would burn and crack and dry, and then burn again, and just keep on until both of my hands, when it was over, were just like raw beefsteaks."[26] Adamson wore his military uniform and officer's cap, but most of the other men were inadequately clad except for their Mae West jackets. Some, including Reynolds, were bare-legged, had no shoes, and paid a terrible price in physical discomfort for thoughtlessly discarding their pants and footwear before leaving the B-17. De Angelis and Whittaker had dark complexions and tanned, but the rest became severely burned and developed open sores that hurt unmercifully.

Early in the ordeal Eddie noticed the little book bulging in one of Bartek's pockets. It was a copy of the New Testament, with Psalms. As days passed with no sign of deliverance, Cherry and Rickenbacker organized devotions in which Cherry addressed prayers to the "Old Master." Eddie had paid little attention to religion since his childhood but now took part in the impromptu services. Despite his misery, Adamson, a self-professed atheist, joined in reading selections aloud. At one point Cherry asked him to repeat a passage from Saint Matthew's Gospel: "Therefore, take ye no thought, saying: 'What shall we eat?' or 'what shall we drink?' or 'wherewithal shall we be clothed?' For these are things the heathen seeketh. But seek ye first the kingdom of God, and His righteousness; and all these things shall be added unto you. Take therefore no thought for the morrow; for the morrow shall take thought for the things of itself. Sufficient unto the day is the evil thereof." Whittaker, also an atheist and the least religious member of the group, felt strangely impressed by these verses and resisted the temptation to taunt his companions for turning to God in their distress.[27]

After the oranges were gone, starvation and thirst became all-consuming. As survivors of similar ordeals discovered, a small amount of food is almost worse than none at all, merely starting gastric juices flowing without easing hunger pangs. The men began to hallucinate about their favorite foods, especially cold, thick milkshakes and hot, juicy hamburgers. Adamson had stuffed an old copy of the *Reader's Digest* in one of his pockets, but the only article not saturated by salt water mentioned the delicious cuisine enjoyed by dirigible pioneer Alberto Santos-Dumont in Paris, and they could not bear to hear about it.[28] In a morbid conversation they thought about cutting off body parts—toes and ear lobes—and attaching them to De Angelis's fishing lines as bait.

On the eighth day, like an apparition materializing out of thin air, a little brown bird came down out of the sky, noisily flapped its wings, and lit on Eddie's hat. Like an omen from heaven, its sudden appearance heralded the uncanniest episode of the raft ordeal and one of the defining moments in Rickenbacker's life. According to accounts that were told and retold among persons awed by the symbolic power of what happened, the bird was a seagull, but Adamson and Whittaker were likely correct in saying it was a swallow or tern because seagulls did not normally fly so far from land in this remote part of the Pacific. If it was indeed a seagull, its identity underscored the seemingly miraculous nature of an event that captured the imagination of millions of people and became an enduring part of the lore resulting from World War II. Ever so slowly and stealthily, as his companions watched with "hungry eyes, famished eyes—almost insane eyes," Rickenbacker began raising his hands toward the bird in an agony of suspense lest it fly away as swiftly as it had appeared. He could not see it but his senses told him where it was perched. "You could have heard a pin drop into the Pacific," he later wrote, trying to recapture the intensity of the moment. With a sudden grasp he closed his fingers around the bird's legs and cupped it in his hands. A brief debate took place whether he should set it free, but there was no escaping the inevitable decision made by the famished men. Wringing the bird's neck and stripping off its feathers, Eddie cut it apart with Cherry's knife, sharing everything but its guts with his companions like a priest at High Mass. The flesh tasted "raw and stringy and fishy," but ravenousness was so compelling that the men ate everything, including the bones.[29] Whittaker later said the bird tasted rank and the muscles were "like iron wires," but Bartek described the meal as "excellent."[30] Attaching the guts to hooks and using a ring as a sinker, they caught two tiny fish, one a mackerel, the other a speckled bass, and gave them to Adamson, who carved them into tiny pieces. Whittaker recalled that "Each of us received a fish steak about an inch square and just a little over half an inch thick."[31]

Eating the bird and the fish only increased their thirst, but soon another seeming miracle occurred, as if to confirm the biblical passages they had read. A squall suddenly appeared on the horizon. As it drew closer, it looked so threatening that they would normally have gone out of their way to avoid it, but instead they paddled furiously in its direction. With its approach, there arose a mighty wind and surging waves. "Then, out of the blackness of the night," Adamson wrote, there "came a blinding flash followed by an ear-bursting crash. More lightning, more thunder, and rain! RAIN! Right on the rafts! It was not a gentle downpour. It came with the extravagant waste of a waterfall."[32] Howling with delight, the men grabbed buckets and empty shell casings from Very guns, stripped off their clothes, and held shirts, pants, and handkerchiefs aloft to wring out the water and squeeze it into the containers. Rickenbacker recalled that Adamson's pants were "the best soaker of the lot." While the rafts "swung crazily back and forth like a Coney Island amusement device," they collected "about a quart and a half" of precious liquid during the fifteen or twenty minutes the squall raged at its height. They would have stored even more except that "a mountain of a wave," as Adamson described it, swamped the vessel occupied by Cherry, Reynolds, and Whittaker, overturning it and costing them some of the precious, lifesaving liquid they had so arduously gathered. Fighting desperately to right the boat and retrieving an aluminum paddle that had been swept overboard, members of the party were left with "about a jigger apiece, which was the sweetest water we had ever tasted," Eddie recalled. "That was our first drink."[33] The drenching also helped them by washing incrusted salt from their sunburned skins and flooding their pores with rainwater. Their dehydrated bodies absorbed the liquid like blotters.

As the rain tapered off, they stored some of it in their Mae West jackets, which contained inner tubes with bicycle valves to admit air. Collecting water in their mouths, they blew it through the valves after squeezing out the air. Cherry siphoned it out of the tubes a mouthful at a time and spat it into empty Very shells from their flare guns. Each casing was about six inches long and the diameter of a quarter. The men initially decided to permit themselves two sips each per day, but their needs were too dire to stick to the plan and the supply quickly disappeared. Adamson and Kaczmarczyk drank first because they were sicker than the rest. After the supply ran out, the men's spirits sank. Their eyes became increasingly bloodshot and burned unmercifully, as if they were full of sand, a result of dehydration and the glare of the sun on the ocean, which had half-blinded them. Hoping to increase their speed and bring them closer to land, Cherry and Whittaker improvised a mast by crossing two oars and stretching an undershirt between them. They kept the oars in place by sitting on the floor of the raft and keeping them apart with their hands, but the experiment cost too much effort for minimal results.

Using pencils on the rafts, Adamson tried to keep track of days by making marks on a roll of canvas. He wrote messages to his wife in a notebook he borrowed from Whittaker. "We do not know where we are or where we are heading," he said, telling her not to grieve but "find some other man who may be even more able to appreciate your fineness than I have." "Oh, my dear, I don't know why I write this," he told her. "You will never see it anyway." He thought he had "made my peace with God," and wrote his last entry on the fourteenth day: "Rick and I are still alive."[34]

That night, tormented beyond endurance by hunger, thirst, and his injured back, Adamson tried to commit suicide by slipping over the side of the raft he was sharing with Rickenbacker and Bartek. In a flash that amazed Bartek, considering Rickenbacker's feeble condition, Eddie sprang across the boat and hung onto Adamson for dear life until Cherry and Whittaker drew the three rafts together and dragged him aboard.[35] Rickenbacker then unleashed the full fury of his deep voice and abrasive tongue, dressing Adamson down with an awesome display of profanity. "It was then that Rick took over," Whittaker declared. "I will not put down all the things he said. They would scorch this paper. But from then on, woe betide the man who appeared about to turn quitter or who did anything to lower the morale of the others."[36] When Adamson apologized, Rickenbacker refused to shake hands with him, telling him he would have to prove his will to live with action, not words. "This was a very difficult thing for me to do," Rickenbacker recalled, "but it was the only weapon I had, to brutalize anyone who seemed to show a weakness or a willingness to give up." Adamson was not the only member of the party to suffer under the lash of Eddie's tongue, saying he "blasted out in thundering wrath when he thought a dose of anger was the best medicine. That the men were sometimes boiling-mad at him did not bother Rick in the least. . . . Lord, how they learned to hate that man!" Rickenbacker upbraided some so abrasively that "they swore they were going to live for one devout purpose only, to bury me at sea."[37]

Whittaker's statement that Adamson's attempted suicide marked the time "Rick took over" was a telling comment about a human drama developing in the ordeal. In a hero-worshiping biography of Rickenbacker that Adamson published soon after the war, he said that Rickenbacker took charge of the party even before it vacated the B-17, "without obviously doing so and without the formal consent of those aboard. To the great credit of Captain Cherry and Lieutenant Whittaker, they took his leadership eagerly and without resentment."[38] As Adamson knew when he wrote it, this statement was untrue. Openly or implicitly, a leadership struggle took place between Rickenbacker and Adamson on one side and Cherry on the other. As captain and pilot of the B-17, Cherry believed he was in command and continued to say so after it sank. Crewmembers shared his feelings, but Adamson and Rickenbacker did not. Despite his increasingly debilitated condition, Adamson claimed that being a colonel made him the highest-ranking officer in the little fleet and entitled him to command. Bartek and De Angelis, both highly loyal to Cherry, regarded Adamson and Rickenbacker as mere passengers. Rickenbacker, a civilian, had no claim to military authority but possessed by far the strongest personality of anyone aboard. It was unthinkable for someone with his determination and sense of self-importance to regard Cherry, whom he had disliked from the beginning, as an equal, let alone a superior. His status as a national hero, Medal of Honor winner, and emissary of Secretary of War Stimson gave him a moral authority possessed by nobody else. Adamson wrote, with good reason, that a man who had led combat pilots in war and been chief executive of an airline in peace "had resources to draw upon in this situation which few men were able to muster." In a preface to Rickenbacker's book, *Seven Came Through,* William L. White commented aptly that he was "a primitive force of nature."[39] It was impossible for an ace of aces who had turned down a two-star generalship to think of Cherry as more than a minor character in a drama in which Rickenbacker, like Captain Ahab, was the main protagonist.

Adamson correctly said, however, that Rickenbacker had "taken charge without obviously doing so and without the formal consent of those aboard." Because of Adamson's status as a colonel, however severe his injuries, he was a convenient power-surrogate for Eddie. Had the aide died, a confrontation would have been inevitable between Rickenbacker and Cherry, who would have had the support of his crew. As long as Adamson remained alive, Eddie had an ally with a claim to military rank higher than that of Cherry, raising the threat of a court-martial if a rescue took place and a military tribunal ruled that Cherry had overstepped his bounds. More than mere personal friendship explains the alacrity with which Rickenbacker bolted across the raft, with a speed that amazed Bartek, to save Adamson's life. By browbeating Adamson, as Whittaker saw, Rickenbacker was overtly taking the reins he had wielded from the mission's inception. Furthermore, by unleashing the full fury of his caustic tongue on crewmembers that showed weakness or lack of resolve, Rickenbacker was not merely trying to strengthen their will to live. He wanted to make them so afraid of his wrath that they would not dare to challenge him in a showdown with Cherry, with whom he had an increasingly bad relationship. The hatred Cherry felt toward Eddie for the rest of his life was that of a man who felt disrespected by a crippled but awe-inspiring figure who refused to yield to his rightful authority.[40]

Nevertheless, Rickenbacker showed the tender side of his nature. Kaczmarczyk became increasingly sick from drinking seawater at night when nobody could see what he was doing. In his delirium he mumbled "Hail Marys" and talked incessantly about a young woman, Coreen Bond, whose picture he carried in his wallet.[41] He frothed at the mouth and shook as if he had ague. His feet became horribly sunburned. Recognizing his agony, Eddie told Bartek to trade places with Kaczmarczyk in the two-man raft and had the sergeant lifted into the one he occupied with Adamson. Cuddling Kaczmarczyk in his arms like a baby, trying to share with him what remained of his body heat, Rick lulled him to sleep for an hour or two but Kaczmarczyk would wake and utter something in Polish about his mother or sweetheart. Occasionally he emitted what Rickenbacker described as "a nightmare moan that seemed to come right out of the dark."[42]

After staying with Rickenbacker about two days, Kaczmarczyk, apparently sensing the approach of death, indicated that he wanted to go back to the tiny vessel with De Angelis. Bartek returned to the bigger raft and Eddie helped move Kaczmarczyk back into the tub. That night, Kaczmarczyk vented a haunting sigh, followed by a silence so profound that Eddie knew he had died. After De Angelis confirmed his diagnosis, Rickenbacker ordered the group—an assertion of authority nobody challenged—to wait until daybreak to determine whether it was certain Kaczmarczyk was gone. At dawn, after the three rafts drew close together, Rickenbacker "checked his heart, checked him in every way I knew how, and pronounced him dead." Cherry, Whittaker, and Adamson reached the same conclusion and attested to Rickenbacker's judgment. Removing Kaczmarczyk's jacket, identification tags, and wallet, and giving them to Cherry for safekeeping, Rickenbacker helped lift the corpse out of the tiny vessel and lower it gently over the side. As it floated away, De Angelis sang Catholic hymns.[43]

Rickenbacker later wrote a mordant epilogue to Kaczmarczyk's death, saying that "a shark hit him" after he "sailed off for forty or fifty feet." He commented that "the shark seems to sense the approach of death, or actual death, because on this particular night there seemed to be twice as many sharks around us as there had been previously, or as there were during the balance of the time." Bartek later denied Rickenbacker's report, but, as he was frank to admit, things happened during the raft episode that he neither wanted to see nor remember. Adamson thought he saw fins protruding ominously from the waves and speeding in Kaczmarczyk's direction as his corpse floated away. Given the reputation of the shark as a scavenger, Rickenbacker probably told the truth.[44]

Nevertheless, sharks did no more harm in the rest of the ordeal except to bump against the floors of the rafts, causing severe pain to buttocks already raw and ulcerated from the effects of salt water. The heat was unbearable, compounding the torture the men endured. Seeking relief, some of them dangled their legs over the sides and even swam around the boats without molestation. They tried to catch fish with their bare hands, only to have them slip away, increasing their frustration. They managed to harvest a few fingerlings, and scraped "sea lice," as Adamson called them, from the sides of the vessels. Flying fish occasionally jumped over the gunwales, providing additional meager fare. Periodic rain that the castaways became more adept at catching and collecting helped keep them precariously alive. Despite the ravages of hunger, however, there were limits beyond which they could not go. Cherry and Rickenbacker both tried drinking their own urine but quickly gave it up. Because of the salt water that the men's bodies absorbed, if for no other reason, they emptied their bladders frequently, usually in a sitting position because they were too weak to stand. Nobody, however, passed solid waste throughout the entire episode, probably because they ate too little to produce it. However ravenous their appetites, some things were impossible for them to stomach. After Cherry caught a small shark with a fish hook and dragged it into his raft, killing it with a knife after a terrific struggle, the taste of its flesh was so putrid that the men threw the carcass back into the ocean. The only result of the episode was a hole that Cherry tore in the floor of his raft by missing with one of his swipes. It was hard to patch and permitted additional salt water to accumulate, exacerbating their already painful sores.

Testifying to the discipline and strong ethical sense of the men, as Kaczmarczyk's burial at sea indicated and as Bartek later attested, was the lack of any inclination to resort to "the custom of the sea"—cannibalism, a practice followed by many desperate men in similar circumstances. Signs appeared, however, that their minds were beginning to crack. Bartek had the small raft to himself for a time after Kaczmarczyk died. "He would loll on his back when the weather was good, sleep, read his Bible, or listen to the talk shouted back and forth between the rafts," Adamson recalled.[45] One day Bartek detached himself from the flotilla for no apparent reason and floated away before paddling back. He could not explain why he went on the brief excursion. Another separation was planned but fruitless. Thinking that routes taken by convoys headed for Australia might be nearer than they were, Cherry, Whittaker, and De Angelis, the strongest members of the crew, disengaged their raft and headed south. Eddie recalled that they "started out about two o'clock in the afternoon. Hours later we could still see them over the horizon, and by morning they had rejoined the little group, stating that it was a physical impossibility to row against the drift, and that they were utterly fatigued from the attempt. At no time were they ever beyond a half or three-quarters of a mile away."[46]

As the ordeal continued, the men grew scraggly beards and lost more and more weight. Rickenbacker felt his gums receding and wheezed when he talked. False teeth a dentist had installed before his trip to England came loose and a "cottony substance" formed under the plate from dried saliva. The only relief he could get was to take it out and rinse it in the sea, "ever mindful that if I let go of those teeth, I would be in a helluva fix."[47] One morning he lost the appliance but managed to recover it before it sank more than a few inches. He began talking to himself and was haunted at night by groans, snores, and shrieks from men having nightmares. In one of his own dreams, he "landed on an island where I found an old friend with a lovely home." His host "put me up in a nice, soft bed and gave me a most delicious breakfast, with an abundance of fruit juices." The house had a telephone with which Rickenbacker called Stimson, asking him to "send a plane for us immediately." When he woke up he found to his "horror and amazement that I was still on the broad Pacific, with its gray mist and that everlasting rocking to and fro that goes on with the swells on any ocean."[48]

The rafts were slowly drifting steadily closer to the Ellice Islands, the only barrier between the castaways and oblivion. Of the nine atolls composing the Ellice group, the most important was Funafuti, which had a large lagoon that made it an ideal location for a naval base. A company of Marines, the PT (patrol torpedo) boat tender USS *Hilo*, five Vought OS2U Kingfisher floatplanes, and four PT boats had occupied it on 2 October in a move by the navy to seize strategic outposts protecting convoy routes to Australia and New Zealand. The PT boats had plywood hulls and Packard engines. Their survival in combat depended on speed and maneuverability. The tender, also known as a mother ship, kept them stocked with supplies and munitions. The Kingfishers were single-engine scout planes designed to be catapulted from a capital ship or take off from water. Ideal for search and rescue operations, they had two separate cockpits for a pilot and a radio operator, a long central pontoon with a "step" to permit takeoffs, and two smaller floats suspended from the wings.

The Japanese were unaware that an enemy naval force had taken control of Funafuti, but the Americans were not sure their presence had gone undetected and the Kingfishers carried out daily patrols of the waters around the base to protect it from surprise attack. Rickenbacker's disappearance was not the primary reason for the close surveillance the Kingfishers maintained, but the possibility that westerly currents prevailing late in the year might be carrying him and his companions near the Ellice chain gave the pilots and radio operators extra incentive to be on the lookout for them.[49]

On the fifteenth or sixteenth day—they were losing track of time—the men in the rafts saw a plane on the horizon and argued whether it was friend or foe. Because it seemed to have a pontoon and a single engine, Bartek, still proficient at aircraft identification despite his delirium, thought it was a Kingfisher, but was in too much of a stupor to make a conclusive judgment. Adamson, also nearly comatose, continued to worry about being captured and forced to divulge what he knew about Operation Torch. He and Rickenbacker renewed their plan of jumping overboard in case Bartek was wrong. Another aircraft of the same type appeared the next afternoon, about five miles away, flying at an altitude of a few thousand feet. Accepting Bartek's opinion that it was American, the men waved frantically and shouted at the top of their lungs. They were devastated when it disappeared, but Eddie tried to console them by saying things would have been much worse had it been Japanese.

The aircraft sightings were the first human contact the castaways had experienced since the beginning of their ordeal. Everybody except Adamson, Bartek, and Reynolds, who were "nothing but skin and bones by this time, which kept them almost in a state of coma," could hardly sleep that night, realizing they were finally coming near an air base, whether friendly or hostile. Six more planes, all of the type already observed, appeared in the next two days, four traveling in pairs. Squalls became more frequent, improving the water supply and reviving the more able-bodied survivors. Small fish resembling sardines appeared in the sur-

436

EDDIE RICKENBACKER

rounding waters, and they caught about thirty of them with their hands. "We ate them alive—at least they were alive when we put them into our mouths," Rickenbacker said. "We crunched them whole and swallowed them." White crabs now clinging to the sides of the rafts met the same fate, although it was not clear they were edible. Nobody cared. Adamson, Bartek, and Reynolds were obviously near death, and "the rest of us were showing an accelerated decline in energy and alertness."[50]

The forms of marine life the men were eating, however, made it increasingly obvious that land was nearby. Arguing that scattered individuals would have a better chance of being spotted by planes now appearing more and more frequently, Cherry decided to take the small raft, detach it from the rest, and go off by himself. Rickenbacker disagreed violently but gave up after an hour-long shouting match and Cherry drifted away without a paddle. Whittaker and De Angelis soon followed, taking Reynolds along in one of the two remaining rafts. Still strong enough to row, Whittaker and De Angelis thought they might reach an inhabited island.[51] Feeling rejected and abandoned, Rick protested bitterly about being left alone with Adamson and Bartek, who were "more dead than alive," but "gave in after some rather harsh words." In his judgment, Whittaker and De Angelis were "not entirely rational."[52]

That November night Rickenbacker slept fitfully, dreaming about his father's death and consoling his mother that he would "never make her cry again." Because the raft had crossed the international date line, it was Friday the 13th when a cold wave crashed over the raft, jarring Rickenbacker awake. Watching Adamson and Bartek as they lay in a stupor, he thought about Adelaide and his sons, who would probably never see him again. He remembered pilots, mechanics, and financial leaders with whom he had associated as CEO of Eastern Air Lines and bade them farewell. His chances of survival seemed negligible. At sunrise a "strong icy downpour" shocked Adamson and Bartek into consciousness. "Such was the will to survive," Adamson later wrote, using the third person, "that the two sick men joined in spreading out rags under the rain, from which Rick squeezed the water into a baling bucket, later transferring it to his life jacket. When the sun drove the clouds away Adamson and Bartek covered up as best they could, and Rick sat in his end of the raft with his soggy and sea-faded hat pulled down over his eyes and a ragged handkerchief drawn across the lower part of his face." At about four o'clock that afternoon, as a squall line approached far to the south, "the silence of sea and space was suddenly ripped apart by the roar of airplane engines," coming from the west. Two "slim silhouettes" came nearer and nearer. Suddenly, Adamson recalled, a pair of aircraft "plunged straight toward the raft."[53]

There was a "tense moment" when Rickenbacker thought that "the barking of machine guns" might punctuate the rhythmic throbbing of the engines. "But no bullets zipped past," he recalled; "instead, the pilots pulled up a few yards above the raft and revealed United States insignia under their wings." The planes zoomed away as the three survivors waved tattered shirts into the air and shouted at the top of what voices they had left. Rickenbacker guessed they were returning to their base to summon help. Actually, they were running low on gas and had to refuel before attempting a rescue. Eddie wondered if they would ever come back as darkness fell with the abruptness characteristic so near the equator, with no sign of aircraft. He worried the raft might be swept away by the oncoming squall before daybreak and never be seen again by the would-be rescuers.

Suddenly the enveloping night became incandescent as red and white flares lit the sky above the raft with blinding radiance. Two lights blinked on the horizon as a PT boat flashed coded signals. After twenty-one harrowing days, rescue was finally at hand.[54]

After the B-17 went down with Rickenbacker aboard, "all available air and sea forces" made search and rescue attempts, but the expanse of water in which the rafts were marooned was too vast for success. The disappearance of Rickenbacker's party, however, was not forgotten and anxiety about Eddie's fate in particular was constantly on the nation's mind. Thousands of newspaper articles, magazine essays, and radio broadcasts paid tribute to him, presuming as time went by that he must have died. Admirers, however, refused to believe he was gone. Joe Williams, a newspaperman and close friend, wrote that "We aren't going to give up on Rickenbacker until we are forced to read the obits. He's the closest thing to Superman it's ever been our thrill to know."[55]

Adelaide was foremost among the faithful. "Eddie will turn up," she said. "He's too old a hand to get lost in any airplane." Two weeks after he disappeared, Arnold sent her a letter of condolence seeming to indicate the search was being called off. Taking a train to Washington, she stormed into his office and "practically tore the decorations off his jacket," demanding that the hunt continue. Arnold promised to prolong it another week.[56] Kingfishers were patrolling the area east of the

Ellice chain with increased intensity as the rafts carrying Rickenbacker and his companions drifted westward toward the archipelago. Bartek had identified them correctly.[57]

Cherry had shown good judgment advocating that the rafts disperse to increase the chances of being discovered. At 16:35 on 11 November, as reckoned west of the international date line, radioman second class Lester H. Boutte, flying in a Kingfisher piloted by Lieutenant (j.g.) Frederick E. Woodward, noticed an irregular object bobbing on the waves. As Woodward approached, they saw that it was a yellow raft with a single occupant. Returning to Funafuti, they guided a PT boat commanded by Lieutenant Alvin P. Cluster to the scene. Its crew rescued Cherry, who said the other rafts were nearby.

That same morning Whittaker, De Angelis, and Reynolds spotted the shoreline of Nukufetau, an atoll sixty miles northwest of Funafuti. Whittaker, with sharks threatening the raft and currents pulling it back to sea, summoned the strength to paddle it over a coral reef and beached it. The men found some coconuts that Whittaker pried open with a sheath knife. They contained more pulp than milk, but Whittaker also killed some rodents with the oar, giving them their first meat in more than three weeks. The next day, they found an abandoned hut and fell asleep on the floor. Early that afternoon outrigger canoes arrived, manned by friendly natives who took them to a nearby village and fed them. A British missionary had dispatched the boats and crews after finding a note dropped by one of the Kingfishers based at Funafuti, asking for help in finding the castaways. The cleric, a coast watcher with a radio, also sent a message to the Marine base that the men had been found. Soon a Kingfisher landed on the lagoon. On board was a medic who gave Reynolds a shot of glucose in time to save his life. Two days later, on 14 November, *Hilo* arrived to take the men to Funafuti.[58]

Rickenbacker, Adamson, and Bartek were already there after a remarkable rescue. Working throughout the night of 11 November, ground crews at Funafuti had readied all five of the Kingfishers to set out at dawn on 12 November to search the area surrounding the location where Cherry had been rescued. Accompanied by *Hilo* and the four PT boats, they closely scanned three areas designated A, B, and C. Late that afternoon, after fruitless hours scanning B and C, two Kingfishers patrolling A sighted a raft with three men aboard. The pilots, lieutenants (j.g.) G. T. Forrest and J. G. Boyd, did not know the identities of the occupants at the time because they were not aware of the radio message to Funafuti from Nukufetau attesting to the safety of Whittaker's party. The Kingfishers were running low on fuel and had to return to their base. Swooping over the raft to display their American insignia as Rickenbacker and his mates waved frantically, Forrest and Boyd noted its location and flew back to Funafuti for help.

Because he had already heard from Nukufetau, Colonel L. L. Leech, the Marine officer in charge at Funafuti, knew that Rickenbacker, the principal object of the search, must be on the raft Forrest and Boyd had spotted. Breaking radio silence for the first time since his force had occupied Funafuti, Leech contacted *Hilo*, still at sea in an undetermined location, with instructions about where the raft had been spotted and an order to send two PT boats that had not yet returned to base to go to the scene as fast as possible. Leech knew the situation was problematic. "Approximately one hour of daylight remained," he wrote in a report about what had happened since Cherry's rescue. "The position of the *Hilo* and PT boats was not known. Visual contact with the raft by an air borne plane was not possible after dark. PT boats could not, except by chance, find the raft after dark without assistance. An additional night in the raft might prove disastrous to the occupants. If the raft were not definitely marked before dark, the problem of relocating it the following morning might consume many precious hours. The sea was calm but there was a heavy ground swell. No boats remaining at the base were capable of reaching the raft in less than five hours under the existing conditions. If a plane landed to pick up the occupants of the raft it could not take off again with the additional weight even though it had suffered no casualty in landing."

Knowing the hazards involved, especially with darkness rapidly descending, Lieutenant (j.g.) William Eadie and Lester Boutte, the radioman who had spotted Cherry, volunteered to search for the raft in Eadie's Kingfisher. Once again it was Boutte who first saw the raft in the glare of a shot from a Very pistol. Dropping two flares to illuminate the scene, Eadie and Boutte settled down on the water near the tiny vessel and climbed out of the single-engine seaplane. Rickenbacker later remembered "how clean and handsome they were, how proud I was to have them as countrymen." Eadie and Boutte saw that Adamson was too badly injured to move by himself and lifted him into Boutte's radio compartment. Lashing Bartek in a sitting position on the leading edge of the right wing, they tied Rickenbacker in the same posture to the one

440

EDDIE RICKENBACKER

on the left. Boutte straddled the area between the wings and central pontoon so he could hang onto the men and keep them stable. Rick and Bartek muttered, "This is heaven," and "God bless the Navy" as they went about their work. Eadie then began taxiing toward Funafuti, about forty miles distant, realizing that if a storm came up the plane would be swamped in the waves.

They had not gone more than a few miles when PT boat 26, commanded by Ensign John M. Weeks, appeared out of the darkness with its twin searchlights piercing the night. It had been delayed by bursting boiler jackets, requiring crewmembers to form a bucket brigade in the engine room. After coming alongside the craft, Eadie and Boutte untied Rickenbacker and Bartek and helped transfer them onto the PT boat's deck over the fantail. Sailors scrambled for the honor of pulling Eddie aboard. When they called him "Mr. Rickenbacker," he bellowed, "Just call me Eddie, boys, but get me on this damned boat!" Eadie and Boutte, thinking Adamson had a fractured spine and should not be moved, kept him on the Kingfisher and accompanied the boat to Funafuti, setting a distance record for taxiing at sea.[59]

Bartek, exhausted, lay in the boat, thinking, "I'm not going to move for another year," but Rickenbacker was too excited to rest. "I've never seen a PT boat before," he said, requesting a tour of the vessel. First, however, he wanted to quench his thirst. Members of the crew warned him not to drink too much too fast, but he ignored them and filled up on water, beef broth, pineapple juice—anything he could lay his hands on. Soon Bartek woke up and drank large quantities of liquid. After taking Rickenbacker around the vessel, seamen took him to Weeks's bunk. Sitting up, he talked excitedly about his experiences on the raft throughout the hours it took the boat to get to Funafuti, where it arrived at 3:00 a.m.

Pharmacist's mates carried Rick and Bartek on stretchers to a makeshift one-room hospital. Both later recalled that the moon was shining through palm trees swaying overhead and it felt like they were in paradise. Their tattered clothing fell apart when attendants stripped it off. Medics washed their salt-encrusted, sunburned bodies and applied soothing agents and sulfa drugs. Rick recalled that his burns and sores "hurt now as they had never hurt on the raft." Adamson, still in the Kingfisher, had diabetes and seemed more dead than alive. Medics gave him a blood transfusion before taking him to the hospital.

Throughout the night "an unquenchable thirst" tortured Rickenbacker, who drank all of the water in a jug beside his bed after being told only to sip. Sleeping fitfully, he dreamed he was still on the raft rocking back and forth. When he awoke the next morning and looked in a mirror, he was dismayed by his loss of weight—he had gone from 180 pounds to 126—and the dirty beard and drooping mustache he had grown. Knowing he would be photographed, he demanded a haircut and shave. By this time *Hilo* had left for Nukufetau to pick up Whittaker, De Angelis, and Reynolds, who were soon reunited with their comrades.

Adelaide's phone rang in New York City, at nine in the morning on 14 November—still 13 November west of the international date line. The caller was Arnold, telling her Eddie was safe. Too overcome to speak, she stammered "God bless you."[60] Meanwhile, hundreds of newspapers exploded with banner headlines, some in letters nine inches high. News of a fierce naval engagement in the Solomon Islands and battles taking place in Tunisia as Operation Torch proceeded took second place to articles about the rescue and photographs of Rickenbacker. Thousands of editorials and radio broadcasts hailed his deliverance. Admirers called him "The Man Who Always Comes Back," "Iron Man Eddie," and "One Ace That Can Get out of Any Hole."[61]

Physicians from American Samoa arrived at Funafuti and decided that all of the men except Reynolds, who was still too debilitated to be moved, should be taken to a naval hospital at Pago Pago. Consolidated Catalinas took them there on 15 November, stopping at an island midway to their destination so they could enjoy a hearty meal topped with pineapple ice cream. Adamson, a special case, made the trip because the benefits of being treated at a top-notch medical facility outweighed the risks of airlifting him. He had blood poisoning because he was allergic to sulfa drugs and received repeated transfusions. Rickenbacker, however, bounced back rapidly. Though gaunt and haggard, he gained twenty pounds in two weeks and toured Tutuila in a jeep. He also sent Stimson a message about his intent to tour American bases in the Southwest Pacific, visit MacArthur at his headquarters (now in New Guinea), and report on the savage battle for Guadalcanal. Arnold agreed to provide air transport when he felt up to going.[62]

A C-87 (military cargo and passenger equivalent of the B-24 bomber) took Rickenbacker to the Fiji Islands by way of Viti Levu and Nouméa, New Caledonia. After reaching Nouméa he was pleasantly surprised to find Colonel H. Weir Cook, who had flown under him in the 94th Pursuit Squadron, commanding the base. After getting only a few hours of sleep, Rickenbacker left Nouméa at 2:00 a.m. on 4 December for Brisbane, where Brigadier General Donald Wilson, chief of staff of the Allied air forces in the Southwest Pacific Theater, was waiting to meet him. Wilson said MacArthur would not permit him to fly to Port Moresby in an unarmed transport plane and was sending a B-17 with a full combat crew. The bomber flew to Brisbane overnight and took off with Rickenbacker on the morning of 5 December, reaching Port Moresby seven hours later after refueling at Townsville.

Rickenbacker did not look forward to delivering Stimson's rebuke but resolved to develop a "mental armorplate" to maintain his composure when he confronted the legendary commander. There was every reason at the time for MacArthur to be inhospitable. Besides bickering with Washington and feeling resentful about shortages of shipping and supplies, he faced a difficult situation trying to stem the Japanese advance across the Owen Stanley Mountains. The enemy came within thirty miles of Port Moresby before turning back for lack of supplies. Having already lost the Philippines, MacArthur feared he would lose his command if the campaign in Papua failed.[63]

The Owen Stanley Range, covered with jungle, loomed forbiddingly in the background as the bomber carrying Rickenbacker approached Port Moresby. It impressed Eddie as "the dust bowl of all creation" because it was covered with bits of red soil blown by winds through valleys in the mountains. Papua's capital was a mere village of squalid, vermin-ridden huts built on stilts above shallow coastal waters. The battered, half-submerged hulk of a cargo ship protruded from the lagoon.[64]

The B-17 landed at Seven-Mile Aerodrome, "a little metal strip in the hills." When the plane stopped at the end of the runway Eddie was amazed to see MacArthur himself, "in his characteristic pose," standing among officers waiting to welcome him. Limping out of the aircraft, Rickenbacker hobbled toward MacArthur as the general came toward him. When they met, MacArthur threw his arms around Rickenbacker's emaciated body and said, "God, Eddie, I'm glad to see you." Caught off guard by MacArthur's "affectionate embrace," he felt the emotional armor he had built around himself melting, disappearing "completely and serenely." MacArthur may have known what his visitor was about to tell him but was also probably moved to compassion as an exhausted Rickenbacker climbed out of the Flying Fortress.[65] Although Eddie recognized the genuineness of MacArthur's response, he was still determined to fulfill Stimson's assignment, but his capacity to perform it, already weakened by his raft ordeal, was further undercut by the unexpected warmth of MacArthur's greeting.

MacArthur insisted on putting him up at his headquarters, which he whimsically called his "shack." Known as Government House, it was actually a large, tastefully landscaped building set on a hill overlooking Port Moresby's harbor, with a breathtaking view of the Coral Sea, a veranda, four bedrooms, and a living room lined with bookshelves. (It also had the only flush toilet in all of New Guinea, installed for MacArthur's exclusive use.) As soon as Eddie was alone with MacArthur, he gave him his message from Stimson, namely that the general "stop trying to generate personal publicity for himself, stop complaining about the limited resources deployed to his theater, and stop criticizing Marshall." Stimson also wanted MacArthur to develop better relations with Admiral Chester Nimitz, whose assigned theater of operations was much larger than the one over which MacArthur presided. Feigning lack of concern, the general listened impassively. Using the personal charm of which he was a master, he treated Rickenbacker royally. Eddie's visit to MacArthur's headquarters transformed a previously distant and sometimes antagonistic relationship into an abiding friendship.

He was particularly pleased about his host's newfound appreciation of air power. Previously skeptical, MacArthur had been impressed by the achievements of General George T. Kenney, a longtime friend of Rickenbacker's who had trained at Issoudun and received the Distinguished Service Cross in World War I. An extremely creative officer, Kenney had revolutionized the inept, disorganized air forces commanded by Major General George Brett at the time MacArthur arrived in Australia from the Philippines. Kenney gave a detailed account of his tactics and innovations to Rickenbacker, who reported a great deal of information to Stimson including how A-20s had used a skip-bombing technique Kenney had conceived, bouncing bombs like pebbles across a pond and hitting Japanese ships at or below the water line. At the time of Rickenbacker's visit, Kenney was arming B-25 bombers with a lethal array of machine guns for coordinated low-level attacks against enemy convoys trying to provision units fighting MacArthur's troops.[66] "You know, Eddie," MacArthur commented, "I probably did the American Air Forces more harm than any man living when I was chief of staff by refusing to believe in the airplane as a war weapon, and I am doing everything I can to make amends for that great mistake."[67]

Rickenbacker helped raise morale among Kenney's airmen by discussing combat tactics with pilots awed by his reputation. After one of them asked how many victories Rickenbacker had scored in World War I, Kenney promised to give a case of Scotch whisky to the first man to break his record. "Put me down for another case," Rick said before departing with Kenney to Australia. "We left amid a lot of grins," Kenney recalled, "but twenty-six was still a long way off." Buzz Wagner topped the list with eight kills when he had gone home two months earlier. The bet between Kenney and Rickenbacker soon became big news among American pilots, setting a mark to emulate.

Rickenbacker regaled MacArthur and his staff with the story of the raft episode. Kenney recalled that it got better every time he heard it, but he never tired of it. He was sorry to see Rickenbacker go because of the tonic effect his visit had produced among his flyers. On 7 December he personally escorted Eddie back to Brisbane, stopping on the way to have him inspect a huge supply depot he had built at Townsville. Major Victor Bertrandais, Rickenbacker's chief mechanic in World War I and a postwar executive with the Douglas Aircraft Company, headed the sprawling facility, staffed by more than 3,000 workers. "He had carte blanche," Kenney said. "All I asked was speed and results."[68]

Rickenbacker left Brisbane in the early hours of 9 December and arrived in New Caledonia in time for breakfast with General Millard Fillmore (Miff) Harmon, a World War I fighter pilot who had served in Pershing's Mexican expedition.[69] A message from Kenney reported the details of a Japanese air attack in which P-39s and P-40s had shot down fifteen enemy planes at the cost of only one "slightly damaged" Airacobra. "Hearty congratulations on your swell day," Rickenbacker replied, "but why in hell did you wait until I left?"[70] Harmon took Rickenbacker on an inspection tour of a base at Espiritu Santo in the New Hebrides Islands, where bombers and fighters were repaired after being damaged in missions to Guadalcanal, 590 miles away. Eddie later told Stimson that the men he encountered were "dreadfully tired because they were trying to do too much with too little," commenting at length about their haggard appearance. "It is almost impossible to conceive the conditions under which our fighting forces are laboring in the cesspool holes and hell holes of the Pacific, both on the ground and in the air," he informed the secretary of war. "Without the privilege of seeing and hearing them on their own grounds you can't penetrate the imagination that deeply and deadly."

Rickenbacker was referring especially to Guadalcanal, the "Green Hell" to which he flew on 10 December after leaving Espiritu Santo. He saw an unforgettable scene as his B-17 crossed "Ironbottom Sound," where fierce naval battles had littered the seabed with sunken American and Japanese ships. The prow of the troopship *Kyusyu Maru,* heavily damaged during a naval engagement in mid-November, protruded like a beached whale among stumps of palm trees lining the shore. Hulks of landing craft were "upside down or on their sides" as Eddie approached Henderson Field, headquarters of the gallant flyers of the "Cactus Air Force" and the epicenter of the conflict that had raged on the island since Leathernecks had stormed ashore in early August. Even from aloft the sight was much more appalling than anything Eddie had seen in New Guinea, where he had not gone far from Port Moresby.[71] On the day before he arrived, the army's 132nd Regimental Combat Team and the 2nd Marine Division, led by General Alexander ("Sandy") Patch, had relieved "hollow-eyed, exhausted and emaciated young men who had grown frightfully old in four months' time," wearing tattered remnants of what had once been uniforms but were now "a mishmash of khaki and green utilities . . . with boondockers held together by what string and remnants of shoelaces they had left." American forces continued to hold only a small perimeter around Henderson Field, named after a flyer killed in the Battle of Midway. To Eddie it seemed like a graveyard with "literally hundreds" of "wrecked and battered" aircraft lining its edges like tombstones. Landing on the metal surface was like taking a roller-coaster ride.[72]

Rickenbacker had dinner with Patch "in a grass-roofed shack, at a table made of rough planks." Afterward they plunged into a dugout as Japanese artillerymen pounded the area around Henderson Field with a howitzer. A flanking party got behind the battery and killed the gunners, temporarily ending the threat. That night, when Brigadier General Edmund B. Sebree, Patch's chief of staff, took Rickenbacker to a tent he had been assigned, Eddie tripped in the darkness and went sprawling in mud up to his knees. Rain came down in torrents, and he could not sleep, "partly because of the drumming of the rain on the canvas, partly because of the mosquitoes of which there were billions." He heard the roaring of cannon and the rattle of machine-gun fire only a few miles from where he lay. Leaving after breakfast the next morning, he was glad to escape with his life. His report to Stimson, vividly describing the appalling conditions he had seen, indicated he was rethinking the "Europe First" strategy he had previously supported.[73]

Upon returning to the hospital in American Samoa, he found that Cherry, Whittaker, De Angelis, and Bartek had already left for the United States but that Reynolds was still too sick to be moved. Adamson, even worse off, had a lung abscess requiring surgery. Looking at Adamson's charts and seeing the desperateness of his situation, he went to his bedside and gave him a stern lecture, telling him that "unless he bucked up and changed his attitude toward life in general, he would probably be there another two or three months" before he could go home on a slow hospital ship. If he took a more positive view, Rickenbacker promised, he would "take him along in my airplane in a hospital bed which I had already arranged for," have his personal physician accompany him to Hawaii, and put him in telephone contact with his wife, Helen.

Rickenbacker had yet one more installation to inspect at Upolu, which before World War I had been a German possession. Flying into its airfield, he noticed the wreck of one of the kaiser's warships still half submerged in the harbor. While he was gone, Adamson had made an amazing recovery, leading the hospital staff to extol "whatever medicine you gave him before you left for Upolu." When he told him to get ready for the flight later that evening, Adamson said, "Thank God." "Yes, thank God," replied Rickenbacker, for whom the raft episode had been a conversion experience, "because He has been riding with you all these many days, and now He has got you well in hand."

Reynolds was also aboard when the plane took off. When it arrived in Hawaii that afternoon, Eddie had an ambulance waiting to take the invalids to a hospital from which Adamson telephoned his wife. Speaking to her, Rickenbacker said, was "a terrific hypodermic." After physicians pronounced Adamson and Reynolds fit to continue, Eddie boarded a plane with them late that night for a 2,500-mile flight to Oakland, California, where Reynolds's parents were waiting at the airport to give their son what he called "one of the most heartrending greetings I have ever witnessed." Smiling broadly and wearing a pith helmet, he pointed an index finger at a cameraman for what became a famous photograph.[74] While an ambulance prepared to take Adamson to a hospital for a full day's rest, Rickenbacker flew to Los Angeles for a joyous reunion with his mother, who met him at the airport with Dewey. She had refused to believe he would not return. After a plane carrying Adamson arrived from

Oakland, Rickenbacker flew to San Antonio, where they landed ahead of schedule. Eddie delayed their departure because he had agreed to meet Stimson and Arnold at Bolling Field at 9:00 a.m. on 19 December and did not want to arrive before they got there.

After an uneventful flight they landed at Bolling Field, which was swarming with dignitaries and top brass including Hap Arnold and Robert Lovett, but Eddie had eyes for only three people: Adelaide, David, and William. The crowd yelled, flashbulbs popped, fighter planes zoomed overhead, and a military band played as he swept them up in his arms. He had been too choked with emotion to say anything when William ran toward him and said "Oh, Daddy, I'm so happy to see you again."

Rickenbacker went immediately to Stimson's office at the recently completed Pentagon Building, to which the secretary of war had moved in mid-November. Presenting him to a roomful of reporters who applauded vigorously, Stimson said, "He is back, and I think there is more of him here than went away." As a gesture of regard, Stimson had Rickenbacker sit in his chair and asked him to speak. With great emotion Eddie recounted the ordeal he and his companions had undergone, including the pathetic story of Kaczmarczyk's death at sea. Telling the newsmen about the dire need for supplies among the troops he had visited, he criticized people who complained about rubber and gasoline rationing, saying that the amount of rubber in a worn-out tire would make possible the production of one of the rafts that had saved the lives of himself and his comrades.[75] Later that day he and his family flew to New York City, where Mayor LaGuardia and a swarm of admirers gave them a noisy reception at LaGuardia Field. The next evening, speaking over a nationwide radio hookup and pointing his finger at an imaginary audience with a look of fierce determination, he said, "We can never approximate the sacrifices our men are making on the battlefront for you."[76]

Not everybody was happy about the publicity Rickenbacker received. The navigator of a Boeing 314 that brought Cherry and other members of his crew back to American overheard one of the men saying, "We stayed alive on that raft just to watch that s.o.b. get all the credit."[77] Nevertheless, Eddie's homecoming had been a national Christmas present, coming as it did when the tide of war seemed to be turning. A year that had begun with staggering Allied defeats had gradually brought a succession of heartening events, including Doolittle's Raid on Tokyo, the Battle of Midway, the British victory at El Alamein, the invasion of

Guadalcanal, the success of Operation Torch, and the Russian victory at Stalingrad. Eddie's return was well timed and the now-famous "seagull episode," which was recounted endlessly in sermons, seemed like an anointment from God. He was no longer a hero but a prophet, consumed by visions he was determined to articulate.

Chapter 18

— ☆ —

New Mandate

Countless letters, telegrams, editorials, radio programs, sermons, and cartoons hailed Rickenbacker's return from the Pacific. Many interpreted it as a sign of divine providence. "When our Great Creator preserved you as His manifestation to the rest of us it demonstrated another miracle . . . to help us on our way to Victory," said a typical message.[1] Clergymen across the nation proclaimed that the seagull episode proved the power of God to intervene in human affairs. Cartoonists competed to find creative ways of showing him as a deliverer from death. The hand of the Almighty rested upon him.[2]

Not merely because of the raft episode but because of its timing, coming so swiftly after his near-death experience in Atlanta, Rickenbacker himself became imbued with a sense of having a divinely ordained mission. Up to this time there is no evidence he had been more than conventionally religious, believing in the Golden Rule but lacking any feeling of a personal relationship with God. Now, the realization that he was still alive, not only after two almost inevitably lethal experiences but also after a multitude of earlier close calls, hit him with terrific force. He had an overriding sense that a Higher Power had spared his life for a purpose. To find that purpose became a consuming passion.

Soon after coming home he dictated three articles about the raft experience for the mass circulation magazine *Life* that became the basis of a best-selling book, *Seven Came Through*. Pervading these publications was a desire to serve others. He insisted that the proceeds—$25,000 for serial rights alone—go to the Army Air Forces Aid Society, which Hap and Eleanor Arnold had established to help families of airmen who had died in the war. He also wanted to do whatever he could to spare victims from ordeals like the one he and his comrades had undergone. In a speech at the Pentagon Building he used all the profanity in his vocabulary demanding that better survival equipment and emergency supplies be installed on airplanes and vessels that might become lost at sea. A partial list of demands included larger rafts, portable sails that could be unfurled on crossed oars, concentrated food, vitamin tablets, sleeping pills, fail-proof flares, steel mirrors for signaling, smoke bombs, radio transmitters, and saltwater-distilling devices.[3]

He wanted his life to be an inspiration for his fellow citizens. Nothing, including *Seven Came Through,* did more to establish his prophetic image than "When a Man Faces Death," an article he published in *American* later in 1943, testifying to his newfound faith in a personal God. He told how his boyhood fear of death had caused him to sob uncontrollably until his father found him and gave him a severe switching. He described wrecks he had survived on the racetrack. He recounted the wing-shredding incident that had almost killed him in World War I. He told about getting lost with ice-covered wings during a Pittsburgh-to-Columbus flight and reaching Toledo almost by accident and with only an eleven-minute supply of gas. He vividly described the Atlanta crash and his agonizing recovery at Piedmont Hospital.

He revealed paranormal events he had experienced, telling how he had seen Bruce and Smythe colliding in mid-air in his mind's eye as he lay on his cot in a hallucinatory state in August 1918; and how Marr, who later told him about the crash, had been amazed by the details he knew about it. He acknowledged his belief in mental telepathy and other psychic phenomena. "Perhaps such things as the control of mind over matter and the transmission of thought waves are tied together," he said, "part of something so big we haven't grasped it yet." The eerie sense of comfort brought by the onset of death led him to an aphorism that "the easiest thing in the world is to die; the hardest is to live," telling readers how often death had approached him like an infinitely alluring angel that he had fought off with sheer determination to live. On the raft, he said, "I called my friends more vile names than I can ever call to mind. I raged at them until they found reason, in the midst of their suffering, to live."

He repeated again and again his conviction that escaping death was a sign that a person was being kept alive for "some purpose, some fulfillment." He wrote about what he called the "Big Radio," a "Thing that keeps all of us flying safely through the fog and night, toward some mysterious and important goal." He affirmed his faith in what he simply called a "Power" and the need to implore It for "aid and for guidance."

He now saw his lifelong habit of carrying talismans as a symptom of his belief in supernatural forces. Even though he had never been "a regular churchgoer," he had carried throughout life a crucifix given him by a little girl before he embarked for France in 1917. "It is almost eaten away now by the salt water of the South Pacific," he said, "but I still treasure it and find comfort in it." He disclaimed self-centeredness by stressing his consciousness that he was part of a greater whole to which it was his responsibility to dedicate himself. "I am not such an egotist as to believe that God has spared me because I am I," he declared. "I believe there is work for me to do and that I am spared to do it, just as you are. If I die tomorrow—I do not fear the prospect at all—I believe my death will have a meaning. It may be only to make others around me to appreciate their own lives even more and use them to better advantage. But it will have a meaning." He urged readers to "live every day as if you will live forever," recognizing "the immortality of the soul." The biggest thing was "to remember the reason to fight and live—others."

He ended his message with a challenge that when the war was over "this country has got to have leadership that is inspired and unselfish . . . We're going to have to find jobs for ten to fifteen million men and women. We've got to rebuild our economy. We've got to lead the world back to reconstruction and peace. Isn't that worth fighting for? Living for? The kids have got it. They've got the will to fight, bleed, and die. They must, when they come home, have the will, under proper leadership, to live, build, create, and keep faith." And, he assured his readers, "most of them are coming home."[4]

The response was overwhelming. He received hundreds of letters, some from people who had escaped near-death experiences, were suffering from intractable diseases, or had been contemplating suicide until Rickenbacker's words made them feel they had been spared for a purpose. One writer had undergone twenty-two operations, from which he had emerged with "great faith that we do not die in this life if our work is unfinished." "I have Hodgkin's disease," wrote a patient at a veteran's hospital, "and after reading what you say I don't think it will get me." Another letter declared that Rickenbacker had written "the most impressive, conceivable revelation on the enigma of life and death ever published." An officer in the Army Engineers wrote that the article had become "a 'bible' to me and accompanies me everywhere. . . . I have done my best to spread its message, and . . . have worn my copy dog-eared." Yet another admirer called his article "the twentieth century version of the Sermon on the Mount."

American received 50,000 requests for reprints. American Viewpoint, an organization Rickenbacker supported financially, gave nearly 400,000 copies to military personnel. John D. Rockefeller Jr. wrote that the article "impressed me profoundly" and arranged to have reprints given to all members of the armed services before they left for overseas duty. "This seems to me one of the most moving and useful human documents I have read in many a day," Rockefeller stated. "It is utterly sincere, wholly without cant and yet breathes a faith born of many unique experiences."[5]

Ironically, Rickenbacker's quest for a mission led him into a speaking campaign that diminished his status in the eyes of many admirers. He came back from the Pacific not merely a messenger of hope but a wrathful Old Testament prophet hurling verbal thunderbolts at special interests, especially labor leaders, accusing them of selfishly undermining production for the war effort. To some degree he was merely continuing the speeches and interviews accompanying his tour of air bases in 1942, attacking complacency, warning that the war would be long, and demanding total commitment to defeating the enemy. Now, however, there was an even stronger bite to his rhetoric. Rickenbacker's ire must have stemmed partly from the physical traumas he had undergone and the exhausting activities he had undertaken for Arnold and Stimson after barely recuperating from the Atlanta crash, but he also felt indignant about seeing ill-prepared and ill-equipped troops fighting the Japanese amid the horrors of Guadalcanal. To understand his feelings, it must be realized that the production miracles that would finally overwhelm Germany and Japan had barely started to materialize when he came home. Observing the terrible results of American unpreparedness to resist the Japanese onslaught, he was furious about what he now perceived as a treasonous lack of total effort on the homefront. Most of all, he was groping toward playing the role to which he believed God had called him after repeatedly sparing him from death.

He did not understand, nor did he care to comprehend, the complexities of mobilizing the resources of a democracy ill-prepared to fight all-out war. The massive industrial buildup taking place in 1942 had imposed stresses on labor and management that were compounded by the fumbling efforts of federal bureaucrats to resolve conflicting priorities under a chief executive who hated to delegate authority or make clear-cut decisions that would alienate established constituencies. The exigencies of mobilization had forced FDR to turn to the giant corporations he had recently condemned and to recruit Republicans like Stimson and Knox to administer military procurement programs, but the way they did so inevitably offended labor leaders who had previously been favored. Bitter infighting ensued between antagonistic interests. Distrust was rife among federal officials, few of whom felt that they had the president's undivided confidence. Stimson's use of a fellow Republican, Rickenbacker, in frequent fact-finding missions resulted in part from his need for his own informants to deal with an administration that kept secrets even from the highest-ranking government officials.[6]

Rickenbacker was too absorbed in his individual sense of mission to take into account the massive industrial upheavals in 1942 as a mitigating factor in the chaos he observed. Conscripting millions of able-bodied men from an overwhelmingly white, male work force had created drastic labor shortages. Trying to deal with this problem, industrialists recruited large numbers of workers unaccustomed to factories and shops. Pouring huge sums of money into making airplanes, tanks, ships, and munitions instead of automobiles, refrigerators, and other consumer goods uprooted untold numbers of people, creating economic turbulence for which the country was manifestly unready. Notwithstanding "no-strike pledges," labor leaders were understandably adverse to giving up hard-won gains they had made in recent years, especially when big business was getting cost-plus contracts from the government and the profits that went with them. Talk of "equality of sacrifice" rang hollow when owners seized opportunities to retake control of work rules and erase gains won by collective bargaining in the 1930s.

Rickenbacker had no concept of problems facing labor leaders trying to enforce discipline among workers who had never belonged to unions or taken part in factory operations. The ability of foremen to buffer conflict between employees and low-level managers shrank as experienced workers flocked to the colors. At General Motors, less than half of 19,000 foremen in 1943 had been working for the corporation for even one year. The increasing prevalence of female and African American workers, through no fault of their own, created unrest as white males tried to relegate them to unskilled and low-paying jobs and keep better ones for themselves. Overwhelmed managers ignored notorious inequities in compensation for comparable jobs, and the overworked National War Labor Board (NLWB), which received up to 15,000 complaints per month, could address grievances only glacially. Housing shortages forced workers to alternate beds and sleep in eight-hour shifts wherever they could find lodgings. Inadequate, outmoded public transport made it difficult for workers to reach workplaces often located far from where they lived. Food prices rose despite efforts by the Office of Price Administration (OPA) to fight inflation. Even though unemployment virtually disappeared, workers wondered what would happen when the war was over, servicemen returned home, and demand for high levels of production shrank. It was only natural to want to feather one's nest while it was possible. The prospect of a postwar economic collapse weighed on the minds of people who had experienced the Great Depression and realized it had not ended until the onset of a preparedness drive in the late 1930s.

In short, situations that Rickenbacker deemed treasonous stemmed from complex realities. He did not credit responsible leaders in the American Federation of Labor (AFL) and Congress of Industrial Organizations (CIO), who recognized the dangers of being called unpatriotic, for doing their best to honor a "no-strike pledge" they had made at the start of the war. Despite their efforts, chaotic conditions that time only gradually straightened out provided opportunities for agitators and opportunists to organize wildcat strikes, slowdowns, sit-downs, "quickie" strikes, and absenteeism that embarrassed organized labor because they impeded war production. The United Auto Workers had to cope with "a new political left" that was "syndicalist in its shop orientation" and motivated by "a highly ideological critique of the war effort." Such radicals, not responsible union leaders, constituted the "labor racketeers" at whom Rickenbacker hurled verbal abuse.

Rickenbacker found a convenient whipping-boy in John L. Lewis of the United Mine Workers, who had resigned as president of the CIO and now quarreled bitterly with its leaders. Lewis was militantly intransigent and seemed indifferent to public opinion. In January 1943, immediately after Eddie returned from the Pacific, thousands of anthracite miners staged a wildcat strike. Lewis eventually expelled the leaders, but many critics thought he had been slow to act. His threats, demands, and nose-thumbing at the NLWB aroused a furious response from federal officials including Roosevelt himself, who had to issue an ultimatum in May after thousands more miners walked out in bituminous coalfields.

"Lewis," a historian later stated, was seemingly "bent on destroying the entire wartime labor program of the government while at the same time discrediting the great majority of laborites who supported it." "Speaking for the American soldier, John L. Lewis, damn your coal-black soul," stated *Stars and Stripes*. Inspired by Lewis's militancy, 50,000 rubber workers defied union leaders by walking out in May 1943 after an unpopular decision by the NLWB. In the same month 24,000 workers walked out at the Chrysler plant in Detroit. Pleas by the United Auto Workers (UAW), headed by Walter Reuther, to be patient until the NLWB responded to their demands, went unheeded. Such occurrences became increasingly common as work stoppages rose from 2,968 in 1942 to 3,752 in 1943 and 4,956 in 1944. "Strikes in coal mining were troublesome," a historian later wrote, "but strikes in shipyards and ammunitions, aircraft, and armaments factories were downright frightening. Strike-reduced coal production, after all, could be made up with additional shifts and overtime. But much delayed military production was lost forever."[7]

Rickenbacker was not alone in condemning the situation. FDR, who abominated Lewis, threatened a government takeover of mines in response to one threatened coal strike. Senator Harry S. Truman said half-seriously that Lewis should be shot. Stimson believed "drastic action" was needed—a National Service Law to prevent "strikes, threats of strikes, excessive turnovers, absenteeism, and other manifestations of irresponsibility." Stimson waged an unsuccessful two-year campaign to convince FDR to adopt a more coercive labor policy. His feelings were no different from those of Rickenbacker, who thought he was carrying out the secretary of war's wishes but wound up with an enduring reputation as a labor baiter.[8]

Rickenbacker briefly became associated with a management-inspired program of voluntary cooperation to prevent absenteeism and work stoppages. Soon after he returned from the Pacific, a movement got underway to create "Hat-in-the-Ring Squadrons" in war-related industries to oppose absenteeism and protect "unrestricted war effort." Rickenbacker decorated employees who were faithful in attendance and job performance with Hat-in-the-Ring pins in ceremonies at defense plants. But the movement lost impetus, indicated by a letter to Eddie from the head of a New York City advertising agency about not getting the plan widely adopted in the aircraft industry.[9]

The collapse of the Hat-in-the-Ring campaign may have resulted in part from less moderate attempts by Rickenbacker to deal with labor problems. Soon after returning from the Pacific, he began vehemently denouncing absenteeism, featherbedding, slowdowns, wildcat strikes, and other activities while speaking to civic clubs, professional organizations, and state legislatures, blaming them on "labor racketeers," an epithet he used with increasing frequency. His first attack came at a dinner of the American Society of Automotive Engineers (ASAE) in Detroit on 22 January 1943, setting a pattern for presentations offensive to organized labor. His emaciated appearance and loose-fitting clothes, the haunted look of his piercing eyes blazing above his hollow cheeks, and the sight of his fingers and hands, scarred by sunburn and salt water, intensified the sting of his rhetoric.

Rickenbacker vividly described the miseries he had witnessed on his Pacific mission. "Oh, men and women of Detroit," he lamented at the ASAE dinner, "if you could only understand what our boys—your boys and mine—are doing in these hell-holes . . . that your way of life may be preserved, and the character that has made this nation great may be carried on, you would not worry about eight hours a day overtime, or double time for Saturdays and holidays. You would not worry about whether you are producing too much per man per day. No, you would and should be grateful for the privilege of offering everything you know how. For none of us are doing so much that we cannot do more. . . . Without victory, social security, old age pensions, hours and wages bills will mean nothing." France, one of his favorite targets, had been a hotbed of labor disturbances and "social legislation, which I am not against," in the 1930s, but the French "failed in the realization that without work and without producing something of value, they could not last. Today they are serfs and slaves of Hitler's hordes." Invoking the hallowed names of the Bataan Peninsula and Corredigor, he implored Americans to "accept your responsibilities with the privileges that you are enjoying. Remember patriotism is a hollow word. Do not let these boys come back from their graves in these hell-holes scattered through the Pacific and other parts of the world and from the depths of the seven seas—do not let them come back and plague you for having failed in your obligation on the home front."

Rickenbacker was disingenuous in saying he was not against the type of social legislation that the French had enacted in the prewar period. Attacking achievements for which legitimate unions had fought in the 1930s, he attributed much of what was wrong on the homefront to "misguided" legislation that made union membership a prerequisite to work, subjecting factory employees to rules and restrictions that hamstrung their ability to contribute as effectively as possible to the war effort. Anticipating the postwar period, he called for laws that would make it unnecessary for returning veterans to join labor unions as a condition of getting jobs. "No, I am not a labor hater," he stated. "I have been laboring for forty odd years—since I was twelve years of age in many lines of endeavor. I came from humble parents. I know the value of honest labor." In his opinion, the effort required for victory had been impeded because the nation had forsaken values stressing individual self-reliance and adopted a cancerous collectivism. "Start today to create and build in yourself and your children—in labor leadership—management leadership—and political leadership that same type of character that will help preserve what your forefathers dedicated to you," he urged. "Then we need not fear that the suffering, the bleeding and dying of our boys will have been in vain."[10]

Rickenbacker elaborated on his feelings in early February in an address at the annual banquet of the Baseball Writers' Association. The War Manpower Commission was considering drafting older persons in "twenty-nine occupational groups," some of whom had five or six children, to enter war-related jobs or face induction into the armed forces. Such action, Rickenbacker said, would do no good because it would force people to work under "racketeers" in closed shops where their ability to do anything useful would be compromised by labor leaders who had never done an honest day's work. Instead of going down such a road, he called for legislation to "free honest labor from those racketeers and parasites that are right now hindering the effort of our workers to do the best they can to win this war." The proper remedy, he said, echoing Stimson's call for a national labor draft, lay in using "the splendid abilities of our local Selective Service Boards" to send such men to paramilitary schools to "be taught an agricultural or industrial skill in the same way that their younger contemporaries are being taught a skill of war," and assign them to war-related work in which they would not have to join labor unions as a prerequisite of employment. Graduates of such training would have "a sobering effect on those malcontents who seem to think it their business to foment strikes and discontent." An honorable discharge, not a union card, should entitle a person who had "risked his life in our behalf" to a job. "What better BONUS could we give our service men than the elimination of their having *to buy the right to work*," he asked, capitalizing and underscoring the words in his text for emphasis. Why should a combat veteran "have to pay exorbitant membership fees . . . under a closed shop agreement?"[11]

Rickenbacker defended his claims with specifics. "In the Boeing factory alone, the day after Christmas, twenty-six per cent of the employees were absentees and our aviators in those hell-holes are crying their eyes out for only a few more Flying Fortresses," he asserted. "In the Douglas plant, there was an absenteeism of eleven thousand employees the day after Christmas—a shocking and deplorable condition." His proposed remedies also became more concrete. Besides drafting "shirkers," he wanted to implement an "incentive plan" rewarding workers for meeting specific production goals instead of paying them by the hour. He urged suspending existing wage and hour laws for the duration of the war. Above all, he objected to paying workers time-and-a-half for overtime. "Let the workingman or any one else make double what they now get—*providing* they earn it," he said. He called for the abolition of union rules that inhibited production and the elimination of compulsory monthly union dues and initiation fees that, in his opinion, constituted a disincentive to work. He declared that unions already had "millions in their coffers. . . . You cannot demand that the mass of common folk shall think only of winning the war if the aristocracy of labor unionism is thinking only of more dues and more power—and the inner clique of bureaucracy is thinking only of a fourth term"—a slap at FDR that could not be missed in the White House.[12]

Rickenbacker went to Washington to defend his ideas in an appearance on 19 March before the Senate Military Affairs Committee. He said he had "discussed the relative merits of the incentive plan versus the 40-hour week and the hourly rate" with plant managers and production experts throughout the country. "In every instance," he said, "they have stated very frankly that there is a difference from 35 to 60 percent in production." The basic problem was not manpower—but *productive* manpower. He thought that "today we have more manpower than we need, if it is properly utilized."

He believed too many able-bodied men between ages eighteen and thirty-eight were working in specialized industrial jobs. Such persons could "be replaced without difficulty because we, today, still have millions of old men and millions of middle-aged women who are anxious and willing to do everything they can, that are in no way at the moment connected with the direct war effort." Jabbing at bureaucracy, he charged, "We have an untold manpower involved throughout the country—and womanpower—trying to take care of thousands of reports from different bureaus, that have no place in a war effort." Regarding absenteeism, Rickenbacker admitted that problems related to housing, transportation, shopping, and sickness caused some of it. Citing the aircraft industry in southern California, however, he claimed that absenteeism in nonunion plants was only half as high as in unionized shops.

Denying claims that he was "a labor hater, a labor baiter," which he called "dastardly," he stressed support in more than 50,000 communications running ninety-two to one in his favor, a few of which came from "heads of labor unions, both A.F. of L. and C. I.O. imploring me to continue to give the racketeers hell." He stressed that piecework—anathema to unions—was not practical in all industries but could be used in 75 percent of war-related plants. Acknowledging the use of piecework formulas in the Soviet Union, he said that this practice, known as Stakhanovism, had "developed faults and had to be modified; the incentives were too intense and wore out the best workers. This must be guarded against." But he believed the United States was "still a long way" from attaining even a modified form of the Russian system. Furthermore, a labor draft would not be needed if his plan were adopted. "The outstanding management problem with most industries," he claimed, "is to find out what their revenue is, with Congress forever unable to make up its mind about taxes, and renegotiation boards calling back quite variable proportions of the profits already made and the job of auditing and the trips to Washington never done. . . . These are matters Congress cannot blame on the Labor unions—they are entirely within its own province and power to rectify."[13]

Critics charged that Rickenbacker was a mouthpiece for the National Association of Manufacturers, which was allegedly grooming him for the White House. One writer charged that he had paid starvation wages as an automobile manufacturer (ignoring that he had been in charge of sales, not payrolls, and that Barney Everitt set company policy) and used scab labor to break a strike at Eastern in 1939 (not mentioning Eddie's encouragement of the International Association of Machinists). Rickenbacker "hasn't missed a trick as the current No. 1 labor-baiter in this country," said a radio commentator, warning that he would have "the same fate as meted out by the American people to Col. Lindbergh. We Americans can shut the door grim and tight when a man we take into our hearts, then plunges a knife."[14]

On the other hand, Rickenbacker's forthrightness sounded presidential to some people. A radio commentator called him "a man of action, a doer of deeds, and accomplisher in two wars of the greatest heroic attainments," adding that "as time goes on, and as we move toward 1944, more and more people will realize that in Captain Eddie Rickenbacker the Republican Party, if it wishes to take advantage of it, has a great presidential candidate." Calling Rickenbacker a "leader who will not compromise with national safety" and "a potential man of destiny," another admirer compared his statements to Calvin Coolidge's declaration that "Where public safety is involved there can be no strikes," predicting that the same political lightning that made Coolidge the Republican vice presidential candidate in 1920 might put Rickenbacker at the head of the party's ticket in 1944.[15]

Rickenbacker received huge amounts of mail, telegrams, and postcards in response to his campaign. Whether it ran ninety-two to one in his favor, as he claimed, is moot, but large numbers of people applauded him. A common thread running through many endorsements was respect for his sincerity. A person who heard his ASAE presentation on the radio said that "One good thing about your speech was that everybody who heard it believes it was right from the heart and done with a great deal of feeling." Another theme was that "The people are restless; they are becoming angry at the muddling incompetence, evident everywhere in Washington from the top down." Writers were concerned that union representatives on the shop floor discouraged individual initiative. Others hated John L. Lewis and ranked him high among the "labor racketeers" Eddie was attacking. "I wish America had ten thousand Rickenbackers to tell such traitors as John Lewis where they stand," said a supporter in Des Moines. "Keep it up."[16]

Nevertheless, Rickenbacker's "two-fisted efforts to keep his kind of America working to the hilt," as one of his admirers called it, damaged his reputation among Americans who had once regarded him as one of the country's greatest heroes. Even some supporters coupled their praise with pleas that he speak with greater moderation. "We agree with you about absenteeism and other activities that do not contribute to the war effort," wrote a California judge. "In this connection, may we suggest that you tone down your direct attacks on labor just a little else the good you are accomplishing may be more than offset by a misinterpretation of your remarks?"[17]

Rickenbacker paid no heed to such well-meaning advice because of a messianic sense that from now on became increasingly prominent in his thinking. Standing out among thousands of letters sent to him was one from two admirers in California saying that they had "listened to your recent radio broadcasts and now we know why you were saved, as we have needed someone in this good country of ours who was not afraid to speak their convictions. . . . The history of our country shows that in every crisis God has always produced a man strong enough for the time and we feel strongly that you were the man for this time."[18] Such tributes confirmed in this man with a mission a passionate belief that God had spared his life, not only in the Pacific, but on many other occasions, for a special purpose, which it was his sacred duty to discover and fulfill, whatever the cost. He spurned all blandishments to run for political office and established a policy of reaping no financial reward from anything he said or wrote. Columnist Ray Tucker grasped the reality by stating that "Rickenbacker has become an evangelist without knowing it. There is an unworldly gleam in his eyes and a quaver in his voice these days." Eddie would have disagreed with only three words—"without knowing it"—in this assessment. He was well aware he had become an evangelist serving a higher cause and relished the role he was playing.[19]

Rickenbacker did not forget that the journey in which he had gone down in the Pacific and been marooned for three weeks was originally meant to have continued around the globe to inspect American military installations in India, China, the Middle East, and North Africa. His sense of destiny led him to conceive a "World Mission" based mainly on a vision of the role American aviation should play after the war. He believed that by commanding the vast ocean of air covering the earth, the United States could establish dominance comparable with what Great Britain had previously wielded on the sea. Others shared his ideas, but nobody championed a new age linking American air power and business enterprise with more vigor.[20]

He spent little time resting from his raft ordeal. His first tasks were to dictate the text of *Seven Came Through* and prepare a report to Stimson, which he delivered to the Pentagon on 25 January 1943. He began by telling Stimson that morale among American forces in the Southwest Pacific was remarkably good despite the terrible conditions under which they were fighting and the limitations of their equipment. Most of the proposals that followed dealt with improving ferrying operations to the theater and enhancing the firepower, bombing ability, and overall performance of aircraft used by Kenney and other air officers. He criticized the quality and inexperience of the crew that had been assigned to him, advocated better training and briefing, stressed the need for better rafts and emergency supplies, and suggested changes in radio and navigational equipment. He made many proposals for improving military aircraft and logistics.

Two parts of his report, however, dealt with broader policy matters. Seeing the Pacific theater at first hand led him to modify the strong "Europe first" emphasis in the report he had given Stimson after visiting England in 1942. MacArthur's views resonated in a statement, "We cannot assume the position or attitude of passively resisting the Japs and throw the full force of our effort into the European theater without running the risk of giving the Japs ample time to reorganize their supply lines and capitalize on the sources of raw material that they have taken in the South Pacific."

His final recommendation was particularly significant, dealing with the role of American aviation, military and commercial, in the postwar world. "In view of the fact that we are spending hundreds of millions of dollars in developing airways throughout the world on property belonging to other nations," he urged, "it is essential that we start today demanding freedom of the air and our own just rights." The United States should receive mandates over islands it had already taken or would seize in the war against Japan and the aerial rights that went with them. But "in view of the selfishness and greed that are already showing their sharp fangs even among our own allies"—a reference to Great Britain—"it is a certainty that not only will we be prohibited the use of the airports that we have built and spent hundreds of millions of dollars on, but will be charged excessive rates for the use of their facilities by those whom we call friends today." The way to prevent future problems was "keeping in operation our military airways throughout the world by our . . . air forces for a period of years, and gradually permit infiltration of commercial services that will eventually take them over." He warned that "if we wait to negotiate until after the war is over, we will have lost our birthright in many places."[21]

Rickenbacker was preaching a gospel pervading the airline industry, which had become an integral part of what Eisenhower later called the "military-industrial complex." Owners and managers hoped for a postwar era in which American passenger and cargo planes would carry Americans and goods to all parts of the world, invading previously closed or severely restricted foreign markets. A battle was already looming about whether Pan American would continue to enjoy "chosen instrument" status, raising the possibility that other carriers, including Eastern, might fly international routes. American ambitions in aeronautics were succinctly expressed by Connecticut congresswoman Clair Booth Luce, whose husband, Henry R. Luce, controlled the *Time-Life-Fortune* empire and championed an "American Century." "American postwar aviation policy is simple," she declared. "We want to fly everywhere!" Such rhetoric menaced the interests of Great Britain, now facing the end of its long domination of world markets coveted by American entrepreneurs.[22]

Despite his busy writing schedule and the rigors of his campaign against "labor racketeers," Rickenbacker felt within a few months that he had recovered sufficiently from his raft ordeal to finish the worldwide mission Stimson had envisioned. During a visit to the War Department early in April 1943, Stimson gave him orders naming him a "Special Consultant" and authorizing him to "visit the stations and installations of the Army Air Forces in North Africa, European Theatre, U.S.A. Forces in the Middle East, U.S.A. Forces in India, Burma and China, and any other areas he may deem necessary for such purposes as he will explain to you in person." Stimson directed that Rickenbacker be given "every possible assistance in the performance of his special duties by all commanders concerned, and he is to be provided with such transportation, both ground and air as he may need and such accommodations as are available."[23]

The sweeping list of places Rickenbacker received authorization to visit masked a covert trip to the USSR. Stimson, though he had not thought originally about having Rickenbacker visit Moscow, became convinced that his knowledge of aircraft would enable him to learn how the Russians were using planes, particularly Bell P-39s, Douglas A-20s, and North American B-25s sent to them under Lend-Lease. Roosevelt, who had conspicuously not taken the secretary of war to Casablanca, had kept Stimson, Marshall, and Arnold out of the loop in formulating policies that had important military implications or overruled them when it suited his purposes to do so. The War Department was especially ill-informed about the Soviet Union because FDR and his closest advisers, particularly Harry Hopkins, did not want to press Stalin too hard lest they alienate him and lead him to make a separate peace with Germany.[24]

Rickenbacker's proposal was well timed with Stimson's viewpoint because of an imbroglio created by Admiral William H. Standley, America's ambassador to Moscow. In March 1943 Standley sparked a major controversy by publicly voicing concern that the Soviet government did not sufficiently appreciate aid the United States had supplied the USSR under Lend-Lease and would not reveal how it was being used. Standley and other persons, including Stimson, had long believed that Roosevelt was too generous in supplying Lend-Lease aid to the Soviets with no strings attached. Standley resented being bypassed about Soviet affairs in general and Lend-Lease aid to the Russians in particular. He was embarrassed by being repeatedly kept in the dark until the last moment about visits to Moscow by American emissaries like Wendell Willkie, bearing important messages Standley knew nothing about. Standley also got no help from American military attachés in Moscow. Colonel Philip R. Faymonville, the intensely pro-Soviet Lend-Lease supply officer, kept information from Standley and was at best indifferent about his desire for American aid to be more strictly administered. Roosevelt was annoyed by Standley's efforts to penetrate Russian secrecy, regarded his publicity leak as a gaffe, and planned to recall him when he found a suitable replacement.

Stimson had originally doubted that the USSR could defend itself against Hitler and believed massive shipments of American aid under the Lend-Lease program would be wasted in the likely event of a Soviet defeat. He also resented the secretiveness of the Russians about their military operations, confiding to his diary that it was "awfully difficult to help people who do that." Roosevelt had repeatedly overruled Stimson's efforts to pressure Stalin to be more open in divulging information. By the time Rickenbacker visited the War Department in April, Stimson had been reassured about Russian military capabilities, particularly after the recent victory at Stalingrad, but was still frustrated by the unwillingness of FDR to pressure the Soviets for information. Roosevelt was negotiating a new Lend-Lease protocol with Stalin, and Assistant Secretary of War Patterson was trying through Hopkins to end priority shipments of materiel to the USSR until it became more cooperative.[25]

Although Rickenbacker's proposal to visit the USSR played into Stimson's hands, the secretary said he would have to clear the project with the State Department. Whether he did so is debatable because he had every reason to think the reaction would be negative. Rickenbacker's crusade against "labor racketeers" had darkened his already bad image at the White House. Roosevelt had not yet met Stalin personally—he would do so for the first time in November at Teheran—and did not want to rock the boat, hoping to impress Stalin with his charm. Letting Secretary of State Cordell Hull know what Rickenbacker had in mind would be likely to get back to FDR and be vetoed. Stimson did not want to share information with Hull anyway and would have discussed Rickenbacker's proposal with him delicately, if at all.

Stimson soon told Rickenbacker that, according to Hull, any visit to Moscow would have to be arranged directly between FDR and Stalin—an obvious impossibility. But an end run was available. Stimson put Rickenbacker in touch with Edward R. Stettinius Jr., a wealthy Republican whom Roosevelt had appointed chairman of the War Resources Board in 1939 for the same reason he had brought Stimson, Knox, and other prominent GOP members into his administration—he needed the support of prominent Republicans and industrialists to help him prepare for war with Germany. Stettinius, chairman of the board of United States Steel, was big business personified. Rising within Roosevelt's entourage, he became Lend-Lease administrator in August 1941. Aircraft supplied to the USSR through the program fell within his jurisdiction. Stettinius had been friendly with Rickenbacker for many years because of their mutual relations with General Motors, the Rockefellers, and Juan Trippe, whose sister Stettinius had married. Sending one of the nation's top experts on aviation to Russia to inspect aircraft provided under Lend-Lease made sense to Stettinius, who approved the project and agreed to keep it secret from Roosevelt and Hull.

Because the USSR would have to clear the proposed visit, Stettinius suggested that Rickenbacker contact Maxim Litvinov, Soviet ambassador to the United States, and General Alexander I. Belyaev, coordinator of Lend-Lease shipments to Russia. Both men were receptive, as they had good reason to be, when Rickenbacker went to their offices. The furor over Standley's claims that Stalin did not properly appreciate American Lend-Lease aid had aroused concern in the Kremlin. Effective aid was finally arriving from America, particularly Bell P-39 Airacobras, which had proved to be excellent antitank weapons. A post-Stalingrad counteroffensive had stalled and the Germans had recaptured Kharkov, making the Soviet government more aware that it needed outside aid. Although Operation Torch fell short of the "second front" Stalin had wanted, the huge bag of enemy prisoners about to be captured in Tunisia was heartening. Knowing American public opinion was becoming restive about supposed Soviet ingratitude for Lend-Lease as a result of Standley's accusations, and that prominent officials were putting pressure on

Roosevelt to be less liberal in supplying the USSR without strings, Stalin decided not only to express thanks for American help—which he did publicly in a May Day address—but also to reveal, at least to some extent, how he was using military equipment supplied by Washington. Litvinov and Belyaev told Rickenbacker they would have to clear his visit with superiors in Moscow, mentioning Foreign Minister Vyacheslav Molotov, but agreed to see what they could do. They said Rickenbacker could expect official word when he reached North Africa about whether his projected visit to Moscow would be welcome.[26]

As Rickenbacker prepared for his journey, Adelaide assembled large quantities of gifts for important people he would meet, including wives and children. She put three dozen pairs of nylon stockings, large quantities of cosmetics, cigarettes, and chewing gum, and—perhaps most important of all—a lot of liquor in his foot lockers. Knowing he would need frequent medical attention, Rickenbacker asked Dr. Dahl, the Atlanta osteopath who had accompanied him on his tour of American air bases for Arnold, to go with him to administer massages and manipulations to keep his aching bones, muscles, and connective tissue as supple as possible. Wanting a plane more comfortable than the B-17, he arranged with Arnold to use a C-54 transport (military equivalent of the DC-4), to take him as far as Cairo. From there a C-87, a converted B-24 Liberator, would carry him the rest of the way.[27]

Flying from Miami to Natal, Rickenbacker thought about the need for the United States to promote business in Latin America after the war, adding to what Trippe and Pan American had already done to weaken British, French, and German interests. He decided American students at all levels should be taught Spanish. Crossing the Brazilian jungle called to mind that Reed Chambers was coordinating a program to gather wild rubber and ship it to America to keep the United Sates from depending too heavily on Malaya and the Dutch East Indies in the postwar era. The entire trip from Miami to Natal to Dakar reminded him of the work Eastern Air Lines was doing for the Air Transport Command in ferrying military personnel and supplies to North Africa in olive-drab planes jokingly called "The Great Chocolate Fleet."[28] Such contributions to the war effort might help Eastern secure commercial rights in the postwar era. At Dakar Rickenbacker discussed with an ATC official the routes used in flying from Natal to Ascension Island, Accra or Dakar, and across Africa—information potentially useful in operating future international air routes.

The early stages of Rickenbacker's African itinerary went from Dakar to Marrakech, Casablanca, Oran, and Algiers. Crossing the Sahara Desert made him think that being forced down in the arid wasteland would make it harder to survive than being marooned on a raft in the Pacific. Landing at Marrakech brought out his anti-Gallic prejudices. "There was a haughtiness about the French people living there I could not understand," he wrote, "because we are their friends, have been for a generation and are trying to help them. . . . Why the French people don't seem to trust us is beyond my comprehension."

At Casablanca he inspected a facility where American and British fighter planes were "tested, assembled, test-hopped and flown to the front." The poverty of Arabs he met appalled him. After a dignitary invited him to dinner, Rickenbacker was disdainful of the etiquette observed at Moroccan functions, bringing a Red Cross nurse to the dinner, ignoring taboos about the presence of women, and refusing to remove his shoes. After breakfasting the next day with an old friend, General Elwood ("Pete") Quesada, who at the time was in charge of the 12th Fighter Command, he went to Oran, where he inspected another air depot and gave a talk praising 3,000 of its personnel for their contributions to the war effort. Wherever he stopped, he met former comrades from World War I working to complete the conquest of North Africa but wishing they were closer to the front. He tried to convince them their noncombatant tasks were extremely valuable.

Flying from Oran to Algiers, he thought about how important four-engine planes would be in operating future commercial air routes and fumed about the army's failure to value air transport before the war. He recalled failing to convince Arnold in 1938 that the Air Corps should order 1,000 DC-4s. Even in 1941, Assistant Secretary of War Patterson had tried to stop the manufacture of military cargo planes, seeing no reason to produce them. A year later, Rickenbacker remembered, the army was desperate for such aircraft, paying the penalty for its "unpardonable stupidity" in delaying production of DC-3s and DC-4s and having to rely on domestic airlines that surrendered half their planes to the ATC. He hoped military authorities had learned their lesson and would remember after the war the help the airlines had provided.

Algiers, located on a hillside overlooking the harbor, reminded him of San Francisco. The bay was crowded with cargo ships, battleships, aircraft carriers, and hulks of half-sunken vessels. After he landed, he dined with some of Eisenhower's senior officers. Air Marshal Sir Arthur

Tedder, who commanded all Allied air forces in the Mediterranean, with Spaatz as his deputy, struck him as "one of the most brilliant mentalities that I had come in contact with for a very long time," unusual praise for Rickenbacker to bestow on a Brit. Still, he regarded Spaatz's subordinate relationship to Tedder as typical of British dominance at this point in conducting operations, intelligence, and logistics, the only exception being that Doolittle had charge of strategic bombing. Rickenbacker realized the intelligence-gathering experience of the British was superior to that of the American, a situation that would require attention in the postwar era. Fortunately, Eisenhower had supreme command and was making things work by putting "the right people in the right places" and using his diplomatic skills to hold things together—a sign, Rickenbacker hoped, that American leadership would become dominant in the future.

Eisenhower was having his hair cut when Rickenbacker went to his headquarters. Eddie approvingly overheard Ike's crusty chief of staff, Walter Bedell Smith, talking about giving British Field Marshal Bernard ("Monty") Montgomery "unadulterated hell and tell him a few things." Eisenhower told Rickenbacker that the final offensive in Tunisia had just begun and things were going better than expected. Ike had received advice from the front "that the roads were jammed with retreating Germans, artillery, and troops."[29]

After his haircut, Eisenhower suddenly got testy, saying a coded message had arrived from Molotov giving Rickenbacker permission to visit Russia. Waving it in Eddie's face, Ike wanted to know "what in Hell was going on." Saying it was a "military secret," Rickenbacker showed the general Stimson's orders and said he would have an unusual opportunity to see how the USSR was using American equipment, adding that he could spy on Soviet air and ground operations. Eisenhower, a firm believer in espionage, was mollified and agreed to detach Major Alden ("Madam") Sherry, who had flown for the 94th Pursuit Squadron in World War I, from Spaatz's staff and have him accompany Eddie as an aide for the rest of the journey. Rickenbacker thus gained the assistance of an old friend who would play the role Adamson had performed in the Pacific mission.[30]

Rickenbacker agreed to take on the unenviable role of bringing bad news to pilots who had been promised they could go home after completing twenty-five missions or 200 hours of combat flying, a commitment Eisenhower's staff had decided was impracticable to fulfill. Knowing that what he had to say would make him unpopular, Eddie volunteered to visit all the airmen affected by the decision and try to brace their morale by telling them how preferable their situation was to the horrors he had observed in Guadalcanal. He would also assure them they would soon be getting new and better planes but warned that it would be impossible to crush Germany until late in 1944 at the earliest. He visited twenty-four groups in one week, talking to as many as six per day for at least forty-five minutes. "I was brutally frank because I was a civilian," he said, admitting the men hated the news, making them angry at him for delivering it.

Leaving Algiers, he saw the end of the Tunisian campaign from aloft. German and Italian troops were surrendering in droves. Rickenbacker naturally attributed the scope of the victory to overwhelming air superiority by Doolittle's bombers, which had destroyed enemy troopships, cutting off all possibility of escape, and to fighter planes that had shot down a large number of Junkers transports. "Thinking about the P-38 and the narrow margin by which it was saved from oblivion the year before at home," he praised the plane's versatility, noting it excelled in fighter combat, high-altitude observation, low-level reconnaissance, photography, dive bombing, and even "slide bombardment," a technique used against Pantelleria, a rocky island honeycombed with underground hangars that had to be eliminated to facilitate the invasion of Sicily.

Flying across Libya to Egypt, he saw the desert littered with burned-out tanks, destroyed artillery pieces, and other remnants of the savage fighting that had driven Germany's Afrika Korps into the Tunisian trap. He visited the 94th Fighter Squadron, now much larger than it had been under his leadership in World War I. Knowing it was stationed in North Africa, he had taken his original Hat-in-the-Ring ornament to a New York City jeweler and ordered 150 exact replicas to pin on members of the unit. Because of the extent to which it had grown, he had to reorder 200 more emblems for enlisted men.

Flying over Egyptian pyramids that he could see from fifty miles away was an unforgettable experience. Outside Cairo he inspected a depot where he saw "thousands of American soldier mechanics, building engines, aircraft and automobiles or repairing or overhauling them . . . on a production line basis, with at least the efficiency of those in Detroit" and "a steel mill and a foundry in the desert which is a living sample of the ingenuity of Americans." He visited hospitals in which he tried to comfort wounded troops, "many of them blind, some with arms or legs off, many with bad burns. I knew that many of the hospitals in the States would be filled for a generation with such men as these after this terrible war was over, and in the face of it all, people back home still wanted to strike and have sit-downs and slow-downs," he stated. "They were, in my opinion, stabbing these boys in the back."

In Cairo he had drinks with Patrick J. Hurley, former secretary of war under Hoover, a supporter of Lend-Lease, and another of the Republicans Roosevelt had brought aboard as war approached in 1940. Now a brigadier general, Hurley, a pompous man with pince-nez glasses and a walrus mustache, had been the only American before Rickenbacker to be invited to visit the Soviet battlefront, providing Stimson with what little he knew about Russian military operations.[31] After advising Rickenbacker about his upcoming trip to Moscow, Hurley asked Eddie whether he hoped to be the Republican nominee for president in 1944 and volunteered to be his running mate. Eddie denied having any political intentions.

From Egypt Rickenbacker flew to India on the C-87 Arnold had promised to provide him. Flying across Palestine, Trans-Jordan, and Iraq, he was aware of following one of the world's most important oil pipelines, owned and operated by the British. He later told an interviewer that the most significant aspect of the American contribution to victory in North Africa was the prospect it created for getting low-cost oil refined in Iran and Iraq. At Abadan he visited "an assembly plant at a large aerodrome which had concrete runways built by Americans as were hundreds of others which I saw in my travels," noting that directly across the river was "one of the largest oil refineries in the world of English ownership." The main purpose of the aircraft plant was to assemble P-39s, A-20s, and Spitfires to be flown by Russian pilots to the USSR. Abadan and Basra were "the two main points on the Persian Gulf and at the head of the greatest supply line in the world." Knowing Britain was weakening, he hoped the United States would take over its interests in the Middle East in the postwar era.

The heat in Iran was "almost unbearable," requiring therapy from Dr. Dahl. At Karachi, Eddie "found a wonderful airport, a fine administration building, built as was inevitably the case at our expense." He hoped America would claim it after the war and was impressed by "a supply depot and an assembly plant for planes going into India and on to China, for Karachi is the crossroad for the African and the Middle East, India,

China, Air Transport and Command Wings." But he was dismayed to see that hundreds of American Vultee Avengers, which had been given the British under Lend-Lease, had been left exposed to the elements, making him indignant that planes built at American expense had been wasted. He thought resentfully about how badly American forces in New Guinea and Guadalcanal had needed such aircraft. Now that Germany and Japan seemed likely to lose the war and the USSR was assuming a steadily increasing role, he had less reason than in 1940 to see Britain as a necessary bulwark against Hitler.

As Rickenbacker journeyed across the Middle East and into South Asia, his Anglophobia surfaced repeatedly. Upon arriving in New Delhi, he noted that the airport, "as usual, was built with American money and by Americans." In Old Delhi and Calcutta he found "the most deplorable conditions imaginable—the squalor, filth and stench were unbearable . . . everywhere throughout India where we stopped the buildings were in dilapidated condition and it seemed to me that no attempt at maintenance or improvement had ever been made," another slam at the Brits. He was angry that food served to American troops under Lend-Lease funding from the United States consisted of "English rations which were frankly a long way from the standards of American rations, and were not sufficient to keep our men in [good] physical condition and health." Of all the places he visited he was most relieved to leave India, having "the distinct conviction and realization that something is definitely lacking when human beings are forced to live in such surroundings and under such conditions." What had England done, he wondered, to alleviate this misery in the crown jewel of the British Empire?

From Calcutta Rickenbacker flew to Chabua, a "little mud hut village" where natives worked for a British-owned tea company, and from which he would fly over the "Hump" into China. At Chabua he met Edgar Snow, a stranded journalist who was desperate to go to China. Knowing Snow's leftist leanings and Marshall's desire for Chiang Kai-Shek to include Mao Tse-Tung's communist forces in the battle against the Japanese, Eddie arranged for Snow to cross the Himalayas in his plane. Writing soon after the war, he praised Snow's books, including *Red Star over China,* which he called "outstanding."[32]

Rickenbacker crossed the Hump in a C-47. The crucial supply line, the only source of aid to China, was operated jointly by the Air Transport Command (ATC) and the China National Air Company (CNAC), led by the Chinese government and Pan American Airways. Rickenbacker believed CNAC was much more efficient than the ATC, partly because of its long familiarity with local conditions and partly because decision making for the ATC took place in faraway Washington. He was critical of the ATC for having pilots ferry planes halfway around the world to India and return to the United States, leaving unseasoned crews to be trained from scratch to fly the Hump with inadequate navigational equipment. He told Stimson that operations over the Hump should be given higher priority, experienced manpower, and better equipment, pointing out that the tonnage of supplies needed to be greatly increased because "every gallon of gasoline, all the oil, ammunition and weapons that go to China" had to cross the mountainous terrain. He advocated shipping 50,000 tons per month and claimed that this level could be reached with effective management.

Looking through broken clouds, he saw parts of the Lido Road being built through northern Burma, using American technicians and native labor. His Anglophobia came through again when he criticized the project as "fundamentally a political effort." He thought it would take at least two years to complete and benefit the Brits, "for it would give them, when completed, transportation facilities from India to China permitting the protection of Siam and Indo-China against any possible aggression on the part of the Chinese Communists." He obviously feared Mao's forces less than continued British influence in the area and called the Lido Road "ridiculous."

After safely crossing the Himalayas, he looked down upon "beautiful countryside with rice paddies everywhere." Discussing operations with volunteer pilots who flew in China under Claire Chennault, a Texan whose views about the offensive capabilities of pursuit planes had made him anathema to American bombing enthusiasts at Maxwell Field, Eddie praised their "Chinese warning net." By radioing information of Japanese takeoffs from one to two hours away, Chennault's "Flying Tigers"—P-40s whose noses were decorated with the eyes and teeth of tiger sharks—were able to climb to 25,000 feet and be ready to intercept enemy aircraft coming in at lower altitudes on bombing runs. Going by car on primitive roads to an aerodrome three hours distant, he praised the efficiency with which some 40,000 Chinese workers, "men, women, and children," had broken large stones into tiny bits to build a runway for two squadrons of B-24s, saying that "they seemed to be a happy and industrious lot." Accommodations at the airport were "extremely good, further evidence of the potential market for manufactured goods of American make." Given effective Chinese leadership, he saw future opportunities for trade if an aerial infrastructure could be built to replace antiquated transportation systems. It was apparent that he had a much more favorable opinion of the Chinese potential for economic development than for that of India. Flying to Kweilin, where he gave his usual speech, wearing a pith helmet, he inspected runways being built on volcanic soil and facilities for bomb storage, maintenance, and overhaul in hollowed-out caves. They were to be used for raids on Tokyo, 1,500 miles away, and Formosa, only 450 miles distant. He admired the diligence of the Chinese workers who had built the base.

Rickenbacker's admiration for the Chinese as a people did not extend to the regime headed by Chiang Kai-Shek. The more he saw of corruption in the Kuomintang, the more disgusted he became. He found that the governor of Yunnan, one of Chiang's cronies, was selling high-grade tungsten ore to the Japanese because of the higher prices he could get from them. Chiang's henchmen were grossly mismanaging Lend-Lease shipments, and pilots flying the Hump were smuggling contraband into China. The situation struck Rickenbacker as another example of Chiang's crooked bureaucracy.

Flying back to Kungming, he heard that a Japanese offensive was underway. He enjoyed listening to radio transmissions between pilots flying P-40s, engaging in a dogfight with Japanese Zeros while defending a formation of B-24s bombing an enemy target. Ten P-40s, seven of them flown by Chinese pilots, were giving a good account of themselves. "There was a lot of screaming and yelling that could be heard over the air," and he heard an American pilot cry with joy when he shot down a Zero. Eavesdropping on the encounter gave Eddie a high opinion of Chinese airmen.

Flying into Chunking, Chiang's squalid capital, he was impressed by the excellence of Chinese irrigation systems that he saw from the air, some of which had been built in the 3rd century BC, but the airport was a nightmare. "It is cut out of the side of a hill and is about 200 ft. wide running along the Yangtze River with a drop of approximately 100 ft. to the water's edge," Rickenbacker wrote. "You come in at one end of it between two hills and it would seem that the wing tips must touch on both sides, it is so narrow." After landing he stayed at American general "Vinegar Joe" Stilwell's residence, for which, he said, the United States was paying exorbitant rent to Chiang's government. He was pleased, however, that a visa had come to the Russian embassy, with a letter from Molotov, granting him permission to visit the USSR.

The enemy offensive had been halted, partly, Rickenbacker learned, because the Japanese had too few planes remaining in Manchuria to reinforce aerial units stationed in China. He gave this information to the Russian embassy, which was grateful to have it. His observations had convinced him "the Chinese theater was primarily an air theater because you cannot serve a British or an American ground army without a port of entry and surface line of supplies which does not exist at that time or in the foreseeable future." The only alternative was to increase fuel supplies over the Hump to make possible a major air offensive and then push the front far enough into eastern China to put bombers within range of the Japanese mainland. He had more hope, however, for a naval offensive in the Pacific that would put American bombers in range to attack Japan from the other direction. "Eventually our navy must invite a knockdown, dragout fight with the Japanese Navy in the open sea, east of the Philippines," he said. "They must demand a fight. This would in all probability develop into the greatest naval battle of the Pacific in the war between Japan and America."

Meetings with Chinese officials in Chunking convinced him all the more of the government's venality, which was well known to Stimson and Marshall. He said it was "unfortunate that the distribution of millions given to China was not controlled by America and used for the benefit of the Chinese people as a whole." Instead, the money was squandered by Chiang's government. The situation was only worsened by conflict between Marshall's protégé, Stilwell, who was chronically at odds with Chiang and called him "Peanut," and Chennault, who supported the dictator.[33] While admitting that Chennault had done a fine job in the early stages of the war, Eddie thought "he should be supported by an able deputy or relieved for no one individual can be permitted to interfere with the overall results and the larger strategy."

Pointedly visiting Madame Sun Yat-sen, a critic of Chiang and widow of the revolutionary leader whom Rickenbacker called the "George Washington of China," he gave her a generous supply of lipstick, cosmetics, and nylon hose. He also distributed gifts at a party held in his honor at the Russian embassy. Such courtesy calls and official functions were among his last activities in China. As the time neared for him to fly back to India, he had mixed feelings about leaving but was optimistic about America's future in China, if only an honest government took power after the war. "With the vast raw material resources that China has and the tremendous reconstruction and development job ahead of them for the next 100 years, I find America in the ideal position to safeguard this market and take cognizance of the desires of the people and help them," he wrote. "This would give us a market for our manufactured products for the next 50 years and for all surpluses of anything, for we naturally complement each other. They have raw materials which we need and we will have the manufactured products which they will demand."

He had hoped to fly directly from Chunking to Moscow but had go by way of India and Teheran because Stilwell, to whom he was to convey a secret message, had been in Washington. Vinegar Joe was still in India on his way back and was not expected to reach China for two weeks, forcing Rickenbacker to fly back across the Hump and meet him at New Delhi. From Chunking he flew to Kungming on the first leg of his trip to India, Teheran, and the USSR. The monsoon season was beginning, and his departure from Kungming was delayed by a flooded runway, giving him a chance to admire Chinese laborers manning "old-fashioned paddle wheels, hand operated, to lift water from one rice paddy to another, a system in use for over 1,000 years. Same is true of the instruments and animals used to plow the fields. They still use the old wooden plow, and the water buffalo to pull it." After the runway was clear for takeoff Rickenbacker flew back across the Hump, thinking that China, in proper hands, "would be one of the greatest countries in the world." Along with other areas he had visited, it could become part of a rising American commercial system built around an international air transport network.

The nature of the secret message Stimson had asked Eddie to give Stilwell in New Delhi is unclear, but they shared their disagreement with FDR's determination to preserve the fiction that China, under Chiang, deserved to be regarded as "the fourth cornerstone of the postwar world order." From New Delhi Rickenbacker flew to Karachi and Teheran, where he met General Donald H. Connolly, head of the Persian Gulf Service Command, which administered the vast supply network to the Soviet Union leading through Iran. Rickenbacker lavished praise on Connolly in his report to Stimson. In Teheran Rickenbacker also met the Turkish ambassador, who asked him "what role his country should play in the war." Rickenbacker said if Turkey would not enter the conflict as a full-fledged belligerent against Germany, as Churchill desired, it should at least permit American and British bombers to use its air-fields to attack targets, including the Ploesti oil refineries in Romania.[34] He was speaking off the record and thought the ambassador knew he was merely a civilian who did not represent FDR. He should have known better, because the conversation nearly produced a diplomatic fiasco. Partly because Germany, despite recent reverses, was still capable of devastating cities like Istanbul, and partly because of a deeply ingrained dislike of Russia and fear of its ambition to have free access through the Dardanelles, Turkey was playing what one historian has called "Operation Footdrag," trying to remain neutral.[35] Recognizing that Turkey was "on the razor's edge," the United States was content to have it do so, even if Churchill was not.[36] As Rickenbacker would soon learn, he should have been more prudent.

On 19 June Rickenbacker, Sherry, and Dahl took off for Moscow with two "hard-eyed" Russians, a navigator and a radio operator, who were aboard the plane in addition to the normal five-man crew. Fearing he was carrying coal to Newcastle, Rickenbacker brought "several cases of a good brand of vodka" to distribute as gifts in the USSR. Flying through a pass in the Elburz Mountains, they followed the west coast of the Caspian Sea, passed Grozny, and landed at Kuibyshev, the site of Moscow's military airport, at about ten o'clock that evening.[37]

Ambassador Standley was unaware that "Rickenbacker was even on the same side of the world as Moscow." He was embarrassed to learn that yet another dignitary from the United States had arrived without having proper notification. He did not know until a few hours before Rickenbacker's plane touched down that the famous aviator was on his way. Hastening to Kuibyshev, he arrived just before the aircraft reached the terminal building. Rickenbacker "climbed down out of the plane with a vigor that belied any remaining illness," said Standley, who knew about the raft episode. On the other hand, he saw that his unexpected guest "was terribly thin, his hatchet face sharpened by the weight loss during his long ordeal afloat." After the two men introduced themselves, Standley asked why Eddie had come to Moscow. He said simply that he was "on a mission for the Secretary of War."[38]

Taking Rickenbacker to Moscow in his official automobile, Standley was amazed by the list of places Stimson had authorized Eddie to visit but was fully cooperative. He thought Stimson felt sorry for him because of his raft ordeal and had sent him on a trip to restore his health, having no idea of Stimson's (or Rickenbacker's) motives. Standley asked, "What do you want to do while you're here, Captain?" "Well, sir," Rickenbacker replied, "first of all, I'd like to visit the Russian Front—then, I want to see as many Russian military airfields as I can—in fact, any military information I can get. And of course, Mr. Ambassador . . . I'd like very much to have an interview with Mr. Stalin." Shaking his head in disbelief, Standley thought that Eddie was still sick and had no idea of the impossibility of what he was proposing. "It is to laugh!" Standley wrote in his diary. He had American military attaché Joseph Michella secure lodging for Rickenbacker and his party.

Standley's worst suspicions seemed to be confirmed the next day when a coded message arrived from Stimson to Rickenbacker. Stimson had been informed by the British ambassador to Iran that "you stated you were enroute Ankara, Turkey, for the purpose of bringing the Turks into the War with the Allies; also, that you would visit Moscow for the purpose of obtaining the use of Soviet air fields for the Allies. You will under no circumstances visit either Turkey or the Soviet Union. In the event that you have already arrived in either of those countries, you will arrange to leave immediately." Not realizing the British ambassador had garbled what Rickenbacker had said, and where he had said it, Standley speculated that "Somewhere along the route, Captain Rickenbacker must have been indiscreet." When he consulted Eddie, however, he learned to his amazement that "arrangements had already been made for him to visit various military airfields and to make other valuable contacts in pursuit of military information." Contacting Stimson, Standley told him Rickenbacker had arrived, took credit for making the arrangements the secretary of war had ordered, and said it would take at least five days to arrange for an exit visa. Meanwhile, Colonel Faymonville, who was on bad terms with Standley, suggested that because the purpose of Rickenbacker's visit had to do with Lend-Lease, he and Michella would take care of things. Michella had already scheduled a cocktail party for Rickenbacker. Washing his hands of the matter, Standley, with good reason, felt put upon. He had in fact already resigned, apparently not realizing that Roosevelt, who sent him a cordial message praising his work and telling him he would be relieved by 10 October, had already been planning to recall him.

At Michella's cocktail party, and at other functions, Rickenbacker endeared himself to the Russians by displaying an enormous capacity to drink vodka without seeming to get drunk. Eddie later said he achieved the feat through sheer will power and knowing how to intersperse bottoms-up drafts of straight vodka with fish, caviar, brown bread, and other food that helped nullify its impact. He claimed he did not like vodka, calling it "liquid fire," and was not normally a heavy drinker—but only a person habituated to alcohol could have done what he did without losing his wits. Trying to keep up with him, a Russian colonel passed out amid cheers from people still on their feet. Rickenbacker's ability to drink Russians into oblivion quickly gave him a legendary status among the Soviets. One of his admirers was Marshal Georgi Zhukov. Because Stalin had promoted Zhukov to deputy supreme commander after his victories against the Germans in 1942, his friendship was a great asset.[39] The way was soon clear for Eddie to visit any installation or military operation he wished.

He found another friend in Andrei Youmachev, who had copiloted a Tupolev ANT-25 that had flown nonstop from Moscow to California in 1937. Youmachev remembered the cordiality with which Rickenbacker had entertained him at a reception in New York City that year on his return to the USSR. He now headed an underground installation near Moscow. When he saw Rickenbacker, he rushed up to him, exclaimed "Ah, Eddie," and gave him a bear hug. Like Zhukov, Youmachev helped Rickenbacker any way he could.

Rickenbacker asked Soviet officials how they dealt with labor problems. He learned that absentees and other workers whose performance was subpar were tried by courts, fined, and shot if their derelictions became flagrant. The piecework system Rickenbacker advocated in America was standard in Russia. Workers that exceeded their quotas were treated like heroes and given special rewards. Rickenbacker had not advocated shooting strikers in America but found the Soviet attitude refreshing.

Meanwhile, he assured Stimson he had not made the statements in Turkey that had been attributed to him. American officials present at Rickenbacker's conversation with the Turkish ambassador to Iran, including General Connolly, wired Stimson to refute the British ambassador's charges, saying that Eddie had been misquoted and had made it clear he was speaking only as a private citizen. According to Rickenbacker, Stimson cabled him to say he was satisfied he had been misrepresented, expressing continued confidence in him and telling him to stay in the USSR until he had finished his mission.

Rickenbacker never had an audience with Stalin but did confer with Molotov in the presence of Litvinov, who had returned home, ostensibly for health reasons. Molotov and Zhukov had already decided to meet Eddie's requests, but he helped his own cause by telling Molotov he would need an interpreter—in other words, a commissar who could observe everything he did. Touring airfields and antiaircraft installations in and around Moscow, he saw hundreds of P-39 Airacobras—"Kobrys," as the Russians affectionately called them—that had been supplied under Lend-Lease. He learned about the high regard of the Soviets for them, not only as interceptors but also because their ruggedness, firepower, and rear-mounted engines made them highly suitable for ground-hugging, tank-busting missions.[40] Stettinius was glad to use this information in his book, *Lend Lease: Weapon for Victory,* published in 1944. Rickenbacker discussed with Russian pilots problems they were having with spark plug points and advised them to ask for gasoline with a higher lead content. Later in his trip he visited a factory where the Russians manufactured Ilyushin Il-2 Shturmovik ground attack planes, being in all likelihood the first American to get such a chance. Seeing them being built gave him valuable information to share when he went home.[41] Tit for tat: he told his hosts about the B-29 bomber program in America.

Meanwhile, he awaited word about when and where he would witness Soviet ground operations. Standley doubted Hitler would launch a major offensive that summer, but Rickenbacker learned that high-ranking Soviet leaders expected one soon. Zhukov told him that Soviet forces had halted two German thrusts at Moscow and said the next attack would probably come from the south. Eddie was soon heading for the front near Kursk.

Flying at an extremely low altitude—100 feet or less—in a DC-3 originally given to the British under Lend-Lease, Rickenbacker was escorted by five Yakovlev Yak-9 fighters.[42] Looking down, he saw well-tilled farms and workers cutting wood for the bitter winter ahead. He admired them for working only a few miles from the front lines. When the Yaks guided him to a sector near Orel, he could see that a major attack was anticipated. Approximately 300,000 workers had dug 3,000 miles of trenches, laid 400,000 mines, and created three lines of fortifications behind which additional troops led by General I. S. Konev were massed. Suddenly, as the Yaks turned, he saw a grass airstrip so cunningly concealed he could barely make it out. Scrutinizing it intently, he discerned camouflaged airplanes hidden among trees. Only someone who knew the location of the field could have found it, even when flying close to the ground.[43]

The DC-3 had barely stopped when a "special navigator" climbed aboard, and it whisked Eddie to another airfield even harder to spot. Because the flight took about twenty minutes, he realized he must be very close to the front lines. Just before the plane touched down he saw woods concealing Douglas A-20s.[44] Taken to the headquarters of the installation, he met the chief engineer and other officers and advised them in detail about characteristics of planes that were causing them trouble. He realized from the questions asked by interrogators that they were not used to flying A-20s and unaware of their special requirements. He felt good about knowing enough to help them and noted that the planes were kept in tip-top shape, removing any doubt in his mind that the Russians were glad to have them—a good thing for Stimson and Stettinius to hear.

I. D. Antoshkin, commander of Soviet air forces in the Orel sector— Eddie thought he looked extremely young for the rank he held—suddenly entered the room and led the group to a mess hall stocked with copious amounts of food and drink, including plenty of vodka. Fortunately, there was a lot of black bread, fish, and oily victuals to mitigate the effects of the "liquid fire." Eddie and his hosts had a far-ranging discussion in which he learned that the Soviets had noticed a decline in the quality of German pilots they were encountering. When he inquired why this was so, they said the most experienced enemy airmen had been returned to Germany to cope with round-the-clock bombing—again intelligence that he thought Arnold, Stimson, and Marshall would want to hear. He slyly remarked that the air raids might be doing something good for the Soviets—a reference to the lack of the "second front" that Stalin wanted so badly—and drew enough of a rise from the airmen to think he had made his point. He also learned that the number of German aircraft in the sector had shrunk by up to 900 planes, making a substantial difference in the balance of forces. On the other hand, the Russians admitted that the remaining German aircraft, numbering about 1,800 to 2,000, were superior in quality and operational efficiency to the 3,000-or so planes the Red Air Force could deploy against them.

After the meal was over and the talking stopped, Eddie's hosts gave him a special treat, a display of acrobatics accompanied by Cossack music. After he declared the performance worthy of a Broadway show, the entertainers played one of his favorite tunes, the "Beer Barrel Polka." The festivities ended at midnight, followed by another meal with yet more vodka. Keeping his senses by mixing drinking and eating as he had done before, he went to bed at an extremely late hour.

He returned to Moscow feeling all the more confident that Americans and Russians could get along after the war. His departure was delayed by a malfunctioning engine, and he had to wait until a new one arrived from Cairo. He spent part of his time enjoying a party at a *dacha* watching nude women swimming on their backs. When the new engine arrived from Egypt, a Russian repair crew installed it in place of the old one with great skill. Standley got up at 4:30 a.m. on 15 July to take Rickenbacker and his party to Kuibyshev. Yak fighters escorted them over Stalingrad, giving them a chance to see the appalling damage caused by the epic battle that had been waged for control of the city. Their route back to America took them to Teheran, Cairo, Marrakech, and, circuitously, out over the Atlantic to London, where, as always, Rickenbacker stayed at the Savoy.

Churchill sent an automobile to bring him to Chequers and report on his trip. At one point, when Churchill appeared to be jesting with him, Eddie said he was ready to leave. Apologizing, Churchill carried on an extended conversation. Rickenbacker urged him to develop the best possible relations with Stalin and gave him a highly sympathetic view of the Soviet Union. His views must have irritated Churchill, who took a realistic view of Stalin and wanted American forces to launch a campaign through Greece and the Balkans to prevent him from getting too deep into Eastern Europe. Eddie also scored no points by predicting to Churchill's face that British voters might remove him from power before the end of the war. He had more satisfactory talks with Harriman, who continued to serve as Lend-Lease administrator but would soon replace Standley in Moscow, and with Winant at the Court of St. James. Winant wanted to arrange for him to present his views to FDR after he returned to America. Eddie doubted that Roosevelt would want to talk with him but told Winant to proceed.[45]

Rickenbacker had amassed much information on his trip and was eager to discuss what he had learned with Stimson, Marshall, and Arnold. Leaving England, he and his entourage flew home via Iceland, Greenland, and Newfoundland. Ultimately he had a complete transcript of his observations and experiences bound in leather, with the imposing title, *World Mission*.[46] He had gone about 55,000 miles in approximately three months and felt satisfied with what he had done He hoped he had helped lay the foundations of a postwar era in which the United States would benefit from forging a partnership with the Soviet Union and a reformed China, while the French and British empires passed into oblivion. He had visited scores of American units and assumed the ungrateful task of telling resentful airmen that they would not be able to go home as soon as they had expected. And he had also scouted the prospects for a vast network of American air routes around the globe, hoping that Eastern and other American airlines would benefit from what he foresaw. A new world order was coming, and he wanted to play an important role as it unfolded.

Chapter 19

— ☆ —

Anticipating Victory

Rickenbacker's role in the postwar era would be paradoxical because he changed from an admirer of the USSR into an impassioned Cold War crusader. Soon after he returned to America, he composed a list of "Assumptions with Regard to Russia." The most important supposition was that "Stalin thinks Russia and the United States are the only countries in the world with any great future. Each can help the other and neither should fear the other. The two great 'have' countries of the world should be able to prosper in peace in spite of all efforts on the part of the 'have not' countries, provided United States 'idealism' does not overcome United States 'realism.'"

The list went into much detail about an American foreign policy based on *Realpolitik*. A basic presumption was that "Stalin is interested only in Russia and how Russia will benefit as a result of any international treaties or other agreements." Another was that "Stalin is . . . no longer interested in the old Bolshevik brand of communism. Russia is swinging distinctly toward the right. Russia is no longer interested in proselyting other countries. . . . Trying to spread world Communism was all right when the U.S.S.R. was a young untried experiment, but is no longer necessary and impractical as well." He believed "Russia is deeply indebted to the United States and will repay all she owes us, with interest. She feels that the United Sates is the only country among the United Nations with no post war ambitions inimical to Russia, but is afraid that the President will lead us into foreign entanglements which forces Russia to watch this administration with suspicion."

He feared "that the administration is playing politics with the war," meaning that "Stalin distrusts Britain's foreign policy under Churchill and is afraid that the United States will allow its foreign policy to be dictated by Churchill and that the United States will be used as a catspaw to pull Britain's chestnuts out of the fire." For the sake of national security the USSR would want to dominate postwar Germany and control a bloc of Eastern European nations—Rickenbacker called it "Russia's pigeon"—stretching from the Baltic through the Balkans and including Czechoslovakia. Rickenbacker saw nothing wrong with this desire, but his hopes for the Soviet Union depended on continued rapprochement with the West.[1]

After returning to America, he told newsmen that "Russia may come out of this war the greatest democracy in the world, while if we continue to move to the left, as we are doing, we may easily be Bolshevist by the end of the war"—a statement reflecting his hostility toward FDR. Telling businessmen in Chicago that the United States should take a conciliatory attitude toward the Soviet Union, he declared that "Communism in Russia . . . is not what I was led to believe it was from Communistic enthusiasts in America and England." He spoke of his admiration for the country and its people and said that as long as the USSR did not try to impose its ideology on other countries there was "no reason why the Russian, English, and American people couldn't get together on a basis that would form the foundation for a lasting peace." Referring to the American and British delay in establishing a second front in Europe, he asked, "if you were in Russia's position, would you have unlimited confidence in us? The answer, obviously, is no." He also liked Stakhanovism. A journalist quoted him as saying that "Incentive payments keep production high and encourage quality work as well. Russia has no absenteeism. A workman who doesn't do his job promptly and well gets fired, and that's that."

Rickenbacker's pronouncements drew mixed reactions. Bryce Oliver, speaking on radio station WEVD, ridiculed Rickenbacker's claim that America was becoming more Bolshevist than Russia. "How can we be turning to the left," Oliver demanded, when the courageous utterances of [Vice President] Henry Wallace only make our press furious?" A critic in Cleveland stated, "Those who see a Bolshevik future for the United States are merely looking through glasses tinted with hate for our President. Their prejudices get the better of their common sense." "Before Eddie and his big business pals start buying tickets for Moscow, we suggest that they find out what happened to capitalists in Russia," declared an editorial in New Jersey. "They got shot." Calling Rickenbacker "the Wily Captain," the *Daily Worker* said he "attempts to utilize the great patriotic exploits of the Soviet workers to substantiate his own anti-labor position."[2]

Other commentators, however, were respectful. Quincy Howe, speaking on radio station WABC, noted, "This visit of Captain Rickenbacker's and the message he's brought back show that the Russians continue to make friends and influence people in our most conservative circles." Sidney Walton, on station WHN, said Rickenbacker's views should not be taken lightly and that it would be a mistake to "dismiss this new attitude of his." Persons who believed big business was anti-Soviet, Walton said, were deceived by appearances. "The big businessmen themselves, the top several dozen American industrial leaders, are as actively pro-Russian as the President, the military chiefs, the Congressional majority, and the majority of the people." Pointing to steel magnate Stettinius, Walton said that Eddie "couldn't possibly have been anti-Russian before and be so pro-Russian as he is now." He was simply in league with capitalists thinking, Howe stated, about making money from good relations with the USSR. In a column, "A Clear-Eyed View of Soviet Russia," a Florida newspaper called Rickenbacker's views "one of the best contributions toward a clear-thinking, hard-headed realistic American view of Russia and a basis for postwar relations." "It would not be at all surprising if within the next few years Russia should take her place on the side of England and the United States as a thoroughly capitalist nation," stated an Oregon newspaper. "Whether Rickenbacker be right or wrong, one thing is certain. If Russia is capable of becoming democratic the proper thing for already existing democracies to do is to encourage the trend rather than dampen it by adopting a dogmatically inimical attitude toward the Russians."[3]

Rickenbacker assembled the notes he had kept during his trip halfway around the earth, with all their political, economic, and military ramifications, and prepared a comprehensive report on what he chose to call his "World Mission" to Stimson soon after returning to America. Without pausing for rest, he set off on his final assignment for him: touring air bases in the last place where American airmen were stationed that he had not already visited—the Alaska–Aleutian Islands Theater. Combat on the far northern frontier had recently ended with the recapture of Attu and Kiska, but it remained a vital corridor of Lend-Lease operations to the Russians through Siberia. Once more Stimson and Arnold gave him carte blanche to "make deviations in your itinerary and proceed to such other places as may be necessary to complete your mission."[4] He also had full cooperation from Soviet officials who had helped arrange his visit to the USSR.[5]

Accompanied by Major Carl H. McClure III of the Army Air Forces, his latest military aide, Rickenbacker left New York on 13 October.[6] Anybody would have been wearied from the long campaign he had recently completed. How he mustered the stamina to tour Alaska and the Aleutians, especially considering that less than a year had passed since his raft ordeal and the ensuing visits to New Guinea and Guadalcanal, is hard to fathom. He meant not merely to fulfill commitments he had made to Stimson before his trip to England in 1942 but also to promote the agenda already apparent in his "World Mission" report—scanning the prospects for domestic airlines, including Eastern, to invade markets in places where the United States had built and paid for a vast network of air bases offering commercial utility in the postwar era. Unlike the other places he had visited, Alaska and the Aleutians constituted a potential gateway for routes to the USSR and China that did not have to cross territory in the British or French empires. The diary that Rickenbacker kept on the upcoming mission shows his alertness to possibilities for air commerce on a meteorologically forbidding but economically exciting new frontier.

On the first leg of his journey he flew to Minneapolis, where Croil Hunter, CEO of Northwest Airlines, threw a cocktail party for him. Before the war Hunter had been a persistent advocate of "Great Circle" routes that would use the curvature of the earth to establish the shortest possible air routes to Siberia and the Orient.[7] After the Japanese attacked Pearl Harbor, Northwest performed impressively for the Ferrying Command and the ATC. Altogether it flew approximately 21 million miles while transporting troops and cargo throughout the far northern theater. It gained a wealth of experience coping with sub-Arctic weather and terrain, made intensive studies of high-altitude flying and deicing, and modified large numbers of aircraft for operations involving intense cold, high winds, and some of the world's fastest-changing weather conditions. Despite constant squabbling with the ATC, Northwest established itself as the most deserving applicant for postwar government favors in the region. As soon as the CAB began considering new route proposals in 1943, Hunter applied for Great Circle routes to the Orient and pushed for access to New York City through Milwaukee and Detroit. Rickenbacker could not be blind to the complementarity of Hunter's

, Eastern's existing route system, and the visions for free
⌐ China and the USSR in his "World Mission" report. Whether
⌐est, a stubbornly independent carrier, would have wanted such
⌐ger at the time is another matter, but access to Rockefeller money
⌐ld have been a major asset to an ambitious enterprise.

Northwest would provide the aircraft and crews for Rickenbacker's upcoming trip. Protocol made it incumbent upon Hunter to entertain a powerful fellow airline executive and send him on his way with a large bash. Extremely important business matters were in the air, however, and it is highly unlikely that Rickenbacker and Hunter failed to discuss them over cocktails at Minneapolis. While Eddie was on his "World Mission," Eastern, Northwest, and fourteen other domestic airlines had subscribed to a joint statement of "International Air Transportation Policy." Its principles had profound implications for the postwar period:

Free and open competition—world-wide—subject to reasonable
   regulation by the appropriate Government agencies
Private ownership and management
The fostering and encouraging by the United States Government
   of a sound, world-wide, air transportation system
Freedom of transit in peaceful flight—world-wide
Acquisition of civil and commercial outlets required in the public
   interest

Two airlines, Pan American and United, had opposed the statement, "urging the operation of all United States international air routes, by a controlled monopoly, as a 'chosen instrument' of the United States Government."[8] The goals adopted by the other airlines, by contrast, constituted a Magna Carta of free trade consistent with the objectives of Rickenbacker's "World Mission" report. Their implementation would give Eastern, Northwest, and other domestic airlines unrestricted access to world markets, using the network of air bases that the United States had built and financed around the globe. Such opportunities must have been on Eddie's mind throughout an arduous trip that was both a scouting expedition and an inspection tour for Stimson and Arnold.

From Minneapolis one of Northwest's crews flew Rickenbacker to Edmonton, the main coordinating base for ATC shipments to Alaska. Departing from Edmonton on 15 October, he went across the snow-capped Wolf Mountain Range to Whitehorse and learned about an oil field at Norman Wells, 500 miles away. Petroleum would be pumped through pipelines to be refined at Whitehorse on the Alaska Highway, a 1,500-mile road from Edmonton to Fairbanks that had been opened in October 1942 after being rushed to completion by army engineers and construction crews. After inspecting an air base at Whitehorse, Rickenbacker flew to Fairbanks, a vital junction on ALSIB (the Alaskan-Siberian Ferry Route) from which the first Lend-Lease flight of A-20 light bombers like the ones he had seen near Kursk had taken off for the USSR on 29 September 1942. Eddie was pleased to hear that the 4,000 enlisted men at Ladd Field got along well with Russians stationed there. From Fairbanks he flew to Nome, where thousands of A-20s, P-39s, P-40s, B-25s, and C-47s were refueled to be sent to the USSR on the "Red Star Line." Two new airports, one with a runway long enough for B-29s (and therefore capable of accommodating large airliners), were under construction near what Eddie called "a real frontier town—rough, ready and muddy." Nome was nearly iced in for the winter, which would make water transport impossible. Commercial aircraft would not be stopped by such conditions but could be temporarily detained by adverse weather, as he learned when he departed for Anchorage ahead of a front that would have kept him socked in for a few days. He was getting a potentially valuable meteorological lesson.

Anchorage, whose population was mushrooming under wartime conditions, was the next stop on his itinerary and the jumping-off point for the Aleutians. After speaking to Americans stationed at Elmendorf Air Base, which had opened in 1940, he flew to Nanek, where he encountered "real Aleutian weather—rain and cold, 300 foot ceiling . . . They say here that if you have 50 feet and can see the end of the runway, you take off." From Nanek he departed for the rocky island of Adak, where army engineers had dammed tidal flats in 1942 to build an airfield capable of supporting operations by B-17s against Japanese-held Kiska. Stopping to refuel at Umnak, 350 miles east of Adak, he found that the "lava rock here makes wonderful runways and roads"—yet more data to assimilate. At Adak the wind blew rain horizontally in sheets.

He continued to the remote island of Attu, where Japanese forces had fought to the death after American forces invaded it amid howling winds in May 1943, recapturing it by the end of the month. Enemy planes were still bombing the island from time to time and alerts took place during his visit. A favorable change in the weather, however, encouraged him that things were not always bad this far north. The island was "as far west as New Zealand," and a general with whom he talked was eager to fly a B-24 from Attu to Hawaii, pointing out that "it's only 2,000 miles and less to Wake Island—it would tie the whole Pacific together," another point for Eddie to ponder. Attu was also close enough to Japan for B-24s to bomb a naval base at Paramushiro, indicating its postwar commercial promise.

From Attu he went to nearby Shemya, which was "very flat and where we are building a 10,000 foot runway for B-29s," again long enough for large commercial airliners to be virtually on Tokyo's doorstep. The splendid weather of the previous day, however, had been replaced by cold rain, wind, and fog. "The flying weather is tough," Eddie wrote, noting that Shemya was the only place in the world where thirty- to forty-mile winds, subzero temperatures, and fog were sometimes present simultaneously. Still, its commercial potential was obvious as a refueling spot on the way from Alaska to Japan.

He was approaching the end of his mission as he overflew Kiska (which the Japanese had abandoned before Americans captured it in August), made a detour to Kodiak, and then returned home via Fairbanks and Edmonton. He and the crew Northwest had provided were grateful for a tailwind as they approached Edmonton, looking eagerly at the lights of the city gleaming in the distance. After reaching New York City, Eddie gave crewmembers $100 each to enjoy themselves. Thinking about the miserable weather they had endured, he joked with them that when the war was over "we must get tough at the peace table with the Russians to be dam [sic] sure they take back Alaska and the Aleutians." While this reference to the blustery outpost made for a good punch line, Eddie's diary was full of information showing the prospects for major American airline operations in a part of the world that was as strategically located commercially as it was militarily.

Not surprisingly, Winant, now back in the United States, had failed to arrange the meeting between Rickenbacker and FDR that he had suggested in London. After Eddie returned from the Aleutians, Winant wanted to renew his efforts, but Rickenbacker told him not to try, saying he would not speak with the president even if asked.[9] His attitude toward Roosevelt had hardened into outright hatred. Before the war, whatever his personal feelings and ideological convictions, he had not engaged in blatant attacks on FDR. Not until after he recuperated from the Atlanta crash and toured American air bases in 1942 had he implied that the president was being dishonest with the American people about how the war was going. Upon returning from the Pacific in 1942, he had dug himself into a deeper hole with FDR by campaigning bitterly against gains made by unions under the New Deal. After coming home from the USSR, he had intimated that Roosevelt was more of a Bolshevik than Stalin. A once-prudent airline leader had not been able to restrain himself from making impolitic statements, and it was not strange that FDR did not want to entertain a man who had gone out of his way to offend him. Rickenbacker had joined Lindbergh in Roosevelt's doghouse.

Whatever the differences between Rickenbacker and Roosevelt, they had common ideas about the future, ones consistent with the principles Eastern and most other domestic airlines had set forth in 1943. Despite his relationship with Churchill, which was now cooling, Roosevelt shared Rickenbacker's attitude toward the British Empire, as did Assistant Secretary of State Adolf A. Berle, who had decided to focus on aviation in his thinking about the postwar world. Like Eddie, Roosevelt and Berle were also opposed to Pan American's hopes of remaining a "chosen instrument" monopolizing commercial air routes between the United States and foreign nations. Recognizing the declining power of Great Britain and the overwhelming lead America would enjoy in aeronautics after the war, FDR and Berle concurred in believing that freedom of air transport should be a major national goal. Preparing to represent the United States at an International Aviation Conference to be held in Chicago in September 1944, Berle wrote a memorandum stating that "Only in America was there enough capital to allow extended private development of civil aviation and even then it was inadequate for the markets to be developed." As a New Deal liberal, he believed that "Planes were expensive and the amount of capital required to develop, build, and maintain them was the equivalent of a public works project in need of government financing."

Rickenbacker, backed by Rockefeller money, did not see the situation the same way. He had deliberately withheld dividends to build substantial cash reserves for Eastern to spend in the postwar era and was too devoted to private enterprise to endorse the "state capitalism" pervading Berle's thinking. Nevertheless, believing that national security and commercial aviation were inseparably connected, Rickenbacker, who had shown no qualms before the war about having airlines protected by the Civil Aeronautics Act or supporting the role played by the WPA in financing airports, had no cause to be concerned about the implications of conceiving aviation as a "public works project in need of government financing." Only minor differences in nuance separated his ideas from Berle's, and he joined the great majority of American airline leaders in wishing Berle and his chief legal assistant, L. Welch Pogue, good luck at Chicago, where they would fight for the principles embodied in the statement of "International Air Transportation Policy" that Eastern and other airlines had endorsed in 1943.[10]

The chief obstacle to American hopes at Chicago was Great Britain, which faced the end of its centuries-old power in international trade. Knowing they would be playing a weak hand at the upcoming conference, the Brits hoped for the united support of their commonwealth partners—Australia, Canada, New Zealand, and South Africa. Canada, however, was determined to pursue its own goals, which were in some respects closer to Berle's objectives than to those of Great Britain. Canada's trump card was its geographical position athwart North Atlantic air routes, giving it control of indispensable bases in Newfoundland and air space that had to be crossed on the shortest and safest route between the United States and Europe.

In the end Britain's main asset at Chicago was its stubbornness, manifested by Lord Philip Swinton, who was determined to defend the aeronautical interests of the British Empire even if it meant pulling out. Despite Rickenbacker's naive hopes, the Soviet Union, which refused to entertain the concept of "innocent passage" over its air space, presented another obstacle. Supporting the United States was a large bloc of countries, including the Netherlands, which still had colonies scattered around the world but knew it was too small to contest American dominance; the Irish Free State, which also had a favorable geographical location on North Atlantic air routes but was hostile to British interests; and the Latin American countries. Berle, who had formidable debating and negotiating skills, effectively exploited the differences between Canada and Britain. At one point, FDR sent a note to Churchill that the prime minister called "pure blackmail."

For a time it seemed that Berle might obtain an "International Air Charter" at Chicago that would force the Brits to sign or walk out. At the last minute, however, FDR, who had been reelected while the conference was in progress and might have given Berle the support he needed, unexpectedly undermined him by removing him from his office as assistant secretary of state. What caused FDR to do what he did is moot. He was extremely ill, and his powers of judgment were weakening. In any event, he hung Berle out to dry. In a final address, Berle put the best face on what the conference had accomplished: laying the foundations of the International Civil Aviation Organization (ICAO), which would be headquartered at Montreal, and securing broad acceptance of five "freedoms" (really privileges) that member nations could observe if they so desired, retaining full control of their air space. Canada, the main winner, emerged from Chicago with Montreal as the nodal center of ICAO and its position in international aviation much strengthened. Britain was also a winner because its intransigence produced an agreement that determination of air routes and the rights or restrictions governing them would be negotiated in bilateral treaties between nations belonging to ICAO. Meanwhile, at least in part because of Roosevelt's change of heart, the United States fell short of attaining its objectives. The results of the conference did not bode well for the international free trade and American dominance of world aviation that Rickenbacker had entertained. His Anglophobia was strengthened, and he had all the more reason to detest FDR.

With the end of his trip to Alaska and the Aleutians, Rickenbacker was free to return to Eastern, which had been administered by Brattain in New York City and Shannon at Miami. Despite wartime restrictions on its domestic fleet and passenger traffic, EAL was still the most lucrative airline in America. Its net earnings for 1943 were $1,426,856; for 1944, $1,499,337. But for excess profits taxes—it was the only American airline required to pay them—its earnings would have increased more than twofold, to $5.77 per share in 1944 instead of $2.54. It had made major contributions to the war effort; in 1944 alone it carried more than 14 million pounds of cargo and 47,000 military passengers for the Air Transport Command. With victory in sight, the ATC no longer needed as many planes to carry troops and materiel and restored service on routes that had been suspended, the most important being St. Louis to Miami. Plans were afoot to buy newer, bigger planes and relegate DC-3s to local service.[11] Whatever his disappointments, Rickenbacker's plate was full as he returned to work at Rockefeller Center.

Some of Rickenbacker's admirers did not want him to go back to the life of an airline executive, hoping he would play an even larger role in national affairs. An increasing number of letters urged him to seek the Republican presidential nomination in 1944. Joseph Patterson, publisher of the *New York Daily News*, was among the most prominent advocates of the idea, but Rickenbacker refused to consider it. He later said he did not feel qualified to be chief executive and would have been unelectable because of his "free-for-all combat with labor racketeers." He probably realized his uncompromising nature and tendency to speak his mind regardless of the consequences would have made the White House an impossible goal. He considered Marshall the best possible choice for president, but Thomas E. Dewey won the Republican nomination and lost to FDR.[12]

Despite spurning all chances to become involved in politics, Rickenbacker spoke out as vigorously as ever on public issues. One of his chief utterances in 1944 was "Masters of Tomorrow," a magazine article in which he predicted that returning veterans would transform the nation by the way they applied the knowledge and maturity they had gained in the war. Put simply, they would reject the misguided attitudes of the 1930s and return to a spirit of self-reliance that, to Rickenbacker's way of thinking, had been subverted by the Great Depression and the New Deal. He wrote glowingly about the jobs that would be available to "magnificent fighting men" he had visited on fronts all over the world. "Aviation, plastics, electronics are in their infancy. These boys have begun to explore them. . . . World trade has never been developed. We have the largest merchant fleet on earth. . . . We are hardly beginning to explore and exploit the secrets of a dozen sciences." Watch out! "You're either going into business with the man who comes back, and make him the heir eventually of your enterprise or you'll find yourself pitted against the toughest competitor or the toughest revolutionary you've ever encountered." He promised that Eastern Air Lines, which aimed "to expand ten to fifteen times," would be in the forefront of providing "a worthy outlet for the zeal and skill of boys who won their wings in the war." Meanwhile, what should the government do? Eddie's prescription was simple: get out of the way, restore solvency, cut waste, practice thrift, and restore "sanity into our national economy."[13]

He did, however, want the government to help veterans get the formal education he had never attained. "Masters of Tomorrow" shows that he had scientific and technical subjects mainly in mind, but others, including English composition and history—if it properly celebrated the principles of the founding fathers—could be valuable too. Differences of opinion existed about how the government should help returning GIs. The American Legion sought legislation providing four years of higher education to "any able-bodied veteran who had 90 days service" in the armed forces. The smaller Veterans of Foreign Wars was afraid such a bill would "consume funds needed for other programs, especially hospitalization," for treatment and rehabilitation of men wounded in battle. The result was an omnibus proposal that met both objectives and provided $20 per month for fifty-two months for ex-servicemen unable to find jobs. The Senate passed the joint resolution overwhelmingly but it got bottled up in a seven-member committee in the House because some representatives did not want to put African American veterans on what they saw as a dole. Three members supported the joint resolution and an equal number opposed it. The swing vote was held by Congressman Frank Gibson of Douglas, Georgia, a supporter of the bill who had gone home at an inopportune time. Nobody knew where he was. Knowing that a search was in progress, Rickenbacker arranged to hold an Eastern flight on the ground at Jacksonville while Gibson was hunted down. After being found, the congressman boarded the plane just in time to reach Washington and cast the deciding vote to bring the measure to the floor. Soon afterward FDR signed the GI Bill of Rights into law in the presence of leaders from the American Legion and the VFW. Rickenbacker was not present, but without his help the ceremony might not have taken place.[14]

Giving veterans a free education did not eliminate one of Rickenbacker's chief concerns about their welfare: that they and their progeny would be saddled with an enormous national debt. Late in 1944, with the Battle of the Bulge raging in Europe and no sign of an early end to the war in the Pacific, Eddie gave a speech to the National Association of Insurance Commissioners in which he made a dramatic proposal. He predicted that the national debt, then estimated at $350 billion, might reach $600 billion in three years of continued warfare that he foresaw. Merely paying the interest on such an enormous obligation, let alone paying it off, would require huge tax increases, sap individual initiative, depress the job market, and complicate the lives of future generations. "It might be better to cancel the debt," Rickenbacker said, and let returning veterans "start from scratch, so that they may win for themselves the great opportunities earlier generations have enjoyed."

The speech aroused a furor among people ranging from bankers to humble citizens who had invested in war bonds, hoping to reap the benefit of the interest they would earn. To one such critic, Eddie replied that "if I were a young man of twenty to thirty, I would much prefer to see this debt cancelled through devaluation or some other appropriate method and have my future free without the strangulating effects that must go with such a future through taxation." He agreed that cancellation "would work a distinct hardship on a lot of people. In fact, it would take up my life's savings as well." Still, he argued, "the wasting of our resources though billions and billions of dollars of needless expenditures has become so commonplace to our people as a whole, including bond holders, savings account depositors and insurance policy owners," that inflation would wipe out any gains they might make from their investment and their assets would be liquidated. "Frankly, at the rate we are going and if the road is long enough, it will become unnecessary to cancel any Federal debt," he indicated, because the country would be bankrupt. "That will surely become automatic as it is taking place today slowly but surely." The main purpose of his speech, he said, was to "awaken people to the realization of what can and will happen to them if they do not start thinking. . . . I assure you that I have no desire to do anyone an injustice."[15]

Rickenbacker's fear that the war would drag on, especially in the Pacific, led him to advocate using any means to shorten it. At Charlotte, North Carolina, he urged "using poison gas to bring Japan to its knees," responding to a critic by saying that the Japanese were inhuman.[16] One place where the war against Japan was dragging on was Burma, where Cherry was now stationed. Lowell Thomas visited it late in the war and learned that Cherry's comrades had mixed feelings about his responsibility for getting lost with Rickenbacker as a passenger. "Some felt he had done the best he knew how. Some thought he had been bullheaded and made a bad mistake." Described as a "bundle of nerves," Cherry said he had "got caught short once," and "by God he was never going to get caught short again."[17]

An airman who gained greater distinction by having his name associated with Eddie was Richard I. Bong, a combat pilot who scored his twenty-sixth and twenty-seventh victories in a sortie near Hollandia, New Guinea, equaling and then surpassing the number Eddie had won in 1918. Rickenbacker promptly fulfilled the commitment he had made while visiting MacArthur's headquarters in 1942 and sent Bong a case of Scotch, but Bong, a teetotaler, would not drink it. Only recently canonized because of the "seagull episode" and his authorship of "When a Man Faces Death," Eddie now received a deluge of letters from clergymen and members of the Woman's Christian Temperance Union (WCTU) and Anti-Saloon League decrying what he had done.

He stood his ground amid the storm. "I come from a family of Swiss descent and was practically weaned on beer, as beer and wines were kept in the house by my father," he wrote an indignant woman, "so while I am not a teetotaler, neither am I a drunkard nor a roué. I indulge whenever I desire and do not enjoy people interfering with my private life, which I consider entirely my own affair."[18]

Bong received the Medal of Honor after scoring his fortieth victory on 17 December 1944, making him America's ace of aces in World War II. Wanting to preserve his life, his commanding officer sent him home, and he married his high school sweetheart. On 6 August 1945, however, he died, crashing on takeoff in a Lockheed P-80 Shooting Star in what should have been a routine flight. Rickenbacker, a devoted Mason, placed a wreath on Bong's grave in Masonic rites at Poplar, Wisconsin, dressed in appropriate regalia.[19]

Controversy erupted over another episode linking Rickenbacker's name with that of a Medal of Honor winner. In 1941 Warner Brothers scored a success with *Sergeant York,* a film directed by Howard Hawks. Gary Cooper played the role of Alvin York, the Tennessee infantryman who came home in 1919 as one of America's greatest heroes, along with Rickenbacker and Pershing, of World War I. After Eddie returned from the raft episode, the idea arose of creating a movie about his exploits, a counterpart of the one about York. Rickenbacker did not object to the honor and arranged to get the best possible deal from Twentieth Century Fox. Preproduction work on the film, called *Captain Eddie,* was underway when the project aroused opposition from unions alienated by Rickenbacker's attacks on "labor racketeers." After failing to prevent the film from proceeding, workers planned to picket showings when it appeared. The final product was a syrupy melodrama, with Fred MacMurray implausibly cast in the starring role, bringing out nothing of the intensity of Rickenbacker's life and experiences. Herbert Hoover tactfully told him that the film did not do justice to his achievements. Despite much careful research that went into its preparation, the script was full of inaccuracies, but Rickenbacker was proud of it and went on tour to promote it, ignoring picket lines, after its premiere at the Ohio Theater in Columbus. He complimented an interviewer for calling it a story about a "thrilling life" in a "thrilling country," praising the United States as "a land where success stories are common," where "any man who is willing to learn and willing to work can have the kind of life he wants."[20]

Despite incurring the wrath of temperance advocates by sending a case of Scotch to Bong, Rickenbacker remained an icon of religious faith. His stature rested partly on a close association he developed with a popular Methodist minister with strong conservative leanings. Late in 1944 Lowell Thomas helped put Rickenbacker in touch with Norman Vincent Peale, the renowned pastor of New York City's Marble Collegiate Church. Peale preached a nondenominational type of Protestant Christianity that was too unsophisticated for intellectuals to admire but highly palatable to persons like Rickenbacker, who cared nothing for theological hairsplitting, had never been a regular churchgoer, and was deeply attracted to a faith stressing an individual relationship with Christ as a personal companion and source of inspiration. Peale saw America as land of opportunity where self-reliant individuals could rise from humble beginnings, as Rickenbacker had done, to fulfill their dreams. He told disciples that "the answer to their troubles lay within themselves, in the divine energy stored within the unconscious, which they had only to tap through affirmative prayer and positive thinking"—a point of view Rickenbacker could readily endorse.[21]

Like Eddie, Peale was a critic of the New Deal, worried about what he saw as a steady drift toward a welfare state. He was allied with powerful business leaders including Standard Oil executive Walter Teagle, retailer Stanley Kresge, and Howard Pew, founder of the Sun Oil Company (Sunoco). In 1945 he launched a magazine, *Guideposts,* similar in format to *Reader's Digest,* featuring short, easily accessible articles celebrating "Americanism, free enterprise, and practical Christianity." He told critics who accused him of crossing the line between church and state that he had no political agenda in mind.[22]

Peale and Rickenbacker soon became friends. In December 1944 Eddie spoke at Marble Collegiate Church about his experiences in the raft ordeal and how it had converted him to believe in a personal relationship with God. His presentation became the first article published in *Guideposts,* "Why I Believe in Prayer." Soon afterward Eddie made a "generous contribution" to *Guideposts,* to which Peale responded, "You will be interested to know that your article is doing a vast amount of good, and is already being quoted widely. You have a tremendous influence, and perhaps you do not even realize the deep affection in which you are held by people everywhere. You are an inspiration to me, also." Responses to the article were so overwhelming that Peale ordered an extra 150,000 reprints. Rickenbacker in turn helped Peale by writing a nationwide letter to prominent business leaders, urging them to support *Guideposts*.[23]

Rickenbacker also began playing a prominent role as toastmaster at banquets and other functions sponsored by religious groups, especially ones involving members of the Rockefeller family. In March 1945, at the invitation of Forrest L. Knapp, general secretary of the World Sunday School Association (WSSA), Eddie presided over one of its dinners at the Waldorf-Astoria. Dignitaries at the speaker's table included Episcopal Bishop Horace W. B. Donegan, Dean Luther A. Weigle of Yale Divinity School, Methodist clergyman Ralph W. Sockman, and Crown Princess Martha of Norway. Weigle sent Rickenbacker an enthusiastic telegram about how well the occasion had gone, "due primarily to your leadership," and the *New York Herald-Tribune* carried photographs of the event showing the prominent role Eddie had played. Soon afterward he helped organize a mass mailing for the WSSA, under his signature, of a letter to business leaders encouraging them to participate in a drive to aid "our postwar task of restoring Christian education in the war-torn countries and of expanding and improving Christian teaching throughout the world." The recruiting campaign gathered an illustrious collection of sponsors, including Harry S. Truman, King George VI of Great Britain, and the presidents of Princeton, Stanford, and Yale universities. Rickenbacker's organizational feat added luster to his image as a moral leader.[24]

He also won acclaim as a philanthropist. As victory drew nearer in Europe, he expressed concern about disabled veterans who might not be able to find jobs. On 1 April 1945 he announced that Eastern would keep open 1,000 jobs for honorably discharged members of the armed forces who had suffered amputations. The New York State Council of Second World War Veterans Organizations passed a resolution hailing his action. "Mere words cannot express our gratitude to you for the consideration that you have shown to ex-servicemen," wrote the council's executive secretary. Other tributes included an award from National Employ the Physically Handicapped (NEPF). Members of the business community were also impressed. Responding to a letter praising Eastern's policy, Eddie said, "When one thinks that it only takes 14,000 to 15,000 employers, large and small, to take one man each it is inconceivable that so few have taken the time to realize this."[25]

Another incident, however, cast Rickenbacker in a much different light. Less than two weeks after he began receiving plaudits for supporting handicapped veterans, he attended an aviation conference at Havana, Cuba, following the 1944 Chicago conclave. Representatives of 57 airlines and 18 countries were about to establish the International Air Transport Association (IATA), a counterpart of ICAO. European airlines (which, unlike American carriers, could form pools and cartels) came prepared to oppose the "Free Skies" policy Rickenbacker had anticipated in his "World Mission." Just before he was to speak at a luncheon, news arrived that Franklin D. Roosevelt had died from a massive cerebral hemorrhage. Showing a conspicuous lack of sensitivity to the potential consequences for Eastern's image, Rickenbacker could not resist being frank, beginning his remarks by saying that the world was better off without FDR and his death was "the best piece of news he had heard in a long time." The diners were so outraged and the repercussions so severe that he had to go home, and Paul Brattain made a hurried trip to Havana to represent Eastern for the rest of the conference.[26] Rickenbacker's feelings about FDR were well known. Paying tribute to him would have been self-evidently insincere, but showing not even a modicum of tact did not bode well for the future.

What had happened? Rickenbacker may have been drinking before the luncheon. The Havana conference may have reminded him uncomfortably of the Chicago meeting, at which British stubbornness and FDR's untimely sacking of Berle had helped doom the "Free Skies" policy Eddie had so ardently wanted. The presence of British and French airline representatives in the Cuban capital may have increased his awareness that their countries were not about to turn over American-built air bases or settle tamely for American aerial hegemony. The postwar world order he had envisioned, dominated by the United States, the Soviet Union, and a reformed China, was already beginning to unravel. Whatever the reason, Rickenbacker's hatred of FDR had spilled over in a regrettable outburst. Paradoxically, he would soon find a new "World Mission" by turning about-face and becoming an outspoken Cold War crusader.

Chapter 20

— ☆ —

Turbulence and Descent

Rickenbacker was probably caught off guard at Havana when he learned about FDR's death. At the time of the conference he was preoccupied by adverse regulatory trends in Washington that had troubling implications for Eastern. Anticipating booming commercial air traffic in the postwar era, the Civil Aeronautics Board (CAB) was committed to fostering competition on routes previously flown by single carriers. In February 1944 the board broke Eastern's grip on traffic along the East Coast by awarding National Airlines, a Florida-based company that Eddie held in contempt, a route from Jacksonville to New York City. As the Havana meeting took place, it was considering a case involving service between the Great Lakes area and the Southeast. In August 1945 it reached a decision that caused wild cheering in Atlanta among employees of Delta Air Lines, crying "Chicago to Miami! Chicago clear to Miami!" Suddenly a carrier whose mainly east-west routes had funneled passengers into Eastern's far larger north-south system was going to compete with EAL on a lucrative vacation route.[1]

Before the war, whatever he felt about FDR and the New Deal, Rickenbacker had shown a pragmatic attitude toward federal airline regulators and enjoyed largely amicable relations with them. Feelings remained cordial after the CAB resumed route awards midway through the war, granting EAL routes from St. Louis to Washington and New York City to Boston, adding New England's largest city to the lucrative route stretching all the way to Miami and Brownsville, the gateways to South America and Mexico. Other significant awards certificated Eastern to fly from Tampa to Miami, removing a dead end at Tampa, and ended restrictions on traffic through Birmingham, giving Eastern easier access to New Orleans. Pending before the CAB were applications by EAL for routes from Detroit to Miami, Pittsburgh to Miami, and an extension of the Miami–Chicago route to Milwaukee and the Twin Cities that would link Eastern and Northwest, possibly resulting from Rickenbacker's tour of Alaska and the Aleutians. Eastern had also asked for a direct flight across the Gulf of Mexico from Miami and Tampa to New Orleans and made applications to serve smaller cities.

Especially important to Eastern were its hopes to become an international airline. It had applied for a route from Washington and Baltimore to Montreal and Ottawa but was particularly intent on establishing service to Havana, Kingston, Mexico City, and Barranquilla, Colombia. It also wanted routes to San Juan and the Panama Canal Zone. Because Eastern wanted at least temporarily to concentrate on gaining a foothold in Latin America—but also to show that Rickenbacker did not desire connections with Great Britain and France—EAL had opted out of competition for North Atlantic routes.[2]

Despite the plums the CAB had given Eastern, its decision to foster competition on two of its most important domestic routes was a bad sign. National and Delta were both small airlines lacking Eastern's financial muscle, but Delta had strong backing from Coca-Cola and R. J. Reynolds and an exceptional leader in C. E. Woolman. Eastern's ability to secure international routes was also in doubt because they were subject to presidential veto, which was likely before FDR's death. By the time Rickenbacker went to Havana, the chances for any connections he might have been contemplating with the USSR and China were also dwindling, giving him additional cause for concern.

Roosevelt's death brought to the presidency a man for whom Eddie had high hopes. Like Rickenbacker, Truman had risen from modest beginnings and fought in World War I, showing leadership and courage in molding an unruly group of soldiers into a model artillery unit. He seemed honest and forthright, a man Eddie he could trust. Displaying no enmity toward Rickenbacker, Truman issued him a presidential citation lavishing praise on Eddie's "exceptionally meritorious conduct in the performance of outstanding services to the United States from December, 1941 to December, 1944," his "great courage and fortitude in the face of the most harrowing physical experiences," and his "unflagging zeal and devotion to the cause of his country."[3]

Intimations of the Cold War were already gathering ominously, threatening the accommodation between the United States and the USSR Rickenbacker desired. Even before he died, Roosevelt was leaning toward curtailing aid to Russia when the war ended. On 11 May 1945, in a move deeply resented by Stalin, Truman canceled unconditional assistance to the Russians and authorized sharp cuts in Lend-Lease supplies. Stalin, who had pledged at Yalta to enter the war against Japan, believed these moves were hostile. During the months that followed, negotiations for a large American loan for Russian reconstruction collapsed.[4] Unlike Eddie, Truman was unwilling to recognize, as a matter of *Realpolitik,* Russia's need for insuring security on its western border by creating a bloc of subservient satellite countries. Considering the enormous damage Germany had inflicted on the USSR, its need for help was obvious to people like Eddie. Instead, Truman showed increasing animosity toward the USSR while "pulling Britain's chestnuts out of the fire," as Rickenbacker had feared.[5]

Walter Lippmann, perhaps the preeminent political columnist of the era, believed like Rickenbacker that Britain and the USSR had deeper conflicting interests than those dividing the United States and the Soviets. Instead of aiming at a balance of power between Britain and the USSR, Lippmann lamented, the United States was becoming Russia's chief antagonist. Like Rickenbacker, Lippmann saw Britain's hand behind America's increasingly hard line.[6]

Rickenbacker's hopes for friendship between the United States and a reformed Chinese government also dimmed despite Truman's efforts to foster compromise between Chiang Kai-Shek and Mao Tse Tung. In December 1945 Truman sent Marshall to China to bring about a "strong, united, and democratic regime." Patrick Hurley, the American ambassador to China, brought Mao and his chief deputy, Chou En-Lai, to Chunking for a meeting with Chiang, but distrust was too strong for a settlement. Tired of dealing with Chiang, Hurley returned home, ostensibly for health reasons, and resisted pressures to return. A civil war, already underway in 1946, eliminated hope that Eastern, or any other American airline, could get routes to China.

Obviously, the views Rickenbacker had expressed in 1943 about the need for U.S.-Soviet cooperation were not shared by Truman and his advisers. Whether American loans to help the USSR recover from World War II would have induced Stalin to act differently in his relations with the United States is subject to debate, but events took a much different course. Stalin and Truman did not like each other when they met at the Potsdam Conference in 1945. Learning about the success of the Manhattan Project at Potsdam—Stalin had already known about the venture from spies—toughened Truman's attitude and increased Stalin's insecurity.[7] Within a short time, hope vanished for the bipolar amity Rickenbacker had advocated.

Rickenbacker himself did an abrupt about-face as tensions mounted between the United States and the USSR, and he saw that he had been mistaken in thinking that Stalin had abandoned communism, whose doctrines Eddie had always condemned. "We are in the same position today as we were in 1935," he said at an American Legion conference in March 1946. "The only difference is that the name then was Adolph Hitler; now it is Joe Stalin." A month later he reluctantly approved Truman's decision to aid Greece and Turkey, calling it "the greatest gamble in the history of the United States" but asserting, "We must take it, for if we don't, Communism will spread and eventually bring about World War III." He supported a military buildup to oppose the growing threat posed by the Soviet Union but was unwilling to commit massive amounts of aid to European nations. Early in 1947 he congratulated Marshall on being appointed secretary of state, but opposed the "Marshall Plan," which was announced shortly thereafter, as "the greatest international gamble America had ever taken."[8]

Eddie had no doubts, however, about the need to combat subversion from within. In 1947 he praised actor Adolphe Menjou for testifying before the House Un-American Activities Committee (HUAC) to help combat communism in the film industry.[9] Early in 1948 Eddie sent his sons, David and William, copies of a recent book that "lays bare the traces of the cancerous Communistic vein throughout mankind's international anatomy as clearly as a surgeon using his scalpel."[10] In a Christmas letter to Laurance Rockefeller, he said that the United States was fighting a cold war on two fronts, one domestic and one international, against "the Communists and their fellow travelers, who have dedicated themselves to the destruction of our American Way of Life."[11]

Rickenbacker's reference to "fellow travelers" was directed against members of the Roosevelt administration suspected of covertly aiding the USSR in World War II. Like his anti-Communist rhetoric, his animosity toward the New Deal was consistent with his prewar feelings, but his public pronouncements, starting with his ill-considered remarks about FDR's death in 1944, manifested a hatred of Roosevelt that had been absent from statements he had made in the 1930s, when he had tried to distinguish between the president and his advisers and avoided attacking him personally. Such pragmatism, which had benefited Eastern's relationship with regulators appointed by FDR, now disappeared. A speech

Rickenbacker gave at East St. Louis in 1948, ostensibly to talk about aviation, turned into a bill of particulars against Roosevelt, alienating a lawyer who had driven from Peoria to hear him speak. Protesting that Eddie had said nothing about aviation, the attorney wrote him a stinging letter declaring he would never fly with Eastern again. Rickenbacker responded tartly that he was merely exercising his freedom of speech and did not care whether people who disagreed with him patronized the airline.[12] Putting his political and ideological views above EAL's best interests became more and more typical of his behavior. After thwarting the attempt by Breech and Hertz to take control of Eastern in 1938, he had stated that by working for "the greatest business in the world" and "the greatest company in the world," he could "serve humanity more completely in my line of endeavor than in any other." Now he seemed to be veering off course.

Major turning points began occurring in Rickenbacker's life in the early postwar era, including the end of his involvement in automobile racing. Since December 1941, when he had shut down the Indianapolis Motor Speedway for the duration of the war into which the United States had just entered, the historic facility had fallen into neglect and disrepair. In November 1945, amid fears among racing fans that it would be torn down and replaced by a housing project, Rickenbacker sold it to Anton ("Tony") Hulman, a businessman from Terre Haute, Indiana, for a reported $750,000. Rickenbacker used the proceeds to deal with a change in federal tax law by paying off a loan. Options for shares of Eastern Air Lines stock he had acquired for $10 per share had appreciated substantially, leaving him with a capital gain that he had to claim. Three-time Indy winner Wilbur Shaw made a notable contribution to saving the speedway by driving around the decaying track in a Solo 500-mile performance, launching a campaign that led to Hulman's buying it from Eddie. Hulman quickly began "rejuvenating" the speedway, beginning a transformation that reestablished it as one of the world's greatest sports arenas.[13]

Rickenbacker sustained a terrible blow when his mother died from pneumonia on 31 March 1946. Earlier that month he had written his son William, now a student at Harvard, that he had "made a hurried trip to California due to Grandmother's serious illness." Elizabeth had meant more to Eddie than anyone else, including Adelaide. "It is rather pathetic to have one grow so old—one who has done so much in the world and given so much to others," he told William. "She seems to have arrived at the end of her rope so to speak, being extremely thin and having no body resistance. She is more or less living on her will power." Eddie said she was "quite rational and had not lost her sense of humor, but there is nothing that can be done for her other than to give her the best medical care and attention." He had arranged to give her round-the-clock nursing care and the best physicians he could find in Los Angeles, but knew her case was hopeless. "As much as I hate to lose her," he felt, "she would be better off to pass along in her sleep and eliminate the suffering of mental anguish which she must be experiencing as she looks back over a long, arduous life." Elizabeth cried when Eddie left the hospital, three days before she passed away, saying "Nobody knows what that boy means to me." A nurse who had attended her told Eddie his mother "met the end bravely and most courageously," but her death devastated him and he turned to God for refuge. "Today is Easter and what a beautiful day," he wrote William on 21 April. "Untold thousands are going to church, which is a wonderful thing because too many of us have gotten away from the simple things in life and that fundamental faith in the Power Above, and we have lost the true beauty of living to a degree."[14]

Another loss did not hit him as hard but was still severe. His longtime friend, Damon Runyon, died from throat cancer on 10 December 1946. Two days later, Rickenbacker, Mike Todd, and Damon Runyon Jr. took Runyon's ashes aloft in a DC-3 and scattered them over Broadway. What they did was illegal, but Eddie did not care, nor did anybody else.[15]

Rickenbacker's friendship with Peale intensified after Runyon's death. When a fire destroyed the *Guideposts* publishing facility at Pawling, New York, on 12 January 1947, Eddie provided funds to help get the magazine up and running again. About a year later Peale thanked Rickenbacker for writing a "wonderful letter" to the national commander of the American Legion on behalf of the periodical. He was also grateful when Eddie arranged for Eastern's planes, which already had Gideon Bibles in their seat pockets, to carry copies of *Guideposts* for passengers.[16]

As the Cold War intensified, Rickenbacker worried about the threat of nuclear war. On 28 February 1950 he responded swiftly to a letter from R. E. Treman, a longtime friend who had fought in World War I. Treman, a resident of Ithaca, New York, greatly admired Peale and was impressed by Eddie's support of *Guideposts*. He was writing on behalf of

Hans Bethe, one of the world's greatest atomic physicists, who taught at Cornell. Bethe was about to visit New York City and wanted to have lunch with Rickenbacker. "Your letter received and I shall be glad to have lunch with Dr. Bethe tomorrow," Eddie wired back.[17]

Bethe had played an important role in the development of "Fat Man," the fusion bomb dropped on Nagasaki in 1945. He also had inside knowledge of efforts being made by Edmund Teller and Stanislaw Ulam to devise a way to create a successful hydrogen bomb. Truman had authorized the creation of such a weapon on 31 January 1950, barely a month before Bethe and Rickenbacker lunched together in New York. What transpired is not clear, but Bethe probably communicated his concern about the terrible dangers involved in the escalating arms race between the United States and the USSR. Eddie's readiness to meet with Bethe stemmed from his growing fear that the world was on the brink of a nuclear war with the USSR, which had successfully tested an atomic bomb on 26 August 1949. Two months after the test, he had learned that Julius and Ethel Rosenberg, spying for the USSR, had stolen atomic secrets for the Soviets. Obviously Rickenbacker and Bethe were not exchanging pleasantries.[18]

Eddie was not simply concerned about the possibility of annihilation. As a fiscal conservative, he was also worried about the staggering cost of the protracted confrontation now taking place. "This 'Cold War' is costing the taxpayers of this country many more billions annually," he told Laurance Rockefeller, "which means ever-increasing taxes that sap the incentive and lifeblood of a great people and a great nation. . . . the day is not far distant when we must take inventory of the remaining assets of this great nation, which will mean changing our habits in accordance with common sense and realism, or we shall continue to go down the highway to bankruptcy."[19]

Fear of atomic war was among the reasons why Rickenbacker acquired a 3,000-acre spread, Bear Creek Ranch, in Hunt, Texas, near Kerrville in the hill country west of San Antonio, thinking it might be a safe haven in a nuclear holocaust. It had a spacious house and a 2,000-acre deer preserve bounded by a ten-foot wire fence. Leaving their apartment at East End Avenue, Eddie and Adelaide rented smaller accommodations at the Park Lane Hotel and spent much of their time at the ranch, from which Eddie commuted to New York to take care of business. He liked to sit on the porch of the ranch house in the evenings and watch deer. He also invited Eastern's board of directors to the property for meetings. "Be sure to bring your swimming trunks because we have a nice swimming hole that can be enjoyed by all," he told Laurance Rockefeller in 1951. Rockefeller later recalled that a director who passed the open door of Eddie's bedroom before turning in for the night saw him kneeling in prayer, so fervent in his devotions that he was oblivious to everything around him.[20]

Visitors to the ranch included William, who joined the Air Force after graduating from Harvard in 1949. He was stationed at Lubbock and drove to see his parents when he was on leave. Adelaide, however, quickly tired of the isolated locality and persuaded Eddie to move back to New York, leaving the property in the custody of East German refugees. Eddie wanted someone he trusted more implicitly to live on the ranch and asked his elder son, David, who had enlisted in the Marines and been a tail gunner in the Pacific theater during World War II, to manage it. After his discharge in 1946, David had taken advantage of the GI Bill of Rights by matriculating at Hamilton College in Clinton, New York. While he was a student there he married Patricia Ann Bowne, who came from nearby Utica. Living on campus in a barracks-type "GI Village," they had their first child, a son named Bryan.[21]

After graduating from Hamilton in 1950, David decided to accept Eddie's invitation. Packing up their belongings in a Plymouth sedan, he, his wife, and their son moved to Texas. Because the ranch was unsuitable for grazing, occupying a wooded canyon along a creek flanked by a steep bluff, Rickenbacker wanted to make it profitable by importing exotic animals—a practice followed by other ranchers in the area—and make it a hunting preserve, building blinds behind which wealthy sportsmen could pay to shoot game. Living in a cabin amid the trees, David and Patricia Ann had their second child, Marcia, who spent her early life on the ranch. Ultimately, however, they got tired of inopportune long-distance telephone calls from Rickenbacker to learn how things were going. After arriving at his Manhattan office early on Sunday mornings—he still worked seven days a week—Eddie made long-distance calls when David and Patricia Ann were trying to sleep in after staying up late on Saturday nights. When they took the phone off the hook Eddie called a caretaker who came to the cabin to roust them out of bed. Eventually he became dissatisfied with its earnings and donated most of the ranch to the Boy Scouts of America in 1957. David and his family moved to Upper Montclair, New Jersey, where he became an account executive with a Wall Street firm, United States Trust Company.[22]

Eddie was highly pleased that William had decided to become a pilot and wanted his younger son to succeed him someday as chief executive at Eastern. During William's training at Lubbock, Eddie advised him to "know and appreciate the mechanics . . . because their appreciation of you at all times may mean the difference between a successful flight and one that is not." He said William was helping the country "to develop the greatest and strongest air power in the world which is basically the salvation of this nation and the future of its people." After William finished training and won his wings—with which Eddie proudly decorated him on 9 February 1952—he flew ferrying missions across the Pacific and became a pilot in a "Gypsy Squadron" that dropped spies behind enemy lines in North Korea, picking them up later from flare-lit beaches.[23]

Eddie himself visited military bases in Korea at the invitation of MacArthur, whom he now idolized. He felt strongly that Truman should have permitted the general to cross the Yalu River to pursue retreating North Korean units and was bitterly critical of the president's decision to sack him in April 1952. He had long since lost respect for Truman and contemptuously called him "the little man in the White House." Awed by MacArthur's "known genius both military and statesmanwise," he ardently wanted him to become president.[24]

Rickenbacker's concerns about communism occupied increasing amounts of his time. Before the war he had traveled incessantly around Eastern's route system keeping close track of its operations; now, because his priorities had changed, he made anti-Communist speeches throughout the country, especially at graduation ceremonies where he received honorary doctorates from colleges and universities. Subversion was constantly on his mind. When a series of crashes took place near Newark International Airport in 1951–52 and protesters demanded that the facility be shut down, Eddie said Communist Party members were distributing leaflets to close the field and told congressional investigators that such a step would benefit only Stalin and his cohorts by inhibiting military traffic.[25]

Like Norman Vincent Peale, Eddie supported Senator Joseph McCarthy's crusade against Communists that had allegedly occupied powerful positions under FDR and Truman. After McCarthy died, Eddie advocated building a monument in Washington in his memory. His admiration for the Wisconsin senator may have been intensified by his image as a Marine tail gunner in the Pacific during World War II, but it was also consistent with that of the American Legion and the Veterans of Foreign Wars, which saw "Tail-gunner Joe" as a champion of "God and Country." Even John F. Kennedy supported McCarthy during his heyday, and Robert F. Kennedy served for a time on his staff. In a major disappointment, Eddie's hopes that MacArthur would receive the Republican nomination for the presidency in 1952 went unfulfilled. After a lackluster performance in hearings on the Korean War, in which he tacitly acquiesced when McCarthy called Marshall a traitor, his prospects faded swiftly and Rickenbacker supported Ohio senator Robert A. Taft's primary campaign against Eisenhower. Eddie told William that Ike had "all the New Deal Republicans supporting him as well as the fringe Democrats and what a menagerie that is." Adelaide took it hard when Eisenhower won a bitterly contested nomination, but Eddie told William that "she, like everyone else, must realize that politics are politics. . . . All we can hope for is that the Lord will endow Eisenhower and his team-mate, Senator Nixon, with the sublime guidance needed to run this land of ours the way it should be run." When Eisenhower won the election in a landslide, Eddie wrote William that he woke up the next morning "with a terrific load off my shoulders, because I have been waiting and battling for twenty years to have such a thing happen. . . . I feel America is back in the hands of Americans again." He went to Washington to witness the inauguration and wrote that "President Ike made an excellent impression."[26]

A few months after Ike took office, Rickenbacker donated a DC-3 that had flown approximately 56,700 hours, emblazoned with the company's peregrine falcon and "Great Silver Fleet" logos and other livery, to the Smithsonian Institution, to which he also gave a Pitcairn Mailwing. These contributions resulted partly from Rickenbacker's friendship with Paul N. Garber, a dedicated curator who was building the world's greatest collection of historic aircraft, but they also reflected Eddie's pride in the contributions Eastern had made to American commercial aviation. Eastern's employees had restored the Mailwing and presented it to Rickenbacker as a personal tribute. Ultimately both planes were suspended from the ceiling of the Gallery of Air Transportation at the National Air and Space Museum, where they remain today.[27]

Eddie was encouraged by Ike's early months in office. He told William that the new chief executive "is certainly moving up on the problems that have accumulated over the last 20 years of New Deal, Fair Deal, and Freakish Deal governments." Early in 1954 Ike invited Eddie to the White House for a stag party with fourteen other men, mostly industrialists or newspaper publishers with a Republican orientation. Robert Kleberg, owner of the King Ranch in Texas and brother of former congressman Richard Kleberg, a longtime friend of Rickenbacker, was among the guests. Ike presented Eddie with an award from the Big Brother Movement, which he had supported for many years.

At the urging of former president Hoover, and in recognition of Rickenbacker's missions for Stimson during World War II, Ike offered to appoint Eddie head of a committee to investigate American intelligence-gathering operations. Rickenbacker volunteered instead to serve as deputy to General Mark W. Clark, a longtime favorite of Eisenhower's who had led the 15th Army Group in the Italian campaign in 1944 and 1945. Rickenbacker and Clark agreed on a division of responsibilities under which Clark went to the Asia and the Pacific and Rickenbacker went to Europe. One of Eddie's missions took him through deep passageways from West Berlin under the eastern part of the city. Touring a tunnel used to tap Soviet communications cables, he eavesdropped on telephone messages between East Germany and Moscow. Using an assumed name, he studied the intelligence operations of the CIA and the army in Switzerland and Italy and held meetings with British agencies, including Scotland Yard's Special Branch—a neat reversal of his rough interrogation in 1916 when he was suspected of being a German spy. He and Clark wrote a top-secret report after their joint assignment, which lasted about three months.[28]

Other activities during the Eisenhower years included being grand marshal of the 1957 Rose Bowl Parade, riding with Adelaide among floats and marching bands and waving at crowds lining the streets of Pasadena. Eddie's friendship with Hoover also drew him back to California to enjoy retreats at Bohemian Grove, a 2,500-acre redwood forest sanctuary north of San Francisco where the ex-president, known as "The Chief," presided over all-male conclaves of conservative industrial and political leaders at which liquor flowed freely amid low humor, performances by popular entertainers, and snide remarks about FDR and the New Deal. Admission to the grounds was by special permission only. William, whose economic and political views were heavily influenced by Eddie's convictions, came to the camp and sat with Eddie in the shade of the redwoods, enjoying the free-flowing alcohol and the fellowship of Roosevelt haters.[29]

Rickenbacker's support for Eisenhower waned because Ike did not dismantle the New Deal. He was particularly offended when Ike supported a guaranteed annual wage for automobile workers in 1955. "Unfortunately . . . over the years we have developed this absolute security idea with all of our give-away programs," he told William, predicting Americans would someday "wake up and find themselves with a planned economy that practically equals a positive dictatorship insofar as their opportunities and privileges are concerned."[30]

He was even more disappointed by the restoration of the Democrats to power in 1960, trying to console himself that the voting public was "divided almost equally" between Kennedy and Nixon and telling William that "it is now the duty and obligation of every one of us to unite and merge behind our new President for the benefit of all."[31] Three years later when Kennedy's life ended tragically in a motorcade at Dallas, Rickenbacker did not repeat what he had done in Havana when he heard about FDR's demise. On 22 November 1963, when he was addressing the St. Louis Chamber of Commerce, someone handed him a note saying an attempt had been made to assassinate the chief executive. Saying he hoped the situation wasn't "serious," Rickenbacker called for a moment of silence. He had been castigating Kennedy's administration and wondered whether he should stop speaking but decided to continue. After he had resumed his remarks, however, he received another message confirming that Kennedy had been assassinated, stopped his speech, and asked his listeners to stand and pray in silence for the stricken leader and his family.[32]

He had risen to the occasion, but an ill-conceived speech in which he had denounced president-elect Kennedy during a route case in which Eastern had much at stake—and which it subsequently lost—had already helped undermine his usefulness to the airline he had once led with great success. Unfortunately, the blunder typified much that had happened to the company in the postwar era.

Many members of the armed services flew for the first time in World War II and became accustomed to the experience. In 1945 expectations were high in the airline industry that veterans would lead the way to a substantial increase in air travel. By 1947 commercial aviation was reeling from unexpected deficits, and the CAB had cut back new route awards. The downturn continued through 1949.

Only one airline—Eastern—prospered amid the hard times. Its net earnings of $5,573,972 for 1947 through 1949 were greater than those of all other American carriers combined, accounting in part for Rickenbacker's making the cover of *Time* on 14 April 1950. Amid a merger mania he refused to acquire less profitable competitors on advantageous terms. "Don't rush it," he said. "I'm going to pick 'em off one by one—they're all heading for bankruptcy." His predictions might have come true but for the onset in June 1950 of the Korean War, which brought recovery to a battered industry.[33]

Even in the late 1940s, however, when Eastern seemed invincible, trouble was brewing. During the prewar years EAL had enjoyed a monopoly on most of its routes, with the notable exception of the heavily traveled corridor between New York City and Washington, on which Eastern competed with American. But things changed radically after the CAB began to award new route certificates in 1943. By 1947 almost all of Eastern's route system had been opened to other airlines. Early in 1946 National began head-to-head competition with Eastern in nonstop Miami-to-New York operations. By this time, Delta was also giving Eastern stiff opposition between Chicago and Miami. In a scramble for taxis in Washington, C. E. Woolman, Delta's genial chief executive, got the last seat available in a cab and Rickenbacker asked if he could sit in his lap. "Well, Eddie," Woolman quipped, "I've been helping support you for years, so I might as well do it some more"—a barbed comment by a former ally who was now a serious rival.[34]

Although avowing he favored fair competition—as he defined it—Eddie resented that Eastern had to share lucrative routes with airlines that needed federal subsidies. His indignation boiled over in 1946 when the CAB denied Eastern a route from Florida to Cuba, Jamaica, Colombia, and the Panama Canal Zone. Storming into the office of CAB chairman L. Welch Pogue, he launched a tirade and pounded Pogue's desk with his fist while sweeping a row of books onto the floor with the other hand. As he left, he winked at Pogue's secretary. What he had done was partly an act—but he was also serious.[35]

His rancor against George T. ("Ted") Baker, founder and CEO of National Airlines, was especially intense because he thought he was a shyster. Like Woolman, Baker had fed traffic into Rickenbacker's system in the 1930s, on Eastern's Jacksonville-to-Miami route, but National, a tiny carrier, was already an annoyance. In 1934 Baker, who had an unsavory reputation for being an alleged rum-runner in the Prohibition era, won an airmail contract from Tampa to Daytona Beach, for which Eddie had neglected to apply. Baker then flew passengers across the peninsula in an "Aerial Taxi" service. But for such blunders by Rickenbacker, National, a shoestring operation whose name belied its puny stature, might not have survived. Baker also capitalized on yet another of Rickenbacker's blunders. Because Eastern's DC-2s often overflew Daytona Beach in the late 1930s due to its small airfield, Baker won temporary authority to carry mail between it and Jacksonville. To Eddie's disgust, the Post Office Department let Baker keep the route after the runway was extended. During the accompanying legal proceedings, Baker charged that Eastern had not done enough to help Tampa become a major air center. Losing his temper, Rickenbacker called Tampa a "dead-end town," producing unfavorable publicity. Baker further offended Rickenbacker by winning a route between Jacksonville and New Orleans and rejecting a buyout by Eastern after intimating that he would be receptive. When Rickenbacker sent Brattain to seal the deal, Baker insulted him by asking why Rickenbacker was sending a boy to do a man's job. "Well," Baker said when Brattain left his office in a huff, "I've just turned down a hell of a lot of money." Eddie's animosity increased in 1944, when the CAB admitted National to the Florida–New York market, and in 1947, when the airline received authority to serve Washington, Baltimore, and Philadelphia as intermediate stops.[36]

Unlike Rickenbacker, who had satisfactory relations with his unionized pilots and mechanics and gave employees the first forty-hour workweek in the industry after the war, Baker hated organized labor. He tried to crush National's chapter of the Air Line Pilots Association during a strike in 1948 by using flagrantly unfair tactics. The CAB so disliked Baker's conduct that it considered disbanding National and dividing its system among other carriers. After Baker backed down, however, the CAB allowed National to survive, partly because it competed with Eastern. As historian of airline unionization George E. Hopkins has stated, Baker was "fortunate in his enemies," particularly Rickenbacker.[37]

However much Baker infuriated him, Eddie realized that National did not have enough capital to be more than an irritant. Delta was much more dangerous. Because of Woolman's unassuming manner, it was easy for Rickenbacker to underestimate him from his lofty perch at Rockefeller Center, but behind his folksiness lay one of the keenest minds in the business. Delta's pilots were unionized, but Woolman quashed a wildcat strike by mechanics in 1947, leaving most of his workers unorganized and therefore easier than Eastern's to handle. Delta also had strong ties with powerful legislators and bureaucrats in Washington because the South was still solidly Democratic, giving Woolman an important advantage over Eastern and its abrasive Republican leader. Woolman was also better at taking advice from his senior executives than Eddie, whose autocratic tendencies intensified after the war. Above all, Delta's leader was relentlessly and intelligently committed to expansion.[38]

Rivalry between Eastern and Delta became a classic case of airline competition after Delta won a Chicago-to-Miami route in 1945. Much of the strategy had to do with aircraft selection, in which Rickenbacker held his own with Woolman for a time but ultimately made mistakes that cost Eastern dearly. Rickenbacker entered the postwar era with numerous DC-3s he hoped to use on short-haul routes while adding newer and bigger planes to serve major markets. The only four-engine aircraft initially available in 1945 for nonstop long-haul routes were reconditioned C-54s (Douglas DC-4s) previously flown by the navy. After negotiations to lease the aircraft fell through, Charles Froesch, Eastern's chief engineer, advised Rickenbacker to buy them outright but Eddie said their $130,000 price tag was too high. Delta, by contrast, seized an early advantage by using war-surplus DC-4s on nonstop runs from Chicago to Miami, capturing passengers who disliked frequent takeoffs and landings at intermediate stops in Eastern's DC-3s. Froesch wisely delayed Rickenbacker's adoption of the Curtiss C-46 Commando, a slow tail-dragger, as a replacement for the DC-3 until delivery problems made its acquisition a dead issue. Rickenbacker, permitting personal feelings to interfere with sound business judgment, wanted to use the Commando partly because he was friends with Curtiss's president, former automobile racer Guy Vaughan. Facing an urgent need for DC-4s after the Commando deal collapsed, Eddie was now forced to buy them but had to pay an average of $170,000 per plane.[39]

Eastern ultimately did utilize thirteen DC-4s, some of them leased, but staked its future on the Lockheed Constellation, a pressurized four-engine aircraft developed by talented engineers including Ward Beman, who conceived its striking combination of a triple tail, high-aspect wing, and a gracefully tapering fuselage.[40] It had excellent operational features, including a cruising speed exceeding 300 miles per hour and space for up to sixty-four passengers, significantly more than the DC-4 could carry. Its chief drawback was that of being the first four-engine airliner requiring a three-man cockpit crew, two pilots and a flight engineer. Despite the extra cost, Rickenbacker was determined to get the plane but had to overcome reluctance by Howard Hughes to sell it because he wanted TWA, which he owned, to monopolize it. Eddie persuaded Hughes to share it with Eastern, arguing that if it was a dud—an unlikely outcome because of its outstanding performance as the C-69 military transport—it would be better for two airlines to share the consequences. Lockheed wanted Eastern to buy twenty of the planes, which had been designated for commercial use as the L-649, but Rickenbacker thought fourteen would be ample for his needs and threatened to resell the six he did not need for knockdown prices if Lockheed remained obstinate.

Rickenbacker falsely claimed that Eastern was the first airline to use the plane—TWA had that honor—but demonstrated its excellence with flair. Merrill, still Eastern's star pilot, set a speed record flying its first Constellation from Burbank, California, to Miami in six hours, fifty-four minutes, scoring a publicity coup. Eastern began using Connies in regular commercial service in June 1947 on the New York–Miami and Chicago–Miami runs, where they overwhelmed DC-4s used by National and Delta. Seeing droves of passengers desert Delta's unpressurized DC-4s forced Woolman to acquire a new aircraft with comparable features, the Douglas DC-6, which needed only a two-man crew and cost less than the Constellation. American and United, however, had accidents using the earliest model of the plane, requiring changes that forced Delta to wait until December 1948 to introduce it on the Chicago–Miami route. In the process, Rickenbacker gained an eighteen-month lead.

Paradoxically, Delta benefited from waiting because the redesigned DC-6B was an excellent aircraft and a worthy competitor to Eastern's L-649s. Rickenbacker upped the ante by adopting the improved Constellation L-749, which had a longer range than Delta's DC-6Bs. He raised the stakes even higher in 1951 when Eastern became the first airline to fly the L-1049A Super-Constellation, a stretched model with eighty-eight seats. Delta had no choice but to adopt the Douglas DC-7, a faster plane of similar size. Baker, like Woolman, used DC-6Bs and DC-7s between Miami and New York. Still, Rickenbacker had succeeded in staying a jump ahead of Delta and National in the late 1940s and early 1950s, helping explain why Eastern prospered in that period.[41]

But Rickenbacker fumbled deciding what midsized plane to adopt to replace the aging DC-3. As in the case of the Curtiss Commando, he had a brush with disaster when he chose the highly touted Martin 2-0-2, which he wanted because of his personal friendship with Glenn Martin—showing again how sentiment influenced his business decisions. Froesch knew the 2-0-2 had structural problems and delayed Eastern's order, but Rickenbacker remained stubborn. Delta rejected the 2-0-2 when engineers visited the Martin plant and reported that "So much is made of weight and space saving that one would think they were designing a piece of luggage instead of an airplane." When the aircraft was introduced, a flange between the inner and outer wing spars cracked under repeated flexing, causing the wings to tear loose when heavily stressed in bad weather. Due to the delay at Eastern, Northwest was not only the first airline to adopt the plane but also the first to experience disaster with it—a crash in which thirty-seven people died. The safety record of the 2-0-2 became so bad that federal officials grounded it. Northwest's pilots distrusted it so much they refused to fly it, and the carrier sold its 2-0-2s at a loss.[42]

Froesch's reservations about the 2-0-2 saved Rickenbacker from a debacle by delaying its acquisition until its flaws became evident. Nevertheless, its grounding plunged Eastern into a crisis because Rickenbacker had invested $11 million in its development and Martin faced bankruptcy. Attempting to salvage the situation, Laurance Rockefeller and Rickenbacker went to the Reconstruction Finance Corporation and tried to persuade its head, Stuart Symington, to bail Martin out by loaning it enough money to redesign the plane. When he refused, Rockefeller and Rickenbacker persuaded former GM executive Charles E. Wilson, now chief of the Office of Defense Mobilization, to meet Martin's payroll while Eddie's longtime financial associate, William Barclay Harding, arranged a reorganization plan with the help of bankers, provided Martin retire. "It was your neck or the company's survival," Eddie laconically told his crestfallen friend. The rescue produced a much better plane, the Martin 4-0-4, which Froesch helped design.

Eastern flew the 4-0-4 for a decade without having a serious accident, and Eddie took credit for its performance. Merrill was fond of it, but many of the company's pilots disliked its cockpit layout, among other peculiarities.[43] Delta's Woolman, who had faced the same problems as Eastern, chose a stopgap measure with Douglas to reconfigure the interior of the DC-3 to hold more passengers and later acquired a plane arguably better than the 4-0-4 by adopting the highly successful Convair 340. National temporarily continued using prewar Lockheed Lodestars with more luxurious appointments before following Delta in adopting the Convair. Because the 4-0-4 did not enter service until 1951, Delta and National came out marginally ahead of Eastern, which continued using unmodified DC-3s on short-haul routes but could not fully exploit their cost advantages because its routes were shorter than Woolman's. Eastern continued to make profits on short-haul routes while waiting for the 4-0-4s only because the aging DC-3s were paid for and fully depreciated. Fortunately, Eastern also continued to monopolize some short-haul routes on which it did not compete with National and Delta.

Aircraft in themselves were not as important as gaining new routes permitting future growth. Rickenbacker thought he scored a coup in May 1946 when the CAB, after two years of debate, permitted Eastern to connect seventy-nine points on its route system with Mexico City through New Orleans, flying directly across the Gulf instead of using a roundabout route through Houston, San Antonio, Corpus Christi, and Brownsville. Rickenbacker and Rockefeller expected the decision to produce $10 million per year in added revenue but this prospect faded when Mexico refused to approve a bilateral treaty with the United States without which the award remained inoperative.

The Mexican debacle typified what happened to Eastern in late 1940s, preparing the way for intensified problems in the next decade. The CAB, influenced by declining traffic from 1947 through 1950, became stingy with new route awards and tried to solve the industry's problems by encouraging mergers. The Great Lakes Service Case to link Louisville, Cincinnati, Columbus, Indianapolis, Toledo, and other cities with Detroit went against Eastern despite repeated appeals, ending in a final defeat in 1948. Efforts to persuade the CAB to give Eastern a route from New York City to Montreal and Quebec fell through, as did attempts to provide service between Washington and Chicago; St. Louis, Chicago, and the Twin Cities; and Tampa–St. Petersburg and Houston via New Orleans. Eastern did not come away empty-handed; by the end of the decade the CAB had given it new routes to cities including Charleston (West Virginia), Pittsburgh, Akron-Canton, Cleveland, and Detroit. These awards, however, were more than offset by CAB decisions admitting additional carriers to routes previously monopolized by Eastern.

Eddie complained that the interlopers got mail subsidies for which Eastern had not applied because it did not need or want them. Conversely, nonsubsidy mail pay that Rickenbacker considered legitimate shrank after the war as the CAB issued show-cause orders proposing rate cuts for Eastern because of its well-earned reputation for being the most frugal airline in the industry. Rickenbacker was infuriated when the rate cuts went into effect. In 1949 his rage spilled over in a well-publicized letter to the Senate Finance Committee in which he offered to operate the entire domestic systems of Delta, National, Chicago and Southern, Capital, and Colonial for $0.65 per ton-mile instead of subsidy rates, averaging $4.45, which they were getting. He estimated that EAL could transport 2,700,000 tons of mail, for which the five firms had received $12 million in 1948, for a mere $1.6 million, saving taxpayers $10.4 million. He professed surprise that the carriers "did not accept this generous offer," knowing that going off subsidy rates would put them out of business while subverting the CAB's desire to foster competition.[44]

As the CAB slowed down new route awards until the industry's economic condition improved, it began permitting carriers to interchange equipment at places where existing routes came together, a practice the Interstate Commerce Commission had used with railroads. Interchanges permitted through passengers to stay on the same plane at a junction point while airlines exchanged pilots and crews. Despite opposition from Eastern, the CAB authorized Delta and TWA to interchange at Cincinnati in 1947. In 1949, in a move that Rickenbacker resented even more because it created transcontinental service he had long coveted, the CAB granted Delta and American an interchange at Ft. Worth, permitting passengers to fly with different airline personnel from Miami and Atlanta to Los Angeles and San Francisco. Eastern had spent much time and effort lobbying to secure one-company service on the same route and felt cheated.

Rickenbacker decided to play the same game, applying for an interchange with Pan American at Miami under which Eastern's planes could fly throughout South America manned by Pan American crews and Trippe's aircraft could fly domestic routes from Miami to various cities with Eastern personnel. An opportunity arose in March 1949 when the governor of the state of São Paulo invited Eddie to visit Brazil and discuss the present and future of aviation in that country.[45] Smelling profits, he got permission from Eastern's directors to make an elaborate goodwill flight to fourteen countries around the perimeter of South America. Nelson Rockefeller, deeply involved in Latin American politics and enterprise, was trying to facilitate a bilateral treaty to give Eastern access to Mexico City, providing an additional motive for the trip.

The expedition lasted thirty days and required much diplomatic and logistical planning. Four department heads, an assistant treasurer, extra crew members, and 6,000 pounds of spare parts made the trip, with newspapermen and publicity agents in tow. The passengers included entertainer Arthur Godfrey, a licensed pilot and promoter of aviation whom Rickenbacker liked. Godfrey took a ukulele along to enliven dull moments.[46]

Taking off from Miami on 1 August 1949, Rickenbacker and his party visited Rio de Janeiro, São Paulo, Montivideo, and Buenos Aries, having a delightful time as they extended "brotherly love and affection from your friends, the people of the United States." They praised an expansion of São Paulo's airport and showed off the Constellation by taking dignitaries on demonstration flights, attending banquets, and sharing expertise with Brazilian airline personnel. Everything went smoothly until they crossed the Andes to Santiago, Chile, where they arrived amid a revolution. Driving to their hotel, they passed "several buses that had been overturned and were ablaze." When Eddie woke up the next morning and looked out his window he saw "howling mobs of citizens fighting with the local police who were throwing tear gas bombs into the crowds." Disregarding danger, they went ahead with some scheduled events; that evening, however, when they came under fire walking down a street, Eddie "decided to leave Santiago in a hurry." The next morning they flew to Lima, taking photographs of the rugged cordillera below. To Eddie's surprise, Harold Tittman, a flyer in the Hat-in-the-Ring Squadron who had been badly wounded in 1918, was now American ambassador to Peru. Leaving Lima the next day, they flew to Bogota, "where a lot of communists existed that were fomenting trouble and revolution and everybody in the town was frightened stiff with the exception of the radical right and communists who were threatening all sorts of dire consequences." Aborting the visit, they flew to Caracas and stayed at a luxury hotel financed by Nelson Rockefeller and his business associates. They also received lavish entertainment at Barranquilla and Mexico City and completed the expedition on 30 August at Miami, where a throng of Eastern employees, their families, and municipal officials greeted them enthusiastically. Eddie said he was "tired but happy."

Eastern could well afford to send him and his party on the expensive junket. Its annual report for 1950 showed $25,108,729 in cash and short-term securities and working capital of $15,738,085. Delta and National had not yet hit their stride in securing new routes, and EAL's net income was a record $5,527,874. Anticipating future aircraft purchases, Eddie negotiated a five-year low-interest line of credit for $30,000,000 from a consortium of banks. The Korean War had created "an unparalleled increase in civilian air traffic," and the Florida vacation trade, which Eddie had worked hard to make into a year-round instead of a seasonal business, was booming.[47]

Considering the CAB's irritation at Rickenbacker's abrasiveness, it was not as hard on Eastern as it might have been. In 1951 it granted the airline a direct route from New York City to San Juan, supplementing its existing route from Miami to Puerto Rico. Constellations flew daylight trips at regular fares and DC-4s offered cut-rate ones at night, drawing a massive influx of Puerto Rican immigrants into New York City. In 1951, after the lavish tour of Latin America, a CAB examiner approved an EAL–Pan American interchange permitting the first-ever one-plane service between Boston, New York City, Washington, Miami, and other destinations including Nassau, Havana, Kingston, Barranquilla, Maracaibo, Panama City, Guayaquil, Lima, Santiago, and Buenos Aires. Eastern also got temporary permission for an interchange service from Miami to the West Coast, sharing equipment with Braniff and TWA. Buoyed by defense-related traffic and cargo operations, net income surged to $7,231,621. Legal complications delayed the start of the interchange to California, but in 1952 profits mounted even higher to $8,513,681.[48]

Nevertheless, Eastern did not get everything Rickenbacker thought it deserved, and he took offense at largesse enjoyed by smaller, less-efficient carriers. He pursued his aspirations for further growth by acquiring Colonial Airways, a financially troubled enterprise. National also wanted Colonial, and Eastern won a bitter merger battle with Baker by using its superior cash reserves to engineer the buyout for more than three times Colonial's estimated book value. Because Colonial served foreign markets including Montreal and Bermuda, approval from the White House was necessary. Accusations of foul play by Baker led Eisenhower to reject the deal, requiring four years of wrangling before the matter was finally settled in Eastern's favor in 1956. Despite adding 3,000 miles to EAL's route system, the victory saddled it with Colonial's debts. Serving a hodgepodge of small northeastern communities increased costs, and a fleet of obsolete DC-3s and DC-4s acquired in the deal—eventually sold off—could not serve short-haul markets as efficiently as Convairs flown by Delta and National.[49]

Delta became an increasing menace in the 1950s. In 1952 it absorbed Chicago and Southern (C&S), whose system linked Chicago, St. Louis, Memphis, and New Orleans on a north-south axis and Houston, St. Louis, and Detroit on a twisting web of routes running southwest and northeast. C&S also had Caribbean routes, making Delta an international carrier for the first time. In addition, the merger gave Delta an influx of managerial talent including W. T. ("Tom") Beebe, a personnel expert who ultimately climbed to president and CEO, and Richard S. Maurer, a shrewd attorney who excelled in arguing route cases. In 1955, partly because of Maurer's deftness in skewering Eastern's courtly but old-fashioned general counsel, Smythe Gambrell, Delta scored a major victory when the CAB authorized it to fly from Atlanta to New York City via Charlotte, Washington, Baltimore, and Philadelphia. By merging with C&S and gaining access to "America's Main Street," as Woolman called the Atlanta–New York route, Delta had become a carrier approaching the size of American, Eastern, TWA, and United. Its fleet was more modern than Eastern's and better able to attain economies of scale.

Rickenbacker's difficulty in acquiring Colonial at an inflated price and the rise of Delta typified a broad range of problems closing in on Eastern, whose cash reserves were shrinking, by the mid-1950s. The CAB tried to reconcile the financial interests of airlines with the convenience of the traveling public by promoting service competition, a game that was hard for Rickenbacker to play because Eastern did not get the large subsidies given many competing airlines. The CAB disliked allowing financially weak carriers to go bankrupt and tried to solve their problems by giving them new routes, a policy that overloaded routes with too many airlines, diluted traffic, and created a need for further subsidies to keep overstrained carriers solvent. With price competition impossible as a matter of principle, the only way firms could compete was by giving passengers more speed, more amenities, and more convenient schedules.

Service competition made sense to the CAB because an old bugaboo, fear of flying, still kept many people on the ground. Airliners incapable of climbing above turbulence spent a lot of time flying at low altitudes in choppy air on short-haul routes, making passengers uncomfortable. Only by giving them comfort and convenience to divert attention from frequent takeoffs and landings, noisy engines, and other distractions could airlines compete with cars, buses, and trains. The CAB's willingness to subsidize companies that pampered travelers flying on overcrowded routes made Rickenbacker's no-frills service, designed to cut costs and boost profits, highly unpopular.

National, kept in business by the CAB to compete with Eastern regardless of its costs, and Delta, whose only unionized employees were its pilots, thrived in a service-oriented industry. Eastern did not, partly because it received low mail pay and had too many short-haul routes but also because Rickenbacker maximized profits by pinching pennies and emphasizing efficiency. He believed his only obligation to the public was offering safe, dependable transportation; running an airline boiled down to "putting asses in seats." He made sure planes arrived at their destination on time by ordering gates closed to travelers who were only a few minutes late, promoting dependability but undermining public relations.[50] To boost earnings, he increased the carrying capacity of Constellations by seating five people abreast, a bad move in a service-oriented industry. "Never have so many paid so much for so little," said Maurice ("Lefty") Lethridge, one of the few executives at Eastern unafraid to speak his mind. Eastern's unionized cabin attendants, including women he had been forced to hire during the war when able-bodied men were in military service, identified with Eddie's hard-nosed attitude. In short, Eastern had made a lot of money because Rickenbacker calculated costs to the last mill, ran short-haul routes with obsolete DC-3s and DC-4s that Eastern owned outright or leased for its seasonal needs, and bought only as many Martin 4-0-4s and Constellations as he absolutely needed. But he paid a heavy price. Because of Eddie's frugality, passengers formed an organization—WHEAL, standing for "We Hate Eastern Air Lines"—to give it bad publicity, a dubious distinction no other carrier could claim.[51]

Complaints about EAL's service abounded. John M. Robinson, a congressman from Kentucky and a member of the House Judiciary Committee, wrote a typical letter saying, "I again wish to call your attention to the extremely poor service that is afforded Eastern Airlines passengers in and out of Washington. You may dismiss this letter as being from a sorehead if you desire. However, in addition to my own experiences I come in contact with many persons who are extremely unhappy about the way they have been treated by Eastern. I can assure you that you are developing public ill will which will be very detrimental to your company in the years to come."[52] African Americans, beginning to fly in increasing numbers, resented conditions harking back to the times when Eastern had flaunted a company banner with crossed United States and Confederate flags. In 1958, Whitney M. Young, dean of Atlanta University, complained to Nelson Rockefeller that Eastern still segregated rest rooms at Washington National Airport.[53]

Rickenbacker's disdain for federal bureaucrats increasingly alienated him from the CAB. An attorney for the agency said Rickenbacker and his lawyers, headed by Gambrell, did not mince words with CAB staff members, telling them to their faces they were incompetent. In Eddie's view, which he did not hide, people worked for the government instead of in private enterprise because they lacked the ability to succeed in business. Incensed by this attitude, CAB officials lectured Eastern's representatives in Washington, saying the company should be more respectful toward federal workers and stop hurting its own interests by being abrasive.[54]

Labor problems increasingly beset Rickenbacker. The worst resulted from a rule adopted by the CAB in 1948 mandating that all passenger aircraft with a maximum takeoff weight exceeding 80,000 pounds have a third member of their cockpit crews with a flight engineer's certificate. Among the planes affected by the rule were Constellations, DC-6s, and DC-7s. This rule, which became effective 31 March 1949, could be met either by using a flight mechanic who would remain frozen in that position or one who was also trained as a pilot and consequently eligible to become a copilot and pilot. Woolman chose the latter course, even though it was more expensive, because he thought it unwise to "put a board on a man's head" by giving him a dead-end job. When Delta absorbed C&S, which had employed flight engineers untrained to be pilots, Woolman gave them a chance to be retrained and thus become eligible for promotion. Those who declined received severance pay aggregating $250,000, a sum Woolman considered well spent. Rickenbacker chose differently, putting crew members of unequal status, representing two different unions, in his cockpits. In all fairness, eight other airlines— American, Chicago & Southern (prior to its merger with Delta), Continental, National, Northwest, Pan American, TWA, and Western—made the same decision. During the late 1950s and early 1960s members of the Air Line Pilots Association (ALPA) and the Airline Flight Engineers Association (AFEA) quarreled so bitterly that cockpit crews sometimes drew lines on the floor to mark jurisdictional boundaries.

Carriers following Eastern's policies established a mutual aid fund to cushion the impact of strikes to which Delta remained immune because it did not follow them. One of a series of walkouts occurred in 1957 at the peak of the winter vacation season, lasting thirty-nine days and providing a temporary bonanza to Delta, which was unaffected. Responding to the recommendations of mediators appointed by Eisenhower and capitulating to union demands, Rickenbacker agreed to put four persons in the cockpits of jet planes Eastern had begun to acquire, resulting in substantial cost increases. Again, he was not alone because Pan American, TWA, and Western adopted the same policy. But they were not competing primarily with Delta.[55]

During work stoppages, even while fuming about unions, Eddie got up early on cold mornings to serve hot coffee to strikers on the picket lines. As always, the hard side of his personality coexisted with a soft heart. His tirades, however, became increasingly terrible to witness and executives quivered under the lash of his tongue. One subordinate was so afraid of Eddie that he put on a suit and tie—even though he was relaxing at home—before daring to speak to him on the telephone. William recalled sitting outside his father's office and hearing him give a fierce tongue-lashing to Brad Walker, a public relations agent. The rumblings coming from behind the closed door reminded him of the lurid atmosphere gathering ahead of a thunderstorm. As Eddie's gorge rose, his profanity resounded and the walls shook from the tumult. Soon, however, he and Walker emerged arm in arm as if nothing had happened. Walker was too accustomed to dealing with him to be unduly disturbed by what he said, but other people were less thick-skinned.[56]

Rickenbacker ran company-wide staff meetings with an authoritarian style that had once been common in an earlier period of business but now seemed anachronistic, particularly to younger employees who did not understand him as Walker did. Eddie believed oral reports required at such conclaves would help people learn to "think on their feet," but many persons who delivered them quaked as they stood at the podium, knowing that Eddie was ready to pounce on them at any moment and demand that they justify what they said. Using his cane, he sometimes gave a speaker "a good hard rap on the leg." Najeeb Halaby, a former naval intelligence officer, attended a staff meeting at Miami Beach as a fact finder and was appalled, telling Laurance Rockefeller he "had never seen a more dictatorial example of centralized management nor such public humiliation of employees."[57]

During the 1950s Rickenbacker, like other airline executives, became increasingly preoccupied with an impending switch from piston-driven to jet-propelled aircraft. The DC-7 had reached the limits of reciprocating engines, with extremely complex power plants that broke down at an alarming rate and required uneconomical amounts of high-octane gasoline. Might not jets, however, be even worse? Rickenbacker was not alone among CEOs who worried about substituting expensive, untried planes for piston-driven models, but he had good reason to worry that the economics of jet transportation would be poorly suited to the plethora of short-stage flights on EAL's system, concentrated east of the Mississippi and lacking the transcontinental routes flown by United, TWA, and American. Halaby, unaware that Eddie and his chief engineer, Froesch, had often been at loggerheads about different aircraft, told Rockefeller they were fighting about a British-built jet, the Vickers Viscount, which Froesch admired, and the Lockheed L-188 Electra, whose turboprop engines had a complicated mixture of jet and propeller-driven components including reduction gears. Halaby thought Eastern should buy three airliners with straight turbojet engines for its New York–San Juan, New York–Miami, and New York–Houston runs, but Eddie chose instead to get forty Electras at a unit cost of $2.4 million, with an option for thirty more. Including spare parts, the order cost $100 million—an immense gamble.

Rickenbacker was not obtuse. C. R. Smith, universally regarded as one of the greatest executives in the industry, ordered thirty-five Electras for American's short-haul routes. Woolman thought seriously about adopting Electras, but American and Eastern had ordered so many that only three, an uneconomical number, were available for Delta. After much debate, Woolman and advisers to whom he listened carefully chose the Douglas DC-8 turbojet over the Boeing 707. When Howard Hughes overreached himself financially, Delta was also able to get three Convair CV-880s, the fastest jetliners built in the late 1950s, from TWA. Woolman, anxious about the new aircraft, said, "we're buying airplanes, that haven't been fully designed, with millions of dollars we don't have, and we are going to operate them with airports that are too small, in an air-traffic control system that is too slow, and we must fill them with more passengers than we have ever carried before." The same fears had troubled Rickenbacker, but Woolman had no choice and took a leap of faith.

Woolman's anxieties were unjustified, and Rickenbacker's decision to go for the Electra turned out badly. Although the Electra ultimately became an outstanding plane and Eastern's pilots enjoyed flying it, early models had a serious flaw causing wing flutter, leading to disaster when Electras acquired by Braniff and Northwest crashed soon after entering service. Amid the resulting clamor, the newly created Federal Aviation Administration (FAA) imposed speed restrictions on Electras that hobbled Eastern's ability to compete with Woolman's DC-8s and CV-880s. Pilots wearing the Delta widget liked to tell passengers to look out their windows at one of Eastern's lumbering Electras as they zoomed past them amid cheers and guffaws. Ironically, Eddie could have had the DC-8s used by Delta but decided to wait for a later model with more powerful engines.[58]

Rickenbacker, spending increasing amounts of time in ideological activities, had resigned as president of Eastern as the jet era opened, giving the position in 1953 to longtime subordinate Thomas F. Armstrong and elevating himself to chairman of the board. Armstrong was merely a loyal figurehead and Rickenbacker continued making important decisions. He had never intended for Armstrong to be president indefinitely because he still hoped William, who was not interested, would become CEO. In 1958 Armstrong stepped down to executive vice president, and Eastern's directors, frustrated by strikes and problems attending the transition to jets, appointed Malcolm MacIntyre, a lawyer who had been undersecretary of the Air Force, to succeed him as president and chief executive officer. Rickenbacker would supposedly continue to chair the board and respect MacIntyre's authority.

Despite the new man's status as CEO Rickenbacker could not give up the control he had wielded for so long and interfered with MacIntyre's attempts to run the company. Eastern's executive hierarchy became split as old-timers took orders from Rickenbacker and newer appointees obeyed MacIntyre. Using aging Constellations, MacIntyre created a shuttle service between Boston, New York, and Washington that guaranteed a seat to anybody who showed up for a flight, even if it meant flying with a single passenger. The innovation was extremely popular and financially profitable, but Eddie opposed it. Arguments between the two executives, both heavy drinkers, sometimes came close to fisticuffs.[59]

One incident above all showed how much Eddie's judgment was deteriorating. Over the years, airmen who had fought in World War I had held reunions of their old units. Responding to an initiative taken by Royal D. Frey of the Air Force Central Museum (now the United States Air Force Museum), Rickenbacker sponsored a preliminary meeting in New York City to plan a grand reunion of all surviving members of the American Air Service in World War I at Wright-Patterson Air Force Base. Together they would form a single organization, and create an Air Force Museum Foundation. At the time, more than 1,200 American veterans of the world's first air war were still alive. After lengthy preparations, 340, along with 200 wives, gathered at Dayton, Ohio, on 24 June 1961. In the next few days, enthusiasm mounted to form a Reunion

Association and an Organizing Committee worked far into the night to prepare a charter to present at a final banquet. Five hundred copies were on the tables by dinner time. After the meal prominent dignitaries gave welcoming addresses and the charter came up for discussion. Naturally, Rickenbacker gave a speech.

Instead of talking about the proposed charter, and oblivious to the fact that he was preaching to the choir, he gave what James J. Sloan, an organizer of the function, called a "diatribe" about the evils of communism and the "treasonous" nature of the incoming Kennedy administration. The speech was interminable, lasting almost an hour and a half. Nearly 600 persons were in the hall when Eddie began speaking. Fewer than 50 remained when he stopped. At one point, when a group got up to leave and Rickenbacker tried to wave them back, a member thumbed his nose at the Ace of Aces. Most of the veterans and their wives went home the next day. A few organizers tried to mobilize what spirit remained for passing the charter but decided it was useless to try.[60]

At about the same time Eastern took a devastating blow in a hotly contested transcontinental route case. Having no routes west of Texas, it had desperately needed to win the proceeding to make efficient use of its aircraft on long-haul transcontinental routes. Instead, the CAB gave Delta and National access to San Diego, Los Angeles, San Francisco, and other western cities while denying Eastern's application. Rickenbacker did not help Eastern's chances by giving a scathing speech in Atlanta attacking president-elect Kennedy before the board handed down its decision.

After the loss, Laurance Rockefeller decided that the only way out was a merger with American, the nation's second-largest carrier after United. Rockefeller wanted to obtain the managerial expertise of C. R. Smith, who was in the twilight of his brilliant career but had powerful connections in Washington through his friendship with Vice President Johnson. Smith came to Rockefeller's office and personally negotiated the details of the merger, but the need for the CAB to approve it aborted the plan. Led by Delta, the rest of the industry attacked the proposal on the grounds that it would create a gigantic enterprise, stifling competition. During the battle, Delta's legal team, led by Maurer, received anonymous tips containing damaging information from disgruntled Eastern employees, showing how badly the war between MacIntyre and Rickenbacker was undermining morale. The case never reached a final decision because it became clear that President Kennedy's brother,

Robert, acting in his capacity as attorney general, would turn thumbs down on the merger on antitrust grounds even if the CAB approved it. The death of the attempt only made things worse, convincing many experts to believe that Eastern's plight was hopeless. Directors who did not want to fire a living legend who had outlived his usefulness wondered what alternative was available.[61]

Chapter 21

— ☆ —

End Game

In 1962, needing a vacation, Eddie took Adelaide to the Far East and Southwest Pacific.[1] Leaving New York on 17 July, they flew to Seattle on a Northwest jetliner. From Seattle the same carrier, which had fulfilled Hunter's aspirations for a northern Great Circle route and was now unofficially known as Northwest-Orient, took them to Anchorage, Shemya, and Tokyo, avoiding Soviet territory. Adelaide wrote a detailed account of the places they visited in Japan, saying its people seemed to "worship General MacArthur." Eddie was greatly impressed by the progress of a people he had earlier called subhuman and later issued a press release proclaiming Japan a coming superpower.[2]

After spending almost two weeks in Japan, they flew to Taiwan, where Chiang Kai-Shek, whom Eddie had loathed in World War II, was heading a government-in-exile. From Taipei the Rickenbackers flew to Hong Kong, where refugees crowded the Crown Colony, still a bastion of the British Empire. By this time Eddie's muscles were cramping so badly he needed osteopathic treatment. Cathay Airways flew them to Bangkok, after which they took Philippine Airlines to Manila, and Eddie inspected Clark Air Force Base.

They took an all-night flight to Sydney on Qantas and proceeded to Melbourne. "Here they have a socialist state, and everybody tries to get on the government payroll," Eddie wrote disapprovingly. "You can imagine a country larger than the United States with resources equivalent to ours 100 years ago. . . . If Australia should ever change to the free enterprise or the incentive way of life, it would be a fantastic development and a great opportunity for young men from any part of the world." In New Zealand they visited Wellington and Auckland and admired the scenery, but he criticized the government, saying that the country was "a welfare state in every sense of the word" and that "young people had no ambition." Auckland's airport was not yet ready for jets, so they took a Pan American DC-7 to Fiji, where they got red-carpet treatment.

The trip now became nostalgic for Eddie. From Fiji they went to American Samoa and visited the hospital where he had recuperated from his raft ordeal. He saw the room in which he had spent ten days recovering from dehydration and malnutrition. After a smooth flight they landed by special request at Canton Island, the elusive target of Eddie's flight from Hickam Field. "Fortunately now they have all the aids in the world on that little atoll," he noted. "We could see the beacon for 75 miles before we reached it." After they landed on a gravel runway Eddie "finally put my foot on the island, and satisfied my twenty year pledge." Canton was now a tracking station for satellites launched in Project Mercury, and he heard a recording of a conversation with John Glenn as he was orbiting above the atoll. After a rough flight to Hawaii, he and Adelaide saw buildings at Hickam Field still scarred by Japanese-inflicted bullet holes and visited the USS *Arizona* memorial.

Airline officials and aircraft manufacturers entertained them throughout their trip. Eddie was amazed by how many old friends greeted him. When they returned to Seattle, Boeing briefed him about a three-engine 727 "Whisperjet" Eastern had ordered. Two months after the trip began, they were back in New York in a happy frame of mind.

But time was running out for Rickenbacker at Eastern. After the failed merger attempt with American, Rockefeller decided change was imperative and appointed four directors to a search committee to hunt for a new CEO. Rickenbacker and MacIntyre did not know what was happening. The committee found its man in Floyd D. Hall, who had risen from the ranks of TWA's pilots to become senior vice president and general system manager. Hall was a protégé of Ernie Breech, who had become chairman of the board at TWA. After leaving Eastern in 1938, Breech had become president of GM's Bendix Aviation subsidiary and helped Henry Ford II rebuild the Ford Motor Company after World War II. Recognizing Hall's talents, Breech was grooming him to take command of TWA after a legal battle was resolved with Hughes, whose stockholdings had been put in a voting trust after he ran up debts on jet aircraft he could not pay. Hall was virtually running TWA while Breech and the airline's president, Charles Tillinghast, spent most of their time fighting Hughes.

Hall was reluctant to give up a bright future with TWA, but as the struggle with Hughes continued unabated, he saw Eastern as a challenge hard to resist. Breech gave him a final push by telling him "nothing is going to satisfy you until you get a chance to take some downtrodden company and put it on its feet. As badly as we'd hate to see you go, and believe me, we don't want you to leave, take Eastern up on their offer." Hall followed Breech's advice.[3]

Meanwhile, soon after returning from his vacation, Rickenbacker dropped a bomb at a board meeting in New York by revealing he had secretly sold 100,000 shares of Eastern stock. It is unclear why he made this damaging admission, which shocked Rockefeller and other directors. Perhaps he was merely manifesting his penchant for being too forthright for his own good, but he may also have wanted to show his lack of confidence in MacIntyre. He had reached a point, he said, where he could no longer keep all of his eggs in the same basket because he could "see too many damned holes in the basket." MacIntyre was livid with rage and demanded to know after the meeting how much money Rickenbacker had made from the sale. "None of your goddamned business!" Eddie snapped. Dumbfounded by what they had just learned, some directors overheard the angry exchange.[4]

Not knowing that a new CEO was waiting in the wings to replace MacIntyre, Rickenbacker did not realize he had sealed his doom by admitting his lack of faith in Eastern's future. Firing MacIntyre, who took the news as a "bitter blow," the directors decided that Eddie had to go too. Hall had not made Rickenbacker's retirement a condition for taking his new position but had made it equally clear that he intended to run the airline. Considering the feuding that had happened in recent years, the directors thought it best to free Hall of the complications likely to occur as long as Rickenbacker continued chairing the board of a carrier in whose future he no longer believed. Having deep regard for Rickenbacker despite his errors and knowing everything he had meant to the company he had built, none of the directors wanted to force him out but reached a consensus that it had to be done.[5]

Rickenbacker soon received an invitation to a meeting at the Hampshire House, a plush hotel on Central Park South where Frederick Turner, a retired telephone executive who had chaired the search committee, had a suite of rooms. All four committee members were waiting when Eddie arrived, an hour and a half late. Probably sensing the purpose of the meeting, he had been drinking. When the directors asked him to retire for the good of the company, he flew into a rage. Elkins, a director from Houston, recalled how Eddie lashed out at each person present, telling them he had built Eastern into a giant among airlines from shaky foundations, that he *was* Eastern, and that he would not bow out voluntarily. A second meeting, again at the Hampshire House, had to take place not long afterward to persuade Rickenbacker to accept the inevitable. This time only two men—Laurance Rockefeller and his chief business manager, Harper Woodward—met with Eddie. Having no choice but to yield to their wishes, he capitulated.[6]

He did so gracefully, sending a teletyped message to "all members of the Eastern Air Lines family," stating, "Today Floyd Hall takes over as president and chief executive officer. . . . We are fortunate to have the services of one of the industry's outstanding young leaders." The announcement said Hall had begun as a pilot—indicating the importance Rickenbacker attached to that distinction—and had, "through study and application, worked his way up through the ranks," another factor that counted heavily in Eddie's estimation. "He thus combines vision with practical 'shirt-sleeves' experience in every phase of modern airline operation, marketing, and management, and is still not afraid of getting a little grease on his hands"—probably a slap at MacIntyre but high praise from a man who had begun his career by learning automotive engineering on the job. "I ask all of you—you youngsters who had more recently joined our ranks as well as you veterans who helped me build Eastern Airlines through the years—I ask all of you to give Floyd Hall the same full measure of loyalty and cooperation you always gave me in the past." Coupled with a statement about Rickenbacker's retirement as chairman of the board, it was a gracious way to go. The signature, "Captain Eddie Rickenbacker," had an endearing quality that his customary sign-off, "Edward V. Rickenbacker" would have lacked. He exited with class.

After passing the torch, he left his suite at 16 Rockefeller Plaza and never entered the building again.[7]

Eastern gave Rickenbacker a suite on the twenty-third floor at 45 Rockefeller Plaza and a chauffeur-driven Cadillac to bring him there in the morning and take him home at night. The door was unmarked. Shepherd had an outer room, working with two secretaries. Rickenbacker's office was "huge," an interviewer stated, estimating it was twenty feet long, "with a giant desk at one end, a ten-foot table crowded with framed autographed photographs and awards—cups and bronze figures and airplanes—at the other." Half a dozen armchairs were scattered here and there. Behind Rickenbacker was "a table piled high with books sent to him or which he had purchased and which he says he has read or is going to read but he hasn't and he isn't." On its surface was a carafe of water from which he drank voraciously with a thirst he could never quench, a residual effect of the dehydration he had suffered in the raft episode. Beyond the table were windows overlooking the Plaza's ice-skating rink and open-air restaurant. Whatever papers he was working on went into his briefcase at the end of the day. Taking them home, he left his desktop clear, showing his lifelong passion for neatness and order.[8]

Freedom from Eastern gave Rickenbacker more time to crusade against "modern liberalism," which, in his view, had replaced the "true liberalism" of individual freedom and initiative. After becoming disenchanted with Eisenhower's brand of Republicanism, and dismayed by the election of Kennedy and Johnson, he had begun calling himself a "conservative" even though he disliked some nuances of the term.

In 1961 he had given a speech, "Conservatism Must Face Up to Liberalism," to the Chicago Economic Club, setting forth the political and economic doctrines in which he believed. Properly speaking, he was closer to being a libertarian but adopted the term "conservative" because it had gained currency across a broad spectrum of political and economic opinion that strongly disapproved of what had happened in America since the onset of the New Deal. His presentation was anchored in Barry Goldwater's book, *The Conscience of a Conservative*, which had been published in 1960 and had a great impact on him. Recognizing his lack of scholarly qualifications, Rickenbacker approached the speech with trepidation, wondering whether members of the intellectually high-powered organization that sponsored it would be interested in what he had to say or prepared for the "challenging, aggressive" way in which he intended to say it. To his surprise, despite "a miserable evening, with snow and sleet," a large crowd of more than 1,000 people gathered to hear him, interrupted him repeatedly with applause, and gave him a standing ovation lasting four minutes.

Rickenbacker's theme was that "modern liberals" had forsaken the tenets inherent in the original meaning of "liberalism," which, as its name implied, was rooted in the concept of human liberty. "Instead of advocating freedom," Rickenbacker declared, modern liberals were "striving to pile up the power of government in Washington." Fortunately, however, a rising tide of opposition was gaining momentum across the land to "resist the encroachment of Federal power." The *Chicago Tribune* published his manifesto in its entirety and a flood of requests for reprints resulted.[9]

On 7 June 1961 Rickenbacker covered some of the same ideas in a speech to the New York Chamber of Commerce. Because of the failure of the recent "Bay of Pigs" invasion, he began with a scathing attack on American policy in Cuba, denying that the term "Cold War" aptly described the conflict in which the United States had been engaged since World War II. He decried Kennedy's failure to enforce the Monroe Doctrine by pledging not to invade Cuba if the USSR removed its missiles. "The world will not respect our rights until we show the world that we shall defend them," he declared. On the other hand, he said that Castro had not created the situation confronting the United States, which had begun "twenty-eight years ago when we recognized a handful of bandits as the lawful government of Russia"—an ironic statement from a man who had ingratiated himself with Litvinov and Molotov in 1943, had wanted Stalin to have a free hand in Eastern Europe, and had dreamed about friendship with the Soviet Union in a bipolar world. Now he charged that America had gone astray because "flaming liberals had just come to power in this country"—a reference to FDR and the New Deal—"and they knew that they could not consolidate their power if the Communist Revolution in Russia collapsed." Ever since the United States had recognized the USSR, "liberals have controlled our foreign policy for the purpose of establishing Liberalism as the dominant theme of our Federal government."

Most of his speech, however, extended what he had already said in Chicago, proclaiming that "modern liberalism" was giving way to a "conservative" movement that had begun to sweep the nation. Even in 1960, despite Kennedy's victory, conservatives had won two seats in the Senate, 20 in the House of Representatives, and about 300 in state legislatures. Goldwater's book had sold almost a million copies. The Young Americans for Freedom had more than 25,000 members on at least 200 campuses. "The battle line has been drawn between two irreconcilable views of government" Eddie proclaimed. "Although the modern liberals derive their name from the Latin word for freedom, their actions and goals have consistently tended to increase the power of the central government. The modern conservatives take individual liberty as their battle cry for they know that individual liberty is imperiled when the government attains unlimited power." He was playing a prophetic role, anticipating the rise of a conservative movement that survived Goldwater's defeat, triumphed when the "Reagan Revolution" created new centers of power in the media, and ultimately reelected George W. Bush in 2004.

Rickenbacker appealed to history to substantiate his claim that modern liberals had hijacked the true meaning of "liberalism." The nation's founders, he said, were "liberals in the true freedom loving sense of the word . . . in their zeal for liberty, they feared the powers of government," which they had surrounded with "a web of limits, checks, balances, and controls." He quoted Washington's statement that: "Government is like fire: a dangerous servant and a fearful master." Every early state constitution, he pointed out, had hedged government with restrictions. Now, "by some queer twist of language, the modern liberals are those who ceaselessly strive to pile up the power of government." His message articulated themes that later became common among neoconservatives: curb the federal government, return power back to the states, and privatize the economy. Modern liberals, he said, had embraced one form of conservatism—conservation of natural resources—but they had "systematically depleted the most precious resource in this nation's inheritance, namely, American freedom."

Echoing Goldwater, Rickenbacker declared that "Freedom is not a physical object. It is a spiritual and a moral environment. . . . The evil of liberalism is its emphasis on material things and its disdain for the spiritual and moral resources that we call liberty. The liberals would sweep aside the Constitutional restraints upon government in a blind rush to supply food, clothes, houses and financial security from birth to death, from the cradle to the grave for everybody." Modern liberals viewed people collectively; conservatives viewed them individually. "The conservative knows that to regard man as a part of an undifferentiated mass is to consign him to ultimate slavery." He again turned to the Founding Fathers, in this case Jefferson and Madison, by stressing the concept, enshrined in the Tenth Amendment in the Bill of Rights and the Virginia and Kentucky resolutions: that the states and the people had delegated powers given to the federal government under the Constitution. "Every time the liberals discover a brand new misinterpretation of the Constitution, every time they invent a new way to circumvent the Constitutional limits of the Federal power," he said, "they pile up more power in Washington at the expense of individual liberty across the land."

Continuing his historical analysis, he asserted that "When Woodrow Wilson told us of the evils of concentrated power, less than 9% of our entire national income was enough to keep all of the Federal and Local governments going." By contrast, in 1960, taxes took "one-third of all of our earnings, and the Federal Government took, controlled and spent 70% of that." Reciting these statistics led Rickenbacker to advocate repealing the Sixteenth Amendment, ironically adopted during Wilson's presidency. Because the principle of income taxes had been enshrined in the Constitution, "the entire gross income of every American is subject to complete Federal confiscation. You have your brackets, exemptions, write-offs, and deductions purely by the grace of Congress. You do not have these protections as a matter of constitutional right. Conservatism must begin the restoration of the American Republic by knocking the 16th Amendment right out of the Constitution. Faint hearts will say that it is impossible but faint hearts thought the American Revolution was impossible too." He ended his speech declaring that "The time is late, the hour is here and it is up to us, the people, you and me."[10]

Despite his rhetoric, Rickenbacker discerned threats to liberty not only from the Left but also from the Right. Like Goldwater, he spurned membership in the John Birch Society, founded in the 1950s by Robert Welch, who had accused Eisenhower of being "either a dupe or a conscious agent of worldwide communism." A deluge of letters from Welch's associates merely increased Rickenbacker's firmness. "If I were a member of any organization or society, I am sure that they would try to cut me in half," he said. "As it is, they cannot touch me."[11]

Despite rejecting the John Birch Society, Rickenbacker had new associates and sought out unaccustomed audiences. He found Billy Ray Hargis, a fire-breathing Oklahoma evangelist, a more suitable ally than Peale in his anti-Communist crusade. Whereas he had previously had little or no respect for the views of women, he now reached out to them because they controlled much of America's wealth, mostly in fixed incomes from pensions and annuities less vulnerable to taxation. He was pleased when women told him they were alarmed by what he said, replying that his main goal was stimulating them to take action. When they asked what to do to help, he urged them to study issues he posed and disseminate his beliefs among their neighbors. He changed in other ways. Having earlier spoken gratis, he began accepting honoraria for his speeches, dividing the proceeds between eight organizations to which he had long been devoted: the Boys' Athletic League; the Boys' Club of

New York; the Children's Village of Dobbs Ferry, New York; the Madison Square Boys' Club; the Boys' Clubs of America; the Big Brothers of America; the Gramercy Boys' Club; and the Boy Scouts of America.[12]

One thing that did not change was Rickenbacker's zest for foreign travel, which he and Adelaide shared. On 2 April 1964 they left New York City to go to Europe and Africa.[13] After they landed in Rome, an executive in Al Italia Airlines drove them to their hotel. Knowledgeable people had warned Eddie that the highway on which they would travel was hazardous because of undisciplined Italian drivers and lax law enforcement. Soon after the Rickenbackers left the airport with their host, they came to an intersection where the driver of a small Fiat tried to cut between the vehicle in which they were riding and the one in front of it. In the resulting collision the Fiat flew into the air, turned over, and ejected a woman who hit the pavement so hard she died instantly, after which "the little car landed upside down on the driver [who] . . . was crushed like an eggshell." Eddie escaped unharmed, but Adelaide's legs were gouged by jagged metal, requiring plastic surgery and skin grafts. After being hospitalized for more than two weeks, she needed eight more days of rest. Rickenbacker managed to avoid publicity about the accident, and her name did not appear in the press. For the moment, however, they had to stay put.

While stranded in Rome they were saddened to learn that Douglas MacArthur, to whom Rickenbacker paid tribute as "one of the most brilliant strategists and generals in all of our history," had died. They were also gravely concerned about the health of Herbert Hoover, who had contracted pneumonia and had a kidney hemorrhage in February, not long before they left New York, but seemed to be bouncing back.[14]

As Adelaide convalesced, Sheppy Shepherd and Curtis Le May, chief of the Strategic Air Command, rearranged their itinerary, during which they had intended to visit officers and personnel at air bases. Because of the time lost in Italy, they also decided not to go to Istanbul. After Adelaide was ready, they flew instead from Rome to Cairo. A military attaché gave them a flight over the Aswan Dam, being built by the USSR because the United States had backed out of the project. Seeing 3,000 Russian technicians "doing a fantastic job," Rickenbacker, disregarding his views about federal spending, denounced the State Department for withdrawing over a cost differential of $25 million, "which is a pittance when compared to the billions we have thrown away in Egypt and other places around the world." Informants had told him that Gamal Abd-Al-Nasser, after overthrowing King Farouk in 1952, had wanted the United States to build the dam but American blundering had driven him to the Soviets, giving them "an open door to all of Africa."

From Cairo the Rickenbackers flew to Nairobi, where dignitaries who hosted them said that long-established residents were fleeing Kenya because the British were about to give it independence and turn it over to forces led by Jomo Kenyatta, who had "murdered many of the white farmers and ranch owners." Instead of hailing the collapse of the British Empire in Africa, which might have been expected after his "World Mission" in 1943, Rickenbacker fumed that thirty-seven former European colonies were gaining nationhood a century before they were ready for it.

He kept up with news from home. In Nairobi a message William had sent to Cairo caught up with him, asking that he send a heartening telegram to Barry Goldwater, who was seeking the Republican presidential nomination and would soon hold a rally in New York City. Rickenbacker sent the wire as soon as he and Adelaide reached Johannesburg, and it reached Goldwater three days before the event. Shepherd reported that 18,000 people had been present and heard the Arizona senator give a "wonderful speech" ending with a standing ovation. She also said that Eddie's telegram, read aloud before the speech, received "the greatest applause next to Goldwater."

Stopping at Salisbury on their way to Johannesburg, the Rickenbackers heard more talk about racial strife in Africa. Eddie wrote that what was then Southern Rhodesia possessed "unlimited resources and potential, but there are not enough whites to create and develop the country." Despite his forebodings, he and Adelaide enjoyed overflying Victoria Falls at low altitude, going up the Zambezi River with a native guide, and picnicking on an island that made them feel "as though we were a million miles from nowhere." Adelaide continued having checkups and treatments as the trip progressed and seemed to be making good progress.

Because of residual pain from her injuries, however, they decided not to visit Great Zimbabwe and proceeded to Johannesburg. On Adelaide's birthday they drove through a nearby game preserve and watched a lioness stalk an impala, kill it, and drag it by the neck into the brush. Rickenbacker spoke in Johannesburg to several hundred Americans and Afrikaners, offering his opinions on international affairs. His speech delighted the audience, which was intent on maintaining apartheid and felt increasingly threatened by the outside world. That evening the American consul general held a reception for the visitors, attended mostly by industrialists. Flying from Johannesburg to Cape Town the next day, Eddie and Adelaide crossed the Kimberley Diamond Mines, which had closed down during World War II and were still inactive pending the installment of a new pumping system. Parliament was in session and the capital was crowded with officials who came to a reception given in honor of the Rickenbackers by the American ambassador. Asked about impressions he had gathered during his trip, Eddie said he believed South Africa had been misrepresented in the United States and that its vast resources offered enormous prospects for future investment but that persons of European descent faced being massacred and driven into the Indian Ocean by a rising tide of black nationalism. He said to the audience that "their only hope was to make a stand and fight." A government official praised him "in glowing terms for my insight into their problems and future and stated they had never met any foreigner who had been in the country only two or three days who knew even one hundredth of what I was able to state." Rickenbacker replied that giving native peoples premature control of Africa would make them "worse off than they have ever been before."

Eddie toured General Motors, Ford, Firestone, and Goodrich factories. At a GM assembly plant he was glad to see that the employees, most of whom were African natives, worked "like Americans used to work." When he asked Firestone officials about their problems, they told him the worst one they faced was "America's sticking their damn nose into our business." After a brief visit to Durban, they returned to Johannesburg and boarded a Lufthansa airliner bound for Frankfurt. During part of the trip the cockpit crew invited Rickenbacker to sit at the controls. "All told it was a beautiful flight," he wrote.

Adelaide slept soundly but her back was hurting when they got to West Germany. Eddie took her to a hospital at Wiesbaden for treatments that did not completely relieve her discomfort but improved her condition. He learned that Goldwater had won a narrow victory in a Republican primary in California but feared his margin of victory over Nelson Rockefeller was "entirely too close for comfort." He also scorned West Germany's "socialistic government. Nobody works on Saturdays or Sundays if they possibly can help it and that is I mean nobody. That goes for every holiday and they have many." Sooner or later the country would "fall apart" if things did not change.

Adelaide felt well enough for them to go to Austria, where they drove through the Vienna Woods, saw the Lipizzaner stallions, and bought a china replica of one of the horses as a Christmas present for Shepherd. Despite Adelaide's injury, the trip was harkening back to their 1922 European honeymoon. Returning to Germany, they visited Munich and continued via Air France to West Berlin, where Eddie met two pilots who had served with the "Flying Circus" during World War I. They enjoyed discussing their experiences and comparing the planes in which they had flown. Taking a helicopter ride, Eddie saw a mound covering the bunker where Hitler "was supposed to have died." He doubted the event had happened as reported and thought *der Führer* might still be alive.

He heard that von Richthofen, Boelcke, and Udet were buried in a graveyard in East Berlin. Taken through Checkpoint Charlie by East German guides, he managed with great persistence—after visiting seven police stations—to get there. Massive locked gates barred the entrance, but he prevailed on a guard to summon the keeper of the facility, with whom he got along so well that he received a tour ending in front of a monument to the Red Baron adorned with nothing but "Richthofen" in large letters. Boelcke's grave had a small headstone, but Udet's had merely a plaque giving minimal information about Eddie's friend, who had mismanaged Nazi aircraft procurement. When Rickenbacker inquired why Udet did not get more notice, his escort said he had disgraced the Luftwaffe and killed himself. The driver of the car in which they were traveling took surreptitious snapshots of Eddie paying his respects to the flyers, but they turned out "so badly blurred as to be useless."

Rickenbacker had not expected "to see how healthy the East Germans looked. They seemed to be well-fed, including the children; fairly well clothed, but they are frustrated-looking." West Berliners told him the Wall gave them a feeling of security from being invaded by East Germany but regretted that it had cut off an influx of skilled people wanting to escape to the West. Before leaving Berlin, he and Adelaide enjoyed a reception aboard a yacht sailing on a lake dividing the two parts of the city. On the western side were "hundreds of thousands of West Berliners—men, women, and children—on the beaches . . . who were enjoying a typical Jones Beach holiday in New York City." On the east side, beyond a line of buoys, were barbed wire, guards, and no bathers. Eddie called East Germany and East Berlin "the greatest concentration camp the world has ever known."

On 15 June the Rickenbackers boarded a Pan American plane for

Hamburg, from where SAS gave them "a perfectly beautiful ride across the Atlantic in a luxurious DC-8 jet with outstanding service." Shepherd was waiting for them at Kennedy Airport late that afternoon, and they took her to dinner at the Regency Hotel, a fine climax for a trip lasting about ten weeks and "full of thrills and excitement," but Eddie worried that Russian and Chinese Communists would divide Africa between them and that the white inhabitants of the continent would be liquidated. In the future, he believed, four great powers would dominate the world: Japan, China, Russia, and a combination of Western Europe and the two Americas—which, if they had foresight, would cling for dear life to South Africa as the last remaining stronghold of free enterprise south of the Sahara.

Goldwater's crushing defeat by Johnson in the 1964 presidential election made Rickenbacker all the more determined to speak his mind. He was particularly incensed about Castro's continuing hold on Cuba, still believing that Kennedy should have removed him from power during the 1962 missile crisis and had violated the Monroe Doctrine by compromising with Khrushchev. In Eddie's estimation, Kennedy had "pulled defeat out of the jaws of victory" by rejecting the advice of hawks like Dean Acheson, McGeorge Bundy, Senators Russell and Fulbright, Curtis Le May, and CIA director John A. McCone, thereby permitting a Communist dictatorship allied with the USSR to remain a base ninety miles from Florida from which to expand Soviet influence throughout the Western Hemisphere. Rickenbacker became a close ally of Dean Clarence Manion of Notre Dame University, who advocated enforcing the Monroe Doctrine by getting rid of Castro through any and all means. Eddie also opposed the Vietnam War as a tragic blunder by Lyndon B. Johnson—the wrong conflict in the wrong place, soaking up immense amounts of money and manpower to perpetuate the mess left behind by the French Empire, which he continued to detest. Why fight a hopeless war in a remote part of the world, he asked, and refrain from military action to remove a much more dangerous menace on America's doorstep? "The obvious solution in Southeast Asia," he thought, would be "for us—the Westerners, the white men, to get out of there." Ultimately Japan, or a Japanese-Chinese alliance, should manage Asia for the benefit of Asians. Despite feeling that the war in Vietnam was a waste of blood and treasure, he condemned campus radicals protesting the conflict, saying they should be drafted into the armed services and given a taste of discipline.[15]

In 1964 Rickenbacker decided to publish an autobiography, not merely to recount his achievements but also to defend his values. He signed an agreement with Booton Herndon, a freelance journalist from Charlottesville, Virginia, who had already produced many such works for other people, to ghostwrite the book. Because Herndon had written two volumes about the Air Force and a memoir of Fulton Lewis Jr., Eddie assumed he had a conservative orientation. In fact, Herndon was a liberal Democrat who disagreed with Rickenbacker's political and economic views but accepted the assignment as a challenge to write a work about a person he believed to be a real American hero.

Rickenbacker chose Prentice-Hall as his publisher because it had a long list of textbooks used in schools. Herndon received a $25,000 advance on royalties—Rickenbacker got $125,000—and signed an agreement stipulating that his role in the project would be strictly anonymous, with only a statement by Eddie expressing "My appreciation to Booton Herndon for his editorial assistance." Rickenbacker also required that Herndon do no independent research for the book, relying only on information and interviews Eddie would give him.

Determined to preserve as much of his record as possible, he rented a tape recorder and relentlessly dictated into it endless copies of speeches, letters, texts of broadcasts, magazine articles, and other things that had been written by or about him. He ordered that an original typed transcript and three carbon copies be made of these documents, which Herndon thought absurd. All of Herndon's interviews with Eddie were similarly taped and transcribed, yielding a mass of material estimated at 2 million words, of which Herndon thought 1.5 million were unnecessary. "Rickenbacker, an uneducated man, reads slowly and haltingly," Herndon observed, "and as a result he spent the better part of a year reading into a mike from nine to five. Don't feel sorry for him, though. Even at 75 he had the energy, and he had the money, too." Eddie kept the originals, gave two copies to the Smithsonian Institution and the United States Air Force Museum, and a final copy to Herndon, who complained it was "often a smeary mess."[16]

Living with relatives in suburban New Jersey, Herndon spent much of the spring and summer of 1965 coming to Rickenbacker's office at 10:00 a.m., taking off an hour for lunch, and returning until 4:45 p.m. He dreaded the sessions because Eddie was abrasive, evasive, and at times insulting. (He also did not refrain from telling outright lies, as when he told Herndon he had written *Fighting the Flying Circus* by himself, with only minimal editorial help from the publisher.) "Though he can be warm and ingratiating," Herndon later wrote, "he is a competitive and aggressive individual who occasionally flies off the handle into bursts of hysterical fury. He is an egomaniac who considers most of us mortals to be beneath him and doesn't hide it. . . . A screaming battle was a kind of emotional cathartic; he felt better afterwards. Me, I hate that kind of thing. I cringe." He worked out his frustration at the end of each day by going to the New York Athletic Club, where he would "sweat it out, then dive in the pool and churn up and down, exhausting the adrenalin." Things got particularly nasty in late July when Rickenbacker thought some of Herndon's questions about his trip to the Soviet Union irrelevant. At one point he got so bitter at Eddie that he turned to leave the office but reconsidered before he got to the door, thinking, "Who would win if I walked out—he or I?" After that point he "never lost sight of the fact that he was an authentic hero with a story to tell, and that I was a dedicated journalist with the mission to tell it." In his mind, "My victory would be in finishing the job and writing this book. I did. That son of a bitch could not keep me from writing this book extolling him as a hero. I won."

Rickenbacker closely scrutinized every word of the book, arguing even about commas and semicolons. However agonizing the process had been Herndon had no cause for complaint about the financial results. By the end of 1968 the book had sold more than 250,000 copies in hardback. Reaching the top of the best-seller lists in eight weeks, it stayed there almost four times that long. "It was Prentice-Hall's biggest money maker of the '67–'68 season," Herndon said, and "the choice of the Literary Guild and several other smaller book clubs." Condensed versions appeared in *True* and *Reader's Digest*. "In addition to the money I have received and will receive," Herndon wrote after earning an initial $50,000, "my professional reputation has been greatly enhanced. It was not only a financial success, but a literary one; reviews have generally been excellent, and only one was bad. Although my name is buried, through prior agreement, everyone in publishing circles knows I wrote it, and, further, gives me full credit for surmounting the difficulties involved."[17]

Rickenbacker stimulated sales by buying large numbers of copies, autographing them, and giving them to libraries, believing that making them available to students would help perpetuate his ideas about the American way of life. He also used the book as a vehicle to gratify his continued zest for predicting the future. The final chapter belied his self-definition as a conservative, being a manifesto of change dealing with the power of technology, allied with individualism and capitalism, to transform the world and penetrate the farthest reaches of outer space. He envisioned hypersonic planes carrying passengers, mail, and freight at 2,000, 4,000, ultimately 25,000 miles per hour. He believed mass aerial transportation at such speeds would help prepare aboriginal and African peoples for full integration into a worldwide family of nations on an equal basis.

Possibly because of the animosity he felt toward Kennedy and Johnson, he was unenthusiastic about the moon race between the United States and the Soviet Union. He thought the Russians should be permitted to win it if they could, predicting that they would bankrupt themselves in the process. He believed the United States should concentrate on orbiting rocket ships that could deliver atomic destruction to its enemies if necessary. He envisioned shuttles blasting off to reach orbiting space stations from which they would be launched on voyages of interplanetary and intergalactic voyages of exploration and discovery. Nuclear-propelled space vehicles would provide passenger, cargo, and mail service to the far reaches of the solar system. Land and sea transportation would be transformed by high-speed monorail systems—he had already ridden a prototype in Seattle—and giant vessels would travel across oceans on "cushions of air."

He predicted computers would regulate vast transportation systems and automobile travel could be rendered accident-proof by remote control. He thought the time would come when all the world's banks would be connected by televised data systems and that electronic scanning would permit huge sums of money to be transferred anywhere in split seconds of time. He foresaw that fossil fuels would ultimately be gone and feared internal combustion engines would seriously damage the earth's atmosphere. The remedy, he thought, was nuclear energy, which would provide a viable means of limitless growth. The power locked in the atom would desalinize seawater and reclaim vast stretches of arid land for agricultural abundance. Fusion would harness the world's oceans, making it possible to mine the seas for endless quantities of minerals. He envisioned enormous progress in electronic communications, but, as a longtime admirer of Professor J. B. Rhine of Duke University, believed that telepathic contact would be an even more effective way to transmit information. He thought of the universe as a vast repository of information that could never be lost and was merely waiting to be accessed. He considered it possible that everything that had ever been thought still existed and was waiting to be regained and interpreted. Humans merely needed to learn how to "tune in."

He believed racial differences would determine the politics of the future and that peace was achievable only by respecting the right of people of various races to control the parts of the earth where they naturally predominated. North and South America, Europe, and Russia would form a culture bloc confronting the rest of the earth, though not necessarily in a warlike manner. His visions in 1943 had not disappeared but merely awaited the end of communism. In the not-far-distant future, Russia would embrace capitalism and become a friend of the United States. Despite the convictions he had expressed in Africa, he predicted that racial minorities would continue to be loyal to America and thought the concept of the melting pot valid, given enough time to materialize. That African Americans might outnumber whites seemed not to trouble him as long as the values he believed in remained dominant.[18]

However wide-ranging his travels, Rickenbacker knew where he wanted to live. He had fallen too much in love with New York City to call anywhere else home. His favorite haunt was the 21 Club, where he had lunch with Hall at the beginning of each month. Ultimately their meetings became less frequent as Eddie's health declined and Hall became increasingly preoccupied with Eastern's affairs. Whenever they met, Hall told Eddie about Eastern's progress and future plans, but only for informational purposes. "I just told him how we were doing," Hall remarked, "and he never offered advice. He never said one word to me about how to run the airline."[19]

Florida ranked second among Rickenbacker's favorite places, partly because he had done so much to transform it during his years promoting tourism and the expansion of airline service to the Sunshine State. A Rickenbacker Causeway connecting Miami with Key Biscayne had already been named for him, but Hall conceived yet another way to honor his memory by enlarging a projected fountain in front of one of Eastern's office buildings in Miami and dedicating it to Rickenbacker. "I wanted to do something for Eddie that people would remember," he said. "I told him I wanted to have a better fountain than what they were going to put out there. I named it the Rickenbacker Fountain and had a bronze cast made of Captain Eddie and we invited him to come down and attend the dedication. We had a big dinner and . . . many employ-ees came from all over to attend the ceremony." Hall recalled that he "really had to twist Rickenbacker's arm to get him to come . . . he said to me, 'why are you building a monument to me? I ain't dead yet,'" to which Hall replied, "Well, I want you to have it before you're dead!" When the event took place on 5 November 1971 Rickenbacker gave an impassioned address, "Americanism versus Communism." In a sentence he underlined for emphasis, he warned that *"a government that is large enough to give you all you want is large enough to take all you own first."*[20]

Death was now claiming increasing numbers of long-cherished friends, many of whom had been Rickenbacker's comrades in the 94th Pursuit Squadron. His brothers Bill and Dewey had both died. An es-pecially tough blow was the death of Reed Chambers on 16 January 1972.[21] Adelaide was in the same situation. Feeling isolated as more and more of her companions passed away, she decided to move to southern Florida because the climate there was more agreeable to her. Still too fond of New York to leave, Eddie let her go, stayed in the metropolis, and visited Adelaide periodically in a villa where servants and relatives watched them as they amused themselves by reading, playing cards, and working on crossword puzzles from the Sunday *New York Times.*[22]

After Eddie came to Florida to celebrate his eighty-second birthday with Adelaide in October 1972, he suffered an encephalitic aneurysm and underwent emergency surgery. Hall visited him at the hospital, talking about how things were going at Eastern but getting no response. Thinking further attempts at communication futile, Hall excused him-self and headed for the door, only to have Rickenbacker follow him, dragging an intravenous feeding pole. "I'll take good care of your air-line, Eddie," Hall said. Looking solemnly at him, the old warrior re-plied, "It's *your* airline now, Floyd."[23]

Incredibly, considering the aneurysm, Rickenbacker recovered well enough to take Adelaide, who was going blind, to Switzerland in July 1973 to be treated by an ophthalmologist. Not long after they arrived in Zurich, Shepherd, who went with them, noticed that Eddie was having trouble breathing and summoned a physician who diagnosed him as having pneumonia and ordered him to be hospitalized. After enduring much pain, he died in his sleep on 23 July. Hall sent one of Eastern's DC-8s, with a full crew of pilots and cabin attendants, to take his ashes, enclosed in a metal container, back to the United States. A memorial service took place at the Key Biscayne Presbyterian Church on 27 July, with Jimmy Doolittle delivering the eulogy. Not long afterward a military honor guard interred Eddie's ashes in Columbus. At the conclusion of the ceremony, jet fighter planes from the 94th Fighter Squadron roared overhead in the "missing man" formation in final tribute to America's Ace of Aces. On 18 May 1974 Lockbourne Air Force Base in Columbus was renamed in Rickenbacker's memory.[24]

Nearly three years later, on February 2, 1977, Adelaide, ninety-two years old and virtually blind, was having dinner with family members in Florida. Suddenly she left the table and painstakingly made her way up a staircase, admonishing those present not to follow her. A few minutes later shots rang out. Rushing to her side, relatives took her to a Miami hospital where she died later that night. "Our grand dame has gone to meet her Captain in the sky," William wrote in a tribute to her.[25]

On 12 June 2000, Richard W. Hoerle, a Columbus resident who had led a successful campaign to issue an airmail stamp in Rickenbacker's honor in 1995, presided at the dedication of a replica of Rickenbacker's boyhood home, built on the grounds of the Motts Military Museum at Groveport, Ohio. Displays included the Duesenberg race car, painted red, white, and blue, in which Eddie had won his first major victory at Sioux City in 1914. People came from as far away as Nova Scotia to attend the ceremony, filled with patriotic pomp. Moments before Hoerle gave a brief synopsis of Rickenbacker's life and achievements, the sound of engines became audible at a distance, growing steadily louder until two F-15 Eagle supersonic jets bearing Hat-in-the-Ring insignia streaked across the site. The noise was earsplitting—a howling, shrieking chant of American airpower paying thunderous tribute to one of its greatest champions. Then, as swiftly as they had come, the warplanes disappeared, leaving only their contrails and a faint reverberation of their presence lingering in the vastness of the sky. An eerie stillness fell, as impressive in its own way as the awesome cacophony the F-15s had created. The turbulence was gone, the air was at peace. A bugler ended the ceremony with "Taps."[26]

Epilogue

— ☆ —

In the Arena

Had Rickenbacker disappeared in 1942 he might have become a male counterpart of Amelia Earhart. The fate of a national hero vanishing without a trace would have been a fit subject for endless speculation. Two famous aviators who became lost seeking tiny atolls in the mid-Pacific about 200 miles apart—the parallel would have been inescapable. Eddie's achievements as a champion automobile racer, combat pilot, airpower advocate, and airline pioneer had made him a person of great consequence in American life before he left Hawaii on a Flying Fortress that never found Canton Island and was ditched at sea. He was a legend when he left and might have been even more of one had he not returned.

But he did return, as indomitable as ever and wearing the mantle of a prophet because of the aura the "seagull episode" had given him. He would remain a public figure for more than thirty years, but was dramatically changed. He had already played the role of a Jeremiah in his tour of American air bases early in 1942, barely a year after sustaining terrible injuries in the Atlanta crash and making an agonizing recovery in Piedmont Hospital. Now, protracted starvation, dehydration, and exposure to the elements had completed his transformation into a zealot driven by a sense that God had repeatedly spared him from death for a reason he could not fathom, wondering why he was alive, and convinced he had a transcendent purpose to fulfill. Whatever he said or did in the rest of his life must be seen in light of what happened to him on the evening in 1941 when he boarded an airliner to give a speech he did not want to make, unaware that the pivotal moment of his life awaited him in a pine forest near Atlanta.

During the postwar years he seemed increasingly out of step with the times. His fierce dedication to the work ethic, his extreme individualism, his opposition to centralized government, and his strictures against organized labor put him at odds with an era in which collectivism seemed to be the wave of the future, liberalism had been redefined, and rugged individualism was deemed anachronistic. His adversative relationships with federal regulators, coupled with his determination to run a no-frills airline at a time when service competition was imperative, led to his downfall. Robert J. Serling, a discerning judge of character who wrote a penetrating history of Eastern Air Lines, called him "a nineteenth-century American trying hard to cope with the twentieth century—a task in which he achieved both magnificent success and dismal failure."[1]

But Rickenbacker lived long enough to witness the onset of a new cycle in government-business relationships more consistent with his outlook than the one with which he was so much at odds. Despite Goldwater's crushing defeat by Johnson, the Arizonan's nomination for president in 1964 was a significant omen of change. Had Rickenbacker lived only a few more years, he could have celebrated the passage of the Airline Deregulation Act in 1978 and cheered the death sentence it imposed on the Civil Aeronautics Board. In 1980 Ronald Reagan was elected president, and the gospel Rickenbacker had preached became political orthodoxy. By the 1990s, with the fall of the Iron Curtain, free-market doctrines reigned in a global capitalist economy and a Democratic president said that the era of big government was over. In 2004 an outpouring of national grief mourned Reagan's death and George W. Bush was reelected president. Historians have overlooked Rickenbacker's role as a prophet of the political and economic change that these developments wrought.

He was also a towering figure in the age of heavier-than-air flight that began at Kitty Hawk in 1903. As one of the greatest combat pilots in the history of aerial warfare and a member of a small group of executives who dominated the formative years of American commercial aviation, he merits a place reserved for pioneers. It is ironic that he ultimately felt obliged to call himself a conservative, because he rode the wings of one of the twentieth century's greatest agents of revolutionary change.

Rickenbacker was in the best sense of the word a tragic hero who endured many ordeals and lost many battles. Had he lived in ancient Greece, a Homer or Sophocles might have seen in him a fitting subject for epic poetry or theatrical drama. His failings, like those of Achilles, are obvious, but his achievements equally so. He was a man of valor who knew that courage could not exist in the absence of fear, the eternal warrior who intuitively realizes that a life well lived is not a state of existence for the timid but a combat zone. He reveled in conflict, seeking the places where wars are waged, issues are debated, and human destiny is decided. It is time to pay him the honor he deserves. If words alone can give Eddie Rickenbacker his due, the well-known speech by Theodore Roosevelt may supply a fitting epitaph:

> It is not the critic who counts, not the man who points out how the strong man stumbled, or where the doer of deeds could have done better. The credit belongs to the man who is actually in the arena; whose face is marred by the dust and sweat and blood; who strives valiantly; who errs and comes short again and again; who knows the great enthusiasms, the great devotions and spends himself in a worthy cause; who at the best, knows in the end the triumphs of high achievements, and who, at worst, if he fails, at least fails while daring greatly; so that his place shall never be with those cold and timid souls who know neither victory nor defeat.[2]

Acknowledgments
— ☆ —

No author is an island apart from the main. One of the hazards of writing acknowledgments is the danger of unintentionally slighting persons who contributed to what is necessarily a collective enterprise. I apologize for any inadvertent omissions. I also take responsibility for any errors I have committed despite having the help of so many people.

I owe much to my agent, Felix C. Lowe, for helping bring my work to fruition. Robert J. Brugger, senior history editor of the Johns Hopkins University Press, had faith in my project from the outset and gave it deeply appreciated support. James O. Wade's editorial acumen sharpened the focus of successive drafts. Gary A. Cantini's formidable talents in computer technology were of inestimable help. Walter J. Boyne and Robert J. Serling were generous with advice and encouragement. Daniel J. Clemons closely read my entire manuscript at a late stage in its composition with a rare combination of critical expertise and boundless enthusiasm. Brian MacDonald provided meticulous copyediting. I also thank Courtney Bond, Christina Cheakalos, Melody Herr, Becky Hornyak, and Amy Zezula for their aid.

William M. Leary helped initiate this work by asking me to write essays about Rickenbacker and Eastern Air Lines for an encyclopedia of commercial aviation. Tom D. Crouch was instrumental in my appointment to a visiting position as Charles A. Lindbergh Professor of Aerospace History at the National Air and Space Museum, giving me a year of free time and easy access to major research repositories. Other historians who aided me in various ways include Thomas Allison, Janet R. Daly Bednarek, Roger E. Bilstein, Mansel Blackford, Robert Casey, Donna M. Corbett, R. E. G. Davies, Virginia P. Dawson, Deborah G. Douglas, Bert L. Frandsen, Larry G. Gerber, C. V. Glines, Michael H. Gorn, Richard P. Hallion, James R. Hansen, Robin Higham, George E. Hopkins, Peter Jakab, Austin Kerr, Roger D. Launius, Edwin T. Layton Jr., Stephen L. McFarland, John H. Morrow Jr., Dominick Pisano, Robert C. Post,

Matthew Rodina, David Bryan Taylor, F. Robert van der Linden, and Rudi Volti. William F. Trimble deserves special thanks for his faith and support as my department chairman.

Dwayne D. Cox, Director of Special Collections and Archives at the Auburn University Library, sustained my efforts to create a major collection of source materials related to Rickenbacker. Nancy Angell Rickenbacker, widow of William Frost Rickenbacker, figured significantly in building the collection by channeling valuable papers, photographs, and memorabilia into it. Joyce Hicks, Martin Olliff, and Brenda Prather helped organize the collection and provided archival expertise. Lynn Williams aided me in accessing archival materials. Other members of the library staff who aided my research include Glenn Anderson, Barbara Bishop, Christine Black, Marcia Boosinger, Boyd Childress, Timothy Dodge, Nancy Noe, Harmon Straiton, and Linda Thornton.

I deeply appreciate interviews granted me by Brian, James, and Marcia Rickenbacker, grandchildren of Eddie Rickenbacker, and Patricia Ann Wrightson, widow of David E. Rickenbacker, dealing with various aspects of their family's history.

I am grateful to Peter D. Laxalt for many things, but particularly for bringing me together with Alan K. Abner, who supplied the intimate grasp of aerial warfare that only a seasoned combat pilot can possess. Floyd D. Hall spent much time discussing his experiences as a pilot and reviewed the events that took place before and after he succeeded Rickenbacker in 1963. Hall also put me in touch with James Elkins, who clarified important details about Rickenbacker's retirement. I thank John F. Bartek, the last survivor of the 1942 raft episode, for visiting Auburn University, giving a talk about the ordeal, and relating his experiences to me in a prolonged interview. Richard W. Hoerle and Captain Hal Nord shared the fruits of their dedication to promoting awareness of Rickenbacker's achievements and keeping the heritage of Eastern Air Lines alive.

Archivists, curators, and librarians, too numerous to mention by name, helped me in my research. I wish, however, to single out Darwin H. Stapleton, Director of the Rockefeller Archive Center, Erik Carlson, Director of the Aviation Collection at the University of Texas at Dallas, and Lyn Ezell of the National Air and Space Museum. I also thank Larry Sall, Director of Libraries at the University of Texas at Dallas, for his role in my selection as Jalonick Memorial Lecturer at that institution.

Hans-Joachim Braun, Alexandre and Danielle Herlea, Alex Keller, Fredy Rey, Rudolf Rickenbacher, Sylvia Waldis Saner, and Henry and Mariette Wydler aided me in European travels. Monique Chapelle enriched my knowledge of European automobiles. David Andersen, Robert and Nancy Ballew, Bettye and Kathy Jo Best, Violet Best, Dante Burgos, Barry Burkhart, Caine Campbell, George R. De Muth, James Holder, Peggy Howland, Daniel K. and Virginia L. Lewis, Colleen and Ed Mallory, William P. McLemore, Kenneth Pepin, Roger Royal, and Alfred Waldis also helped me in numerous ways.

I am grateful to William E. Mock, M.D., an opthalmologist, for valuable advice about Rickenbacker's visual impairment and to J. David Hagan, M.D., an internist, for discussing with me the probable effects of the prolonged dehydration that Rickenbacker suffered in his 1942 raft ordeal.

As always, my deepest debt of gratitude is to my wife, Pat, a constant companion throughout nearly fifteen years of living with Eddie Rickenbacker as our guest. She was my chief research associate, made countless Xerox copies, climbed rugged Swiss terrain, toured French battle sites, brought me meals when she could not pry me away from the computer—I cannot possibly do justice to the manifold ways in which she supported my work. She is my very best friend and richly deserves having this book dedicated to her.

Notes

— ☆ —

Abbreviations

ERP-AU: Eddie Rickenbacker Papers, Auburn University Special Collections and Archives, Auburn, Alabama

EVRD-1918: Diary kept by Edward V. Rickenbacker in 1918; copy at United States Air Force Museum, Wright-Patterson Air Force Base, Dayton, Ohio

EVRD-J-M 1919: Diary kept by Edward V. Rickenbacker, January–March 1919, copy supplied by Daniel J. Clemons, Escondido, California

EVRED-1919: Engagement Diary kept by Rickenbacker in 1919, copy at United States Air Force Museum, Wright-Patterson Force Base, Dayton, Ohio

EVRP-LC: Edward V. Rickenbacker Papers, Library of Congress, Washington, D.C.

EVRR: Edward V. Rickenbacker, *Rickenbacker* (Englewood Cliffs, NJ, 1967), autobiography of Rickenbacker, ghostwritten by Booton Herndon

EVRS: Edward V. Rickenbacker Scrapbooks, Auburn University Special Collections and Archives, Auburn, Alabama

FFC: Edward V. Rickenbacker, *Fighting the Flying Circus* (New York: Frederick P. Stokes Company, 1919), Rickenbacker's World War I memoirs, ghostwritten by Laurence La Tourette Driggs

FFCL: Edward V. Rickenbacker, *Fighting the Flying Circus,* edited by W. David Lewis (Chicago: Lakeside Press, 1997), a revised and abridged version of the original text

Leighton Interviews: Interviews by Isabel Leighton of people who had long known Rickenbacker and his wife, Adelaide, conducted for Eureka Pictures, Inc., in preparation for production of *Captain Eddie,* a film about Rickenbacker (Twentieth Century Fox, 1945), Auburn University Special Collections and Archives.

"Life Story": "Life Story of Captain Edward V. Rickenbacker," a two-volume document based on interviews with Rickenbacker held to assist Twentieth Century Fox in filming *Captain Eddie.* Thurber Special Collections Department, Ohio State University, Columbus

PACC: Preliminary typewritten accounts, in EVRP-LC, box 91, of Rickenbacker's World War I experiences, supplied by Rickenbacker to Laurence La Tourette Driggs

R-H Tapes: Transcribed taped interviews of Rickenbacker by Booton Herndon, 1965, with copies of accompanying documents provided by Rickenbacker, at United States Air Force Museum, Wright-Patterson Air Force Base, Dayton, Ohio

TGSFN: The Great Silver Fleet News, magazine published by Eastern Air Lines

Preface

1. William M. Leary, *Aerial Pioneers: The U.S. Air Mail Service, 1917–1927* (Washington, DC: Smithsonian Institution Press, 1985), 85, 214–15, 208–9. Also see www.centennialofflight.gov.essay/Government Role/navigation/POL13.htm.

2. On the army's dirigible program in the mid-1930s, see Maurer Maurer, *Aviation in the U.S. Army, 1919–1939* (Washington, D.C.: Office of Air Force History, 1987), 217, 238. James R. Hansen provided advice on this matter.

3. Wiley Post and Harold Gatty, *Around the World in Eight Days: The Flight of the "Winnie Mae"* (1931; repr., New York: Orion Books, 1989), 159 and unpaginated appendix with facsimile copy of Gatty's log book.

Prologue. A Boy and His Flying Machine

1. The account that follows is based on EVRR, 1–2, 11–12, and R-H Tapes, reel 1, side 1, and reel 15, side 2.

Chapter 1. Starting Line

1. Unless otherwise specified, information in this chapter about William Rickenbacher, his wife, Elizabeth Basler Rickenbacher, and their children is derived from Marian Pflaum Darby, *The Inspiration and Lives of Elizabeth Basler Rickenbacher and William Rickenbacher* (Columbus, OH: privately published, 1963), used with permission of Richard W. Hoerle, copyright holder.

2. Letter from Ruth Haener, Staatsarchiv des Kantons Basel-Landschaft, Liestal, Switzerland, to author, 8 October 1998; Lionel Gossman, *Basel in the Age of Burckhardt* (Chicago: University of Chicago Press, 2000), 30–48. On Swiss values, see Georg Theurer, *Free and Swiss* (Coral Gables, FL: University of Miami Press, 1970).

3. J. P. Zwicky, "Die Familie Rickenbacher von Zeglingen"; Kory L. Meyerink, "Rickenbacher Research Report"; and letter from William Woys Weaver, genealogist, all materials shared with author by William F. Rickenbacker, son of Edward V. Rickenbacker; Gossman, *Basel,* 68, 113, 212.

4. *Industries of Ohio: Columbus, Historical and Descriptive Review, Business and Businessmen in 1878* (Columbus: Historical Publishing Company, 1878), 262; *History of*

Franklin and Pickaway Counties, Ohio (Columbus, 1880), 589; *Columbus City Directory for 1880* (Columbus: G. J. Brand & Co., 1889), 319.

5. La Vern J. Rippley, *The Columbus Germans* (Baltimore: Society for the History of the Germans in Maryland, 1968), 3, 16–19, 35–36, 42.

6. Theurer, *Free and Swiss*; La Vern J. Rippley, *The German-Americans* (New York: Twayne Publishers, 1976), 85; Stephen P. Halbrook, *Target Switzerland* (Rockville Center, NY: Sarpedon Publishers, 1998), 17–19. Halbrook points out that the Swiss did not convert their cantonal militias into a standing army until after the Franco-Prussian War.

7. Darby's *Inspiration and Lives* contains a photocopy of the page from the Bible on which the entries were made.

8. William's employment history and changes of residence can be traced in Columbus city directories throughout the 1880s and early 1890s. They correlate with national trends discussed in Rendig Fels, *American Business Cycles, 1865–1897* (Chapel Hill: University of North Carolina Press, 1959), 159–71. On the Rickenbacher family's financial problems during this period, see Darby, *Inspiration and Lives*, 21–27. The house in which Edward was born no longer exists; a motel stands on the site.

9. Descriptions and photographs of the house, located at 1334 East Livingston Avenue, at various points in its history are in the Historical Preservation Files of the Ohio Historical Society, Columbus, Ohio. The dwelling still stands and is one of three buildings in Columbus (along with the Ohio State Capitol and the Ohio Theater) listed as a National Historic Landmark. Because it is in a rundown neighborhood and could not be moved, a furnished replica was built on the grounds of Motts Military Museum, Groveport, Ohio. Richard W. Hoerle, who led the restoration drive and found the cost of the house in local records, has supplied me with a floor plan.

10. Unless otherwise indicated, information about Rickenbacker's youth from this point on is based on EVRR, 1–18, valuably supplemented by R-H Tapes, reel 1, sides 1 and 2.

11. See particularly Dixon Wecter, *The Hero in America: A Chronicle of Hero Worship* (New York: Scribner's, 1941). Virtually all of the heroes discussed by Wecter, except Theodore Roosevelt, came from agricultural or small-town backgrounds. On streetwise behavior by urban children at the turn of the twentieth century, see David Nasaw, *Children of the City* (New York: Anchor Books, 1985).

12. Jacob H. Dorn, *Washington Gladden: Prophet of the Social Gospel* (Columbus: Ohio State University Press, 1967), 69–71, 307–9, 311.

13. Alfred E. Lee, *History of the City of Columbus*, 2 vols. (New York and Chicago: Munsell & Co., 1892), 2:315–37; Henry L. Hunker, *Industrial Evolution of Columbus, Ohio* (Columbus: Ohio Historical Society, 1958).

14. Page Smith, *The Rise of Industrial America* (New York: McGraw-Hill, 1984), 508–33; H. Wayne Morgan, *William McKinley and His America* (Syracuse, NY: Syracuse University Press, 1963), 152–82.

15. *History of St. John's Evangelical Protestant Church, 1872–1974* (Columbus: privately published, n.d.), 1–16. Statements by Rickenbacker that the church was Lutheran are incorrect.

16. Cecelia E. O'Leary, *To Die For: The Paradox of American Patriotism* (Princeton, NJ: Princeton University Press, 1999), 172–93.

17. "Life Story," 2:396, expressing Rickenbacker's resentment of beatings by his father.

18. Hans C. Adamson, *Eddie Rickenbacker* (New York: Macmillan Company, 1946), 13–14; R-H Tapes, reel 1, side 1.

19. Clipping from *Ohio State Journal* (Columbus), 26 February 1919, EVRS 1 (1913–19).

20. E. Anthony Rotundo, *American Manhood* (New York: Basic Books, c. 1993), 31–55.

21. "Laborer's Skull Fractured by Two Blows with Level" and "Charge of Murder Will Probably Be Put against Negro," *Columbus Evening Dispatch*, 18, 19 July 1904; "Victim Can't Recover," *Columbus Citizen*, 19 July 1904; "Skull Broken by Murderous Blow," *Ohio State Journal* (Columbus), 19 July 1904.

22. "Gaines Claims He Hit in Self-Defense," *Ohio State Journal* (Columbus), 21 July 1904; "Rickenbacher Was after Him with a Knife," *Columbus Evening Dispatch*, 21 July 1904.

23. "Rickenbacher Is Close to Death," *Columbus Citizen*, 25 August 1904; "Wm. Rickenbacher Takes Nourishment" and "To Aid Rickenbacher's Family," *Columbus Evening Dispatch*, 23 July, 2 August 1904.

24. "Rickenbacher Dies" and "William Gaines Is Found Guilty," *Columbus Citizen*, 26 August, 27 October 1904; "Victim of Assault Dies," *Columbus Evening Dispatch*, 26 August 1904; "Rickenbacher Is Dead," *Ohio State Journal* (Columbus), 27 August 1904; Indictment for Manslaughter, Doc. No. 7747, Franklin County Court of Common Pleas, with accompanying notation of verdict, 17 December 1904. Craig D. Walley provided valuable assistance on legal aspects of the case.

25. Compare conflicting accounts in EVRR, 16–18, and Finis Farr, *Rickenbacker's Luck: An American Life* (Boston: Houghton Mifflin, 1979), 8. Farr, the first person to set the record straight on the circumstances of William Rickenbacker's death, mistakenly states that he died on 4 August 1904.

26. Thomas Hine, *The Rise and Fall of the American Teenager* (New York: Avon Books, 1999), 139–48.

27. David Gelernter, *Machine Beauty: Elegance and the Heart of Technology* (New York: Basic Books, 1998).

Chapter 2. Ignition

1. Unless otherwise noted, the discussion of Rickenbacker's experiences that follows is based on EVRR, 28–34; R-H Tapes, reel 16, side 1, and reel 39C, side 1; and Ad-

amson, *Eddie Rickenbacker,* 55–67. On the location of the Evans Garage, see *Columbus City Directory,* vol. 31 (Columbus, OH: R. L. Polk & Co., 1907), 369, 1178–79, 1185.

2. For pictures and descriptions of cars mentioned here, see Nick Baldwin et al., *World Guide to Automobile Manufacturers* (New York: Facts on File, 1987), 294, 387–88; Beverly Rae Kimes and Harry Austin Clark Jr., *Standard Catalog of American Cars, 1805–1942,* 3rd ed. (Iola, WI: Krause Publications, 1996), 819, 890–91, 1105–7; Edward L. Throm and James S. Crenshaw, *Popular Mechanics Auto Album* (n.p.: Popular Mechanics Auto Press, 1952), 48; Clarence P. Hornung, *Portrait Gallery of Early Automobiles* (New York: Harry N. Abrams, n.d.), plate 27; and George H. Dammann and James A. Wren, *Packard* (Osceola, WI: Motorbooks International, 1996), 8–19.

3. Gardner Hiscox, *Horseless Vehicles, Automobiles, Motor Cycles Operated by Steam, Hydro-Carbon, Electric and Pneumatic Motors* (New York: Norman W. Henley & Co., 1901); Throm and Crenshaw, *Auto Album,* 61–64; Waverley advertisement in Clay McShane, *The Automobile: A Chronology of Its Antecedents, Development, and Impact* (Westport, CT: Greenwood Press, 1997), photographic section following p. 37.

4. Throm and Crenshaw, *Auto Album,* 43–60; Kimes and Clark, *Standard Catalog,* 1297–1301, 1454–55; Rudi Volti, "Why Internal Combustion?" *American Heritage of Invention and Technology* 6, no. 2 (Fall 1900): 42–47.

5. John B. Rae, *The American Automobile Industry* (New York: Twayne Publishers, 1984), 19.

6. R-H Tapes, reel 39C, side 1.

7. Ibid., 16–19.

8. John C. Villaume, "The ICS Story: 65 Years of Educational Service," and other materials supplied to author by Lackawanna Historical Society and ICS Learning Systems, Scranton, Pennsylvania. I am grateful to Mary Ann Moran, Director, Lackawanna Historical Society, and Linda Yantorn, administrative assistant for ICS, for their help.

9. Adamson, *Eddie Rickenbacker,* 61.

10. List of Principals and Assistant Principals, International Correspondence Schools, *Fifteenth Anniversary Exercises and Banquet, October 16, 1891–1906* (Scranton, PA: International Textbook Company, 1906), 22–23.

11. See particularly Eugene S. Ferguson, *Engineering in the Mind's Eye* (Cambridge, MA: MIT Press, 1992), 49, 137. Robert Fulton stated, "the mechanic should sit down among levers, screws, wedges, wheels, etc. like a poet among the letters of the alphabet, considering them as the exhibition of his own thoughts; in which a new arrangement transmits a new idea to the world." Cynthia Owen Philip, *Robert Fulton: A Biography* (New York: Franklin Watts, 1985), vii.

12. Monte A. Calvert, *The Mechanical Engineer in America, 1830–1910: Professional Cultures in Conflict* (Baltimore: Johns Hopkins Press, 1967), esp. 105, 124; Robert Kanigel, *The One Best Way: Frederick Winslow Taylor and the Enigma of Efficiency* (New York: Viking, 1997), 93–147.

13. Howard Gardner, *Frames of Mind: The Theory of Multiple Intelligences,* 10th an-

niversary ed. (New York: Basic Books, 1983), 129. Gardner's work has been of fundamental importance in my study of Rickenbacker's developing abilities. He was also well endowed with other types of intelligence identified by Gardner, including visual-spatial and bodily-kinesthetic. For a masterful synthesis of the type of intelligence discussed here, see Ferguson, *Engineering and the Mind's Eye*.

14. See particularly Griffith Borgeson, *The Golden Age of the American Motor Car* (New York: W. W. Norton & Company, 1966), 62–82, and Borgeson's essay on Miller in Ronald Barker and Anthony Harding, eds., *Automobile Design: Twelve Great Designers and Their Work* (Warrendale, PA: Society of Automotive Engineers, Inc., 1992), 199–223.

15. Richard E. Barrett, *"Made in Columbus" Automobiles* (Columbus, OH: Columbus Historical Society, 1994), 2. Another authoritative work lists forty-five Columbus marques; see Kimes and Clark, *Standard Catalog*, 1608.

16. Barrett, *"Made in Columbus" Automobiles*, 3; Kimes and Clark, *Standard Catalog*, 558; advertisement of Frayer-Miller car at the Antique Automobile Club of America Library, Hershey, Pennsylvania.

17. R-H Tapes, reel 2, side 1.

18. Copy of Ohio State University transcript of Lee Ambrose Frayer, in author's possession.

19. Barrett, *"Made in Columbus" Automobiles*, 3, 6.

20. R-H Tapes, reel 2, side 1.

21. Ibid.

22. "Dyke's Instruction Number One," *Dyke's Automobile and Gas Engine Encyclopedia for 1910* (Chicago: Goodheart-Wilcox, 1951) 2–9.

23. R-H Tapes, reel 16, side 1.

24. R-H Tapes, reel 39C, side 1. On the composition of Babbit metal, see Peter Lafferty and Julian Rowe, *Dictionary of Science* (London: Brockhampton Press, 1994), 56. Isaac Babbit, an American, invented the alloy in 1839.

25. Joan E. Ames, *Mastery: Interviews with 30 Remarkable People* (Portland, OR: Rudra Press, 1997), 2.

26. B. Eugene Griessman, *The Achievement Factors* (New York: Dodd, Mead & Company, 1987), 28–60.

27. EVRR, 34–35; R-H Tapes, reel 2, side 1.

28. Quoted in Stephen Kern, *The Culture of Time and Space, 1880–1918* (Cambridge, MA: Harvard University Press, 1983), 113.

29. Marshall M. Kirkman, *Operation of Trains*, vol. 3 of *The Science of Railways*, 12 vols. (New York and Chicago: World Railway Publishing Company, 1896), 142.

30. Robert A. Smith, *A Social History of the Bicycle* (New York: McGraw-Hill, 1972), 17–33; Tom D. Crouch, *The Bishop's Boys: A Life of Wilbur and Orville Wright* (New York: W. W. Norton & Company, 1989), 108–9.

31. Smith, *Social History*, 143–71.

32. Roger Hicks, ed., *The Encyclopedia of Motorcycles* (San Diego: Thunder Bay

Press, 2001), 9–10, 140–41, 228, 266; Patrick Hook, ed., *Harley-Davidson: The Complete History* (London: PRC Publishing, 2002), 47.

33. "America's Motor Car Speed Records," *Motor* 22, no. 5 (August 1914): 43, 45; Don Berliner, *Victory over the Wind: A History of the Absolute World Air Speed Record* (New York: Van Nostrand Reinhold Company, 1983), 15–16.

34. Ivan Rendall, *The Checkered Flag: 100 Years of Motor Racing* (Secaucus, NJ: Chartwell Books, Inc., 1993), 12–16.

35. "America's Motor Car Speed Records," 43, 45; Beverly Rae Kimes, "The Vanderbilt Cup Races, 1904–1910," *Automobile Quarterly* 6, no. 2 (Fall 1967): 185. I have drawn heavily on Kimes's article in relating the events that follow. On Vanderbilt's relationship to Cornelius Vanderbilt, see Arthur T. Vanderbilt II, *Fortune's Children: The Fall of the House of Vanderbilt* (New York: Morrow, 1989), esp. 116–17.

36. Robert Casey, "The Vanderbilt Cup, 1908," *Technology and Culture* 40, no. 2 (April 1999): 359.

37. Kimes, "Vanderbilt Cup Races," 185–90. On the history of the cars mentioned, see Baldwin et al., *World Guide*, 103–4, 128, 370–71, 447–48.

38. EVRR, 35; R-H Tapes, reel 39B, side 2.

39. Casey, "The Vanderbilt Cup," 361; R-H Tapes, reel 2, side 1; E. V. Rickenbacher and J. C. Burton, "The Loyal Legion of Speed," *Motor Age* 28, no. 14 (30 September 1915): 5–10; John E. Blazier and Tom Rollings, *Forgotten Heroes of the Speedways: The Riding Mechanics* (undated, unpaginated booklet), Indianapolis Speedway Hall of Fame Museum.

40. "Life Story," 1:62–63; EVRR, 36–37.

41. On the history of the De Dietrich, see Baldwin et al., *World Guide,* 133.

42. EVRR, 38–39.

43. Casey, "The Vanderbilt Cup," 359–60; Kimes, "Vanderbilt Cup Races," 190–92.

44. See, for example, *Omaha Sunday Bee,* 2, 4 October 1910, from which I have quoted here.

45. The developments traced here are related at greater length in Charles E. Tuttle, "Columbus Buggy Company," *Carriage Journal* 15, no. 4 (Spring 1978): 386–91, and 16, no. 1 (Summer 1978): 7–14, and Richard E. Barrett, *"Made in Columbus" Automobiles,* 7–17.

46. R-H Tapes, reel 2, side 1, and reel 3, sides 1 and 2, on which the ensuing developments are based. On the importance of drawing in engineering practice, see Ferguson, *Engineering and the Mind's Eye,* 97–102.

47. R-H Tapes, reel 3, side 2. On the distinction between an invention and an innovation, see John J. Staudenmeier, *Technology's Storytellers: Reweaving the Human Fabric* (Cambridge, MA: MIT Press, 1985), 55–61.

48. "National Show Best of All," "News Events of the Chicago Show Week," and "A Pictorial Review of Coliseum Show Exhibits," *Motor Age* 15 (January–April 1909): 1–19.

49. See pictures of the car in Kimes and Clark, *Standard Catalog,* 564. As Kimes and Clark state, the Buggy Company opposed the concept of an annual model change and chided other manufacturers for pursuing it.

50. Donald Finlay Davis, *Conspicuous Production: Automobiles and Elites in Detroit, 1899–1933* (Philadelphia: Temple University Press, 1988), which develops at length the argument made here.

51. For the details of a thermo-syphon cooling system, see Andrew L. Dyke, *Dyke's Automobile and Gasoline Engine Encyclopedia,* 4th ed. (St. Louis: A. L. Dyke, Publisher, 1915), 178.

52. James J. Flink, *America Adopts the Automobile, 1895–1910* (Cambridge, MA: MIT Press, 1970), 70–71. Flink calls physicians "the most innovative single group in the adoption of the automobile in the United States. The local doctors were invariably among the first persons to purchase cars in any community."

53. R-H Tapes, reel 42, side 1. Bryan had toured southern Illinois in a Benz touring car while campaigning for president against William McKinley in 1896, and intensified his use of automobiles in 1900 against the Republican ticket of McKinley and Theodore Roosevelt. Flink, *America Adopts the Automobile,* 69.

54. R-H Tapes, reel 3, side 1.

55. Ibid., reel 39D, side 1.

56. On the types of forced circulation systems used at this time, driven by geared, centrifugal, and rotary pumps, see *Dyke's Encyclopedia,* 181.

57. The account presented here attempts to reconcile two different versions of what happened, as related in EVRR, 51, and a letter from Coffeen to Rickenbacker, 19 June 1955, EVRP-LC, box 9, folder marked "'C' Miscellany." According to EVRR, Frayer offered Eddie the Omaha job while he was still in Arizona. Coffeen's reminiscences, which Rickenbacker did not challenge in a response dated 23 June 1955, provide the most convincing explanation of what actually took place.

58. John C. Schneider, "Omaha Vagrants and the Character of Western Hobo Labor, 1887–1913," *Nebraska History* 63, no. 2 (Summer 1982): 255–72.

59. Tommy R. Thompson, "The Great Omaha Train Robbery of 1909," *Nebraska History* 63, no. 2 (Summer 1982): 216–31.

60. Susanna Rodell, "How Stock Cars Became Icons of Americana," *New York Times,* 21 May 2000.

61. R-H Tapes, reel 3, side 2. Rickenbacher stated that Frayer had been the first person in America to put the steering wheel on the left side of the automobile. I have been unable to validate or disprove this claim.

62. On Coffeen's racing background and his role in training Rickenbacher, see "Omaha Driver Wins 300-Mile Race at Home," *Omaha Bee,* 6 July 1915.

Chapter 3. Acceleration

1. "The Roads to Red Oak Town," *Red Oak (IA) Express,* 24 June 1910.

2. *Red Oak (IA) Express,* 3 June 1910.

3. W. W. Merritt, *A History of the County of Montgomery from the Earliest Days to 1906* (Red Oak, IA: Express Publishing Company, 1906), 220–27. Information supplied by Bettie McKenzie, Director, Montgomery County Historical Society, who was of great assistance to me during a visit to Red Oak, where I toured Pactolus Park.

4. "Immense Crowd Attend Races," *Red Oak (IA) Express,* 24 June 1910.

5. Ibid.

6. On the Cole marque, see Kimes and Clark, *Standard Catalog of American Cars,* 350–54.

7. On the Chalmers-Detroit, a lineal ancestor of the Chrysler, see ibid., 270.

8. On the race at Red Oak, see R-H Tapes, reel 3, side 2, and reel 39C, side 2, on which I have drawn extensively in the account that follows.

9. *Atlantic Telegraph,* 1 July 1910. The E.M.F. (Everitt-Metzger-Flanders), which would figure significantly in Rickenbacher's later career, was a medium-priced car produced in Detroit by Byron F. ("Barney") Everitt, William Metzger, and Walter Flanders. Kimes and Clark, *Standard Catalog,* 532–34, shows pictures of the touring model Rickenbacher drove in the five-mile race.

10. Originally a high-wheel buggy-type automobile capable of only thirty miles per hour, the Staver-Chicago became a conventional four-cylinder automobile in 1910. Kimes and Clark, *Standard Catalog,* 1386.

11. "Automobile Races—Grand Opening of the Omaha Speedway," "Auto Speedway Is Improved by Rain," "First Auto Races on New Track of Speedway Association," and "Car Wrecked, Driver Doherty Is Injured," *Omaha World-Herald,* 2, 9, 11, 12 September 1910.

12. Arvid E. Nelson, *The Ak-Sar-Ben Story* (Omaha: Johnson Publishing Company, 1967), 1–87.

13. "Ak-Sar-Ben to Put Auto Races in Festival," "Fast Time at Motor Races," and "Reichenbacher Repeater," *Omaha Bee,* 15 September and 3, 4 October 1910; "Glory and Dust at the Motor Speedway" and "Scores Made at New Speedway Yesterday," *Omaha World-Herald,* 3 October 1910.

14. On Oldfield, see William F. Nolan, "You Knew Him . . . Barney Oldfield," *Automobile Quarterly* 1, no. 1 (Spring 1962): 22–30, 101, and Nolan's *Barney Oldfield: The Life and Times of America's Legendary Speed King* (New York: Putnam, 1961).

15. R-H Tapes, reel 3, side 2, and reel 39C, side 2.

16. Adamson, *Eddie Rickenbacker,* 97–98.

17. Ibid., 98–99; R-H Tapes, reel 11, side 1.

18. EVRR, 57; Kimes and Clark, *Standard Catalog,* 564.

19. On the early history of the Indianapolis Speedway, see Jack C. Fox, *The Illustrated History of the Indianapolis 500, 1911–1994,* rev. ed. (Speedway, IN: Carl Hung-

ness & Associates, 1994), 10–11. On Fisher, see Jerry M. Fisher, *The Pacesetter: the Untold Story of Carl G. Fisher* (Fort Bragg, CA: Lost Coast Press, 1988).

20. See the extended analysis in W. David Lewis, "Divergent Cultures: The American Response to European Dominance in Automobile Racing, 1895–1917," *ICON: Journal of the International Committee for the History of Technology* 7 (2001): 1–34.

21. Visitor brochure, Brooklands Speedway, 1993; Howard Johnson, *Wings over Brooklands: The Story of the Birthplace of British Aviation* (London: Whittet Books, 1985), 9–31; David McDonald, *Fifty Years with the Speed Kings* (London: Stanley Paul, 1961), 15–16.

22. Rendall, *The Checkered Flag*, 60–61.

23. Peter Helck, "Twenty-Four Hours to Go: A Saga of the Dirt-Track Grinds in America," *Automobile Quarterly* 5, no. 1 (Summer 1966): 24–25, 56–67.

24. Russ Catlin, "54 Bittersweet Years of the AAA Contest Board: American Motorsport Goes Big Time," *Automobile Quarterly* 20, no. 4 (1982): 393–98.

25. Ibid.

26. EVRR, 56.

27. L. Spencer Riggs, *Pace Cars of the Indy 500* (Fort Lauderdale, FL: Speed Age Inc., 1989), 8.

28. Erwin Lessner, *Famous Auto Races and Rallies* (Garden City, NY: Hanover House, 1957), 23–29.

29. Fox, *Illustrated History of the Indianapolis 500,* 24–27. Harroun's black Marmon six, bearing a large gold numeral 32, is today in the center of the main floor in the Hall of Fame Museum, Indianapolis, Indiana.

30. EVRR, 57.

31. Riggs, *Pace Cars,* 10–11.

32. Ibid., 31–32; Fox, *Illustrated History of the Indianapolis 500,* 28–31; EVRR, 151–53; "Ralph De Palma's Glorious Failure," typescript of article by Rickenbacker for *Esquire* magazine, 1962, EVRP-LC, box 128. On De Palma's life and career, see William F. Nolan, "Ralph De Palma," *Automobile Quarterly* 2, no. 3 (Fall 1963): 264–71.

33. The account of these developments in EVRR, 57, based on faulty memory on Rickenbacker's part or a desire to gloss over an ill-fated association with a second-rate racing group, indicates mistakenly that he went directly to Des Moines to work for Fred and August Duesenberg.

34. It is likely that "Mrs. Marshall" was Elizabeth Walton Marshall, wife of Chicago architect Benjamin H. Marshall, who designed the Drake Hotel. Benjamin Marshall was devoted to horse racing, belonged to the Chicago Automobile Club, and had social ties with flyers including Italo Balbo, all congruent with an interest in motor sport. Newspaper clippings, Marshall file, Chicago Historical Society; Mae Felts Herringshaw, ed., *Clark J. Herringshaw's City Blue Book of Current Biography* (Chicago: American Publishers' Association, 1913), 228; and article about Marshall in John Zukowsky, ed., *Chicago Architecture, 1872–1922: Birth of a Metropolis* (Munich: Prestel-Verlag, 1987), 277–88.

35. The account given here is based on local newspapers at the Iowa State Historical Society in Des Moines, all published during the summer of 1912. Among others, see *Harlan Tribune*, 10, 17 July; *Marshalltown Times-Republican*, 3, 5, 7, 8, 9, 10, 11 August; *Mason City Globe-Gazette*, 10, 17, 19, 26 September and 3, 8 October.

36. *Mason City Globe-Gazette*, 17 September and 8 October 1912.

37. Minutes, AAA Contest Board, 24 October 1912, Hall of Fame Museum, Indianapolis, Indiana.

38. Griffith Borgeson, *The Golden Age of the American Racing Car* (New York: W. W. Norton, 1966), 48–52; Don Butler, *Auburn-Cord-Duesenberg* (Osceola, WI: Motorbooks International, 1992), 5–43; J. L. Elbert, *Duesenberg: The Mightiest American Motor Car*, rev. ed. (Arcadia, CA: Post-Era Books, 1975), 24–25; Brock Yates, "Duesenberg," *American Heritage* 45, no. 4 (July–August 1994): 88–99; miscellaneous photos, newspaper clippings, and publicity releases, Duesenberg Collection, Iowa State Historical Society, Des Moines.

39. Because the Duesenbergs could not afford to purchase forgings, they made their own, requiring manual work of the type about which Rickenbacker spoke.

40. Adamson, *Eddie Rickenbacker*, 110.

41. Fox, *Illustrated History of the Indianapolis 500*, 32–35.

42. *Columbus Sunday Dispatch*, 29 June 1913, clipping in EVRS 1; "Rickenbacker Speeds Up with a Mason Car," typescript of article from *Ohio State Journal* (Columbus), 30 June 1913, Franklin Count–Columbus Metropolitan Library.

43. Ralph Mulford, "Racing with Lozier: A Memoir," *Automobile Quarterly* 7, no. 4 (Spring 1969): 367–81.

44. J. W. Lehman, "Mulford in a Mason Wins 200-Mile Race at Columbus," *Motor Age*, 10 July 1913, 10.

45. "Galveston 300 Mile Race," National Automotive History Collection, Detroit Public Library; Adamson, *Eddie Rickenbacker*, 111–12.

46. Adamson, *Eddie Rickenbacker*, 111–12; R-H Tapes, reel 39C, side 2. Adamson's account of an incident in the St. Paul race, in which Rickenbacker lost control of his car attempting to pass Louis Disbrow (the car somersaulted in the air and landed upside down after smashing through a fence), crawled out after the crash, walked virtually unhurt back to the Duesenberg pit, and received a standing ovation, is erroneous. The incident, or something like it, did occur, but the driver involved was Billy Chandler, another member of the Duesenberg team.

47. Box 23 of EVRP-LC contains a typewritten list, "Rickenbacker Automobile Racing Record," with additions in Rickenbacker's handwriting, showing the dates, locations, distances, cars, and results of all of Rickenbacker's races between 4 October 1911 and 16 November 1916. I have relied on this list unless evidence from primary sources contradicts it.

48. Adamson, *Eddie Rickenbacker*, 112.

Chapter 4. Full Throttle

1. "Review of Record Breaking Santa Monica Races," *Horseless Age*, 11 March 1914, 395–402; photograph, EVRR, facing page 76. Jerry E. Gebby, "Mercer at Indy," *Antique Automobile* 47, no. 2 (March–April 1983): 26–31. The caption accompanying the photo of Richenbacher contains two errors, stating that the crash happened at the 1913 Vanderbilt Cup Race at Santa Monica, where the 1914 Vanderbilt Cup and Grand Prize races constituted a single venue. Rickenbacher was not involved in the Vanderbilt Cup Race but competed for the Grand Prize. Ferdinand Roebling and Washington Roebling II, members of the illustrious family responsible for such famous structures as the Brooklyn Bridge, were among the founders of the Mercer Automobile Company.

2. Fox, *The Illustrated History of the Indianapolis 500*, 36–39; Jerome T. Shaw, "France Sweeps the Boards at Indianapolis," *Horseless Age*, 3 June 1914, 855–64; Lessner, *Famous Auto Races*, 129–31.

3. R-H Tapes, reel 39D, side 1.

4. "22 Entries for Sioux City 300-Mile Race," *Horseless Age*, 1 July 1914, 5. EVRS 1 contains a mass of clippings about the sweepstakes, on which the account that follows is based.

5. "Rickenbacker Captures First Place," unidentified Sioux City newspaper, 4 July 1914, EVRS 1; R-H Tapes, reel 39D, side 1. The taped interview and a corresponding passage in EVRR state that another driver, T. C. Cox, was killed in this race because of a glancing collision with Rickenbacher's car. The incident actually happened in the second running of the same race at Sioux City in 1915.

6. R-H Tapes, reel 39D, side 1.

7. *Horseless Age*, 9 September 1914, 386. For a different account of the Beachey-Rickenbacker race, asserting that Beachey won, see Ann Holtgren Pellegrino, *Iowa Takes to the Air* (Sioux City, IA: Aerodrome Press, 1980), 186–87, with photograph. The discrepancy stems from the handicap imposed on Beachey, without which he would have been the victor.

8. Rickenbacker Automobile Racing Record, EVRP-LC, box 23.

9. "De Palma's Mercedes Wins Both Elgin Races," *Horseless Age*, 26 August 1914, 306–9; R-H Tapes, reel 11, side 1, and reel 39D, side 1; Peter Helck, "The 1914 Race for the Elgin National Trophy," *Horseless Carriage Gazette* 37, no. 3 (May–June 1975): 32–35, with maps of the course and artwork by Helck; Peter Helck, "The Races for the Elgin National Trophy," ibid., 36–38.

10. Lowell Thomas, *Good Evening Everybody: From Cripple Creek to Samarkand* (New York: Morrow, 1976), 66–67. Thomas misdates the race as having occurred in 1910 when he was a student at Valparaiso University. Because he associates the race with Wishart's death, it is clear that it took place in 1914 when Thomas was a student at the Chicago-Kent School of Law and also worked as a reporter for the *Chicago Evening-Journal*. See W. David Lewis, "Lowell Jackson Thomas," in Kenneth T. Jackson,

Karen Markoe, and Arnold Markoe, eds., *The Scribner Encyclopedia of American Lives* (New York: Charles Scribner's Sons, 1998), 1:786–88. I am grateful for the help of the late Fred D. Crawford, who was writing a biography of Thomas before his death.

11. Adriano Cimarosti, *The Complete History of Grand Prix Motor Racing* (London: Aurum Press Limited, 1997), 42–45; Beverly Rae Kimes, "Peugeot: A Family Affair," *Automobile Quarterly* 4, no. 4 (Spring 1966): 415–16.

12. R-H Tapes, reel 4, side 2.

13. EVRR, 62. On Miller's career, see Mark L. Dees, *The Miller Dynasty: A Technical History of the Work of Harry A. Miller, His Associates, and His Successors,* rev. 2nd ed. (Moorpark, CA: Hippodrome Publishing Company, 1994), and Borgeson, "Harry Miller," 199–223.

14. "Maxwell Builds Seven Racing Cars," *The Automobile,* 25 February 1915, 388; "Maxwells Designed for 105 M.P.H.," in ibid., 25 March 1915, 528–30; undated clipping from unidentified newspaper, "Rickenbacker Is to Fly Maxwell Colors," EVRS 1.

15. Baldwin et al., *World Guide,* 316–17.

16. "The Problems of Kerosene," *The Automobile,* 30 March 1916, 573–76.

17. R-H Tapes, reel 4, side 2; "Resta Wins Grand Prize," "Resta Wins Again," and "The Winning of the Grand Prize," *The Automobile,* 4 March 1915, 398–99, and 11 March 1915, 446–48.

18. "Resta Wins Again—Takes Vanderbilt" and "Resta's Generalship Won Vanderbilt," *The Automobile,* 11 March 1915, 446–47, and 18 March 1915, 512–13; Rickenbacker Automobile Racing Record, EVRP-LC, box 23.

19. R-H Tapes, reel 4, side 2; "Only 30 Stops in Venice Race" and "Oldfield and Carlson Win at Tucson," *The Automobile,* 25 March 1915, 561; Rickenbacker Automobile Racing Record, EVRP-LC, box 23.

20. Adamson, *Eddie Rickenbacker,* 128. On the Blitzen Benz and its record-breaking performances, see "America's Motor Car Speed Records," *MoToR* 22, no. 5 (August 1914): 47. As this source indicates, Robert (Bob) Burman set a land speed record of 141.732 miles per hour in the Blitzen Benz at Daytona Beach on 23 April 1911, eclipsing a previous mark of 131.275 set by Barney Oldfield in the same vehicle at the same place on 23 March 1910. Rickenbacker admitted that he "never had any real experience with the Benz." R-H Tapes, reel 4, side 2.

21. R-H Tapes, reel 4, side 2.

22. Ibid.; Fox, *Illustrated History of the Indianapolis 500,* 40–43.

23. Adamson, *Eddie Rickenbacker,* 130, 136.

24. "Holiday Racing on the Speedways," *Horseless Age,* 7 July 1915, 2–3. On the difficulty of a racer's regaining focus after an interruption, see Ernie Pyle, *Home Country* (New York: William Sloane Associates, Inc., 1947), 150.

25. Adamson, *Eddie Rickenbacker,* 131.

26. "Rickenbacher and O'Donnell Again at Omaha," *Horseless Age,* 7 July 1915, 3.

27. Robert Cutter and Bob Fendell, *The Encyclopedia of Auto Racing Greats* (Englewood Cliffs, NJ: Prentice-Hall, 1973), 7.

28. "Two Racing Co.'s Formed," *The Automobile,* 23 September 1915.

29. Adamson, *Eddie Rickenbacker,* 135.

30. Rickenbacher and Burton, "Loyal Legion of Speed."

31. Adamson, *Eddie Rickenbacker,* 132–33.

32. R-H Tapes, reel 4, side 2; M. P. Shattuck, "Low Speed Marks Providence Century," *Horseless Age,* 1 October 1915, 312–14.

33. Copy of *Motor Age* article in EVRP-LC, box 23.

34. Kimes and Clark, *Standard Catalog,* 1442; "Stutz Withdraws from Racing Indefinitely," *Horseless Age,* 1 November 1915, 430.

35. Catlin, "54 Bittersweet Years of the AAA Contest Board," 402–4.

36. James M. Laux, *The European Automobile Industry* (New York: Twayne Publishers, 1992), 62–63.

37. For the best available biography of Fisher, see Fisher, *The Pacesetter,* which, however, says little about his role in the Indianapolis Speedway after 1919 and nothing about the Prest-O-Lite or Speedway teams discussed here.

38. "1916 Racing Cars at Sheepshead," *The Automobile,* 11 May 1916, 844–47, with analysis of changes incorporated in the new Maxwells. Streamlining was becoming increasingly common in motor sport before World War I. Pictures of cars used in successive Indy 500s between 1911 and 1916 show how bodies offered less resistance to airflow. See, for example, photographs in Fox, *Illustrated History of the Indianapolis 500,* 24–45.

39. R-H Tapes, reel 5, side 1.

40. EVRR, 67–68; Oney Fred Sweet, "It Wasn't My Fault That a Valve Broke," clipping from unidentified newspaper, EVRS 1. I could not find a copy of the rule book.

41. Jerome T. Shaw, "And What about Racing in 1916?" *Horseless Age,* 1 March 1916, 177–78; Fox, *Illustrated History of the Indianapolis 500,* 44.

42. Clipping from *Motor Age,* 13 April 1916, EVRS 1.

43. "Rickenbacker Slips Away to Dixie to Wed a Movie Star," clipping from unidentified, undated newspaper, probably April 1916, EVRS 1.

44. "Maxwell Wins Trophy: Short Events Are Won by Peugeots—Limberg Killed" and "Limberg Killed in Metropolitan Event," *The Automobile,* 18 May 1916, 879–85; R-H Tapes, reel 11, side 1.

45. "Rickenbacher's Nerve Unshaken by Narrow Escape, Did Rare Bit of Driving," clipping from unidentified newspaper, EVRS 1; Adamson, *Eddie Rickenbacker,* 139–40.

46. "Maxwell Wins Trophy," *The Automobile,* 18 May 1916; "Maxwell Wins Metropolitan Race," *Horseless Age,* 15 May 1916.

47. "Life Story," 1:152.

48. Fox, *Illustrated History of the Indianapolis 500,* 44–47.

49. Sweet, "It Wasn't My Fault That a Valve Broke."

50. "Resta Enters in Omaha Race," "Some Inside Dope Heard among the Rail

Birds at the Speedway," "Two New World's Record Are Made," "Annual Omaha Auto Derby to Be Held Today," and "Resta Wins the Omaha Derby," *Omaha Bee,* 23 June and 10, 11, 15, 16 July 1916. Among the founders of the Crawford Automobile Company was Mathias Peter Möller, a Danish immigrant who became more famous by manufacturing pipe organs.

51. "Rickenbacker Wins the Montmarathon," undated clipping, EVRS 1; "Life Story," 1:138–39.

52. "Aitken Makes Clean Sweep," *The Automobile,* 14 September 1916, 463–54; "Life Story," 1:140–41; Rick Popely, with L. Spencer Riggs, *Indianapolis 500 Chronicle* (Lincolnwood, IL: Publications International, Ltd., 1998), 21.

53. Rickenbacker later stated that he had actually earned "more than $60,000" in 1916 because of "extras" that other members of the team did not receive, including endorsements for "gas, oil, and so forth." R-H Tapes, reel 39E, side 1.

Chapter 5. Shifting Gears

1. Anonymous, *The History and Development of the Sunbeam Car, 1899–1924: A Souvenir of a Quarter of a Century of Sunbeam Success and Service* (Wolverhampton, UK: Sunbeam Motor Car Company Limited, 1924), 23–31; Peter King, *The Motor Men: Pioneers of the British Car Industry* (London: Quiller Press, n.d.), 105–6.

2. On the Weightman fortune, which ranked among the thirty largest in America between 1901 and 1914, see Kevin Phillips, *Wealth and Democracy: A Political History of the American Rich* (New York: Broadway Books, 2002), 51.

3. J. C. Burton, "Magnates of Speed," *MoToR* 28, no. 2 (May 1917): 75–78.

4. "Life Story," 1:150.

5. R-H Tapes, reel 39F, side 1; John R. Breihan, Stan Piet, and Roger S. Mason, *Martin Aircraft 1909–1960* (Santa Ana, CA: Narkiewicz/Thompson Publishers, 1995), 5–13; Wayne Biddle, *Barons of the Sky* (New York: Henry Holt, 1991), 44–67.

6. R-H Tapes, reel 39F, side 1. Dodd was assigned to the 1st Aero Squadron from 15 March 1916 to 15 March 1917. In September 1916, when the unit was headquartered at Columbus, New Mexico, he took command to replace Benjamin Foulois, who was assigned to temporary duty in Washington before becoming aviation officer of the Southern Department at Fort Sam Houston, Texas. James J. Sloan, *Wings of Honor: American Airmen in World War I* (Atglen, PA: Schiffer Publications, 1994), 404; Ernest La Rue Jones Papers, United States Air Force Historical Research Agency, Maxwell Air Force Base, Montgomery, Alabama, file 168.65011-22, entry for 22 September 1916. Dodd may have been flying between New Mexico and San Diego, where the Signal Corps Aviation School was located. I am grateful to Bert Frandsen for advice on this subject and supplying the citation for the Ernest La Rue Jones Papers.

7. "Peugeot Wins Road Classics," *The Automobile,* 22 November 1916, 872.

8. "Rickenbacker Wins at Ascot—Duesenberg Takes 150-Mile Race—Cooper Is Second and Pullen Third," *The Automobile*, 7 December 1916, 959.

9. "Resta Confirmed as Champion," *The Automobile*, 7 December 1916, 958.

10. "Rickenbacker Is Europe-Bound: Expected to Bring Back Cars; Name Withheld," clipping from undated, unidentified magazine, EVRS 1. For a photograph and diagram of the Fiat in which Duray set the record at Ostend, see Peter J. R. Holthusen, *The Fastest Men on Earth: 100 Years of the Land Speed Record* (Gloucestershire, UK: Sutton Publishing Limited, 1999), 17.

11. "Rickenbacher Signs Up with Phil. Millionaire," clipping of 9 December 1916 from unidentified newspaper, Biography Collection, Franklin County–Columbus Metropolitan Library, Columbus, Ohio; "Rick Sails to Bring Back Two Fast Cars: Eddie Rickenbacker Starts for England, France and Italy in Quest of Speediest Autos, Planning to Wear 1917 Speed Crown," clipping from unidentified newspaper, 12 December 1916, EVRS 1.

12. Adamson, *Eddie Rickenbacker*, 149.

13. Copies of passport and visa supplied by Frank Hammelbacher, Flushing, New York, cited with his permission.

14. Adamson, *Eddie Rickenbacker*, 147–50; R-H Tapes, reel 39E, side 2.

15. A. G. Waddell, "When Scotland Yard Shadowed an Ace," *Radco Automotive Review*, September 1929, in EVRP-LC, box 128.

16. R-H Tapes, reel 39E, side 2; Douglas H. Robinson, *The Zeppelin in Combat*, rev. ed. (Sun Valley, CA: John W. Caler, 1966), 190–203.

17. George R. Sims, "The Savoy Extension," *London Observer*, 30 October 1910; Stanley Jackson, *The Savoy: A Century of Taste* (London: Frederick Muller, 1979), 60–62.

18. On class distinctions in Great Britain that Rickenbacker abominated, see Barbara Tuchman, *The Proud Tower: A Portrait of the World before the War, 1890–1914* (New York: Ballantine Books, 1966), 3–59, 351–403.

19. "Rickenbacker in Europe for King Motor Company," clipping from *Atlanta Journal*, 4 February 1917, EVRS 1.

20. R-H Tapes, reel 39E, side 2; "Sunbeam Cars," http://Sunbeam Cars.local history.scit.wlv.ac.uk/Museum/Transport Cars/Sunbeam.htm, accessed 24 June 2004, with map of Moorfield Works; Colin Campbell, *The Sports Car: Its Design and Performance* (Cambridge, MA: Robert Bentley Inc., 1955), 230–31.

21. R-H Tapes, reel 39E, side 2, and reel 39F, side 1; Howard Johnson, *Wings over Brooklands: The Story of the Birthplace of British Aviation* (London: Whittet Books, 1985), 9–31; McDonald, *Fifty Years with the Speed Kings*, 15–16; brochure, Brooklands Speedway, 1993.

22. John Milton Cooper Jr., *The Warrior and the Priest: Woodrow Wilson and Theodore Roosevelt* (Cambridge, MA: Harvard University Press, 1983), 315.

23. "Life Story," 1:162–65.

24. "Plans to Enlist Race Drivers for Aviation," *New York Times*, 18 February 1917, sec. 3, p. 2.

25. "Auto Racers Would Be Air Fighters," undated clipping from unidentified newspaper, EVRS 1.

26. "Life Story," 1:166–68; R-H Tapes, reel 39E, side 1.

27. "Life Story," 1:166–68; R-H Tapes, reel 39E, side 2; Barbara W. Tuchman, *The Zimmermann Telegram* (New York: Viking Press, 1958).

28. EVRR, 83–84.

29. Cooper, *The Warrior and the Priest,* 318–22.

30. EVRR, 84–85.

31. Fox, *Illustrated History of the Indianapolis 500,* 12.

32. R-H Tapes, reel 15, side 2.

33. Edward M. Coffman, *The War to End All Wars: The American Military Experience in World War I,* paperback ed. (Madison: University of Wisconsin Press, 1986), 46–53; John J. Pershing, *My Experiences in the First World War,* paperback ed. (New York: Da Capo Press, 1995), 1–40.

34. Installment from Christian ("Chris") Sinsabaugh, *"Who, Me?" My AUTO-biography,* in EVRS 3 (1936–40); R-H Tapes, reel 39E, side 2. Sinsabaugh, a newspaperman, covered the automobile industry.

35. R-H Tapes, reel 39E, side 2. For a photograph and brief history of the *Baltic,* see William H. Miller Jr., *The First Great Ocean Liners in Photographs* (New York: Dover Publications, 1984), 28–29.

36. Gene Smith, *Until the Last Trumpet Sounds: The Life of General of the Armies John J. Pershing* (New York: John Wiley & Sons, Inc., 1998), 149–51; Donald Smythe, *Pershing: General of the Armies* (Bloomington: Indiana University Press, 1986), 13.

37. EVRR, 87.

38. Pershing, *My Experiences,* 42–44; Donald Smythe, *Pershing: General of the Armies* (Bloomington: Indiana University Press, 1986), 14.

39. R-H Tapes, reel 39F, side 1; "Life Story," 1:171–72.

40. Pershing, *My Experiences,* 43–46; Smythe, *Pershing,* 15; account of Rickenbacker interview with French reporters published in *Chicago Herald,* 2 September 1917, clipping in EVRS 1.

41. Photograph from *Los Angeles Examiner,* June 1917, and "American Commander and His Men Are Honored Abroad," *Chalmers Illustrated News,* 1 August 1917, clippings in EVRS 1; Smythe, *Pershing,* 15–18; Smith, *Until the Last Trumpet Sounds,* 152; Pershing, *My Experiences,* 46–52; EVRR, 89; "Life Story," 1:72; R-H Tapes, reel 6, side 2. Some details in the Herndon interview conflict with the account in "Life Story," which I have followed because it dates from 1943, when Rickenbacker's memory was probably clearer than in 1965.

42. R-H Tapes, reel 6, side 2, and reel 39F, side 1; "Life Story," 1:173–74.

43. R-H Tapes, reel 6, side 2.

44. "Rickenbacker U.S.A. Soldier," *Motor Age,* 26 July 1917, citing article in *l'Auto* datelined Paris, 4 July 1917; "Rickenbacker to Take Up Aviation," *Wheeling (WV) Register,* 19 August 1917, clippings in EVRS 2 (1920–35); Farr, *Rickenbacker's Luck,* 42.

45. Smith, *Until the Last Trumpet Sounds,* 155–60; Smythe, *Pershing,* 33–44.

46. "Life Story," 1:174.

47. "Through Rick's Eyes: Former Racing Champion Writes 'Tribune' Man of Viewing the Big Fight at Pershing's Side," clipping from *Chicago Tribune,* 30 December 1917, EVRS 1.

48. Smythe, *Pershing,* 30–31.

49. Douglas MacArthur, *Reminiscences* (New York: Da Capo Press, 1964), 59. On Pershing's affair with Resco, see Smythe, *Pershing,* 296–301.

50. William L. Mitchell, *Memoirs of World War I* (New York: Random House, 1956).

51. William L. Mitchell, "Rickenbacker: The Ace of Aces of the A.E.F.," *Liberty,* 17 May 1930, 20, copy in vertical files, National Air and Space Museum, Washington, D.C.; James J. Cooke, *Billy Mitchell* (Boulder, CO: Lynne Rienner Publishers, 2002), 64.

52. Mitchell, "Rickenbacker," 20–21; William L. Mitchell, "Rickenbacker: The Ace of the American Expeditionary Force," in Frank C. Platt, ed., *Great Battles of World War I* (New York: Weathervane Books, 1966), 90.

53. "Life Story," 1:174–75; R-H Tapes, reel 39F, side 1.

54. "Life Story," 1:308–9; R-H Tapes, reel 39F, side 1.

55. "Life Story," 1:175; Farr, *Rickenbacker's Luck,* 44. On the establishment of the base, see Maurer Maurer, ed., *The U.S. Air Service in World War I,* 4 vols. (Washington, DC: U.S. Government Printing Office, 1978), 1:58, and Rebecca Hancock Cameron, *Training to Fly: Military Flight Training, 1907–1945* ([Washington, DC]: Air Force History and Museums Program, 1999), 148–49. Rickenbacker's statement that Mitchell selected the site on this trip is untrue; a commission headed by Raynal C. Bolling had already chosen it.

56. "Life Story," 1:175–76; R-H Tapes, 26 February 1965.

57. Sloan, *Wings of Honor,* 32–36.

58. R-H Tapes, reel 6, side 2, reel 39F, side 1, and 26 February 1965; "Life Story," 1:176–77; EVRR, 89–90. For Mitchell's own account, see Mitchell, "Rickenbacker—The Ace of the American Expeditionary Force," 91.

59. Cameron, *Training to Fly,* 149–54. On this training method, see also James Norman Hall, *High Adventure* (Boston: Houghton Mifflin, 1918), 25–26.

60. R-H Tapes, reel 15, side 2, and reel 39F, side 1.

61. "Life Story," 1:177; EVRR, 90–91; clippings from *Chicago Tribune,* 30 December 1917, and *Pittsburgh Leader,* 30 January 1919, EVRS 1.

62. Maurer, *The U.S. Air Service in World War I,* 1:93, 97.

63. Quoted in James J. Cooke, *The U.S. Air Service in the Great War, 1917–1919* (Westport, CT: Praeger, 1996), 20. See also Charles Woolley, with Bill Crawford, *Echoes of Eagles* (New York: Dutton, 2003), 54.

64. R-H Tapes, reel 39F, sides 1 and 2; Geoffrey Perret, *Old Soldiers Never Die: The Life of Douglas MacArthur* (New York: Random House, 1996), 230; Richard G. Davis, *Carl A. Spaatz and the Air War in Europe* (Washington, DC: Smithsonian Institution Press, n.d.), 3–5. Spatz ultimately changed his name to Spaatz.

65. Bert Frandsen, *Hat in the Ring: The Birth of American Air Power in the Great War* (Washington, DC: Smithsonian Books, 2003), 42–43.

66. R-H Tapes, reel 6, side 2; "Life Story," 1:179–82; EVRR, 93–94.

67. Headquarters American Expeditionary Forces, Special Order No. 185, 10 December 1917, copy in Edward V. Rickenbacker Collection, United States Air Force Museum, Wright-Patterson Air Force Base, Dayton, Ohio.

68. R-H Tapes, reel 6, side 2; "Life Story," 1:182–84.

69. Headquarters, Line of Communications, Special Orders, 3 January 1918, copy in Rickenbacker Collection, United States Air Force Museum.

70. On Meissner's background, see Frandsen, *Hat in the Ring*, 27–30. Frandsen has been of great help to me regarding Meissner's relationship with Rickenbacker.

71. R-H Tapes, reel 6, side 2; "Life Story," 1:184–85; EVRR, 95.

72. Headquarters U.S. Troops, Paris, American Expeditionary Forces, Special Order No. 40, 19 February 1918, copy in Rickenbacker Collection, United States Air Force Museum.

Chapter 6. Takeoff

1. Irving B. Holley Jr., *Ideas and Weapons: Exploitation of the Aerial Weapon by the United States during World War I* (1953; repr., Washington, DC: Office of Air Force History, 1983), 37–46; Maurer, *U.S. Air Service in World War I,* 1:51; Samuel Taylor Moore, *U.S. Airpower* (New York: Greenberg Publishers, 1958), 52.

2. John S. D. Eisenhower, *Intervention! The United States and the Mexican Revolution* (New York: W. W. Norton & Company, 1993), 254–57; Herbert M. Mason, *The Great Pursuit: Pershing's Expedition to Destroy Pancho Villa* (1970; repr., New York: Smithmark Books, 1995), 103–19, 221–22; Enrique Krauze, *Mexico: Biography of Power* (New York: Harper Collins, 1997), 328–29.

3. Frandsen, *Hat in the Ring*, esp. 3. On the Lafayette Escadrille and Lafayette Flying Corps, see James Norman Hall and Charles Bernard Nordhoff, eds., *The Lafayette Flying Corps*, 2 vols. (Boston: Houghton Mifflin Company, 1919), and Dennis Gordon, *The Lafayette Flying Corps: The American Volunteers in the French Air Service in World War One* (Atglen, PA: Schiffer Publishing Ltd., 2000).

4. Arthur Sweetser, *The American Air Service: A Record of Its Problems, Its Difficulties, Its Failures, and Its Final Achievements* (New York: D. Appleton and Company, 1919), 79.

5. Cooke, *U.S. Air Service in the Great War,* 25–26; Smythe, *Pershing,* 60–65.

6. "Life Story," 1:312; James J. Hudson, *Hostile Skies: A Combat History of the American Air Service in World War I* (Syracuse, NY: Syracuse University Press, 1968), 54–55.

7. Alexander McKee, *The Friendless Sky: The Story of Air Combat in World War I* (London: Souvenir Press, 1962), 203–4; Philip Flammer, *The Vivid Air: The Lafayette Escadrille* (Athens: University of Georgia Press, 1981); Sloan, *Wings of Honor,* 16–31.

8. Flammer, *Vivid Air,* 161–83; Sloan, *Wings of Honor,* 87–92.

9. Martin Gilbert, *The First World War: A Complete History* (New York: Henry Holt and Company, 1994), 375–405; Smythe, *Pershing,* 74–80.

10. Frandsen, *Hat in the Ring,* 55–57.

11. Ibid., 8–9.

12. Sloan, *Wings of Honor,* 101–4; Harold Buckley, *Squadron 95* (Paris: Obelisk Press, 1933), 26–29.

13. EVRD-1918, copy at United States Air Force Museum. In *Wings of Honor,* 108, Sloan states that Rickenbacker did not begin keeping the diary until August 1918 and that the entries prior to that time are unreliable because they were written from memory. I have found no evidence for this claim. Entries in the diary can easily be correlated with information in other primary and secondary sources.

14. EVRD-1918, entries for 2–4 March; Buckley, *Squadron 95,* 30–31.

15. EVRD-1918, entries for 5–7 March; Hall and Nordhoff, *Lafayette Flying Corps,* 1:280–81.

16. Buckley, *Squadron 95,* 32.

17. Ibid., 32–33; EVRD-1918, entries for 9, 10 March; Frandsen, *Hat in the Ring,* 22–25.

18. Hall and Nordhoff, *Lafayette Flying Corps,* 1:328–38.

19. Flammer, *Vivid Air,* esp. 16–17; Flint O. DuPre, *U.S. Air Force Biographical Dictionary* (1964; New York: Franklin Watts, Inc., 1965), 145–56; Herbert Molloy Mason Jr., *The Lafayette Escadrille* (1964; repr., New York: Smithmark Publishers, Inc., 1995), 279.

20. The discussion that follows is based largely on Richard P. Hallion, *Rise of the Fighter Aircraft, 1914–1918* (Baltimore: Nautical & Aviation Company of America, 1984).

21. The curatorial files of the Department of Aeronautics, National Air and Space Museum, Washington, D.C., contain a mass of material on the Nieuport 28 and the Gnome Monosoupape engine. See also Bert L. Frandsen and W. David Lewis, "Nieuports and Spads: French Pursuit Planes and American Airpower in World War I," *History of Technology* 21 (1999): 189–202.

22. Edward H. Sims, *Fighter Tactics and Strategy, 1914–1970,* 2nd ed. (Fallbrook, CA: Aero Publishers, Inc., 1972), 3–22.

23. EVRD-1918, entries for 11, 13–17 March; Buckley, *Squadron 95,* 35.

24. EVRD-1918, entries for 18, 19, 21, 22 March.

25. Buckley, *Squadron 95,* 36; Sloan, *Wings of Honor,* 108–9, 129.

26. John Keegan, *The First World War* (New York: Alfred A. Knopf, 1999), 392–406; Gary Mead, *The Doughboys: America and the First World War* (Woodstock, NY: Overlook Press, 2000), 208–18.

27. Gilbert, *First World War,* 406–10; Coffman, *War to End All Wars,* 154–55; EVRD-1918, entries for 23–26 March.

28. EVRD-1918, entry for 27 March; Jack R. Eder, ed., *Let's Go Where the Action Is: The Wartime Experiences of Douglas Campbell* (Knightstown, IN: JaaRE Publishing, Inc., 1984), 50. The account in *FFC,* 1–10, about how Lufbery announced his choice of Rickenbacker and Campbell is fictional, having been written by the book's ghost-

writer, Laurence La Tourette Driggs, who also misdated the sortie by saying that it occurred on 6 March.

29. The flying suit, designed by Sidney Cotton, an Australian, was called a "Sidcot" by the British. American units called it a "teddy bear suit." A specimen is displayed at the Wings over the Rockies Air and Space Museum, Aurora, Colorado.

30. On developments that follow, see EVRD-1918, entry for 28 March, and the initial pages of a preliminary account (PACC) that Rickenbacker wrote for Driggs. On the relationship between PACC and *FFC*, see Lewis, "Historical Introduction," in *FFCL*, lxiii–lxxii.

31. On this procedure, see *FFC*, 56–57, and annotation by Lewis in *FFCL*, 71–72. For an account of the steps involved, see also W. E. Johns, *Fighting Planes and Aces* (London: John Hamilton, n.d.), 16.

32. Mitchell, *Memoirs of World War I*, 62. For descriptions of the terrain between Villeneuve and Rheims, see ibid., 19–65. I have supplemented the account presented here with personal observations of the area on a visit to Rheims, Epernay, Vertus, Villeneuve, Chalons, and Suippes in August 1999.

33. Ibid., 23.

34. John Cook, *The Book of Positive Quotations* (Minneapolis: Fairview Press, 1993), 411.

35. Emile Gauvreau, *The Wild Blue Yonder* (New York: E. P. Dutton, 1944), 68–71.

36. EVRD-1918, entries for 29, 30 March; Maurer, *U.S. Air Service in World War I*, 1:171, 284.

37. EVRD-1918, entry for 31 March; photograph in Charles Woolley, *First to the Front: The Aerial Adventures of 1st Lieutenant Waldo Heinrichs and the 95th Aero Squadron, 1917–1918* (Atglen, PA: Schiffer Publishing Ltd., 1999), 75.

38. James Norman Hall, *My Island Home: An Autobiography* (Boston: Little, Brown and Company, 1952); Paul L. Briand Jr., *In Search of Paradise: The Nordhoff-Hall Story* (New York: Duell, Sloan & Pearce, 1966); Hall and Nordhoff, *Lafayette Flying Corps*, 1:256–58; Flammer, *Vivid Air*, 136–39, 156, 173, 187; Mason, *Lafayette Escadrille*, 213–18, 259–70, 276–78, 283–84.

39. Hall and Nordhoff, *Lafayette Flying Corps*, 1:382–384; Flammer, *Vivid Air*, 142, 144, 151, 173, 186; Molloy, *Lafayette Escadrille*, 218–19, 249, 258–70, 283.

40. Hall and Nordhoff, *Lafayette Flying Corps*, 1:354; Flammer, *Vivid Air*, 120–21, 147–50, 173.

41. EVRD-1918, entry for 1 April; EVRR, 288; R-H Tapes, reel 15, side 2.

42. R-H Tapes, reel 15, side 2.

43. *FFC*, 15–16.

44. EVRD-1918, entry for 2 April; *FFC*, 16–17.

45. EVRD-1918, entry for 4 April.

46. Flammer, *Vivid Air*, 118–19, 124, 148, 173; EVRD-1918, entries for 4, 5 April.

47. EVRD-1918, entry for 11 April.

48. EVRD-1918, entry for 6 April.

49. Interview with Bert Frandsen by author. Operationally the First Pursuit Group was under the jurisdiction of the 8th French Army Corps. Liggett delegated much of his authority over aviation to Mitchell, and for all intents and purposes Americans had charge of operations.

50. *FFC*, 20.

51. On aircraft insignia and markings in World War I, including Rickenbacker's, see Eric Lawson and Jane Lawson, *The First Air Campaign: August 1914–November 1918* (Conshohocken, PA: Combined Books, 1996), 51–55.

52. William F. Rickenbacker informed me that his father wanted his name pronounced to rhyme with "hacker." On the circumstances of the change, which I cannot date precisely, see W. David Lewis, "Edward V. Rickenbacker," in William M. Leary, ed., *The Airline Industry* (New York: Facts on File, 1992), 398.

53. "'Gimper,' Flier Stopping at Nothing, Definition Given by Eddie Rickenbacker" and "Proving That a Gimper Is Far from a Cuckoo Bird," clippings from *Detroit News*, 21 July and 17 August 1918, EVRS 1.

54. EVRD-1918, entries for 12, 13 April.

55. Mitchell, "Rickenbacker: The Ace of the American Expeditionary Force," 93.

56. Unless otherwise noted, details of the sortie that follows are from *FFC*, 21–26, and the corresponding account in PACC.

57. R-H Tapes, reel 15, side 2.

58. *FFC*, 26–27; Maurer, *History of the U.S Air Service in World War I*, 1:284; Alan Winslow, "No Parachutes," *Liberty* 10, no. 8 (25 February 1933): 11, and no. 9 (4 March 1933): 18. For the best account of the episode, see Frandsen, *Hat in the Ring*, 90–93.

59. Mitchell, *Memoirs of World War I*, 192.

60. EVRD-1918, entries for 14–17 April.

61. EVRD-1918, entry for 18 April; typescript, 16 November 1918, dictated by Rickenbacker, in PACC; *FFC*, 28–29.

62. EVRD-1918, entries for 20, 21 April; Coffman, *War to End All Wars*, 144–48.

63. Typescript dictated by Rickenbacker, 16 November 1918, PACC; *FFC*, 50–52; EVRR, 103.

64. EVRD-1918, entries for 26, 28 April.

65. On the sortie discussed here, see particularly a typescript dictated by Rickenbacker, 16 November 1918, PACC, from which the quotation is taken.

66. *FFC*, 41.

67. Typescript dictated by Rickenbacker, 16 November 1918, PACC.

68. EVRD-1918, entry for April 29.

69. *FFC*, 60.

70. Typescript dictated by Rickenbacker, 16 November 1918, PACC.

71. Ibid.; EVRD-1918, entry for May 15.

Chapter 7. Learning Curve

1. Buckley, *Squadron 95*, 51–54. On the color schemes used by the French, see R. L. Cavanagh, "The 94th and Its Nieuports, 15 April–11 June 1918," *Cross and Cockade Journal* 21, no. 3 (Autumn 1980): 200.

2. Dave English, *Slipping the Surly Bonds: Great Quotations on Flight* (New York: McGraw-Hill, 1998), 100.

3. Hall and Nordhoff, *Lafayette Flying Corps*, 1:169–70; EVRD-1918, entry for 3 May.

4. Details of the sortie that follows are included in the typescript dictated by Rickenbacker, 18 November 1918, PACC. See also *FFC*, 60–61.

5. Anthony Bruce, *An Illustrated Companion to the First World War* (London: Michael Joseph Ltd., 1989), 187.

6. EVRD-1918, entry for 7 May.

7. Hall, *My Island Home*, 203–9; Briand, *In Search of Paradise*, 62–65 and illustrations following p. 44.

8. Briand, *In Search of Paradise*, 65–67; typescript dictated by Rickenbacker, 18 November 1918, PACC.

9. James Norman Hall, *Flying with Chaucer* (Boston: Houghton Mifflin, 1930).

10. Maurer Maurer, "Another Victory for Rickenbacker," *Airpower Historian*, April 1960, 117–24.

11. Buckley, *Squadron 95*, 113.

12. On the events that follow, see typescript dictated by Rickenbacker, 26 November 1918, PACC, and compare with *FFC*, 113–20.

13. Various sources deal extensively with the circumstances surrounding Lufbery's death. Among others, see Hall and Nordhoff, *Lafayette Flying Corps*, 336–37; Gordon, *Lafayette Flying Corps*, 295–96; and Frandsen, *Hat in the Ring*, 103–6.

14. Obituary, "O. J. Gude Jr.," *New York Times*, 7 December 1944.

15. For a discussion of this problem, see Dave Grossman, *On Killing: The Psychological Cost of Learning to Kill in War and Society* (Boston: Little, Brown and Company, 1995).

16. Davis had joined the 94th Pursuit Squadron on 1 April 1918. He was killed in action on 2 June while helping escort a British bomber squadron across the front lines. Gordon, *Lafayette Flying Corps*, 123.

17. Ibid., 295–96; Mitchell, *Memoirs of World War I*, 198–202; Royal D. Frey, "A.E.F. Combat Airfields and Monuments in France, WWI," *American Aviation Historical Society Journal* 17, no. 3 (1972): 196.

18. Mitchell, *Memories of World War I*, 198–202; Eder, *Let's Go Where the Action Is*, 66–67, with photograph of the burial.

19. Eder, *Let's Go Where the Action Is*, 66.

20. "Down in Flames," undated transcript in PACC. As later indicated, this episode was the first part of what became *FFC* to be drafted by Rickenbacker. The document, filed among the reports used by Laurence LaTourette Driggs in ghostwriting

Rickenbacker's wartime memoirs, differs from the others in being undated, double-spaced, and considerably more polished, indicating that Driggs had revised Rick's earlier draft. It appears in only slightly modified form in *Fighting the Flying Circus*, 81–90, immediately before the chapter pertaining to Lufbery's death, which actually occurred two days earlier than that of Kurtz. As indicated in EVRD-1918, entry of 23 May, shooting down the German plane (an Albatros D-V) in the sortie with Chambers and Kurtz gave Rickenbacker his third confirmed victory.

21. For a synopsis of the developments discussed in this chapter, see Frandsen and Lewis, "Nieuports and Spads," 189–202.

22. Frandsen, *Hat in the Ring*, 98–102. For an extended account of the episode, see PACC, 18 November 1918, corresponding closely with what Meissner said about it. The account in *FFC*, upon which historians have relied, contains inaccurate embellishments added by Rickenbacker's ghostwriter, Driggs. On the identity of the German plane, see Norman L. R. Franks and Frank W. Bailey, *Over the Front: A Complete Record of the Fighter Aces and Units of the United States and French Air Services, 1914–1918* (London: Grub Street, 1992), 60–61.

23. For the best available account of this episode, see PACC, 25 November 1918. *FFC*, 72–81, contains embellishments by Driggs that do not appear in the original document dictated by Rickenbacker. For valuable commentary on the sortie, see Walter J. Boyne, *Aces in Command: Fighter Pilots as Combat Leaders* (Washington, DC: Brassey's, 2001), 38–39.

24. EVRD-1918, entry of 17 May 1918.

25. Ron Dick, *American Eagles: A History of the United States Air Force* (Charlottesville, VA: Howell Press, Inc., 1997), 35.

26. PACC, 29 November 1918; *FFC*, 117–19; Buckley, *Squadron 95*, 71–72.

27. Frandsen, *Hat in the Ring*, 106, citing Meissner Diary, 3 June 1918; PACC, 29 November 1918; *FFC*, 110–15; EVRD-1918, entry for 30 May; Cavanagh, "The 94th and Its Nieuports," 204–5.

28. Woolley, *First to the Front*, 114.

29. Bert L. Frandsen, "Nieuport 28: Broken Wings in the Pursuit Group," *W.W.1 Aero: The Journal of the Early Aeroplane*, no. 165 (August 1999): 38–42. See also Frandsen, *Hat in the Ring*, 107–10.

30. Frandsen, *Hat in the Ring*, 110–12.

31. Ibid., 113–14; Smythe, *Pershing*, 143–44; Hudson, *Hostile Skies*, 56–57; Pershing, *My Experiences*, 2:50; Mitchell, *Memoirs of World War I*, 205. Understandably, Pershing and Mitchell glossed over the details of the episode and did not reveal the disputes involved.

32. Frandsen, *Hat in the Ring*, 114–15; transcript, Court-Martial No. 127115, 24 February 1919, Record Group 153, National Archives, provided by Frandsen; EVRD-1918, entry for 4 June; Sloan, *Wings of Honor*, 131. In *The Hat in the Ring Gang: The Combat History of the 94th Aero Squadron in World War I* (Atglen, PA: Schiffer Publishing, Ltd., 2001), Charles Woolley speculates that Huffer was cashiered because of

his "non-performance" in the episode leading to Lufbery's death. I have followed Frandsen's interpretation.

33. For an extended discussion underlying this analysis, see Herbert L. Frandsen Jr., "First Pursuit Group in the Great War: Leadership, Technology, and the Birth of American Combat Aviation" (Ph.D. dissertation, Auburn University, 2000), 197–240.

34. Harold E. Hartney, *Up and At 'Em* (Harrisburg, PA: Stackpole Sons, 1940), 114–35; Frandsen, *Hat in the Ring,* 121–33.

35. Frandsen, *Hat in the Ring,* 124–34.

36. Alfred F. Hurley, *Billy Mitchell: Crusader for Air Power* (New York: Franklin Watts, Inc., 1964), 34.

Chapter 8. A Matter of Luck

1. Quentin Reynolds, *They Fought for the Sky* (New York: Rinehart & Company, Inc., 1957), ix.

2. Terry C. Treadwell and Alan C. Wood, *German Knights of the Air, 1914–1918: The Holders of the Orden pour le Merite* (New York: Barnes and Noble, 1997). Eighty-one pilots received the decoration, which was discontinued after 1918.

3. Boyne, *Aces in Command,* 1–9; Robert S. Johnson and Martin Caidin, *Thunderbolt!* (New York: IBooks paperback edition, 2001), xiv.

4. John H. Morrow Jr., *The Great War in the Air: Military Aviation from 1909 to 1921* (Washington, DC: Smithsonian Institution Press, 1993), 281–95, 310–29; Christopher Shores, Norman Franks, and Russell Guest, *Above the Trenches: A Complete Record of the Fighter Aces and Units of the British Empire Forces, 1915–1920* (London: Fortress Publications, Inc., 1990), 6–10.

5. Franks and Bailey, *Over the Front,* 6–7.

6. Morrow, *Great War in the Air,* 295–310; Norman L. R. Franks, Frank W. Bailey, and Russell Guest, *Above the Lines: A Complete Record of the Fighter Aces of the German Air Service, Naval Air Service, and Flanders Marine Corps, 1914–1918* (London: Grub Street, 1993), 5–10.

7. Franks et al., *Above the Lines,* 5–10.

8. Ibid., 187–89; John H. Morrow Jr., *German Air Power in World War I* (Lincoln: University of Nebraska Press, 1982), 109–11.

9. Shores et al., *Above the Trenches,* 76–78, 255–57; Franks and Bailey, *Over the Front,* 160–62, 170–71.

10. Franks and Bailey, *Over the Front,* 55–57; James J. Hudson, *In Clouds of Glory: American Airmen Who Flew with the British during the Great War* (Fayetteville: University of Arkansas Press, 1990), 9–22; Frederick Libby, *Horses Don't Fly: A Memoir of World War I* (New York: Arcade Publishing, 2000).

11. Eder, *Let's Go Where the Action Is,* 21–28, 62–67.

12. Franks and Bailey, *Over the Front,* 68; Eder, *Let's Go Where the Action Is,* 70–71; PACC, 27 November 1918.

13. EVRD-1918, entry for 28 May; PACC, 27 November 1918; Eder, *Let's Go Where the Action Is,* 71; *FFC,* 107–8.

14. "My Fifth Victory," PACC, 28 November 1918; *FFC,* 110–15. The title of the section in PACC was changed to "Jimmy Meissner Again" in *FFC* to eliminate confusion because of the fact that the next chapter, "America's First Ace," tells how Campbell got credit for his fifth victory before the one that Rickenbacker scored on 30 May could be confirmed.

15. "Lieutenant Campbell Becomes America's First Ace," PACC, 29 November 1918; *FFC,* 120–26; EVRD-1918, entry for 31 May 1918.

16. Eder, *Let's Go Where the Action Is,* 72–74.

17. Franks and Bailey, *Over the Front,* 29; Eder, *Let's Go Where the Action Is,* 75–77; PACC, 29 November 1918; *FFC,* 140–50.

18. Gilbert, *First World War,* 406–15; George B. Clark, *Devil Dogs: Fighting Marines of World War I* (Novato, CA: Presidio Press, Inc., 1999), 62–94; John Toland, *No Man's Land* (New York: Konecky and Konecky, 1980), 244–52.

19. Frandsen, *Hat in the Ring,* 139–40.

20. Bruce, *An Illustrated Companion to the First World War,* 324–25.

21. World War I aviation experts Dan Abbott, James Davilla, and Leonard E. Opdycke have advised me in this matter. The Parabellum machine gun was a German equivalent of the British Maxim gun, lightened to enhance its effectiveness in the air. It was often used by observers in reconnaissance planes, including Rumplers. See Bruce, *An Illustrated Companion to the First World War,* 282.

22. PACC, 30 November 1918; EVRD-1918, entries for 1–7 June.

23. PACC, 1 December 1918; EVRD-1918, entries for 8, 9 June.

24. John Keegan, *The First World War* (New York: Alfred A. Knopf, 1999), 407–8; Clark, *Devil Dogs,* 112–13; Gina Kolata, *Flu: The Story of the Great Influenza Pandemic of 1918 and the Search for the Virus That Caused It* (New York: Farrar, Straus and Giroux, 1999), 9; Coffman, *War to End All Wars,* 221–22.

25. EVRD-1918, entries for 9–13 June.

26. PACC, 1 December 1918; EVRD-1918, entry for 18 June.

27. Richard P. Hallion, *Strike from the Sky: The History of Battlefield Air Attack, 1911–1945* (Washington, DC: Smithsonian Institution Press, 1989), 19–25.

28. EVRD 1918, entry for 19 June.

29. Ibid.

30. Among other accounts of observation balloons in the war, see Stephen Pope and Elizabeth-Ann Wheal, *The Macmillan Dictionary of the First World War* (New York: Macmillan, 1997), 57.

31. EVRD-1918, entry for 24 June; PACC, 1 December 1918; James Streckfuss, "Wounded in Action: The Story of Harold H. Tittmann, Jr.," *Over the Front* 3, no. 3 (Autumn 1988): 244.

32. PACC, 1 December 1918.

33. John Mosier, *The Myth of the Great War: How the Germans Won the Battles and How the Americans Saved the Allies* (New York: HarperCollins, 2001), 320–23.

34. EVRD-1918, entries for 26 June–2 July.

35. Frandsen, *Hat in the Ring*, 150–63 Sloan, *Wings of Honor*, 133–34; Treadwell and Wood, *German Knights of the Air*, 179–80; EVRD-1918, entry for 2 July 1918.

36. PACC, 3 December 1918; EVRD-1918, entries for 4–6 July; Sloan, *Wings of Honor*, 130. For an elaborate but inconclusive discussion of whether Rickenbacker flew the same Spad throughout the rest of the war or had two planes with the same numeral, see H. L. Elman, "'Old Number One'—Rickenbacker's Spad," *Journal of the Society of World War I Aero Historians* 9, no. 3 (Autumn 1968): 244–56.

37. PACC, 3 December, 1918; EVRD-1918, entries for 7–10 July. On the circumstances dictating the move to Saints, see Frandsen, *Hat in the Ring*, 170.

38. EVRD-1918, entries for 11–14, 17 July; Toland, *No Man's Land*, 313–15; PACC, 3 December 1918.

39. On the importance of the process Rickenbacker was undergoing, see Boyne, *Aces in Command*, 42–43.

40. Among many accounts of these developments, see particularly Toland, *No Man's Land*, 315–50, and Coffman, *War to End All Wars*, 222–27.

41. For an extended discussion of the Spad XIII, see Frandsen, "The First Pursuit Group," 455–65. Among many other analyses of the planes, see Jack M. Bruce, "Spad Story," part I, *Air International* 10 (May 1976): 237–42, and part II (June 1976): 289–312; "Spads VII and XIII," *World War 1 Aero* 107 (December 1985): 7–47, by the same author; and Roland W. Richardson, "Spad XIII," *The Aerospace Historian* 27 (Winter 1980): 257–60. The National Air and Space Museum, Washington, D.C., has a large curatorial file about the Spad XIII.

42. Frandsen, "First Pursuit Group," 441, 495–99, 513–19; Frandsen, *Hat in the Ring*, 189–92.

43. Frandsen, "First Pursuit Group," 481, 521.

44. Ibid., 404–9, 437, 520–28.

45. EVRD-1918, entries for 19–27 July.

46. EVRD-1918, entry for 31 July; Frandsen, "First Pursuit Group," 521–22.

47. EVRD-1918, entry for 1 August; Frandsen, "First Pursuit Group," 522–23.

48. EVRD-1918, entries for 4–6 August.

49. EVRD-1918, entry for 8 August; R-H Tapes, reel 7, side 1.

50. PACC, 4 December, 1918; EVRD-1918, entry for 17 August; EVRR, 120; Sloan, *Wings of Honor*, 131–32. The autobiography erroneously states that the episode in which Smythe and Bruce were killed occurred on a Sunday and gives a slightly different account of other details, as does *FFC*, 227. I have relied, as always in such cases, on the diary entry and transcribed report in PACC. The episode was partly responsible for Rickenbacker's enduring belief in extrasensory perception, precognitive dreams, and other psychic phenomena. On the dubious rationale for Ameri-

can policy in failing to use parachutes, see Maurer, *U.S. Air Service in World War I,* 1:200.

51. EVRD-1918, entries for 18, 19 August; Toland, *No Man's Land,* 351–73.

52. EVRD-1918, entries for 21–25 August.

53. EVRD-1918, entries for 24, 26 August. For the corresponding chapter in Rickenbacker's published memoir, see *FFC,* 81–90.

54. PACC, 4 December 1918; Frandsen, *Hat in the Ring,* 198–99; Hartney, *Up and At 'Em,* 200.

55. EVRD-1918, entries for 4–8 September; PACC, 4 December 1918; Adamson, *Eddie Rickenbacker,* 204–5.

56. PACC, 4 December 1918.

57. Hartney, *Up and At 'Em,* 202.

58. PACC, 4 December 1918.

Chapter 9. Climax

1. Smythe, *Pershing,* 179–81; Coffman, *War to End All Wars,* 262–78.

2. Frandsen, *Hat in the Ring,* 202–4; Hartney, *Up and At 'Em,* 257–58.

3. EVRD-1918, entries for 9–16 September; Smythe, *Pershing,* 181–86. Among other accounts of the American victory, see Coffman, *War to End All Wars,* 278–83, Toland, *No Man's Land,* 417–25; and Gregor Dallas, *1918: War and Peace* (Woodstock and New York: Overlook Press, 2000), 60–63.

4. EVRD-1918, entry for 13 September; PACC, 5 December 1918; R-H Tapes, reel 39F, side 2; Frandsen, *Hat in the Ring,* 214.

5. Fransden, *Hat in the Ring,* 215; EVRD-1918, entry for 14 September; PACC, 5 December 1918, confirmation of victory in General Order No. 8, 22 September 1918, paragraph 4 in *Gorrell's History of the American Expeditionary Forces Air Service, 1917–1919,* M990, series E, vol. 12, National Archives, Washington, D.C.

6. EVRD-1918, entry for 15 September; PACC, 5 December 1918; General Order No. 6, 17 September 1918, paragraph 4, *Gorrell's History.*

7. EVRD-1918, entry for 16 September; PACC, 5 December 1918.

8. Coffman, *War to End All Wars,* 301–6; Forrest C. Pogue, *George C. Marshall: Education of a General, 1880–1939* (New York: Viking Press, 1963), 175–79; David McCullough, *Truman* (New York: Simon & Schuster, 1992), 125–27.

9. Mitchell, *Memoirs of World War I,* 253; Hartney, *Up and At 'Em,* 239–49; Norman S. Hall, *The Balloon Buster: Frank Luke of Arizona* (c. 1928; repr., New York: Arno Press, 1972), 1–68; Frandsen, "First Pursuit Group," 541–43, 577–79; Frandsen, *Hat in the Ring,* 218–21.

10. Frandsen, "First Pursuit Group," 579–83; Frandsen, *Hat in the Ring,* 221–23; Hartney, *Up and At 'Em,* 166; Hall, *Balloon Buster,* 69–104; PACC, 6 December 1918. On Rickenbacker's desire to have Luke transferred to the 94th, see R-H Tapes, reel 7, side 1.

11. EVRD-1918, entries for 19–23 September; R-H Tapes, reel 7, side 1; Frandsen, *Hat in the Ring,* 227–28.

12. Frandsen, "First Pursuit Group," 591; Sloan, *Wings of Honor,* 131–32, showing dates of appointment to the 94th Pursuit Squadron.

13. Frandsen, "First Pursuit Group," 591; Aaron Norman, *The Great Air War* (New York: The Macmillan Company, 1968), 507; Stephen Longstreet, *The Canvas Falcons: The Men and Planes of World War I* (1970; repr., New York: Barnes & Noble Books, 1995), 252; Boyne, *Aces in Command,* 50.

14. EVRD-1918, entry for 24 September.

15. R-H Tapes, reel 11, side 1, and reel 14, side 2; Adamson, *Eddie Rickenbacker,* 206–7.

16. PACC, 6 December 1918. Confirmation of Rickenbacker's victory over the Halberstadt came quickly, on September 27. He did not receive official credit for the Fokker until 15 November. See General Orders 10 and 26, cited in *Gorrell's History.*

17. R-H Tapes, reel 7, side 1; Hartney, *Up and At 'Em,* 269. For an acute analysis of Luke, see Boyne, *Aces in Command,* 48–50.

18. Hartney, *Up and At 'Em,* 268–79; Hall, *Balloon Buster,* 144–83. Both of these sources contain affidavits signed by villagers at Murvaux testifying to the details of Luke's death, as does Laurence La Tourette Driggs, *Heroes of Aviation* (Boston: Little, Brown, and Company, 1929), 292–96. Driggs also provides transcribed reports by officers of the American Service who visited Murvaux in January 1919. Nevertheless, controversy continues about the circumstances.

19. Hall, *Balloon Buster,* 183–88, with copy of citation.

20. Hartney, *Up and At 'Em,* 276.

21. R-H Tapes, reel 7, side 1, and reel 20, side 1.

22. PACC, 6 December 1918; Coffman, *War to End All Wars,* 306.

23. PACC, 6 December 1918; R-H Tapes, reel 11, side 1. A better-known evocation of the spectacle in *FFC,* 269, often quoted in secondary works because of its literary quality, was written by Driggs.

24. R-H Tapes, reel 11, side 1.

25. Ibid.; Frandsen, "First Pursuit Group," 613.

26. Coffman, *War to End All Wars,* 300, 304–14; Toland, *No Man's Land,* 428–38.

27. Mitchell, *Memoirs of World War I,* 258–59; Frandsen, *Hat in the Ring,* 239.

28. PACC, 7 December 1918.

29. Ibid.

30. Longstreet, *The Canvas Falcons,* 253.

31. "Rickenbacker's Ambition," *Cleveland Press,* 20 November 1918, clipping in EVRS 1.

32. Adamson, *Eddie Rickenbacker,* 213–14. A similar story relating to Major Carl A. Spaatz receiving the same treatment as Kirby is in all likelihood apocryphal because Spaatz was stationed with the 94th between 1 and 9 September 1918, before Hart-

ney put Rickenbacker in command of the unit. See Sloan, *Wings of Honor,* 132. On Spaatz's visit to the squadron, see Richard G. Davis, *Carl A. Spaatz and the Air War in Europe* (Washington, DC: Smithsonian Institution Press, 1992), 6. Davis mistakenly calls Rickenbacker a major, a rank he did not attain until after the war.

33. PACC, 8 and 10 December 1918; Franks and Bailey, *Over the Front,* 30, 68; Sloan, *Wings of Honor,* 130–32. On the Hannover and LVG observation planes, see Peter Gray and Owen Thetford, *German Aircraft of the First World War* (London: Putnam & Co., Ltd, 1962), 432, 484.

34. Noel C. Shirley, "Leigh Wade: Test Pilot," *Over the Front* 21, no. 3 (Autumn 1980): 243. Bert Frandsen kindly called this article to my attention.

35. PACC, 10 December 1918; Franks and Bailey, *Over the Front,* 68; Sloan, *Wings of Honor,* 135.

36. EVRD-1918, entries for 11–17 October; Adamson, *Eddie Rickenbacker,* 213–14. On Meredith's identity and Rickenbacker's relationship with her, see Farr, *Rickenbacker's Luck,* 63–74.

37. Paul F. Braim, *The Test of Battle: The American Expeditionary Forces in the Meuse-Argonne Campaign* (Newark: University of Delaware Press, c. 1987), 126–29; Smythe, *Pershing,* 212–19.

38. EVRD-1918, entry for 10 October; PACC, 10 December 1918; "Air Battle Staged for Motion Pictures: Rickenbacker in Sham Fight with a Real German Plane over American Lines," *New York Times,* 24 November 1918, clipping in EVRS 1. Because Rickenbacker merely identified the film producer as a "Captain Cooper" (as Driggs did also in *FFC,* 321–22), authors of subsequent works have sometimes assumed that the person in question was Merian C. Cooper, an adventurer, explorer, and cinematic pioneer who later became famous for producing such films as *King Kong* and *The Quiet Man.* As indicated in the newspaper clipping cited here, the film producer was Edwin H. Cooper. Merian Cooper did participate in World War I as a member of the 20th Bombardment Squadron. He was wounded in action on 26 September 1918, became a prisoner of war, and was still in captivity when the mock battle took place. Colonel David T. Zabecki, an authority on Merian Cooper's experiences in World War I, has advised me in this matter.

39. The De Havilland DH-4, usable either as an observation plane or light bomber, was one of four European models selected for production in the United States in 1917. By 1918 it was obsolescent, having been superseded by the De Havilland DH-9, but the Bureau of Aircraft Production decided to manufacture it in quantity and send it abroad because it was the only American-built warplane ready for mass production. Known as "Flaming Coffins" because of the vulnerability of the fuel tank, which was directly behind the pilot, they illustrated the shortcomings of the American approach to making aircraft for a war in which aircraft design changed rapidly in response to demands from the front, a situation to which European manufacturers were better able to adapt. See the critical analysis in Holley, *Ideas and Weapons,* 127–32.

40. Woolley, *The Hat in the Ring Gang*, 192, containing verbatim copies of reports filed by Rickenbacker.

41. PACC, 11 December 1918; EVRD-1918, entries for 26, 27 October.

42. "E. Rickenbacker, L. A. Ace, Who Is in War Hospital," from unidentified Los Angles newspaper; "Airman Denies Engagement: Captain Rickenbacker Says He Is Not to Wed Movie Actress," *Portland Oregonian*, 17 November 1918; "Star Enthusiastic Motorist," *Kansas City (MO) Journal*, 30 March 1919, clippings in EVRS 1.

43. George Seldes, *Witness to a Century: Encounters with the Noted, the Notorious, and the Three SOBs* (New York: Ballantine Books, 1987), 75–76.

44. PACC, 12 December 1918; James S. Alford, "The History of the First Fighter Group, vol. 1: The First Pursuit Group in World War I," 175–77, unpublished manuscript, Air Force Historical Research Agency, Maxwell Air Force Base.

45. Thomas Kunkel, *Genius in Disguise: Harold Ross of The New Yorker* (New York: Random House, 1995), 53; *FFC*, 351–52.

46. Among varying accounts of the closing stages of the Meuse-Argonne campaign and the diplomatic complexities leading to the Armistice of 11 November 1918, see Braim, *Test of Battle*, 137–70; Smythe, *Pershing*, 212–13; and Toland, *No Man's Land*, 474–593. On Rickenbacker's activities, see EVRD-1918, entries for 1–7 November.

47. The account of Driggs's background and early career that follows is based on an unpublished typewritten autobiography that he wrote for a family genealogy, kindly supplied to me by Mrs. Laurence (Ethel) La Tourette Driggs II, of Easton, Maryland.

48. "Fourth Arm in Warfare," *Outlook*, 21 March 1917.

49. This expedition resulted in an admission by Hindenburg that "The American infantry won the World War in the Battle of the Argonne" and a subsequent trial at Chaumont at which the "Runaway Correspondents"—Lincoln Eyre, Frederick A. Smith, C. C. Lyon, Herbert Corey, and George Seldes—were arraigned by General Dennis Nolan on behalf of the judge advocate general on the orders of General Pershing for violating orders by making a fact-finding trip into Germany starting 21 November 1918. Seldes discussed the episode in no less that three books: *Witness to a Century*, 96–101; *You Can't Print That!* (New York: Payson & Clarke, Ltd., 1919), 24–40; and *Even the Gods Can't Change History* (Secaucus, NJ: Lyle Stuart, 1976), 23–27. See also Emmet Crozier, *American Reporters on the Western Front, 1914–1918* (New York: Oxford University Press, 1959), 268–78. The charges against the reporters were withdrawn, but the story they brought back was censored. The significance of the episode is that Ludendorff's statement refuted Adolf Hitler's later claim that the German army was not defeated in the field but by forces on the home front.

50. Alford, "History of the First Fighter Group," 184–85; EVRD-1918, entries for 9, 10 November.

51. "How Peace Came to First Pursuit Group," *Out of Control* (newsletter published by members of the group), 1, no. 2 (19 November 1918), Crocker Manuscript Collection, Lafayette College, Easton, PA, provided by Bert Frandsen; Alford,

"History of the First Fighter Group," 186–87; Hartney, *Up and At 'Em,* 236; *FFC,* 357–58.

52. *FFC,* 359–60. Purporting to be Rickenbacker's evocation of what happened, the account described what Driggs had witnessed.

53. PACC, 16 December 1918.

Chapter 10. Homecoming

1. Robert H. Zieger, *America's Great War: World War I and the American Experience* (Lanham, MD: Rountree and Littlefield, 2000), 165; Smythe, *Pershing;* Cooke, *Billy Mitchell,* 99–100, 105–6; Mitchell, *Memoirs of World War I,* 289, 294; Sloan, *Wings of Honor,* 123; *Gorrell's History,* M990, series E, vol. 12, National Archives.

2. Boyne, *Aces in Command,* 51.

3. History of 94th Pursuit Squadron, Air Force Historical Research Agency; *Gorrell's History,* M990, Series E, vol. 12, National Archives; Hartney, *Up and At 'Em,* 278.

4. Copy of agreement between Rickenbacker and Driggs, 16 November 1918, ERP-AU; "Laurence La Tourette Driggs," autobiography provided by Ethel S. Driggs (see chapter 9, note 47), 173; PACC.

5. R-H Tapes, reel 7, side 2.

6. Ibid.; manuscript diary of Lieutenant Joseph K. Eastman, a member of the 94th Pursuit Squadron provided by Bert Frandsen, entries for 19, 21 November 1918.

7. EVRD-1918, entry for 24 November; Eder, *Let's Go Where the Action Is,* 79–81.

8. Briand, *In Search of Paradise,* 69–88; Hall, *Flying with Chaucer*; Maurer, "Another Victory for Rickenbacker."

9. Eastman diary, entries for 21, 29 November 1918.

10. "Laurence La Tourette Driggs," 175; Frandsen, "First Pursuit Group," 358–71; Frandsen, *Hat in the Ring,* 136–37; EVRD-1918, entries for 1, 2 December. Frandsen shared a transcript of the court-martial proceedings with me.

11. EVRD-1918, entries for 13–15 December; Frandsen, "First Pursuit Group," 1–3.

12. EVRD-1918, entries for 17–25 December. The manuscript Rickenbacker gave Driggs is the source frequently cited PACC.

13. "Laurence La Tourette Driggs," 175–76.

14. EVRD-1918, entries for 26–31 December; R-H Tapes, reel 7, side 2.

15. EVRD-J-M 1919, entries for 1, 2 January. Daniel J. Clemons, a Rickenbacker aficionado, kindly shared this extremely valuable document with me.

16. "A History of Sunbeam," http://sunbeam.org.au/history, accessed 24 June 2004.

17. EVRD-J-M 1919, entries for 4, 9, 10 January. On developments related to zeppelins that I have mentioned, see Douglas H. Robinson, *The Zeppelin in Combat:*

A History of the German Naval Airship Division, 1912–1918 (Sun Valley, CA: John W. Caler Aeronautica, 1966), 284–96, and Douglas Botting, *The Giant Airships* (Alexandria, VA: Time-Life Books, 1981), 70–71, 75–79.

18. R-H Tapes, reel 7, side 2; "Laurence La Tourette Driggs," 176.

19. EVRD-J-M 1919, entries for 14–21 January.

20. R-H Tapes, reel 7, side 2.

21. EVRD-J-M 1919, entry for 21 January.

22. "Eddie Rickenbacker May Race in Spokane If Sport Is Revived," *Spokane Chronicle*, 18 November 1918; "Rickenbacker to Quit Racing," *Cleveland Press*, 26 December 1918; "$200,000 Offer Is Made [to] Eddie Rickenbacker," *Los Angeles Herald*, 30 December 1918, clippings in EVRS 1.

23. "Rickenbacker Lands in New York," *Columbus Citizen*, 1 February 1919; "Rickenbacker Tells of Air Force Need," *New York Sun*, 7 February 1919, clippings in ibid.

24. "Rickenbacker to be Whistled into New York: Auto Plants Announce Intention of Tooting at Top Pitch to Welcome Ace," *Tulsa (OK) Democrat*, January 24, 1919, clipping in ibid.

25. Sinsabaugh, *Who? Me*, EVRS 3; EVRD-J-M 1919, entries for 31 January, 1, 2 February.

26. The hotel known as the Waldorf-Astoria at the time of the ceremony held for Rickenbacker in 1919 was not the one that exists today but a composite structure consisting of two adjoining buildings, 11 and 13 stories high respectively, between 33rd and 34th streets. See Kenneth T. Jackson, ed., *The Encyclopedia of New York City* (New Haven: Yale University Press, 1995), 1232–33.

27. EVRR, 138–39; R-H Tapes, reel 7, side 2; Leonard Mosley, *Lindbergh: A Biography* (Garden City, NY: Doubleday, 1976), 73; *New York Times*, 4 February 1919, 4; EVRD-J-M 1919, entry for 3 February. See also "Wings of Victory Presented to Rick," undated clipping about the banquet with a photograph of the wings, and "Rickenbacker, Ace of Aces, No Fairy Tale Hero," *Waco (TX) Herald*, 9 March 1919, EVRS 1. Daniel J. Clemons suggested to me the possible connections between Orteig's presence at the banquet and his subsequent announcement of the Orteig Prize.

28. EVRD-J-M 1919, entries for 10–16 February; "House Stops Quibbles to Honor Captain Rickenbacker," clipping from *New York Journal*, 12 February 1919, and "Ace Hoped to Fly across Ocean: Capt. Rickenbacker, Expressing Feasibility of Transatlantic Flight, Tells of Disappointment in Not Being Ordered to Fly," *Evening Sun*, 27 March 1919, EVRS 1.

29. EVRD-J-M 1919, entries for 17, 18 February; "Eventful Trip for Rick," *Zanesville (OH) Signal*, 17 February 1919; "Life Has Been Just One Autograph after Another for Rickenbacker," *Columbus Dispatch*, 17 February 1919; "America's Ace of Aces Is Honored with Mammoth Street Parade," *Columbus Citizen*, 17 February 1919; "Rickenbacker Given Royal Welcome Home: Thousands Throng Streets in Rain and Snow 2 Hours to Give Rick Big Greeting," *Ohio State Journal*, 18 February 1919; "Ova-

tion Given Greatest Ace" and "The Stroller," clippings from unidentified Columbus newspapers, in EVRS 1.

30. "Rick Is Going; He's Sorry," unidentified Columbus newspaper, 18 February 1919, and "Knights of Columbus Ball Tomorrow," *New York Sun*, 23 February 1919, clippings in EVRS 1; EVRD-J-M 1919, entries for 22, 26 February; "Laurence La Tourette Driggs," 175–76; interview of Ethel S. Driggs by author.

31. EVRD-J-M 1919, entries for 22, 27 February; "Rickenbacker Will Aid 5th Liberty Loan Drive," *Philadelphia North American*, 16 February 1919, datelined New York, 15 February; EVRR, 140; Jimmy Breslin, *Damon Runyon* (New York: Bantam Doubleday Dell Publishing Group, Inc., 1991), 180–82.

32. "Flying Will Always Have the Sporting Element," *New York American*, 9 March 1919, EVRS 1.

33. EVRD-J-M 1919, entries for 28 February, 1 March.

34. "Governor, Mayor, 'All' to Greet Capt. Eddie Rickenbacker: Rickenbacker Due in Detroit Monday Morning," *Detroit News*, 2 March 1919, clipping in EVRS 1; clipping in *Anaconda (MT) Standard*, 9 March 1919, EVRS 1; EVRD-J-M 1919, entries for 2, 3 March.

35. EVRD-J-M 1919, entries for 4–14 March.

36. EVRED-1919, entry for 22 March 1919.

37. "Prominent Men Pay Tribute to Rick," *Columbus Citizen*, 27 February 1919, EVRS 1.

38. EVRED-1919, entries for 22–25 March; "Urges Airdrome in Boston" and "Famous Ace Thrills Audience," clippings from *Boston Transcript*, 25, 26 March 1919, EVRS 1; EVRR, 140–41.

39. EVRED-1919, entries for 27–31 March; "Rickenbacker Wins His Way into Our Hearts," *Springfield Republican*, 28 March 1919, EVRS 1.

40. "Rickenbacker a Platform Ace as Well as in Air," "Capt. Eddie Rickenbacker," and "Capt. Rickenbacker's 'Ace' Lecture Thrills," clippings from unidentified newspapers, 2 April 1919, EVRS 1.

41. Farr, *Rickenbacker's Luck*, 104, 137, 142, 170, 292, 341.

42. Ben Yagoda, *Will Rogers: A Biography* (New York: Alfred A. Knopf, 1993), 215.

43. Entries for April in EVRED-1919.

44. "American Ace Urges Native Land to Develop Airplane," *Dayton Herald*, 7 May 1919; "World-Famous Airmen Meet for First Time," *Dayton Journal*, 8 May 1919, EVRS 1.

45. "American Ace Urges Native Land to Develop Airplane"; "World-Famous Airmen Meet"; "Rickenbacker Holds Hearers: American Ace Does Not Talk of Himself but Relates Deeds of Others," *Detroit News*, 5 May 1919; "Ace of Aces Is Modest Hero: Captain Rickenbacker . . . Gives Credit to Comrades," *Kansas City (MO) Post*, 15 May 1919, EVRS 1.

46. "Rickenbacker Ill: Cannot Speak Here," *St. Paul Dispatch*, 22 May 1919; "Voice

Lost: Ace of Aces Cancels Talk," *St. Paul News,* 22 May 1919; "Rickenbacker's Ailment," *Oklahoma City Oklahoman,* 28 May 1919, EVRS 1; EVRR, 142.

47. "Ebert Field Planes to Do Honor to Capt. Rickenbacker" and "Rickenbacker Tells of Exploits Which Won for Him 'Ace of Aces' Title," *Little Rock Arkansas Democrat,* 24, 27 May 1919; "Captain Rickenbacker Is Given Rousing Reception," *Memphis Commercial Appeal,* 27 May 1919, EVRS 1; EVRED-1919, entry for 29 May.

48. Farr, *Rickenbacker's Luck,* 97. Farr did not connect the tour, which he discusses in pp. 87–97 of his biography, with the Fifth Liberty Loan Drive, apparently not realizing it was the mission for which the War Department had summoned Rickenbacker back to the United States instead of permitting him to remain at Koblenz with the 94th Pursuit Squadron.

49. EVRR, 142.

50. Popely, with Riggs, *Indianapolis 500 Chronicle,* 24–25; "Thrilling Kaleidoscope of Events Like Day at Front Says Famous Ace," *Los Angeles Examiner,* clipping in EVRS 1.

51. "Top Notch Airmen Home Ungreeted," *New York Sun,* 1 June 1919; EVRED-1919, entry for 3 June; photograph of banquet in photogravure section of *New York Times,* 15 June 1919; "Elsie's Not Engaged to Ace Rickenbacker: Actress Says It's Not So but She Wishes It Might Be," *Ohio State Journal* (Columbus), 30 July 1919, EVRS 1; Lee Alan Morrow, "Elsie Janis: 'A Comfortable Goofiness,'" in Robert A. Schanke and Kim Marra, eds., *Passing Performances: Queer Readings of Leading Players in American Theater History* (Ann Arbor: University of Michigan Press, 1998), 151–72.

52. Clippings from *Boston Record,* 18 May 1919; *The Broadside,* May 1919; *Philadelphia Public Ledger,* 24 May 1919; *The North American,* 24 May 1919; *The Dial,* 31 May 1919; *New York Tribune,* 24 May 1919, *Bookseller,* 1 June 1919, and *Toronto Globe,* 5 July 1919, EVRS 1.

53. Clipping from *Cincinnati Enquirer,* 4 February 1919, EVRS 1.

54. Edward Behr, *Prohibition: Thirteen Years that Changed America* (New York: Arcade Publishing, Inc., 1996), esp. 78–80. Ironically, as Behr indicates, Rickenbacker's home state of Ohio was a hotbed of sentiment for Prohibition, and no city was more prominent in its inception than Columbus, many of whose political leaders supported it publicly but abhorred it privately, intending to profit from it illegally if it became law.

55. Thomas A. Rumer, *The American Legion: An Official History, 1919–1989* (New York: M. Evans and Company, 1990), 8–77; R-H Tapes, reel 15, side 1; Jonathan Shay, *Odysseus in America: Combat Trauma and the Trials of Homecoming* (New York: Scribner, 2002), 40; R-H Tapes, reel 15, side 1.

56. EVRR, 137, states that in 1919 "Publishers were after me to have my story 'ghosted' by any one of a number of prominent writers. I refused them too, although later I did write my memoirs of World War I, *Fighting the Flying Circus.*" This statement, of course, is untrue, as is Rickenbacker's claim on the same page that

he was "pretty nearly broke" or actually bankrupt as he stated to Booton Herndon, the ghostwriter of his memoirs, in R-H Tapes, reel 8, side 1. The discussion of this period in Farr, *Rickenbacker's Luck*, 97–121, referring at one point (p. 103) to Rickenbacker's "dwindling bankroll," is also misleading. Apparently neither Farr nor Herndon knew about the advances and royalties Rickenbacker received from the serial and book rights to *Fighting the Flying Circus*.

57. EVRED-1919, entry for 25 May; "Rickenbacker Tells of Exploits Which Won for Him 'Ace of Aces' Title," *Little Rock Arkansas Democrat*, 27 May 1919, clipping in EVRS 1.

58. EVRED-1919, entries for 2, 4, 5, 9 June.

59. EVRR, 137; Bernard F. Dick, *City of Dreams: The Making and Remaking of Universal Pictures* (Lexington: University Press of Kentucky, 1997), 10–72; Richard Koszarski, *An Evening's Entertainment: The Age of the Silent Feature Picture, 1913–1928* (New York: Charles Scribner's Sons, 1990), 86–87; "Priscilla Dean," in Kalton C. Lahue, *Ladies in Distress* (South Brunswick and New York: J. S. Barnes and Company, 1971), 74–82.

60. EVRED-1919, entries for 11–17 June.

61. "Same Old Rick" and untitled article from *Los Angeles Evening Herald* and *Los Angeles Times*, 21 June 1919, EVRS 1.

62. Photograph of Rickenbacker and accompanying article, *Los Angeles Record*, 21 June 1919; "Here Is Program for Welcoming Army Ace," *Los Angeles Examiner*, 21 June 1919; "L. A. Greets Rickenbacker," "Same Old 'Rick,' Same Old Style," and "Program for Rickenbacker Celebration," *Los Angeles Evening Herald*, 21 June 1919; "Rickenbacker Smiles Joy at L.A. Ovation . . . 300,000 Cheer Hero Aviator" and "Whole City Turns Out to Honor Rickenbacker," articles from unidentified Los Angeles newspapers, 21, 22 June 1919, EVRS 1.

63. EVRED-1919, entry for June 26. A photograph showing Rickenbacker with Sennett and Syd Chaplin, EVRR, section following p. 76, is misdated as having been taken in 1913.

64. EVRED-1919, entries for 26, 27 June; "Captain Rickenbacker Visits City: Predicts Great Future for Flying," *San Francisco Examiner*, 28 June 1919; "Rickenbacker Lunch Guest of Auto Row," *San Francisco Call*, 28 June 1919; "America's Chief Ace Visits City," *San Francisco Chronicle*, 28 June 1919, clippings in EVRS 1.

65. EVRED-1919, entries for 29 June–6 July; "Greeting an Ace," *Tacoma News-Tribune*, 2 July 1919; "Elaborate Cover for Menu for Rickenbacker Banquet," "Joyous Welcome for Yankee Ace," and "Tacomans Present Diamond Pin to Eddie Rickenbacker," *Tacoma Ledger*, 2, 4 July 1919; "Rickenbacker to Be Honor Guest" and "Eddie Rickenbacker in Buick at Tacoma Races," *Seattle Post-Intelligence*, 2, 13 July 1919; "Seattle Honors Ace This Evening," *Seattle Times*, 2 July 1919; "Seattle Showers Honors on Captain Rickenbacker," *Seattle Daily Times*, 3 July 1919; "Rickenbacker Back in Tacoma," "Captain Rickenbacker, Premier Ace, Is Here," "Captain Eddie Rickenbacker on Visit to Seattle as Honor Guest," "America's Ace of Aces Tells War

Experiences," undated clippings from unidentified newspapers in Seattle-Tacoma area, July 1919, EVRS 1. Farr, *Rickenbacker's Luck*, 103, erroneously states that Rickenbacker was offered only $150.00 for flying over Mount Tacoma during his visit to the area, indicating that Rickenbacker, allegedly short of cash, "feared that the meanness of this offer might be an indication of what he was really worth on the market." See EVRED-1919, entry for 5 July. Such an offer would have been insulting to Rickenbacker.

66. R-H Tapes, 9 March 1965, reel 8, side 1; Farr, *Rickenbacker's Luck*, 122–23; "Rickenbacker Lunch Guest at Auto Row," *San Francisco Call*, 28 June 1919; and "Elsie's Not Engaged to Ace Rickenbacker," *Ohio State Journal* (Columbus), 30 July 1919, EVRS 1.

67. EVRED-1919, entries for 7–11 July. I am indebted to Sharon Steinberg of the Connecticut Historical Society Museum, Hartford, Connecticut, for providing information to me about the Bill family.

68. "*Predictions* by Captain Eddie Rickenbacker, Banff, Canada, June, 1919," typed manuscript in Thurber Special Collections Department, Ohio State University, Columbus.

69. Promenade decks became features of lighter-than-air travel in the 1920s and 1930s. Rickenbacker did not indicate how he expected heavier-than-air planes to accommodate them.

70. For perspective on the technocratic utopianism implicit in this and other passages in Rickenbacker's speech, see Joseph J. Corn, *The Winged Gospel: America's Romance with Aviation* (New York: Oxford University Press, 1983), and *Imagining Tomorrow: History, Technology, and the American Future* (Cambridge, MA: MIT Press, 1986). The theme of city blocks, or indeed entire cities, covered with roofs, walkways, and other structures, originating in the works of H. G. Wells, became a staple theme of science fiction works and motion pictures during the period in which Rickenbacker was speaking. It reached a climax in Isaac Asimov's *Foundation* series, which envisioned the entire planet being so covered.

71. On the development of such entities, see Adrianus D. Groenwege, *Compendium of International Civil Aviation*, 2nd ed. (Montreal: International Aviation Development Corporation, 1996), 43–44.

72. In *Rickenbacker's Luck*, 108, Farr aptly compares the conclusion of Rickenbacker's speech with Rudyard Kipling's short story, "With the Night Mail."

73. EVRED-1919, entry for 12 July.

Chapter 11. Domestic Front

1. EVRR, 136; R-H Tapes, reel 39G, side 1.
2. EVRED-1919.
3. "'Rick' Plans New Plane to Cross Pacific," clipping from *Los Angeles Examiner*,

29 June 1919, EVRS 1. Ince had offered the $50,000 prize contingent upon starting in Venice, California. In a long statement about his intention to compete for the prize, Rickenbacker said that "Aviation today offers no impossible problems" and that "The start from the Pacific Coast has a strong appeal to me as I feel bound to Los Angeles and Venice by many close and intimate ties."

4. Martin Caidin, *Barnstorming: The Treat Years of Stunt Flying* (New York: Duell, Sloan and Pearce, 1965); Paul O'Neil, *Barnstormers and Speed Kings* (Alexandria, VA: Time-Life Books, 1981), 6–73.

5. Leary, *Aerial Pioneers*, 30–112, 160–70. Even Aeromarine–West Indies Airways, which carried passengers seeking to escape the territorial bounds of the United States to imbibe alcohol legally after the onset of Prohibition, was only in the planning stage in 1919 and did not begin flight operations until October 1920, after securing a mail contract. Leary states that in this period, except for Aeromarine and two even smaller carriers, "American commercial aviation did not exist." See also T. A. Heppenheimer, *Turbulent Skies: The History of Commercial Aviation* (New York: John Wiley & Sons, 1995), 5–8.

6. EVRED-1919. For an extended discussion of Rickenbacker's activities during this period, based on the same source, see Farr, *Rickenbacker's Luck*, 109–21. On the problems of the Curtis Aeroplane and Motor Company in 1919, see Louis R. Eltscher and Edward M. Young, *Curtiss-Wright: Greatness and Decline* (New York: Twayne Publishers, 1998), 26–29.

7. EVRED-1919, entries for 10 June and 6 October 1919. In *Rickenbacker's Luck,* 121, Farr draws an unwarranted distinction between the two propositions by saying that under the one made at Sandusky (misdated by Farr as occurring on 9 June) the plan "had been to run up a car in someone else's shop, to be identified with Rick only by a label as it rolled out the door." The entry indicates that Rickenbacker could have been a stockholder and part-owner of the enterprise had he so chosen.

8. EVRED-1919, entries for 7–15 October.

9. Donald Finlay Davis, *Conspicuous Production: Automobiles and Elites in Detroit, 1899–1933* (Philadelphia: Temple University Press, 1988).

10. R-H Tapes, reel 39G, sides 1 and 2; Robert Szudarek, *How Detroit Became the Automotive Capital* (Warren, MI: Typocraft Company, 1996), 341. A hiatus in Rickenbacker's scrapbooks between 1919 and 1922 and the discontinuation of his diaries after 1919 makes it difficult to trace his whereabouts during that period except from scattered letters in his papers (EVRP-LC) at the Library of Congress and interviews with Herndon in the R-H Tapes.

11. Letter from Chambers to Rickenbacker, 20 December 1919, EVRP-LC, box 9, folder marked "C-I Miscellaneous 1916–1961." On Schroeder's background and achievements see Lester D. Gardner, *Who's Who in American Aeronautics,* 2nd ed. (New York: Gardner Publishing Co., Inc., 1925), 16–17, and materials in vertical files, National Air and Space Museum, Washington, D.C. The congressional proceedings mentioned by Chambers led to the Army Reorganization Act of 1920,

which perpetuated the Army Air Service but kept it a subordinate entity within the United States Army.

12. Letter from Chambers to Rickenbacker, 12 March 1920, EVRP-LC, box 9, folder marked "C-1 Miscellaneous, 1916–1961."

13. Letter from Chambers to Rickenbacker, 21 April 1920, in ibid.

14. Maurer, *Aviation in the U.S. Army, 1919–1939,* 39–52. For a positive assessment of the act as a forward-looking though limited step in the development of American airpower, see Robert P. White, *Mason Patrick and the Fight for Air Service Independence* (Washington, DC: Smithsonian Institution Press, 2001), 48–52.

15. "The Log of an Aluminum Air Liner," *U.S. Air Service* 3, no. 6 (July 1920): 17–19.

16. Leary, *Aerial Pioneers,* 117–27, containing an extended account of the history of the Junkers F.13, and Larsen JL-6; R-H Tapes, reel 23, sides 1 and 2.

17. Leary, *Aerial Pioneers,* 121–27; EVRR, 168.

18. R-H Tapes, reel 23, side 1, and reel 39F, side 1. The time when this venture took place is difficult to determine. Rickenbacker said that it occurred "after Harding became President." If this statement is literally true, the flight could not have occurred until after Harding was inaugurated in March 1921. It is possible that a blizzard occurred in Nevada that late in the winter season. On the other hand, Rickenbacker may have meant that the episode took place after Harding was elected but before he actually took office. It could not have taken place during the winter of 1921–22 because the Rickenbacker Motor Company had already started operations by that time and Rickenbacker was too busy with other responsibilities.

19. Farr, *Rickenbacker's Luck,* 130–31. The opening three games of the World Series were played at Brooklyn on 5–7 October, making it possible to determine the approximate time the reconciliation occurred. See *The Baseball Encyclopedia,* 10th ed. (New York: Macmillan, 1996), 2859.

20. Kimes and Clark, *Standard Catalog,* 1346; folder marked "Sheridan," Antique Automobile Club of America Library, Hershey, Pennsylvania (hereafter AACA Library).

21. R-H Tapes, reel 23, side 1, and reel 39G, side 2; Bob Considine, "Captain Eddie," *Cosmopolitan,* July 1945, 116, copy in EVRP-LC, box 128; Kimes and Clark, *Standard Catalog,* 1346.

22. R-H Tapes, reel 23, side 1; "Forced to Earth in Storm," clipping from *Chattanooga Times,* 8 July 1923, EVRS 2.

23. Edward V. Rickenbacker, "Is General Pershing Wrong?" *U.S. Air Service* 3, no. 3 (April 1920): 14–16.

24. Ireland's relationship with Rickenbacker is discussed in Farr, *Rickenbacker's Luck,* 83–85. On the events surrounding Mitchell when Rickenbacker visited Washington, see Burke Davis, *The Billy Mitchell Affair* (New York: Random House, 1967), 65–112, and Maurer, *Aviation in the U.S. Army,* 115–21.

25. Copies of materials submitted by Everitt to Michigan Securities Commission, 23 July 1921, in exhibits filed by Rickenbacker "In the Matter of Protest Relating to

Income Taxes for the Calendar Year 1923"; letter from Byron F. Everitt to Ricken-backer, 23 July 1921; promissory note to Everitt for $181,884.73 signed by Ricken-backer on 23 July 1921; and agreement between Everitt and Rickenbacker signed by both parties on 25 July 1921, all in ERP-AU.

26. White, *Mason Patrick,* 56. After Patrick's nomination was approved by the Senate and he assumed his post on 7 October, Mitchell submitted an organizational plan that would have put him, not Patrick, in effective control of the Army Air Service. When Patrick vetoed the document, Mitchell submitted his resignation but rescinded it when Patrick expressed his willingness to accept it. These developments left Patrick in full control, beginning a chain of events leading to Mitchell's court-martial in 1925.

27. "Building Up the Tired Business Men," *Detroit Free Press,* 16 June 1915; "De-troit Athletic Club, 1915–1960," booklet commemorating the Club's Forty-fifth An-niversary; "We Old Timers," *Detroit News,* 10 April 1940; "Sons in Fathers' Sanctum," *Life,* 17 March 1950; and other materials in folder, "Detroit Athletic Club, Miscel-laneous Material, I," Burton Historical Collection, Detroit Public Library.

28. Article, title missing, from *The Automobile,* 11 August 1921, research files of Beverly Rae Kimes, *Automotive Quarterly* headquarters, Kutztown, Pennsylvania (here-after referred to as Kimes Research Files); "Rickenbacker Obtains Detroit Plant," *Automobile Trade Journal,* November 1921, 64, Rickenbacker File, AACA Library. I ap-preciate permission from Kimes to use extensive notes she gathered for her article, "Hat in the Ring: The Rickenbacker," *Automobile Quarterly* 13, no. 4 (1975): 418–35.

29. "Twenty-second National Automobile Show," Kimes Research Files.

30. "The Rickenbacker Plan for Breaking in New Territory," in unidentified busi-ness magazine, May 1924, copy in EVRP-LC, box 128.

31. Leary, *Aerial Pioneers,* 127.

32. EVRR, 145, 172–73. On Stinson, see Roger E. Bilstein, *Flight Patterns: Trends of Aeronautical Development in the United States, 1918–1929* (Athens: University of Geor-gia Press, 1983), 60–61, 65, 68, 71–72.

33. "Rickenbacker Produces Ten a Day," "1,000th Car for Rickenbacker," "Rick-enbacker Output Grows," "2,500 Rickenbackers Produced," "Rickenbacker Deliv-ered 3,000th Car Last Week," "Rickenbacker Car on Radio Tour," "Rickenbacker Six Makes a Record," and "Pelletier Joins Rickenbacker," *Automobile Topics,* 4, 18 March, 20 May, 17 June, 9, 23 September, and 2 December 1922, Kimes Research Files.

34. Edward V. Rickenbacker, "The New Transportation," *The Ace* 3, no. 7 (July 1922): 9, brought to my attention by Deborah G. Douglas.

35. "From Steve Hannagan," Leighton Interviews; Farr, *Rickenbacker's Luck,* 104, 109, 122–23.

36. EVRR, 146; "Second Session with Mrs. Rickenbacker" and "From Steve Han-nagan," Leighton Interviews; Farr, *Rickenbacker's Luck,* 124–25; Joseph S. Freeman, "Prodigal Son: The Whirlwind Career of Russell Clifford Durant," *Automobile Quar-terly* 40, no. 3 (August 2000): 47–52.

37. Interview with William F. Rickenbacker by author; Freeman, "Prodigal Son," 53; articles of indenture between William C. Durant and Guaranty Trust Company of New York, 31 December 1918, and final California divorce decree of 10 July 1922, ERP-AU; letters from William C. Durant to Adelaide Frost Durant, 12 May and 21 December 1918, in notes taken from records supplied by Nancy Angell Rickenbacker, Francestown, New Hampshire, 1995, in author's possession.

38. "Ethel Wilhelm," Leighton Interviews; interview by author with Patricia Ann Wrightson (widow of David E. Rickenbacker, first son of Edward V. Rickenbacker).

39. Leighton, best known for editing *The Aspirin Age: 1919–1941* (New York: Simon and Schuster, 1949), interviewed a number of people who knew Rickenbacker, particularly his wife Adelaide, in preparation for a film, *Captain Eddie,* released by 20th Century-Fox in 1945. Leighton's seventy-five-page document is a valuable source about various phases of Rickenbacker's life.

40. EVRR, 146.

41. "Initial Interview with Mrs. Rickenbacker," Leighton Interviews.

42. "Ethel Wilhelm," in ibid.

43. Interview with William F. Rickenbacker by author; "Ethel Wilhelm," Leighton Interviews.

44. "The Opening of a New Chapter in My Book of Life," diary kept by Rickenbacker during honeymoon with Adelaide from 16 September through 27 November 1922, ERP-AU, entry for 16 September. All quoted material in the discussion that follows is taken from the diary unless otherwise indicated.

45. R-H Tapes, reel 7, side 2.

46. Ibid.

47. ERP-AU has a color transparency of the watercolor, made with permission from Nancy Angell Rickenbacker.

48. Burton Historical Collection, Detroit Public Library, envelope marked "Detroit—Apartment Houses H-J, Miscellaneous Material."

49. W. A. P. John, "Champion Race Driver, Premier Ace of America's Air Forces, Motor Magnate, Sums up the Career of Edward V. Rickenbacker," *MoToR,* May 1923, 48, 112, 114, 116, 118, 120, 122.

50. Memorandum from Everitt to stockholders of the Rickenbacker Motor Company, 2 November 1922, in Rickenbacker File, AACA Library. The net profit of $360,806 comes from a table of comparative earnings of the Velie, Stephens, R&V, Dort, Stutz, and Rickenbacker companies for 1922 and 1923 in a proposal made by H. A. Holder of C. A. Pfeffer and Associates, Inc., in April 1924 to merge the six enterprises (hereafter "Merger Proposal") in ERP-AU.

51. "All Rickenbacker Officers Reelected—5000 Cars Made," datelined Detroit, 6 January 1923, in *Motor Age,* 11 January 1923; "Rickenbacker Celebrates the First Year at New York Show," *Motor Age,* 18 January 1923, clippings in Rickenbacker File, AACA Library.

52. Accurate statistics about the annual production of Rickenbacker cars are ex-

tremely elusive. The figure in *Moody's Industrials* comes from Kimes Research Files. The same figure, based on a copy of an advertisement by the Rickenbacker Motor Company in *The Magazine of Wall Street,* is given in *The Hat in the Ring,* official news publication, Rickenbacker Car Club of America, Inc., 5, no. 12 (Spring 1980), and Ken Gross in "The Car Worthy of Its Name," *Special Interest Autos* 28 (March–April 1977): 27. Another authoritative source, however, states that only 2,262 Rickenbackers were produced in 1922; see Kimes and Clark, *Standard Catalog,* 1291.

53. "Rickenbacker Increases Capital," datelined Detroit, 17 March 1923, in *Motor Age,* clipping in Rickenbacker File, AACA Library; handwritten materials and "10,000th Rickenbacker," clipping from *Automotive Industry,* July 12, 1922, Kimes Research Files.

54. Miscellaneous materials, Rickenbacker File, AACA Library.

55. Advertisement, "What Car to Buy?," "Rickenbacker Makes Enclosed Line Its Regular Production," and "Rickenbacker Statement," both datelined 26 May 1923, clippings from *Motor Age* in Rickenbacker File, AACA Library.

56. Gross, "The Car Worthy of Its Name," 27; clipping, "Rickenbacker to Make Only Four-Wheel Brake Models," datelined 11 August 1923, and advertisement, "It Sure Is Tough On the Tag-Alongs," 26 September 1923, both from *Motor Age,* Rickenbacker File, AACA Library.

57. Among numerous discussions of the priorities involved, see particularly Kimes, "Hat in the Ring," 428–29, and Gross, "The Car Worthy of Its Name," 27. On the Heine-Velox, see Kimes and Clarke, *Standard Catalog,* 694.

58. *4-Wheel Brakes: The Greatest Improvement in Automobile Engineering since the Inception of the Self-Starter—13 Years Ago* (Detroit: Rickenbacker Motor Company, 1923), copy in Historical Research Files, 1921–27, National Automotive History Collection, Detroit Public Library. See also "Rickenbacker Adopts 4-Wheel Brake Model," unpaginated clipping from *Automotive Industries,* 28 June 1923, and "Rickenbacker Adopts Four-Wheel Brakes," *Automobile Topics,* 30 June 1923, 653–55, Kimes Research Files.

59. Full-page advertisement, 1924 Studebaker Files, AACA Library.

60. EVRR, 148.

61. E. J. Finney, *Walter E. Flanders: His Role in the Mass Production of Automobiles* (Berkeley, CA: privately published, 1992), 29–32.

62. Beverly Rae Kimes, "E-M-F and LeRoy," *Automobile Quarterly* 17 (1979): 359.

63. "Rickenbacker Sales Continue to Mount" and "Rickenbacker to Redouble," clippings from *Automobile Topics,* 1 September and 17 November 1923, Kimes Research Files; "Merger Proposal" (see endnote 3) and "Special File Confidential," ERP-AU.

64. Edward V. Rickenbacker, "What I Saw in Europe," *MoToR,* January 1924, 110–12, copy in Kimes Research Files.

65. EVRR, 147.

66. Letter from B. F. Everitt to Rickenbacker, 24 December 1923, with canceled note, ERP-AU.

67. "Rickenbacker Announces Prices of 1924 Models," *Automotive Industries,* 27 December 1923, Kimes Research Files.

68. "Cognoscenti Cheers Rickenbacker Copy," *Automobile Topics,* 22 March 1924, Kimes Research Files.

69. Cullen Thomas, "Chrysler: The Early Years," *Automobile Quarterly* 6, no. 1 (Summer 1967): 91–94; John Lee, *Standard Catalog of Chrysler* (Iola, WI: Krause Publications, 1990), 20; Vincent Curcio, *Chrysler: The Life and Times of an Automotive Genius* (New York: Oxford University Press, 2000), 307–22.

70. Curcio, *Chrysler,* 326; Lee, *Standard Catalog of Chrysler,* 30–31.

71. J. E. Schipper, "New Rickenbacker Vertical Eight Will Supplement the Six," *Automotive Industries,* 26 June 1924, 1369–72, and "Rickenbacker Presents New Vertical Eight," *Automobile Topics,* 28 June 1924, copies in Rickenbacker File, AACA Library; Gross, "The Car Worthy of Its Name," 29, with detailed list of specifications.

72. Kimes and Clark, *Standard Catalog,* 488–90, 626–29, 655, 1316–17, 1442–44, 1495–98.

73. "Possibilities of a Rickenbacker Combination," 7 July 1924, ERP-AU.

74. "$23,000,000 Merger Is Subject of Meeting," *Automobile Topics,* 18 October 1924, Kimes Research Files; "Rickenbacker Company Now Controls Trippensee Corp.," clipping from *Motor Age,* 15 January 1925, Rickenbacker File, AACA Library.

75. *The Whole Works,* illustrated booklet, 1925, copy from private collection of Robert and Jill Duquette, owners of a 1926 Rickenbacker Phaeton, Wilton, New Hampshire; Stephen G. Ostrander, "A Car Worthy of Its Name," *Michigan History Magazine,* January–February 1992, 25–27, with photograph of main plant from Michigan State Archives, Lansing, Michigan.

76. "Rickenbacker Company Now Controls Trippensee Corp." and "Trippensee Uses Sub-Assembly Methods in Building Sedan Bodies," *Automotive Industries,* 1 March 1923, Rickenbacker File, AACA Library.

77. Memoranda issued 24 June 1924, EVRP-LC.

78. Undated memorandum, "To All Distributors and Associate Distributors," ERP-AU.

79. Resignation of Banta mentioned in Kimes Research Files; "Defer Dividend Payment," clipping from *Motor Age,* 22 January 1925, AACA Library; Financial Statement of Rickenbacker Motor Company, 31 December 1924, in EVRP-LC, box 23.

80. "Displacement of Rickenbacker Six Is Increased—Eight Unchanged," *Automotive Industries,* 1 January 1925, Rickenbacker File, AACA Library.

81. "Report of Around the World Flight by Airplane," in Around-the-World Flight Papers, Air Force Historical Research Agency, Maxwell Air Force Base; Lowell Thomas, *The First World Flight* (Boston: Houghton Mifflin Company, 1925), 297.

82. Russ Catlin, "The Inimitable Mister Baker," *Automobile Quarterly* 13, no. 1 (1975): 38–51; *The Hat in the Ring* (Rickenbacker Motor Company Magazine) 1, no. 1 (March 1925), and Charles C. Proche, "A Hat in Every Ring: Captain Eddie and

His Electric Career," *Car Life*, October 1961, unpaginated copies in Kimes Research Files; Gross, "The Car Worthy of Its Name," 30.

83. Riggs, *Pace Cars of the Indy 500*, 32–33.

84. EVRR, 146–47, states that the child was born 4 January 1925, with no indication that he was adopted. I have not been able to ascertain the place of David Edward Rickenbacker's birth or the date on which his parents adopted him.

85. Curcio, *Chrysler*, 323–35, quoting in part from Edward D. Kennedy, *The Automobile Industry: The Coming of Age of Capitalism's Favorite Child* (New York: Reynal & Hitchcock, 1941); Kimes, "A Hat in the Ring," 433–35; Gross, "The Car Worthy of Its Name," 30.

86. Beverly Rae Kimes, "1926 Rickenbacker Super Sport: Captain Eddie's Swiftest Flight of Fancy," *Road and Track*, January 1987, 76–81; "Rickenbacker Super Sport" brochure, Kimes Research Files; Kimes, "A Hat in the Ring," 433.

87. Kimes, "A Hat in the Ring," 434–35; docket entries, *Columbia Axle vs. Rickenbacker Motor Company*, equity case 1747, United States District Court, Detroit, in National Archives, Great Lakes Region, Chicago, supplied by Beverly Watkins, archivist; "Rickenbacker Sale Authorized" and "Rickenbacker Plant Auction November 28," *Automobile Topics*, 13 August and 22 October 1927, Kimes Research Files; Kimes and Clark, *Standard Catalog*, 1292, estimating that the company made only 571 cars in the 1927 model year—but did not necessarily sell that number. Statistics from *Moody's Industrials* (see Kimes Research Files) indicate that the enterprise made 34,549 automobiles in its six-year history. An estimate in *The Hat in the Ring*, the official news publication of the Rickenbacker Car Club of America, 5, no. 12 (Spring 1980), supplied by Lyle and Nell Rose Corey, antique automobile collectors from Granada, Mississippi, sets the figure at 34,796.

88. R-H Tapes, reel 39G, side 2.

89. EVRR, 149.

Chapter 12. Frustrations

1. *Butte (MT) Daily Post*, 13 July 1923, clipping in EVRS 2.

2. John William Leonard, *Who's Who in Engineering: A Biographical Dictionary of Contemporaries, 1922–1923* (New York: John W. Leonard Corporation, 1923), 58; *Who's Who in America* (Chicago: A. N. Marquis Company, 1944), vol. 23 (1943–44): 48; Glenn Dale Angle, *Airplane Engine Encyclopedia: An Alphabetically Arranged Compilation of All Available Data on the World's Aircraft Engines* (Dayton, OH: Otterbein Press, c. 1921), and *Engine Dynamics and Crankshaft Design* (Detroit: Airplane Engine Encyclopedia Company, c. 1925); U.S. Patent No. 1,670,294, 22 May 1928, based on specification filed 27 July 1925.

3. "New Air Motor Given Tryout," undated clipping from unidentified newspaper; "New Driggs Coupe Takes the Air," *Detroit Free Press*, 29 August 1926; P. Whit-

comb Williams, "New Plane Presages Ship for Home Use," *Los Angeles Sunday Times*, 26 September 1926; Harold J. Wymer, "Rickenbacker Engine Test-Flown," *Aero Digest*, October 1926, 332, all in EVRS 2. Janet R. Daly Bednarek provided me much-appreciated information about Driggs. His birth name was Polhemus and he was not related to Laurence La Tourette Driggs.

4. Joseph P. Juptner, ed., *U.S. Civil Aircraft* (Los Angeles: Aero Publishers, 1962), 1:69–71.

5. Henry Ladd Smith, *Airways: The History of Commercial Aviation in the United States* (Washington, DC: Smithsonian Institution Press, 1991), 94–102; Nick Komons, *Bonfires to Beacons: Federal Civil Aviation Policy under the Air Commerce Act, 1926–1938* (Washington, DC: Smithsonian Institution Press, 1989), 65–88; R. E. G. Davies, *Airlines of the United States since 1914* (Washington, D.C.: Smithsonian Institution Press, 1988), 16–55; Donald R. Whitnah, "Air Mail Act of 1925," and William M. Leary, "Air Commerce Act of 1926," in Leary, *The Airline Industry*, 12–13, 20–21.

6. Albert LeShane Jr., "Florida Airways," *American Aviation Historical Society Journal* 22, no. 2 (1977): 123–25; Davies, *Airlines of the United States*, 49; "Skeletal Outline of the Events Connected with Florida Airways and Mr. Virgil Edwards Chenea, and Terminating in the Founding of PAA," supplied by Matthew E. Rodina Jr., who owns a large research collection on the history of seaplanes and the origins of Pan American Airways.

7. EVRR, 175.

8. LeShane, "Florida Airways," 123–25.

9. "An Invitation to Participate in the Initial Financing of the Florida Airways Corporation," prospectus supplied by Rodina.

10. "Plans Airways to Link Entire South. Florida Line Only Entering Wedge for System," clipping from unidentified newspaper datelined Nashville, Tennessee, 4 January 1926, EVRP-LC, box 9, folder marked "E. V. Rickenbacker—C-I Miscellaneous 1916–1961."

11. Fisher, *The Pacesetter*, 139–207; Frederick Lewis Allen, *Only Yesterday: An Informal History of the 1920s* (1931; repr. New York: Perennial Classics Edition, 2000), 234–43; Ann Armbruster, *The Life and Times of Miami Beach* (New York: Alfred A. Knopf, 1995), 5–49.

12. "Ford's Commercial Planes Off," "Ford's 'Tin Geese' Laid Up for Week," "Three of Ford Passenger Planes Badly Damaged," and "'Tin Geese' Slightly Hurt," clippings in EVRS 2; "Skeletal Outline," 5–6.

13. LeShane, "Florida Airways," 128–29; information provided by Rodina; "Personal History" and letter from Brooks to Hart, 21 May 1926, Arthur Raymond Brooks Papers, National Air and Space Museum Annex, Suitland, Maryland, box 3, folders 4 and 5.

14. "Skeletal Outline," 7.

15. EVRR, 176; LeShane, "Florida Airways," 131–32; Betsy Braden and Paul Hagan, *A Dream Takes Flight: Hartsfield International Airport and Aviation in Atlanta* (Athens: University of Georgia Press, 1989), 34–36.

16. "Skeletal Outline," 6–7; letter from Dennis to Brooks, 30 June 1926, Brooks Papers.

17. EVRR, 176.

18. Allen, *Only Yesterday,* 243–44; Armbruster, *Life and Times of Miami Beach,* 50–52; Fisher, *The Pacesetter,* 301–3.

19. Marilyn Bender and Selig Altschul, *The Chosen Instrument* (New York: Simon and Schuster, 1982), 83–106; Wesley Phillips Newton, "Juan T. Trippe," in Leary, *The Airline Industry,* 466–469. Rodina has provided insight about the effects of the hurricane; see also LeShane, "Florida Airways."

20. "Skeletal Outline," 8–9; Braden and Hagan, *A Dream Takes Flight,* 39.

21. George W. Cearley Jr., *Eastern Air Lines: An Illustrated History* (Dallas, TX: privately published, 1983, 1985), 7–9. On Pitcairn's life and career, see Frank Kingston Smith, *Legacy of Wings: The Story of Harold F. Pitcairn* (New York: Jason Aronson, Inc., 1981), and William F. Trimble, *High Frontier: A History of Aeronautics in Pennsylvania* (Pittsburgh: University of Pittsburgh Press, 1982), 124, 147–48, 173–78.

22. A. Scott Berg, *Lindbergh* (New York: Putnam, 1998), 3–6, 112–31; John William Ward, "Charles Lindbergh: His Flight and the American Ideal," in Carroll W. Pursell, ed., *Technology in America: A History of Individuals and Ideas,* 2nd ed. (Cambridge, MA: MIT Press, 1990), 211–26.

23. The Burton Historical Collection at the Detroit Public Library has numerous documents and newspaper clippings about Clancy's efforts to secure the Medal of Honor for Rickenbacker.

24. Fisher, *The Pacesetter,* 307–8; EVRR, 152–53.

25. Interview with Laurance S. Rockefeller by author.

26. Alfred P. Sloan Jr., *My Years with General Motors* (Garden City, NY: Doubleday & Company, 1964), 268–69; obituary of Lawrence P. Fisher, *New York Times,* 4 September 1961; Kimes and Clark, *Standard Catalog,* 218, 842–43; Walter M. P. McCall, *80 Years of Cadillac LaSalle* (Osceola, WI: Motorbooks International, 1982), 110; Maurice Hendry, "Cadillac Led V-8 Development" and "Model 314 Cut Ties with the Past," in Mary Sieber and Ken Buttolph, eds., *Standard Catalog of Cadillac, 1903–1990* (Iola, WI: Krause Publications, 1995), 20–23, 31–32; Stephen Bayley, *Harley Earl and the Dream Machine* (New York: Alfred A. Knopf, 1983), 36–42.

27. Sloan, *My Years,* 269; Riggs, *Pace Cars of the Indy 500,* 36–37; James D. Bell, "Companion Car to Cadillac," *Automobile Quarterly* 5, no. 3 (Winter 1967): 305–6.

28. "Ed Rickenbacker Now on LaSalle Executive Staff," clipping from unidentified newspaper, EVRS 2.

29. Interview with William F. Rickenbacker by author; EVRR, 150; Berg, *Lindbergh,* 175.

30. "Address by Captain E. V. Rickenbacker to Eastern Air Lines Employees at Hialeah, Florida, November 24, 1937," p. 9, in vol. 1 of staff speeches by Rickenbacker, given to author by Floyd D. Hall, now in Auburn University Archives, Auburn, Alabama.

31. Farr, *Rickenbacker's Luck*, 156–58; EVRR, 162–63.

32. "50 Million Cars in 20 Years Ace's Prediction," *Milwaukee Journal*, 6 February 1928; "Rickenbacker Sees Speed as Enemy of War," undated clipping from unidentified newspaper, Houston, Texas, EVRS 2.

33. Clipping from *Los Angeles Examiner*, EVRS 2.

34. "War Ace Names Lowry Field Ideal Airport Site," *Rocky Mountain News*, 16 February 1928; "Rickenbacker Sees 50,000,000 Autos in U.S. by 1950," clipping from undated Kansas City newspaper; "Predicts an Age of Super-Speed," undated clipping from unidentified El Paso newspaper, EVRS 2.

35. "Tradition Impedes State, Flyer Avers; Rhode Island Must Awaken to Save Industries, Asserts Capt. E. V. Rickenbacker," EVRS 2.

36. "Foresees Dozen Airfields Here," clipping from unidentified Boston newspaper, 23 March 1928, EVRS 2.

37. "Cadillac Reports Large Sales Increase," clipping from *Jersey City Journal*, 21 March 1928, and undated clipping from *Detroit Free Press*, EVRS 2; McCall, *80 Years*, 119–28; Kimes and Clark, *Standard Catalog*, 219–20; Sieber and Buttolph, *Standard Catalog of Cadillac*, 23.

38. McCall, *80 Years*, 119; U.S. Department of Commerce, *Statistical Abstract of the United States, 1929* (Washington, DC: Government Printing Office, 1929), 385.

39. William F. Rickenbacker, personal files, Francestown, New Hampshire, used with permission of his widow, Nancy Angell Rickenbacker.

40. Wesley Phillips Newton, *The Perilous Sky: U.S. Aviation Diplomacy and Latin America, 1919–1931* (Coral Gables, FL: University of Miami Press, 1978), 125–56; Berg, *Lindbergh*, 174–75; Donald R. Whitnah, *Safer Skyways: Federal Control of Aviation, 1926–1966* (Ames: Iowa State University Press, 1966), 44; Barnaby Conrad III, *Pan Am: An Aviation Legend* (Emeryville, CA: Woodford Press, 1999), 52, 55.

41. Quoted verbatim in EVRR, 164.

42. EVRR, 154–55; Popely, with Riggs, *Indianapolis 500 Chronicle*, 40–41.

43. "Life Story," 1:452–55.

44. Farr, *Rickenbacker's Luck*, 159–60; Sloan, *My Years*, 431–32.

45. McCall, *80 Years*, 129–35; *Statistical Abstract, 1929*, 385.

46. EVRR, 178; Farr, *Rickenbacker's Luck*, 166; Marc Dierikx, *Fokker: A Transatlantic Biography* (Washington, DC: Smithsonian Institution Press, 1997), 132–34; Sloan, *My Years*, 423–25.

47. Dierikx, *Fokker: A Transatlantic Biography*, 48–136; Henri Hegener, *Fokker: The Man and the Aircraft* (Letchworth, UK: Harleyford Publications, Ltd., 1961), 36–84.

48. Introduction by Rickenbacker to Anthony H. G. Fokker and Bruce Gould, *Flying Dutchman: The Life of Anthony Fokker* (New York: Henry Holt and Company, 1931), 3–4.

49. In addition to Dierikx, *Fokker*, and Hegener, *Fokker*, see William M. Leary, "Henry Ford and Aeronautics during the 1920s," in William M. Leary, ed., *Aviation's Golden Age: Portraits from the 1920s and 1930s* (Iowa City: University of Iowa Press,

1989), 1–17; Lesley Forden, *The Ford Air Tours, 1925–1931* (New Brighton, MN: Aviation Foundation of America, 1973), 22, 27–28.

50. Robert J. Serling, *Legend and Legacy: The Story of Boeing and Its People* (New York: St. Martin's Press, 1992), 13–15.

51. Farr, *Rickenbacker's Luck*, 162; Sloan, *My Years*, 423–26.

52. Photograph in Hegener, *Fokker*, 74; "For Aviation Mechanics," 1929, EVRP-LC, box 100.

53. "More Sunshine, Said Rickenbacker," typescript of article from *Automobile Topics*, 15 March 1930, EVRP-LC, box 100.

54. The McNary-Watres Act was one of the most significant pieces of legislation in the history of American commercial aviation. Among numerous accounts of the act and the circumstances under which it was passed, see Smith, *Airways*, 156–66; Komons, *Bonfires to Beacons*, 347–79; and F. Robert van der Linden, *Airlines and Air Mail: The Post Office and the Birth of the Commercial Aviation Industry* (Lexington: University Press of Kentucky, 2002), 106–36.

55. Edward V. Rickenbacker, "We Can Go Forward without a Nurse," *U.S. Air Service,* June 1930, 21–25, in EVRP-LC, box 100.

56. Dierikx, *Fokker,* 137; EVRR, 179.

57. Hegener, *Fokker,* 77.

58. On developments preceding and after the announcement, see 70th Cong., 1st sess., S.R. 3878, 2 April 1928, and H.R. 12675, 4 April 1928; 71st Cong., 1st sess., H.R. Report 2568, 16 February 1929; and a mass of documentation in EVRP-LC, box 11, folder marked "E. V. Rickenbacker, Congressional Medal Award." The entire controversy is ably summarized in Farr, *Rickenbacker's Luck*, 162–64. In the same connection, see also S. E. Liggett, "Rickenbacker Given Honor: Heroic Efforts in France Are Finally Recognized by War Department," undated clipping from *Detroit Free Press* in Rickenbacker File, Burton Historical Collection, Detroit Public Library.

59. Program of award ceremony and other documents in EVRP-LC, box 11, folder marked "E. V. Rickenbacker Congressional Medal Award."

60. Dierikx, *Fokker,* 136–38; Roy Allen, "Fokker Is 75—or If You Prefer, 82," *Airways* 1, no. 1 (March–April 1994): 25; Hegener, *Fokker,* 76–77.

61. "Life Story," 1:451–52. Rickenbacker misdated the episode as happening in 1929. EVRS 2 contains numerous clippings pertaining to the accident. See also "Col. Rickenbacker, War Ace, Limps From Fall in Sleep," *New York World,* 11 September 1930, clipping in National Automotive Collection, Detroit Public Library, and Farr, *Rickenbacker's Luck,* 167. William F. Rickenbacker, the probable source of Farr's statement that Rickenbacker had "come home after a drinking bout," confirmed the cause of the accident in an interview with me.

62. Dominick A. Pisano, "The Crash That Killed Knute Rockne," *Air and Space / Smithsonian* 6, no. 5 (December 1991–January 1992): 88–93; Dierikx, *Fokker,* 140–41.

63. Pisano, "Crash That Killed Knute Rockne," 92–93; Dierikx, *Fokker,* 141–43;

Eric Schatzberg, *Wings of Wood, Wings of Metal: Culture and Technical Choice in Airplane Materials, 1914–1945* (Princeton, NJ: Princeton University Press, 1999), 133.

64. Schatzberg, *Wings of Wood.*

65. Farr, *Rickenbacker's Luck,* 167–68.

Chapter 13. Comeback

1. The best account of these developments is van der Linden, *Airlines and Air Mail,* 84–186.

2. Biographical sketch of Cord in Lee Beck and Josh B. Malks, *Auburn and Cord* (Osceola, WI: Motorbooks International, 1996), 42–43; George E. Hopkins, "E. L. Cord," in Leary, *The Airline Industry,* 123–25; Farr, *Rickenbacker's Luck,* 170–71.

3. Van der Linden, *Airlines and Air Mail,* 229.

4. Among other accounts, see Kenneth S. Davis, *FDR: The New York Years, 1928–1933* (New York: Random House, 1979), 331–34, and Robert J. Serling, *Eagle: The Story of American Airlines* (New York: St. Martin's / MAREK, c. 1985), 39–41.

5. Farr, *Rickenbacker's Luck,* 171–75; Serling, *Eagle,* 42–43; van der Linden, *Air Lines and Air Mail,* 228–34; Rudy Abramson, *Spanning the Century: The Life of W. Averell Harriman, 1891–1986* (New York: W. Morrow, 1992), 201–6.

6. J. Mel Hickerson, *Ernie Breech: The Story of His Remarkable Career at General Motors, Ford, and TWA* (New York: Meredith Press, 1968), 78–81; EVRR, 182–83; Sloan, *My Life,* 426–27.

7. Van der Linden, *Airlines and Air Mail,* 250–253.

8. B. Douglas Craig, *After Wilson: The Struggle for the Democratic Party, 1920–1934* (Chapel Hill: University of North Carolina Press, 1992), 270–95; Robert F. Burk, *The Corporate State and the Broker State: The Du Ponts and American National Politics, 1925–1940* (Cambridge, MA: Harvard University Press, 1990), 143–277. On the development of the Liberty League, see also Frederick Rudolph, "The American Liberty League, 1934–1940," *American Historical Review* 56 (October 1950): 19–33, and George Wolfskill, *The Revolt of the Conservatives: A History of the American Liberty League, 1934–1940* (Boston: Houghton Mifflin Company, 1962).

9. EVRR, 182, 184.

10. David D. Lee, "Airmail Episode of 1934," in Leary, ed., *The Airline Industry,* 23–26.

11. Among other articles on Rickenbacker's statement, see "'Legalized Murder,' Rickenbacker Holds in Deaths of Air Mail Flyers," *Columbus (OH) Sunday Dispatch,* 18 February 1934, and "Hits 'Legalized Murder,' Rickenbacker Comments of Army Flyers' Deaths," *New York Times,* 19 February 1934, clippings in EVRS 3.

12. F. Robert van der Linden, *The Boeing 247: The First Modern Airliner* (Seattle, WA: University of Washington Press, 1991); Rene J. Francillon, *McDonnell Douglas Aircraft since 1920* (London: Putnam, 1979), 16–17, 165–71.

13. Francillon, *McDonnell Douglas Aircraft since 1920*, 17; Hickerson, *Ernie Breech*, 82–83.

14. R-H Tapes, reel 25, side 1; "Air-Mail Mark Set In the Final Flight," *New York Times*, 20 February 1934; clippings including "Rickenbacker Sets Air Mark," *Detroit News*, 19 February 1934, and David P. Sentner, "Rickenbacker Flies Airmail Across Country in 13 Hours," *New York Journal*, 19 February 1934, in EVRS 2. Sentner, an International News correspondent, was a passenger on the DC-1. For an extended account of the flight by Rickenbacker himself, see "Army Planes Unfit . . . Boys Are Sacrificed," clipping EVRS 2 from *Washington Post*, 20 February 1934. I am indebted to Matthew Rodina for providing me with a mass of materials pertaining to the flight, too numerous to cite here.

15. Folder marked "Transcontinental Record, 1934," EVRP-LC.

16. "Army Planes Unfit" and "Rickenbacker Sets Air Mark," clippings in EVRS 3.

17. See particularly Robert J. Serling, "Unsung Hero: Frye of TWA," *Airways* 3 (May–June 1996): 24–26.

18. Kenneth S. Davis, *FDR: The New Deal Years, 1933–1937* (New York: Random House, 1986), 361. For account of the episode crediting the Army Air Corps with doing a praiseworthy job of carrying the airmail, see DeWitt S. Copp, *A Few Great Captains: The Men and Events That Shaped the Development of U.S. Air Power* (Garden City, NY: Doubleday, 1980), 155–221.

19. "Rickenbacker Asks President to Oust 'Traitorous' Officials," *Washington Times*, 13 March 1934; "Rickenbacker Halted after Rapping FDR," in unidentified newspaper, 17 March 1934; and other clippings in EVRS 3.

20. David D. Lee, "Airmail Act of 1934," in Leary, *The Airline Industry*, 22–23; W. David Lewis, ed., *Airline Executives and Federal Regulation: Case Studies in American Enterprise from the Airmail Era to the Dawn of the Jet Age* (Columbus: Ohio State University Press, 2000). 8.

21. Hickerson, *Ernie Breech*, 84–89.

22. Letter from Rickenbacker to William Randolph Hearst, 31 March 1934, quoted in clipping from unidentified, undated newspaper, EVRS 3.

23. Hickerson, *Ernie Breech*, 90–91; "16 Will Fly to Miami and Return Today: Rickenbacker in Charge of Dawn-to-Dusk Trip Preceding 8-Hour Service to Florida," *New York Times*, and "Rickenbacker in Air Dash to Miami," *Detroit Evening Times*, both dated 13 November 1934; "Gales Deprive Rickenbacker of Flight Mark," *New York World Telegram*, "16 Reach Miami in 8 ½ Hr. Hop," *Los Angeles Evening Post*, "Rickenbacker Cheerful in His Defeat," *New York Journal*, "Noted Airman Ends Futile Quest for Record," *New York American*, and "Florida Flight Misses Record," *New York Sun*, all dated 14 November 1934; "Back the Same Day, Anyway," *Richmond News-Leader*, 15 November 1934, and other clippings in EVRS 3.

24. Hickerson, *Ernie Breech*, 91.

Chapter 14. Apex

1. Unless otherwise noted, the account of Eastern's early history that follows is based on Smith, *Legacy of Wings*; "History of Eastern Air Lines," an unpublished twenty-seven-page manuscript of unknown authorship in Rockefeller Archive Center, Sleepy Hollow, New York, Record Group 2; W. David Lewis, "Eastern Air Lines," in Leary, *The Airline Industry*, 22–23; and Robert J. Serling, *From the Captain to the Colonel: An Informal History of Eastern Airlines* (New York: Dial Press, 1980), 8–84.

2. Kenneth Munson, *Airliners between the Wars 1919–39* (New York: Macmillan, 1972), 36, 117–19; H. A. Taylor, "The Uncompetitive Condor," *Air Enthusiast* 6 (March–June 1978): 94–106.

3. Hickerson, *Ernie Breech*, 84–89.

4. EVRR, 189–90; Hickerson, *Ernie Breech*, 85; "History of Eastern Air Lines," 19–25, Rockefeller Archive Center.

5. Serling, *From the Captain to the Colonel*, 117–18.

6. "History of Eastern Air Lines," 24–25, Rockefeller Archive Center.

7. Peter W. Brooks, *The Modern Airliner* (1961; repr., Manhattan, KS: Sunflower University Press, 1982), 80–83; Arthur Pearcy, "Douglas Commercial Two," *Air Enthusiast* 19 (August–November 1982): 60–77.

8. Francillon, *McDonnell Douglas Aircraft*, 178–91; Henry M. Holden, *The Legacy of the DC-3* (Niceville, FL: Wind Canyon Publishing, Inc., 1997), 63–94; Serling, *From the Captain to the Colonel*, 118–20; reminiscences of the DC-2 by former EAL pilots in *REPArtee* (Retired Eastern Pilots Association, Goodyear, AZ), Summer 1995, 36–41.

9. Serling, *From the Captain to the Colonel*, 122–23.

10. Wilbur H. Morrison, *Donald W. Douglas: A Heart with Wings* (Ames: Iowa State University Press, 1991), 84–86; Serling, *Eagle*, 77–102.

11. An enormous literature exists about the DC-3. For representative accounts, see Francillon, "Douglas DC-3 and Derivatives," in Francillon, *McDonnell Douglas Aircraft*, 230–63; Douglas Ingells, *The Plane That Changed the World* (Fallbrook, CA: Aero Publishers, 1966); and Arthur Pearcy Jr., *Fifty Glorious Years* (New York: Orion Books, 1985).

12. Comparative statistics for 1936 and 1937, North American Aviation, Inc., Annual Report to Stockholders, 1937.

13. Serling, *From the Captain to the Colonel*, 123–29.

14. The Will Rogers Memorial and Public Library, Claremore, Oklahoma, has thousands of documents pertaining to the committee and the role Rickenbacker played in it.

15. Unless otherwise noted, material about Merrill and his flights is based on Jack L. King, *Wings of Man: An Informal Biography of Captain H. T. "Dick" Merrill* (Glendale, CA: Aviation Book Company, 1981).

16. Interview of Nancy Angell Rickenbacker, widow of William F. Rickenbacker, by author.

17. Despite drawing upon King's *Wings of Man* for some details about the flight of the "Lady Peace," my account of the episode is based primarily on Gregory C. Krohn's more carefully researched "Lady Peace Mission," *Armchair Aviator* 2, no. 4 (May 1973): 19–31, 47, provided to me by Matthew Rodina.

18. Cover photo in *The Great Silver Fleet News* [*TGSFN*] 3, no. 8 (April 1938), showing presentation of the trophy by FDR.

19. Comparative statistics in North American Aviation, Inc., Annual Report to Stockholders, 1937.

20. Memorandum of Ernest R. Breech to Rickenbacker, 12 October 1935, Henry Belin du Pont Papers, Eleutherian Mills Historical Library, Wilmington, Delaware, box 88, accessed with help from Marjorie G. McNinch.

21. Memoranda, Rickenbacker to Breech, 10, 14 June 1937, and transcript of telephone conversation of 14 June 1937, in "NAA Special Correspondence," copies in author's possession from files shared by Nancy Angell Rickenbacker.

22. R-H Tapes, reel 25, side 1; Serling, *From the Captain to the Colonel,* 132–33.

23. Farr, *Rickenbacker's Luck,* 186; Hickerson, *Ernie Breech,* 55–56.

24. Hickerson, *Ernie Breech,* 91–96; *Time,* 14 March 1938, 60, 62.

25. EVRR, 190–92; *Business Week,* 12 March 1938, 17; *Time,* 14 March 1938, 60, 62; Sloan, *My Years,* 427.

26. Letters from William Barclay Harding to Laurance S. Rockefeller, 4, 9 March and 28 April 1938, Rockefeller Archive Center, Record Group 2.

27. R-H Tapes, reel 39I, side 2; *Time,* 14 March 1938, 60–62.

28. *Business Week,* 12 March 1938, 17.

29. Sloan, *My Years,* 365–66; R-H Tapes, reel 39I, side 2; EVRR, 192–94.

30. R-H Tapes, reel 39I, side 2; EVRR, 194–95.

31. "EAL Celebrates Tenth Anniversary with Banquet," *TGSFN* 3, nos. 9–10 (May–June 1938): 7–11.

32. "EAL Participates in National Air Mail Week," *TGSFN* 3, nos. 9–10 (May–June 1938): 2–4, 6.

33. "Capt. Rickenbacker's Message," in *TGSFN* 3, nos. 9–10 (May–June 1938): 1.

34. *TGSFN* 3, nos. 6–7 (February–March 1939): 5; 4, no. 7 (November 1939): 8–9; 4, no. 8 (December–January 1940): 7; 5, no. 1 (February–March 1940): 30–31; and 5, no. 3 (Vacation Edition 1940): 2–3; Peter Collier and David Horowitz, *The Rockefellers: An American Dynasty* (New York: Holt, Rinehart and Winston, 1976), 217–18; interview of Laurance S. Rockefeller by author.

35. Nick A. Komons, *The Cutting Air Crash: A Case Study in Early Federal Aviation Policy* (Washington, DC: Federal Aviation Administration, 1973); Komons, *Bonfires to Beacons,* 277–379; Robert Burckhardt, "Air Transport Association," and Dominick A. Pisano, "Edgar S. Gorrell," in Leary, ed., *The Airline Industry,* 28–29, 189–91.

36. In addition to the sources cited in the preceding note, see my essay, "Ambivalent Relationship: Airline Executives and Federal Regulation," in Lewis, *Airline Executives and Federal Regulation,* 11–12.

37. Arnold E. Bridden et al., *FAA Historical Fact Book: A Chronology, 1926–1971* (Washington, DC: Department of Transportation, Federal Aviation Administration, 1974), 40; Smith, *Airways,* 357–59; Nick A. Komons, "Civil Aeronautics Administration," and Donald R. Whitnah, "Civil Aeronautics Board," in Leary, *Airline Industry,* 101–8. For the text of the law, see *United States Statutes at Large,* 75th Cong., 3rd sess., 1938, 985–1030.

38. Davies, *Airlines of the United States,* 202.

39. EVRR, 218–23; "A Triumph for Eastern Air Lines" and "Flying Down to Rio," *TGSFN* 3, no. 12 (August 1938): 1, and 4, no. 1 (September 1938): 9–12.

40. Annual Report of Eastern Airlines, 1938, 9; Davies, *Airlines of the United States,* 203.

41. "EAL Inaugurates Tampa, San Antonio Routes," *TGSFN* 4, no. 2 (December 1938): 3–5.

42. "Wings across the Border," *TGSFN* 4, no. 4 (May 1939): 1–7.

43. "Airmail Via 'Windmill,'" *TGSFN* 4, no. 6 (September 1939): 13–14; "Seen at Washington's National Aviation Forum," *TGSFN* 5, no. 3 (Vacation Edition, Summer 1940): 23; Carroll V. Glines, *Airmail: How It All Began* (Blue Ridge Summit, PA: TAB Books, 1990), 136.

44. Annual Reports, Eastern Air Lines, 1941, 5–6, and 1942, 1–2.

45. Annual Reports, Eastern Air Lines, 1938–41; "The Annual Family Conference of Eastern Air Lines' Employees," addendum to 1939 annual report.

46. *Aviation Week* article printed in *TGSFN* 6, no. 2 (Summer 1941): 16; "Sea Island Joins Family of EAL Resorts," with accompanying photographs, and "EAL Celebrates Its 13th Anniversary May 1," *TGSFN* 6, no. 1 (Spring 1941): 18–19, 40; "EAL Flag Presented United Daughters of the Confederacy," *TGSFN* 4, no. 8 (December 1939–January 1940): 5. On the origin of the EAL flag, see "Speaking of Flags," *TGSFN* 4, no. 4 (May 1939): 34.

47. "Powers Behind the Throne at Miami," "Miami Executive Roll Call," and other articles in *TGSFN* 4, no. 6 (September 1939): 17–33, 37–38, 40. Routine maintenance was performed at airports throughout the system, particularly at Newark International Airport.

48. "Atlanta . . . Gateway to the South," *TGSFN* 4, no. 2 (December 1938): 39–44.

49. "A Closeup of EX NY," *TGSFN* 4, no. 8 (December 1939–January 1940): 26–27.

50. Kenneth Jackson et al., eds., *The Encyclopedia of New York City* (New Haven: Yale University Press, 1995), 1015; Ric Burns and James Sanders, with Lisa Ades, *New York: An Illustrated History* (New York: Alfred A. Knopf, 1999), 450–55.

51. Serling, *From the Captain to the Colonel,* 156.

52. "EAL's New Home . . . Rockefeller Center," *TGSFN* 5, no. 3 (Vacation Edition, 1940): 1, and "A Building Is Named," *TGSFN* 6, no. 4 (Post-Autumn Edition, 1940): 1–3.

53. Francis Sill Wickware and Charles J. V. Murphy, "Eddie Rickenbacker," *Life* 7, no. 7 (3 July 1939): 59–65; photographs in *TGFSN,* numerous issues, 1937–41; Leighton Interviews, 23, 38–39.

54. Interviews with William F. Rickenbacker, Bryan A. Rickenbacker (son of David E. Rickenbacker), and Patricia Ann Wrightson (first wife of David F. Rickenbacker) by author.

55. Angus MacDonald, "Out of Season: William Frost Rickenbacker, 1928–1995," *The St. Croix Review* 27, no. 4 (August 1995): 1–12; interviews with William F. Rickenbacker, Bryan Rickenbacker, and Patricia Ann Wrightson by author; correspondence by author with Marie-Louise Perri (half sister of William F. Rickenbacker), Las Vegas, Nevada; Leighton Interviews, 36–37.

56. McDonald, "Out of Season," 9; interview with William F. Rickenbacker by author.

57. Leighton Interviews, 75–76.

58. On most of the personal characteristics described here, see Leighton Interviews. Rickenbacker's addiction to tobacco is mentioned in Farr, *Rickenbacker's Luck,* 167, stating that Rickenbacker "smoked cigarettes like a testing machine in a cancer laboratory."

59. Wickware and Murphy, "Eddie Rickenbacker," 61.

60. The bust is now displayed at Motts Military Museum, Groveport, Ohio.

61. David K. Vaughan, "Technology and American Values: Juvenile Aviation Adventure Series of the 1930s," *Journal of Popular Literature* 1, no. 1 (Spring–Summer 1985): 102–16.

62. Edward V. Rickenbacker, *Ace Drummond* (Racine, WI: Whitman Publishing Company, 1935), copy in Thurber Special Collections Department, Ohio State University Library.

63. Don Rogers, "Rickenbacker—Air Lines Wizard," *Scribner's Commentator,* June 1941, 45–52, copy in EVRP-LC, box 128; "Capt. Rickenbacker's Life Dramatized over Network" and report from EAL's Chicago office, *TGSFN* 4, no. 5 (June–July 1939): 1, 38–39.

64. William Randolph Hearst Jr., with Jack Casserly, *The Hearsts: Father and Son* (New York: Roberts Rinehart Publishers, 1991), 116.

65. Letter from Laurance S. Rockefeller to Edward C. Romph, 1 February 1939, Rockefeller Archive Center, Record Group 2.

66. "Leslie P. Arnold Named to Assist Capt. Rickenbacker," *TGSFN* 5, no. 1 (February–March 1940): 1, 28–29.

67. Hearst, *The Hearsts,* 116.

68. Wickware and Murphy, "Eddie Rickenbacker," 65.

69. R-H Tapes, reel 39I, side 2; EVRR, 155–56; Popely, with Riggs, *Indianapolis 500 Chronicle,* 50–51.

70. Interview with Birdie Bomar by author; W. David Lewis and Wesley Phillips Newton, *Delta: The History of An Airline* (Athens: University of Georgia Press, 1979), esp. 346.

71. King, *Wings of Man,* 220–21.

72. Serling, *From the Captain to the Colonel,* 132.

73. Stuart D. Brandes, *American Welfare Capitalism, 1880–1940* (Chicago: University of Chicago Press, 1976).

74. "EAL Credit Union Declares 6% Dividend," *TGSFN* 4, no. 3 (January–February 1939): 14; "EAL Credit Union Flourishes," *TGSFN* 4, no. 6 (September 1939): 27; "EAL's Credit Union Nears Second Anniversary," *TGSFN* 4, no. 8 (December–January 1939–40): 13; "New York Credit Union Holds Annual Meeting," *TGSFN* 5, no. 1 (February–March 1940): 25; "Miami Credit Union Doubles Strength Annually," *TGSFN* 5, no. 4 (Autumn 1940): 15.

75. "Capt. 'Eddie' Announces Christmas Appreciation Fund," *TGSFN* 4, no. 2 (December 1938): 2; "Board Approves Stock-Purchase Plan," *TGSFN* 4, no. 3 (February–March 1939): 7; "'Complete Security Plan' Is Proving Popular," *TGSFN* 4, no. 5 (June–July 1939): 30.

76. George E. Hopkins, *The Airline Pilots: A Study in Elite Unionization* (Cambridge, MA: Harvard University Press, 1971), best covers the origins and development of the ALPA in this period.

77. EVRR, 207.

78. Serling, *From the Captain to the Colonel*, 153–54.

79. "Flight-Steward Fledglings," *TGSFN* 4, no. 5 (June–July 1939): 27; "Latest Class of Flight-Stewards Reports for Duty," *TGSFN* 5, no. 2 (April–May 1940): 25; "Eastern Carries the Male!," *TGSFN* 6, no. 1 (Spring Edition, 1941): 41–44.

80. "Presenting . . . EAL's 'Million-Milers'!" and "Eastern Air Lines' 'Million-Miler' Captains," *TGSFN* 4, no. 3 (February–March 1939): 13, 19, 22–25; R-H Tapes, reel 39K, side 2.

81. Whitnah, *Safer Skyways*, 102.

82. Jason Hicks, "Edward V. Rickenbacker's Fight to Improve the Aviation Infrastructure in the 1930s," 10–11, unpublished research paper, Auburn University; R-H Tapes, reel 39K, side 2; King, *Wings of Man*, 140–51. King misstates the nature of the injury Merrill sustained, saying merely that he lost some teeth.

83. Hicks, "Rickenbacker's Fight," 11–12; Whitnah, *Safer Skyways*, 127–32, 163.

84. "Legionnaires Honor Captain Rickenbacker and Themselves," *TGSFN* 3, no. 3 (November 1937): 6; Hicks, "Rickenbacker's Fight"; Whitnah, *Safer Skyways*, 106.

85. "Statement Made by Capt. E. V. Rickenbacker," *TGSFN* 3, no. 1 (September 1937): 13; John Ingle, "Years Ago—Eastern's First Airline Crash," *REPArtee* (magazine of the Retired Eastern Pilots Association), 20, no. 3 (Winter 1999–2000): 71–73; "EAL Wins Fourth Consecutive Safety Award," *TGSFN* 5, no. 1 (February–March 1940): 41.

86. EVRR, 210–12.

87. Wickware and Murphy, "Eddie Rickenbacker," 59.

88. Serling, *From the Captain to the Colonel*, 144–45.

Chapter 15. Pivot

1. Cooke, *Billy Mitchell*, 269–70; Hurley, *Billy Mitchell: Crusader for Air Power*, 135; Ruth Mitchell, *My Brother Bill: The Life of General "Billy" Mitchell* (New York: Harcourt, Brace and Company, 1953), 339–42; R-H Tapes, reel 10, side 1.

2. "Rickenbacker Would Free Aviation of Politics: Disagrees on Policy with Gen. Mitchell," *Charlotte (NC) Observer*; "Rickenbacker Urges Pacific Air Travel," *San Bernardino (CA) Daily Sun*; "Airline to Japan Rickenbacker Aim," *New York Times*, all dated 4 October 1934, clippings in EVRS 2.

3. R-H Tapes, reel 10, side 1; Cooke, *Billy Mitchell*, 7–8.

4. "Rickenbacker Would Free Aviation of Politics."

5. "Life Story," 2:554.

6. Williamson Murray, *Strategy for Defeat: The Luftwaffe, 1933–1945* (Roysted, Hertfordshire: Eagle Editions Ltd., 2000), 15.

7. Elizabeth-Anne Wheal, Stephan Pope, and James Taylor, *Encyclopedia of the Second World War* (Edison, NJ: Castle Books, 1989), 191, 307; R-H Tapes, reel 7, side 2.

8. EVRR, 261; R-H Tapes, reel 7, side 2; "Life Story," 2:553–54.

9. Interview with Adelaide Rickenbacker, Leighton Interviews.

10. Ibid., 29–30; the caricatures are now displayed at the United States Air Force Museum.

11. R-H Tapes, reel 7, side 2. On Vansittart, see Winston S. Churchill, *Memoirs of the Second World War* (New York: Houghton Mifflin Company, 1949), 82.

12. R-H Tapes, reel 7, side 2.

13. Ibid.

14. Wayne S. Cole, *Charles A. Lindbergh and the Battle against American Intervention in World War II* (New York: Harcourt Brace Jovanovich, 1974), 31–40.

15. R-H Tapes, reel 10.

16. The Rickenbackers sailed for Europe on 25 June 1938 and returned on 1 August. "Rickenbackers Sail" and "'Captain Eddie' and Family Welcomed Home," *TGSFN* 3, no. 11 (July 1938): 2, and no. 12 (August 1938): 13.

17. On Roosevelt's unpopularity in the aviation industry, stemming not only from the airmail crisis of 1934 but also from his budget cutting at the expense of air safety, see Dominick A. Pisano, *To Fill the Skies with Pilots: The Civil Pilot Training Program, 1939–46* (Urbana: University of Illinois Press, 1993), 24.

18. In this connection, see William L. O'Neill, *A Democracy at War: America's Fight at Home and Abroad in World War II* (New York: Free Press, 1993), 16; Thomas M. Coffey, *Hap: Military Aviator* (New York: Viking, 1982), 192.

19. On 12 January 1939, Roosevelt sent Congress a request to spend $525 million for military spending, $300 million of which was earmarked for aircraft; Pisano, *To Fill the Skies with Pilots*, 2.

20. "50,000 Planes Can't Be Wrong, by Captain Eddie V. Rickenbacker as told to Gardner Harding," *Collier's* 103, no. 16 (29 April 1939): 9–10, 60–61.

21. Pisano, *To Fill the Skies with Pilots,* 1–33.

22. "Norway Trip, July 12, 1939 to September 5, 1939," diary kept by Adelaide Rickenbacker, ERP-AU.

23. See, for example, Paul H. Wilkinson, New York City, to EVR, 25 September 1939, in EVRP-LC, folder marked "W–2 Miscellaneous 1916–1961."

24. The full text of Rickenbacker's address is contained in *TGSFN* 4, no. 7 (November 1939): 1–6.

25. Letter from Ida L. Tuve, Washington, D.C., to EVR, 27 September 1939, EVRP-LC, folder marked "T-Miscellaneous 1916–1961"; letter from Frank B. Wilson, New York City, to EVR, 27 September 1939; letter from Ken Wilhelm, Alamosa, Colorado, to EVR, 28 October 1939; and letter from Daniel Willard to EVR, 3 October 1939, all in EVRP-LC, folder marked "W–2 Miscellaneous 1916–1961."

26. The synopsis of events here is based largely on Martin Gilbert, *The Second World War: A Complete History,* rev. ed. (New York: Henry Holt and Company, 1989), 1–102. On the Scandinavian campaign, see Adam R. A. Claasen, *Hitler's Northern War* (Lawrence: University Press of Kansas, 2001), 62–140.

27. "Rickenbacker Tells Hub U.S. Has No Place in War," *Boston Evening American,* 3 June 1940; "Rickenbacker Sees U.S. in War If Allies Hold Out 3 Months," *New Orleans Tribune,* 7 June; "A Big Day in Evansville History," *Evansville Courier,* 24 August 1940; "U.S. Will Fight in Spring, Says Rickenbacker," *Chicago Tribune,* 24 August 1940; "U.S. Aid Vital to Beat Nazis," *Atlanta Constitution,* 26 August, 1940, EVRS 3.

28. Letter from Robert E. Wood to Rickenbacker, 15 August 1940, with attached materials, and reply from Rickenbacker to Wood, 19 August 1940, copies in EVRP-LC, folder marked "America First Committee." Rickenbacker's opposition to shipping combat planes to Europe was widely shared in the Army Air Corps; see Copp, *A Few Great Captains,* 463–67.

29. Letter from R. Douglas Stuart Jr. to Rickenbacker, 7 September 1940, EVRP-LC, folder marked "America First Committee."

30. Telegrams dated 3, 27 December 1940, in ibid.

31. "Defense Unity Urged by F.D.R.; Rickenbacker Says U.S. to Enter War," *Ohio State Journal* (Columbus), 11 December 1940; "Rickenbacker Avers U.S. Will Enter War in 1941," *Buffalo (NY) Courier Express,* 24 December 1940; "U.S. Seen at War by Rickenbacker," *Bronxville (NY) Review Press,* 26 December 1940, clippings in EVRS 3.

32. *AFC Bulletin* 14, dated 21 January 1941, and letter from Rickenbacker to Augustus L. Richards, Greenwich, Connecticut, 8 May 1942, in ibid.

33. Davis, *FDR,* 19; Henry L. Stimson and McGeorge Bundy, *On Active Service in Peace and War* (New York: Harper & Brothers, 1948), 343; Coffey, *Hap,* 221–23.

34. James MacGregor Burns, *Roosevelt: The Soldier of Freedom* (1956; repr., New York: Smithmark Publishers, 1996), 27–29; Pisano, *To Fill the Skies with Pilots,* 28.

35. "Celebrating Capt. Eddie's Golden Birthday Anniversary," *TGSFN* 6, no. 4 (Post-Autumn Edition, 1940): 43.

36. "World's First Airlines Terminal," "As the Camera Saw the New York Yuletide

Party," "Honoring the Flying Cadet," and "Capt. Eddie Accepts New La Guardia Field Hangar," *TGSFN* 5, no. 6 (Winter 1940–41): 1, 10, 21, 32–33; Eastern Air Lines Annual Report, 1941.

37. Thomas Kessler, *Fiorello H. LaGuardia and the Making of Modern New York* (New York: McGraw-Hill, 1989).

38. Ibid., 132–33, 270–91.

39. This account of the origins and development of what became known as La-Guardia Field is based mainly on Kessler, *LaGuardia*, 432–35, and John R. Tunis, *Million-Miler: The Story of an Air Pilot* (New York: Julian Messner, Inc., 1942), 129.

40. R-H Tapes, reel 39J, side 2; interview by author with James Hoogerwerf, a retired Delta Air Lines pilot familiar with the sinking of the runways Rickenbacker had anticipated.

41. David Gelernter, *1939: The Lost World of the Fair* (New York: Avon Books, 1995), 2.

42. Serling, *Eagle*, 133–37.

43. "The Story of EAL at Newark Is the Study of Growth," "Growth of EAL's Radio at NK Is Saga of Miracles," and accompanying photographs in *TGSFN* 4, no. 7 (November 1939): 28–33.

44. "New York Municipal Airport–LaGuardia Field," *TGSFN* 5, no. 3 (Vacation Edition, 1940): 59.

45. Cover photograph, "New York's Little Flower Christens the Mexico Flyer," "EAL Inaugurates Service from New York Municipal Airport–LaGuardia Field," and "EAL 'At Home' at LaGuardia Field," *TGSFN* 5, no. 2 (April–May 1940): 1–3.

46. "Baltimoreans Who Inspected LaGuardia Airport," *TGSFN* 5, no. 3 (Vacation Edition, 1940): 38–39; "Celebrating Capt. Eddie's Golden Birthday Anniversary," *TGSFN* 5, no. 4 (Autumn 1940): 43; "World's First Airlines Terminal" and "Honoring the 'Flying Cadet,'" *TGSFN* 5, no. 6 (Winter 1940–41): 1, 21.

47. EVRR, 236; *New York Times,* 26 February 1941.

48. For perspective on the relationship between Birmingham and Atlanta, see W. David Lewis, *Sloss Furnaces and the Rise of the Birmingham District: An Industrial Epic* (Tuscaloosa: University of Alabama Press, 1994), 379, 432–33, 436, 466, 483, 508.

49. "Life Story," 1:429; account of Dixon's life, Gubernatorial Papers, Alabama Department of Archives and History, Montgomery.

50. Damon Runyon and Walter Kiernan, *Capt. Eddie Rickenbacker: Complete Life Story,* 26, vertical files, National Air and Space Museum.

51. Jan Morris, *Manhattan '45* (New York: Oxford University Press, 1987), 171–72; Jackson et al., *Encyclopedia of New York City,* 890–91.

52. Domestic airlines began serving alcoholic beverages in the 1950s to boost traffic. Pan American had served them much longer. See Lewis and Newton, *Delta,* 311.

53. For a discussion of the mass transportation systems built in New York City in the late 1930s, see Robert A. Caro, *The Power Broker: Robert Moses and the Fall of*

New York (New York: Vintage Books, 1975), 499–575. For descriptions of LaGuardia Field, see "Air Terminal Deluxe," *Aviation* 38 (November, 1939): 20–21; "Fiorello's Windflower," *Fortune* 22 (August 1940): 38–44, 84; Samuel E. Stott, "New York's Municipal Airport," *Mechanical Engineering* 67 (February 1940): 103–11; "New York City Municipal Airport, North Beach, Long Island, NY," *Aero Digest*, November 1939, 32–26; R. L. Taylor, "A Reporter at Large: An Airport with a View," *New Yorker* 16 (1 June 1940): 46–52; and John Walter Wood, *Airports: Some Elements of Design and Future Development* (New York: Coward-McCann, Inc., 1940), 111–18. I am indebted to Deborah G. Douglas for providing me with copies of these materials. On the history of the terminal, see Douglas's Ph.D. dissertation, "The Invention of Airports: A Political, Economic and Technological History of Airports in the United States, 1919–1939" (University of Pennsylvania, 1996), 377–86.

54. Ric Burns and James Sanders, with Lisa Ades, *New York: An Illustrated History* (New York: Alfred A. Knopf, 1999), 439, 446; Jan Morris, "When Great Ships Came In," *New York Times*, 25 January 1998, sec. 15; Jackson et al., *Encyclopedia of New York City*, 1275–76. That the weather had cleared is indicated by a subsequent report made by the Civil Aeronautics Board, cited in note 57. On the spectacle of New York City's waterfront at nightfall, see photographs and selections from John Dos Passos, Thomas Wolfe, and Carl Sandburg in Robert Gambee, *Manhattan Seascape: Waterside Views around New York* (New York: Hastings House, 1975), 192–95.

55. Originally there were six hangars. By the time of Rickenbacker's flight there were eight.

56. Holden, *Legacy of the DC-3*, 100; Kenneth Munson, *Airliners between the Wars, 1919–39* (New York: Macmillan, 1972), 164–65.

57. Unless otherwise noted, all details of the flight are based on *Report of the Civil Aeronautics Board . . . of an Accident Involving Civil Aircraft of the United States NC 28394, which Occurred Near Atlanta, Georgia, on February 26, 1941* (Washington: Government Printing Office, 1941), supplied by Edmund Preston.

58. EVRR, 236.

59. "Lawsuit Kept Pearson Off Ill-Fated Airliner," *Atlanta Journal*, 28 February 1941, clipping in EVRS 3.

60. "Airliner Overdue with 16 On Board," *New York Times*, 27 February 1941; "Littledales Both Editors," *New York Sun*, 28 February 1941, clipping in EVRS 3.

61. See procedure specified in Tunis, *Million-Miler*, 146–50.

62. Serling, *From the Captain to the Colonel*, 121–22. On Thomas's background, see "Copilot Thomas' Body Sent Home," *Atlanta Constitution*, 1 March 1941, clipping in EVRS 3.

63. *Report of the Civil Aeronautics Board*, 6–7.

64. For a detailed history of Washington-Hoover Field and the origins and development of Washington National (now Ronald Reagan) Airport, see James M. Goode, "Flying High: The Origin and Design of National Airport," *Washington History* 1 (Fall, 1989): 4–25, 98–99, provided by Deborah G. Douglas.

65. *Biographical Directory of the United States Congress, 1774–1989,* Bicentennial edition (Washington, DC: Government Printing Office, 1989), 723.

66. *Report of the Civil Aeronautics Board,* 8.

67. R-H Tapes, reel 39K, side 1, and reel 46, side 1; "Life Story," 1:425–30.

68. The ensuing discussion of expectations concerning pilots is based on interviews by author with Bishop Simpson, an Eastern Air Lines Mechanic who was a member of the party that discovered the crash site the day after the accident; with Perry Hudson, former chief pilot of Eastern Air Lines, who flew for Eastern at the time of the crash; and with Floyd D. Hall, who began his career as a pilot and ultimately became chief executive officer of Eastern Air Lines.

69. Interview with Floyd D. Hall by author.

70. *Report of the Civil Aeronautics Board,* 8–10.

71. Hall showed me such an altimeter and demonstrated how it was set.

72. On the techniques involved in such an approach, see William M. Leary, "Instrument Flying and Radio Navigation," in William M. Leary, ed., *Infrastructure and Environment,* vol. 1 of *From Airships to Airbus: The History of Civil and Commercial Aviation* (Washington, DC: Smithsonian Institution Press, 1995), 109.

73. Interview with Floyd D. Hall by author.

74. "Plane Crash Probe Hears Expert," *Atlanta Journal,* 4 March 1941; interview with Floyd D. Hall by author.

75. *Report of the Civil Aeronautics Board,* 13–22. This document shows that when Perry left Washington, Airway Traffic Control gave him an altimeter setting (above sea level) of 28.94 inches of mercury. When Perry contacted the Atlanta control tower, this reading was corrected to 30.23. When the plane's altimeters were recovered, one of them was set at 30.33 and the other at 29.92.

76. R-H Tapes, reel 13; EVRR, 237.

77. EVRR, 237.

78. Bradley R. Rice, "Flashback: A Romantic Slice of Clayton County History," *Metro South,* Spring 1988, 14–16.

79. Photographs of plane at crash site, ERP-AU.

80. Among many newspaper clippings pertaining to the crash, all in EVRS 3 and dated 28 February 1941, see "7 Die in Georgia as Airliner Crashes 6 Hours Out of New York," unidentified newspaper; "Crash Victims Voice Thanks for Being Safe," "Little Light Thrown on Cause of Crash," and "Morrow Is Still Atremble at Tragedy," all from *Atlanta Constitution;* "Crash Victims' Bodies Sent Home for Funeral," "Pilot Perry's Funeral to Be Held Saturday," and "Probing the Air Wreck," from *Atlanta Journal;* and "Air Crash Inquiries Begin," from *New York Sun.* Other clippings include "Plane Crash Probers Due Wednesday," *Atlanta Journal,* 1 March 1941; "Airline Mystery Victim Requires Double Coffin," *Atlanta Journal,* 2 March 1941; "Atlanta Airliner Kept Flying Low after Clipping Trees Quarter Mile from Scene of Crash, Bird Hunters Discover," *Atlanta Constitution,* 2 March 1941; "Plane Crash Probe Hears Expert," "Residents Near Air Crash Spot Will Testify," and "Silver Sleeper's Last

Five Minutes," *Atlanta Journal*, 4 March 1941; "Two Witnesses Declare Weather Not Cause of Fatal Air Crash," *Atlanta Constitution*, 7 March 1941; and "Salute to Rick," from unidentified newspaper, 10 March 1941. See also "7 Dead, 9 Injured in Crash of Plane outside Atlanta," *New York Times*, 28 February 1941.

81. R-H Tapes, reel 13; interview with Birdie Bomar.

82. R-H Tapes, reel 13; EVRR, 237. The extent of Rickenbacker's injuries is revealed in a report by Edward E. Kaplan, M.D., Bendiner & Schlesinger X-Ray Laboratories Inc., Third Avenue & Tenth Street, New York City, to Dr. H. S. Schwartz, 53 E. 61st St., New York City, 14 August 1941, copy in ERP-AU.

83. R-H Tapes, reel 13.

84. Ibid.

85. Joint interview with Bishop Simpson and Perry Hudson by author.

86. Ibid.; R-H Tapes, reel 13.

87. McRae's father had been cofounder of the hospital, formerly the residence of a wealthy Atlanta family, when it opened as a sanitarium in 1905. Interview with Diane Erdeljac, Curator, Piedmont Hospital Archives, by author.

88. R-H Tapes, reel 13.

89. Ibid.; EVRR, 244–45; interview with William F. Rickenbacker by author.

90. "Rickenbacker Honored by Greensboro–High Point Citizens" and "'Captain Eddie' Honored by Miami University," *TGSFN* 6, no. 2 (Summer 1941): 13–16, 41; R-H Tapes, reel 39K, side 1; EVRR, 444.

91. R-H Tapes, reel 13, and reel 46, side 1; EVRR, 245–48.

92. Photograph of departure at Atlanta Historical Society; clipping from *New York Sun* datelined 26 June 1941; EVRS 4 (1941–November 1942); "The Eastern Air Lines Family Also Serves," *TGSFN* 6, no. 3 (Vacation Issue 1941): 1–4.

93. "Capt. Eddie Returns Home" and "Capt. Eddie Smacks the Ball," *TGSFN* 6, no. 3 (Vacation Issue, 1941): 2, 4.

94. "Wings to Forty Million Americans," *TGSFN* 6, no. 1 (Spring 1941): 35, 38.

Chapter 16. Call to Duty

1. Peter Young, ed., *The World Almanac Book of World War II* (New York: World Almanac Publications, 1981), 91–111; Martin Gilbert, *Churchill: A Life* (New York: Henry Holt and Company, 1991), 679–700; Samuel Eliot Morison, *The Battle of the Atlantic, September 1939–May 1943*, vol. 1 of *History of United States Naval Operations in World War II* (1947; repr., New York: Castle Books, 2001), 45–64; Peter Calvocoressi, Guy Wint, and John Pritchard, *The Penguin History of the Second World War* (New York: Penguin Books, 1999), 164–95; Williamson Murray and Allan R. Millett, *A War to Be Won: Fighting the Second World War* (Cambridge, MA: Harvard University Press, 2000), 91–123.

2. Clippings from *New York Sun*, 26 June 1941, and unidentified Hyannis (MA)

newspaper, 4 September 1941, in EVRS 4; articles in *TGSFN* 6, no. 1 (Spring 1941): 7, 15, 35, 54–58, 61–66, and no. 2 (Summer 1941): 1, 3–4, 9–11, 29, 31, 34, 53, 55, 59, 67–68; Reginald M. Cleveland, *Air Transport at War* (New York: Harper & Brothers, 1946), 111; James D. Carter, "The Early Development of Air Transport and Ferrying," in Wesley Frank Craven and James Lea Cate, *The Army Air Forces in World War II* (Chicago: University of Chicago Press, 1948), 1:324.

3. Thomas A. Rumer, *The American Legion: An Official History, 1919–1989* (New York: M. Evans and Company, Inc., 1990), 236–41.

4. Wayne S. Cole, *Charles A. Lindbergh and the Battle against American Intervention in World War II* (New York: Harcourt Brace Jovanovich, 1974), 142–85; Berg, *Lindbergh*, 408–32; Leonard Mosley, *Lindbergh: A Biography* (Garden City, NY: Doubleday & Company, Inc., 1976), 262–302.

5. Clipping from *Marietta (GA) Daily Journal*, 5 September 1941, EVRS 4.

6. Clipping from *Asheville (NC) Times*, 27 November 1941, in ibid.

7. Farr, *Rickenbacker's Luck*, 208–9.

8. On the developments that follow, see numerous sources including Young, *World Almanac Book of World War II*, 119–36, and Williamson and Millett, *A War to Be Won*, 120–68.

9. Farr, *Rickenbacker's Luck*, 207–8.

10. Wheal, Pope, and Taylor, *Encyclopedia of the Second World War*, 485–86.

11. Farr, *Rickenbacker's Luck*, 208–9.

12. Berg, *Lindbergh*, 431–32; Mosley, *Lindbergh*, 303–12.

13. Bob Considine, "On the Line," clipping from *New York Daily Mirror*, 12 December 1941, EVRS 4.

14. Farr, *Rickenbacker's Luck*, 209–10.

15. Eric Larrabee, *Commander in Chief: Franklin Delano Roosevelt, His Lieutenants and Their War* (New York: Simon and Schuster, 1987), 224–25.

16. Berg, *Lindbergh*, 433–39.

17. Dik Alan Daso, *Hap Arnold and the Evolution of American Airpower* (Washington, DC: Smithsonian Institution Press, 2000), 169–73; EVRR, 272–73.

18. Clipping from *Minneapolis Tribune*, 9 March 1942; "Hold Fire, Shoot Straight Is Rickenbacker's Advice," clipping from *Kenton (OH) News-Republican*, 11 March 1942, EVRS 4.

19. EVRR, 272–73; Franks and Bailey, *Over the Front*, 45–46.

20. Lee Kennett, *For the Duration: The United States Goes to War, Pearl Harbor–1942* (New York: Charles Scribner's Sons, 1985), 181–83.

21. Clipping from *New York World-Telegram* datelined Atlanta, 26 February, EVRS 4.

22. Clippings from *Tampa Tribune*, 11 March, and *Savannah News*, 12 March 1942, ibid.

23. Clippings from *Clayton (GA) Advocate, Columbia (SC) Gazette, Florence (SC) News, Raleigh (NC) News and Observer, Meridian (MS) Star, Jackson (MS) News* and *Clarion-Led-*

ger, *New Orleans Times-Picayune, Shreveport Times, Oklahoma City Oklahoman* and *Will Rogers Field News, Gallup (NM) Independent,* and *Los Angeles News,* 13–16 March, ibid.

24. EVRR, 275–76.

25. Clipping from *Long Beach (CA) Press-Telegram,* 26 March 1942, EVRS 4; Robert F. Dorr, "94th Pursuit Squadron," *Wings of Fame,* vol. 4 (London: Aerospace Publishing Ltd., 1996), 29; confidential letter from Rickenbacker to Arnold from Spokane, Washington, 29 March 1942, R-H Tapes, reel 50, side 2.

26. Clippings from *Oklahoma City Oklahoman, Los Angeles Herald and Express, Los Angeles Examiner, Long Beach Press-Telegram, San Francisco News,* and *Seattle Times,* 19, 26, 27 March, in EVRS 4.

27. Confidential letter from Rickenbacker to Arnold, 29 March 1942, R-H Tapes, reel 50, side 2.

28. Ibid.; clippings from *Salt Lake City Tribune,* unspecified date in late March 1942; *Pueblo (CO) Chieftan,* 1 April 1942; *Grand Junction (CO) Sentinel,* 1 April 1942; *Wichita (KS) Beacon,* 2 April 1942; and *Memphis (TN) Press-Scimitar,* 2 April 1942, EVRS 4.

29. Clippings from *Eureka (CA) Times,* unspecified date in April 1942; *Braymer (MO) Bee,* 16 April 1942; *Albany (NY) Times-Union,* 18 April 1942; *Albany (NY) Knickerbocker News,* unspecified date in April 1942, ibid.

30. Clippings from *Aberdeen (WA) World,* 28 March 1942; *Spokane (WA) Chronicle,* 30 March 1942; *Newport News (VA) Press,* 8 April 1942, and *Pacific Coast Register,* unspecified date in April 1942, ibid.

31. Clipping from *New York World Telegram,* 13 April 1942, ibid.

32. Copy in R-H Tapes, reel 50, side 2.

33. Young, *World Almanac Book of World War II,* 151–59; Morison, *The Battle of the Atlantic,* 127–28.

34. "WPB Can't Find the Steel: No Engines Possible for Big Cargo Planes," undated clipping from *Washington (DC) News;* clippings from *Christian Science Monitor* (Boston), 29 July 1942; *Detroit Free Press,* 30 July 1942; *Nashville Times-Banner,* 29 July 1942; *San Francisco Chronicle,* 30 July 1942, EVRS 4.

35. "Rickenbacker Blasts Cargo Plane Project, Joins Other Air Experts in Telling Obstacles," *Chicago Tribune,* 29 July 1942; "Rickenbacker for Kaiser as 'Sky Boat' Chief," *San Francisco Call-Bulletin,* 9 August 1942, ibid.

36. Clippings from *Medford (OR) Mail Tribune,* 30 July 1942; *Cincinnati Enquirer,* 2 August 1942, quoting Lippmann; *Plainfield (NJ) Courier News,* 3 August 942, ibid.

37. Robert W. Rummel, *Howard Hughes and TWA* (Washington, DC: Smithsonian Institution Press, 1991), 77–82.

38. Morison, *Battle of the Atlantic, 1939–1943,* 409.

39. EVRR, 280–81; Wheal, Pope, and Taylor, *Encyclopedia of the Second World War,* 91–92.

40. Gerald Astor, *The Mighty Eighth: The Air War in Europe as Told by the Men Who Fought It* (New York: Donald I. Fine Books, 1997), 14.

41. Stephen L. McFarland and Wesley Phillips Newton, *To Command the Sky: The Battle for Air Superiority over Germany, 1942–1944* (Washington, DC: Smithsonian Institution Press, 1991), 35–38; Geoffrey Perret, *Winged Victory: The Army Air Forces in World War II* (New York: Random House, 1993), 110–15.

42. Perret, *Winged Victory,* 115–20.

43. "Rickenbacker Lauds U.S. Planes," *St. Paul (MN) Dispatch,* 31 August 1942, and "Rickenbacker Answers Critics of U.S. Fighters and Bombers," *Boise (ID) Statesman,* undated but referring to the same radio address, EVRS 4.

44. Astor, *Mighty Eighth,* 31–33; Norman Franks, *Aircraft versus Aircraft: The Illustrated Story of Fighter Pilot Combat from 1914 to the Present Day* (New York: Barnes & Noble Books, 1999), 122–25; David Donald., ed., *American Warplanes of World War II* (New York: Barnes & Noble Books, 2000), 128–34, 221–24; "American-Built Bombers, Medium and Attack, Are Rated the Best," *St. Louis Post-Dispatch,* 6 September 1942, quoting Seversky, clipping in EVRS 4.

45. "Critics of American Planes Challenged," *Denver Post,* 9 September 1942, clipping in EVRS 4.

46. "World War Ace Lauds U.S. Planes," undated clipping from *San Francisco Examiner,* ibid.

47. For the full text of Rickenbacker's speech, see "An Open Address to Hitler, Benito and Tojo . . . By Capt. Eddie Rickenbacker," *Miami Daily News,* 12 September 1942, EVRS 4.

48. Clippings (all from 1942) from *Conneaut (OH) News Herald,* 12 September; *New York Journal-American,* 14 September; *Cedar Rapids (IA) Gazette,* 14 September; *Tampa News,* 14 September; *Jacksonville Times-Union,* 16 September; *Anderson (SC) Independent and Tribune,* 21 September, in ibid. For further favorable comment, see "Rickenbacker Assails Critics of U.S. Planes," *Los Angeles Times,* 11 September, "Critics," *Chicago Calumet,* 15 September; and "Quality of Airplane Depends on the Job Designed to Do," *San Jose (CA) Mercury-Herald,* 15 September, EVRS 4.

49. Copies of letter from Stimson to Rickenbacker and order mandating cooperation with him in R-H Tapes, reel 50, side 1.

50. The analysis that follows is based on McFarland and Newton, *To Command the Sky.*

51. R-H Tapes, reel 35, contains the full text of Rickenbacker's report. Because virtually everything in the discussion that follows is based at least in part on this document, I have cited in the notes other sources that provide background indispensable to understanding the details of Rickenbacker's visit.

52. See also Juliet Gardiner, *"Overpaid, Oversexed, and Over Here": The American GI in World War II Britain* (New York: Canopy Books, 1992), 64–72, 162.

53. Astor, *The Mighty Eighth,* 15–42; Theo Boiten and Martin Bowman, *Battles with the Luftwaffe: The Bomber Campaign against Germany, 1942–1945* (New York: Harper-Collins, 2001), 10–12; David R. Mets, *Master of Airpower: General Carl A. Spaatz* (Novato, CA: Presidio Press, 1997), 121–37; Richard G. Davis, *Carl A. Spaatz and the Air War*

in Europe (Washington, DC: Smithsonian Institution Press, 1992), 67–116; Stephen E. Ambrose, *Eisenhower: Soldier, General of the Army, President-Elect, 1890–1952* (New York: Simon and Schuster, 1983), 180–81; Henry L. Stimson and McGeorge Bundy, *On Active Service in Peace and War* (New York: Harper & Brothers, 1947), 426.

54. Henry Probert, *Bomber Harris: His Life and Times* (London: Greenhill Books, 2001), 178; Gardiner, *"Overpaid, Oversexed, and Over Here,"* 64–69.

55. On the diplomatic and public relations skills shown by Eisenhower in this period, see Ambrose, *Eisenhower*, 171–88, and *The Supreme Commander*, paperback ed. (Jackson: University of Mississippi Press, 1999), 78–81. On relations between American GIs and the British public, see particularly Gardiner, *"Overpaid, Oversexed, and Over Here."*

56. On Leigh-Mallory's tactics and the Dieppe raid, see I. C. B. Dear and M. R. D. Foot, eds., *The Oxford Companion to World War II* (Oxford: Oxford University Press, 1995), 242, 298–99, 310, 677, 949.

57. For a searching critique of the American prejudice against wood in aircraft production as opposed to metal, see Schatzberg, *Wings of Wood*. On the Mosquito, see Dear and Foot, *Oxford Companion to World War II*, 546.

58. Martin Gilbert, *Churchill: A Life* (New York: Henry Holt and Company, 1991), 726–29; Mark M. Boatner III, *The Biographical Dictionary of World War II* (Novato, CA: Presidio Press, 1999), 145, 519. Churchill also revealed the impending North African invasion to Stalin at the Moscow meeting, which had taken place in mid-August 1942 between visits to Cairo.

59. On Winant's background and the circumstances of his appointment as ambassador to Great Britain, see Kenneth S. Davis, *FDR: The War President, 1940–1943* (New York: Random House, 2000), 113–14.

60. The Royal Air Force Museum at Hendon has a copy of the report Trenchard gave to Rickenbacker and a curator showed it to me during a research trip to the museum in 1993.

61. On this point Rickenbacker was reflecting the views of Spaatz, who recognized that bombers were useless unless their crews were trained for combat and that all of the airmen reporting for duty in England lacked such training. See Davis, *Carl A. Spaatz*, 104.

62. For a map of 8th Air Force bases in operation by August 1942, see ibid., facing p. 85.

63. R-H Tapes, reel 48, side 2.

64. On the characteristic location of the blind spots, see R-H Tapes, reel 48, sides 1 and 2.

65. On this point, see ibid.

66. Ambrose, *Eisenhower*, 196–97, and *The Supreme Commander*, 101–3.

67. EVRR, 294–95. The statement in this source that Rickenbacker left England on 11 October is erroneous. His report to Stimson (see R-H Tapes, reel 35, side 1) states more credibly that he left London on Thursday, 8 October.

Chapter 17. Pacific Mission

1. Perret, *Old Soldiers Never Die*, 320–21 and 623, n. 34, based on Farr, *Rickenbacker's Luck*, 241. Although Farr's biography of Rickenbacker is not closely documented, there is no reason to doubt Perret's analysis. A mass of correspondence that I found in William F. Rickenbacker's study in Francestown, New Hampshire, shortly after his death in 1995, shows that he worked closely with Farr during the writing of *Rickenbacker's Luck*. As Perret indicates, William was the probable source of information divulged to Farr, based on knowledge gained from his father.

2. Perret, *Old Soldiers Never Die*, 292–307. On the intensity of Marshall's efforts to send supplies and reinforcements to MacArthur, see Forrest C. Pogue, *George C. Marshall: Ordeal and Hope, 1939–1942* (New York: Viking, 1966), 232–60. For a scathing critique of MacArthur's capabilities, see Richard Connaughton, *MacArthur and Defeat in the Philippines* (Woodstock, NY: Overlook Press, 2001).

3. The narrative that follows is based mainly on published sources including Adamson, *Eddie Rickenbacker*, 258–80; W. David Lewis, "The Rescue of Eddie Rickenbacker," *Air and Space / Smithsonian* 13, no. 3 (August–September 1998): 64–73; EVRR, 296–302; Edward V. Rickenbacker, *Seven Came Through: Rickenbacker's Full Story* (Garden City, NY: Doubleday, Doran and Company, Inc., 1943), 6–20; James C. Whittaker, *We Thought We Heard the Angels Sing: The Epic Story of Those Who Were with Eddie Rickenbacker on the Plane Lost in the Pacific* (Philadelphia: Blakiston, 1943), 19–45; N. W. Emmott, "Navgoof: A Plunge in the Pacific," in undated issue of *Litton Avionics Newsletter*, vertical files, National Air and Space Museum; unpublished materials including "Interrogation of Captain William T. Cherry, Jr., December 11, 1942," from Air Transport Archives, supplied by Matthew Rodina; "Life Story"; and the following unpublished eyewitness accounts, all in Auburn University Archives: an unpaginated handwritten diary by Rickenbacker prepared during and after his mission; "Pacific Mission: As Related by Captain Edward V. Rickenbacker," dictated by Rickenbacker for Eureka Pictures, Inc., in 1943 as a working document in connection with the making of a film, *Captain Eddie*, released by Twentieth Century Fox in 1945, pp. 5–24; interviews between representatives of Eureka Pictures and John J. De Angelis, 8 July 1943, and John F. Bartek, 21 July 1943, in the same collection; and transcribed texts of a presentation made by John F. Bartek at Auburn University on 19 July 1999, followed by a three-hour taped interview with Bartek on 20 July 1999. Details from these sources are so inextricably interwoven that repeated references to the same materials would be superfluous. I have therefore documented the account sparingly, citing direct quotations or specific details requiring further comment or drawing upon other sources not mentioned here.

4. EVRR, 296, mistakenly identifies the plane as a Sikorsky Clipper. Information supplied by Matthew Rodina shows that it was a Boeing 314 used to shuttle VIP passengers on missions to Hawaii.

5. Wilbur D. Jones Jr. and Carroll Robbins Jones, *Hawaii Goes to War: The Aftermath of Pearl Harbor* (Shippensburg, PA: White Mane Books, 2001).

6. Herbert S. Zim, *Air Navigation* (New York: Harcourt, Brace and Company, 1943), 227–43.

7. Bartek interview.

8. "Life Story," 2:671.

9. Bartek interview.

10. Adamson, *Eddie Rickenbacker,* 260.

11. Bartek interview.

12. Carl Oates, *Canton Island: Aerial Crossroads of the Pacific* (McLean, VA: Paladwr Press, 2003), 106–9; "Canton Island, Phoenix Group, South Pacific," document dated 1 August 1962, Miscellaneous Rickenbacker Papers, ERP-AU; Ronald W. Jackson, *China Clipper* (New York: Everest House, 1980), 165–79, on American assertion of sovereignty and preparations for a Pan American base; "Canton Island Base Finished in Record Time," "Civilization Comes to Canton," and "Canton Island to Have Hotel," *Pan American Air Ways* magazine, September–October 1939, 20, supplied by Matthew Rodina.

13. Adamson, *Eddie Rickenbacker,* 273.

14. Bartek interview.

15. A source in addition to those cited in note 3 is John F. Bartek, with Austin Pardue, *Life Out There: A Story of Faith and Courage* (New York: Scribner's, 1943), a transcript of a taped recording that Bartek had no chance to edit, which contains details that Bartek disavows. Again, I have limited myself to citing direct quotations or specific details that seemed worthy of further comment.

16. "Pacific Mission," 28.

17. Whittaker, *We Thought We Heard the Angels Sing,* 45.

18. Adamson, *Eddie Rickenbacker,* 287.

19. "Pacific Mission," 32.

20. Adamson, *Eddie Rickenbacker,* 281; Oates, *Canton Island,* 108.

21. See particularly the discussion of sharks in Ellen J. Prager and Sylvia A. Earle, *The Oceans* (New York: McGraw Hill, 2000), 222–30.

22. Whittaker, *We Thought We Heard the Angels Sing,* 56.

23. "Pacific Mission," 29–31.

24. Ibid., 32–33.

25. Ibid., 34.

26. Ibid.

27. Whittaker, *We Thought We Heard the Angels Sing,* 54–55.

28. Adamson, *Eddie Rickenbacker,* 288.

29. Ibid., 289–90; "Pacific Mission," 53–54.

30. Whittaker, *We Thought We Heard the Angels Sing,* 60; Bartek interview.

31. Whittaker, *We Thought We Heard the Angels Sing,* 61.

32. Adamson, *Eddie Rickenbacker,* 292.

33. "Pacific Mission," 57–61.

34. Adamson, *Eddie Rickenbacker,* 298–99.

35. Bartek interview.

36. Whittaker, *We Thought We Heard the Angels Sing,* 69–70.

37. Adamson, *Eddie Rickenbacker,* 282–83; "Pacific Mission," 47–48.

38. Adamson, *Eddie Rickenbacker,* 271.

39. W. L. White, introduction to Rickenbacker, *Seven Came Through,* viii.

40. Cherry, now deceased, steadfastly refused to be interviewed by me despite repeated efforts to persuade him to do so. An intermediary quoted him as saying that he "had never talked about that God-damned son of a bitch while he was alive" and "would not talk about that God-damned son of a bitch after he was dead," repeating the epithet for emphasis.

41. Later Coreen Bond Shenck, Corona, California, with whom I corresponded in January 1999.

42. "Pacific Mission," 39.

43. De Angelis interview.

44. "Pacific Mission," 36–41; Bartek interview.

45. Adamson, *Eddie Rickenbacker,* 285.

46. "Pacific Mission," 68. Rickenbacker stated that he encouraged the three men to go on this futile mission. De Angelis said that Rickenbacker forbade the men to go but they defied his will. De Angelis interview. On the practice of cannibalism in similar circumstances, see Neil Hanson, *The Custom of the Sea* (New York: Wiley, 1999).

47. "Pacific Mission," 70.

48. Ibid., 75–76.

49. Samuel Eliot Morison, *Aleutians, Gilberts and Marshalls, June 1942–April 1944,* vol. 7 of *History of United States Naval Operations in World War II* (1951; repr., Edison, NJ: Castle Books, 2001), 78–79; William Breuer, *Devil Boats: The PT War against Japan* (Novato, CA: Presidio Press, 1987), 3–4; David Donald, ed., *American Warplanes of World War II* (New York: Barnes & Noble Books, 1995), 248–49; information provided to author by United States Navy Archives, Washington, D.C.

50. "Pacific Mission," 85–86.

51. Whittaker, *We Thought We Heard the Angels Sing,* 107.

52. "Pacific Mission," 87–88.

53. Adamson, *Eddie Rickenbacker,* 303–4.

54. "Pacific Mission," 91–93.

55. Clippings and cartoons from *Washington Post,* 24 October 1942; *Washington Times-Herald,* 25 October 1942; *Columbus (OH) Citizen,* 26 October 1942; and *Manchester (NH) Union,* 9 November 1942, among hundreds of such items in EVRS 5 (October–November 1942).

56. Interview with William F. Rickenbacker by author.

57. Commanding Officer, United States Marine Corps, Headquarters Defense

Force, Funafuti, "Report of Rescue of Captain Rickenbacker and Party, 11–12 November, 1942," 15 November 1942, Cynthia White /Lester Boutte Papers, ERP-AU. Unless otherwise noted, all of the material that follows relating to the base at Funafuti and the rescue of Rickenbacker and other members of the raft party are based on this four-page report. White is the daughter of Lester Boutte, who figured prominently in the narrative that follows. The document came from the personal papers of Boutte, which were bequeathed to White, who generously permitted the Auburn University Archives to make copies of the original documents.

58. Whittaker, *We Thought We Heard the Angels Sing,* 113–31.

59. Breuer, *Devil Boats,* 81–82. Breuer's account, which is consistent with the "Report of Rescue," provides valuable supplementary details about the rescue operation. Among various accounts of the rescue written or dictated by Rickenbacker, see particularly Rickenbacker, *Seven Came Through,* 67–72. Early newspaper articles about the rescue mistakenly state the aircraft involved was a Consolidated Catalina, an error perpetuated in Farr's *Rickenbacker's Luck.* For a fuller discussion, see W. David Lewis, "Rickenbacker Revisited," *Aviation History,* May 1999.

60. "Ace's Elated Wife Never Lost Faith," *New York Journal-American,* 14 November 1942, EVRS 4.

61. Clippings and cartoons from *Boston American,* 14 November 1942, devoting entire first page to articles about the rescue; *Stamford (CT) Advocate,* 14 November 1942; *Boston Sunday Post,* 14 November 1942; *Washington Post,* 16 November 1942, and undated issue of *Tyler (TX) Morning Telegraph,* among hundreds of other items in EVRS 4 and 5.

62. Unless otherwise noted, all details about Rickenbacker's itinerary from the time he left the hospital at American Samoa until his return to the United States are taken from "Pacific Mission," containing a typescript of Rickenbacker's letter of transmittal to Secretary of War Henry L. Stimson, 25 January 1943, and "Confidential Report to Secretary of War, Hon. Henry L. Stimson from E. V. Rickenbacker. Subject: Visit to Pacific. Dated: January 25, 1943," in R-H Tapes, reel 36, sides 1 and 2. On the trip from Funafuti to Tutuila, see also Rickenbacker, *Seven Came Through,* 75–76.

63. Harry Gailey, *MacArthur Strikes Back: Decision at Buna, New Guinea, 1942–1943* (Novato, CA: Presidio Press, 2000), 155–92; Perret, *Old Soldiers Never Die,* 292–327; Desmond Flower and James Reeves, eds., *The War, 1939–1945: A Documentary History* (New York: Da Capo Press, 1997), 717.

64. Rickenbacker, *Seven Came Through,* 80–81; Flower and Reeves, *The War, 1939–1945,* 705–6.

65. Perret, *Old Soldiers Never Die,* 301; R-H Tapes, reel 36, side 1.

66. Thomas E. Griffith Jr., *MacArthur's Airman: General George C. Kenney and the War in the Southwest Pacific* (Lawrence: University Press of Kansas, 1998), 1–96; George C. Kenney, *General Kenney Reports: A Personal History of the Pacific War* (1949; repr., Washington, DC: Office of Air Force History, 1987), xi–xviii, 3–134.

67. R-H Tapes, reel 36, side 1. See also Griffith, *MacArthur's Airman,* 96.

68. Kenney, *General Kenney Reports,* 152–54. Kenney's statement that Rickenbacker visited MacArthur's headquarters in late November and that he took him back to Brisbane on 28 November is incorrect. As the itinerary given in Rickenbacker's subsequent report to Stimson indicates, he arrived at Port Moresby on 5 December and departed on 7 December. In late November he was still in the hospital in American Samoa recovering from the effects of his raft ordeal. He could not have recuperated from the raft ordeal in time to have Thanksgiving dinner with MacArthur and his staff, as Kenney indicates.

69. Boatner, *Biographical Dictionary of World War II,* 205.

70. Kenney, *General Kenney Reports,* 161.

71. William J. Owens, *Green Hell: The Battle for Guadalcanal* (Central Point, OR: Hellgate Press, 1999), esp. 15, 226–27. Among many books written about the Guadalcanal campaign, see particularly Richard B. Frank, *Guadalcanal: The Definitive Account of the Landmark Battle* (New York: Penguin Books, 1990), a superbly detailed account that merits its subtitle.

72. R-H Tapes, reel 36, sides 1 and 2. Rickenbacker's statement that he arrived at Guadalcanal on 10 December and his subsequent assertion that Patch had taken charge of the troops on the island "the day before I landed," which accurately dates the transfer of command to Patch from Marine General Alexander Vandegrift, confirm the accuracy of the other dates given in the itinerary he provided to Stimson on 25 January 1943.

73. Rickenbacker, *Seven Came Through,* 87–88.

74. Photograph in ibid., facing page 54.

75. R-H Tapes, reel 50, side 2; EVRR, 336–37.

76. Photograph in *Rickenbacker, Seven Came Through,* facing page 55.

77. Oates, *Canton Island,* 109.

Chapter 18. New Mandate

1. Letter from Frank V. Martinek, Chicago, to Rickenbacker, 21 December 1942, EVRP-LC, folder marked "E. V. Rickenbacker, Letters M-1, 1916–1961." There are hundreds of such letters scattered throughout the Library of Congress collection.

2. A collection of such cartoons is contained in EVRS 5.

3. EVRR, 340–42; Rickenbacker, *Seven Came Through,* esp. 96–97; interview by author with Floyd D. Hall, who was an officer in the Air Transport Command present at the speech Rickenbacker delivered at the Pentagon Building; Edward V. Rickenbacker, "Eddie Rickenbacker's Own Story," *Life,* 25 January 1943, cover and 19, and "Pacific Mission," Part I, *Life,* 25 January 1943, 20; Part II, *Life,* 1 February 1943, 78; Part III, *Life,* 8 February 1943, 94.

4. Edward V. Rickenbacker, "When a Man Faces Death," *American* 136, no. 5 (November 1943), copy in EVRP-LC, box 128.

5. Contents of folder marked "Magazine Articles—Comments 1916–1961," EVRP-LC, box 20.

6. Numerous studies of Roosevelt have emphasized his inability to delegate undivided responsibility, his fondness for playing off divergent factions against one another, and a deviousness that was apparently deeply imbedded in his character despite his admirable traits. For a pioneering analysis, see James MacGregor Burns, *Roosevelt: The Lion and the Fox* (New York: Harcourt, Brace, 1956). An excellent study bearing on the same issue praises Burns as "the only prominent scholar to look seriously at the less admirable side of Roosevelt's character." See William L. O'Neill, *A Democracy at War: America's Fight at Home and Abroad in World War II* (New York: Free Press, 1993), 438, n. 2. O'Neill published his book before Thomas Fleming, *The New Dealers' War: F.D.R. and the War within World War II* (New York: Basic Books, 2001), an unsparing attack on Roosevelt's capacity for duplicity. David Stafford, *Roosevelt and Churchill: Men of Secrets* (Woodstock, NY: Overlook Press, 1999), emphasizes the same theme. For a firsthand analysis of bureaucratic infighting in wartime Washington, see Bruce Catton, *The War Lords of Washington* (New York: Harcourt, Brace, 1941). On Stimson's own situation in being kept in the dark by Roosevelt on important issues, see Stimson and Bundy, *On Active Service in Peace and War,* 333, with the telling statement that "Although he . . . established effective working relations with its leaders, Stimson never became one of the special intimates of the administration, and he occasionally felt that the President listened too much to men who were not his direct constitutional advisers." The statement goes on to indicate Stimson's dependence on Harry Hopkins, with whom Stimson fortunately had good relations, in communicating with FDR.

7. Nelson Lichtenstein, *Labor's War at Home* (Cambridge: Cambridge University Press, 1982), 82–135, and *The Most Dangerous Man in Detroit: Walter Reuther and the Fate of American Labor* (New York: Basic Books, 1995), 211; Melvyn Dubofsky and Warren van Tyne, *John L. Lewis: A Biography* (New York: Quadrangle / The New York Times Book Company, 1977), 389–440; Robert H. Zieger, *John L. Lewis: Labor Leader* (Boston: Twayne Publishers, 1998), 133–49.

8. Stimson and Bundy, *On Active Service in Peace and War,* 480–88. For a critical analysis of Stimson that goes far toward explaining congruities between his thinking and that of Rickenbacker, see Larry G. Gerber, *The Limits of Liberalism: Josephus Daniels, Henry Stimson, Bernard Baruch, Donald Richberg, Felix Frankfurter and the Development of the Modern American Political Economy* (New York and London: New York University Press, 1984), 22–34.

9. Instructional Booklet, "Uncle Sam's Hat in the Ring Squadron: Challenging the Absentee Problem and Promoting Unrestricted War Effort"; letter from James A. Simpson, partner in Lange, Simpson, Brantley & Robinson law firm, Birmingham, Alabama, to Rickenbacker, 23 December, 1942; letter from R. I. Ingalls Jr., Vice Chairman of the Board, Ingalls Shipbuilding Company, to Rickenbacker, 9 February 1932; correspondence between General Motors, Delco-Remy Division, Ander-

son, Indiana, and Rickenbacker beginning 9 January 1943; letter from E. V. Rickenbacker to Alayne Fisher, Adel Precision Products Corporation, 10 February 1943; letter from Marguerite Shepherd to Roy Booker, Atlanta, GA, 17 February 1943; letter from Fletcher D. Richardson, President, Campbell-Ewald Company, Inc., New York City advertising firm, to EVR, 10 May 1943; and many other materials in EVRP-LC, box 15, folder marked "E. V. Rickenbacker—Hat-in-the-Ring & Rickenbacker Groups."

10. "Address at SAE Dinner," Detroit, Michigan, 22 January 1943, EVRP-LC, folder marked "Speeches 1943."

11. "Baseball Writers' Association, Annual Banquet—February 7, 1943, by Eddie Rickenbacker," in ibid.

12. Edward V. Rickenbacker, "America Must Return to Fundamentals," address before the New York State Legislature, 11 February 1943, in ibid. The speeches cited here represent only a sampling of addresses given by Rickenbacker from January through April 1943 in the same folder, dealing with the same themes.

13. "Statement of Capt. Eddie Rickenbacker," Hearings before the Committee on Military Affairs, U.S. Senate, 78th Cong., 1st sess., S. 666, "A Bill to Provide for the Successful Prosecution of the War through a System of Civilian Selective Service with the Aid of the Selective Service System," Part II, 19 March 1943 (Washington, DC: Government Printing Office, 1943), 439–45.

14. "Rickenbacker Will Have Fate Like Lindbergh's," based on broadcast by Clifford Evans on radio station LLIB, in *Radio Reports, Inc. Manuscript Service,* 8 February 1943; "Rickenbacker's Labor Record as Employer Denounced," *Radio Reports,* 17 March 1943, based on radio broadcast, "Our Daily Bread," by Tom Van Dyke on station KPAS, Pasadena, California. Van Dyke was a member of the Los Angeles Industrial Union Council of the CIO. The broadcast indirectly went so far as to implicate Rickenbacker with the Ku Klux Klan. For a hostile editorial, based on the erroneous assumption that aspirations for the presidency underlay Rickenbacker's campaign against "labor racketeering," see "Rickenbacker for President?" *New Republic* 108, no. 7 (1943): 196–97.

15. "Rickenbacker Seen as Leader Who Will Not Compromise with National Safety," broadcast by Arthur Hale on radio station WOR, *Radio Reports,* 18 February 1943; "Close Compared Rickenbacker with Jefferson," broadcast by Upton Close on radio station WOR, *Radio Reports,* 11 April 1943. See also "Rickenbacker's Remarks on Labor 'Most Refreshing Yet,'" *Radio Reports,* 20 March 1943.

16. Letters from William Benson Mayo, Detroit, Michigan, 26 January 1943; from T. J. Williams, Eddyville, Iowa, 13 November 1943; from John Adams, Battle Creek, Michigan, 23 December 1942, to Rickenbacker; Paul Mallon of *Los Angeles Examiner,* quoted in letter from Adolphe Menjou, Beverley Hills, California, to Rickenbacker, 19 February 1943, EVRP-LC, folders marked "E. V. Rickenbacker . . . Miscellaneous 1916–1961."

17. Letter from Judge Russ Avery, Los Angeles, CA, to Rickenbacker, 15 February 1943, EVRP-LC.

18. Letter from Mr. and Mrs. J. S. Woffington, San Jose, CA, to Rickenbacker, 23 February 1943, EVRP-LC, folder marked "E. V. Rickenbacker W–2 Miscellaneous 1916–1961."

19. EVRR, 377.

20. The account that follows parallels the chapter entitled "Russian Mission" in EVRR, 347–90, which does not provide the original rationale underlying the venture (aggrandizing the postwar role of American commercial aviation) but contains many of the details provided here. Unless otherwise noted, however, the narrative presented, full of details that do not appear in EVRR, is based on a series of transcribed interviews in the Rickenbacker Papers at the United States Air Force Museum covering reels 27, 28, 29, 30, and 31. Although Rickenbacker gave these tapes to Booton Herndon, ghostwriter of the autobiography, in April 1965, Herndon did not conduct the interviews, which, according to Rickenbacker, were based on "documentary evidence previously recorded but not taped by me, only from memory." The only clue to the identity of the interviewer is a reference by Rickenbacker to a person named "Walter" in one of the tapes. Internal evidence indicates that the material was recorded soon after the events transpired.

21. "Pacific Mission," report submitted by Rickenbacker to Stimson, 25 January 1943, text included in R-H Tapes, May 5, 1965, reel 36, side 1.

22. Lewis, "Ambivalent Relationship," 15–16.

23. R-H Tapes, reel 50, side 2.

24. On Stimson's need to use Hopkins as an intermediary with Roosevelt, see Stimson and Bundy, *On Active Service in Peace and War*, 333–34.

25. Much of the discussion here and in the following paragraphs is based on George C. Herring Jr., *Aid to Russia, 1941–1946: Strategy, Diplomacy, the Origins of the Cold War* (New York: Columbia University Press, 1973), 80–109; Hubert P. van Tuyll, *Feeding the Bear: American Aid to the Soviet Union, 1941–1945* (Westport, CT: Greenwood Press, 1989), 1–62; William H. Standley and Arthur A. Ageton, *Admiral Ambassador to Russia* (Chicago: Henry Regnery Company, 1955), 255–349; Von Hardesty, *Red Phoenix: The Rise of Soviet Air Power, 1941–1945* (Washington, DC: Smithsonian Institution Press, c. 1982), 86, 88, 100, 126.

26. R-H Tapes, reel 27. Most of the information in my discussion of the early stages of Rickenbacker's mission comes from this source.

27. The C-54 "Skymaster" used by Rickenbacker was probably the C-54A, introduced in January 1943, but could have been an earlier model, seating twenty-six passengers, which first saw service in 1942.

28. For a detailed summary, see Robert J. Serling, *When the Airlines Went to War* (New York: Kensington Books, 1997), 162–70.

29. For an overview of Operation Torch from its inception to the victory in Tunisia, see Rick Atkinson, *An Army at Dawn: The War in North Africa, 1942–1943* (New York: Henry Holt, 2002).

30. On Eisenhower's dedication to spying, see Stephen E. Ambrose, *Ike's Spies: Eisenhower and the Espionage Establishment* (Garden City, NY: Doubleday, c. 1981).

31. Russell D. Buhite, *Patrick J. Hurley and American Foreign Policy* (Ithaca: Cornell University Press, 1973), 82–133.

32. Rickenbacker's praise for Snow and *Red Star over China* is particularly significant because it shows that he did not fear the consequences of a takeover in China by Mao Tse-Tung at this time.

33. Differing views of Stilwell are presented in Barbara Tuchman, *Stilwell and the American Experience in China, 1941–1945* (New York: The Macmillan Company, 1970), and Jonathon Fenby, *Chiang Kai-Shek: China's Generalissimo and the Nation He Lost* (New York: Carroll & Graf, 2004), 370–426.

34. On Churchill's efforts to persuade Turkey to enter the war against Germany, see Winston S. Churchill, *Memoirs of the Second World War* (New York: Bonanza Books, 1978), 676–78, 733–34, 774–77.

35. Edward Weisband, *Turkish Foreign Policy, 1943–1945: Small State Diplomacy and Great Power Politics* (Princeton, NJ: Princeton University Press, 1973), esp. 146–66.

36. Selim Deringil, *Turkish Foreign Policy during the Second World War: An "Active Neutrality"* (Cambridge: Cambridge University Press, 1989), 144–65.

37. Regarding a number of details about the flight, I have followed Standley and Ageton, *Admiral Ambassador to Russia*, 386. An account of the trip in EVRR contains several errors, misdating it as occurring on 19 July, calling Kuibyshev "the capital of Russia while Moscow was under siege," and saying that the plane landed at about 1:00 p.m., which is impossible considering the length of the flight from Teheran. A message received by Standley stated that Rickenbacker's plane landed at Kuibyshev on 19 June at 19:57. The message further informed Standley that Rickenbacker and his party would be brought to Moscow the following day.

38. For Standley's account of Rickenbacker's visit, on which I have drawn heavily in this paragraph and the narrative that follows, see Standley and Ageton, *Admiral Ambassador to Russia*, 386–89. See also R-H Tapes, reels 32 and 33.

39. For a brief sketch of Zhukov's career, see Dear and Foot, *Oxford Companion*, 1300–1301.

40. On the reasons why the Russians held the P-39 in high regard, see Hardesty, *Red Phoenix*, 141.

41. On the Shturmovik, a two-seat armored attack plane with superb tank-fighting abilities, see ibid., esp. 169–76; David Mondey, ed., *The International Encyclopedia of Aviation* (New York: Crown Publishers, 1977), 207–8, and Christopher Chant, *The World's Greatest Aircraft* (Edison, NJ: Chartwell Books, Inc., 1999), 368.

42. The Yak-9 was a light, highly maneuverable fighter plane. See Mondey, *International Encyclopedia of Aviation*, 196. Rickenbacker was witnessing Russian preparations to stem a massive German offensive, beginning on 5 July 1943. The titanic battle that resulted ended Hitler's offensive capabilities on the eastern front. See David M. Glantz and Jonathan M. House, *The Battle of Kursk* (Lawrence: University Press of Kansas, 1999). On the role played by Soviet aircraft in the battle, see Hardesty, *Red Phoenix*, 149–79.

43. Rickenbacker's observations can be closely compared with Hardesty, *Red Phoenix*, 152.

44. The Douglas A-20 was a twin-engine attack bomber, also used as a night fighter, of which 3,125 went to the USSR under Lend-Lease and other arrangements. Various models existed and it is not clear which one Rickenbacker observed. See Donald, *American Warplanes of World War II*, 87–93.

45. R-H Tapes, reel 33, side 1.

46. This copy is included in EVRP-LC.

Chapter 19. Anticipating Victory

1. Edward V. Rickenbacker, "Assumptions with Regard to Russia," 27 September 1943, in miscellaneous documents shared with me by Nancy Angell Rickenbacker.

2. On Rickenbacker's pro-Russian views, see numerous clippings in EVRS 7 (29 April 1943–22 February 1944) and "This War Is Not Over," press release, 17 August 1943, in vertical files, National Air and Space Museum. For adverse reactions see transcript of broadcast by Oliver, 20 August 1943, *Radio Reports*, ERP-AU; clippings from *Cleveland (OH) Press*, 19 August 1943, *Camden (NJ) Evening Courier* (undated), and *Daily Worker*, 19 August 1943, in EVRS 7.

3. Transcripts of broadcasts by Howe, 17 August 1943; Thomas, 17 August 1943; and Walton, 21 October 1943, *Radio Reports*, ERP-AU; clippings from *Escanaba (MI) Press* (undated), *Jacksonville (FL) Journal*, 19 August 1943, and *Albany (OR) Democrat-Herald*, 20 August 1943, in EVRS 7.

4. War Department, Headquarters of the Army Air Forces, Orders No. 1, dated 10 August 1943, ERP-AU. See also R-H Tapes, reel 34.

5. "Memoranda to Rickenbacker from Meredith," 27 and 28 October 1943, ERP-AU.

6. The extended account of Rickenbacker's journey that follows is based on a detailed memorandum from McClure to Rickenbacker summarizing the trip, dated 2 November 1943, and Rickenbacker's own "Notes from Diary on Trip to Alaska and the Aleutians, 1943," both in ERP-AU. See also R-H Tapes, reel 34.

7. On Hunter, see W. David Lewis, "Croil Hunter," in Leary, ed., *The Airline Industry*, 236–40, and William M. Leary, "Northwest Airlines," in ibid., 319–21; biographical sketch of Hunter by Lewis in John A. Garraty and Mark C. Carnes, eds., *Dictionary of American Biography*, supp. 8, 1966–70 (New York: Charles Scribner's Sons, 1988), 291–93. Advice from Donna M. Corbett aided me in the discussion that follows.

8. Sixth Annual Report of Eastern Air Lines, Inc., 1943, 5–6.

9. EVRR, 419.

10. The analysis of the background and conduct of the Chicago conference presented here is based on Jordan A. Schwarz, *Liberal: Adolf A. Berle and the Vision of an American Era* (New York: Free Press, 1987), 216–53.

11. Annual Reports, Eastern Air Lines, 1943–45.

12. Letters from John R. Todd, Pomona, California, and W. P. Winslow, Pontiac Motor Division, Pontiac, Michigan, to Rickenbacker, 23 February and 3 March 1943, EVRP-LC, folder marked "E. V. Rickenbacker T-Miscellaneous 1916–1961"; R-H Tapes, reel 40, side 1, and reel 49, side 1. Many letters to Rickenbacker in 1943 and early 1944, urging him to seek the presidency, are scattered throughout various folders in EVRP-LC.

13. Edward V. Rickenbacker, "Masters of Tomorrow," *American Magazine,* June 1944, copy in EVRP-LC, box 128.

14. Herbert Malloy Mason Jr., *VFW: Our First Century, 1899–1999* (Lenexa, KS: Addax Publishing Group, c. 1999), 107–10. For a history of the bill, see Michael J. Bennett, *When Dreams Came True: The GI Bill and the Making of Modern America* (Washington, DC: Brassey's, 1996).

15. Clipping from *New York Times,* 5 December 1944; letters from Frederick H. Wappler, Flushing, New York, to Rickenbacker, 7 December 1944, and from Rickenbacker to Wappler, 12 December 1944, in EVRP-LC, folder marked "E. V. Rickenbacker W-1 Miscellaneous, 1916–1961."

16. Letter from G. Ray Jordan, D.D., to Rickenbacker, 20 May 1944, and reply from Rickenbacker to Jordan, 22 May 1944, EVRP-LC, in folder marked "E. V. Rickenbacker Miscellaneous W-2, 1916–1961," which contains a large sheaf of correspondence pertaining to the controversy.

17. Lowell Thomas, *Back to Mandalay* (New York; Greystone Press, c. 1951), 193–94.

18. Letters from Raymond C. Acheson to Rickenbacker, 26 April 1944, and Rickenbacker to Mrs. Napoleon Girard, 12 June 1944, in EVRP-LC, box 28, folder marked "E. V. Rickenbacker W.W. II Activities—Bong."

19. Carl Bong and Mike O'Connor, *America's Ace of Aces: The Dick Bong Story* (Mesa, AZ: Champlin Fighter Museum Press, c. 1985), containing photograph mentioned here.

20. Letter from Herbert Hoover to Rickenbacker, 25 June 1945, Rickenbacker Collection, Hoover Presidential Library, West Branch, Iowa; "Report to the Nation," broadcast on radio station WABC, September 2, 1945, EVRP-LC, box 7, folder marked "Broadcasts, 1933–1948." The Ohio Historical Society has a copy of the script. The film is unavailable for public sale because of copyright restrictions. The author witnessed a private showing in Columbus in 1995 through the courtesy of Richard W. Hoerle. For a negative evaluation of the film, see Alun Evans, *Brassey's Guide to War Films* (Washington, DC: Brassey's, 2000), 35.

21. Carol V. R. George, *God's Salesman: Norman Vincent Peale and the Power of Positive Thinking* (New York: Oxford University Press, 1993).

22. Ibid., 103–7; for a critical view of *Guideposts,* see Seldes, *Witness to a Century,* 76–77.

23. Letters from Peale to Rickenbacker, 15 December 1944, 13 February, 3 May, and June 5 1945, EVRP-LC, box 15, folder marked "E. V. Rickenbacker—'Guideposts.'"

24. Letters from Forrest L. Knapp to Rickenbacker, 3, 8 March and 18, 30 April 1945; Luther A. Weigle to Rickenbacker, 21 March 1945; correspondence between Rickenbacker and Madame Chiang Kai-Shek, 28 August 1945 and 27 November 1946, EVRP-LC, folder marked "E. V. Rickenbacker World Sunday School Assn. World Council Christian Association"; letter from Lord Mackintosh of Halifax, London, England, to Rickenbacker, 22 November 1950, in EVRP-LC, box 15, folder marked "E. V. Rickenbacker M-1 Miscellaneous 1916–1961."

25. Letters from Howard W. Whyte to Rickenbacker, 14 April 1945, and C. J. Wilcox to Rickenbacker, 20 November 1945, EVRP-LC, folder marked "E. V. Rickenbacker Miscellaneous W-2, 1916–1961"; "Captain Eddie Rickenbacker Transcription for NEPH Week, 3–9 October 1948." in EVRP-LC, box 7, folder marked "Broadcasts, 1933–1948."

26. Robin Higham, "International Air Transport Association," in Leary, ed., *The Airline Industry,* 243–44; IATA Annual Report for 2005 (Tokyo, Japan, 2005), 4; Serling, *From the Captain to the Colonel,* 203–4.

Chapter 20. Turbulence and Descent

1. Lewis and Newton, *Delta,* 104–6.

2. Eastern Air Lines, Annual Report for 1944.

3. R-H Tapes, reel 50, side 1. See also EVRR, appendix following p. 447.

4. Herring, *Aid to Russia, 1941–1946,* 144–275.

5. Van Tuyll, *Feeding the Bear,* 137–38.

6. Ronald Steel, *Walter Lippmann and the American Century* (New York: Vintage Books, 1989), 420–21.

7. Buhite, *Patrick J. Hurley and American Foreign Policy,* 162–281; Stanley Weintraub, *The Last Great Victory: The End of World War II, July/August 1945* (New York: Dutton, 1995).

8. Letters from Rickenbacker to Marshall, 27 January 1947, EVRP-LC, folder marked "E. V. Rickenbacker M-1 Miscellaneous 1916–1961," and from Robert E. Wood to Rickenbacker, 5 May 1948, EVRP-LC, folder marked "E. V. Rickenbacker W-2 Miscellaneous 1916–1961"; Martin Walker, *The Cold War: A History* (New York: Henry Holt, 1995), 47–52.

9. Menjou-Rickenbacker letters, EVRP-LC, folder "M-1 Miscellaneous, 1916–1961"; for Menjou's testimony, see Eric Bentley, ed., *Thirty Years of Treason: Excerpts from Hearings before the House Committee on Un-American Activities, 1938–1968* (1971; repr., New York: Thunder's Mouth Press/Nation Books, 2002), 119–35.

10. Letter from Edward V. Rickenbacker to William Rickenbacker, 7 February 1948, in W. F. Rickenbacker, ed., *From Father to Son: The Letters of Captain Eddie Rickenbacker to His Son William from Boyhood to Manhood* (New York: Walker and Company, 1970), 83–84, original copy in ERP-AU.

11. Christmas greeting from Rickenbacker to Laurance Rockefeller, December

1951, Rockefeller Archive Center, folder marked "Eastern Air Lines Correspondence 1941–1957."

12. Letters from Richard T. Carter to Rickenbacker, 24 August 1948, and Rickenbacker to Carter, 30 August 1948, EVRP-LC, folder marked "E. V. Rickenbacker C-1 Miscellaneous 1916–1961."

13. R-H Tapes, reel 39K, side 1; "Indianapolis Motor Speedway," at http://racing .ballparks.com/Indianapolis; "Oldtimers Name Hulman as Speedway's Most Influential Person," at http://ims.brickyard.com/500news/1999/oldtimers~052599 .html; Popely, with Riggs, *Indy 500 Chronicle*, 6, 78.

14. Letter from Edward V. Rickenbacker to William F. Rickenbacker, March 18, 1946, in W. F. Rickenbacker, *From Father to Son*, 55–58, original copy in ERP-AU; letter to Rickenbacker from Lena Kleist, a nurse who had attended his mother, 3 April 1946, Miscellaneous Papers, Rickenbacker Collection, ERP-AU; Farr, *Rickenbacker's Luck*, 285.

15. Jimmy Breslin, *Damon Runyon: A Life* (New York: Bantam Doubleday Dell Publishing Group, Inc., 1991), 394–98; Farr, *Rickenbacker's Luck*, 285.

16. Broadcast, "One Book for One World," 7 December 1946, EVRP-LC, box 7, folder marked "Broadcasts 1933–1948"; Serling, *From the Captain to the Colonel*, 230; letters from Peale to Rickenbacker, 19 May 1947, 1 April 1948, 19 April 1950, and sheaf of correspondence in 1957 about Rickenbacker's receiving the "Guideposts Award," EVRP-LC, box 15, folder marked "E. V. Rickenbacker—Guideposts."

17. Letters from Treman to Rickenbacker, 28 February and 15 April 1950, and telegram from Rickenbacker to Treman, 1 March 1950, EVRP-LC, folder marked "E. V. Rickenbacker T-Miscellaneous 1916–1961."

18. Richard Rhodes, *The Making of the Atomic Bomb* (New York: Simon and Schuster, 1986), 417–20, 579–80, 754–56, 772–78; Richard Rhodes, *Dark Sun: The Making of the Hydrogen Bomb* (New York: Simon and Schuster, 1995), 364–68, 433.

19. Christmas letter from Rickenbacker to Rockefeller, December 1951, Rockefeller Archive Center, folder marked "Eastern Air Lines Correspondence 1941–1957."

20. Interviews with Patricia Ann Wrightson and Laurance Rockefeller by author; information gathered by the author during visit to the ranch.

21. R-H Tapes, 22 June 1965, reel 40, side 1; "Biographical Sketch of David E. Rickenbacker," Miscellaneous Notes, ERP-AU.

22. R-H Tapes, reel 40, side 2, and reel 42, side 1; interviews with Patricia Ann Wrightson, widow of David Rickenbacker, and with Bryan and Marcia Rickenbacker, son and daughter of David and Patricia Ann Rickenbacker, by author; "Biographical Sketch of David E. Rickenbacker," ERP-AU; letter from Edward V. Rickenbacker to Laurance Rockefeller, 10 September 1951, Rockefeller Archive Center, folder marked "Eastern Air Lines Correspondence 1941–1957"; visit by author to ranch.

23. Letter from Edward V. Rickenbacker to William F. Rickenbacker, 11 January 1951, in W. F. Rickenbacker, *From Father to Son*, 117–22, original copy in ERP-AU;

R-H Tapes, reel 42, side 1; interview with Nancy Angell Rickenbacker, widow of William F. Rickenbacker, by author.

24. Letter from Edward V. Rickenbacker to William F. Rickenbacker, April 21, 1952, in ibid., 146–47; letters from Rickenbacker to MacArthur, 4 March 1944, 21 January 1949, and 23 April 1951, EVRP-LC, folder marked "E. V. Rickenbacker M-1 Miscellaneous 1916–1961."

25. William M. Leary, "Death from the Skies: The Newark Air Disasters of 1951–1952," in Janet R. Daly Bednarek and Tom D. Crouch, eds., *1998 National Aerospace Conference: The Meaning of Flight in the 20th Century* (Dayton, OH: Wright State University, 1999), 369–81.

26. Arthur Herman, *Joseph McCarthy: Reexamining the Life and Legacy of America's Most Hated Senator* (New York: Free Press, 2000); Geoffrey Perret, *Jack: A Life Like No Other* (New York: Random House, 2001), 158, 230; Perret, *Old Soldiers Never Die*, 569–77; George, *God's Salesman*, 182; letter from Rickenbacker to MacArthur, 10 July 1952, EVRP-LC, folder marked "E. V. Rickenbacker M-1 Miscellaneous 1916–1961"; letters from Edward V. Rickenbacker to William F. Rickenbacker, 16 July, 20 October, and 6 November 1952, and 26 January 1953, in W. F. Rickenbacker, *From Father to Son*, 155–60, 162–63, 175–77, original copies in ERP-AU.

27. Accession materials given to author by F. Robert van der Linden, Curator of Air Transportation, National Air and Space Museum; photograph in Serling, *From the Captain to the Colonel*, following p. 248; C. D. B. Bryan, *The National Air and Space Museum* (New York: Harry N. Abrams, Inc., 1979), 15, 98, 109–12.

28. R-H Tapes, reel 39M, side 1.

29. Interview with Nancy Angell Rickenbacker by author. On the Grove and the conclaves Hoover hosted there, see Richard Norton Smith, *An Uncommon Man: The Triumph of Herbert Hoover* (New York: Simon and Schuster, 1984), 207, 233–35, 364, 388, 405.

30. Letter from Edward V. Rickenbacker to William F. Rickenbacker, 6 July 1955, in W. F. Rickenbacker, *From Father to Son*, 193–98, original copy in ERP-AU.

31. Letter from Edward V. Rickenbacker to William F. Rickenbacker, Christmas 1960, in ibid., 198–200.

32. R-H Tapes, reel 41, side 1.

33. Eastern Air Lines, Annual Reports for 1947, 1948, and 1949; Serling, *From the Captain to the Colonel*, 211.

34. W. David Lewis and Wesley Phillips Newton, "C. E. Woolman," in Leary, ed., *The Airline Industry*, 509.

35. Interview with L. Welch Pogue by author.

36. Brad Williams, *The Anatomy of an Airline* (Garden City, NY: Doubleday, 1970), 41–47.

37. George E. Hopkins, "Fortunate in His Enemies: George T. Baker, National Airlines, and Federal Regulators," in Lewis, ed., *Airline Executives and Federal Regulators*, 213–41.

38. Lewis and Newton, *Delta,* 107–68, 211–61.

39. Serling, *From the Captain to the Colonel,* 206–7; Lewis and Newton, *Delta,* 112.

40. Walter J. Boyne, *Beyond the Horizons: The Lockheed Story* (New York: St. Martin's Press, 1998), 137–38.

41. Cearley, *Eastern Air Lines,* 26–31; Lewis and Newton, *Delta,* 114–18, 145, 150, 245; Serling, *From the Captain to the Colonel,* 209–22; Williams, *Anatomy of an Airline.*

42. Charles E. Anderson, "The 'Martinliner,'" *American Aviation Historical Society Journal* (1962): 120–25; Serling, *From the Captain to the Colonel,* 223–24; Lewis and Newton, *Delta,* 121.

43. Serling, *From the Captain to the Colonel,* 225–26.

44. "Comments on Air Mail Subsidy and Competition," 4 April 1949, attached to Eastern Air Lines, Annual Report for 1949; EVRR, 402.

45. The account that follows is based on an extended description of the trip by Rickenbacker in R-H Tapes, reel 39, sides 1 and 2.

46. Arthur J. Singer, *Arthur Godfrey: The Adventures of an American Broadcaster* (Jefferson, NC, and London: McFarland & Company, Inc., Publishers, 2000), 133.

47. Eastern Air Lines, Annual Report for 1950.

48. Ibid.

49. Serling, *From the Captain to the Colonel,* 244–51.

50. Interview by author with William M. Leary, a former dispatcher for Eastern who ultimately became an eminent historian of aviation.

51. Serling, *From the Captain to the Colonel,* 226, 277.

52. Letter from Robinson to Rickenbacker, Rockefeller Archive Center, folder marked "Eastern Air Lines Correspondence 1958–1973."

53. Young to Nelson Rockefeller, 18 July 1958, in ibid.

54. Interview with Irving Roth, a retired CAB attorney, by author.

55. Lewis and Newton, *Delta,* 306–7; Lewis, "Eastern Air Lines," 164; Nick A. Komons, *The Third Man: A History of the Airline Crew Complement Controversy* (Washington, DC: Federal Aviation Administration, 1987). Delta was not the only airline to use pilots trained as flight engineers for the third cockpit position; Braniff, Capital, Northeast, and Panagra did also. As Komons points out, the need to use four-person cockpit crews had been phased out by the end of 1964—by which time Rickenbacker had been forced to retire.

56. Interview with William F. Rickenbacker by author.

57. Najeeb E. Halaby, *Crosswinds: An Airman's Memoir* (Garden City, NJ: Doubleday, 1978), 155–57. Rickenbacker defended the meetings in R-H Tapes, reel 37.

58. Serling, *From the Captain to the Colonel,* 269–73. For a detailed analysis of the Electra, see Robert J. Serling, *The Electra Story: Aviation's Greatest Mystery* (Garden City, NY: Doubleday, 1963). On Woolman and Delta, see Lewis and Newton, Delta, 262–82.

59. Serling, *From the Captain to the Colonel,* 348–72, 383.

60. Sloan, *Wings of Honor,* 14–15.

61. Interview with Laurance S. Rockefeller by author; Lewis and Newton, *Delta*, 283–302, 340; Serling, *From the Captain to the Colonel*, 310–47.

Chapter 21. End Game

1. The narrative that follows is based on Adelaide's "Diary Covering the Orient and the Southwest Pacific Trip" and Eddie's "The Continuation of the Orient and South Pacific Trip with Mrs. Rickenbacker," R-H Tapes, reel 44, side 1, and reel 45, sides 1 and 2.

2. R-H Tapes, reel 46, side 2.

3. Interview with Floyd D. Hall by author, supplementing information in Serling, *From the Captain to the Colonel*, 379–82. Hall corrected a statement by Serling that he had made Rickenbacker's dismissal a condition of his becoming CEO.

4. Serling, *From the Captain to the Colonel*, 382.

5. Interviews with Floyd D. Hall and Laurance S. Rockefeller by author.

6. Interview with James Elkins by author; Serling, *From the Captain to the Colonel*, 383–84. Elkins, a member of the search committee who attended the first meeting, resolved confusing details in Serling's account by pointing out that that two separate meetings took place at the Hampshire House, the first involving Rickenbacker and the four original members of the search committee and the second involving Rickenbacker, Rockefeller, and Woodward.

7. Serling, *From the Captain to the Colonel*, 384–85.

8. Booton Herndon, "Narrative Report on Writing *Rickenbacker*," Booton Herndon Papers, Virginia Commonwealth University, Richmond, Virginia. Bonnie Herndon, widow of Booton Herndon, kindly provided me a copy of this fifty-two-page essay, from which I have quoted with permission from the Virginia Commonwealth University Archives.

9. R-H Tapes, reel 50, side 1; EVRR, 424–25. On the origins and development of postwar conservatism in the United States, see particularly George H. Nash, *The Conservative Intellectual Movement in America since 1945* (Wilmington, DE: Intercollegiate Studies Institute, 1998). The term "conservatism" was not universally popular among adherents of the movement, which, as Nash indicates (see p. 170), contained a "philosophic gap between traditionalism, with its stress on the restraint of man's will and appetites, and libertarianism, with its zeal for individual freedom and (implicitly) *self*-assertion." In this dichotomy Rickenbacker was clearly more a libertarian than a traditionalist, particularly because his radical faith in technological change was implicitly revolutionary in its tendency. As far as I am aware, he did not call himself a conservative until about the time Goldwater's *The Conscience of a Conservative* appeared in print.

10. Copy of speech in R-H Tapes, reel 50, side 1.

11. Letters from Welch to Rickenbacker, 1 August 1963, and Rickenbacker to Welch, 7 August 1963, followed by letters in the same month from Rickenbacker to Nathaniel E. Adamson Jr., Stillwell J. Conner, Ralph E. Davis, William J. Grede, A. G. Heinsohn Jr., Fred C. Koch, N. Floyd McGowin, Robert H. Montgomery, and Louis Rothenburg, EVRP-LC, box 32, folder marked "E. V. Rickenbacker—John Birch Society, 1963."

12. EVRR, 426–27.

13. The narrative of his extended trip that follows is based on "Rickenbacker's Diary of His Trip through Africa and Several Other Countries during April, May and June, 1964," R-H Tapes, reel 47, sides 1 and 2 and reel 48, side 1.

14. Smith, *An Uncommon Man*, 427.

15. On relationships between Kennedy and hawkish advisers, see Evan Thomas, *Robert Kennedy: His Life* (New York: Simon and Schuster, 2000), 209–39, based on fresh research in previously untapped sources. On Rickenbacker's opposition to the war in Vietnam, see EVRR, 438.

16. I used the set of copies at the United States Air Force Museum.

17. Interview with Bonnie Herndon by author; "Narrative Report." Herndon wrote such a narrative report for every book he ghostwrote, using the essays for teaching journalism classes. On Rickenbacker's claiming sole authorship of *Fighting the Flying Circus*, see R-H Tapes, reel 29, side 1.

18. R-H Tapes, reel 17, side 2 (see also EVRR, 428–43).

19. Interview with Floyd D. Hall.

20. Ibid.; "Americanism versus Communism," address by Edward V. Rickenbacker, Miami, Florida, 5 November 1971, in vol. 3 of a three-volume collection of Rickenbacker's staff presentations given by Hall to author, now in Auburn University Archives.

21. "Officers Assigned to the 94th Aero Squadron during W.W.I, 1917, 1918, 1919, Addresses and Status as of about 1970," document at United States Air Force Museum; obituary of Reed Chambers, *New York Times*, 18 January 1972.

22. Interviews with Marcia Rickenbacker and Patricia Ann Wrightson by author.

23. Interview with Floyd D. Hall.

24. Serling, *From the Captain to the Colonel*, 457–60; interviews with William F. Rickenbacker, Marcia Rickenbacker, Patricia Ann Wrightson, and Floyd D. Hall, correcting some details in Serling's account; notes taken on folder, "WFR Written Pre-Printed EVR Death Notice," at home of Nancy Angell Rickenbacker, Francestown, New Hampshire, 15 August 1995, including obituary of Edward V. Rickenbacker by William F. Rickenbacker in *National Review*, 17 August 1973, in author's possession.

25. Interviews with William F. Rickenbacker and Patricia Ann Wrightson; newspaper clippings and correspondence from collection at home of Nancy Angell Rickenbacker, Francestown, New Hampshire, copied by author.

26. Program of ceremony in possession of author, who was present.

Epilogue. In the Arena

1. Serling, *From the Captain to the Colonel*, 309.

2. Theodore Roosevelt, *History as Literature and Other Essays* (1941; repr., Port Washington, NY: Kennicat Press, Inc., 1967), 143–44 (from Roosevelt's address, "Citizenship in a Republic," given at the Sorbonne in Paris, 23 April 1910).

Essay on Primary Sources
— ☆ —

The most obvious primary source about Rickenbacker's life is his autobiography, *Rickenbacker* (Englewood Cliffs, NJ: Prentice-Hall, 1967), which he did not write. As I have indicated, Booton Herndon, a veteran freelance journalist, ghostwrote it after conducting numerous interviews with Rickenbacker in 1965. Despite Herndon's skills—the book would not have been reprinted seven times in hardback within less than a year of its initial publication, and in numerous paperback editions thereafter, had it not been so effectively written—it is marred by numerous errors and misrepresentations stemming from Rickenbacker's desire to aggrandize his image for posterity and hide developments that embarrassed him. Being forced to retire unwillingly from a major airline whose growth he had nurtured for almost three decades in an industry in which he justly ranked among the foremost pioneers intensified his determination to tell Herndon only what he wanted him to hear, a fact reinforced by denying Herndon the right to conduct further research on his own. As a national hero whose name had been a household word among millions of people, Rickenbacker wanted to be a role model to future generations. His memoir is a minefield that I have tried to use sparingly, but no coherent account of his life could be written without recourse to it. I have corrected as many errors and falsifications as I could, ignored material that seemed unbelievable, and retained information I have no reason to doubt after consulting as many primary sources as humanly possible in nearly fifteen years of research on this epic figure.

Closely connected with the autobiography is a massive corpus of typed transcripts resulting from the interviews Herndon conducted with Rickenbacker in 1965, the "R-H Tapes" that appear so frequently in my endnotes. Made from double-sided tape recordings, duplicate sets are located at the United States Air Force Museum (from which I obtained xerographic copies for a fee) and the Library of Congress. Although the material in the transcripts lies behind the condensed account Herndon provided in the autobiography, its greatly amplified richness and depth of detail valuably supplements the book that he ghostwrote. Over the years I have increasingly admired Herndon's devoted professionalism as a journalist determined to "get the story" as accurately as possible, given the constraints and imperatives under which he worked. His relentless questioning (cross-examining might perhaps be a more appropriate word) of Rickenbacker under exceedingly frustrating circumstances helped me greatly in weighing what to believe, what to disbelieve, and what to ignore in the reams of information he amassed. He deserves high praise for his perseverance in telling the epic story of a man he genuinely admired despite being offended by his personality and abominating his ideological convictions. Despite Eddie's crusty, combative manner and the patent falsity of some of the things he said, including his claim that he had written *Fighting the Flying Circus* by himself, Herndon accurately (at least to me) perceived him as an authentic American hero whose story deserved to be told, whatever the injured feelings and frustrations he had to endure in telling it.

The transcripts on which Herndon based the autobiography are doubly valuable because they contain verbatim copies of reports Rickenbacker wrote after completing his missions for Arnold and Stimson, speeches he made, articles he contributed to pulp magazines, and other documents he had accumulated throughout his long and incredibly active life. Herndon considered transcribing such materials a waste of time and money, but they have been a godsend to me, sparing me the need to track them down in untold numbers of places. Besides, Rickenbacker's prose style pervades them, which it might not have done in versions prepared by government bureaucrats, editors, and other persons who would likely have modified these texts to bring them in line with a more conventional style or even eliminated material they might have found offensive.

As noted, Rickenbacker's memoirs of the role he played in World War I, published as *Fighting the Flying Circus,* were ghostwritten. Laurence LaTourette Driggs, who gave the book its name, was an eloquent writer whose graceful prose made it a classic, though not necessarily an accurate account of its subject. Awed by aces, about whom he wrote incessantly, and wanting to put Rickenbacker in the best possible light, Driggs embellished his achievements, gave false information in some cases, and added extraneous material on his own volition. Fortunately, however, Driggs based most of the book on Rickenbacker's 1918 diary and dated reports by Rickenbacker, presumably dictated to an adjutant, that are written in a modest, sometimes self-effacing style that adds to their credibility. Wherever possible in writing about Rickenbacker's wartime experiences I have relied on the diary, the manuscript of which is available at the United States Air Force Museum (there is also an excellent typewritten transcription at the Wings over the Rockies Air and Space Museum, Aurora, Colorado) and carbon copies of the reports, in box 91 of the Rickenbacker Papers at the Library of Congress.

The Air Force Museum also has an "Engagement Diary"—an appointment journal and daybook—that Rickenbacker kept throughout much of 1919, except for January through mid-March and early November through the rest of the year. This document makes it possible to trace Rickenbacker's daily activities and correct misstatements he made in his 1965 interviews with Herndon, who perpetuated them in ghostwriting the autobiography. Finis Farr used the Engagement Diary in writing *Rickenbacker's Luck: An American Life,* but misunderstood some of its contents. In a godsend to my own work, Daniel J. Clemons, an extremely knowledgeable collector of Rickenbacker manuscripts and memorabilia, generously made available to me a diary Rickenbacker kept from 1 January through 14 March 1919, without which I would not have known much that happened during that brief but extremely important period in Eddie's life.

The Library of Congress has the largest collection of Rickenbacker Papers currently in existence. I studied its contents intensively when I was Lindbergh Professor of Aerospace History at the National Air and Space Museum in 1993–94 and returned for shorter visits thereafter. It is impossible to present more than a brief description of the riches the collection contains, including thousands of letters, telegrams, and manuscripts filed by Rickenbacker's secretary, Marguerite Shepherd. Most of these materials are in folders marked alphabetically by last name of sender or recipient from 1916 through 1965, but some of them are in folders devoted to specific topics, including Rickenbacker's racing career, his reception of the Medal of Honor, the transcontinental speed record he helped set in 1934, his brief membership in the America First Committee, his return from the raft episode in 1942, the role he played in Norman Vincent Peale's *Guideposts* magazine, and his rejection of membership in the John Birch Society. The files that are alphabetically arranged include a vast number of messages expressing joy about Rickenbacker's return from the raft episode, praising or condemning him for his campaign against "labor racketeers" in 1943, and telling him about inspiration derived from "When a Man Faces Death," published during the same year in *American* magazine.

Other folders include the cache of letters from Reed Chambers in 1920 that aroused Rickenbacker's interest in aircraft manufacturing after he had strongly committed himself to making automobiles, a list of the dates and results of every automobile race in which Rickenbacker participated on the AAA tour, letters documenting Rickenbacker's enduring loyalty to International Correspondence Schools, texts of radio broadcasts Rickenbacker made throughout his career, comments by columnists and radio commentators responding to his attacks on labor practices and pronouncements on foreign policy after his return from the Soviet Union, correspondence between Rickenbacker and actor Adolphe Menjou regarding Menjou's testimony to the House Un-American Activities Committee about Communists and the film industry, and letters showing the care he took in answering messages from young people, to whose interests he was intensely devoted. The reports Rickenbacker gave to Driggs for November–December 1918, located in box 91, permitted me to have more-trustworthy accounts of his activities and sorties in World War I than the ones in *Fighting the Flying Circus* and to edit a new edition for R. R. Donnelley & Sons Company's American Classics Series (Chicago: Lakeside Press, 1997) that eliminates much extraneous text added by Driggs and provides a "Historical Introduction" and annotations.

Besides possessing a complete set of the Rickenbacker-Herndon interviews, the United States Air Force Museum, Wright-Patterson Air Force Base, Dayton, Ohio, also has copies of orders relevant to Rickenbacker's service in World War I, materials pertaining to stages of his life including the 1942 raft episode, and a large collection of Rickenbacker photographs.

The most valuable product of my research at the National Archives in Washington, D.C., was a history of the 94th Pursuit Squadron in collection M990, series E, volume 12, part of a series of Army Air Service unit histories coordinated after World War I by Colonel Edgar S. Gorrell. The Great Lakes Branch of the National Archives, headquartered in Chicago, supplied district court records pertaining to the bankruptcy of the Rickenbacker Motor Company.

Rickenbacker subscribed to a clippings service and amassed untold thousands of newspaper and magazine clippings relating to his career, dating from 1913 to the end of his life. He donated the resulting twenty-six scrapbooks to the National Air and Space Museum, which kept them in its annex at Suitland, Maryland, where they were extremely difficult for me to use in cramped quarters. The impossibility of my taking notes on more than a fraction of the material they contained led the Museum to donate them to the Special Collections and Archives Department of my home institution, Auburn University, in return for its help in microfilming their contents. Without convenient access to these scrapbooks I could not have discovered a wealth of information about Rickenbacker contained throughout this book, which might otherwise never have appeared in print. Along with transcripts of the Rickenbacker-Herndon interviews, they constitute perhaps the single most valuable source upon which this biography is based, and I am extremely grateful to the National Air and Space Museum for its kindness.

The National Air and Space Museum has vertical files containing huge quantities of materials pertaining to noteworthy figures in aviation; curatorial files on noteworthy aircraft including the Nieuport 28 and Spad XIII; and a complete set of annual reports of Eastern Air Lines, collected by curator of air transport R. E. G. Davies. All of these resources figured importantly in my research. The Suitland annex has the Arthur Raymond Brooks Papers, which contain a wealth of material pertinent to the history of Florida Airways. This collection was valuably supplemented by an outline history of that company by Victor Chenea, who succeeded William A. Robertson as head of operations, provided to me by Matthew Rodina, an authority on the history of seaplanes, the development of Pan American Airways, and many other topics relevant to this book.

The Special Collections and Archives Department at Auburn University's Ralph Brown Draughon Library has a vast and constantly growing collection of Rickenbacker Papers, of which the scrapbooks just mentioned are only a part. Other materials include "The Opening of a New Chapter in My Book of Life," a honeymoon diary Rickenbacker kept from 16 September through 27 November 1922; more than 1,000 photographs of and pertaining to Rickenbacker; typescripts of extended interviews with persons who had known Rickenbacker for many years, conducted by Isabel Leighton for Eureka Pictures and Twentieth-Century Fox in preparation for filming *Captain Eddie*; copies of *The Great Silver Fleet Newsletter* from 1935 through 1941; transcripts of interviews by various persons, including military interrogators, with John F. Bartek, William C. Cherry, John J. de Angelis, Frank Reynolds, and James C. Whittaker about what happened during the Pacific raft episode in 1942; and the Cynthia White Papers, generously donated by the daughter of Lester Boutte, the airman who first spotted Rickenbacker's raft and helped rescue him, which contain message traffic and other information from the Marine base at Funafuti before, during, and after the rescue of Rickenbacker and other persons who had been stranded at sea during the raft episode.

The department also possesses "Pacific Mission," Rickenbacker's own account of the raft episode; travel diaries kept by Adelaide Rickenbacker during extended trips to various parts of the world with her husband; copies of the original letters published by William F. Rickenbacker in *From Father to Son*; manuscript records documenting critical stages in the history of the Rickenbacker Motor Company; a copy of the contract executed by Rickenbacker and Driggs on 16 November 1918 specifying the terms under which Driggs wrote *Fighting the Flying Circus*; three bound copies of presentations given by Rickenbacker to staff members of Eastern Air Lines; film footage about various phases of Rickenbacker's career, including his travels in the Southwest Pacific after recuperating from the raft episode; and other documents and materials too numerous to mention. The collection will grow appreciably in the near future when I give the Special Collections and Archives Department the notes and xerographic files I have collected during my research for this book. I also depended heavily on the Library's microfilm files of the *New York Times* and other newspapers; official government documents, including the records of congressional hearings in which Rickenbacker testified; patent reports (particularly important with regard to the "plane for the masses" developed by Rickenbacker and Glenn D. Angle); and *United States Statutes at Large,* with copies of airmail legislation.

Bert L. Frandsen, who wrote a doctoral dissertation under my direction at Auburn University about the history of the 1st Pursuit Group (subsequently published by Smithsonian Institution Press in 2003 as *Hat in the Ring: The Birth of American Air Power in the Great War*) owns a mass of primary documents that he generously shared with me, including a manuscript diary kept by Lieutenant Joseph Eastman, a member of the 94th Pursuit Squadron, and a transcript of the court-martial proceedings brought against Major Jean W. F. M. Huffer, both of which greatly illuminate what happened to Rickenbacker and the 94th Pursuit Squadron between 11 November and 31 December 1918. Frandsen also shared with me his formidable expertise about the Nieuport 28 (including its wing-stripping problems) and the Spad XIII.

Frank Hammelbacher, of Flushing, New York, a dealer in manuscripts and memorabilia, owns a copy of the passport Rickenbacker obtained before his voyage to England in 1916, showing all the countries he expected to visit and containing stamps of various police stations to which he reported, and generously made it available to me.

Ethel Driggs of Easton, Maryland, daughter-in law of Laurence LaTourette Driggs, owns a Driggs Family Genealogy including a extended typed autobiography that he contributed to it, rich in information about his background, his tours of British and American air bases in France, and his association with Rickenbacker, leading to the ghostwriting of *Fighting the Flying Circus,* and kindly made this extremely valuable source available to me.

I conducted much of my research about Rickenbacker at a large number of archives, libraries, and historical societies not yet mentioned in this essay. Such is their number that I must inevitably mention some of them. I begin with the Rockefeller Archive Center, located in Sleepy Hollow, New York, whose holdings include a manuscript on the early history of Eastern Air Lines, correspondence relating to the role Laurance Rockefeller played in the enterprise, and letters containing criticisms of Eastern's management under Rickenbacker in the late 1950s and early 1960s. Darwin H. Stapleton, director of the RAC, gave me free access to these records. Unfortunately, the bulk of Eastern's business records were apparently destroyed after the company went bankrupt in 1991.

The Thurber Special Collections Department of Ohio State University in Columbus has "Life Story of Captain Edward V. Rickenbacker," a thick two-volume document based on interviews with Rickenbacker held to assist Twentieth Century-Fox in filming *Captain Eddie.* Other valuable materials include a collection of speeches by Rickenbacker, particularly "Predictions," the address he gave at Banff Springs, Alberta, Canada, in 1919, and a copy of Rickenbacker's "big-little" book, *Ace Drummond* (Racine, WI: Whitman Publishing Company, 1935), intended for young readers.

The Ohio Historical Society, headquartered at Columbus, has city directories documenting the places of residence and occupations of Elizabeth Basler Rickenbacher, William Rickenbacher, and other members of the Rickenbacher family in the late nineteenth and early twentieth centuries; and a filmscript of *Captain Eddie.* Columbus newspapers available on microfilm contain information about the death of William Rickenbacher in 1904 and efforts by citizens to restore the house at 1334 East Livingston Avenue in which Edward Rickenbacker grew up, which is one of three buildings in Columbus identified as a National Historic Landmark. Because these efforts were unsuccessful (another one is now in progress), a replica of the house was built at Motts Military Museum in Groveport, Ohio, at the initiative of Richard W. Hoerle. The museum also has memorabilia relating to Rickenbacker. The Franklin County–Columbus Metropolitan Library has files of newspaper clippings about various phases in Rickenbacker's life and career.

Marian Pflaum Darby's booklet, *The Inspiration and Lives of Elizabeth Basler Rickenbacker and William Rickenbacker,* privately published in 1963, is based largely on information provided to Darby, Edward V. Rickenbacker's niece, by Elizabeth Basler Rickenbacher, her grandmother. It is the only available source of information about the family life of the Rickenbachers and their children, and was made available to me by Richard W. Hoerle, who owns the copyright. Darby obtained genealogical data about the Rickenbacher family from Swiss relatives and cantonal officials and visited Switzerland in further quest of related materials. I followed her footsteps in that country, obtained further genealogical materials, and visited Zeglingen and its environs, including Forderes Ried, the chalet in which Elizabeth Basler grew up.

The Des Moines, Iowa, Public Library has newspaper clippings and other materials pertaining to Rickenbacker's residence in Iowa in 1912–14. The Iowa State Library and Iowa State Historical Society, both headquartered in the same building, have small collections of materials relating to the Mason and Duesenberg motor car companies and large newspaper files making it possible to trace the appearances at county fairs in 1912 of the Flying Squadron racing team and study the organization and logistics of small-time automobile racing in the early twentieth century. Minutes of the American Automobile Association Contest Board at the Hall of Fame Museum at the Indianapolis Motor Speedway record the suspension of Rickenbacker's license to compete on the AAA Tour and provide the names of the towns in which Rickenbacker competed as a member of the Flying Squadron. Newspapers filed at the Blue Earth (Minnesota) Public Library contain dramatic information about one of the events in which he participated without AAA sanction. The Sioux City (Iowa) Public Library has newspaper and other records documenting the 300-mile sweepstakes in which Rickenbacker won the first major victory of his career as a professional automobile racer on 4 July 1914. The track at which the race occurred, in nearby North Sioux City, South Dakota, is now overgrown by a cornfield surrounding a private airport once known as Rickenbacker Field, but traces of the racing facility, including a tunnel under the infield, are still faintly visible.

The Red Oak Public Library and Red Oak Historical Society, Red Oak, Iowa, have newspaper files and other primary source materials documenting hostility between residents and the railroad, horse racing, enthusiasm for automobiles, and the background and running of the first automobile race of Rickenbacker's career in June 1910. Pactolus Park, in which he raced, remains in thriving condition as a county fair site.

Four consecutive years of the *Omaha Bee,* acquired on microfilm by Auburn University from the Omaha Public Library, contain valuable information about local automobile dealers and automobile races held in and near the city from 1909 through 1912, when Rickenbacker lived and worked there. The library also provided copies of articles from the 1910 *Omaha World-Herald* documenting a series of races Rickenbacker won and materials relating to the early history of the annual Ak-Sar-Ben festivals. Other newspaper files pertinent to his racing career, as already noted, are available at the Library of Congress. Fair grounds that I visited in Nebraska, Iowa, and Minnesota evoke the atmosphere in which Rickenbacker competed.

The Herbert Hoover Presidential Library, West Branch, Iowa, has a large collection of correspondence between Hoover and Rickenbacker, particularly relevant in the post–World War II period when the two men had become close friends living near each other in New York City. Along with sources in Auburn University's

Department of Special Collections and Archives, the Hoover Presidential Library's files also contain information about Rickenbacker's visits to the Bohemian Grove sanctuary in California.

The Burton Historical Collection at the Detroit Public Library has files pertaining to the Detroit Athletic Club, Indian Head Village, and the effort from 1927 through 1930 to secure the Medal of Honor for Rickenbacker. The National Automotive History Collection, located in the Detroit Public Library, has a number of sources pertinent to Rickenbacker's racing career, including the rules governing the 300-mile Sioux City Sweepstakes that he won on 4 July 1914. The Henry Ford Museum, at Dearborn, Michigan, possesses large files of automotive magazines including *Horseless Age, Motor Age, MoToR,* and *The Automobile,* and an impressive number of historic race cars and aircraft, some of which figured, directly or indirectly, in Rickenbacker's life. The private collections of Joseph Gertler, an automobile and aviation enthusiast who resides in northwest Florida, contain files of other early automobile magazines including *American Chauffeur.*

The national headquarters of the Antique Automobile Club of America, at Hershey, Pennsylvania, has a mass of information about early American marques, drawings and illustrations, articles about noted drivers, and other subjects relevant to the history of motor sport. The publishing headquarters of *Automobile Quarterly* at Kutztown, Pennsylvania, has the research notes gathered by Beverly Rae Kimes for her article, "Hat in the Ring: The Rickenbacker," published by the *Quarterly* in 1975, which she kindly opened to me. Her notes include a large number of articles from newspapers and trade journals pertaining to the history of the Rickenbacker Motor Company.

The Eleutherian Mills Historical Library, Wilmington, Delaware, has a collection of reports Rickenbacker made to Henry Belin du Pont at the time Eastern Air Lines was controlled by General Motors, as well as correspondence between the two men.

The Will Rogers Memorial and Public Library, Claremore, Oklahoma, has many boxes of letters, publicity announcements, reports, and other materials documenting Rickenbacker's role in raising funds to memorialize Rogers after his fatal crash with Wiley Post at Point Barrow, Alaska, in 1935.

The Gubernatorial Papers at the Alabama Department of Archives and History, Montgomery, Alabama, contain valuable information about Governor Frank W. Dixon's service in World War I that was helpful in showing why Rickenbacker reluctantly accepted a speaking engagement in Birmingham leading to his near-fatal crash near Atlanta on 26 February 1941. Dr. Deborah G. Douglas, curator of the MIT Science Museum, Cambridge, Massachusetts, and an authority on the history of American airports, possesses a wealth of information, including newspaper clippings and magazine articles about the origins of LaGuardia Airport, which she generously made available to me. The archives of Piedmont Hospital, Atlanta, Georgia, possess information about Rickenbacker's recovery from the crash and his treatment by Floyd W. McRae Jr., M.D. Diane Erdeljac, director of the archives, helped me access this information.

Materials at the Royal Air Force Museum, Hendon, United Kingdom, include a document written by Air Marshal Hugh. G. Trenchard about the use of airpower against Germany, a copy of which Rickenbacker transmitted to Secretary of War Henry L. Stimson.

The Special Collections Department at Virginia Commonwealth University, Richmond, has custody of extended essays Booton Herndon wrote after each of his ghostwriting projects, including the one he prepared after the publication of Rickenbacker's autobiography. Bonnie Herndon, Booton Herndon's widow, made available to me the text of his essay about the experience of interviewing Rickenbacker, and related to me the frustrations he endured.

Interviews with persons who played significant roles in Rickenbacker's life were important primary sources in my research. I was probably the last person to interview William Frost Rickenbacker, in October 1994, before he died from cancer in March 1995. He gave me a wealth of extremely candid information about his famous father and his mother, Adelaide Frost Durant Rickenbacker. Nancy Angell Rickenbacker, William Rickenbacker's widow and sole executrix of his estate, gave unsparingly of her time in repeated interviews and led me to dealers in manuscripts and ephemera from whom Auburn University obtained many of the materials in its Rickenbacker Papers. The university acquired many others from Mrs. Rickenbacker herself, including furniture from Rickenbacker's office at Rockefeller Center, now in my office in Thach Hall. Other members of the Rickenbacker family who granted me valuable interviews include Patricia Ann Wrightson, David E. Rickenbacker's widow; James and Bryan Rickenbacker, her sons; and Marcia Rickenbacker, her daughter. Letters from Marie-Louise Perri, William F. Rickenbacker's half sister, supplied information about his birth parents.

William F. Rickenbacker's study at his former residence in Francestown, New Hampshire, to which I was permitted free and unrestricted access by Nancy Angell Rickenbacker, contained materials relating to his search to discover the identities of his birth parents after his adoptive parents died. Documents in his desk, which had been used by his father at Rockefeller Center and now belongs to Auburn University, revealed the role Mr. Rickenbacker played in encouraging Finis Farr to write *Rickenbacker's Luck: An American Life*. Files belonging to Mrs. Rickenbacker also contained her father-in-law's "Assumptions with Regard to Russia," dated 27 September 1943. What happened to all these documents after Rickenbacker died in 1995 is unclear, but the Department of Special Collections and Archives at Auburn University has the research notes I took on them.

Laurance S. Rockefeller, chief investor in Eastern Air Lines, gave me two highly informative interviews about his relationship with Rickenbacker and the chain of events leading to the failed merger attempt with American Air Lines in 1963. Floyd H. Hall, who took the helm at Eastern late in 1964, gave me repeated personal and telephone interviews that were immeasurably valuable in understanding the process by means of which he became Eastern's chief executive officer, his meetings with Rickenbacker in the years following his retirement, the arrangements he made for a work of sculpture honoring Eddie at Eastern's headquarters in Miami, a visit he paid to him during his hospitalization for an aneurysm in 1973, and the provisions he made to have Rickenbacker's body returned to America after he died in Switzerland in 1973. James Elkins, a director who served on the search committee that recommended Hall to lead Eastern and was present at the first meeting at the Hampshire House at which Eddie was asked to retire, clarified the sequence of events that forced him from office. L. Welch Pogue, who had chaired the Civil Aeronautics Board in the period following Rickenbacker's return from his missions in World War II, provided the details of a stormy meeting with him after Eastern had failed to win a coveted route award, discussed Rickenbacker's difficulties in dealing with a service-oriented industry, and admonished me to remember that Rickenbacker was a "great man and a great American."

Bishop Simpson, a mechanic for Eastern Air Lines, and Perry Hudson, a pilot, who participated in the search for the wreckage of the plane in which Rickenbacker crashed in 1941, provided much information in personal and telephone interviews about their experiences, as did Birdie Bomar, a registered nurse who visited Rickenbacker at Piedmont Hospital. Mrs. Bomar, now deceased, also told me about Rickenbacker's generosity to her and her husband, Richard Bomar, a pilot for Eastern Air Lines who returned wounded from World War II.

I could not gain access to transcriptions of interviews conducted by Robert J. Serling with a large number of individuals who figured importantly in the development of Eastern Air Lines because he had returned them to the company and they were apparently destroyed along with Eastern's business records after the carrier went bankrupt. Serling's "informal history," *From the Captain to the Colonel,* contains much information derived from these interviews, including a penetrating character analysis of Rickenbacker. Correspondence and telephone interviews with Serling figured importantly in my work. He went to great lengths to help me secure an interview with William T. Cherry, who resolutely refused to talk about the raft episode. Cherry did, however, discuss it with a class of seventh-grade students at a reunion of raft survivors at Ames, Iowa, in 1985. His extended remarks, which were filmed, provide valuable insight about the part he played in the ordeal. The Cynthia White Papers at Auburn University contain correspondence and other materials pertaining to the reunion. A highly revealing transcript of testimony that Cherry gave to superior officers in the Air Transport Command is also among Auburn's holdings, provided by Matthew Rodina.

As I have already said, visits to places associated with Rickenbacker's life were valuable sources of firsthand evidence. Insights gained from visiting Apremont, Bar-le-Duc, Chalons, Montsec, Rheims, Seicheprey, and other places where Rickenbacker served in France, the Brooklands Motor Speedway at Weybridge in Surrey, and the Savoy Hotel in London, which has its own archives, facilitated a better understanding of what Rickenbacker saw and experienced in World War I.

Published works (for places and dates of publication, see my endnotes) were also important primary sources in my research. Jack C. Fox, *The Illustrated History of the Indianapolis 500, 1914–1994* contains a mine of essential details regarding races, racers, race cars, times, and orders of finishes that I could not have done without. William L. Mitchell's *Memoirs of World War I* and his essay, "Rickenbacker—The Ace of the American Expeditionary Force"; Harold Buckley's *Squadron 95*; Jack R. Eder's edited work, *Let's Go Where the Action Is: The Wartime Experiences of Douglas Campbell*, consisting mainly of entries from Campbell's diary; Alan Winslow's article, "No Parachutes," *Liberty* 10, nos. 8 and 9 (1933); and Harold E. Hartney's *Up and At 'Em*, among a few, were indispensable sources based on eyewitness experiences, however carefully historians must use them. Charles Woolley's *First to the Front: The Aerial Adventures of 1st Lieutenant Waldo Heinrichs and the 95th Aero Squadron, 1917–1918* and *The Hat in the Ring Gang: The Combat History of the 94th Aero Squadron in World War I* contain mainly firsthand reports transcribed verbatim and also offer a wealth of photographs. Norman L. R. Franks and Frank W. Bailey, *Over the Front: A Complete Record of the Fighter Aces and Units of the United States and French Air Services, 1914–1918*; Norman L. R. Franks, Frank W. Bailey, and Russell Guest, *Above the Lines: A Complete Record of the Fighter Aces of the German Air Service, Naval Air Service, and Flanders Marine Corps, 1914–1918*; Christopher Shores, Norman Franks, and Russell Guest, *Above the Trenches: A Complete Record of the Fighter Aces and Units of the British Empire Forces, 1915–1920*; and James J. Sloan, *Wings of Honor: American Airmen in World War I* are all noteworthy for the mass of primary details they contain. The merits of the essays accompanying them are also considerable.

Beverly Rae Kimes and Harry C. Clarke, *Standard Catalog of American Cars*, which has gone through various editions, contains a mine of information relevant to Rickenbacker's experiences in racing and the automobile industry, in addition to thousands of photographs of yearly makes and models. Alfred P. Sloan Jr.'s *My Years with General Motors* contains valuable information about the managerial role Sloan played in General Motors and how he assisted Rickenbacker's takeover of Eastern Air Lines in 1938. Hans Christian Adamson's worshipful *Eddie Rickenbacker*—how could he have written dispassionately about a man who had saved his life?—contains a valuable eyewitness account of the raft episode, as does James C. Whittaker's *We Thought We Heard the Angels Sing: The Epic Story of Those Who Were with Eddie Rickenbacker in the Plane Lost in the Pacific*. Rickenbacker's *Seven Came Through* is also a firsthand account published soon after the ordeal. George Seldes, *Witness to a Century: Encounters with the Noted, the Notorious, and the Three SOBs* is a highly opinionated work containing useful details about the author's experiences with Rickenbacker.

The works cited here are only a partial list of the voluminous primary sources on Rickenbacker I have consulted. Taken together, whatever their individual shortcomings might be, they offer a fresh and comprehensive look at an epic life that merits much attention.

Index

— ☆ —

Angle, Glenn D., 282, 283
anti-Germanic sentiment, 235
Antique Automobile Club of America (AACA), 55
Antoshkin, I. D., 481
"Arena of the Sky, The" (speaking tour), 230–33
armistice, 215–17, 218
Armstrong, Thomas F., 527
army, service in: application for transfer, 128; awards, 139, 219, 301–3; as chief engineer, 106–9; as driver, 98–104; over enemy lines during, 121–25; gunnery training, 109–10; pilot training, 104–6; promotions, 140, 145–46, 168–69, 195–96, 210, 234; self-doubt and, 127. *See also* 94th Aero Pursuit Squadron
Army Air Corps, 356
Army Air Forces (AAF): change of name of, 384; defense of H. Arnold, 397–401; fleet of, 395–96; Kaiser plan and, 394; in New Guinea and Solomon Islands, 403; tour of bases of, 386–90, 401–2, 405–13, 415–16, 442–43. *See also* 8th Air Force
Army Air Forces Aid Society, 450
Army Air Service: Chambers and, 246; combat records of, 162; French training and, 104–5; leadership struggles in, 141, 155–56; Menoher and, 247; 94th squadron and, 131; round-the-world flight and, 278
Arnold, Henry H.: Alaska-Aleutian Islands Theater and, 486–87; Army Air Forces Aid Society and, 450; defense of, 397–401; ER and, 356, 386, 390, 394–95; fighter planes and, 396, 397; Lindbergh and, 386; J. Montgomery and, 288; reports to, 389; search for ER and, 438–39; speed record and, 250
Arnold, Leslie P., 345
Ascot Speedway, Los Angeles, 90
"Assumptions with Regard to Russia" (Rickenbacker), 484–85
Astor, Gerald, 395
Aswan Dam, 538–39
Atkinson, Bert: career of, 115; 1st Pursuit Wing and, 184; Hartney, Bonnell, and, 179–80, 193; Lufbery and, 118; Nieuports and, 155; 95th squadron and, 121; patrols ordered by, 117; promotion of, 186; Spad incident and, 176–77
Atlanta, Georgia, 286–87, 337–38, 368
Atlantic, Iowa, 48
Attu Island, 489–90
autobiography, work on, 543–45

autogiro, xii, 319–20
automobile manufacturing. *See* Rickenbacker Motor Company
automobile racing: beginnings of, 28; closed tracks, 53, 56; dangers in, 35–36; early years of, 30–33; first experiences, 46–48; innovations in, 62, 82; internationalism of, 88; in Iowa, 46–49; in Nebraska, 49–50; in Ohio, 50, 51–52; professional drivers and, 55–56; safety regulations for, 55–56, 60; types of, 49, 53; Vanderbilt Cup Races, 31–36, 71–72, 90; vehicle standards and, 80–81. *See also* Indianapolis 500-mile race; professional race driver, career as
aviation: articles about, 299–301; big business and, 310; cockade on planes, 129; competition on routes in, 501; desire for career in, 242, 243; in Europe, 265, 267; fatal accidents in 1936, 332; first experiences with, 89–90; on future of, 239–41; government regulation of, 332–34; issues in, in Washington, 252; jet transportation and, 525–26; making money in, 242–43; postwar era and, 463–64, 491–92, 512–13; speeches about, 256–57, 292–93, 294; U.S. and, 111, 112–13. *See also* airmail routes; air power; Civil Aeronautics Board (CAB); *specific airlines*
Aylesworth, Merlin H., 295

B. P. Pond Lyceum Bureau, 230, 237
Baer, Paul, 162
Bailey, Fred C., 59, 60
Baker, Erwin G., 278
Baker, George T., 513–14, 516, 521. *See also* National Airlines
Baker, Hobie, 129
Baker, Newton D., 226–27, 231
Baldwin, Stanley, 355–56
balloon-busting, 173–75, 191–94, 198–99, 200–201, 203–4, 207, 212
Baltic (ship), 99, 250
Banta, A. J., 277
Barney, T. B., 260
Bartek, John F., 416–19, 422–23, 431–37, 440–42, 447
Baselland, Basel, Baselstadt, Switzerland, 3, 5
Basler, Anna, 7
Basler, Rudolph, 5–6
Baylies, Frank, 162
Beachey, Lincoln, 68
Bear Creek Ranch, Texas, 507–8
Beebe, W. T., 522
Behncke, David L., 348

Belleau Wood, 167, 171, 175
Bellefonte, Pennsylvania, ix–x, 247
Bell P-39 Airacobras, 395, 396, 466, 480
Belyaev, Alexander I., 466, 467
Beman, Ward, 515
Bendix Aviation, 317
Berle, Adolf A., 491–93
Bertrandais, Victor, 445
Bethe, Hans, 507
Biddle, Charles J., 225
Bill, Charles G., Dorothy, and Ruth, 238, 241
Bingham, Hiram, 302
Birmingham, Alabama, 368–69, 381
Bishop, Billy, 269
Black, Hugo, 312
Black-McKellar Act, 320, 321
Blair, Frank, 281, 289–90
"Blitzen Benz" (race car), 51, 72
Blodgett, Richard A., 142
Bockholt, Ludwig, 223
Boeing, William E., 238
Boeing planes: B-17C, 416, 418, 420; B-17D,
    419; B-17 Flying Fortress, 395, 398, 403–4,
    405, 411–12; B-314 Clipper, 416; 247, 322
Boelcke, Oswald, 119, 162, 198, 541
Bomar, Birdie, 376
Bong, Richard I., 496, 497
Bonnell, Geoffrey H., 157–58, 179–80
Boutte, Lester H., 439, 440
Bowne, Patricia Ann, 508
Boyd, J. G., 439–40
Boyne, Walter J., *Aces in Command*, 196, 218
brakes, four-wheel, 271–73
Brancker, Sefton, 268
Braniff, Thomas, 334
Brattain, Paul, 324, 500, 514
Breech, Ernest R., 309–10, 314, 317–18,
    320–21, 328–29, 330, 531
Brett, George, 444
Briey Iron Basin, 125
Britain. *See* England
Brooklands Speedway, England, 53–54, 95
Brooks, Arthur R., 286
Brown, Walter F., 312, 316, 320
Bruce, Alexander, 182
Bruce-Brown, David, 57–58
Bruske, Paul Hale, 71, 72
Bryan, William Jennings, 42–43
Buck, Gene, 96
Buckeye Motor Company, 25–26
Buckley, Harold, 154
Burckhardt, Jacob, 3
Burgess, Lewis, 98
Burman, Bob, 30, 66, 78, 81

Burt, Andrew, 59
Burtis, Preston, 69
Byrd, Richard E., 298, 302
Byron, William D., 372, 375

Cadillac (car), 292, 293
calculated risk management, 198
Calhoun, Blanche, 10, 44
Campbell, Douglas: in Alert Room, 131;
    competition with, 159, 162–63, 164–66;
    flights with ER, 122, 136; on Lufbery, 149;
    94th squadron and, 234; orders for, 109;
    return to France by, 220; return to U.S. by,
    222–23; victories of, 132–33, 134
Canada, 492, 493
Canadian Colonial Airways, 370
Candler Field, 286, 373, 374
Canner, C. W., 59, 60
Cannon, Joe, 228
Canton Island, 416, 419, 420, 531
Captain Eddie (film), 497, 597n39, 622n3
"Captain Eddie" nickname, 232, 234
Carlson, Billy, 71, 72
Carpenter, Walter F., 310
Casablanca, Morocco, 468
Casgrain, Wilfred V., 154
Castro, Fidel, 542
Caudron (biplane), 105
Certificate of Public Convenience and
    Necessity (CPCN), 333–34
Chalmers-Detroit Motor Car Company, 47
Chalons, France, 123, 128, 262
Chambers, Reed: aircraft manufacturing
    and, 245–46; balloon-busting and, 174,
    201; as C.O., 222–23; death of, 547; down-
    ing of enemy by, 203; first meeting of,
    108; 1st Pursuit Group and, 245; Florida
    Airways and, 283–89; 94th squadron and,
    116; on patrol with, 149–50; promotion of
    ER and, 195; Saunders and, 209; sorties
    of, 130, 131–32, 205–6; as witness to vic-
    tory, 153
Chaplin, Charlie, 238
Chapman, Charles W., Jr., 136, 142
character traits, of ER: accident-proneness,
    11; Anglophobia, 94, 268, 472, 473;
    arrogance, 18; artistic inclinations, 13;
    attention, need for, 10–11; "boy culture"
    and, 12–13; fear of mortality, 11, 13, 451;
    Francophobia, 265–66; intelligence, 25,
    342; introspection and, 178, 189; music,
    love of, 10, 13; negative, 319, 341–42, 382;
    positive, x, 161–62, 319, 341–42. *See also*
    drinking; superstitious behavior

Frayer, Lee A.: Buckeye Motor Company and, 25; Columbus Buggy Company and, 36, 37–38; Firestone-Columbus and, 39–40; Indianapolis race and, 52, 57–58; as mentor, 27–28; Oldfield and, 50, 51; as racer, 26, 32, 33; retirement of, 58
Frayer-Miller Racing Team, 28, 32
Frayer-Miller vehicles, 25, 26, 28
Frederick A. Stokes Company, 229
Fritz, Larry, 315
Froesch, Charles, 323, 515, 526
Frost, Stoel Meech, 258
Frye, Jack, 313, 314, 316, 317
Funafuti atoll, 435–36
future, predictions about, 239–41, 545–46

Gaines, William, 14–15
Gambrell, Smythe, 522, 524
Garber, Paul N., 510
gasoline engines, 21–22, 23–24
gas warfare, 173
Gatty, Harold, xi
Geiger, Roy, 446
General Aviation Corporation, 299, 314, 317
General Aviation Manufacturing Corporation, 305–6
General Motors (GM): aviation and, 296, 317; Breech and, 309; deals with, 296, 299; employment at, 291–93, 294; FACA and, 298–99; FDR and, 311; North American Aviation and, 309–10, 320; resignation from, 306; Sheridan car and, 249, 250; in South Africa, 540. *See also* Breech, Ernest R.; Eastern Air Lines (EAL); Sloan, Alfred P.
Gengoult, France, 141–42, 153, 156, 167, 263
George VI, 327, 499
Gerard, Paul, 139
Germany: Berlin, trip to, 263–65; cruise to, 358; defeatism in army of, 187–88; defensive strategies of, 142–43, 161; hyperinflation in, 264; invasion of Soviet Union by, 382; Luftwaffe, 354–55, 384; Orden Pour le Merite, 159; Poland and, 359, 360; as primary target, 410; relations with U.S. in WWI, 95, 97; submarines of, 385, 390–91, 394
GI Bill of Rights, 495
Gibson, Frank, 495
Gifford, Sarah, 12, 23
"Gimper," 130
Gladden, Washington, 8
Glendale, California, 314

Global Mission (Arnold), 401
Godfrey, Arthur, 519–20
Goering, Hermann, 264–65, 354
Goldwater, Barry, 534, 535, 539, 540, 542
Gorrell, Edgar S., 332
Gould, Leslie, 328
Goux, Jules, 60–61, 65
Grant, Alfred, 198
Grant, Harry, 36
Great Britain. *See* England
"Great Circle" routes, 487–88, 530
Green, Edward, 109, 142, 143, 182
Green, Fred W., 302
Green, Ralph, 379
Greiner, Art, 57
Griffith, Beverly, 324
"grinds," 49, 55
Guadalcanal, 446–47
Gude, Oscar Jay, 109, 147–48
gunnery training, 121; at Cazaux, 109–11

Haig, Alexander, 101
Halaby, Najeeb, 525, 526
Hall, Floyd D., 531–32, 533, 546–47
Hall, James Norman: book by L. Driggs and, 223; capture of, 140, 142–45; crash of, 127–28; ER and, 136–37; Lafayette Escadrille and, 130; 94th squadron and, 126, 129; return from captivity, 220; victory of, 138
Hannagan, Steve, 256, 257, 260
Hannover CL-V observation plane, 205, 206, 209
Hansell, Nils, 375
Harding, Warren G., 231, 248–49
Harding, William Barclay, 330, 517
Hargis, Billy Ray, 537
Harkness, Harry, 81
Harmon, Millard, 117, 220, 445
Harriman, W. Averell, 307, 308, 409, 482
Harris, Arthur, 404, 406, 407–8
Harroun, Ray, 57, 58, 70–71
Hartney, Harold E.: L. Driggs and, 214; Huffer and, 221; Larsen JL-6 and, 247; Luke and, 192–93, 198–200; Medal of Honor for ER and, 302; Nieuport and, 157; promotion of ER and, 194–96; Rembercourt and, 184–85; St. Mihiel salient and, 186–87; 27th squadron and, 179
Hartsfield, William B., 286
Harvest Classic races, 85–86
Hat-in-the-Ring campaign, 456–57
Hat-in-the-Ring emblem, 130, 272, 276, 278, 302, 388, 390

Keys, Clement M., 320
Kilner, W. G., 96
Kimes, Beverly Rae, 273, 279
King, Ernest J., 386
Kirby, Maxwell, 205, 208, 215
Kiska Island, 490
Kleberg, Robert, 511
Knabenshue, Roy, 1
Knapp, Forrest L., 499
Knight, Harry, 57
Knowlton, Hugh, 329, 330
Knox (car), 51
Knox, Frank, 363, 364
Knudsen, William S., 328, 329, 330, 364
Koblenz, Germany, 221–22
Kohlstaat, H. H., 30
Kriemhilde Stellung, 202
Kurtz, Paul B., 109, 149–50

Laass, Jack H., 283
labor and management, criticism of, 453–55, 456–62
labor unions, 348–49
Lady Peace (Vultee V-1A), 326–27
Laemmele, Carl, 236–37
Lafayette Escadrille, 112–13, 130
Lafayette flyers, 112, 113–14, 157
Lafayette Flying Corps, 112–13
LaGuardia, Fiorello H., 109, 338, 365–66, 367, 448
LaGuardia Field, 367, 369–70, 371
Lardner, Ring, 232
Larsen, John M., 246, 248
Larsen JL-6 (plane), 246–48, 256
LaSalle (car), 290–91
Leahy, William D., 386
Lear, Oscar, 25
LeBlond Aircraft Company, 283
Lebowitz, Allan, 376
Leech, L. L., 440
Lehman, Robert H., 307, 309
Leigh-Mallory, Trafford, 407
Leighton, Isabel, 259
Leland, Henry, 230
Le May, Curtis, 538
Lend Lease: Weapon for Victory (Stettinius), 480
Lethridge, Maurice, 523
Lewis, Dave, 84
Lewis, John L., 455–56
Libby, Frederick, 162
Liberty Bonds, 220, 229, 230, 231. *See also* "Arena of the Sky, The" (speaking tour)
Liberty League, 311–12
Liggett, Hunter, 134, 141, 209, 215

Limberg, Carl, 81
Lindbergh, Charles A.: airmail contracts and, 312; DC-1 and, 314; decline in popularity of, 383–84; flight to Paris by, 289, 294; goodwill flight of, 291; Medal of Honor for ER and, 302; Orteig Prize and, 227; trips to Germany by, 356; WWII and, 386
Lippmann, Walter, 387, 393, 503
Littledale, Clara Savage, 371, 376
Littledale, H. A., 371
Litvinov, Maxim, 466, 467
Lockheed planes: Constellation (L-649, 749, and 1049A), 515–16; L-10 Electra, 321, 322; L-188 Electra, 526–27; P-38 "Lightning," 397, 412, 470
Locomobile (car), 21, 31, 35, 102
London, England, 223, 267–68, 355–56, 358
Longuyon, France, 220
Loomis, William, 174
loop antenna, 373–74
Los Angeles, California, 237–38, 292
Lovell, Walter, 128
Lovett, Robert S., 364
Low, Seth, 109, 121, 129
Luce, Clair Booth and Henry R., 464
Ludendorff, Erich von, 114, 121, 167, 171, 176, 178, 187–88
Lufbery, Raoul (Luf): career of, 117–18; death of, 147–49; J. Hall and, 145; Lafayette Escadrille and, 113–14, 130; memoir of, 219; sortie over German lines, 121–25; victories of, 162
Luftwaffe, 354–55, 384
Luke, Frank, Jr., 188, 191–94, 198–200, 303
Lynd, William L., 416, 417–18, 419

MacArthur, Douglas, 102, 209, 414–15, 443–44, 509, 510, 538
Machado, Gerardo, 288
MacIntyre, Malcolm, 527, 532
Manion, Clarence, 542
Manufacturers Contest Association (MCA), 56
Mao Tse Tung, 503
March, Peyton C., 113
Maria, Juan Gadala, 376
Marmon Wasp (race car), 57–58
Marr, Kenneth: Hartney and, 194–95; Independence Day celebration and, 176; Lafayette Escadrille and, 130; as leader, 180; 94th squadron and, 126, 129, 156; visit to ER by, 181
Marshall, George C., 191, 386, 414–15, 504

Martin, Glenn, 89–90, 393, 516, 517
Martin planes: 2-0-2, 516–17; 4-0-4, 517–18
Mason (car), 60–61, 64
Mason, Edward R., 60–61
"Masters of Tomorrow" (Rickenbacker), 494–95
Maurer, Richard S., 522, 528
Maxwell Motor Company team, 70–72, 74, 75
Maxwell Special (race car), 76, 78–79, 82, 84, 86
Maytag, Frank and Elmer, 60
McCarthy, Joseph, 509
McClure, Carl H., III, 487
McClure Syndicate, 229, 230
McCook Field, 245
McKinley, William, 9, 11
McNary-Watres Act (1930), 300, 301, 307, 312, 320
McRae, Floyd W., Jr., 378–79, 380–81
Medal of Honor, 197, 301–3, 343
Meissner, James A.: in Alert Room, 131, 132; assignment of, 115; flights of, 163–64, 166, 174; as friend, 116; gunnery training and, 109–10; Hannover plane and, 209; 94th squadron and, 220; 147th squadron and, 180; rescue of, 207–8; return to U.S. by, 222–23; wing stripping and, 151, 154
Menjou, Adolphe, 504
Menoher, Charles T., 226, 247, 252
Mercedes (car), 57–58, 69, 84
Mercer (car), 64
Meredith, Lois, 208, 213
Merrill, Henry Tyndall, 325–28, 347, 348, 350, 516
Metropolitan Trophy, 80, 81, 82
Metzger, William, 244
Meuse-Argonne offensive, 191, 198, 200–205, 213
Mexico Flyer, 368, 370–77
Meyer, Eugene, 71
Miami, Florida, becomes EAL's second headquarters, 337
Miami Beach, Florida, 285
Michella, Joseph, 478
Milch, Erhard, 264–65, 354
Miller, Harry, 25, 70
Miller, James E., 104, 107, 115, 117, 220
Miller, John M., 335
Miller, William J., 25
"Million Dollar Guard," 107, 113
Mills, Ogden, 101
Mitchell, John, 109, 163–64, 216
Mitchell, William B. (Billy): apology of, 249; assignment of, 113; death of, 353, 354; *Drachen* and, 192, 207; as driver for, 103–4;

enemies of, 303; 1st Army Corps and, 129; first sortie and, 133; Foulois and, 155–56, 158; on Huffer, 221; independent air force campaign of, 252; Meuse-Argonne offensive and, 202, 203–4; Pershing and, 183–84, 218; promotion of, 186; promotion of ER and, 145, 195–96; public rebuke by, 184; service of, 141; St. Mihiel salient and, 188; strafing and, 173; in Toul sector, 102–3
Mitsubishi Zero (plane), 395, 396
Mixter, George, 283
Molotov, Vyacheslav, 467, 469, 475, 479–80
Monroe Doctrine, 542
Montgomery, John K., 287–88
Montgomery, Lillian Tolliver, 293–94
Montmarathon race, Tacoma, Washington, 84–85
Moore, Clarence, 371, 374, 376
Moraine-Saulnier (monoplane), 105
Morgan, Anne, 283
Morison, Samuel Eliot, 394
Moross, Ernest A., 72
Moses, Robert, 366
Motor Age award, 77
movie project, 236. See also *Captain Eddie* (film)
Mulford, Ralph, 62, 66, 67, 68, 84, 238
Mussolini, Benito, 266
Myers, T. E. (Pop), 290, 295

name, of ER: "Captain Eddie" nickname, 232, 234; middle, 353; spelling of, 76, 129–30
Narragansett Park, Providence, Rhode Island, 77
National Airlines, 501, 513–14, 522–23
national debt, speech on, 494–95
National Defense Act (1920), 246
National War Labor Board (NWLB), 455, 456
navigators, 417
Nelson, Donald, 393
Newark International Airport, 365, 367
New York American, article for, 229
New York Automobile Show, 255, 274, 277
New York City: airport for, 365–67; EAL and, 338; life in, 236, 306, 345–46, 546, 547; move to, 296
Nieuport 28 (plane): availability of, 115; performance of, 135, 137; Pershing and, 114; virtues and flaws of, 118–19, 155, 156–58; wing stripping and, 144, 151–55, 164
Nimitz, Chester, 444
94th Aero Pursuit Squadron: buddy system

and, 205; as C.O. of, 196–97, 204–5; death
of ER and, 548; departure of Meissner
and, 180; first sortie of, 130–33; as flight
leader, 145–47; Gerard visit to, 139–40;
as Hat-in-the-Ring, 130; insignia of, 129;
at Medal of Honor ceremony, 303; misfortunes in, 133–36; in North Africa, 470;
ordered to active duty, 128–29; reconnaissance missions of, 188; return to U.S.
by, 234; Spads for, 179; strafing missions
of, 187, 188; successes of, 218–19; at
Villeneuve, 115, 116; visit to, 388. *See also*
combat victory
95th Aero Pursuit Squadron, 115, 116–17,
121, 141–42
Nome, Alaska, 489
noninterventionism, espoused by ER, 356,
359–60, 383
North Africa, 413, 468–71
North American Aviation, Inc., 308–10, 313,
317, 320
North American P-51 Mustang (plane),
397, 412
Northcliffe, Lord, 214
Northwest Airlines, 487–88, 517, 530
Norton, Fred, 181
nuclear war, threat of, 506–7
Nukufetau atoll, 439
Nutt, Alan, 202, 203

observation balloons, attacking. *See* balloon-
busting; *Drachen*
O'Donnell, Eddie, 62, 68, 74, 75
Oldfield, Barney: at AAA banquet, 226; AAA
Contest Board and, 56; as auto racer, 30,
50–51, 65, 66; as bicycle racer, 29; on ER,
52; Maxwell Motor Company team and,
71, 72; speech attended by, 388
Oliver, Bryce, 485
Omaha, Nebraska, 44–45, 49–50, 74–75, 84
103rd Pursuit Squadron, 114, 128, 388
147th Aero Pursuit Squadron, 157–58, 172,
179–80
O'Neill, Thomas, 14
Orteig, Raymond, 227
Oscar Lear Company, 25, 26–27
Owen Stanley Range, 443

Pacific, the: aircraft sightings in, 436–37;
bird and, 429; devotions and, 428; ditch-
ing of plane in, xii, 422–23; flight from
Hawaii to Canton Island, 416–21; hunger
and, 428–29; mental state in, 434–35;
power struggle in, 431–33; in rafts in,

423–26, 430, 434, 437; recovery from, 442;
rescue from, 437–41, 450; search and, 427,
438; sharks and, 425–26, 433–34; storm
in, 429–30; sunburn and, 427–28; tour of
stations in Southwest, 442–48
Packard (car), 21–22, 266
Pactolus Park track, Red Oak, Iowa, 46, 47
Palmyra Island, 420, 421
Pan American Airways, Inc.: "chosen instrument" status of, 463–64; founding of, 287–
88; interchanging of equipment with, 519,
521; International Air Transportation Policy
and, 488; Lindbergh and, 294; Mexico City
and, 334, 335; stewards and, 349
Paris, France: family visit to, 358–59; flight
of Lindbergh to, 289, 294; honeymoon in,
261–62, 265, 267; leave in, 171, 208, 213;
surgery in, 177, 181, 183
passport application, 92
Patch, Alexander, 446
Patrick, Mason M., 155, 254
Patschke, Cyrus, 67
Patterson, Joseph, 493–94
Peale, Norman Vincent, 498, 506
Pearl Harbor, 385, 387, 416
Pearson, Drew, 370–71, 372
Pelletier, LeRoy, 274, 280
Perret, Geoffrey, 415
Perry, James A., Jr., 370, 372–73, 374–75
Pershing, John J.: "All-American drive" and,
186, 187–88; as army chief of staff, 253–54;
aviation and, 103; court-martial of Huffer
and, 221; as driver for, 101–2; in Europe,
98, 99, 100; 1st Division of, 208; Foulois,
W. Mitchell, and, 155; March and, 113;
Meuse-Argonne offensive and, 191, 202,
204; Mexico and, 112; J. E. Miller and,
107; W. Mitchell and, 183–84; removal of,
from active command, 208–9; testimonial
from, 231; 3rd Army of Occupation, 218
Pétain, Philippe, 101
Peterson, David M., 126, 129, 130, 131,
132, 180
Peterson, Ralph, 293–94
Peugeot (car), 69–70, 75–76, 78, 84, 88–89
Peugeot racing team, 69–70, 86, 89
Pfalz D-III, 137
Pickens, Will, 56, 72
Piedmont Hospital, Atlanta, 378–81
pilot training: advanced, 110–11; as ground
officer, 109; gunnery training for, 109–10;
at Issoudun, 107; with Nieuport 28, 119–
20; on own, 107–8; at Tours, 104–6;
at Villeneuve-les-Vertus, 115

ment in automobile manufacturing by, 242–45, 253–56, 269–81; marriage of, 260–61, 339–40; painting of, by Christy, 343; prophet, role as, 239–41, 549–50; raft ordeal in Pacific Ocean, 423–38; self-esteem of, 139; setting of transcontinental speed record by, 314–15; severely injured in crash near Atlanta airport, 374–77; special missions of, in WWII, 386–90, 401–15, 442–48, 462–83, 486–90; victories of, in automobile racing, 47–50, 67–68, 74–77, 81–82, 84–85, 90; victories of, in WWI, 136–39, 143, 149, 151, 153, 163–64, 189–90, 201, 203, 204–8, 210, 212, 220; wins control of EAL, 328–31; wins Medal of Honor, 197, 301–3

Rickenbacker, Marcia (granddaughter), 508
Rickenbacker, William Frost (son): adoption of, 293–94; Air Force and, 508, 509; Hoover and, 511; Merrill and, 326, 327; personality and parenting of, 339–41; return of ER and, 448
Rickenbacker Blood and Plasma Bank, 380
Rickenbacker engine, 282
Rickenbacker Motor Company: debts from, 280–81; decline of, 272–73, 274–75, 276–77, 280, 282; financial status of, 270; idea for production of car and, 242, 243–44; incorporation of, 253, 254–55; marketing plan of, 255–56; merger opportunities for, 275–76; Model C series, 274; models of, 270–72, 277–78; production of cars of, 252–53; prototype for, 244–45; Series D, 277–78; Series 8-A, 275, 276–77, 279; Super Sport 8, 279–80; tooling up for production by, 256; travels for, 270
Rickenbacker's Luck (Farr), 622n1
riding mechanics, 32–33
Riggenbach, Anton Ludwig Niklaus, 3
Riggenbach, Christoph, 3
Riggenbach, Christoph Johannes, 3
Riggenbach, Niklaus, 3
Robertson, William A., 284, 287
Robinson, John M., 523
Rockefeller, John D., Jr., 453
Rockefeller, Laurance: drinking by ER and, 345; EAL and, 329–30, 332; forcing ER out of EAL, 533; Martin and, 517; merger and, 528; religion of ER and, 508; Rockefeller Center and, 338; search committee and, 531
Rockefeller, Percy, 283
Rockne, Knute, 305
Roe, A. V., 53, 95

Rogers, Will, xi, 232, 304, 324
Rooney, Tom, 80
Roosevelt, Franklin D.: administration of, 454; aviation and, 316, 357; Berle and, 492–93; big business and, 310–13; character traits of, 627n6; Churchill and, 409; on death of, 500; Joint Chiefs of Staff of, 386; J. Lewis and, 455, 456; Lindbergh and, 383; MacArthur and, 414, 415; Merrill and, 328; neutrality acts and, 356; nomination of, 308; Pearl Harbor and, 387; views on, 485, 490–91, 504–5; War Department and, 464; WWII and, 363, 364, 384–85
Roosevelt, Philip J., 115, 180
Roosevelt, Quentin, 109, 177–78, 179
Roosevelt, Theodore, 50, 95, 214, 551
Roosevelt, Theodore, Jr., 362
Rose, Mauri, 346
Rose Bowl Parade, as grand marshal in, 511
Rosenberg, Julius and Ethel, 507
Rosenfeld, Jesse S., 375
Ross, Harold, 212
Rouen, France, attack on, 398, 405–6
Royce, Alexander B., 330
Ruggles, N. J., 61–62
Rumpler C-IV observation plane, 167–71
Runyon, Damon, 222, 229, 230, 345, 506
Russia, Bolshevik takeover in, 114. *See also* Soviet Union
Ruth, Babe, 388
Ryan, Alan A., 78
Ryan, John D., 225

Saints, France, 177
San Francisco, California, 238, 249
Santa Monica, California, 64
Saunders, Raymond, 209
Savoy Hotel (London), 93–95, 223, 267, 269, 482
Schiff, John, 329
Schoenhair, Lee, 285
Schroeder, Rudolph, 245, 246
Schwab, Charles, 275
Scotland Yard, 92, 93, 96, 100, 224–25, 511
Sebree, Edmund B., 446
Second Battle of the Marne, 179
Seicheprey, France, 134
Seldes, George, 212, 213, 214, 346
self-promotion, ER's zeal for, 211–12, 324–25
Sennett, Mack, 238
Sergeant York (film), 497
Serling, Robert, 352, 550
Seven Came Through (Rickenbacker), 432, 450
Shannon, Sidney, 324, 337